Also by the same authors:

THE OPERA
A History of Its Creation
and Performance: 1600-1941

Men of Music

THEIR LIVES, TIMES, AND ACHIEVEMENTS

Wallace Brockway & Herbert Weinstock

REVISED AND
ENLARGED EDITION

SIMON AND SCHUSTER · NEW YORK

COPYRIGHT © 1939, 1950, 1958 BY SIMON AND SCHUSTER, INC.

PUBLISHED BY SIMON AND SCHUSTER, INC.

ROCKEFELLER CENTER, 630 FIFTH AVENUE

NEW YORK 20, N. Y.

TWELFTH PRINTING

REVISED AND ENLARGED EDITION

MANUFACTURED IN THE UNITED STATES OF AMERICA
BY AMERICAN BOOK—STRATFORD PRESS, INC., NEW YORK

To
Lillian Brockway Simmons
and
Edna O. Weinstock

Introduction to the Revised Edition

Eleven years have elapsed since we finished the manuscript of Men of Music, *and in those years the book has run through eight printings. It was one of the end products of many years of an all but uninterrupted conversation about arts and letters. The book appeared, and the conversation went on, particularly about music. We discussed not merely what we had already written and published, but also what might have gone into it had it been the ideal book we had always wanted to write. We took into account both criticisms received and our own evolving opinions. By the time it became obvious that a ninth printing was demanded, we felt that* Men of Music *needed to be corrected in detail, brought down to date, and enlarged. This Revised Edition is the result of that feeling.*

The phrase "corrected in detail" needs qualification. We did not try to recast the entire volume to fit our changed (and ever-changing) opinions about the multifarious data that had passed through our minds. Rather, the hundred or so small corrections affected chiefly minor facts. Recently unearthed bits of information were occasionally inserted. Rarely did we alter a judgment—in fact, we did so only when we ourselves found a passage we could not read without blushing. For instance, the curious are invited to compare our present evaluation of the Verdi Requiem with the casual dismissal of that high work of genius in the First Edition. On the other hand, in the matter of enunciating points of view that many have found unpalatable we remain unreconstructed.

Bringing Men of Music *down to date was a much easier task than we might have envisaged had we known, eleven years ago, that we would be doing it. Of the twenty-one composers to whom, in the First Edition, we devoted a chapter apiece, two of the three who were living then are living still. Richard Strauss, whose demise many years earlier would have left music none the poorer, died in 1949. Reports of a new symphony from the octogenarian Jean Sibelius crop up constantly—as they did a decade ago. And we still wait for Igor Stravinsky to equal the greatness of his early years. Sibelius appears to have created little or nothing since our chapter was written. Strauss and Stravinsky have been busy, and their latest activities have been faithfully recorded.*

Bringing Men of Music *down to date on Strauss and Stravinsky has lengthened it, but an added chapter, on Hector Berlioz, is a more considerable enlargement. Hearing more and more of his music through the years had brought us inevitably to the decision that he belonged among those great creators portrayed and criticized in* Men of Music. *We were, even in our First Edition, somewhat reluctant to omit him, but our excuse at that time was perfectly valid. He was, eleven years ago, so little played that we could not, without dishonesty, have pretended to judge him. Times have changed, though not enough. Unfortunately, several of Berlioz's greatest compositions were available to us only in recorded excerpts or in score. But it is a good sign that while we discussed and wrote this new chapter it was possible to hear Berlioz's music (including an uncut performance of* Roméo et Juliette) *on the radio or play it on the gramophone.*

WALLACE BROCKWAY
HERBERT WEINSTOCK

New York
February 22, 1950

Acknowledgments

For the opinions and statements in this book, the authors are alone responsible. They feel indebted, however, to numerous friends and well-wishers for invaluable practical assistance. They wish to thank Richard L. Simon for many illuminating suggestions. Margaret Sloss, who read the manuscript as it was written, and pulled the authors back from the brink of not a few absurdities, has their lasting gratitude. They owe much to the stimulating editorial comment of the late Henry H. Bellamann and Robert A. Simon. Ben Meiselman was of great assistance in preparing the index. Finally, Bart Keith Winer undertook the job of reading complete page proofs of the book, and at the last moment removed various unintentionally humorous touches.

For the revised edition Jacques Barzun's criticisms of the added chapter on Berlioz have been invaluable.

Table of Contents

INTRODUCTION TO THE REVISED EDITION   vii

I. THERE WERE GREAT MEN BEFORE BACH   3

Ancestors of Western music. Dunstable and the English polyphonists. The Flemings. Josquin hints for preferment. A bad influence. Palestrina the God-intoxicated. Saves music from decadence and extravagance. The Improperia and the Missa Papae Marcelli. Wife and money troubles. Di Lasso, dramatist in tone. A success story. Mixed motives. Seven penitential psalms. Victoria the devout. Spanish rhythms. The climax of unaccompanied vocal polyphony in Palestrina, Di Lasso, and Victoria. Close of a period.

II. JOHANN SEBASTIAN BACH   22

Bach's fame. A musical clan. Childhood. Foreign influences. Stubbornness. Life in Weimar. Appearance. An epitomizer of forms. A duke's servant. Cantatas. The greatest organist. Cöthen. The Well-Tempered Clavichord. *The "Brandenburg" Concertos. Leipzig. The Magnificat. The* St. Matthew Passion. *A stickler for rights. The B minor Mass. More cantatas. Secular compositions. Bach's sons. Frederick the Great and his theme. Musical puzzles. Blindness and death.*

III. GEORGE FRIDERIC HANDEL   53

A child prodigy. Johann Mattheson. Almira, Handel's first opera. Italy. Domenico Scarlatti. Success. Hanover and London. Purcell, England's greatest composer. George I and a false legend. The Water Music. *Cliques and stage battles. Big box office. Handel clings to tradition. Esther, the first English oratorio. Alexander's Feast. Misfortunes and illness. Handel as clavier composer. Failure after failure. A chain of masterly oratorios. Messiah. The* Firework Music. *Twelve thousand people attend a rehearsal. Blindness and death. Handel as a British vice and glory.*

IV. CHRISTOPH WILLIBALD VON GLUCK   85

The Renaissance produces opera. It degenerates in France and Italy. Opera as a social gathering. Gluck's childhood. He writes conventional successes. Visits Handel in London. Marries well. Is knighted by the Pope. Reforms ballet. Meets a librettist with ideas. Orfeo ed Euridice. Relapse. Alceste. The importance of the overture. Iphigénie en Aulide. *Marie Antoinette and Sophie Arnould.* Armide *and a famous feud.* Iphigénie en Tauride. *Reforms. Failures. Social old age. Entertains the Mozarts. Disobeys doctor's orders.*

v. FRANZ JOSEF HAYDN   102

Parliament pays a bill. St. Stephen's and a brutal dismissal. A famous singing teacher. Karl Philipp Emanuel Bach. Haydn marries the wrong wife. The Esterházys. A phlegmatic genius. Excellent working conditions. An indiscretion. Haydn meets Mozart. And loses his job. Goes to England. Becomes the idol of London. The "Salomon" Symphonies. Haydn teaches Beethoven. As a symphonist. Gott erhalte Franz den Kaiser. The Creation. *Its fading luster.* The Seasons. *Apotheosis and death. The rediscovery of Haydn. His string quartets. His lasting greatness.*

vi. WOLFGANG AMADEUS MOZART   124

The rococo. Most dazzling of child prodigies. Leopold Mozart. Maria Theresa. Tours. A boy writes operas. Finds Salzburg intolerable. Grows up. Violin concertos. Mannheim and the Webers. Back to imprisonment in Salzburg. The Archbishop kicks him out. He marries. Die Entführung. *Gluck. Poverty and extravagance. Mozart as a piano composer. The concertos. Symphonies. Freemasonry. Plays quartets with Haydn.* Le Nozze di Figaro. *Success in Prague.* Don Giovanni. *A triumph. Hints of the coming century. The three master symphonies.* Die Zauberflöte. *A mysterious visitor and the Requiem. Death. Mozart's overtowering greatness and limitations.*

vii. LUDWIG VAN BEETHOVEN   162

The French Revolution. A hero. Childhood. Helpful friends. Escape to Vienna. Beethoven's notebooks. Noble patrons. Slow development. Early piano sonatas. The First Symphony. The nineteenth century opens. The "Heiligenstadt" Testament. Physical afflictions. The mystery of the "Immortal Beloved." Piano concertos. Napoleon and a symphony. More piano sonatas. Strange career of Fidelio. *Its overtures. Beethoven writes the Fifth Symphony. The Violin Concerto. M. Lesueur cannot find his head. Overtures. The Seventh Symphony. Goethe. Beethoven as puritan.* Wellington's Victory. *Apotheosis. Last piano sonatas. The* Missa solennis. *The Ninth Symphony. Death. The string quartets.*

VIII. CARL MARIA VON WEBER 208

Relation to Constanze Mozart. Trouping childhood. Wild oats. Early operas. Life in Prague. Captures Germany with patriotic songs. Der Freischütz, *the first romantic opera. The* Conzertstück *as program music. Spontini stages a spectacle. The failure of* Euryanthe. *Beethoven speaks. Weber learns English. Composes* Oberon. *Ill treatment in London. Triumph of* Oberon. *Dies away from home.*

IX. GIOACCHINO ANTONIO ROSSINI 226

Wagner visits a retired dictator. Childhood in eighteenth-century Italy. Early operas. Writes a smash-hit song. An impresario and his mistress. The Barber of Seville. *Rebellion in Naples. Rossini marries. Advice from Beethoven.* Semiramide. *The siege of Paris. Balzac likes* Moïse. *High finance.* William Tell. *The monarch of opera abdicates. Olympe Pélissier.* Stabat Mater. *A gay old age. Death.*

X. FRANZ PETER SCHUBERT 248

Unconscious tragedy. Genius and intellect. Mastersongs and doggerel. Limitations. Poverty and adoring friends. Masterpieces at eighteen. The "Schubertians." The "Forellen" Quintet. Schubert fails with opera. Syphilis. The "Unfinished" Symphony. Tales of romance. Composes for piano. The song cycles. The C major Symphony. Sees Beethoven. Death and a monument.

XI. FELIX MENDELSSOHN-BARTHOLDY 267

A happy life. The wonder child. A Midsummer Night's Dream. *The rediscovery of Bach. Mendelssohn conquers England.* Fingal's Cave. *Writes the "Italian" Symphony. Renovates Düsseldorf. Leipzig, the Gewandhaus, and Robert Schumann.* St. Paul. *Mendelssohn listens to Rossini. A romantic marriage. The King of Prussia is difficult. The "Scotch" Symphony. Again* A Midsummer Night's Dream. *The Violin Concerto.* Elijah. *Queen Victoria. Death. Mendelssohn rejudged.*

XII. ROBERT SCHUMANN 292

Heredity and romanticism. Studies law. Quarrels with Friedrich Wieck. Papillons. *Romance and obstacles. Founds a journal. The Davidsbündler.* Carnaval. *Arrival of Mendelssohn. Wieck is obdurate. Schumann visits Vienna. Finds Beethoven's pen and a Schubert symphony.*

Marries Clara. Fantasiestücke *and* Kreisleriana. *The great songs. Flaws as a symphonist. Fails as a pedagogue. Signs of mental decay.* Genoveva. *The Piano Concerto. Tragedy and death. Schumann's reputation.*

XIII. FRÉDÉRIC-FRANÇOIS CHOPIN   314

Fame and self-limitation. Childhood in Poland. Weltschmerz. *Paris in the 1830's. Noble patrons. Valses. Liszt and polonaises. Another Polish dance. Pedagogy. Études. Mendelssohn's criticism. Chopin's failure as a pianist. Liaison and romance. Nocturnes. Scherzos. George Sand. Hell in Majorca. A vigorous corpse. Preludes. Four mad children. The masterly Fantaisie. Break with George Sand. Doting women. Purgatory in England. Death from consumption.*

XIV. HECTOR BERLIOZ   338

Retarded recognition. A country childhood. Assaults on the Prix de Rome. An idée fixe. *A marvelous Opus 1. The* Symphonie fantastique. *Sojourn in Italy. Marriage. A spot of Byronism. The mighty Requiem. Cellini and Shakespeare. Funeral weeds.* Wanderjahre. *Faust damned. Setbacks. Visits to London.* L'Enfance du Christ. *A mammoth opera. More Shakespeare. A classical romantic. Problems and answers.*

XV. FRANZ LISZT   374

A figure of legend. The master virtuoso. Early amours. Chopin and Paganini. Love and Mme d'Agoult. Swiss interlude. Liszt conquers Thalberg. Triumphal tours. Creates the piano recital. Lola Montez et al. Liszt's children. Weimar and the Princess. He renounces the world. Becomes an international celebrity. A fine conductor. Enthusiasm for Wagner. Almost marries. Becomes an abbé instead. A vie trifurquée. *Ten thousand pupils. Death. An estimate.*

XVI. RICHARD WAGNER   395

Social position of composers. Biography as detective story. Admiration for Weber. Wagner writes a bloodcurdling libretto. Composes two operas. Begins to attract creditors. Marries Minna. Das Liebesverbot *finishes an opera company. Riga and machinations. Flight by sea. Beginnings of* Der fliegende Holländer. Rienzi *and success. The* Leitmotiv. *Composes* Tannhäuser, *which is tepidly received. Quarrels with Minna. More creditors. Writes the* Lohengrin *libretto. Toys with revolution. Exiled. Fails to conquer Paris. More love affairs.* Lohengrin *fails. The* Ring *librettos. Wagner leads musical life of Zurich.*

*Pamphleteering. Mathilde Wesendonck and the Asyl. Enter Cosima
von Bülow. The* Ring *progresses.* Tristan. *The Paris* Tannhäuser
*fiasco. More wanderings. A fairy prince. Revolution in Munich. Wagner
composes* Die Meistersinger. *Marries Cosima. Completes the* Ring.
Builds the Festspielhaus. The first Ring. Parsifal. *The Wagner
legend.*

XVII. GIUSEPPE VERDI   445
*Verdi the patriot. Early years. Marriage. First opera a success. Death of
wife and children. Triumph of* Nabucodnosor. *Troubles with the
censors. The Villa Sant' Agata. Giuseppina Strepponi.* Rigoletto. Il
Trovatore. Camille *and* La Traviata. *Failure and fiasco. Verdi
becomes a war cry. Marries Giuseppina. Enters parliament. St. Petersburg and* La Forza del destino. *The Khedive wants an opera.* Aïda.
*The Requiem. Thirteen years of silence. Arrigo Boïto. Two Shake-
spearean masterpieces. Dawn of the twentieth century.*

XVIII. JOHANNES BRAHMS   469
*"The three B's." Brahms speaks. Childhood in the slums. Potboilers.
Joseph Joachim. The Schumanns.* New Paths. *Schumann dies. Brahms
and Clara. Brahms' psychology. A court musician. The First Piano
Concerto. Re-creates the variation form. Moves to Vienna. As chamber
composer. Brahms and romance.* Ein deutsches Requiem. *Waltzes
and Hungarian dances. Elisabeth von Herzogenberg. The Franco-
Prussian War. The "Haydn" Variations. Brahms as lieder composer.
Four symphonies. Visits Italy. The Violin Concerto. A degree and the*
Akademische Festouvertüre. *A famous beard. Von Bülow. Brahms
meets Tchaikovsky. The "Double" Concerto. The last piano pieces.*

XIX. PIOTR ILYICH TCHAIKOVSKY   502
*A neurotic child. A petty official. Studies music. The Rubinsteins.
Moscow. Tchaikovsky writes a symphony. The affaire Désirée Artot.
The Five.* Romeo and Juliet. *The First Piano Concerto. Von Bülow
plays in Boston. Bizet vs Wagner. Nadejda von Meck and Antonina
Miliukova. Tchaikovsky marries. Grim tragedy. Ballets. The Fourth
Symphony.* Eugen Oniegin. *Italy. The Violin Concerto. World fame.
The Fifth Symphony.* Pique-Dame. *Break with Nadejda. Tchaikovsky
visits the United States. The* Nutcracker. *The* "Pathétique." *Cholera.*

XX. CLAUDE-ACHILLE DEBUSSY   529
*"Musicien français." Paris and tradition. Childhood. The Conserva-
toire. Visits to Moscow.* L'Enfant prodigue. *Composes songs. The*

Prix de Rome. A Wagnerian. La Damoiselle élue. *Russian and Javanese music.* Green-eyed Gaby. L'Après-midi. *The String Quartet. The first Debussyans. Pierre Louÿs. More songs. First marriage.* Nocturnes. "M. Croche." *Maeterlinck, Mary Garden, and Georgette Leblanc. The leitmotiv and* Pelléas. *Second marriage. Piano compositions.* La Mer. *Concert tours.* Chouchou. Le Martyre de Saint-Sébastien. *D'Annunzio.* Images. Préludes. *The World War.* Études. *Death.*

XXI. RICHARD STRAUSS   556

Decline of a giant. Prodigious youth. Von Bülow. Early works. Don Juan. *Influence of Wagner.* Tod und Verklärung. *As conductor and discoverer. Egypt and an opera. As lieder composer. Marriage.* Till Eulenspiegel. Also sprach Zarathustra. *A touch of megalomania.* Don Quixote. *A monument to bad taste. Berlin, Nikisch, and Wilhelm II.* Feuersnot *and the critics. What is the* Sinfonia Domestica? Salome. Elektra. *Strauss visits the United States.* Der Rosenkavalier. Ariadne auf Naxos. *Decline and fall. A Nazi? A lesson from Rossini.*

XXII. JEAN SIBELIUS   574

False picture of Finland. Ancestry and boyhood. Law and music in Helsingfors. Germany and education. En Saga. *Marriage. Epic inspiration.* The Swan of Tuonela. *A government grant. The First Symphony and Tchaikovsky. A patriotic gesture. The Second Symphony and the Violin Concerto. Moves to Järvenpää. The Third Symphony. Miscellanea.* Pohjola's Daughter. *Illness.* Voces intimae. *The controversial Fourth. Sibelius visits the United States. The First World War. The Fifth Symphony. Revolution and a siege. Under fire. The Sixth Symphony and the Seventh. Sibelius at seventy-four; at eighty.*

XXIII. IGOR STRAVINSKY   594

Russian composers and academies. Rimsky-Korsakov. Two short orchestral pieces win Diaghilev. L'Oiseau de feu. Petrouchka. *Piano compositions. Nijinsky and* Le Sacre du printemps. *A riot in the Champs-Élysées. Neoclassicism.* Le Rossignol. *Experiments.* Les Noces *and catharsis. Devitalization.* Oedipus Rex. *Jean Cocteau. The* Symphonie de psaumes. *A genius of emptiness. Music for Ringling Brothers and Billy Rose. The later symphonies.* Orpheus *and an opera in English. The future of music.*

INDEX   613

MEN OF MUSIC

Dull-Useful Information
for Conscientious Readers

Titles of compositions are given in their original form except where common usage forces the English translation. Thus, we speak of *The Well-Tempered Clavichord*, not *Das Wohltemperirte Clavier;* of *La Traviata*, not *The Strayed One*.

The word *clavier* is used throughout for all immediate ancestors of the piano. The authors found that discriminating narrowly between clavicembalo, clavichord, clavier, harpsichord, and spinet would involve discussions of timbre and mechanism not within the scope of this book.

Chapter I

There Were Great Men
Before Bach

THE fierce, blinding sun of the high Renaissance was beating down on papal Rome when Giovanni Pierluigi da Palestrina, the greatest of the old composers, was writing Masses for worldly and splendor-loving pontiffs. Around him flowed the variegated life of sixteenth-century Italy, given its pattern, texture, and color by this phenomenal upsurge of human ambition. Everywhere artists were celebrating the victory of the senses: sculptors were exploring with rediscovered candor the contours of the human body; painters were transforming their peasant mistresses into the Mother of God; architects were masking the harsh Gothic face of the cities with gracious temples and colonnades, and philosophers were dreaming of Plato, that prince of pagan poets whom a blasphemous humanist had actually proposed for sainthood. In the midst of all these busy sensualists ostensibly re-creating the classic past, but in reality creating the modern world, Palestrina was patiently putting the finishing touches to the Gothic edifice of medieval music.

By Palestrina's time music was an exceedingly complicated affair. Like every other art, it had developed slowly and painfully from meager beginnings. From the ritual grunts of savages it had evolved with geologic slowness into an adjunct of the Greek drama. Whether, if we knew how to perform it, Greek music would appeal to us or not we can never know, for, as a wise English critic has said, "All the research in the world will not enable us to understand the Greek musician's mind."

From a strictly pragmatic point of view, music blossoms at that moment in the fourth century when Ambrose, Bishop of Milan, decided to regulate the singing for the services in his diocese. The Ambrosian chant—the first thoroughly recognizable ancestor of music as we hear it—is the leanest and most solemn adaptation of the Greek modes, the ancestors of our modern scales. This somber singing can still be heard in certain Milanese churches, but today we are more familiar with the elaboration of St. Ambrose's system known as the Gregorian chant, which largely superseded the older musical service at about the beginning of the seventh century. Some think that St. Gregory, the greatest Pope of the early Middle Ages, sponsored, or even devised, the innovation; less romantic historians believe that he was too busy with barbarians, heretics, and plague to bother with ideas about music.

For a thousand years the music of the Church was rigidly melodic: that is, it attained its ends without the use of harmony as we conceive it today. The troubadours and minnesingers accepted unquestioningly this purely horizontal tradition of music, and lavished their imagination on the melody and words. But neither these gay itinerant musicians nor the formulators of primitive counterpoint (whoever they were) can be called real composers.

The Renaissance, which exploited the individual ego, gave birth to the composer with a name. Until then men had been content to submerge their names in anonymous giving of their talents: the musician was as nameless as the altar boy swinging the censer. In the Middle Ages music had no separate identity: it was as much an accessory of the sacred rite as Greek music was of the drama. Definitely, purposely, a part of some greater whole, it was designed to recede. It is no coincidence that the first pieces of self-sufficient music are (with few exceptions) not anonymous: they were still written for the Church, but the composer had begun to think of his music as a living thing he had created.

Considering the exalted and ancient lineage of the other arts, it comes as a shock to find that the first composer, in the modern sense of the word, was an Englishman who died in 1453. This man, John Dunstable, is an almost mythical figure, a sort of English Orpheus who was even credited with the invention of counterpoint—a feat obviously beyond the abilities of a single individual. Also, for no apparent reason, he has been confused with St. Dunstan, an Archbishop of Canterbury who had died more than four centuries before. Add that he was even confused with another English composer of his time, and was reputedly astrologer and mathematician, and this sums up what is known of the man who was probably Geoffrey Chaucer's most gifted artistic contemporary. Little of Dunstable's music survives, and he might have vanished from history altogether if it had not been for his long and fruitful association with Continental musicians of his age, whose successors—especially the Flemish masters—evidently studied his methods to great advantage.

Dunstable's suave and euphonious style tended temporarily to soften the harsh contours of the music of the Flemings. But Jean de Okeghem reverted to the austerity of earlier Flemish music, while vastly increasing its technical resources. Okeghem has been called the greatest music teacher of all time, and in his relentless pursuit of a new methodology has been likened to the modern experimentalist, Arnold Schönberg. This is by no means a forced comparison, for the purely esthetic results of their efforts are, in both cases, open to question.

Like many another outstanding theoretician, Okeghem was fulfilled in the work of his pupils, the greatest of whom was Josquin Des Prés. Coming upon Josquin after mingling with his still shadowy predecessors is like emerging suddenly into the light of day: he is recognizably a modern man, an erratic genius whose checkered career extended well into the sixteenth century. He was born in the dawn of a new age, when the Turks swarming into Constantinople and Gutenberg devising the printing press helped to liberate forces that would destroy the Middle Ages. Josquin emerges from the mists as a singer at Milan in 1474. He was then about thirty years old, and it seems probable that his sophistication was already such that even the excessive splendor of the court of the Sforzas could not overawe him. For he was no stranger to court life, as he himself testifies: he had studied under Okeghem at the royal chapel of Louis XI. As he left the then cheerless city of Paris with a whole skin, we may be sure that he did not make the sour French monarch the butt of those practical jokes for which he later became notorious.

Within the next decade or so, Josquin made a leisurely progress through the burgeoning duchies of northern Italy, where beauty-loving and neurasthenic princes welcomed good musicians with the extravagant warmth of those lush and expansive times. He finally arrived at Rome, which was for two hundred years to be the center of the musical world, and became a singer in the papal chapel, thus choosing a road to fame that became stereotyped with his successors. Perhaps the choristers in the Pope's service lived aloof from the dissolute life of Renaissance Rome, but if they came much into contact with that grand old rake, Innocent VIII, or his even more riotous successor, Alexander VI, they must have witnessed some of the most colorful and improper scenes in the history of even the Eternal City. Here, despite the obvious distractions of Borgian Rome, Josquin worked on his first book of Masses—probably some of them were sung in the Sistine Chapel with the composer himself taking part.

Louis XI had died, Charles VIII had climaxed a humiliating career by mortally bumping his head, and that brilliant matchmaker, Louis XII, was firmly seated on the French throne before Josquin wandered back to Paris to seek preferment. At first he had to live on glory and promises: his first book of Masses, published in 1502,* was received with great acclaim, and though Louis XII began to hint cheerfully about church benefices, these failed to materialize. Josquin was no respecter of the person of the Most Christian King, and dared to jog his memory. Being commissioned to compose a motet for performance in the King's presence, he chose two telling phrases from the Psalm cxix—"Let Thy words to Thy servant be remembered" and "My portion is not in the land of the living"—for his contrapuntal embroidery. He received a benefice.

Josquin died in 1521. Later composers, exploiting even further the devices he had used and the styles he had vivified, crowded his music out of the churches with motets and Masses of their own. For almost four hundred years Josquin has been hardly more than a name. Yet the most painstaking musicologists, after piecing together the pitifully sparse details of his life, round out their labors by unanimously acclaiming him a genius. Although rarely performed, a sufficiently large amount of his music survives for us to visualize him three-dimensionally as a composer. He widened the scope of musical art unbelievably: he advanced and subtilized the technical resources of his predecessors; more important still, he discovered that music can be made the vehicle of varying human emotions. Even the most baroque of Josquin's works, though full of higher-mathematical intricacies, are nevertheless expressive— the music of a man who felt deeply and made spacious melodies. What sets him above the earlier masters—and, indeed, above most

---

* Although the first printed music antedates this by a quarter of a century, Josquin was the earliest composer to have a complete printed volume of his music published.

composers—is precisely this richly varied expressiveness. His music possessed a powerful appeal for his contemporaries, who invariably referred to him as "the wonderful" or "the marvelous" Josquin. Luther, a good judge of music, and himself a composer of sorts, said, probably of Josquin's less intricate style (for this downright reformer had little use for musical monkeyshines), that others were mastered by notes while Josquin did what he pleased with them.

Josquin's effect on music was not wholly salutary: his associates and followers—particularly the Flemings—admired him most as a superb craftsman, and tended to forget the more purely musical excellences of his style. Uncritically digesting his technique, they then began at the point beyond which prudence and taste had prevented Josquin from venturing, and went on to create monstrous complexities, at which, finally, the Pope himself began to shudder.

For almost two hundred years the Holy See had been vaguely disturbed by the growing elaborations and often glaring inappropriateness of the music for the services. The complaints were numerous: secular tunes and even words were used; different sets of words were sung simultaneously, and at times the style was so florid that the words, lost in the mazes of ornamentation, were completely incomprehensible. Imagine a solemn High Mass sung to the tune of *Oh! Susanna*, with the tenors crooning *Kiss Me Again* and the basses growling *Asleep in the Deep*! This is the sort of thing we might still hear if an affronted and conscientious Pope had not moved to reform these evils.

Reform was in the air. The Council of Trent, originally convened to checkmate Luther's criticisms by a general house cleaning, was reconvened in 1562 by Pius IV, after a recess of ten years. Among what they doubtless considered far weightier matters, the fathers of the conclave found the degraded state of church music worthy of their august consideration. Therefore, with the Pope's emphatic approval, two cardinals* were appointed in 1564 to see that sacred music was once more made sacred. At first the situation seemed so hopeless that there was talk of restricting the

* One of them was Carlo Borromeo, the greathearted Archbishop of Milan. A nephew of Pius IV, he almost justified the institution of papal nepotism by those noble deeds that led to his being sainted, twenty-five years after his death in 1584, by Paul V.

musical services to the traditional body of plainsong. It is possible that this deadening remedy had already been seriously considered when a man was found who could evolve an idiom both artistically mature and ecclesiastically acceptable.

Giovanni Pierluigi da Palestrina, the man who saved the art of music, was thirty-nine years old at this time. Like the magnificent Leonardo, he had taken as his own the name of his native village, where he was born in either 1525 or 1526. Palestrina is, and doubtless was, a drowsy and picturesque little town nestling in the craggy fastnesses of the Sabine Mountains. The composer's parents were people of substance in this obscure place, holding their land in fee of the powerful Colonna family. It is probable that one of the Colonnas took notice of the child, and persuaded his parents to let him enter the papal service. At any rate, we know that as early as his twelfth year Palestrina was living in Rome, and serving as a choirboy in the basilican church of Santa Maria Maggiore.

After seven years in Rome Palestrina returned to his native town with a life appointment as organist and choirmaster of the cathedral, offices carrying the revenues of a canonry. His fortunes were on the upgrade. Three years later, his marriage to a local heiress diverted a fat dowry his way. Shortly afterwards, Giovanni Maria del Monte, Cardinal Bishop of Palestrina, became Pope as Julius III—an event of prime importance in the ascending sequence of Palestrina's fortunes. Almost immediately the new Pope appointed his organist choirmaster of the Julian Chapel, the nursery for future Sistine singers. Palestrina dedicated his first book of Masses to the Pope, who responded by giving him a life appointment as a singer in the papal chapel, thus enabling him to give up his exacting duties at the Julian.

In March, 1555, Julius III died, and the next month Cardinal Cervino was elected to succeed him, assuming the curiously archaic name of Marcellus II. Unfortunate in life—he had enjoyed the papacy but three weeks when he died, probably poisoned—he was singularly fortunate in his post-mortem fame, for Palestrina's greatest Mass was named for him. Giovanni Pietro Caraffa followed the luckless Marcellus, and as Paul IV connected himself inextricably with the most exquisite refinements of the Inquisition, to which, as a Neapolitan, he was peculiarly fitted to lend his inventive genius. One of his first acts was to rescind Palestrina's "life" appointment in the Sistine: the morbidly devout pontiff could not brook the idea of a married man singing in the Vatican.

Palestrina interpreted his dismissal as a personal slight (though two other married members of the choir were let out at the same time), and his health suffered. The niggardly pension that Paul assigned him could scarcely compensate for his loss of prestige, though his injured feelings were somewhat assuaged by his appointment to succeed the renowned Di Lasso as musical director of St. John Lateran, "of all churches in the world the mother and head." However, this position seemed to be better than it actually was: the music was not well endowed, and Palestrina was constantly at loggerheads with his employers, who do not seem to have appreciated him. This impossible situation was terminated by his resignation in 1560, possibly with the intention of devoting himself exclusively to composing. Sorely disturbed though he was by the undignified bickering at the Lateran, he yet composed, in the *Improperia* for the Good Friday service, the work that raised him to a pre-eminence that went almost unchallenged until his death.

The *Improperia* brought Palestrina so much acclaim that he was besieged simultaneously by requests for more compositions and by appeals to re-enter the service of the Church. The compositions were forthcoming in profusion, but he hesitated to return to masters who had treated him so ambiguously. After eight months of unemployment, however, he consented to return to Santa Maria Maggiore, to lead the choir in which he had sung as a child. Here he remained for six years.

The fanatical Paul IV died in 1559, and there ascended the throne of St. Peter one of the most amiable figures of the late Renaissance, Giovanni Angelo de' Medici. This cultured and enlightened philosopher, known as Pius IV, was evidently deeply impressed by Palestrina's music, for he requested that the *Improperia* be copied into the manuscript books of the Sistine Chapel. It is possible that the simplicity and genuine piety of these Good Friday pieces led the Pope's commissioners to turn to Palestrina in solving the crisis created by the ultimatum of the Council of

Trent. But it is impossible to verify the old tale that it was the *Missa Papae Marcelli* that won them over.

This Mass, the most famous piece of Renaissance music, is as shrouded in legends and conflicting traditions as the *Mona Lisa*. Among a welter of data there are many absurdities and few authenticated facts. The most preposterous story attributes the composition to Pope Marcellus I, a thoroughly unmusical gentleman who was martyred early in the fourth century. It seems likelier that Palestrina composed it in 1562, and submitted it to Cardinal Borromeo and his associate two years later. Even the date and place of the first performance are not known with certainty: some say Santa Maria Maggiore heard it first; others favor a private audition at the palace of one of the commissioners, followed by a performance at the Sistine, in the presence of the Pope himself, on June 19, 1565.

We are on firm ground, however, in regard to the ultimate reception accorded this great masterpiece, for here the question refers not to a contradiction in data, but to the inherent grandeur of a peak in art comparable to the Sistine frescoes. If Pius IV did not really say that the *Missa Papae Marcelli* was comparable to the music heard by St. John the Divine during his vision of the New Jerusalem, he should have said it. After all, it is merely a florid Renaissance way of saying exactly what critics have been saying ever since. But the making of heavenly melodies was not very profitable, and Palestrina welcomed the largess of wealthy clerics and noblemen.

In 1565, Palestrina's friend Pius IV died; he was succeeded the following year by the cantankerous Inquisitor General, Michele Ghislieri, who assumed the name of Pius V. This thoroughly morose monk (the last sainted pope) reappointed Palestrina to the Julian Chapel in 1571, this time as choirmaster. Meanwhile, the composer's creative genius was at flood: Masses, motets, and sacred madrigals flowed from his pen unceasingly, and apparently without effort. Two of the madrigals commemorated the signal victory of the allied Venetian, Spanish, and papal navies over the Turks at Lepanto.

Palestrina's sobriety of character must have made him welcome in the more serious ecclesiastical circles of the time. His intimacy with Filippo Neri, the founder of the Order of Oratorians, dates from the year 1571, when the future saint* is said to have invited him to conduct the musical services at Neri's own church. These services came to be known as oratorios because they were performed in an oratory: the term "oratorio" was not applied to a particular form of music until 1600. Neri, who seems to have been free of the more forbidding qualities usually connected with saints, became the composer's lifelong friend.

Despite Palestrina's many friends among the powerful and holy of the Renaissance—a list of his dedications reads like a sixteenth-century *Almanach de Gotha*—his life was cheerless and pinched. His wife and two musically promising sons died within a few years of each other, and he was left with one rascally boy who not only plagued him during his life, but also, as his father's musical executor, damaged his musical reputation after his death. His second marriage, at the age of fifty-six, could not well have been a romantically happy one: he needed money and someone to preside over his household. The woman of his choice was a widow in comfortable circumstances, and presumably in need of the same human companionship that Palestrina craved. He took over a fur-and-hide business she had inherited from her first husband, and made a decided go of it, buying much valuable real estate with his profits.

The last seventeen years of Palestrina's life were marked only by domestic vicissitudes; officially, through his honored connections with the Vatican, he had achieved the utmost distinction the Renaissance had to offer a musician. Others might be better rewarded, but the fact remained that Palestrina's offices gave him the tacit dictatorship of the musical world. Only a technical question of seniority of service kept him from the position of master of the papal choir. He issued his works with almost calendar regularity, though not in the sumptuous format that distinguished the publications of certain of his contemporaries who enjoyed the patronage of a mere king or duke—the Popes were not so munificent to their musicians as to their painters and sculptors.

Palestrina was not one of the most prolific composers: he left only ninety-three Masses, five hundred motets, four books of madrigals, hymns, and offertories for the whole Church year, three

---

* Palestrina numbered at least three saints among his acquaintance—Carlo Borromeo, Pius V, and Filippo Neri.

books of Magnificats, three of litanies, three of lamentations, and two of sacred madrigals—a mere trifle compared to the incredible output of his well-kept contemporary, Orlando di Lasso. But the percentage of excellence is amazingly high: Palestrina seldom fell below his own standards, which were uncompromising. Occasionally a composition written to order did not please the great personage for whom it was intended. When the learned builder-Pope, Sixtus V, heard the Mass *Tu es pastor ovium,* he remarked dryly that Palestrina seemed to have forgotten the *Missa Papae Marcelli.* But even this hypercritical pontiff was won over by *Assumpta est Maria,* as well he might be, for it is barely, if at all, inferior to the Marcellan Mass.

Sir Donald Tovey has pointed out that Palestrina, like Spinoza, was a God-intoxicated man. His secular compositions are negligible in number, but in his Church music he did not invariably follow the letter of the regulations laid down by the Council of Trent. He frequently used secular tunes for sacred texts: for instance, he used the folk melody *L'Homme armé* as the basis for two Masses. He set another Mass to the tune of a French love song. However, his intense devotional fervor so spiritualized these lay melodies that all trace of their vulgar origin was removed.

Palestrina gave music a new kind of beauty based on an understanding of integral structure. His predecessors, even the greatest of them, had been content to solve specific technical problems without conceiving them in relation to the total effect. Some of them had given beautiful and expressive melody to each voice, and had ingeniously carried these single threads through a complicated labyrinth, producing a rich fabric of sound. But in their single-minded pursuit of correct horizontal development of the separate voices, they failed to relate them vertically in such a way as to produce harmonically beautiful chords. We have no evidence that the ugly discords of the great Flemings were intentional.

In the rather barren controversies that rage perennially over the comparative worth of various compositions by a single master, and which are particularly unprofitable in the case of a composer so rarely performed as Palestrina, the vote is always divided. The *Missa Papae Marcelli* is by no means unchallenged in its pre-eminence: at least three other Masses compete for highest place. *Assumpta est Maria,* for instance, has been compared (with complimentary intent) to the *Sistine Madonna*. But now that the recording companies and the radio have thrown their enormous weight on the side of the Marcellan Mass, it seems destined to hold its place in popular estimation as the greatest composition before Bach. Nowadays, when the link with Palestrina is becoming ever more tenuous, it is increasingly difficult to enjoy him fully without the act of faith that is the very essence of the creed he illuminates. For Palestrina is, above all else, other worldly, and therefore, to the vast majority of our contemporaries, he must necessarily seem remote; by the same token, his esthetic is as difficult to enter into as that which reared a Buddhist stupa or fashioned a T'ang vase. The *Missa Papae Marcelli* sums up, in a way that only an expert can appreciate, but everyone can feel, what was best in the music of the time. If you are not conditioned to be moved by its applicability as part of revealed truth, you can at least savor it as the voice of a particular moment in history—that frozen, baffling eternity known as the Middle Ages.

In the dedication to Gregory XIII of his fourth book of Masses, Palestrina shows a lively sense of his own gifts as a composer. His contemporaries already regarded him as one of the fountainheads of music. One of them, the Spaniard Victoria, so admired him that he not only imitated the Italian master's musical style, but is said to have copied his somber clothes and the cut of his beard. In 1592, a group of accomplished north-Italian composers presented a collection of vesper psalms to Palestrina, with a dedication that reflects the reverence in which he was held during the last years of his life. Its language is extravagant, and would be fulsome if addressed to any lesser personage: "As rivers are naturally borne to the sea as their common parent and lord, and rest in its bosom as the attainment of their own perfection, so all who profess the art of music desire to approach thee as the ocean of musical knowledge to testify their homage and veneration."

During his last years, his responsibilities somewhat lightened, Palestrina continued, as was his oft-expressed intention, to create music for the greater glory of God. Old age did not stem his creativeness, and he was preparing his seventh book of Masses for publication when he died, on February 2, 1594. His intimate friendship with Filippo Neri lends plausibility to a legend that he died in the saint's arms.

Palestrina was buried in the old basilica of St. Peter's, but his tomb was moved during the demolition of the church, and no longer exists. Records preserve the epitaph, its Latin sonorousness aptly saluting the greatness of his achievements:

JOANNES PETRUS ALOYSIUS PRAENESTINUS
MUSICAE PRINCEPS

With the *Missa Papae Marcelli* there began the last phase of purely vocal contrapuntal development, enriched by later works of the Prince of Music himself and his most eminent contemporaries —Orlando di Lasso and Tomás Luis de Victoria. Di Lasso worked mainly in Germany, and therefore fell little under the influence of Palestrina: a native of Flanders, he summed up the accomplishments of the Flemish school. Victoria, however, spent much time in Rome, and consciously modeled his compositions after the great Italian's. During the last third of the sixteenth century, when all three of these men were prodigally pouring forth a flood of masterpieces, they divided the domain of music among them. Although they cannot be considered rivals, they offer endless material for comparison and contrast. Palestrina was a lyric tone poet of the lineage of Raphael and Mozart; Di Lasso was a dramatist in tone, related to Michelangelo and Bach; Victoria, finally, was a sort of Spanish Palestrina, but endowed with the passion and mystical tenderness of his countrymen.

Of this peerless constellation, Di Lasso had the most eventful life. His was the first really big success story in music. Noble patrons competed for the honor of employing him: he started out as the favorite of a Gonzaga, and ended up at the court of Munich in the softest musical berth in Europe. The pomp and glitter of his life is rather like Leonardo's. He spent his vacations running pleasant diplomatic errands for his powerful patrons. Everything conspired to produce for him those ideal circumstances for which every composer yearns.

Orlando was born at Mons, in what is now Belgium, about 1530. Even at the age of nine he had progressed so far musically, and had so angelic a voice, that he was thrice abducted, the third time by agents of Ferdinand Gonzaga, Viceroy of Sicily. His lifelong habit of consorting with noblemen was formed early, and after his

he spent several years fancying the high society of
Rome.

Naple's bent was, from the first, secular. Unlike Palestrina,
...d his entire life in the papal service, Orlando held only
... church appointment, and that early in his life: the direc-
...he choir at St. John Lateran. He left this post to resume his
...ings with a highborn friend, and may even have reached
...d before settling temporarily at Antwerp in 1555. In that
... he brought out his first two publications, a book of madrigals,
mostly on verses by Petrarch, and a collection of madrigals, chansons, and villanelle, with four motets trailing after. These *juvenilia*,
which are characterized by bold chromatic devices, annoyed Dr.
Charles Burney, the foremost English music critic of the eighteenth
century, into calling Orlando "a dwarf on stilts" as compared with
Palestrina.

Orlando cannily dedicated his first book of motets to the future
Cardinal de Granvella, and that rising statesman promptly
recommended him to the attention of Albert V, Duke of Bavaria.
It was at the brilliant court of the Wittelsbachs, at Munich, that
Orlando passed most of his life. At first only a court singer (he had
to learn German before assuming heavier responsibilities), he already drew a larger salary than the *Kapellmeister*. He married a rich
Bavarian girl. Within an amazingly short time after his arrival in
Munich he himself was *Kapellmeister* and one of the Duke's most
trusted ambassadors. And in 1570 the Emperor Maximilian II
ennobled him.

Orlando's fame soon spread throughout Europe, and he was
received with great enthusiasm wherever he went. Even though he
enjoyed incomparable working conditions at Munich, it is difficult
to understand how he found time to produce the stupendous body
of his music. One year he was in Venice finding singers for the
ducal chapel, another year in Paris hobnobbing with Charles IX,
himself an amateur musician; another time he journeyed to Ferrara to present Alfonso II with a book of madrigals. The Italian
ruler received him coldly, and to save the artistic credit of an Este
the Florentine ambassador intervened in Orlando's behalf. A
slight to this composer was an international incident.

An exuberant love of fun endeared Orlando to a Paris ruled
by Valois and Medici. The judicious Abbé de Brantôme spoke of

some music he had written at Catherine de' Medici's o.
most melodious he had ever heard, while Charles IX's ad
became so intense that he offered to engage Orlando as a c.
musician at a fabulous salary. He declined the honor, bu\
tinued on such friendly terms with the royal family that Henri
the last of the Valois, gave him a pension and special privileges
publishing his music in France.

The truth is that Orlando needed no favors from foreign poten-
tates. His salary at Munich was more than lavish, and the conditions under which he worked literally have no parallel. His job
was simple: to write as much as he wished in whatever style he
chose. The only thing the Duke asked for himself was to be on
hand when Orlando's works were performed. The many musicians
who thronged the court of Albert V were at Orlando's beck and
call: in the realm of music he was as absolute as the Duke was in
affairs of state. If Orlando wrote a Mass, he could order its immediate performance in the ducal chapel; if he wrote a madrigal,
the chances were that it would be sung at a court gathering the
same evening. Here the ideal circumstances of demand and immediate performance were realized as they never have been since.

While fortune kept her fixed smile turned on Orlando, he continued to issue Masses, Magnificats, *Deutsche Lieder*, and chansons
in bewildering abundance. Albert V died in 1579, and his son,
Orlando's close friend, succeeded him as William V. Albert's
lavishness left the treasury depleted, but Orlando did not suffer—
on the contrary, his salary was doubled within the next few years.
Meanwhile, the Jesuits got at the Duke, and their influence slowly
seeped into the court, blotting out the old gay life, and making
William so unpleasant that history has nicknamed him the Pious.
Orlando, as a clever courtier, must have responded to this re-
vivalism, and yet in 1581 his villanelle are still overflowing with
the very essence of comic drama—hold, indeed, the germs of
opéra bouffe. The Duke's bigotry seemingly imposed few restrictions
on Orlando, and more than ever he wrote magnificently, with
subtlety, expressiveness, freedom, and boundless audacity.

In 1584, the annual procession of the Sacrament through the
streets of Munich on Corpus Christi was threatened by a thunder-
storm. For some moments—the whole incident reads like a fine
page from *South Wind*—it seemed that the ceremony would have to

be held indoors. The Sacrament was carried to the porch of the Peterskirche, and the choir began to intone Orlando's motet *Gustate et videte*. Suddenly the storm abated, the sun shone brightly. On the theory that this meteorological miracle had been brought about by the music, this same motet was thereafter sung during outdoor processions as a deterrent to storms.

The last decade of Orlando's life was marked by a growing sobriety of attitude. His fifth book of madrigals, published in 1585, revealed this change. Like some of his earlier efforts in this genre, they were settings of Petrarch, but the overdone chromaticism of the early pages now gave way to a purer diatonic style. It was as though he was censuring himself for his youthful extravagances, and subjecting his gifts to more rigorous discipline. But the strength of strength's prodigy began to fail, and 1586 passed ominously without a publication. The Duke noticed Orlando's failing health, and presented him with a country house to which he might retire from the strenuous ritual of court life.

Baseless fears for the future of his family were sapping the composer's vitality. His mind became increasingly disturbed—he seems to have suffered attacks of real insanity. At times, he refused to speak to anyone, and was unable to recognize his wife. The court physician treated him, and temporary recovery followed. But he brooded constantly on death, and spoke so bitterly that the patient Duke became enraged, and was calmed only by the intercession of Orlando's faithful wife. His blackest humors passed as unreasonably as they had come, and he was able for a time in 1594 to resume his duties at court.

On May 24, Orlando dedicated his *Lagrime di San Pietro* to Clement VIII. It was his swan song, and before its publication he died, on June 14, 1594, little more than five months after his peer Palestrina.

Orlando is one of the most difficult composers to analyze: not only did he write almost two thousand works, but he wrote them in a bewildering multiplicity of styles. If he were performed as often as Wagner, it would take many months of ceaseless listening merely to hear all of him; as it is, he is performed even less than Palestrina. His works range from ribald, actually bawdy chansons (which blushing editors permit us to see only in bowdlerized versions) to some of the most sublime devotional music ever written. Between these extremes are pieces expressing every subtle shade of emotion. The large number of compositions that lie at the opposite poles of this gamut suggests a manic-depressive personality at work, and there are passages in Orlando's life itself that give color to this hypothesis. It remains unexplained why this exuberant wisecracker and punster, whose letters to Duke Albert are full of excessive high spirits, ended his life of unrelieved good fortune as a near-insane melancholic. Needless to say, this emotional seesawing does not detract from the greatness of his music.

In surveying the vast and elevated domain carved out by Orlando's genius, critics have espied few of those isolated peaks that crown the Palestrinian landscape. The altitude is consistently very high, but the slopes are gentle: there is no *Missa Papae Marcelli*, no *Assumpta est Maria*. There is, nevertheless, general agreement that Orlando's setting of the seven penitential psalms is his greatest single work. In the musical language of God-directed contrition and sorrow, Orlando has never been excelled by anyone, has been equaled, perhaps, only by the Bach of the *St. Matthew Passion*. In these poignant lamentations, all earthiness and ribaldry have been burned out by searing emotion, and what remains is the very distillation of sublimity.

Tomás Luis de Victoria is the third of this great trio of sixteenth-century religious composers. He was born at Ávila, probably about 1540. As the birthplace of St. Teresa—she may have known Victoria personally, for she mentions his brother Agustín in one of her books—Ávila calls to mind the inextricable mingling of music and religiosity in late Renaissance Spain. Mystical and ascetic, sensual and ecstatic, St. Teresa fills a unique niche in hagiology, and resembles closely but two other figures in history: El Greco and Victoria. The latter, though influenced by Palestrina, never lost the dark, intensely Spanish quality that some find repellent, others magnificent. The mixture of spiritual ecstasy and lasciviousness in his compositions has often reduced the sacred-music experts to a state of silent embarrassment. Critics have been similarly tongue-tied before certain of El Greco's canvases.

Unlike most of his contemporaries, Victoria never had to free himself from the bonds of Flemish pedantry, with its endless elaborations and frequently empty scrollwork: from the beginning he used a simple and expressive style. It had flowered first in Palestrina's motets, but Victoria molded it into something entirely new. His motets, though less gracious and less contrapuntally clever than Palestrina's, overflow with warmth, masculine tenderness, and mystical ardor.

Victoria was a priest. He, rather than Palestrina, was the paragon sought by the reforming fathers of the Council of Trent: he never composed a secular piece or used a secular theme. He inscribed a book of motets and psalms not to a living patron, but "to the Mother of God and to All the Saints." In dedicating a book of Masses to Philip II of Spain, he said that he had been led by instinct and impulse to devote himself exclusively to church music. At the same time, he bade farewell to composing, saying that he was determined to resign himself to the contemplation of divine things, as befitted a priest. He made this vow in 1583, but the urge to create was too strong, and before he died, almost thirty years later, he had published many other volumes.

Victoria was happy in his patrons, whose generosity enabled him to issue his compositions in sumptuous folios that quite outshone the publications of his contemporaries. His severely devout nature recommended him to Philip II, who in 1565 sent him to Rome to continue his musical studies. Here he became a chaplain-singer, and eventually choirmaster, at the Collegium Germanicum, Loyola's bulwark against Lutheranism. He worked at the Collegium for more than a decade, leaving in 1578 to become chaplain to Philip's sister Maria, widow of the Emperor Maximilian II.

Victoria's relations with the Empress were close. He remained in her service until her death in 1603, and the liberal pension she left him in her will evidences her esteem. A profoundly devout woman, she took up her residence in Madrid at the convent of the Franciscan nuns known as Descalzas Reales, and Victoria's duties included leading its choir. The Empress' daughter Margaret joined this barefoot order in 1584, and it was to this princess that he dedicated a great *Officium defunctorum*, written for the funeral of her mother. He survived the Empress but eight years, during which he was chaplain to the Archduchess Margaret, and died on August 27, 1611.

In forming our judgment of Victoria, we are not embarrassed

by the overwhelming output of an Orlando. The Spaniard was
not a prolific composer: he left less than two hundred separate
compositions. The most striking characteristic of his music is its
hint of Moorish influence: it sometimes uses those harmonic and
rhythmic devices which, however metamorphosed and cheapened,
are to this day the unmistakable hallmark of Spanish music. Victoria, even in his imitation of Palestrina, retained his special native
quality: his Spanishness is as obvious as that of Albéniz or Falla,
though it is asserted less blatantly.

No less Spanish is Victoria's pervasive mysticism, which occasionally borders on hysteria. He was very sure of his mission. In the
dedication of the *Canticae beatae Virginis*, one of his most ecstatic
outpourings, he declared that his aim was to compose music solely
as a means for raising men's minds by pleasant stages to the contemplation of divine truth. No music would be more likely to accomplish such a purpose than Victoria's, though cynical ears may
hear in it sounds more descriptive of Mohammed's paradise of
houris than of a seemly Christian heaven.

The death of Tomás de Victoria in 1611 brought to a close the
great age of unaccompanied vocal polyphony. Music had gone
far since that almost mythical past when St. Ambrose devised his
chants, but even in its complex development it had kept to substantially the same road. The great musical trinity who lifted their
art to equality with painting and sculpture, and added to the
splendor of the dying Renaissance, were better composers than
Okeghem and Josquin. They handled richer materials with more
freedom, with more sweep and emotional depth, than the old
Flemish masters. With all their multifarious gifts, they had summed
up twelve hundred years of technical progress, and had set up
enduring monuments to the past. The sound of their own mighty
cadences, as well as their very position in history as the inheritors
and fulfillers of the great tradition of ecclesiastical music, deafened
them to the feeble murmurs of the new music coming to life around
them. The first opera—a puny infant—was performed while two
of them were still alive.

Palestrina, Orlando, and Victoria closed a period with such
finality that no further development in unaccompanied vocal
polyphony was possible. Their own followers, obscure men all,

were feeble, ineffectual, and anticlimactic. Music, to develop further, needed innovators, experimentalists with motivations and compulsions different from those which had unleashed the creative drive of the great vocal contrapuntalists. It took a hundred years of experimentation with new forms and new techniques to produce, in Johann Sebastian Bach and George Frideric Handel, men comparable in stature to the master polyphonists of the sixteenth century.

Chapter II

Johann Sebastian Bach

(Eisenach, March 21, 1685–July 28, 1750, Leipzig)

O NE of the most dangerous of pastimes is nominating a man for first place among the musical immortals. For this supreme honor there are rarely more than three candidates, and the war between their adherents wages perpetually in the living rooms of the land. Like three eternally recurring cards in the musical deck, Bach, Beethoven, and Mozart are dealt out with a monotonous regularity that enrages a Handel or Wagner cultist. However, there can be no doubt that a vote taken today would favor Johann Sebastian Bach for first or, just possibly, second place.

The growth of Bach's fame is in itself a story of absorbing interest. All but forgotten for almost a century after his death, he was discovered by a coterie of nineteenth-century musicians much as classical antiquity had been discovered by the scholars of the Renaissance. Mozart and Beethoven had both drunk deep at the inexhaustible well of Bach's technique, but it remained for Mendelssohn and Schumann to preach the greater Bach. They saw him not merely as a magnificent textbook, but also as the creator of manifold and incomparable beauty. From Germany the good tidings spread to England, and then rapidly throughout the rest of the Protestant world. Bach, as pre-eminently the glory of Protestant music as Palestrina is of Roman Catholic, had to wait longer for recognition in Latin countries.

What had begun as the jealous enthusiasm of a group came to delight the entire confraternity of musicians throughout the civilized world. In 1850 the Bach Gesellschaft, a society to publish the complete corpus of Bach's surviving works (few of which were published during his lifetime), was founded, with twenty-three royal patrons, and subscribers from a dozen countries, including the United States. This stupendous undertaking required forty-nine years for its completion, and was carried out under several editors of varying competence. Brahms said that the two greatest events of his lifetime were the founding of the German Empire and the completion of the Bach Gesellschaft's publications. With numerous other partial editions of Bach's output, the Gesellschaft served to disseminate his compositions so effectively that today the sun never sets upon his empire.

All this tremendous to-do would have nonplussed the industrious old town musician whose mortal greatness culminated when a king deigned to give him a theme for improvisation. For Johann Sebastian Bach never once fancied himself as anything so unlikely as the greatest composer in the world. He was merely carrying on the family trade (seven generations of Bachs had already included more than fifty cantors, organists, and town musicians), and doing his job as well as he knew how. What differentiated him from Uncle Christoph or Cousin Johann Valentin was simply that he happened to be the greatest musical genius the world has ever known.

There is no evidence to prove that the far-flung Bach clan realized that Johann Sebastian was much better than they were: even his son Karl Philipp Emanuel dismissed him as "musical director to several courts and in the end cantor at Leipzig"—in short, a common, garden variety of Bach. It must be realized, however, that this was in itself high praise, for the Bachs were the most renowned musical family in Germany, having cornered the musical market in at least half a dozen towns. One branch of this prolific family settled at Erfurt, near Leipzig, and so identified themselves with the musical life of the town that many years after the last of them had departed, "Bach" remained a synonym for any musician plying his trade there.

The great Johann Sebastian was born on March 21, 1685, at Eisenach, the capital of the tiny duchy of Saxe-Eisenach. The associations of the town were such that it was as if fate itself had had a hand in choosing his birthplace. For here, in the four-hundred-year-old Wartburg, which dominated the town from its lofty eminence, Luther had made his epochal translation of the Bible into German, and had lightened the long hours by singing the simple, rugged hymns that he loved. Here he had come from the Diet of Worms, for which he had written *Ein feste Burg ist unser Gott*, that battle hymn of militant Protestantism which Heine called the "*Marseillaise* of the Reformation," and which Bach was to know well and to use as the theme of one of the best loved of his cantatas. But Eisenach boasted an even more venerable tradition, for in the Wartburg, then the seat of boisterous Thuringian land-graves, had taken place in 1207 that memorable contest of minne-singers which Wagner immortalized in *Tannhäuser*.

Johann Sebastian's father, Johann Ambrosius, one of the Erfurt Bachs, had come to Eisenach as town musician in 1671, succeeding another member of his ubiquitous tribe in that post. Their clan-nishness is typified by the fact that Johann Ambrosius twice mar-ried women already related to him by marriage. Johann Sebastian was the eighth and last child of the first marriage. Of the amazing, almost miraculous precocity that gives the story of Mozart's early childhood an air of legend, Bach showed no trace during his boy-hood in Eisenach. We know that he entered the local *Gymnasium*, where he was by no means a star pupil; we assume, but do not know, that he received his first clavier lessons from his father.

In 1695, shortly after both his parents died, Bach was sent to the little village of Ohrdruf, in the depths of the Thuringian Forest. Here life was even quieter than at Eisenach, and from his organ bench at the Lutheran Michaeliskirche one of Bach's elder brothers presided over the musical destinies of the pious burghers. In this remote hamlet there was no call for the secular music that Johann Ambrosius had practiced at Eisenach. The school where Bach completed his formal education was known for its theological bias and grave atmosphere; though no pains were spared to ground its pupils in the humanities, Ohrdruf's was primarily a stern school of character. Its lessons had a profound, lifelong effect on Johann Sebastian: the lad who had nodded over his catechism at Eisenach now took to his heart the simple trusting faith that was to flower in the greatest devotional music the world has ever heard.

Johann Sebastian continued his clavier lessons with his brother, and—what had an even more important effect on his life and his art—began to play the organ. This "king of instruments," though used in Christian churches as early as the fifth century, developed a literature comparatively late, and only came into its own during the seventeenth century. No interpretive art boasts a more majestic and continuous tradition than German organ playing. It flowers with Reinken and Buxtehude, whom Bach heard and revered, and runs unbroken through Bach and Handel down to Albert Schweitzer, humanitarian, doctor, theologian, and Bach scholar. The Germans were so devoted to the organ that many forms of music developing in Italy and France during the seventeenth century gained little headway in Germany.

Clavier music in seventeenth-century Germany developed only less rapidly than organ music. Essentially Latin in its origins, it was until late a secondary interest that consumed the lighter inspirations of the great German masters of organ composition. Johann Sebastian's brother owned a collection of clavier works by his teacher, Johann Pachelbel, Böhm, Buxtehude, and others. For some unknown reason, the use of these pieces was refused the boy, who thereupon secretly took them from the music cabinet, and copied them out on moonlit nights. This six-month task was the beginning of his lifelong custom of transcribing music that he wished to study. When the vast amount of music Bach copied is added to the noting down of his own compositions, it is little wonder that he eventually became blind.

In 1700, when Bach was fifteen years old, and his brother no longer found it convenient to house him, it happened that Lüneburg, more than two hundred miles away, was in need of a good soprano. The lad, whose sweet treble had already secured him a paid job in the Ohrdruf choir, made the long journey, and was promptly accepted as choirboy at the Michaeliskirche. The three years he spent in Lüneburg broadened his musical horizon immeasurably, though the most vitalizing contacts were outside the town itself. His own church was pedestrian in its services, but at the near-by Katharinenkirche the eminent Georg Böhm sat at the organ console. Already Johann Sebastian had copied some of this man's work, and now there is little doubt that he came to know him personally. It was probably at Böhm's suggestion that Bach once trudged the thirty miles to Hamburg to hear the venerable Johann Adam Reinken, a master of florid organ effects whose influence is strong in some of Bach's early works.

Now, too, Bach was exposed to other than purely German influences. In the notable music library of the Michaeliskirche he suddenly came upon a new world of musical delight. The foreigners—Orlando, Monteverdi, Carissimi, and many others—brought him news of a more urbane civilization than the one he knew. And at near-by Celle, an imitation Versailles whose Francophile duke ate his German food to the accompaniment of elegant

French music played by French musicians, Bach caught the dim reflection of a brilliant culture, beside which Eisenach, Ohrdruf, and Lüneburg were uncommonly, Teutonically stodgy. During his many visits to the ducal *Schloss* he may sometimes have taken his place at the clavier. At all events, the French music he heard there, including both orchestral suites and the tinkling clavier suites of Couperin *le grand*, profoundly influenced him. Not only did he delight in this suave and polished Latin idiom, but his own Italian Concerto, French Suites, and other curiously un-German pieces show that he understood it.

But Lüneburg, despite its many extraneous attractions, did not offer the opportunities Bach desired for bettering himself financially and professionally. In 1702, when he was only seventeen, he was actually elected organist at a neighboring town, but its overlord imposed his own candidate on the electors. A job in the private band of the reigning Duke of Saxe-Weimar's younger brother was in itself a makeshift, though it brought him into contact with one of the most interesting minor figures in the musical life of the times. This was his master's younger son, Johann Ernst, a precocious talent whose violin concertos were so beautiful and so professionally made that three of them later adapted by Bach for clavier were attributed to Antonio Vivaldi, the Paganini of the eighteenth century.

While still employed at Weimar, Bach made the first of those journeys to inspect an organ that occur with increasing frequency throughout the rest of his life. Although he was but eighteen years old, his fame as an organist had reached the ears of the good men of Arnstadt, and after he had tried out the instrument they promptly offered him a position.

Bach's new duties were not unusually onerous, but included one he always resented: training the choristers. He did not suffer tribulations silently: he was a vocal and irascible man even at the age of twenty. Growing dissatisfaction with his singers precipitated an incident that does much to correct the widespread false picture of Bach as a gentle old hymn-singing fogy entirely surrounded by children. He had reached such a stage of exasperation with his charges that they began to resent his attitude. One night, as he was returning home from the *Residenzschloss*, he was attacked by several of them. One, hurling a pungent epithet at him, began to belabor him with a stick, but the young organist defended himself so ably with his sword that the ruffians retired discomfited. The fracas came to the notice of the town authorities, and Bach was called to account for his unconventional behavior. Nothing came of the incident, but he was now embarked on his long career of alternately explaining his doings to, and defying, stiff-necked officials.

These controversies were the trivia of a musical life that at Arnstadt began to find its own direction. It is not known where or when Johann Sebastian wrote down his first compositions, but certain it is that the first typical fruits of his genius belong to his stay at Arnstadt. These compositions bespeak a learner, not one who has mastered his craft. The scoring of his first cantata, for instance, is overheavy and highfalutin. One of these Arnstadt pieces, though slight musically, deserves mention as Bach's only essay in out-and-out program music. A clavier *Capriccio on the Departure of His Beloved Brother*, it summons up the apprehensions and regrets of farewell, and imitates vividly the hurly-burly of the coachyard.

Again, as at Lüneburg, Bach found the most enduring inspiration away from the scene of his official duties. In October, 1705, his employers granted him a month's leave of absence so that he could go to hear the most famous organist of the day, Dietrich Buxtehude. Installing his cousin as deputy organist, he set out on the three-hundred-mile journey to the old Hanseatic port of Lübeck. So widespread was the fame of Buxtehude's *Abendmusiken*, or evening church concerts, that it threatened the supremacy of Hamburg in the north-German musical world. Bach was so held in the magical thrall of Buxtehude's dazzling technical display that when he finally tore himself away, three months had passed.

Back among the staid Arnstadters, their organist exhibited the effects of his hegira with stupefying eloquence. Their beloved organ, which had been wont to give forth only the most conventional sounds, now emitted such audacities, such swirling and unchurchly arabesques, that they were struck dumb. Bach had annexed many of Buxtehude's extravagances, and had outstripped him in improvisation. These modernisms might have served him well in a more sophisticated musical center, but in Arnstadt they bordered on heresy. Once again he was haled before the authorities, and the accumulated grievances burst out in a relentless catechism. Why had he outstayed his leave? Why was he so stubbornly neglecting his choirmasterly duties? Why did he introduce monstrosities into the simple Lutheran tunes? Why, finally, had he had a "strange maiden" in the organ loft? Bach's answer to the first three questions was—after some hemming and hawing—to terminate his now thoroughly unpleasant connection with the Michaeliskirche.

Bach next went to Mühlhausen, another little center of Thuringian life, where he had secured the post of organist at the Blasiuskirche. Although his stipend here was no larger than in Arnstadt, he regarded this change as a promotion, for his predecessor had been a man of some distinction. And now a timely legacy enabled him to marry the "strange maiden." She was his cousin, Maria Barbara Bach, and they were married on October 17, 1707, remaining in Mühlhausen less than eight months after their marriage. To this period, however, belongs the only cantata Bach composed that was published during his lifetime: *Gott ist mein König*. Doing his duty by his new congregation was fraught with difficulties, but this time Bach's role was that of the innocent bystander. The little town was in the grips of a feud between the orthodox Lutherans and a kill-joy sect known as Pietists. Much of the squabbling centered on the church music: the orthodox wanted it just as it was, and the Pietists did not want it at all. Bach was caught between them, and had practically reached his wit's end when an opportunity occurred to return to Weimar. The Mühlhausen authorities accepted his resignation only on condition that he continue to supervise the enlargement of the organ he had himself requested.

As they rush from the railway station to the houses of Goethe and Schiller, and perhaps remember to visit the scenes of Liszt's declining years, visitors to Weimar are likely to forget Bach's fruitful years there. Weimar itself has forgotten Bach—not even one of those ubiquitous bronze plaques marks his possible dwelling. Yet it was at Weimar that he reached his zenith as a composer for the organ; here, too, he produced the brilliant "Vivaldi" Concertos and many cantatas, some of them only a shade less masterly than those of his last period. Finally, Weimar saw the birth of two of his three famous sons—Wilhelm Friedemann and Karl Philipp Emanuel.

Bach's position at Weimar was that of court organist and chamber musician to the reigning Duke, Wilhelm Ernst, brother to the now deceased prince who had first invited Bach there. His new employer was a petty tyrant whose tolerance barely extended beyond his own person. A childless, dour man, he had a lively sense of his duty to keep the lower classes in their place, and his actions suggest that to him anyone not in the *Almanach de Gotha* belonged among them. For his own pleasure he supported a court orchestra, where Bach alternated between the clavier and the violin, but his public emphasis was all on church music. Bach, therefore, was largely employed in the court chapel, an overdone baroque creation whose theatricality was by no means as foreign to the florid, ill-considered virtuosity of his earlier toccatas as some Bach experts would lead us to believe. Pompously peruked and accoutered in the regular livery of the Duke's servants, Bach sat at the organ every Sunday outdoing Buxtehude, while the gloomy prince and his respectfully morose court looked on from the loges.

Nothing that we know about Wilhelm Ernst can convince us that he was able to distinguish between the compositions of Bach and those of any other musician. He had hired the best organist available, and that, according to the convention of the times, meant someone who would compose, improvise, and adapt the music he played. The Duke was scarcely the man to appreciate that his ears were hearing the toccata transformed from the collection of magnificent fragments that had satisfied Buxtehude into a perfectly molded whole, in which brilliant cascades of sound were built into a vast architectural form. Buxtehude left the toccata a showpiece; Bach made it into a perfect vehicle for exalted musical ideas. Such a composition as the massive D minor Toccata and Fugue would in itself have made a deathless reputation for a lesser composer, but in Bach's case it is only one of many peerless works. His treatment of the toccata illustrates, at a comparatively early stage of his career, his phenomenal capacity for saying the last word in the musical genres he used.

It has been said that Bach invented no musical form. This is true only if *invented* is interpreted literally, for he borrowed nothing that he did not transmute beyond recognition. To take the most striking case, who would credit the invention of what he himself called the passacaglia to anyone but Bach? True, Girolamo Frescobaldi and Buxtehude had composed fine passacaglias. Bach used the form only once, but in this Passacaglia in C minor he is as different from them as they are from the nameless Juan Diego who *invented* the Spanish folk rhythm they borrowed. This grave and measured dance, certainly one of the most superbly conceived creations in all music, affords the unique example of a composer using a form once, exploiting its utmost possibilities, and then abandoning it.

It is always a shock to turn from Bach's lofty creations to a consideration of the humdrum details of his everyday life. Weimar must have been an uncongenial place for a man of his touchy disposition. The Duke treated him as a servant, and even failed to appoint him *Hofkapellmeister* when the post fell vacant; his neighbors treated him just as they would the cobbler or the apothecary. And why not? No one observing Bach in the bosom of his family, laboring over his manuscripts, or trudging to the *Schloss* would have had the slightest reason to suspect this bumbling fellow, with his short neck, protruding jaw, slanting forehead, and almost comically misshapen nose, of being even a cut above the other five thousand folk in Weimar. He loved his wife, was well started on his extraordinary career as a father (he begat a grand total of twenty children), and never had to scrimp too much. In an age when façade counted for much, Bach was neither handsome nor clever nor highborn nor rich—and the good people of Weimar were not music critics.

While it is difficult to interpret Bach's motives from the documentary evidence, it is clear that after five years in Weimar he was prepared to consider bids from other quarters. Now the Liebfrauenkirche at Halle invited him to succeed Handel's teacher as its organist. After some complicated negotiations, he finally turned down the offer because the salary was less than he was already receiving at Weimar. Further, the Duke disliked anyone leaving his service, and chose this particular moment to make him *Konzertmeister* and raise his pay. The authorities at Halle, resorting to the time-honored reasoning of *post hoc, propter hoc*, accused Bach of temporizing with them to force the Duke's hand. He answered this probably unjustified charge in a letter that was both temperate and dignified, saying in part:

"To insinuate that I played a trick upon your worshipful Collegium in order to compel my gracious master to increase my stipend here is unwarranted; he has always been so well-disposed to me and my art that, certes, I have no need to use Halle to influence him. I am distressed that our negotiations have not reached a satisfactory conclusion, but I would ask whether, even if Halle offered me an emolument equivalent to my stipend here, I could be expected to leave my present situation for the new one."

Bach's position placed him under obligation to compose "one new piece monthly," and so brought his attention back to the cantata form he had already tried with indifferent success at Arnstadt and Mühlhausen. Now he collaborated with another member of the ducal household, Salomo Franck, a numismatist with a flair for letters, in the production of no fewer than thirty sacred cantatas in three years—a pious Gilbert-and-Sullivan partnership that was crowned with great success. The Duke unloosed his purse strings to provide paper (then a luxury) for these works. Although none of them is as impressive as the best cantatas of Bach's last period, almost all contain fine single numbers, and at least one achieves an internal unity that places it high among his smaller compositions. This—the popular *Gottes Zeit ist allerbeste Zeit*—is thoroughly German in its directness and simplicity. It follows the text with great sensitivity, and the statement is so personal that some experts think that Bach also wrote the words. *Gottes Zeit*'s tragic and poignant utterance has evoked any number of fantastic interpretations: Rutland Boughton, composer of the perennially popular English opera, *The Immortal Hour*, believes that it represents the funeral of Christianity!

The Duke of Saxe-Weimar's dynastic plans now began to influence the course of Bach's life. He had no children, and his heir presumptive was unmarried. In 1714, taking Bach along, he paid a ceremonial visit to the Landgrave of Hesse-Cassel, in search of a wife for this nephew. Matrimonially, the visit was a fizzle, but it gave Bach an opportunity to play before the music-loving Landgrave and his son Frederick, the future King of Sweden. Bach's performance on this occasion was so brilliant that, in the words of one of the audience, "His feet, flying over the pedals as though they were winged, made the notes reverberate like thunder in a storm, till the Prince Frederick, *cum stupore admiratus*, pulled a ring from his finger, and presented it to the player. Now bethink you, if Bach's skilful feet deserved such a bounty, what gift must the prince have offered to reward his hands as well?"

Two years later, Wilhelm Ernst made another ceremonial visit, this time to Duke Christian of Saxe-Weissenfels. The occasion was a great hunting party arranged in honor of Christian's thirty-fifth birthday, and his cousin of Weimar commissioned his *Konzert-meister* to compose an appropriately jolly piece. The result was Bach's first secular cantata, *Was mir behagt*, an allegorical and mythological work which produced such an effect that Christian had it performed again thirteen years later when he made Bach his honorary *Kapellmeister*. If such Olympian celebrities as Diana and Pan seem out of place in Bach, it will be recalled that he had been studying contemporary French and Italian works that made abundant use of mythological machinery.

The same year Bach returned to Halle to inspect and perform on the new organ at the Liebfrauenkirche. The rancor of the Collegium was entirely dissipated, and Bach was regaled at a Teutonic feast of epic proportions: "Eggs boiled in brine, cold meats, ox tongues, and saveloys, washed down with Rhenish and Franconian wine and beer." During his six-day visit, coachmen and a staff of servants were at his constant disposal. Clearly, Bach's dignified estimate of himself as a personage had led the Halle authorities to treat him as one.

Bach's reputation as an organist was growing apace. The staging of a contest between him and Louis Marchand, organist to Louis XV, began to be discussed. As Handel's interests lay almost exclusively in England, this would have brought together the two most noted Continental organists of the day. Marchand's part in the business seems to have been confined to a great deal of preliminary boasting, but when Bach arrived in Dresden, where the bout was to take place, and Marchand accidentally heard him improvising, his assuredness collapsed, and he fled from town by the first post chaise. Commenting on this ignominious retreat, Dr. Burney wrote, "It was an honor to Pompey that he was conquered by Caesar, and to Marchand to be only vanquished by Bach."

This bloodless conquest took place during a crisis in Bach's life.

It had all begun when Wilhelm Ernst finally persuaded a respectable and well-dowered widow to marry his heir, Ernst Augustus. This lady's brother, Prince Leopold of Anhalt-Cöthen, a gifted musical amateur, met Bach at his new brother-in-law's palace, and was so impressed by his genius that he forthwith offered him the position of *Kapellmeister* at Cöthen. Several considerations prompted Bach to entertain the offer. As a member of the ducal household he was hedged in by a thousand irritating restrictions, not the least of which forbade him to visit the heir presumptive and his wife, with whom the Duke was constantly quarreling. In defiance of this ukase, Bach's friendship with Ernst Augustus and his consort continued on so intimate a footing that the Duke became suspicious. Any chance of closing the rift between Bach and his employer was precluded when the Duke passed over Bach's head in appointing a new *Kapellmeister*, the highest musical honor in his gift. Smarting from this indignity, Bach proceeded to his triumph at Dresden, and came back with his mind made up. He informed Prince Leopold of his willingness to leave Weimar, and the deal was closed in August, 1717.

When Bach applied for his release, the Duke was furious. Innately opposed to change as something inherently wrong, he saw in the threatened departure of one of his best musicians a determination on his heir's part to interrupt the smooth tenor of his life. He refused. Bach insisted, and on November 6 the Duke placed him under arrest. During his incarceration, which lasted almost a month, Bach seems to have imitated the examples of Cervantes, Bunyan, and other geniuses who suffered imprisonment, by continuing to work at his art. The one thing he did not do was change his mind. Torture being out of fashion, the Duke had to give in, and on December 2 he granted this stubborn servant permission to go elsewhere. On that date Bach's official career as an organist came to an end. Little more than a week later, he was settled at Cöthen.

The move was a drastic one. From a worldly point of view, it meant promotion, more prestige, and more pay. Bach had always coveted the title of *Kapellmeister*, and for some years had needed an income more nearly commensurate with the demands of a rapidly growing family. The attitude of his new patron was like a tonic to his flagging spirits. At Weimar he and his family had been cooped up in such narrow quarters that his own health and that of his children had been imperiled. At Cöthen, as the friend rather than the servant of Prince Leopold, he seems to have settled with his family in the *Schloss*. After the rigors of court life in Weimar, Bach must have looked forward to Cöthen as a blessed dispensation.

But Cöthen proved to be a mixed blessing. Pleasant shelter it was, but Bach paid for it by renouncing the most solemn duty he had laid upon himself: to dedicate his art to the service of God. In Cöthen this was literally impossible, for the official Calvinism of the dynasty allowed only the sternest, most unadorned hymns to be sung in chapel. There was no call for the cantatas and chorales that until then had tapped the purest sources of Bach's genius. Willy-nilly, he had to turn to the secular art practiced by his father and grandfather, and provide music for the players in the court band, in which the Prince himself played the clavier, violin, or viola da gamba. Simultaneously he—the most famous organist of the age—found himself without constant access to an organ worthy of his supreme talents. All this meant that, at the age of thirty-two, Bach had to learn to function in a new world.

Bach did not completely lose touch with the world he had abandoned. His celebrity as an organist and authority on the instrument itself brought him constant invitations from other towns. Less than a week after his arrival at Cöthen, he was off to Leipzig to inspect the new organ in the Paulinerkirche. His report bristles with rare knowledge of acoustics and details of organ manufacture. More picturesque are the records of his visit, in 1720, to Hamburg, where the seemingly imperishable Reinken was still active. Probably Bach went there to compete for the vacant post of organist at the Jacobikirche, and as Reinken was one of the judges, played before the ninety-seven-year-old master. After the younger man had improvised for a good hour on a theme Reinken himself had once used, this mighty voice from the past spoke, "I thought this art was dead, but I see it still lives in you." Eventually the Jacobikirche organ was offered to Bach, but he declined it, chiefly because of his loyalty to Prince Leopold.

If, despite this loyalty, Bach really was looking for other employment in Hamburg, there were two reasons. First, there was in Cöthen no Lutheran school where he could send his children. Second, the town became crowded with sad memories for him when, on returning from a trip to Carlsbad with the Prince, he found his wife dead and already buried. Of the seven children she had borne him, four survived, and the task of caring for them fell on him alone, for the eldest was a twelve-year-old girl. Less than a year and a half later, he led Anna Magdalena Wilcken to the altar. His new bride, though only twenty, was a court singer earning half as much as Bach himself. What was in every sense an excellent match turned out to be a happy marriage, for Anna Magdalena was a good housekeeper, a good stepmother, and a good musician. She bore him thirteen children, including his third famous son, Johann Christian, the "English" Bach. She was his faithful companion and helpmeet until his death, and survived him for ten years.

Meanwhile, Bach did not forget his children's musical education. Wilhelm Friedemann, always his favorite, was the first to receive instruction. The little exercise book his father wrote out for him is still preserved. Partly from these exercises, headier fare was soon provided in twenty-four preludes and fugues for the clavier. With a second set compiled at Leipzig in 1744, these were published after Bach's death as *The Well-Tempered Clavichord*. This title, indicating Bach's secondary purpose in composing them, is less mysterious than it sounds. "Tempered" merely means "tuned," and so *The Well-Tempered Clavichord* is Bach's pronunciamento against the old system of tuning instruments which, as H. C. Colles pithily observes, "made the instruments beautifully in tune in certain keys, the more usual ones, and quite unbearable in others." By writing this series of pieces, one for each major and minor key, Bach forced upon the old-fashioned tuners that modern system which prepares the instrument for playing in any key.

If *The Well-Tempered Clavichord* had done nothing more than revolutionize tuning, it would still be worth a paragraph in any history of music, for much of the effectiveness of the instrumental music of the eighteenth century and later depends upon the ability to shift from one key to another without catastrophic sound effects. But it is as revolutionary musically as technically. These preludes and fugues, starting out as exercises for children, have, like Chopin's etudes, been graduated from the studio to the concert hall, where their popularity shows unflagging vitality. Nor is this only because of the many-sidedness of the task they set the performer.

In sheer musical quality, in variety of mood, and in unceasing inventiveness, they are scarcely matched in the entire field of keyboard literature. With these "Forty-eight" and the partitas and French and English Suites, Bach raised the clavier to a position of pre-eminence that its descendant—the modern piano—has sustained to this day.

The Well-Tempered Clavichord has had a varied and amazing career, some of which would have delighted the pedagogue in Bach. Not only is it a favorite with virtuosos and their audiences, but it is also used as a textbook in the study of harmony, counterpoint, and fugue. Although Schumann called it the "musicians' Bible," many have dared to violate the sacred text. The unfortunate "Forty-eight" have been adapted for other instruments, transcribed, and probably even sung. Needless to say, they have not escaped the lush orchestrating hand of Dr. Leopold Stokowski. But the first prelude of the first set has suffered the strangest fate of all. Using it as an accompaniment to the text of the *Ave Maria*, the composer of *Faust* was inspired to add a honeyed soprano obbligato. But even in this form the prelude is indestructible—Gounod's *Ave Maria* is among the most popular songs ever manufactured.

Another favorite from the Cöthen period is the set of six concertos written at the request of Christian Ludwig, Margrave of Brandenburg, an obscure younger son of the House of Hohenzollern. These stirring, vibrant pieces represent Bach's first excursion into purely instrumental music on a large scale. They are not concertos in the modern sense; that is, they are not for a solo instrument accompanied by the rest of the orchestra. Rather, they are more like *concerti grossi*, in which several instruments have more important roles than the balance of the ensemble. The "Brandenburg" Concertos exhibit Bach as a tireless experimentalist, constantly trying new effects, testing the color of various instrumental combinations, and indulging his own concepts of form. The "Brandenburg" at their best tremble on the brink of being orchestral music in the modern sense, and only Bach's way of conceiving the parts vocally keeps them from being so. André Pirro, whose study of Bach's esthetic is definitive, has flatly called them symphonies. Of the six, the third has long been the most popular. Scored for strings and clavier, it consists of two vigorous allegros—bracing instrumental polyphony that moves to irresistible rhythms. All the others have contrasting slow movements and, with the exception of the sixth, are scored for strings, wind instruments, and clavier. The andante of the second is of a serene and unearthly loveliness that even Bach himself has not often equaled. These are but isolated beauties in five small masterpieces (for the first is by comparison uninspired) that Schweitzer has called "the purest products of Bach's polyphonic style."

The *Well-Tempered Clavichord* and the "Brandenburg" Concertos by no means complete the tally of Bach's instrumental works. There exist, in bewildering profusion, pieces for clavier, violin, and various ensembles. In discussing these, confusion worse confounded arises from the impossibility of establishing their chronological order, and from the absurdity of the names applied to many of them by editors and publishers. As enjoyment of these delightful pieces does not depend on knowing when they were written, or why one is called a French Suite rather than a partita, solving these puzzles can safely be left to the musical Dr. Dryasdusts. Bach himself was too busy for such minutiae; he did not scruple to move a whole section from a secular into a sacred cantata written more than a decade later. His borrowings from himself were sometimes made with ludicrous results, and only a hair divides his worst transplantations from Handel's callously putting Agrippina's words and music into Mary Magdalene's mouth. And he borrowed from others, too—notably some of the best melodies in the *St. Matthew Passion*. Bach was not composing for his biographers: he was always devising a cantata for the Duke of Saxe-Weimar, finishing a suite for Prince Leopold, or piecing together a Passion for the Leipzig worthies—he was like a newspaperman with a perpetual deadline.

All of Bach's instrumental music, except that for the organ, belongs in spirit to his happy years at Cöthen, whether written there or at Leipzig. French Suites, English Suites, partitas, and concertos—most of them contain music of rare quality, for Bach could not write long without achieving some memorable measures. Occasionally he strikes a note of grandeur, as in the last movement of the second partita for violin alone—the sublimely built chaconne, as varied, as perfect, and as lifting as a great Gothic cathedral. But the adjectives that best describe most of this instrumental music—delightful, charming, sprightly—are not those commonly applied to the greatest music. Compared to the Bach of the B minor Mass and the *Matthew Passion*, they are lightweight. They are the diversions of a man whose deepest and most intense inspirations were of a religious nature. The Italian Concerto has the feckless gaiety of a man enjoying his vacation. The French Suites echo the heeltaps of Versailles. The concerto for four claviers is a delicious excursion into pure melody.

But the conception of an unrelievedly pious Bach dies hard. He loved his life in Cöthen, even though he could not write religious music there. The idea that he was unhappy in Cöthen is the invention of earnest souls who insist upon standing up for his better nature, which they must have unrelieved. Actually, seven years after leaving Cöthen he was still writing wistfully of his life there: "Its gracious Prince loved and understood music, so that I expected to end my days there." In this same letter, he revealed the true cause of his departure: "My *Serenissimus** married a Bernburg wife, and in consequence, so it seemed, his musical *inclination* abated, while his new Princess proved to be an *amusa*." This lady, whom Prince Leopold took as his consort a week after Bach's marriage to Anna Magdalena, disliked music, and resentment of the time her husband gave to it soon changed to jealousy of Bach. Leopold's growing coolness fortified the composer in his wish to move to a town where his children could attend a Lutheran school.

In 1722, Johann Kuhnau, one of the earliest composers of program music, died, leaving vacant the cantorate of the Thomasschule in Leipzig. Although this was not at the time a very important post, six candidates presented themselves, including the redoubtable Georg Philipp Telemann, musical autocrat of Hamburg. Telemann, whose candidacy was a mere political maneuver, was unanimously elected, but preferred to return to Hamburg and enjoy an increased stipend. Bach then entered the field, but the electors' second choice fell upon one Graupner, a nonentity employed as *Kapellmeister* at Darmstadt. His employer refused to release him, however, and Bach was then chosen because, as the electors explicitly said, no one better offered himself. By May, 1723, he and his family were settled in their new home.

In Leipzig, Bach entered seriously upon his career as a litigant.

* The italicized words in quotations from Bach have been left in the language and form in which he wrote them.

His official duties as cantor of the Thomasschule, an ancient academy for poor students who were trained to sing in the choirs of the four principal city churches, would, under ideal conditions, have made him musical dictator of Leipzig. But such conditions were lacking: there was nothing in the rules and regulations of the Thomasschule that clearly defined the cantor's office, and Bach's conception of his duties differed widely from what the rector and other officials expected of him. He was to furnish a cantata for the Thomaskirche and the Nikolaikirche on alternate Sundays—he favored the Thomaskirche. He was to teach Latin to the scholars, and to supervise their choral training—he either neglected these duties or delegated them to others. These omissions led to constant and protracted bickering, acrimonious letters exchanged, appeals to the Elector of Saxony, and picayune feuds over questions of precedence and prerogative. Bach, who had gone to Cöthen partly because he coveted the title of *Kapellmeister*, felt that a cantorate and many of its duties were beneath his dignity: he salved his vanity by acting as though he were still a *Kapellmeister*, and by calling himself *Director Musices*.

When Bach arrived in Leipzig, the opera, founded there as early as 1693, was in a decayed state, and folded up several years later. Otherwise, the town was already launched on its stately career as one of the musical centers of the world. During Bach's lifetime there was founded a small civic society of instrumentalists, and from this humble origin grew the Gewandhaus concerts, which have numbered among their conductors Mendelssohn, Nikisch, and Furtwängler. A more cosmopolitan life than was common to the rest of Germany existed at Leipzig because of the great trade fairs that were held there annually. The many foreigners who came to these, and the town's large leisure class combined to produce a more sophisticated culture than that to which Bach had been used.

Bach celebrated his first Christmas in Leipzig by performing one of his masterpieces—the Latin Magnificat. On Christmas Eve, it was the pleasing custom at the Thomaskirche—one continued well into the nineteenth century—to stage a sort of mystery play of the birth of Christ. Bach's contribution to the fete was his largest church work up to this time: it is scored for a five-part chorus, soloists, and full orchestra, as that term was then interpreted. It is rarely heard, for its qualities have less appeal than those of the

B minor Mass and the *St. Matthew Passion*. The fact that Bach was setting Latin words may well have prompted him to use an aloof, objective style which owes much to the technically tight Italianism of the times. There is nothing personal or reflective about the Magnificat: it depends for its effect on its flawless formality, its unearthly jubilance, and its florid conduct of the voices. It is, of all Bach's works, the one best meriting the oft-repeated sneering comment on his music—"golden mathematics."

For ten years or more, Bach's fight for prestige and ideal conditions for producing his music went on at a jog trot, though his field of controversy was slowly widening. He got off to a bad start by inheriting a feud with the University authorities from his predecessor. It involved the ex officio right of the Thomascantor to conduct certain services in the Paulinerkirche, or University church. After two years of fruitless warfare with its musical director, Bach appealed to the Elector, who instantly commanded the University to answer Bach's charges. As their reply was unsatisfactory in certain details, Bach sent to the Elector the longest letter extant from his pen. Its Jesuitical casuistry elicited from Augustus the Strong a fence-straddling reply worthy of the oracle of Delphi. It indicated the separate provinces of the *Stadtcantor* and his opponent, but left the boundary between them vague. Therefore, when the Electress Christiane Eberhardine died, the feud took a new turn, as neither rival had a clear title to the right to conduct the memorial service for her august and truly lamented majesty. This time Bach won: on October 17, 1727, seated at a clavier in the organ loft of the Paulinerkirche, Johann Sebastian triumphantly conducted one of his less distinguished compositions.

Less acrimonious, but involving finer music, was a misunderstanding with the Nikolaikirche, always the stepchild of Bach's conscience. Among his duties was that of providing the Thomaskirche and the Nikolaikirche on alternate years with special Good Friday music known as a Passion. In applying for the cantorate, he had composed a Passion to prove his abilities, and had performed it in the Thomaskirche on Good Friday, 1723. The authorities of the Nikolaikirche, which had missed its turn in 1722, were eagerly awaiting the Holy Week of 1724, when they were suddenly confronted with programs announcing that the Passion would again be performed in the Thomaskirche. They protested, and Bach answered that their facilities were inadequate: the gallery was too small, and the organ was a wreck. By immediately tending to these matters, the authorities forced Bach's hand, and on Good Friday, 1724, the Nikolaikirche heard the *St. John Passion*.

This was the first of possibly five Passions that Bach wrote, of which two unquestionably authentic ones remain. A third, though in his handwriting, is probably a copy of a work by another composer. When Bach died, his manuscripts were divided among the members of his family, the Passions falling to Karl Philipp Emanuel and Wilhelm Friedemann. The methodical younger son cherished his share, and the *John* and *Matthew* are therefore preserved. But the ne'er-do-well Wilhelm Friedemann lost the three entrusted to him. His loss of these has given rise to a literature of conjecture as to their nature and quality that almost equals the commentaries on the existing Passions.

Bach was not fortunate in the libretto for the *John Passion*. He used, in addition to direct quotations from the eighteenth and nineteenth chapters of the Gospel according to John, parts of a poetic paraphrase of the same material by Barthold Heinrich Brockes, a Hamburg town councilor. Despite its confused and feeble character, Brockes' libretto was much favored by other eighteenth-century composers, including Handel. Bach attempted to improve on Brockes, and achieved passages whose absurdity surpasses even the original. His work on the text clearly evidences the harried spirit of a man writing against time, and the music itself shows traces of the same hurry. The whole work produces a certain disjointed effect that certainly was not part of the composer's plan. But the *John Passion* was written as part of a church service in which every circumstance conspired to bridge what modern concertgoers may feel are gaps in the formal structure.

The *John Passion* opens with a massive chorus done in Bach's largest manner. It is, with the possible exception of the alto aria, "*Es ist vollbracht*," the most effective section of the work. Certain portions are positively operatic in their impact, notably in the Golgotha music, where the mighty catechism of the full chorus is answered by a solo voice, producing a moment of piercing, intolerable tragedy. Although the rest of the *Passion* is not at this intense pitch, there are many surpassingly fine pages evoking despair and triumph, interspersed with passages of the most appealing tenderness. And yet, with its many excellences, the *John Passion* has a way of creaking at the joints: the episodes succeed each other without cumulating. The work in its present state was twice revised by Bach; even so, it remains a stringing together of musically unequal units.

The *St. Matthew Passion* leaves no such impression of makeshift. From the first moment, when the choral floodgates are flung open, to the tragic revery at Christ's tomb, this tremendous drama, which is scored for three choruses, two orchestras, two organs, and soloists, and which takes three hours to perform, is deeply felt, flawlessly designed, and magnificently achieved. First produced at the Thomaskirche in 1729, it shows such unfailing command of the material that it lends weight to the well-attested theory that another Passion, now lost, intervened between it and the *John Passion*. The *Matthew* is, by comparison, a revolutionary work.

In the first place, Bach was not plagued by a poor libretto. Christian Friedrich Henrici, a local postal official who wrote under the name of Picander, had collaborated with him as early as 1725, and now provided a workmanlike and thoroughly adequate text, which, considering the abject state of German poetry at the time, was no mean task. It was so exactly what Bach needed that we can assume that Picander was an amiable man who probably was happy to take any reasonable suggestion from his collaborator. He cleverly devised the *Matthew Passion* libretto so that the two sections are contrasted dramatically: the first is lyrical, reflective, almost a commentary, until, in its closing moments, Judas' betrayal of Christ foreshadows the swiftly moving catastrophe of the second section. The tragic problem is set in part one: in part two it is resolved. In this *Passion*—Bach's supreme flight in the purely German manner—the collaborators limn the Christ loved by the simple Lutheran congregations, the human being who suffered for their redemption, rather than the God incarnate glorified in the ultramontane splendors of the B minor Mass.

The key to the vastness of the *Matthew Passion* is Bach's profound conception of the Christ. In the *John Passion* he made no attempt to differentiate musically between the words of Christ and those of the other actors in the drama; in the *Matthew* His voice is distinguished from the others by having a string accompaniment, one that adds luminosity and warmth to the tonal color whenever He speaks. Bach's sensitive response to text is evident in many works, but in the *Matthew Passion* he surpassed himself. At no point has he failed the slightest promptings of the words: the merest syntactical shift finds its counterpart in some subtle alteration in musical texture. Yet it is never precious or *over*subtilized: the design persists, the structure coheres. If at any moment Bach seems to clothe his text too realistically (and it must be admitted that the musical cockcrow strains the integrity of the structure), he recovers himself immediately by some miraculous touch.

The *Matthew Passion* was received with a bewilderment of which one of Bach's pupils has left an account: "Some high officials and well-born ladies in one of the galleries began to sing the first Choral with great devotion from their books. But as the theatrical music proceeded, they were thrown into the greatest wonderment, saying to each other, 'What does it all mean?' while one old lady, a widow, exclaimed, 'God help us! 'tis surely an Opera-comedy!'" Such a reception, which must have been Bach's common lot as a composer, was not calculated to improve his touchy disposition, and his wrangling with the authorities vexed them so that when the councilors met to appoint a new rector, one of them expressed the fervent hope that they would "fare better in this appointment than in that of the cantor." Their pent-up anger at Bach's grand manners and arrogant disregard of his pedagogical duties finally burst forth in a threat to sequestrate his moneys.

But if the town fathers were fed up, so was Bach. It is certain that by October, 1730, he was ready to relinquish the cantorate and go elsewhere. It is to his straining at the leash that we owe the most personal of his extant letters, written to Georg Erdmann, a childhood friend who was then the Tsarina's agent at Danzig. "Unfortunately," Bach wrote, "I have discovered that (1) this situation is not as good as it was represented to be, (2) various *accidentia* relative to my *station* have been withdrawn, (3) living is expensive, and (4) my masters are strange folk with very little care for music in them. Consequently, I am subjected to constant annoyance, jealousy, and persecution. It is therefore in my mind, with God's assistance, to seek my *fortune* elsewhere. If your Honor knows of or should hear of a *convenable station* in your town, I beg you to let me have your valuable *recommendation*. Nothing will be wanting on my part to give *satisfaction*, show diligence, and justify

your much esteemed support. My present *station* is worth about
700 kronen a year, and if the death-rate is higher than *ordinaire-
ment*, my *accidentia* increase in *proportion*; but Leipzig is a healthy
place, and for the past year, as it happens, I have received about
100 kronen less than usual in funeral *accidentia*. The cost of living,
too, is so *excessive* that I was better off in Thuringia on 400 kronen."

After his bill of complaints, with its pettifogging note, Bach
passes to a newsy paragraph about his home life: "And now I must
tell you something of my domestic circumstances. My first wife
died at Cöthen and I have married again. Of my first marriage
are living three sons and a daughter, whom your Honor saw at
Weimar and may be pleased to remember. Of my second marriage
one son and two daughters are living. My eldest son is a *studiosus
juris*, the other two are at school here in the *prima* and *secunda
classis*; my eldest daughter as yet is unmarried. My children by my
second wife are still young; the eldest boy is six. All my children
are born *musici*; from my own *familie*, I assure you, I can arrange a
concert *vocaliter* and *instrumentaliter*; my wife, in particular, has a
very clear soprano, and my eldest daughter can give a good account of herself too."

But things cleared up. The bumbling old rector, whose dotage
had been unequal to the task of suppressing faction, was succeeded
by a man of very different stripe, Johann Matthias Gesner. A man
of generous affections and wide taste, and himself a leader of the
new humanism that was warming the intellectual currents of
eighteenth-century Germany, he immediately appreciated Bach,
and exerted his sympathetic nature to soothe the troubled waters.
For nearly five years the cantor enjoyed comparative calm, almost
as if he were gathering strength for the bitter controversies of the
late thirties.

In 1729, Bach was appointed honorary *Kapellmeister* to his old
friend, Christian of Saxe-Weissenfels. About this time, he began
going frequently to Dresden, ostensibly to take his favorite son,
Wilhelm Friedemann, to the opera, but actually to canvass possibilities for advancement at the Elector's court. Here he met the
now-forgotten, but then world-famous, Johann Adolf Hasse, and
his dazzlingly lovely wife, Faustina. Hasse was *Hofkapellmeister*, and
divided the honors of the royal opera with Faustina, he as composer, she as prima donna. It is doubtful that Hasse cared more for

Bach's compositions than the Thomascantor did for his. Bach's attitude toward opera in general is summed up in his "Well, Friedemann, shall we go to Dresden and hear the pretty tunes?" In 1731, when he was there to hear the *première* of one of Hasse's operas, he gave a recital at the Sophienkirche, after which the *Hofkapellmeister* joined the chorus of those who hymned Bach as the king of organists. This recital, coming after seven years' retirement as an organist, launched Bach on a new career of trips to near-by towns to "examine and display" organs.

In 1733, Augustus II, Elector of Saxony and King of Poland, passed to whatever reward comes to a man who has begotten three hundred and sixty-five illegitimate children. During the period of mourning decreed by the court, less music was used in the churches, and Bach's duties were therefore light. He used his leisure to concoct a Latin Kyrie and Gloria—parts of the Mass common to the Roman and Lutheran services—that might aptly accompany a request to a Catholic sovereign for the office of *Hofcompositeur*, a distinction that would strengthen his hand in Leipzig. Unfortunately, the gift and petition found Augustus III immersed in the troubled waters of Polish politics, and Bach had to wait three years for his appointment. Although the Kyrie and Gloria seem never to have been performed for Augustus, this did not deter Bach: in five years he welded them into a structure so vast that it could never be performed as part of any church service. This was his supreme masterpiece.

The B minor Mass is the greatest composition ever written. Its sustained sublimity would seem to predicate Bach, the very vessel of divine inspiration, creating it whole in one mighty surge. Actually, it was composed and arranged in an amazingly desultory manner. If, as many believe, it was finished in 1740, it had taken as long to complete as *The Last Judgment*. But Bach, unlike Michelangelo, had not been working exclusively on his masterpiece: quite literally, he did it in his spare time. It does not even consist of entirely new material—though the samples he had sent to Augustus III did: throughout, he borrowed copiously from himself. Of the twenty-six divisions of the Mass, several are adaptations from sacred cantatas, and at least one had its ultimate source in an unquestionably secular piece. Naturally, a work put together in this fashion does not have the same kind of unity as a Mozart symphony or a Beethoven quartet. But it is doubtful whether the conglomerate text of a Mass demands this kind of unity. What holds the B minor together, and gives the impression of a unifying design, is its consistently Bachian character.

The Mass opens with a five-part fugue, 126 bars long, whose severe and uncompromising woefulness prepares the least aware for this fearsome journey into a new musical world. The very form of this Kyrie sets it apart from the intimate German utterances of the cantatas and Passions: we hear once again, after more than a century, the accents of Palestrina. Luther suddenly recedes into the remote distance, and the vast, impersonal voice of Rome is heard. As the huge liturgical machine gets under way, Spitta says, "The solo songs stand among the choruses like isolated valleys between gigantic heights, serving to relieve the eye that tries to take in the whole composition." Bach moves among the complexities of the text with perfect ease, and even at that part of the Credo where the Nicene Fathers fell into doggerel keeps to the lofty plane. And when the text itself is most dramatic, as in the *Resurrexit*, when the tragic despair of the *Crucifixus* is dissipated in an outburst of ecstatic joy, Bach creates page after page of a majestic intensity unequaled in music.

The history of the B minor Mass is unique. Never given in its entirety during Bach's lifetime, it did not have its first complete performance until well into the nineteenth century. Today it is the most famous, and possibly the most popular, of his larger compositions. Bach Societies everywhere devote much of their time and energy to "working up" the B minor, most often with indifferent success. The Bach Festival, at Bethlehem, Pennsylvania, annually presents it with pious attention to detail; it attracts capacity audiences from all over the world.

In glaring contrast to the ever-growing popularity of the Mass is the unworthy fate of the vast majority of Bach's vocal works. Of more than two hundred cantatas, as well as a considerable miscellany of pieces going under other names, but few have been performed in the United States. Yet these, far more than the Passions and the B minor Mass, represent the intimate side of Bach's creative nature; not only did he earn his daily bread by composing them (sometimes at the rate of one a week), but they were themselves the bread of life to him, based as they are on those simple

Lutheran hymn tunes that were his first musical loves. The cantatas, too, rather than the Passions and the great Mass, give us the most varied and nearly complete picture of Bach as a vocal writer. They were composed for every Sunday and great feast of the church year, and range from the most solemn and poignant lamentations to canticles of pure joy. Some are mystical and contemplative, others so dramatic that they lack only action to be operas.

Those few cantatas that have been made accessible through occasional performances, transcriptions, and recordings are masterpieces in small. The Easter cantata, *Christ lag in Totesbanden*, is a stark frenzied commentary on the death sacrifice of the Son of God. In *Ein feste Burg*, Bach, with the foursquare Gospel in his hand, thunders forth his simple German credo. And in portions of *Wachet auf* the music reaches such passionate heights that it has been called the greatest love music before *Tristan und Isolde*. The choice of the cantatas performed has admittedly been fortuitous: there is every reason to believe that the untapped remainder is an inexhaustible supply of great music. One of the reasons heard most frequently for not giving these works is that Bach did not know how to write for the voice. This is merely an excuse for singers too lazy to learn more than the bare fundamentals of their craft. Some difficulties arise from the fact that notes now represent a much higher pitch than they did in Bach's day. Even allowing for this, his vocal music at its most complex is not unsingable; rather, it is the most rewarding a conscientious singer can hope for, as it exploits the fullest resources of the human voice.

Only twenty-four of the cantatas are written to secular texts, and even many of these are predominantly religious in feeling. But in a few of them Bach shows a refreshingly topical slant. The "Coffee" Cantata satirizes a Leipzig that, when coffee was still a fad of the wealthy, boasted eight licensed coffeehouses. *Der Streit zwischen Phoebus und Pan* strikes a more personal note because of its connection with Johann Adolf Scheibe, a voluminous composer and criticaster Bach had blackballed for a job, and who took his revenge by indicting the bases of his enemy's musical style. Bach, in lampooning Scheibe as Midas, got back at him much as Wagner was to scuttle his enemies in *Die Meistersinger*. Scheibe, however, probably reflected the bafflement of even the more cultured among Bach's audience when exposed to his complex style.

"This great man," Scheibe wrote, after the conventional tribute to Bach's prowess at the organ, "would be the wonder of the universe if his compositions displayed more agreeable qualities, were less turgid and sophisticated, more simple and natural in character. His music is exceedingly difficult to play, because the efficiency of his own limbs sets his standard; he expects singers and players to be as agile with voice and instrument as he is with his fingers, which is impossible. Grace notes and embellishments, such as a player instinctively supplies, he puts down in actual symbols, a habit which not only sacrifices the harmonic beauty of his music but also blurs its melodic line. All his parts, too, are equally melodic, so that one cannot distinguish the principal tune among them. In short, he is as a musician what Herr von Lohenstein* used to be as a poet: pomposity diverts them both from a natural to an artificial style, changing what might have been sublime into the obscure. In regard to both of them, we wonder at an effort so labored, and, since nothing comes of it, so futile."

As Bach, reviving *Phoebus und Pan* in 1749, satirized a new adversary as Midas, it is probable that he became reconciled with Scheibe. Less happy was the outcome of a long and bitter controversy with Gesner's successor as rector of the Thomasschule, Johann August Ernesti. Although his reputation as a classical scholar has justly dwindled, there is no doubt that Ernesti stood forth as one of the leaders in the movement to free institutions of learning, as Charles Sanford Terry says, "from the standards of the age in which they originated, from the classical trammels of the Renaissance, and the theological bonds of the Reformation. . . ." As Ernesti naturally tried to shift the Thomasschule's emphasis from music to a general curriculum, his activity conflicted with the cantor's personal interests. Bach was unconsciously shunted into the position of a pigheaded opponent of the *Zeitgeist*, for, after sifting all the petty details of this dreary tug of war, it is clear that the equally pigheaded Ernesti was on the side of progress. After keeping the rector, the cantor, the students, and sundry town busybodies in an uproar for several years, the struggle seems to have died of sheer inanition. Or perhaps Bach's appointment as *Hofcompositeur* in 1736 salved his injured feelings, and made his ad-

* D. C. von Lohenstein (1665–1684) wrote numerous wooden dramas.

versaries feel that they had best not proceed farther against so lofty a personage.

Augustus III asked Baron Karl von Kayserling to deliver the long-delayed appointment to the composer. This envoy's insomnia called forth one of Bach's most delightful clavier works. Kayserling, a man of culture, kept a private musician named Goldberg, a pupil of Bach and his son Friedemann. For this David, whose chief duty was to relieve his wakeful hours with cheerful melodies, the amiable Saul commissioned Bach to supply a new musical balm, and the result has been known ever since as the "Goldberg" Variations. They doubtless performed their work well, and Kayserling affectionately referred to them as "my variations." He paid off like a true grandee, sending Bach one hundred louis d'or in a golden goblet. The insinuating and delicious suite has had a notable progeny, for from it stem the tremendous *"Eroica"* and "Diabelli" Variations of Beethoven and, less directly, Brahms' achievements in the form.

In giving the title of *Hofcompositeur* to Bach, Augustus III had set the official seal on a creative faculty that was well-nigh spent. In 1736 the master still had fourteen years to live, but aside from a mere handful of cantatas and a few finishing touches on the B minor Mass, his vocal work was behind him. The Dresden appointment was far from an empty honor: it involved frequent attendance at court on ceremonial occasions. Bach was often away playing and testing organs. In his spare time he was editing and arranging his works, preparing for death by putting his remains in order, as great men often do. He paused from his labors in 1744 to complete the second part of *The Well-Tempered Clavichord*, which had been composed as study pieces for his second family just as the first part had been written for his elder children.

The widespread ramifications of his first family, as well as the educational needs of his second, now took up more and more of Bach's time. Wilhelm Friedemann, first at Dresden and then at Halle, seemed to be starting the brilliant career his doting father hoped for him (mercifully he managed to check until after the old man's death an un-Bachian talent for loose living that finally wrecked his life). Johann Gottfried Bernhard was less considerate. After running out on his organist's job—and numerous debts—he disappeared, and when next heard of had died of fever. Karl

Philipp Emanuel, though less endowed with native genius than
Wilhelm Friedemann, had inherited his father's steadfast character, and at an early age was on the way to becoming the most distinguished musician of his generation.

In 1740 Karl Philipp Emanuel, though technically a Saxon subject, accepted a post at the court of Frederick the Great, who was
about to launch an attack on Augustus III, Austria's ally. He was
on excellent terms with the flute-playing King, whom he often
accompanied, and was promoted in 1746 to the position of *Kam-
mermusikus*. When Emanuel's first son was born, Bach doubtless
would have gone to Berlin to attend the christening had not Frederick chosen that very month—November, 1745—for investing
Leipzig. Bach had to wait two years to see his first grandson. Taking Wilhelm Friedemann with him, he set out for the Prussian
capital. Emanuel, who was proud of his father, knew the music-
loving sovereign would appreciate Bach's playing, and informed
the King that he was coming.

When told of Bach's arrival in Potsdam, Frederick was just sitting down to participate in his usual evening concert. He rose
excitedly, and exclaimed, "Gentlemen, old Bach is here!" Commanded to join the King at once, Bach appeared in his traveling
clothes. Frederick greeted him warmly, high-flown compliments
were exchanged, and the old cantor was brought face to face with
an instrument he had never seen before—a piano. He immediately
sat down and improvised fugally on a theme that the King gave
him there and then. He disliked the instrument, but gave so magnificent a performance that Frederick invited him to return the
next day, give an organ recital, and again attend him in the
evening.

Back in Leipzig, prompted both by his admiration of the King's
theme and his eagerness to advance Emanuel's fortunes by a diplomatic stroke, Bach composed a musical gift for Frederick. Using
the theme as the basis of several complicated fugues and canons,
and adding a grateful flute part, Bach devised the so-called *Musikalisches Opfer*, had it engraved, and sent the first sections to Potsdam
with an unusually flowery letter of dedication. It is problematical
whether Frederick, who collected great men as an entomologist
collects specimens, quite realized that he was crowning the mortal
career of the greatest of all composers.

Bach did not forget the King's theme. It haunted his mind, and he finally arrived at the idea of using a condensed version of it as a guinea pig to be subjected to every possible contrapuntal operation. He called these experiments simply "counterpoints," and there is not a scrap of evidence that he ever intended them to be played. He did not even specify the medium for which they were intended—if, indeed, they were intended for anything more than object lessons. But his editors got hold of these "counterpoints," as well as some fragments that have no earthly connection with them, and published the odd assortment as *Die Kunst der Fuge*. It has been adapted for solo piano, for two pianos, for string quartet, for orchestra. And it has been selected by Bach cultists as the very ark of their covenant with an esoteric Johann Sebastian of their own imagining.

Heading those amused at this sanctification of the "counterpoints" would undoubtedly be Bach himself. The truth is that most of these diabolically clever solutions of contrapuntal puzzles are thankless in performance, while the few with real musical appeal do not sufficiently relieve the crushing tedium of listening to *Die Kunst der Fuge* as a whole. The less extravagant fugues rank with the best in *The Well-Tempered Clavichord*, but they are not enhanced by being played with others of which Parry said, "Bach possibly wrote them just to see if it could be done; he certainly would not have classed them as musical works unless as extremely abstruse jokes."

The fact that *Die Kunst der Fuge* breaks off abruptly—in a fugue on the notes B A C H (B is B flat, H is B natural in German notation)—tells dramatically the failure of Bach's health. Whether he became blind at this point, or, what is more likely, suffered a paralytic stroke, is not known. The certain facts are that by the summer of 1749 he was so incapacitated that there was talk of appointing his successor as *Stadtcantor*, and that in January of the following year he entrusted his tired eyes to the knife of the "Chevalier John Taylor, Opthalmiater." It is difficult to say whether Taylor was a quack or was consistently called in too late, but his principal claim to fame is that he operated with varying degrees of unsuccess on three of the greatest men of the eighteenth century—Bach, Handel, and Gibbon.

On July 18, after six months of darkness prescribed by Taylor as a postoperative requisite, during which Bach chafed at the inactivity and reacted poorly to the dosage, he definitely rallied. It was then decided to admit light into the sickroom, and test his sight. He could distinguish objects in the room and the faces of his anxious family. But the excitement was too much for him: a few hours later he had a stroke. For ten days he lay unconscious and in a raging fever. Toward evening, on July 28, 1750, he died. Before his burial, three days later, the town councilors had appointed his successor at the Thomasschule.

At the time of his death, Bach was known throughout Germany, but as his fame was chiefly that of an organ virtuoso, it did not endure into an age when the organ ceased to dominate music. He was soon forgotten by everyone except his family and a few of his pupils. His small estate, consisting mainly of musical instruments, theological tomes, and household furnishings, did not suffice to maintain his widow and four children who were still minors. Four of his grown children seem not to have lifted a finger to help Anna Magdalena. Karl Philipp Emanuel was the sole exception: he took the youthful Johann Christian to live with him, and helped to form that facile talent which later made "the English Bach" London's most popular composer of Italianate opera. Anna Magdalena survived her husband for ten years, and died in the poorhouse. The site of Bach's grave was lost for almost a hundred years, and his body was recovered late in the nineteenth century only by a clever piecing together of records. The inscription that now marks his sepulture is even more stark than that on Palestrina's:

JOHANN SEBASTIAN BACH

1685–1750

Chapter III

George Frideric Handel

(Halle, February 23, 1685–April 14, 1759, London)

EXCEPT for the fact that Handel and Bach were born only a month apart, and both in Saxony, they had nothing in common but genius. Bach was a small-town musician who devoted his unsurpassed gifts mainly to the service of the church; Handel wrote for a metropolitan audience, and spent most of his life in the world's largest city. If he was not precisely obscure, Bach's fame was limited to Germany except among professional musicians; Handel was for many years the most celebrated composer alive. Time has commented ironically on this situation. The fame of the Thomascantor keeps growing, and shows no sign of slackening this side of deification, but the great god of the eighteenth century has fallen from his pedestal. The stricken deity lies neglected while the world comes perilously near to overrating Bach—if such a thing is possible. We hear little of the greater Handel, and too much of that little in bad superproductions of *Messiah*.

George Frideric Handel,* unquestionably one of the greatest musicians the world has ever known, was born at Halle on February 23, 1685. His father, Georg Händel, was a rich barber-surgeon, and one of the town's leading citizens. At the age of sixty-one he married as his second wife a clergyman's daughter, and George Frideric was the first surviving child of this union of highly respected and thoroughly mediocre parents, in whose veins flowed not a single drop of musical blood. The old barber-surgeon was not only unmusical—he had an aversion to musicians, and was determined that his son should become a lawyer. Nevertheless, a relentless artistic urge drove the child to find an outlet for his musical cravings, and in some way (just how, nobody knows) he learned to play the organ and the clavier. When he was seven years old, his father, who was court surgeon at Weissenfels, took him there on a visit. He played the organ for the Duke, who was so delighted at the lad's obvious talent that he advised his amazed and nettled surgeon to get the boy a music teacher.

* The form in which, from 1719 to his death, he himself signed his name.

At Halle they found the very man—Friedrich Wilhelm Zachau, organist of the Liebfrauenkirche. Romain Rolland, a close student of seventeenth- and eighteenth-century music, testifies to the talents of this forgotten musician. From the first, the relations between master and pupil were of the warmest. Zachau instantly recognized the child's gifts, and lavished the greatest care on training him as both instrumentalist and composer. But his most valuable service to Handel, as it turned out, was introducing him to the music of other lands, particularly Italy. While studying with Zachau, Handel seems to have begun composing with the unstinted fluency he never lost. When the brilliant pupil needed refreshment, a visit to Berlin was arranged. The eleven-year-old boy apparently made this considerable journey alone, and was received cordially at court, which was enjoying a flicker of brilliance under the dashing leadership of the Electress Sophia. Evidently Handel had influential sponsors, for he was commanded to play before their Electoral Highnesses. They were so impressed by his pyrotechnics at the clavier that the Elector offered to send him to Italy for further study. But Georg Händel was enraged by the idea, and ordered his son's immediate return to Halle. Probably while on the way home, the lad was overtaken by news of his father's death on February 11, 1697.

Five years later, after preparatory studies, Handel entered the University of Halle as a law student, in deference to his father's wishes. Thereafter he did not strain his filial piety: a month after matriculating, he accepted a temporary appointment as organist at the Domkirche. Only a recognition of his extraordinary gifts could have persuaded the tight-lipped Calvinists to give this responsible position to a seventeen-year-old college boy not of their faith. The youthful Georg Philipp Telemann, even in 1702 well on the way to becoming the most prolific of composers, passed through Halle about this time, and wrote a eulogy of the "already famous Handel." It was on the cards that his native town could not long hold this prodigious boy. In 1703, probably after consulting Zachau, he responded to the lure of Hamburg, the capital of German opera.

The musical tsar of this busy seaport was the notorious Reinhard Keiser, then at the height of a variegated career. Handel naturally gravitated to Keiser's opera house, where he was soon playing the violin and imbibing the fecund ideas and lyric melodies of this vest-pocket Mozart. It is probable that Handel's relations with Keiser were on a rather formal basis, but he found a warm though capricious friend in Johann Mattheson, another law student who had turned to music. A man of wide versatility, Mattheson sang, composed, and conducted. When deafness caused him to abandon these activities, he turned to writing, and left behind him more than eighty books containing invaluable source material about the music of his epoch, as well as contributions to musical theory that are still significant.

Handel and Mattheson had much to offer each other, and their common youth made interchange easy. Handel was eager to know all about the workings of an opera house bulwarked by a quarter century of brilliant achievement. Mattheson, who had already had an opera produced, willingly played the city mentor to the new-comer, whose genius he immediately—and enviously—sensed. They became inseparable, and when Mattheson went to Lübeck to try out as Buxtehude's successor at the Marienkirche, Handel accompanied him. When they heard that the new organist was required to marry Buxtehude's daughter, they took one look at the *Fräulein*, and then did what Bach is said to have done a few years later—ran as fast as they could.

Mattheson's *Cleopatra*, produced sumptuously in 1704, caused a stir quite out of proportion to its musical worth: it was such a popular success that Keiser's star temporarily waned. Mattheson, who fancied himself declaiming the romantic lines of Antony, installed Handel in the conductor's place at the clavier, and himself resumed the conducting only after dying on the stage. One day, Handel, no longer able to brook Mattheson's overweening vanity, refused to relinquish his place. Violent words and fisticuffs were exchanged, and the audience fanned the flames by taking sides in a lusty Hamburger fashion. After the curtain was rung down, the erstwhile friends, followed by the enthusiastic audience, repaired to the Gänsemarkt, and fell to with their swords. Numberless millions might have been deprived of the "Hallelujah" Chorus and the "Largo" had not Mattheson's sword shattered against a button on Handel's coat. This anticlimax seems to have stopped the actual fighting. After a sullen truce of some weeks, they were reconciled, and with a gala celebration began the rehearsals of Handel's first opera.

Almira, which had its *première* on January 8, 1705, with Mattheson as first tenor, was notable for the splendor of its sets. Although written to an absurd and bombastic libretto, it had many dramatic high spots which Handel had treated with delightful freshness and the sure touch of a born writer for the stage. It was a smash hit, ran for almost seven weeks, and was retired only because Handel wished to mount his second opera, *Nero.* * Keiser, who had turned the book of *Almira* over to Handel because he was too lazy to write music for it himself, was enraged by the success of the parvenu. He and his cronies set about to destroy the one man who could have rehabilitated the tottering fortunes of their opera house, and succeeded in driving him from Hamburg.

Not that he would have remained, anyway. His somewhat languid interest in Italy had been whetted by a meeting with Giovan Gastone de' Medici, the dissolute but music-loving tag end of the once illustrious Florentine family. Only one thing could have induced this gay prince to linger in murky, bourgeois Hamburg—the opera. Much taken by Handel's talents and personality, he tried to persuade him to migrate south. But the young composer did not act upon this urging until the machinations of his enemies and the decline of the opera house made him realize that Hamburg was no longer the best arena for his efforts. So, sometime before the Christmas of 1706, he decided to stake all on an Italian hegira. He set out armed with a paltry two hundred ducats and a letter to Giovan Gastone's brother Ferdinand.

Stopping in Florence merely long enough to pay his respects to the Medici, compose twenty cantatas, rewrite part of *Almira*, and begin a new opera, Handel posted to Rome, doubtless pondering the stinginess of Ferdinand, who had once answered Alessandro Scarlatti's plea for a loan by saying, "I will pray for you." The Holy City, where opera was under a papal ban, was little more generous, and Handel was soon back in Florence with the completed score of his new opera, *Rodrigo.* Ferdinand, who had tired of Scarlatti's learned and melancholy music, sponsored its production, and so enthusiastic was he over this lighthearted work that he loosed his purse strings, and presented its composer with fifty pounds and a set of dishes. Having successfully set an Italian text and mastered the flowing Italian vocal style, Handel turned his

* *Love Obtained Through Blood and Murder,* or *Nero,* ran for three nights.

thoughts to Venice, still lit by the late sun of the Renaissance. Here, in 1637, had been built the first public opera house, and it was still the most opera-loving city in the world.

But Venice turned a cold shoulder to Handel's hopes. The doors of its fifteen opera houses remained shut against him, though high society lionized him as a virtuoso. Alessandro Scarlatti's son Domenico, destined to revolutionize the bases of keyboard style, and to eclipse the fame of a father deified by the connoisseurs of the eighteenth century, first heard Handel at a costume ball. After listening spellbound to the masked performer, he exclaimed, "That must either be the famous Saxon or the Devil!" The friendship thus warmly inaugurated endured for many years. But of decisive importance in shaping Handel's career were encounters with Prince Ernst Augustus of Hanover and the English envoy to Venice, the Duke of Manchester. The former engineered Handel's appointment as *Kapellmeister* to his brother, the Elector of Hanover, later George I of England. Manchester pressed him to seek his fortune in England, and promised to help him when he got there.

Handel did not take advantage of these invitations immediately. Instead, he traveled southward with Domenico Scarlatti, and once again laid siege to the papal capital. Glowing reports of the high excellences of *Rodrigo* had preceded him, and this time the Roman nobles vied with each other for the honor of entertaining him. The Arcadian Academy, a society of a few artists and many dilettantes, feted the dashing Saxon, and two of its most lavish patrons were his hosts. Prince Ruspoli built a private theater in his palace for the *première* of Handel's first oratorio, *La Resurrezione*, which was really an opera disguised to evade the papal ban. Its overwhelming success set all Rome talking, and Handel was prompted to try his hand at another oratorio. But though produced under the even more distinguished patronage of Cardinal Ottobuoni, nephew of a Pope, and furnished with a libretto by another cardinal, *Il Trionfo del tempo e del disinganno* fell flat, partly because the music was too difficult for the orchestra assembled by the renowned Corelli, Ottobuoni's concertmaster. The work haunted Handel's imagination, and almost fifty years later his last oratorio was called *The Triumph of Time and Design.*

Ever on the search for preferment and sympathetic understanding of his music, Handel now drifted to Naples, where the story of social success and lack of solid opportunity was repeated. For a time this child of the North surrendered to the lure of the southern paradise, storing his phenomenal memory with its catchy folk tunes. But the only ponderable result of a year's stay developed from a meeting with Cardinal Grimani, the Imperial Viceroy. This cultivated scion of a princely Venetian family gave him the libretto for his next opera, *Agrippina*, and laid plans for its production at the theater the Grimani controlled in Venice. The certainty of a public performance under such propitious circumstances roused Handel from his languor, and in three weeks he had completed the score. With the precious manuscript in his traveling bags, he returned to Rome, and lingered there until time for the new opera to go into rehearsal.

On December 26, 1709, *Agrippina* began a spectacular run of twenty-seven nights at the theater of San Giovanni Crisostomo. It was, beyond question, the best opera Handel had yet written, and as Venetian approval was the touchstone of musical success, his Italian reputation was made. The echoes of the frantic applause carried Handel's name across Italy and throughout Europe, and in Venice itself he was more important than the Doge. He had justified his rash invasion of Italy, which now lay prostrate at his feet. But he had no settled future, and while he was pondering the next step Prince Ernst Augustus of Hanover intervened. Night after night this already stanch Handelian had sat entranced in the royal loge at the Crisostomo. The manifold beauties of *Agrippina* convinced him more than ever that Handel was the man for his brother's court. He urgently renewed his invitation, and this time Handel accepted.

Hanover offered as ideal conditions as any musician could hope to find in eighteenth-century Germany: the most beautiful opera house in the country and a perfectly drilled corps of singers and instrumentalists. This happy state of affairs had been brought about by the unwearying efforts of Agostino Steffani, one of the most remarkable figures of the age. This charming Venetian—a jack-of-all-trades with a touch of genius for each—was still officiating as *Kapellmeister* when Handel arrived. They had met in Italy, and had struck up a cordial relationship based on mutual esteem. It is not known whether Steffani graciously yielded place to the younger man, or whether misunderstandings with his orchestra and singers forced his hand. In any event, Handel soon became *Kapellmeister* with his predecessor's blessing. Although their contact had been fleeting, Steffani's influence was decisive in the final molding of Handel's Italian manner, and Handel never forgot this debt.

The new *Kapellmeister*'s first act was to ask for leave of absence to go to England. Why did he go? Probably plain restlessness and curiosity—a desire for new worlds to conquer. England was wearing her gloomiest autumnal aspect when he landed on her shores. Everything was against him. He did not know a word of English. The few German musicians resident in London looked upon the newcomer as a source of danger to their embattled positions. And in Queen Anne's England music was in a state of coma brought about by a chain of lamentable circumstances and a dearth of national talent. The structure of English music, founded on so fair a base by Dunstable, gaining high-vaulted nave and transepts with Orlando Gibbons and William Byrd, and crowned with a gleaming spire by Henry Purcell, had suddenly collapsed.

Fifteen years before Handel's advent in 1710, Purcell had died prematurely. It is idle to speculate what he would have done if he had lived longer. In his single opera, *Dido and Aeneas*, he achieved perfection; though an indefatigable writer for the stage, he never wrote another true opera. He was too busy with anthems, catches, chamber pieces, organ voluntaries, and the other occasional music demanded by the exigencies of his numerous official positions. No matter whether examined through a microscope or a telescope, Purcell is a baffling figure. Artistically speaking, he is a sport: he had no recognizable ancestors; more, no heirs claimed his rich musical estate, though Handel borrowed what he pleased of it. Indeed, Handel's "Englishness" is exactly that borrowing, and is betrayed in his mighty choral effects, his widely spaced harmonies, and the pungent utterances of his woodwinds and brasses. The overwhelming choruses conceived by the Saxon invader, and sung at vast tribal festivals these past two hundred years, have served to blot out Purcell's fame. Yet he was a very great composer, far ahead of the resources of his age, speaking in a voice that was at once unmistakably his own and that of Restoration England. No one has less deserved obscurity.

Musically, then, England was a sorry place when Handel arrived there. The drying up of the national genius had left the field vacant for foreigners. Thus far, however, though English society loved Italian opera, no company had been successful in establishing itself. There were plenty of good singers available, but no composers of sufficient talent to make society venture out among the footpads and murderers who infested the London streets and lanes at night. Drury Lane and the Queen's Theater in the Haymarket were in such rank sections of town that the diminishing audiences feared for their lives going to and from the opera. Frequently pockets were picked and noses broken in the theaters themselves. With box-office receipts steadily falling, and society forsaking town in despairing ennui, it was evident that only a novelty of high quality would save the day. Handel was exactly the man to fill the bill.

The astute impresario of the Queen's Theater, Aaron Hill, clearly recognized the desperate situation he was in, and as soon as Handel arrived, commissioned him to set a preposterous libretto based on Tasso's *Gerusalemme liberata*. Within a fortnight Handel gave Hill a masterpiece, and this, under the title of *Rinaldo*, was first presented to an unsuspecting London on February 24, 1711. Its success was beyond Hill's wildest dreams: overnight Handel added England to his empire. In vain did Addison, himself the producer of an unsuccessful opera, fulminate against *Rinaldo;* in vain did Steele, with an ax to grind in the concert field, come to his friend's aid. *Rinaldo* ran through the town like wildfire: society danced it, whistled it, warbled it—and even returned to London to hear it. Between the *première* and June, it played fifteen times to packed houses. John Walsh, who published the score, made so much money out of it that Handel remarked bitterly that Walsh should compose the next opera, and he would publish it.

Although Handel continued to compose operas for a quarter of a century, he never surpassed *Rinaldo*. He himself pronounced the air "*Cara sposa*" the best he ever wrote; "*Lascia ch'io pianga*," which he borrowed note for note from *Agrippina*, is scarcely less fine. These lamentations are not, however, characteristic of the opera as a whole: *Rinaldo* brims over with a bright youthful passion that Handel lavished on his scores but, seemingly, not on his personal relationships. It sounds like the music of a young man very much in love, but outside of a not very well attested story of a passing fancy for a singer who had sung in *Rodrigo*, there is not a scrap of evidence that Handel ever submitted to the tenderer emotions. Indeed, except for Sir Isaac Newton, Handel seems to have been the most unemotional man in eighteenth-century England.

At the end of the season, Handel reluctantly left Piccadilly's hospitable drawing rooms, and returned to assume his duties at Hanover. It was a decided letdown after the feverish activity of London, and the opera house, which alone might have made life tolerable for him, was closed. A year later, he applied for another leave of absence, which was granted graciously enough, for the Elector was willing to have so welcome an ambassador of good will in England, where he hoped shortly to reign. Handel was cautioned, however, to return in a "reasonable time." His interpretation of this vague phrase was the most elastic in history: with the exception of flying visits to the Continent and Ireland, he remained in England until his death almost half a century later.

Handel's return was marked by the unsuccessful performance of a rather dull opera he had begun in Hanover. *Teseo*, his next production, was a great success, due both to its superb music and the excellent libretto furnished by Nicolò Haym, who thus began a long and happy collaboration with his great countryman. The libretto was dedicated to Richard Boyle, Earl of Burlington, the most distinguished art patron of the age, and already, at seventeen, an intelligent admirer of Handel's music. After hearing *Teseo*, he invited Handel to take up his abode at Burlington House. Here he came into contact with the social and intellectual elite. Pope and Gay were intimates of the house, the former delicately tasting the music he was to extol, years later, in *The Dunciad*.

But an even more august personage was to shed her favor on Handel. While *Teseo* was still playing to crowded houses, he was setting his first English text, to celebrate the approaching birthday of Queen Anne. The lonely and embittered daughter of James II was so delighted with this *Birthday Ode*, and with the *Te Deum* Handel composed for the fetes in honor of the Peace of Utrecht, that she settled an annual pension of two hundred pounds on him. Poor Anne, whose energies were too often spent in securing petty revenge, was happy to make England seem a paradise for the favorite musician of the Elector of Hanover, whom she detested. But Handel was backing the wrong horse. In August, 1714, Anne did the one thing that has immortalized her: she died. On the same day the hated Hanoverian was proclaimed King.

At first Handel had every reason to fear that his slighted master would retaliate. His name was pointedly missing from among those commanded to compose music for the coronation, and though he kept his pension, he was not summoned to court. But George I loved music passionately—even Thackeray's superb vilification grants that. In 1715 the news that Handel had written another delightful opera was too much for the King: he sulkily missed the first performance, but showed up at the second with two fantastic German ladies (his mistress and his half-sister), and thereafter came regularly during the balance of the opera's run. He and Handel were then formally reconciled.

The bare facts of this reconciliation, which had such bright results for English music, did not please the romancemongers. They told a charmingly whimsical story that is still treasured in the great human hearts of the broadcasting companies. According to this idyl, in 1715 things became so strained that His Majesty's benevolent Master of the Horse thought of a quaint stratagem. While George was making one of his frequent progresses down the Thames, Handel and a band of musicians were to follow closely in another barge, and play music that would melt the King. And everything fell out just as the kindly old official had planned. George was so enchanted with the music that he embraced Handel, and forgave him completely.

There is only one thing wrong with this story: it is not wholly true. Part of the *Water Music* was written and performed in 1715, part in 1717, after the reconciliation between Handel and the King. Instead of being sprung on George as a surprise, the 1715 portions were played at his command for a party on the Thames. He liked it so well that he had it repeated during the evening, though each performance lasted more than an hour. Even in the much truncated form in which the *Water Music* is played to-day (as originally published in 1740 it had twenty-five movements), it can be heard again and again without losing its freshness.

Handel never composed anything more English than the *Water Music*. It is shot through and through with English feeling; it is fashioned with jaunty English rhythms and bold, simple harmonies. The hornpipe, which is one of the most effective sections of the suite, utilizes a form that reaches back at least to Ben Jonson's England. The suite concludes with a robust allegro deciso brimming over with the gusto of living, and full of high, singing brasses that would have delighted Purcell. Written several years before the "Brandenburg" Concertos (the third of which it resembles in rhythmic heartiness), the *Water Music* is the oldest orchestral piece in the standard repertoire. It is difficult to conceive of an age that will not yield to its vigorous masculine beauty.

Handel's reconciliation with George I had doubled his pension. Further to emphasize his favor, the King appointed him music master to the royal granddaughters—an honor, but scarcely a pleasure. And when the sovereign, disgusted with English ways, decided in 1716 to go home to Hanover—he even threatened never to return—he took Handel with him. For the composer this German sojourn was one of almost complete inactivity: the King was too busy with politics and the chase to think about music. Handel paid a visit to Halle, where he saw his mother, and generously relieved Zachau's widow, who had been left in penury. He made a sentimental journey to Ansbach to see his old university chum, Johann Christoph Schmidt, and found him and his large family in pitiable circumstances. Handel's warm sympathies were roused, and as he needed a sympathetic friend to manage his affairs, he invited Schmidt to accompany him to England. Schmidt accepted, and so successfully did the arrangement turn out that he soon became indispensable to his benefactor. He shortly brought over his entire family, and they all seem to have lived with Handel. One of the sons, whose name was anglicized to John Christopher Smith, gradually took over his father's duties as Handel's general factotum. It was to this John Christopher, himself a prolific composer and accomplished organist, that Handel dictated his music when he could no longer see to write. He was warmly attached to the Schmidts. Once, having removed old Schmidt's name from his will in anger, he replaced it with that of John Christopher and tripled the legacy. For Handel, to whom love seemed a stranger, was the most affectionate and appreciative of men.

Handel returned empty-handed to England early in 1717, without even waiting to hear the first performance, in Hamburg, of the sole fruit of his German visit—a Passion based on the same text Bach later used for parts of his *John Passion*. Not only does this work not merit mention in the same breath with Bach's great Passions, but it shows that Handel's genius was not congenial to the sentiments of German Pietism. As he never showed the slightest interest in his Passion, he probably realized that this type of music was not in his province. Poles apart from the profoundly subjective Bach, Handel was too much the magnificent extrovert ever to be a truly religious composer.

Handel's return coincided with a lull in the furore for opera, and for a while he was at a loose end. More, he was in financial difficulties. It is true that he had his pension and fees for teaching the princesses and a few noble pupils, but such an income was nothing to a man who had learned to live lavishly from the high society in which he moved. But, as always, he had a windfall. He met James Brydges, Earl of Carnarvon, an amiable scoundrel who for years had enjoyed the best graft in England as Paymaster of the Forces. The Earl had amassed an immense fortune, and in 1712 had begun the building of Canons, a vast palace near London, reputed to have cost £230,000. The magnificence of life at Canons, and particularly of its musical establishment is thus described by Defoe:

"The chapel hath a choir of vocal and instrumental music, as in the Chapel Royal; and when his grace goes to church, he is attended by his Swiss Guards, ranged as the yeomen of the guards; his music also plays when he is at table; he is served by *gentlemen* in the best order; and I must say that few German sovereign princes live with that magnificence, grandeur, and good order."

The director of the music at Canons was the competent but pedantic Dr. Johann Christoph Pepusch, later to become famous as arranger of *The Beggar's Opera*. Poor Pepusch had no chance at all after his patron met Handel. He got his walking papers in short order, and Handel moved in. Here, in surroundings which were, even for him, of unprecedented luxury, he lived quietly, spending most of his time playing on the clavier or the organ. He occasionally staged a masque in the private theater or gave a formal recital for his master's guests. In 1719, when the Earl was created Duke of Chandos, Handel hymned the great event in a group of cantatas—the "Chandos" Anthems. These little-known works, based almost entirely on the Psalms, are in effect sketches for the vast religious dramas of his later years. The choruses are big and imposing—monumental on a small scale.

In 1720, Handel published his first book of *Pièces pour le clavecin*, which were originally noted down for the studies of the little princesses. The character of these pieces obviates any real comparison with *The Well-Tempered Clavichord*: Bach opened up a new world of design, while Handel was content to follow safely in the steps of Domenico Scarlatti and Couperin. A second book of *Pièces*, published in 1733 (without Handel's permission), is equally conventional. His clavier compositions are apt to disappoint the listener used to the prodigally ornamented polyphonic schemes of Bach. Handel's are unaffectedly barren in harmony, and their simple plan of successive tonics and dominants at first suggests lack of imagination. These suites, and particularly the second book, were in effect but sketches for Handel's own performance. They may be filled out in imagination, if the hearer wishes, with the wealth of improvisatorial ornament that flowed torrentially from Handel's fingers.

But this does not mean that the suites cannot be enjoyed precisely as they stand. On acquaintance, their very simplicity and Doric leanness invest them with vigorous beauty, and eventually one finds oneself going back to them again and again. The fifth suite in the first book contains the air and variations known familiarly but absurdly as "The Harmonious Blacksmith." The seventh suite in this book, conceived in the grand style Handel most often reserved for his great choruses, contains a magnificent passacaglia that is ever effective in the many arrangements that have been made of it. Finally, in the G major Chaconne, from the second suite of Book II, rich variety is created by slight changes in pattern—a typically Handelian method. It is another essay in the grand style, opening maestoso, going on its way in many moods —scamperingly, playfully, pathetically—and ending in a swirling cascade of rolling notes. There is nothing in this music that would baffle a first-year theory student, and its effect is magical. It illuminates Beethoven's judgment: "Go and learn of him how to achieve great efforts with simple means."

Handel's yearning for the stage bore fruit early in 1720, when he set John Gay's *Acis and Galatea*, which contains one of his most jocose and engaging airs (for a bass!), "O ruddier than the cherry."

The same year, probably to a poem by Pope (not one of his happiest flights), he composed *Haman and Mordecai,* for which the Duke of Chandos was said to have given him £1000. Both of these were masques, and were doubtless first produced in the private theater at Canons. Handel then put them aside, and years later produced much expanded versions of them. But they were still the characteristic efforts of a composer working leisurely under the patronage of a benevolent prince. Even while he was fashioning these trifles, a scheme was under way that was destined to uproot him forever, and throw him into the hurly-burly of opera management.

Disgusted with the trash that was still holding the London stage, an aristocratic clique under the direction of the Duke of Newcastle floated a shareholding company that was called, by George I's permission, the Royal Academy of Music. It was characteristic of the age of the South Sea Bubble and other vast money-making schemes that an artistic venture, designed to make London the capital of opera, should have been put on a speculative basis. The entire stock issue of £50,000 was quickly subscribed, each share costing £100 and entitling its owner to a permanent seat in the house. As early as 1719, Handel, to whom the active musical direction had been entrusted at the King's suggestion, was in Germany hiring singers for the great enterprise. Everything was done on a lavish scale. There were associate composers; there were official librettists, including Handel's favorite collaborator, Haym; and, finally, as stage manager, the directors secured the services of John James Heidegger, called "the Swiss Count." If not one of the most romantic figures of the time, Heidegger was surely one of the most picturesque. His ugliness was a byword, but fortunately it was matched by a resourcefulness that amounted to genius. The warm friendship between him and Handel had begun in 1713, when the kindhearted Swiss had saved the run of *Teseo* after a dishonest manager had absconded with the box-office receipts.

The first season of the Royal Academy of Music opened not with an opera by Handel, but with a confection by an insignificant fourth-rater. It ran six nights, and then the season really opened, on April 27, 1720, with *Radamisto,* one of the loveliest and most melodious of Handel's scores. None of the celebrated stars hired by Handel had yet arrived, and the difficult role of Zenobia was probably sung by the very adequate, but familiar, Anastasia Robinson. King George and his entourage occupied the royal box, and society stormed the rest of the house, even gallery seats going as high as forty shillings. But the music did not need the glamour of new stage personalities to get across. For almost two months the Haymarket Theater was the scene of nightly near riots by wildly enthusiastic audiences. Once more the notes of Handel were on every lip. The shareholders were delighted.

At the moment of Handel's triumph forces were gathering for his destruction. Led by his former friend, the Earl of Burlington, they included those exquisites who did not consider the large-bodied German the most appropriate apostle of pure Italian art. Burlington now went abroad to find the real thing, and brought back with him Giovanni Battista Buononcini, almost as supreme on the Continent as Handel was in England. This affected but talented Italian became the spearhead of the growing cabal against the man who had re-established England's prestige in music. Fate played into his hands: the opera Handel had designed to inaugurate the season of 1721 fell flat, despite its fine melodies and the magnificent roulades of the most sensational *castrato* of the hour, Senesino. The society that had hailed Buononcini's *Astarto* the season before wanted more music in this lighter vein. Buononcini was ready. The success of two tuneful operas, produced in rapid succession, took the town by storm, and drove most of fashionable society into his camp. Momentarily at least, Handel was crowded off the stage.

Buononcini was rashly content to rest on his laurels. He roused himself from his luxurious sloth during the next year only to write the anthem for the funeral of the great Duke of Marlborough. Meanwhile, Handel was deploying his forces for a final struggle with his epicene opponent. Great general that he was, he realized that London could not be reconquered by fine music alone. He therefore sent to Venice for Francesca Cuzzoni, already at twenty-two so famed that on the basis of her reputation alone he offered her £2,000 a year. But the ugly soprano proved so intractable and arrogant that he once threatened to throw her out of a window if she did not sing the way he wanted her to. Taming Cuzzoni was worth the trouble, for her brilliant performance in the *première* of *Ottone*, on January 12, 1723, helped Handel to regain his pre-

eminence. Although Buononcini remained in London for another
decade, even producing an occasional work with some success, he
quietly faded out as an effective rival to the all-conquering Saxon.
And yet, a dispassionate observer will agree with the epigram John
Byrom struck off in the heat of the controversy:

> *Some say, compared to Buononcini*
> *That Mynheer Handel's but a ninny;*
> *Others aver that he to Handel*
> *Is scarcely fit to hold a candle.*
> *Strange all this difference should be*
> *Twixt tweedle-dum and tweedle-dee.*

Up to this point Handel had shown himself superior only in kind
to Buononcini.

Until 1724 Handel had been content to fit his happy inspirations
into the creaking formal patterns of conventional Italian opera.
Furthermore, he had responded like a weather vane to every
breeze. Even at the height of the struggle with Buononcini, he
emulated his rival's style. Now, however, without sloughing off the
absurd conventions that were to hold opera in chains until Gluck
rebelled against them, he invested the old forms with a new expressiveness. *Giulio Cesare* and *Tamerlano*, both produced in 1724,
suffered from weak librettos, but even so Handel worked wonders
with them. The recitatives are dramatic revelations of character,
and *Tamerlano*, indeed, built up to such a tremendous climax of
pathos that the sophisticated and reasonable audiences were sent
home weeping.

But circumstances prevented Handel from exploring farther this
rich new vein, even had he wanted to. Despite the quality of its
music and the most starry casts in Europe, the Royal Academy of
Music was tottering. The generalissimo of this vast enterprise was
desperate. Cuzzoni and Senesino drew such fabulous salaries that
only nightly capacity audiences could satisfy them and the shareholders. And attendance was falling off. Instead of retrenching,
Handel decided to stake everything on a single throw of the dice
by importing Faustina Bordoni, Cuzzoni's only rival. In contriving
to bring together the two most famous sopranos in Europe, Handel
adumbrated the exploits of P. T. Barnum. He was a man without
fear: he put them both in his new opera, *Alessandro*, which opened

with great *réclame* on May 5, 1726. As it ran until the end of the season, it began to seem that Faustina's salary of £2,000 a year was well spent.*

If the contest between Handel and Buononcini was a spectacle, that between Cuzzoni and Faustina was a sideshow. For two whole years, music played second fiddle at the Haymarket. The audiences divided into Cuzzonites and Bordonites: not since the days of the Empress Theodora and the Hippodrome riots between the Blues and the Greens had faction run so high. Footpads and hooligans mixed with the operagoers, and took sides in the rowdy demonstrations. Unquestionably the two most important events of the year 1727 were the death of George I in a post chaise on a lonely German road and the public hair-pulling match between the rival queens of song on the night of June 6.

In the midst of all this hubbub Handel solemnly became a British subject.

One of the new Englishman's first duties was to provide the anthems used at the coronation of George II, in October, 1727. The next month, as a further compliment to his adopted country, he presented a new opera, *Riccardo Primo*, a fantastic hash based remotely on the adventures of Richard the Lionhearted. He dared to use his rival prima donnas in the cast again, but the public would have none of Richard. Handel played every trump in his hand, but even his belated nationalism peeping from under an Italian domino could not save the Royal Academy. The following January the happy collaboration of Gay and Pepusch successfully exploited, in *The Beggar's Opera* (which included tunes lifted brazenly from Handel), a vein of nationalism that paid real dividends. But Handel was still too immersed in Italianism to draw the moral from its overwhelming success. He saw his few remaining patrons flocking to the Little Theater in Lincoln's Inn Fields. While Gay and Pepusch were pioneering in musical comedy, and packing them in with broad ditties sung in English and strung together by rollicking dialogue, the master opportunist at the Haymarket could do nothing better than compose another—and then another—Italian opera. Both of these contained much excel-

---

* After two seasons Faustina returned to Italy. Later she became as well acquainted with Bach as she had been with Handel. She died in 1783 at the age of ninety.

lent music, but they could not save the situation. In June, 1728, the last season of the Royal Academy ended with a huge deficit.

Still Handel clung to Italian opera. Having lost a fortune for the Academy shareholders, he now decided to risk his own and Heidegger's. Accordingly, early in 1729, after leasing the King's Theater, he made another Continental foray in search of singers. He lingered in Venice until news that his mother had suffered a paralytic stroke made him squeeze his huge frame into the first post chaise. At Halle he found her in a pitiable state—blind, crippled, and mortally ill. In a life singularly free of emotional attachments, Handel had lavished all his love on his mother. To see her thus stricken dejected him immeasurably, and when, at this juncture, Wilhelm Friedemann Bach arrived bearing an invitation from his father in Leipzig, Handel was too depressed to accept. These two giants of eighteenth-century music never met.

Reluctantly bidding what he must have known was a last farewell to his mother (she died the following year) Handel returned to London, and busied himself with managerial problems. So arduous and hectic were these that not until a fortnight before the opening did he finish his first offering of the season. Haste played him false: the opera was a makeshift that deservedly failed. And, in fact, the new management's entire first season was an unmitigated failure despite the singers Handel had imported. The season of 1730-31 was more successful, due as much to the drawing power of Senesino as to the revival of several Handel favorites. *Poro*, a new work, was actually declared by connoisseurs to be the finest opera he had yet composed. Not a single performance failed to pay. The old magic was working once more. But even it could not contend against the weather, of which there was a vast deal in May, 1731. The King's Theater was the last in London to surrender to an unprecedented heat wave.

The next season opened dully, and was languishing along unprofitably when there took place an event, not in itself important, that changed the direction of Handel's life and altered the face of English music. Bernard Gates, one of his warm admirers, arranged a birthday surprise for Handel—a revival of *Haman and Mordecai*, the masque composed for the private theater at Canons a decade before. Little did the forty-seven-year-old composer realize, as he listened to the children of the Chapel Royal performing his long-neglected work, that from it he would seize an idea whose development would make his place secure among the greatest masters of music long after his Italian operas had fallen into undeserved oblivion. And when a second performance drew loud plaudits from a picked audience, Handel's only reaction was a decision to produce an enlarged version at the Haymarket. He planned to have it sung by the children of the Chapel Royal, who had given so excellent an account of themselves in the Gates revival. But as soon as the news spread, there were vociferous protests from moralists and churchmen. They had protested until they were blue in the face about the bawdy farces filling the playhouses. They were on firmer ground in objecting to a Biblical drama in an opera house. Gibson, the learned and austere Bishop of London, brought matters to a head by forbidding the performance. This was more than an empty ukase, for the Chapel Royal was under his jurisdiction. Handel circumvented the ban by a technicality: he further revised *Haman and Mordecai*, named it *Esther: an Oratorio in English*, and presented it on May 2, 1732, at the Haymarket, but without scenery, costumes, or stage business. On the fourth night the royal family attended in state, and from then on *Esther's* complete success was assured.

It was not at once apparent that oratorio would ultimately dislodge Italian opera from its firm hold on the English heart. In fact, Handel's next two experiments in disguised opera were disheartening, despite the increasing impressiveness of his choruses. *Deborah* was a dead failure, and the measured success of *Athalia* was due mainly to the fact that it was produced for university celebrations at Oxford. Here Handel was welcomed with noisy admiration by students and dons alike, but his own enthusiasm was dampened when he learned that the doctorate of music the University intended to confer on him would cost him £100. He declined the honor.

Until 1738 Handel's interest in oratorio was definitely a sideline, and he remained generally faithful to his old love. But Italian opera proved a faithless wench. Affairs at the Haymarket went from bad to worse, and the rise of an opposition opera under the sponsorship of Frederick, Prince of Wales (historically a mere incident in the bitter feud between George II and his heir), brought the Handel-Heidegger management to the brink of disaster. The new venture, housed in the Lincoln's Inn Fields Theater, drew away from the Haymarket its brightest stars—Senesino and Cuzzoni—and also secured the services of Porpora, the most celebrated singing teacher of the age, and the peerless *castrato*, Farinelli. Porpora, who was also the official composer of this "Opera of the Nobility," might not compose as effectively as Handel, but the Prince's patronage secured the most fashionable audiences possible, and his singers were more brilliant than those the Haymarket could muster. In July, 1734, Handel and Heidegger bowed to the inevitable, and closed their doors. Porpora immediately leased the Haymarket, which was a better house than Lincoln's Inn Fields.

As a businessman Handel was as resilient as ever: knowing full well that Lincoln's Inn Fields was inadequate in every respect, he nevertheless took it, and boldly planned his coming season. His new opera house was seated in little better than a garbage dump, and was a catchall for London's lowest denizens; his once splendid galaxy was sadly depleted, and the King's halfhearted patronage availed nothing against the Prince of Wales' spirited championing of Porpora. Handel revived a few operas at Lincoln's Inn Fields, but the response was worse than poor—all London was flocking to the Haymarket, where the one and only Farinelli was warbling inimitably in *Artaserse*, the masterpiece of Faustina's husband, Johann Adolf Hasse. Nor did a move, in December, 1734, to a new theater in Covent Garden help matters much. The exquisite melodies of *Alcina* could not leave the English heart completely untouched, but generally speaking, Handel's ill luck continued throughout 1735. And now, to make matters worse, the robust Saxon frame was assailed by the first of a cumulation of ailments that were to trouble the latter days of this amiable glutton. He was fifty, and had never had the prudence to husband his strength.

Back from taking the waters at Tunbridge Wells, Handel devoted himself feverishly to setting the finest libretto that ever fell to his lot—a version of Dryden's *Alexander's Feast, or the Power of Music*. He completed the oratorio in twenty days, and shocked conservative musicians by hiring a nineteen-year-old English boy as leading tenor. This youngster, John Beard, was finally to lift Handel from the financial morass as effectively as Farinelli had lifted Porpora's company. *Alexander's Feast* was a triumph. Dryden had written this most Dionysiac of English odes in a single night: Handel's setting has the same controlled abandon, the full flavor of a classic bacchanal. Handel, whose English was so broken and halting that he was a laughingstock among the cruel wits of the town, honored Dryden's beautiful lines with a perfect understanding that wove for them a sumptuous and entirely appropriate garment of song.

But *Alexander's Feast* only momentarily stemmed the flood of disaster. Even good luck was against Handel. When custom required him to write wedding music for the Prince of Wales, he did his duty so well that the Prince was won over to his side in the War of the Opera Houses. But by winning the Prince he lost the King, who declared pettishly that where his son went he was never seen. The effect on musical London was simple: Covent Garden and the Haymarket exchanged audiences. And both companies rushed headlong toward failure. Handel's health became alarming: his frantic efforts to shore up his collapsing fortunes were succeeded by an obstinate spell of the most abject depression. As Covent Garden dragged to its miserable end, the composer was smitten with paralysis. His entire right side was affected, he was in agony, and for a moment it seemed that his mind was going. While he was in this fog of mingled physical and mental anguish, Covent Garden closed its doors. Ten days later, Porpora too was forced to the wall.

And now the threat of imprisonment was added to Handel's other woes. He was bankrupt, and though most of his creditors were well disposed toward him, at least one of them acted toward the fallen impresario with malignant severity. Possibly Handel's official position enabled him to escape debtors' prison. In any event, after giving promissory notes to his creditors, he painfully took ship for the Continent. He lingered at Aix-la-Chapelle for some months: the paralysis gradually left him and the clouds lifted from his mind. When he returned to England in November, 1737, he was, to all intents and purposes, completely cured. He found London in gloom: Caroline, the beloved wife of George II, was dying. To his sorrow, Handel's first task proved to be her funeral anthem. Not since the days of Tomás Luis de Victoria's elegy on the death of his august patroness had so majestic a threnody been composed. Under such solemn auspices did the disgraced composer win back his place in the fickle affections of the people.

But his misfortunes dragged on. Heidegger, the new lessee of the Haymarket, staged two new Handel operas early the next year. London stayed away, not maliciously, but because Italian opera had momentarily worn out its welcome. Handel's inability to meet his notes so enraged one of his creditors that he was again threatened with debtors' prison. At this juncture he was reluctantly persuaded to permit a benefit concert in his behalf. Fashionable London, which had so frankly left him in the lurch as soon as his entertainment bored them, turned out en masse as if to make amends. One thousand pounds was collected, and with this sum Handel was able to pay his persecutor, and tell him off in a spate of mixed German and English invective.

In the summer another proof of Handel's place in public esteem was provided when the astute Jonathan Tyers, manager of the Vauxhall Gardens, London's most fashionable resort, commissioned Louis-François Roubilliac, a kind of latter-day Bernini, to make a statue of Handel for the Gardens. Tyers would never have spent the £300 unless he had been certain that it was good business. Even if the public stayed away from his operas, Handel was the idol of the hour. Nobody's music was more popular at the Gardens: the band nightly played excerpts from his works. Of course, Tyers reaped a golden harvest. As for poor Handel, all he got was a silver ticket of general admission to the Gardens, engraved by Hogarth.

Handel reacted to these signs of friendliness with a terrific spurt of energy. In April, Heidegger had staged *Serse* at the Haymarket. This new work had been a clever attempt to muscle in on the new territory opened up by *The Beggar's Opera*. But despite a really funny libretto and appropriate music, *Serse* (which looks forward to the *opéra comique* rather than backward to *The Beggar's Opera*) had not caught the public fancy. It contained the aria "*Ombra mai fu*," which as far as is known evoked no curtain calls opening night. It was just another Handel tune. It got no publicity in the eighteenth century. Suddenly, in Queen Victoria's time, it was taken up, and, as "Handel's Largo" or "The Largo from Xerxes," now holds a vast public. As performed today (in the wrong tempo), it is peaceful and majestic, almost solemn in mood; its popularity is something of a mystery. What Handel thought of it is not known, but as he had a habit of using his favorites over and over, the fact that "*Ombra mai fu*" appears in only one opera tells its own story.

The failure of *Serse* finally convinced Handel that his struggle to keep Italian opera on the boards was futile. At the age of fifty-three, he boldly started at the top of another musical leaf. But love dies hard, and during the next three years he worked intermittently at two operas. These, tuneful though they are, seem half-hearted and stillborn. Handel allowed them to be produced carelessly by hack singers: he was busy making history with the oratorio.

Had Handel died in 1738, he would not now be reckoned among the titans of music. As far as their value to posterity is concerned the first fifty-three years of his life must be counted as a tragic waste. In cold fact, some of his finest inspirations lie buried in those crumbling operatic scores that seem unlikely ever to be revived except as lifeless curiosities. The blame for this neglect must be laid unqualifiedly at Handel's own door. He was content to acquiesce in the traditional scheme of Italian opera—a succession of barely related numbers having no integral connection with the libretto, itself usually a piece of extravagant and high-flown nonsense. It seems doubtful that he ever conceived of the opera as a dramatic unity—in any event he never achieved it. Many of his arias and concerted numbers attain momentary dramatic integrity, and a surprisingly high percentage of them are as lovely and appealing now as the day they were written. The best airs have a springtime spontaneity that is lacking in the otherwise more impressive later works. But so long as recitalists confine their exhaustive investigations to the compositions of Oley Speaks, Liza Lehmann, Ernest Charles, and other modern masters, it seems unlikely that audiences will ever know that Handel wrote more than ten or twelve songs.

Had Handel died in 1738, what now would be salvaged? Probably nothing more than the "Largo," "The Harmonious Blacksmith," and the *Water Music*. In short, he would belong among those small masters who on rare occasions outranked themselves. He would be classed among the Rameaus and Corellis and Galuppis, with their *Tambourins* and *Weinachtskonzerts* and *Toccatas*. Once in a while that discoverer of buried treasure, Bernard Herrmann, would dignify the business of broadcasting by presenting one of the *Concerti grossi*,* the best of which challenge comparison with the "Brandenburg" Concertos. But that strange marriage of names —Bach and Handel—would never have been heard. Handel would have been, in musical history, just another of that group of eighteenth-century immortals—Alessandro Scarlatti, Hasse, Porpora, and Jommelli—unjustly massacred in the operatic revolution of Christoph Willibald von Gluck.

But Handel in 1738 had more than twenty years to live. Without worrying about a career that lay in ruins, he set about creating— or piecing together—a new musical form. Just as he had stubbornly kept on producing Italian operas long after the public lost interest in them, he now began literally forcing oratorios on his audiences. There was bitter resistance. He made and lost fortunes, and triumphed in the end only because he happened to die on an upswing. It is only fair, however, to observe that the reaction in favor of these magnificent creations eventually drew to them the largest and most enthusiastic audiences in the history of music.

Although Handel had already tentatively explored the possibilities of oratorio, it was not until 1739 that he turned his back on Italian opera, and finally made oratorio the main business of his life. His new career began inauspiciously enough. Having leased the King's Theater, he produced *Saul* and *Israel in Egypt* within a few months of each other. The indifference that greeted these works is inexplicable: the solemn and majestic Dead March from *Saul* would alone immortalize this work, while the monumental *Israel in Egypt*, now heard all too rarely, does not lack partisans who hold it more sublime than *Messiah*. It is so vast in its proportions that Handel waited seventeen years before reviving it. The thunder of its choruses rolls almost constantly, unfolding the awful chronicle of Exodus with epic grandeur. With the surest of instincts, Handel rigorously limited the use of solo voices, doubtless realizing that they could not sustain the dread cadences of the narrative. Of course, as the choruses now used in *Israel in Egypt* are usually at full war strength, outnumbering the orchestra at least five to one, it has become almost impossible to hear the oratorio as Handel conceived it, with chorus and orchestra of equal size. Sir

* Although not yet published in 1738, most of the twelve masterly *Concerti grossi* of Opus 6 had doubtless been composed.

Donald Tovey, who produced *Israel in Egypt* in Handel's way, called "The people shall hear and be afraid" the "greatest of all Handel's choruses."

Depressed in mind and purse by the failure of these oratorios, Handel withdrew once more to the smaller Lincoln's Inn Fields Theater. Strangely enough, the very people who had disdained to hear *Saul* and *Israel in Egypt* at the King's Theater plowed their way through the noisome muddy lanes to the large hovel that housed Handel's new undertaking. There was war with Spain, and the martial flourishes of the *Ode for St. Cecilia's Day* stirred the bellicose Londoners. Soon the town was belligerently droning Dryden's worst lines:

> The TRUMPETS *loud Clangor*
> *Excites us to Arms*
> *With shrill Notes of Anger*
> *And Mortal Alarms.*
> *The double double double beat*
> *Of the thund'ring* DRUM
> *Cryes, heark the Foes come;*
> *Charge, Charge, 'tis too late to retreat.*

For a time, money poured in. Then came an intense cold wave, so persistent and unprecedented that it is still known as the "great frost of 1740." Handel, whose enterprises had once succumbed to heat prostration, tried to make the theater as coldproof as possible, and wooed his frozen patrons with a new work of exceeding charm—*L'Allegro, il Penseroso, ed il Moderato.* Charles Jennens, who contrived this potpourri, used parts of Milton's two poems, and added a third section by himself—a tasteless procedure typical of an age which preferred Nahum Tate's bowdlerized versions of Shakespeare to the originals. This work failed, and so did Handel's final fling at opera the next autumn. The weary old man withdrew into himself, and none but his intimates saw him for almost a year. In the drawing rooms of Piccadilly they were saying that Mr. Handel was through.

Suddenly, in November, 1741, he emerged from his shell, and sailed for Ireland at the invitation of the Lord Lieutenant. He was traveling heavy—in his luggage was the manuscript of *Messiah*, which he had composed the previous summer in little more than three weeks. In Dublin, he was received everywhere with an acclaim that quickened his chilled blood. He produced several of his compositions with growing success. Late in March, the first playbills announcing *Messiah* appeared in Dublin, and on April 13, 1742, it was produced at Neal's Music Hall in Fishamble Street. Scenes of wildest enthusiasm occurred at this performance, and it seems strange that Handel waited until June to repeat it. This day turned out sultry, but heat did not deter the Irish: Neal's was packed to the roof. Two cathedral choirs sang the mighty choruses superbly, and the notorious Mrs. Cibber, who had created the role of Polly Peachum in *The Beggar's Opera*, sang the air "He was despised" with such devout tenderness that the Reverend Dr. Delany exclaimed, "Woman! for this thy sins be forgiven thee!"

Messiah is Handel's masterpiece, and among the unquestioned masterpieces of music it towers like a mighty alp. In this rarefied atmosphere only the tremendous massif of the B minor Mass reaches higher. With the *Matthew Passion*, *Messiah* crowns the devotional aspiration of the Protestant genius. From the foursquare orchestral introduction to the great concluding chorus, "Worthy is the Lamb," the oratorio is sustained on the loftiest level of musical invention and spiritual nobility. Unity though *Messiah* is, it contains many separate airs which lose little in being performed alone. The two tenor airs after the introduction are so moving that one hearing *Messiah* for the first time, and unaware of Handel's stanchless melodic inventiveness, might fear that his best work is at the beginning. But *Messiah* is like a palace in which wonderment grows at every step, and the mere recital of its treasures is wearisome. That outburst of tremendous joy, the "Hallelujah" Chorus, which brought cocky little George II to his feet in spontaneous homage, has lost none of its overpowering vitality in two centuries. Handel believed it was divinely inspired: "I did think I did see all Heaven before me—and the great God himself." The pathos of "He shall feed His flock" and "I know that my Redeemer liveth" is not lost even on an unbeliever. The truth is that *Messiah*, like any transcendent work of genius, escapes the boundaries of creed and nation.

The British did not take to *Messiah* at once. When Handel returned from Dublin, he was not so simple as to begin his London season with a work he had first produced in Ireland. He presented, instead, an entirely new oratorio, *Samson*, which under the King's patronage enjoyed the brilliant success it well deserved. This time the librettist had bowdlerized Milton's *Samson Agonistes*, a poem from which Handel wrung the utmost dramatic value. Although it is Handel on a large scale, and contains such memorable numbers as "Fixed in His everlasting seat" and "Total eclipse," it is not of *Messiah* caliber. And yet, the very people who had acclaimed *Samson* received *Messiah* coldly. In vain did George II do homage—London barely supported five performances of Handel's masterpiece in six years. For once, the composer was so annoyed that he took to his bed, and somewhat later had recourse to the waters at Tunbridge Wells.

It took a national celebration to rouse Handel from his lethargy. On June 27, 1743, the King happened to be with his armies at Dettingen, a tiny Bavarian village. Here he chanced to meet a much larger French army, and in some inexplicable way won the only victory of his brief career as a soldier in the field. A tremendous celebration with trumpet and drum was in order, and Handel rose to the occasion with the specially composed *Dettingen Te Deum*, which was performed on a terrifyingly large scale in the Chapel Royal. Needless to say, this *Te Deum* was the only important result of George II's great victory at Dettingen.

During the next two years. Handel was busy producing both sacred and secular oratorios, only one of which is still stageworthy. Most of these are museum pieces, but *Semele* is really delicious throughout. Unhappily, the lovely "Where'er you walk" exerts a fatal attraction on every proud possessor of a tenor voice. As sung by John McCormack, it comes through as the high lyrical flight that Handel wrote. *Semele* provoked a modest show of interest, but the machinations of rival impresarios (who were still true to opera) wooed away his patrons, and the productions that followed it soon dissipated not only the meager profits from *Semele*, but also those from his Irish tour. And so, in April, 1745, Handel was once more forced into bankruptcy, and went automatically to drink what must by then have been the very bitter waters of Tunbridge Wells. Pain racked his body, and this time there were those who said that Mr. Handel was going mad.

But again he disappointed his enemies. He rose triumphant to scourge the Stuart uprising—the sad lost cause of the Young Pretender—in the vengeful strophes of the *Occasional Oratorio*, and a little more than a year later he hymned the victor of Culloden with a masterpiece, *Judas Maccabaeus*. It would take a Jesuit to find any real resemblance between the noble hero of the Maccabees and the bloody Duke of Cumberland, the butcher who had finally saved England from the Stuarts. Nor is there any reason to suspect that Handel saw any resemblance. However, in the stirring chorus "Glory to God," the old composer rose loftily to the patriotic demands of an England that had treated him shabbily for years. And *Judas Maccabaeus*, with its intensely expressed national feeling, turned the English into true if tardy Handelians, and so they have remained ever since.

Because Judas Maccabaeus was the first Jewish figure to be represented favorably on the English stage, the Jews crowded Covent Garden during the entire run of the oratorio. Handel's fortunes were completely rehabilitated, and as a grateful compliment to his new patrons (as well as what he thought was a shrewd business move), the rest of his oratorios, except one, were based on stories from Jewish history and legend. The writing of these took most of his creative energy from the summer of 1747 to that of 1751. Although he did not hit another real winner until *Jephtha*, the last of these, every one of them, with the possible exception of *Alexander Balus*, contains melodies and choruses of enduring beauty. *Joshua* has the lyric "Oh, had I Jubal's lyre," *Susanna* the exquisitely tender "Ask if yon damask rose be fair," and *Jephtha* the perennial favorite, "Waft her, angels." Such instances could be many times multiplied. Handel himself said that the chorus "He saw the lovely youth," from *Theodora*, was the finest he ever composed, and complained bitterly that the oratorio was not better attended. "There was room enough to dance there when that was performed," he declared. George II remained faithful, but so little social importance attached to his person that often he was almost alone in the theater.

But if London was cold to these novelties from the pen of its aging musical arbiter, it lined his pockets* when he revived those works which were already on their way to becoming staples of the English fireside. *Hercules*, now gone from the repertoire, was a

---

* In his otherwise simply appointed house in a fashionable section, Handel collected some fine paintings, including several Rembrandts.

great favorite in the eighteenth century. *Judas Maccabaeus* by itself made a fortune for Handel. But *Messiah*, the history of whose popularity is still being written, eventually outstripped its rivals, even during his lifetime. Things came to such a pass that it was almost necessary to declare a national holiday when Mr. Handel, seated in majesty at the organ, conducted his masterpiece.

But the phenomenal vitality that had driven this mighty engine for sixty-four years was beginning to dry up. Gout tortured Handel's massive body, and every motion was agony. His sight was failing rapidly. Early in 1749, the King asked him to perform what proved to be his last official duty—the composition of music for a celebration of the Peace of Aix-la-Chapelle. The result was the celebrated *Firework Music*. When it was rehearsed in Vauxhall Gardens on April 21, over twelve thousand people paid two shillings sixpence each to hear it, and held up traffic over London Bridge for three hours—probably the most stupendous tribute any composer ever received. The performance, six days later, was even more spectacular. A fantastic victory temple was erected in the Green Park, a noted French pyrotechnician was employed to devise the fireworks, 101 brass cannon were provided for the royal salute, Handel was given a band larger than a modern symphony orchestra, and the bill for everything was handed to the Duke of Montagu, who died three months later. In fact, everything was done to hide the truth that the Peace of Aix-la-Chapelle was an empty victory for England. All London was crowded into the Green Park: the little brass cannon roared, the fireworks fizzled, and finally the victory temple burst into flames. The one unquestioned success was the music.

The *Firework Music* ranks just below the *Water Music*, which it strongly resembles, with its emphatic rhythms and noisy, eloquent brasses, though here, as always, Handel knew how to ring the changes on his own quotations. The idyllic largo, which he called *La Paix*, breathes the very essence of a world into which peace has come. Both the *Firework* and *Water* suites, so admirably scored for open-air performance, evidence Handel's delicate sense of acoustics.

In May, 1749, Handel repeated the *Firework Music* in the first of those charity concerts which have ever since linked his name inextricably with that of the Foundling Hospital. The next year he began the famous annual series of benefit performances of *Messiah*, the proceeds of which—never less than £500, and once as much as £1000—likewise went to the Hospital. His last years were spent in thinking up ways of helping this favorite charity, to which he willed a copy of *Messiah*, and he served as a governor of the institution for many years. As Hogarth was likewise a governor, the Foundling Hospital was served by the two greatest geniuses in England.

In August, 1750, Handel made his last trip to the Continent. He was sixty-five years old, and must have wanted to see the scenes of his childhood for the last time. Just outside The Hague his coach overturned, and he was severely injured. After convalescing, he proceeded to Halle, where he found Wilhelm Friedemann Bach—whose illustrious father had died only a few months before—presiding in Zachau's place at the Liebfrauenkirche organ. Handel was soon back in London. At first he was too sick to work, but in January began to compose his last oratorio, *Jephtha*. While he was working on the final chorus of the second part, "How dark, O Lord, are Thy decrees," he received the first serious warning of impending blindness. Despite the ministrations of three doctors, his sight grew dimmer rapidly, and on January 27, 1753, the *Theatrical Register* told the tragic outcome: "Mr. Handel has at length, unhappily, quite lost his sight." Rather confused records suggest that John Taylor, who did his worst on Bach, also operated unsuccessfully on Handel's eyes.*

Handel the composer was through. But though the creative spark was extinct, the old man did not give up. He was the greatest of living organists, and almost until the last day of his life continued his wonderful virtuoso performances. In 1753 he played all of his organ concertos from memory. Year after year he revived his oratorios to packed houses, conducting and accompanying them at the organ. At last, after years of disappointment and bad luck, he had acquired the touch of Midas. Better still, he was loved by all London: by 1759 the figure of this enormously fat old man, scarcely able to walk a step unassisted, seemed almost as much part of the landscape as the Tower and Westminster Abbey. He celebrated his seventy-fourth birthday in the midst of his most successful season. On April 6, with mastery unimpaired, he pre-

* One eminent authority, however, believes that Handel retained a vestige of sight until his death.

sided at a performance of *Messiah* at Covent Garden. Yet all was not well. In one section he faltered, but recovered himself adroitly. Scarcely had the final amen been sung when he fainted, and was carried to his house in Brook Street. As he lingered in his last agony, he said, "I want to die on Good Friday in the hope of rejoining the good God, my sweet Lord and Saviour, on the day of his Resurrection." Actually, he died early in the morning of Holy Saturday, April 14, 1759.

Handel had expressed in his will a desire to be buried in the Abbey, and his wish was enthusiastically carried out. Six days after his death, at eight o'clock in the evening, he was lowered into his place among England's great, in the presence of three thousand uninvited mourners, while the combined voices of the Gentlemen of the Chapel Royal and the choirs of St. Paul's and the Abbey sang the dirge.

The best proof of Handel's unique sovereignty over English music was furnished by his posthumous glorification. That at his death he was well beloved and greatly honored is unquestioned; a few years later, he was a god, or in less pagan parlance, a saint. The official canonization took place in 1784, when a five-day commemoration was arranged on an unprecedented scale. George III, assisted by a committee of noblemen, was the moving spirit of the fete, during which *Messiah* was given twice in the Abbey. So elaborate were the ceremonies that Dr. Burney wrote an account of them some months later, to which Dr. Johnson contributed the dedication to the King. It proved to be the Grand Cham's last effort, and before the pamphlet actually appeared he too was dead. The Handel Commemoration was the death knell of the eighteenth century: even as the mighty amens of *Messiah* rolled away into silence, the first premonitions of the French Revolution were rumbling across the Channel.

Although popular enthusiasm for Handel continued unabated, it was not until 1857—the year of the Indian Mutiny—that the English actually got around to staging the first of the well-known festivals that have been the admiration and despair of critics, according to their points of view. The lamentable story of this musical elephantiasis can be compressed into the fact that while Handel himself presented *Messiah* with a chorus and orchestra numbering about thirty performers each, at recent festivals the chorus has swollen to four thousand voices "supported" by an orchestra of five hundred pieces. The Gargantuan scale of these performances is not so fatal to Handel's intention as the flagrant disproportion of the choral and orchestral elements. The directors of these festivals, from Sir Michael Costa to Sir Henry J. Wood, might well have remembered that Handel himself, supreme master of the grand effect, never, except in the single instance of the *Firework Music*—an outdoor performance—set out to make as much noise as possible.

However, to offset this gaudy festival picture, England boasts a thriving and intelligent Handel Society which, since 1882, has presented most of the oratorios under the direction of excellent musicians. Germany has contributed an edition of Handel edited by the great enthusiast Chrysander, which falls short of the magnificent Gesellschaft Bach, but is nevertheless a monument to one man's untiring industry and patient research. In America, however, popular knowledge stops short with *Messiah*—occasional presentations of a few other works do not alter the fact that Handel is, in this country, the most neglected of the truly great composers. Bach, now that he is widely known, is unlikely ever to give place to another on that high seat to which public esteem has exalted him. But the day cannot be far distant when familiarity with the manifold facets of Handel's genius will elevate him to his rightful place a small step below that of his great contemporary.

Chapter IV

Christoph Willibald von Gluck

(Erasbach, July 2, 1714–November 15, 1787, Vienna)

T HE Renaissance, which invented so many things, also invented
opera. It all happened quite accidentally. The legend is—and
for once the legend is true—that at the dawn of the seventeenth
century Count Bardi and a group of smart young Florentines, wistful for the past, decided to stage dramatic adaptations of Greek
myth as the Greeks had staged Aeschylus and Euripides. They
fondly believed they had found the Greek formula—and who
knows?—maybe they had. Believing that the ancient actors had
declaimed their lines in a style halfway between speech and song,
they invented recitative, that is, they guided the rising and falling
cadences of the players by means of musical notes. Whenever they
felt inclined to interrupt the narrative, they wrote a set piece either
for the singing voice or to accompany dancing, which ultimately
developed into the operatic aria and the operatic ballet respectively. In the glorious sunset of Italian vocal polyphony, Count
Bardi's young men showed their independence, and possibly some
real knowledge of the role and nature of the music used at Greek
dramatic performances, by adopting a simple homophonic style.
With doubtless a full appreciation of the many-voiced, ingeniously
interwoven music Palestrina had lately brought to a triumphant
maturity, they nevertheless chose the single spare line of accompanied melody.

A few years after these experiments at the Palazzo Bardi, Claudio
Monteverdi shrewdly made use of the tentative form that had been
evolved. He was more talented and resourceful than the first pioneers of opera: several musical ideas that were eventually made
much of appear in his operas in rudimentary form. He wrote the
first operatic duet. He even sired a remote ancestor of the Wagnerian leitmotiv. The rest of his technical accomplishments may
be left to the musical archeologist. What concerns us is that he
wrote, in both his operas and his madrigals, some music that can
still be heard by courtesy of something better than mere historical
curiosity. His *L'Incoronazione di Poppaea* has recently been revived

with modest success: it is probably the earliest opera to survive the discriminating hand of time.

Until 1637, when the first public opera house was opened in Venice, opera was the plaything of the nobility. Then the people took it up, and before the end of the century Italy was dotted with opera houses. Within a hundred years it became the principal distraction—and besetting sin—of the Italians, because it allowed such ample scope to the national gift for facile melody. As it increased in popularity, opera changed its character. Abandoning the archaic dramatic gusto of Monteverdi, it tended to become prettified and overelaborate—a mere showpiece for the fantastically flexible voices of the times. This coincided with the discovery that *castrati*, originally used to enhance the sexless character of religious music, could outdo even their most spectacular female rivals in coloratura tricks. Some of the music written for these freak voices is so difficult that it can no longer be sung. By the end of the seventeenth century, Italian opera had degenerated into a contest between rival songbirds, and had lost the little dramatic integrity it once had.

In France, things were no better. Opera, which became the vogue under the iron dictatorship of Louis XIV's Italian favorite, Jean-Baptiste Lully, did not suffer from the empty contests of *castrati* (who never flourished in France), but fell into the hands of the masters of stage effects. Lully's operas, which often possess single numbers that are most moving and impressive, are dramatically absurd—the attention is inevitably distracted by the goings-on of the ponderous stage machines. Hannibal crosses the Alps, rivers overflow their banks, cities go up in smoke, fountains play; of a piece with these bewildering scenic cataclysms, the meaningless plot goes cluelessly on.

Italian opera at its most inane held the rest of Europe in a stranglehold. In the German-speaking countries, Italians and Italianized natives ground out servile imitations of the Southern pattern. In England, Purcell, the one man with a marked talent for dramatic music, wrote a single opera, and died young. *Dido and Aeneas* had no progeny: the Italians therefore annexed England as easily as they had Germany. Handel, complacently accepting the conventions of opera as he found it, was not able to beat the Italians at their own game. His genius for the dramatic found its proper scope only when he abandoned opera for oratorio, in which he invented his own conventions.

It has often been asked why opera, which almost from its inception recruited the services of first-rate composers, languished so long and so smugly in a state of complete inanity. The answer is that its patrons liked it just as it was. Even more than today, the opera was then a social affair. People went to see and to be seen, to watch the amazing stage business as children watch a circus, and to take sides in the quarrels between rival *castrati* and prima donnas. The noble and the moneyed sipped beverages in their loges, diced, or played cards, and discussed politics. The famous Président de Brosses considered the opera merely a distraction from a too great passion for chess. These much admired eighteenth-century bluestockings and *philosophes* turned their languid attention to the stage only when some unwieldy engine was erupting over a papier-mâché Pompeii, when a Faustina or a Farinelli was carrying a tortuous roulade beyond the compass of the human ear, or when a hummable tune they already knew from a dozen previous operas was being resung. With such excellent diversions, why should operagoers have ever asked for anything more? As a matter of fact, they eventually got something more not because they asked for it, but because the feeble protests of a few musical progressives, hitherto lost in the din of rattling chessmen, grinding wheels, and screeching sopranos of both sexes, finally found, in Christoph Willibald von Gluck, a champion with vigor and genius.

Gluck's vigor is easier to account for than his genius: his parents came from peasant stock with a long tradition as upper servants to the nobility. They were of mixed German and Bohemian blood. The father was a forester, and seems to have been in much demand, for he was constantly on the move. Until his eighteenth year, when he went to Prague, Gluck led a more or less outdoor life, picking up scraps of education where he could. Of his youth nothing beyond the usual assortment of cut-and-dried conjectures is known. It is not even certain what he did in Prague outside of supporting himself by giving music lessons and playing the organ, but it is fairly obvious that he had already acquired a haphazard musical education. Also, in Prague he must have heard opera, particularly the works of the most popular composer of the day— Johann Adolf Hasse, the fortunate husband of the lovely Faustina.

These slick musical nosegays, the favored vehicle of the peerless *castrato*, Farinelli, made a deep impression on Gluck.

In 1736, Gluck went to Vienna, where he was received into the palace of Prince Lobkowitz, his father's liege lord, as a chamber musician. In the capital he was exposed to nothing but Italianate music, and within a year was off to Milan in the private orchestra of a Lombard noble of exalted rank. Here he took what were probably his first serious musical lessons from Giovanni Battista Sammartini, who has come in for a lot of jingoistic praise in recent years as a precursor of Haydn—who, though invariably generous in his estimates, summed him up as a "bungler." The effect on Gluck of Sammartini, primarily an instrumental composer, was rather enigmatic: after studying with him for four years, Gluck wrote his first opera, *Artaserse*, to some shopworn doggerel by Metastasio, the busiest librettist of the age. The music is lost, yet it is easy to imagine what it must have been like—not too good an imitation of Hasse further obscuring the tortuosities of a long and rambling libretto. But it got Gluck a big following, and he found in it the idiom he was to use more or less unquestioningly for the next thirty years.

By 1745 Gluck had composed ten operas, all of which were enthusiastically received by the uncritical Italian audiences. They contained no hint of any dissatisfaction with the established mode of writing opera. Only one of them, *Ipermestra*, survives in entirety, and it shows the feebleness of the technique he was content to use. Yet his fame spread widely, and late in 1745 he was invited to London to compose operas for the Haymarket Theater. If the noble lessee of the Haymarket hoped that Gluck would initiate a renascence of Italian opera in England, he was sadly mistaken. Gluck's stage pieces were too wishy-washy for the sharpened taste of London audiences, used now to the richer diet of Handel's great oratorios. Tovey flatly says, "Gluck at this time was rather less than an ordinary producer of Italian opera," and there is no mystery about his failure in England.

Handel received Gluck with bearish good humor, and roughly consoled him for his ill fortune, remarking cynically that he had taken too much trouble for English audiences, who understood music only when it sounded like a big drum. But this was Handel in one of his notorious half-truthful moods, and he was probably being as serious as when he said, "Gluck knows no more counter-point than my cook." (The cook, incidentally, was an excellent bass singer, who had appeared successfully in many of Handel's operas, and was doubtless harmonically aware.) But there was a deep truth underlying Handel's flippancy: Gluck was always tech-nically insecure, and even years later, after he had mastered the fundamentals of his mature style, his technique often limped be-hind his intentions.

Up until his London visit, Gluck's success had been so uniform that he had had no reason to examine the esthetic bases of his art. He was a shameless writer of *pasticci*, those monstrous hashes made up of pieces taken from older works and set to a new libretto. But he took Handel's criticism to heart, and his failure with London audiences gave him even greater pause. The man's complacency was jolted. He reacted characteristically: endowed with a keen mind, he was slow on the uptake, and had to mull ideas over for years before taking action. His bitter London experience and his admiration for Handel and, to a lesser degree, for Jean-Philippe Rameau, whom he met in Paris at about the same time, influenced the forming of his mature style—twenty years later. In the mean-time, he went on grinding out imitation Hasse that could have been produced by a man who never stopped to think at all.

Until 1761—that is, for more than fifteen years—the history of Gluck's mind is one of silent growth, so silent, in fact, that few realized that anything at all was happening to him. To all out-ward appearance, he continued his humdrum round, turning out ephemeral stage pieces of all sorts. His mediocre compositions being much in demand, he traveled extensively; at home in Vienna, he was often about the court. All this activity was superficial. Actu-ally, he was educating himself, pondering the esthetic bases of dramatic music, and gradually coming to those conclusions that would revolutionize the whole art of opera. He was studying for-eign languages and letters, and gaining a working knowledge of French by writing *opéra comique*. Finally, he was cultivating an ac-quaintance among the *cognoscenti*. In short, his own innate bent toward things intellectual, stultified in his extremely active youth, was now asserting itself.

Even Gluck's choice of a wife reflects his ruling mental passion: Marianne Pergin, whom he married in 1750, was no beauty. Their marriage, though childless (according to Dr. Alfred Einstein because of a venereal infection Gluck had contracted from a wanton singer), was apparently happy, doubtless because Frau Gluck was something of an Aspasia. One of the few surviving double portraits of a composer and his wife shows Gluck and his Marianne at table, enjoying a drink together. His marriage is important from a musical point of view mainly because his wife's dowry freed him forever from money worries, so that when his phlegmatic development was at last consummated, he could write the operas he wanted without fear of the economic consequences.

Gluck shared with Mozart the not very high distinction of receiving the Golden Spur, a low-grade papal order. Unlike Mozart, who never paraded his insignificant knighthood, he thenceforth signed himself Ritter von Gluck. Appropriately, he received his Golden Spur not for one of his great operas, but for a tawdry piece of musical fustian. It merely happened that Benedict XIV, really quite an astute man otherwise, took a fancy to the mediocre opera called *Antigono*. But the Golden Spur was the least important incident of Gluck's Roman sojourn of 1756, for here he joined the circle of Cardinal Albani, and met Winckelmann, the inspired resuscitator of a fake classicism. Even though Winckelmann's Greece was unlike anything ever on land or sea, it profoundly attracted Gluck. It was a convention of Italian opera to set almost nothing but classical subjects, but the classicism of Gluck's mature operas shows a glimpse of antiquity that, however distorted, could only have come from the epochal *Geschichte der Kunst des Alterthums*, which was then being conceived in Winckelmann's gigantic but mistaken intellect.

Gluck is always called the reformer of opera: it is not so well known that he first tried his hand at reforming ballet. In trying to understand why his first thunderbolt was cast where it was, it must be remembered that the date of *Don Juan* (1761), his great ballet and the first of his mature works for the theater, coincided with Noverre's impassioned plea for a reformed ballet. This noted French dancer and ballet master, while revolutionizing the actual technique of ballet dancing, wanted dramatic music and eloquent action. Anyone who has suffered through that long-drawn-out Chopinesque swoon known as *Les Sylphides* can understand what Noverre was up against. Although he did not dance in it, and in fact had nothing to do with it, *Don Juan* effectually answered his plea. To start with, the librettist-choreographer had cleverly retold Molière's *Le Festin de pierre* in danceable terms. With a suddenness that has led many to the improbable conclusion that he changed overnight, Gluck produced music showing that the ideas which had been brewing so long in his mind had at last fermented. He went far toward making the music and the story one, mainly by throwing overboard the meaningless conventions that had been the curse of ballet music. Almost for the first time in its history, the stage had recruited a composer willing and able to place his brains as well as his purely musical talents at its disposal.

Having experimented successfully with ballet, Gluck turned back to opera. Hitherto he had set little else than Metastasio, whose librettos had not only cornered the market, but were used over and over again. But with their tortured conceits and lifeless artifice, these were not suitable for the musical dramas Gluck was contemplating. At this juncture, Raniero da Calzabigi, one of Metastasio's most outspoken critics, turned up with the right sort of libretto. The initiative for this happy collaboration came from Calzabigi, and there are writers who believe that he, rather than Gluck, should be credited with the reform of opera. But it is not reasonable to assume that in 1762, when Gluck wrote *Orfeo ed Euridice*, he should suddenly have pulled an eminently successful dramatic opera out of the blue: Calzabigi merely touched fire to well-seasoned kindling.

Orfeo ed Euridice, while retaining much of the old-style diction, departed from Metastasio in telling a simple story in dramatic terms. The sweet singer Orpheus mourns his dead wife, Eurydice; the gods permit him to bring her back from the Elysian Fields if he will not look at her before they reach daylight. But Eurydice's pleadings force him to break his vow, and she dies again. In defiance of the classical legend, Calzabigi then has Amor restore her to life, and the opera ends happily, not without loss of dramatic verity. Care has been taken to give each character music that really expresses him—music that subtly changes with each new situation. But we must listen carefully to realize that we are hearing dramatic music—must listen with innocent ears. We must not expect to hear the protagonists shouting at the top of their voices as in Wagner and Strauss. This is drama as the ancients knew it—

decorous, stylized, restrained. We must discard temporarily the conventions of modern music drama, and judge *Orfeo ed Euridice* and Gluck's five other masterpieces within the framework of their times.

But to respond to the purely musical charm of Gluck no such adjustment is needed. *Orfeo* is an excellent introduction to the greater Gluck. Unfortunately for him who is being introduced to this noble style, however, it opens unpromisingly with one of Gluck's dullest overtures, anything but expressive of what is to follow. But after the brief first act comes a scene Gluck never surpassed in dramatic intensity: Orpheus, finding his way to the Elysian Fields blocked by a chorus of Furies, pleads with the infernal sentinels to allow him to pass. As his ineffably poignant song proceeds, they interrupt him with shouts of "No!" The exquisite strains reduce even them to submission, and the gates open. Almost immediately, before the spell of this superb scene has worn off, we hear the serene and solemn "Dance of the Blessed Spirits," the most affecting music Gluck ever composed for instruments alone. The thin, pure line of the flute achieves a particular kind of magic here—the essence of that fabled "peace which passeth all understanding"—that is unique in the whole realm of music. Here Gluck, whose gifts are not always purely musical, stands on the loftiest heights with the very greatest of the masters.

After the two magnificent scenes of the second act, almost any third act would have seemed flat. *Orfeo*'s suffers undeservedly both from its position in the opera and from the fact that the libretto trails off into an absurd, tacked-on happy ending. Gluck might better have rung the curtain down as Eurydice dies—except for one thing: the deathless aria *Che farò senza Euridice*. By modern standards, this is not a very dramatic aria: measured, for instance, against the *Liebestod*, it sounds lyric rather than dramatic. The point is that sung in the proper tempo,* and by a real artist, it is irresistible, and seems the only possible expression of Orpheus' grief. As Alfred Einstein has well said, "It is devoid of pathos because . . . it transcends all expression." After this great melody has been sung, those who have the heart may remain to witness, in

---

* Gluck himself admitted that taking the aria at a wrong tempo would reduce it to a merry-go-round tune, and critics, enlarging on this point, have said that taken a shade faster, it might better be sung to joyful words—"I've found my Eurydice," for example.

the concluding ballet and general jollification, the very inanities against which Gluck had struck the first blow in this selfsame opera.

Orfeo ed Euridice was first produced at Vienna on October 5, 1762. It was received coldly, but within a year a strong reaction in its favor set in. By 1764 it had become so popular that it was used at the coronation of the Archduke Josef as King of the Romans at Frankfort, where the young Goethe, who was on hand for the ceremonies, heard it. It brought Gluck so much money that in the same year he was able to give up the position of *Hofkapellmeister* Maria Theresa had conferred on him ten years before. He raised his style of living, moving from a comfortable but unpretentious house into a splendidly appointed one in a fashionable quarter of Vienna. Now, instead of taking the next logical steps after *Orfeo*, Gluck immediately reverted to the old-fashioned opera, and even gave Metastasio a special order for a libretto. For the next five years Gluck served up silly confections and gave singing lessons at court, one of his pupils being the young Archduchess Marie Antoinette.

In 1766 Gluck began to write *Alceste* to a Calzabigi libretto. By examining the probably ghostwritten dedication, we can see that Gluck had not wasted the years since *Orfeo*: he had raised his previously nebulous feelings about operatic reform to the conscious level. This brief revolutionary manifesto is one of the most important documents in musical history. "My purpose," he writes firmly, "was to restrict music to its true office, that of ministering to the expression of the poetry, and to the situations of the plot, without interrupting the action, or chilling it by superfluous and needless ornamentation." And further, "I thought that my most strenuous efforts must be directed toward a noble simplicity, thus avoiding a parade of difficulty at the expense of clearness. I did not consider a mere display of novelty valuable unless naturally suggested by the situation and the expression, and on this point no rule in composition exists that I would not have gladly sacrificed in favor of the effect produced."

Gluck carried out these ideas in *Alceste* with such relentless logic that he all but alienated the world of Vienna, where it was first produced on December 16, 1767. The plot was even more stark than that of *Orfeo*: King Admetus must die unless he can find a substitute; Alcestis, his wife, offers her life for his, and Admetus recovers. When Alcestis dies, Admetus prepares to kill himself. Apollo appears, and revives Alcestis. This story offered situations more dramatic than those of *Orfeo*, and Gluck fully exploited them. The overture marks another step in his reform. In the dedication he had written, "My idea was that the overture should prepare the spectators for the plot to be represented, and give some indication of its nature." This the *Alceste* overture, with its slow, solemn, and elevated cadences, does perfectly. While the necessity of an appropriate overture has long been a commonplace of opera, it must be borne in mind that previous to *Alceste* most overtures had been mere irrelevant curtain raisers. Even before this one melts into the first scene, the curtain is up. Besides the overture, only two excerpts can be familiar to even the most faithful concert-goers. The first is Alcestis' grand scene of renunciation in the first act—"*Divinités du Styx,*"* which by its nervous, sensitive changes of tempo exquisitely mirrors the heroine's shifting emotions. The other is Saint-Saëns' potpourri of ballet tunes from the opera, which was yesterday a hackneyed stand-by of pianists of recital and subrecital stature.

Like *Orfeo ed Euridice*, *Alceste* got a chilly reception at the *première*. Probably voicing the consensus, one member of the audience said, "For nine days the theater has been closed, and on the tenth it opens with a Requiem." Everybody was annoyed with Gluck: his confreres resented his attack on their style of opera; the singers were vexed because this unadorned music gave them no chance to display their incredible agility, and the audience was bored because it could not hear the singers exercise. Gluck's patrons trickled away: scarcely anyone encouraged him to persist in his great effort. But he had found his métier—and he was a very stubborn man when he finally made up his mind. Even as his critics and enemies multiplied, he turned once more to Calzabigi for the libretto of an opera that would shock them even further.

Paride ed Elena is not the best of Gluck's operas, but it is in one sense the most dramatic. Or at least Calzabigi and Gluck intended it to be. The dramatic crux is the conflict, or antithesis, between two civilizations, the Spartan and the Phrygian. Helen is a pure, high-minded, and chaste Grecian maid, Paris a voluptuous and impulsive Trojan youth. The librettist even altered the legend,

* The opening words of the aria in the later French version of *Alceste*.

making Helen Menelaus' fiancée rather than his wife, in order to make her more than ever a goody-goody. Unfortunately, the action does not measure up to the grandiose scheme of racial contrast. As Cupid promises Helen to Paris early in the first act, the only reason her four acts of prudish protest are not anticlimactic is that the opera has no climax. The music, by its finely drawn contrasts, partly saves the stupid plot. The alternation of numbers in varying modes is highly effective, and the love music is, for Gluck, convincingly erotic. Paris' passionately yearning "*O del mio dolce ardor,*" still a prime favorite in the recital hall, is one of the great love songs of all times, but it is a pity that in this long five-act opera the musical climax should occur in the first act.

Considering its palpable defects, it is no wonder that *Paride ed Elena* was a failure. Gluck made matters worse by defying public, colleagues, critics, and singers in another dedicatory blast. After defending *Alceste* and calling its detractors pedants, he flings down the gauntlet: "I do not expect greater success from my *Paride* than from *Alceste*, at least in my purpose to effect the desired change in musical composers; on the contrary, I anticipate greater opposition than ever; but, for my part, this shall never deter me from making fresh attempts to accomplish my good design." And he winds up this dedication to the Duke of Bragança with the courtierlike avowal that he is ready to take it on the chin from the general public so long as he has one Plato to encourage him.

In reality, Gluck was bitterly disappointed at the public's apathy and open hostility. Nor were his feelings assuaged when Calzabigi generously shouldered the blame for *Paride ed Elena*. But whereas Calzabigi had won his own battle—diminishing Metastasio's predominance—Gluck had reached a stalemate. After 1770, when *Paride* was first produced, it became obvious to him that Vienna was invincible in its stupidity. He then began to look toward Paris, which had already been put in a receptive mood by the declamatory style of Rameau. So seasoned a courtier as Gluck had no difficulty in pulling the proper wires, and we soon find him on the friendliest terms with the Bailli du Rollet, secretary of the French embassay in Vienna. In the back of his mind was the fact that his former pupil was now the pampered and all-powerful wife of the Dauphin Louis.

Du Rollet, besides being a first-rate wangler, also had literary ambitions, which the politic Gluck was pleased to further. The Frenchman now became his librettist, presenting him in 1772 with *Iphigénie en Aulide*, a curious hodgepodge of Racine, legend, and Du Rollet. Gluck started to work on this at once, and by the end of the year the collaborators prayerfully forwarded the first act to Antoine d'Auvergne, a director of the Opéra. D'Auvergne answered at once, saying that he would like to produce the opera, but would do so only if the Chevalier Gluck would undertake to write five more operas for him. By these exacting terms he doubtless hoped to deter a man who was almost sixty years old. On the other hand, the reason he gave for the proviso—that one Gluck opera would drive all competitors from the stage—was so flattering to the composer's thirsting ego that he decided to force the issue. Realizing that he was too old to guarantee five more operas, he induced Marie Antoinette to command the staging of *Iphigénie en Aulide*. His royal friend did her work so well that by the end of 1773 he received an invitation to come to Paris to direct the opera on his own exceedingly favorable terms.

Early in 1774, Gluck and his wife, with his highly talented niece, whom they had adopted some years before, set out for Paris. They stopped in Karlsruhe to visit the poet Klopstock, then at the height of his fame, and by early spring were in the French capital. Gluck worked himself to a shadow during the rehearsals of *Iphigénie*: there were all the usual difficulties with singers, orchestra, and managers, and on several occasions Marie Antoinette had to soothe ruffled feelings all round. The peerless Sophie Arnould, who was to sing Iphigenia, was so intractable that once Gluck threatened to return to Vienna if she did not follow instructions. But ultimately all obstacles were overcome: the most dangerous critics were placated in advance, and even the savage Jean-Jacques Rousseau, for long the champion of Italianate opera, was won over by carefully directed flattery.

On April 19, 1774, *Iphigénie en Aulide* was produced at the Opéra. Gluck must have risen to conduct with a mind full of doubts and questions. Would Arnould, as usual, sing off pitch? Was Legros really too ill to do justice to the tempestuous role of Achilles? Would the phlegmatic Larrivée, by some miracle, make Agamemnon come to life? During rehearsals Gluck had torn his hair as Larrivée listlessly walked through the part, but the baritone had said loftily, "Wait till I get into my costume—you won't recognize me then." But when, at dress rehearsal, Larrivée was as wooden as ever, Gluck had called out, "Oh, Larrivée, Larrivée, I recognize you!" And finally there was the problem of Vestris, *le dieu de la danse*, who had once boasted that the three greatest men in Europe were Frederick the Great, Voltaire, and himself. If he had had his own way, *Iphigénie en Aulide* would have been more ballet than opera. One by one, Gluck had squelched his demands, even refusing his piteous appeal for a chaconne at the end of the opera. "Whenever did the Greeks dance a chaconne?" Gluck had asked witheringly. But Vestris was not to be withered. "Oh, didn't they?" he replied haughtily. "So much the worse for them!"

Iphigénie triumphed at once. Despite certain glaring absurdities in the libretto, and not a few arid stretches in the music, Paris momentarily took the Chevalier Gluck to its heart. At the *première* the overture, generally considered the finest he composed, was enthusiastically encored. At one point the music and action were so convincing that some hotheaded officers in the audience were ready to rush onto the stage and rescue Iphigenia. The score is rich—almost too rich—in fine airs, which sometimes come in clusters of three, thereby tending to interrupt the flow of the action. Although there were disturbing errors of taste in Alexander Smallens' revival some years back of what might more appropriately have been called *Iphigénie en Philadelphie*, enough of Gluck's intention came through to convince the audience that it was having an esthetic experience of the first rank. The whole effect of the opera is one of archaic grandeur, sustained by sculptured declamation and a loftiness of effect that rarely falters even when purely musical inspiration flags.

The witty Abbé Arnaud had remarked of one bit from *Iphigénie*, "With that air one might found a religion," and, indeed, the Parisians were not slow in founding one, its devotees being known as Gluckists, though all Paris did not worship at this shrine. Some months later, Gluck was ready with a French version of his *Orfeo*, with the hero's part transposed for Legros, a tenor, as there was no male contralto to sing the part as originally written. This change of key spoiled many of Gluck's finest effects,* but the Parisians liked *Orphée et Eurydice* even better than *Iphigénie*. On the crest of this unflawed success, with his celebrity growing by leaps and bounds, Gluck returned to Vienna to receive from Maria Theresa a brevet as court composer. In 1774, at the age of sixty, he had become the leading musician of Europe.

The next year, however, found Gluck in poor spirits. He had several important projects under way, one of them a French version of *Alceste*. He busied himself remodeling two flimsy operas of his earlier period. Neither interested the Parisians, though Marie Antoinette, now Queen of France, had asked for them. Gluck was present when the first of these was given, but he lay perilously near to death in Vienna when the other was produced, and so was spared a repetition of the bitter spectacle of public apathy. He returned to Paris on his recovery, and the following spring was recompensed for all his recent disappointments by the success, negligible at first, but ever increasing, of the French *Alceste*. Unhappily, in one of his absences from Paris the meddlers at the Opéra commissioned François-Joseph Gossec—a young Belgian whose fame is kept verdant by an immortal and ninth-rate gavotte, and by the fact that he first used the clarinet in a score—to write an extra character—Hercules—into the third act of *Alceste*, where it has remained to this day.

In 1777, Gluck produced *Armide*, the libretto of which had been adapted from Tasso's *Gerusalemme liberata* by Molière's collaborator and erstwhile rival, Philippe Quinault, for the use of Louis XIV's dictatorial favorite, the former Italian busboy, Jean-Baptiste Lully.† Nor had a century on the shelf improved the libretto—it was more old-fashioned, and certainly just as diffuse. Armida in her magic garden is a sort of seventeenth-century Kundry, and her natural playmates are demons, knights-errant, warlocks, and fairies. It is useless to pretend that Gluck was entirely successful in setting Quinault's libretto—the bewildering change of scene and the stage properties got in the way of the music all too often. Nevertheless, though *Armide* does not hold together, and is less rich in memorable airs than some of Gluck's other operas, it shows him as not

---

* In modern revivals, the role of Orpheus is always sung—in the original key—by a woman.

† Handel had also used Quinault's libretto for his *Rinaldo*.

only a starter but a developer of character. The influential critic, La Harpe, entirely missed the point in stigmatizing the part of Armida as "a monotonous and fatiguing shriek from beginning to end." What Gluck had really done with considerable success was to sacrifice purely musical beauty to the demands of dramatic characterization—a romantic attitude that has found its ultimate logic in Strauss' *Elektra*.

Armide touched off the fuse of the most notorious strife in musical history—the war between the Gluckists and the Piccinnists. It embroiled everyone in Paris with the exception of Gluck and the frightened and confused Niccola Piccinni, who had originally been imported to cross swords with the great Austrian—and to add to the gaiety of nations. Far too much has been made of this quarrel. It is true that all sorts of bigwigs—Marie Antoinette, Mme Du Barry, Voltaire, and Rousseau—were involved in setting the stage for the pitched battle, and anyone reading the journals of the time would conclude that nothing else was talked of. Actually, the principals refused to fight: Gluck not only scrapped a partially completed version of *Roland* when he heard that the conspirators had given Piccinni the same libretto, but consistently refused to admit that there was any rivalry between him and the Italian; Piccinni, who had his share of talent and taste, was loud in his admiration of Gluck. Eventually, however, the unwilling protagonists were tricked into setting the same libretto—*Iphigénie en Tauride*. Piccinni offered his profound apologies to Gluck, and the whole feud shortly died of inanition.*

Gluck was sixty-five years old when *Iphigénie en Tauride*, the last of his six great operas, was first performed. He was fortunate in securing, for this final masterpiece, the best libretto he ever had, adapted from Euripides with singular faithfulness by an obscure poet, Nicolas-François Guillard. For once, Gluck was freed from supplying appropriate music to absurd mythological hocus-pocus. The story is refreshingly straightforward: when Iphigenia offers to take her brother Orestes' place on the sacrificial altar, her nobility is rewarded by the gods; she is rescued by Orestes' faithful friend, Pylades, and the tyrant who had ordered the sacrifice is slain. Age had steadied rather than weakened Gluck's hand, and the only

---

* The Gluckists claimed the victory, for Piccinni's setting of *Iphigénie en Tauride* fell far short of Gluck's—as Piccinni was the first to acknowledge.

criticism of the score (if criticism it be) is that it lacks those catchy melodies which have served to keep Gluck's fame alive in public esteem. Otherwise the Tauric *Iphigénie* is the perfect and magnificent realization of his operatic theories—simple music that effectively, inevitably clothes the text. His achievement here is all the more impressive since several of the most dramatically apt numbers were borrowed from earlier works, borrowed with such nicety of discrimination and adapted to their new surroundings with such a sure touch as to completely transform them.

It was this quality of intelligence, of seeing the shape of an opera whole, that drove Gluck to the innovations that constitute his historical importance. In sheer musical genius he was not measurably superior to the best of his now forgotten contemporaries, except in the few instances when he was carried beyond his own powers by the force of the drama. His actual idiom differs but little from theirs, and so there is no exaggeration in Vernon Lee's judgment: "Musical style, in its musical essentials, was unaltered by Gluck's reforms." His aims were all in the direction of dramatic verity and continuity. Stated bluntly, his was a scissors-and-paste job: he moved certain elements around, dropped others, and made inserts of his own. He saw, for instance, that the time-honored *da capo* aria, with its automatic reprise, was fatal to all dramatic movement: he dropped it. He saw that clavier-accompanied recitative interrupting the orchestral language was quite as fatal to his purpose: he dropped the clavier, incidentally creating the modern opera conductor, for the clavierist had previously given the beat.

Iphigénie en Tauride was Gluck's last success—almost his last effort. Shortly afterwards, he wrote *Echo et Narcisse*, and for the first time in years, the directors of the Opéra, with ominous prescience, dared to bargain with him about the price. They were right: *Echo et Narcisse* failed miserably, infuriating Gluck and losing money for the management. He would have fled to Vienna at once, but he was in bed recovering from a stroke of apoplexy. He was worn out from hard work and years of rich food and drink: the lustrous gray eyes were dimmed; the brown hair was silvery white, the thick bull neck withered, the towering frame stooped. Before reaching Vienna, in October, 1779, he suffered several more slight strokes.

Gluck's last years were uneventful. He had no financial worries: not only was his wife wealthy, but he had himself made a large fortune. Furthermore, he had his salary as court composer at Vienna and an annual pension of six thousand livres from Marie Antoinette, which he had been drawing since 1774. He and his wife lived happily if rather lonesomely (their adopted daughter's death, some years earlier, had affected them both deeply) in a spacious house in the Rennweg. They occasionally entertained with some splendor: Catherine the Great's son, the future Paul of Russia, and his wife called in 1781, and the next year the Mozarts dined with them. Nothing resembling the friendship between Mozart and Haydn resulted, but the two composers genuinely admired each other: Gluck listened to *Die Entführung aus dem Serail* with sympathetic delight; Mozart haunted the rehearsals of *Iphigénie en Tauride* (not disdaining to get a few pointers for *Don Giovanni*), and even composed a set of variations on a Gluck theme.

Musically, Gluck was all but comatose. He toyed with the idea of writing music for one more Calzabigi libretto—*Les Danaïdes*—but abandoned it shortly, turning it over generously (but without the playwright's authorization) to his protégé, Antonio Salieri, whom he allowed to announce the work as a joint product of their pens. When the opera was a hit, Gluck was even more kind to Salieri: he publicly stated that his only share in the work had been advice. But when the rightfully indignant Calzabigi protested against this highhanded use of his libretto, Gluck was silent. He had nothing to say—there was no effective defense possible, and besides, he was too ill to reply. He now saw no one. Under the strictest medical care because of recurring strokes, he was deprived of the last pleasures of the aged. This was worse than death to Gluck, and one day when his wife's back was turned, he downed a liqueur. Feeling nothing the worse, he went for a drive. Before reaching home, he had another seizure, and before the day was over he was dead. It was November 15, 1787, and Gluck was seventy-three years old.

Chapter V

Franz Josef Haydn

(Rohrau, March 31, 1732–May 31, 1809, Vienna)

I N 1795 England was well embarked on that bloody and protracted strife with France that was to end on the field of Waterloo some twenty years later. It was a black year, characterized by
bread riots and widespread famine. There were threats against the
life of the younger Pitt, whose indomitable spirit alone kept the
war going. In October, a hungry mob howled at poor crazy George
III on his way to open Parliament. Everyone except the ministry
wanted peace, and it seemed that the brave English nation could
think of nothing but its misery. Parliament was the scene of acrimonious debate on matters of the gravest import. And yet, at a
time when the most trivial motion was made a pretext for embarrassing the government in the voting, the battling Whigs and To-
ries agreed to honor an Austrian* composer's claim for one hundred
guineas. For the creditor was Franz Josef Haydn, who had lately
given the people of England such musical fare as they had not enjoyed since the days of George Frideric Handel.

Of course, some of the more old-fashioned squires may have
muttered that the bill was not in the best of taste. It was well
known that Herr Haydn had carried away a small fortune from
the island, not to speak of a talking bird of inestimable value. A
more fastidious man, going off with such spoils, might well have
hesitated to bill the royal family for the unique honor of appearing
at twenty-six command performances.

But the truth is that the excellent businessman who presented
the claim was anything but a fastidious gentleman. He was a peasant, with a peasant's shrewdness and realism about money matters.
That is the fundamental thing to remember about Josef Haydn,
Mus. D. (Oxon), *Kapellmeister* to His Serene Highness Prince
Esterházy, and the music that he made. Even in his silkiest peruke
and most brocaded court suit he never forgot his poor and humble
origins and, far from trying to gloss them over, proudly described

* The idea that Haydn had some Croatian blood has now been thoroughly
discredited.

himself as something made from nothing. His father was a wheel-wright, his mother a cook; both families were completely undistinguished.

Haydn's father lived at Rohrau, in Lower Austria, and there, in a poor, almost squalid, house that is still standing, the composer was born on March 31, 1732. Both of his parents loved music, the father playing the harp by ear. Their leisure hours were often spent singing the local folk melodies that Haydn himself was to use as thematic material. The child showed such a lively interest in this homemade music, and sang so sweetly, that at the age of six he was carried off to near-by Hainburg by a distant relative who there served as schoolteacher and choirmaster. His preceptor, though unnecessarily harsh, grounded him in the fundamentals of violin and clavier, and trained his voice so well that two years later, when the music director of St. Stephen's at Vienna was passing through Hainburg, and heard Haydn sing, he asked to have the boy for his choir. Permission was granted, and Haydn became a Viennese at the age of eight.

So much legend has clustered around Haydn's life in St. Stephen's choir school that it is no longer possible to disentangle fact from fiction. Boiled down to their bare essentials, these often pointless stories testify not only to his extreme poverty, but also to his intense love of music. The choirmaster, whose sole interest was to keep his establishment running on the smallest possible amount of money, did little to encourage Haydn's obvious talent. He was a cruel and exacting slave driver, and it is amazing that his stern, repressive measures did not crush the boy's high spirits. There was never any love lost between the two, and when Maria Theresa complained of Haydn's voice, which was beginning to break, the choirmaster was glad to seize upon the first pretext for dismissing him. When Haydn was accommodating enough to cut off another chorister's pigtail, and was summarily thrown out, the director doubtless congratulated himself on having washed his hands of an insolent practical joker.

Thus, at the age of seventeen, Haydn found himself alone and friendless in the streets of Vienna. This was not quite so bad as it sounds, for though almost a century was to elapse before Johann Strauss made Vienna the symbol of *Schwärmerei*, it was already the scene of gaiety and good fellowship. Musicians of all ranks enter-

tained their patrons and friends with open-air serenades, often
scored for full orchestra. Vienna was organized like a luxury liner,
with half the population devoted to the full-time business of entertaining a benevolently disposed nobility. The streets were full of
friendly people, who were too busy having a good time to stand on
ceremony. One of them—a tenor with a wife and child—met
Haydn disconsolately roaming about, and generously offered him
a bunk in his humble attic. For three years Haydn's efforts to stave
off hunger were no more interesting or distinguished than those of
any young man in his position: he sang in church choirs, took part
in street serenades, and helped out the music at weddings, funer-
als, and other festal occasions. All this time he studied hard: he
learned theory backward and forward, and practiced the clavier.
He got hold of six of Karl Philipp Emanuel Bach's clavier sonatas,
and studied them so thoroughly that they became the backbone
of his own style. In crystallizing the sonata form, Karl Philipp
Emanuel had in one respect outdone his illustrious father, who
evolved nothing, but perfected forms already at hand. Haydn himself, in both his quartets and symphonies, developed the new form
far beyond anything achieved earlier, but its fundamental architecture he owed to the pioneer. Quick to give praise where it was
due, he freely admitted this debt, and Bach returned the compliment by proclaiming Haydn his one true disciple.

Spurred on by his studies in theory and his increasing command
of instrumental resources, Haydn had begun to compose. Most of
his very early works, including a comic opera for which he received the splendid sum of twenty-five ducats, are lost. An indifferent Mass, for which, as one of his firstborn, Haydn had a sneak-
ing partiality, survives. It must be admitted that these first flights
add little to his stature as a composer, and at the time added less to
his purse. He even had to accept menial jobs to make ends meet.
For several years he gave music lessons to a young Spanish blue-
stocking whose general education was being supervised by "the
divine Metastasio." Haydn's meeting with this stuffy but kindly
old bachelor set in motion a train of events that determined the
entire course of his life. For Metastasio introduced him to another
stuffy old bachelor, Niccola Porpora, "the greatest singing master
that ever lived." Haydn aspired to study with him, but had nothing to offer in payment except his services as valet and accom-

panist. Porpora, whose penny pinching was notorious, drove the hardest possible bargain.

Working for Porpora was probably the toughest job Haydn ever filled. Porpora was an irascible old man, embittered by his fruitless rivalry with Handel, unsuccessful quest for high preferment, and the obvious truth that his great days were mostly behind him. Haydn had to bear the brunt of his spleen. But between brushing the *maestro*'s filthy clothes and accompanying the Venetian ambassador's mistress at her singing lessons, he somehow managed to get the information he wanted. George Sand has amusingly embroidered the few facts known about this strange relationship in her long but rewarding musical novel, *Consuelo*. Although Haydn, with his usual generosity, admitted his debt to Porpora, it was actually less artistic than social—through him he met many wealthy noblemen and celebrities, among them Gluck, already famous for a long series of conventional operas, but not yet embarked on his stormy career as a reformer. More important to Haydn was a rich Austrian squire, Karl von Fürnberg.

Von Fürnberg, a man of artistic tastes, who entertained lavishly at his country house outside Vienna, invited the needy young man to assume the direction of the music at Weinzierl. Haydn accepted with alacrity, and in 1755 initiated his long career as a household musician. He was at Weinzierl less than a year, but in that brief time wrote a series of eighteen pieces for strings, which he labeled indifferently *divertimenti*, nocturnes, and cassations. Basing them on the conventional orchestral suite, he gradually refashioned them in the light of the formal hints he had taken from the sonatas of Karl Philipp Emanuel Bach. In this way, Haydn slowly made something new out of the suite, bringing into being, according to the instruments used, his conceptions of the string quartet and the symphony. Naturally, he did not effect this transformation at one sitting or without getting ideas from other composers: the gap between one of the Weinzierl pieces and the "Oxford" Symphony of his last period is enormous. He made many false starts (some of them delightful) before evolving the four-movement symphony and quartet that until yesterday were the formal norms for these media.

Haydn returned to Vienna with money in his pocket and prestige increased. He came perilously near to becoming a fashionable singing and clavier teacher. After three years, during which he seems to have sacrificed his creative ambitions to ready-money teaching and performing jobs, he was rescued by Von Fürnberg, who recommended him to Count Maximilian von Morzin, a Bohemian grandee who kept a country establishment far beyond his means. Von Morzin engaged Haydn as his music director and composer at the niggardly salary of two hundred florins yearly—about $100. His new master kept him a scant two years, during which he returned to composition, producing a mass of miscellaneous pieces that have mostly been forgotten.

Now twenty-eight years old, and good Viennese bourgeois he had become, Haydn bethought himself of taking a wife. There were three stumbling blocks in the way of his marriage: his stipend was too meager to support even a frugal bachelor; Count von Morzin never kept a married man in his employ, and the girl of Haydn's choice—a barber's younger daughter—entered a convent. None of these warnings could shake his determination: he wanted to get married, and nothing could stop him. Accordingly, when the calculating barber suggested his elder daughter as a second choice, Haydn rose to the bait. On November 26, 1760, he led the elder Fräulein Keller to the altar. She was three years his senior—and a highly unreasonable woman. From the beginning, this loveless marriage was doomed to failure. Fortunately, Haydn was not a very emotional man, and marrying a harridan could not break his spirit. There were no children to hold them together, and after a few years a separation was quietly arranged, though he continued to support her.

Von Morzin had no opportunity to apply to his musical director his odd rule about married men. His creditors denied him that luxury. Early in 1761, he was obliged to retrench, and his musicians were among the first dismissed. Luckily for Haydn, just before the collapse Prince Pál Antal Esterházy visited Von Morzin, and was greatly impressed by Haydn's compositions and by his conduct of the band. He at once offered him a place in his own musical establishment, and so, when he was dismissed, Haydn went almost immediately to the Esterházy estate at Eisenstadt.

Haydn was to remain in the service of the Esterházys until the dawn of the nineteenth century. Because of the medieval temper of the Hungarian squirearchy, as well as the idiosyncrasies of his masters, he was practically a prisoner in the country for almost thirty years. Very occasionally, when he had an acute attack of wanderlust, he resented this enforced isolation. But he was not a man to beat his wings against the bars in senseless fretting—he was inclined to take life as he found it. As a peasant who had come up in the world, homely philosophy was definitely his line, and he almost invariably stuck to it. A Beethoven or a Mozart could not have brooked the soul-sapping monotony of petty court life—either they would have revolted by running away, or would have stifled their anguish in tragic masterpieces. But Haydn was content, even when his fame had spread throughout Europe, to remain the perfect upper servant perfectly performing his daily duties.

Judged by ordinary standards, Haydn was emotionally a vegetable. After leaving Rohrau at the age of six, he seems to have displayed only the most perfunctory interest in his parents. Their deaths apparently left him untouched. His attitude toward his brothers, two of whom were musicians, might be described as one of polite interest. As we have seen, his marriage was entered into without romance, and turned out a complete failure. He was far advanced in his forties before he really fell in love, if indeed such a strong term can be applied to his businesslike passion for a young married woman, almost thirty years his junior. In fact, Haydn's recorded connections with women invariably have a touch of the comic about them.

A clue to Haydn's sparse emotional life is to be found both in the wearisome multiplicity of his official duties and in the very quality of the vast amount of music he composed. To paraphrase Buffon, the music was the man. He was well balanced, genial, sensible, a little pedantic, and did not wear his genius on his sleeve. In short, just the sort of person to get along with a temperamental master and win the affection of his colleagues—the perfect *Kapellmeister*. There was something in Josef Haydn that liked being a functionary: he took even the deification he underwent in his old age as the just deserts of a man who had done his job faithfully and well.

When Haydn first took up his residence at Eisenstadt, he found his duties comparatively light. The musical establishment was small, and besides, he was at first only assistant *Kapellmeister*. In less than a year, however, Prince Pál Antal died, and was succeeded by his more ostentatious brother, who immediately began to expand in all directions. His Serene Highness Prince Miklós Jozsef Esterházy of Galánta, Knight of the Golden Fleece, was known, with the curious understatement of the eighteenth century, as "the Magnificent." Decked out in his renowned diamond-studded uniform, he would be perfectly at home on a De Mille set. When he made his triumphal entry into Eisenstadt after succeeding to his resounding title, the festivities lasted a month, and were on an imperial scale.

But Prince Miklós had something more than a baroque side to his nature. Like all the Esterházys, he loved music, and wanted his artists to be the best in Europe. Accordingly, when his old *Kapellmeister* died in 1766, he promoted Haydn to the post. It turned out that this was a far more important position than his predecessor had held, for Haydn was soon presiding over the musical household of the most spectacular country place east of Versailles. In 1764 the Prince, bored with his two-hundred-room manor at Eisenstadt, had begun a vast Renaissance château directly inspired by a visit to Versailles. Whether Prince Miklós actually aimed at putting Louis XV's nose out of joint will never be known, but it is certain that he dropped eleven million gulden transforming an unhealthy marsh about thirty miles from Eisenstadt into the fairy palace of Esterház. The cleverest gardeners worked miracles with its unpromising environs, strewing them with the elegant commonplaces of eighteenth-century landscaping: grottoes, hermitages, classical temples, kiosks, artificial waterfalls, and —of course—a maze. The park was copiously stocked with game; the streams were sluggish with fish. But more important than these were the spendthrift provisions for musical and theatrical entertainment: the opera house accommodating four hundred spectators and the marionette theater equipped with every imaginable contrivance.

As *Kapellmeister* of one of the most hospitable magnificoes of the age, Haydn held no sinecure. The detail work was tremendous, and despite his fertility, composing must have taken up only a tithe of his time. To get a picture of Haydn's schedule, imagine Toscanini composing almost everything he plays, acting as music librarian, seeing that the instruments are in repair, and sending written reports of his players' conduct to the board of directors of the National Broadcasting Company. Even when the master was away, Haydn had to give two concerts a week to guarantee against the musicians absenting themselves without leave, and to keep them in concert trim. And when Prince Miklós had a houseful of distinguished guests (which was much of the time), Haydn's duties kept him on the run from early morning until the last candle was snuffed.

Haydn spent almost a quarter of a century at Esterház, occupying three rooms in the servants' wing. His relations with the Prince were as warm as the difference in their ranks allowed. True, while still assistant *Kapellmeister*, Haydn had been reprimanded for—of all things—dilatory attention to his duties. And once he made the tactical blunder of mastering the baryton, a kind of viola da gamba on which his master fancied himself a virtuoso. Instead of being pleased, the Prince was annoyed to find a rival in the field. Haydn then showed his native diplomacy by abandoning the baryton except to write some two hundred pieces for it, pieces carefully calculated not to expose the Prince's limitations. He was unfeignedly fond of his patron. After Prince Miklós' death, he wrote:

"My Prince was always satisfied with my works; I not only had the encouragement of constant approval, but as conductor of an orchestra I could make experiments, observe what produced an effect and what weakened it, and was thus in a position to improve, alter, make additions or omissions, and be as bold as I pleased; I was cut off from the world, there was no one to confuse or torment me, and I was forced to become *original*."

Between Haydn and his musicians the friendliest feelings always prevailed. The junior members of his staff, many of whom studied with him, were the first to refer to him as "Papa Haydn." In truth, he was a father to all his musicians, and was always ready to plead their case. One of the more delicate subjects was obtaining leave for the men, practically cut off from their families by the Prince's morbid affection for Esterház. With rare humorous tact, Haydn once presented a vacation plea by writing the "Farewell" Symphony, in the finale of which the men blew out the candles on their music stands, and stole out, one by one. Until, as Michel Brenet says, "Haydn, alone at his desk was preparing, not without anxiety, to go out too, when Nicolas Esterhazy called him and announced that he had understood the musicians' request and that they might leave the next day."*

But though Haydn and his men craved an occasional vacation, life at Esterház was not too monotonous, and working conditions were—for the period—excellent. Haydn went to work originally for four hundred florins a year, a figure which was almost doubled before Prince Miklós died. Considering that he had no personal expenses, the fact that he saved a mere pittance during a quarter century at Esterház is eloquent of an extravagant wife. But Frau Haydn was not entirely to blame. When the composer was almost fifty, he became involved with the wife of one of his violinists. Little Signora Polzelli, a vocalist briefly employed at Esterház, was only nineteen when Haydn met her. She did not love her husband, and there is little evidence that she cared for the bluff old Austrian. Soon, however, things came to such a pass that the lovers were exchanging pledges that they would wed when death released them from their partners. Polzelli died after a polite interval, but Haydn's wife was disobliging enough to linger until 1800, at which time the now rather faded siren got Haydn to sign a promise to leave her an annuity of three hundred florins. Whereupon she married an Italian, for the money had been her only object all along. Before forcing the promise of an annuity, she had for years been milking Haydn, probably on the strength of an old indiscretion. Only once did he complain, after he had sent her six hundred florins in one year.

The *affaire* Polzelli seems to have been the only wild oat Haydn sowed at Esterház. His mere routine duties ruled out excesses; the special entertainments for the Prince's eminent guests made self-denial mandatory. The gallant Prince Louis de Rohan, later the scapegoat of the "affair of the diamond necklace," stopped at Esterház in 1772, and delighted his host by comparing the château to Versailles. The next year, Maria Theresa was entertained at a three-day festival, for which Haydn composed the delightful symphony that still bears her name. And so it went, with the palace a scene of constant revelry and music-making. Or Prince Miklós might tear himself away from Esterház for the pleasure of exhibiting his band and its increasingly famous leader. Sometimes he

* In 1939 the Boston Symphony Orchestra, attired in eighteenth-century costume, enacted this scene, with Dr. Koussevitzky as Haydn.

took them to Pressburg, where the Hungarian diet met; one year they went to the imperial palace at Schönbrunn, where Haydn conducted one of his own operas as well as the music at a state dinner. When the Grand Duke Paul of Russia visited Vienna in 1781, Prince Miklós and his orchestra were on hand. Some of Haydn's operas were performed, and the indefatigable *Kapellmeister* composed the six "Russian" Quartets in Paul's honor. The Grand Duchess, who was extremely fond of his music, presented Haydn with a diamond-studded addition to his already imposing collection of royal and noble snuffboxes.

But infinitely more important than Haydn's contacts with the most imposing stuffed shirts of the era was his meeting with Mozart. This was more than a mere momentary crossing of paths. It was a mutual recognition of genius that affected the work of both men, and thus left an imperishable mark on music. Each had something of the highest value for the other, and it is no mere coincidence that their masterpieces were composed after their meeting. They saw each other rarely, but for collectors of great moments be it known that on at least two occasions they sat down to play quartets together, once with Karl Ditters von Dittersdorf and their now forgotten rival, Johann Baptist Wanhal.

And so the years passed gently over Haydn's head. Suddenly, in September, 1790, Prince Miklós died, and the world Haydn had known for almost thirty years came to an end. The new Prince, less interested in the arts than most of the Esterházys, disbanded the musicians—and Haydn, at fifty-eight, was out of a job. This was no great tragedy, for his beloved patron had left him an annual pension of one thousand florins, to which Prince Antal now generously added four hundred more. It might seem that with an assured annual income of almost twice his stipend from Prince Miklós, Haydn was better off financially than ever. But this was not the case. Not only did the bonuses Prince Miklós had given him for special compositions cease, but also he was obliged to live at his own expense. And life in Vienna, to which he naturally gravitated, was expensive. On the other hand, his already great fame brought many pupils flocking to his door, and considerable sums were coming in from his publishers.

For the man who had once been reprimanded for loafing on the job had really produced during his life at Esterház a vast body of compositions. Unlike Hasse, who may possibly have been cheated of immortality when the great Dresden fire destroyed almost all his manuscripts, Haydn, though he lost many scores in a fire at Esterház in 1779, had already published so much that his fame would have been secure if he had never written another note. Roughly speaking, while there he had composed over twenty operas, about ninety symphonies, and more than sixty quartets, besides small orchestral works, pieces for clavier and other solo instruments (including a glass harmonica and a musical clock), chamber music of all varieties, and Masses and other works for solo and concerted voices.

Almost without exception, Haydn's early vocal works are now outside the living repertoire, if, indeed, they were ever in it. Most of them were written to be performed at Esterház, and were born and died there. Haydn himself seems to have had mixed feelings about the operas. On the one hand, he could write with naïve conceit to his Viennese publisher: "If only the French could know my operetta *L'Isola disabitata* and my last opera *La Fedeltà premiata*! I am sure such works have never yet been heard in Paris, perhaps not even in Vienna." The answer is that by 1781, when this letter was written, the French and the Austrians had heard far too many such operas, and Gluck had already won his battle against them. Haydn, who had been taught to write opera according to the old-fashioned recipes of Alessandro Scarlatti and Hasse, was in a saner frame of mind six years later, when he was invited to compose an opera for Prague:

"You ask me for a comic light opera," he wrote. "Certainly, if you are willing to reserve for private use some vocal work of my composition. But if it is intended for performance in the theater at Prague, then I cannot serve you, for all my operas are written for the special conditions of Esterház, and could not produce elsewhere the effect I have calculated upon for this setting. It would be otherwise if I had the inestimable good fortune to be able to compose for your theater upon a completely new libretto. Though, there again, I should run too many risks, for it would be difficult for anyone—no matter whom—to equal the great Mozart. That is why I wish that all music lovers, especially the influential, could know the inimitable works of Mozart with a profundity, a musical knowledge, and a keen appreciation equal to my own. Then the nations would compete for possession of such a treasure. Prague must hold fast so precious a man—and reward him. For without that, the history of a great genius is a sad one, and gives posterity little encouragement to follow the same course. That is why so much fine and hopeful talent unfortunately perishes. I am full of anger when I think that this unique genius is not yet attached to a royal or imperial court. Forgive this outburst: I love the man too much."

Haydn's affection for Mozart was reciprocated. In 1790, when he was invited to visit London, Mozart tried to dissuade him from going. "Oh, Papa!" he exclaimed (though momentarily he seemed like the wise parent), "you have had no education for the wide, wide world, and you speak too few languages."

"My language is understood all over the world," Haydn replied dryly. For he was determined to go. Salomon, the London impresario, had suddenly burst in upon him several days before, saying, "I have come from London to fetch you. We will settle terms tomorrow." That morrow came, and like Satan displaying the nations of the world from the mountaintop, Salomon unrolled his little plan. Haydn heard, was tempted, and fell. Salomon guaranteed him £900 if he would make the trip. The only difficulty, from Haydn's point of view, was that he had to pay his own traveling expenses. However, Prince Esterházy advanced him the money, and after providing for his wife by selling a little house in Eisenstadt that Prince Miklós had given him, Haydn set out for London in mid-December. Mozart, on hand to see him off, burst into tears. "This is good-by," he sobbed. "We shall never meet again." And, indeed, before Haydn returned to Vienna Mozart was dead.

At fifty-eight, the composer set out on his travels with the naïve curiosity of a child. The Channel crossing was rough. "I remained on deck during the whole passage," he wrote, "in order to gaze my fill at that huge monster, the ocean. So long as it was calm, I had no fears, but when at length a violent wind began to blow, rising every minute . . . I was seized with a little alarm and a little indisposition." He landed at Dover, and arrived in London on New Year's Day, 1791. He was received like a sovereign prince: his fame had been trumpeted before him, and the clever Salomon had used the press to raise public interest to fever pitch. His lodg-

ings were besieged by ambassadors and great nobles, and invitations came pouring in by the hundreds. The inescapable Dr.
Burney called, and firmly presented him with an ode of welcome.
In view of the fact that the terms of his contract called for twenty
especially written compositions, including six symphonies, he
finally had to move into the country to elude his pertinacious
admirers. Unhappily he had arrived in the midst of one of those
wars of the impresarios in which Handel had received so many
noble scars, and thus his opening concert was delayed. Slurring
squibs about him appeared in the newspapers, and doubtless the
announcement of an actual date for the first concert narrowly
averted a question being asked in Parliament.

All criticism was silenced by the overwhelming success of the
first concert. The adagio of the symphony (now known as the
"Salomon" No. 2) was encored—in those times a rare proof of
enthusiasm. And when the Prince of Wales appeared like a resplendent apparition at the second concert, the newspapers
changed their tone. Blending sycophancy with true admiration,
they now referred to "the sublime and august thoughts this master
weaves into his works." The shrewd Salomon was assisting at an
apotheosis. Crowds were turned away from the Hanover Square
Rooms for every concert, and Haydn's benefit on May 16 realized
£350—almost twice the take Salomon had guaranteed. The first
week of July, Haydn journeyed up to Oxford (or, as he wrote it,
Oxforth), which, at Burney's recommendation, had offered him a
musical doctorate. At the second of the three concerts given there
in his honor, the lovely symphony in G major he had written some
years before was performed instead of a new work. Ever since
known as the "Oxford" Symphony, this delicious musical kitten
appealed immediately to the lettered dons and young fashionables.

Haydn was enormously pleased—and a bit flustered. After he
received his degree, he acknowledged the applause by raising his
doctor's gown high above his head so that all could see it, saying
in English, "I thank you." He must have been a rather comic
figure, though he wrote home in great glee, "I had to walk around
in this gown for three days. I only wish my friends in Vienna might
have seen me." Like so many famous men, he was decidedly below
middle height. His thickset, flabby body was carried on absurdly
short legs. And his face was far from prepossessing, though its fea-

tures, except for an underslung Hapsburg jaw, were regular. His swarthy skin was deeply pitted by smallpox, and his nose was disfigured by a growth he stubbornly refused to have removed even when John Hunter, the ablest surgeon of the epoch, offered to perform the operation. Haydn realized that he was ugly, and preened himself on the fact that women fell in love with him "for something deeper than beauty."

Susceptibility to women as women made Haydn rather uncritical of them. One was "the most beautiful woman I ever saw"; another, "the loveliest woman I ever saw." These were but glances: his affections were directed toward Mrs. John Samuel Schroeter, a widow of mature years. What began as music lessons ended as something far more intense: she was soon addressing her elderly music master as "my dearest love." As for Haydn, he cherished a packet of her letters until his death, and once said, "Those are from an English widow who fell in love with me. She was a very attractive woman and still handsome, though over sixty; and had I been free I should certainly have married her."

It may be that Mrs. Schroeter's matronly charms played their part in keeping Haydn in London. At any rate, he dallied there until June, 1792—a full year and a half after his arrival—and then set out for the Continent. He traveled by way of Bonn, where the young Beethoven presented himself, and submitted a cantata for criticism. Haydn's generous praise may well have spurred Beethoven to study in Vienna. In December, Beethoven began to take lessons from Haydn. From the beginning, they misunderstood each other: the young musical rebel puzzled Haydn, while the impatient Beethoven rather unfairly regarded his aging teacher as a fogy. Haydn was too old to realize the scope and significance of Beethoven's music—to him certain aspects of it seemed senseless license. But in the course of years, Beethoven came to appreciate his teacher's musical genius. Yet, the relationship between the two men was nothing more than a protracted casual meeting—they were never actually friends, and their influence on each other was negligible. Beethoven said flatly, "I never learned anything from Haydn."

Wanderlust—and a dazzling new contract from Salomon—called Haydn back to England after a year and a half in Vienna. He arrived in London in February, 1794, and it is worth recording that he carefully chose lodgings near Mrs. Schroeter's house. This is the single tantalizing scrap of knowledge preserved about Haydn's love affair during this second visit. Warm though London had been to him when he first reached England, it now offered him an adulation it had lavished on no composer since Handel. After six new symphonies had been performed, the public clamored for a repetition of the first set. His benefit concert netted him £400. The royal family took him up: George III, whose first loyalty to Handel never flagged, was somewhat restrained in his ardors, but the Prince of Wales invited Haydn to Carlton House twenty-six times. It was for these performances that Haydn presented to Parliament his famous bill for the extremely modest sum of £100.

Again Haydn found it difficult to tear himself away: he remained in England for more than eighteen months, playing the social game heavily. During the summer of 1794 he moved leisurely from one spa or country seat to another. His diary is bare of references to music: he was much exercised over the character of Mrs. Billington, the actress, whose frank memoirs were the current scandal. He remarked on the national debt, preserved the Prince of Wales' favorite recipe for punch, and looked in at the trial of Warren Hastings. Not even the price of table delicacies escaped his omnivorous curiosity: "In the month of June 1792 a chicken, 7 s.; an Indian (a kind of bittern found in North America), 9 s.; a dozen larks, 1 coron [crown?]. N. B.—If plucked, a duck, 5 s." Haydn relished a good joke, and the best ones he heard also went into his diary. Certain lines about the comparative morals of English, French, and Dutch women are too graphic for publication. So, busily jotting down fresh items along the way, he returned to Vienna early in September, 1795.

With this second London visit, Haydn wrote finis to his career as a symphonist. That career, extending over more than thirty-five years, had produced no fewer than one hundred and four separate symphonies, many of high quality, but less notable for their variety. The fact that his earliest trial balloons are worthless museum pieces is easily explained: learning to write for the orchestra was to Haydn a slow and painful process completed comparatively late in life, and he had no models. He literally evolved the symphony from the orchestral suite and the clavier sonatas of Karl Philipp Emanuel Bach by laborious trial and error. The wonder is that he found the essential symphonic form as quickly as he did: to perfect it (within his recognized limitations, of course) took years. For almost a quarter of a century he continued to write symphonies for his small court orchestra, many of which are delightful and witty, and almost all of which are within the same narrow range. Their individuality rests on thematic variety alone.

The more Haydn's life and compositions are examined, the clearer it becomes that Mozart provided the stimulus for his emancipation from the stiffness of his earlier manner. The difference between even the finest of Haydn's pre-Mozartian symphonies—the "Farewell" and *La Chasse*," for example—and a richly mature work like the "Oxford" is not an obvious one: from first to last, the personality of Josef Haydn dominated, and limited, his symphonic conceptions. But in the later works this personality expressed itself through more ample resources—richer orchestration and untrammeled handling of musical ideas. With Mozart, Haydn finally brought the purely classical symphony as far as it could go without becoming something else. In the twelve "Salomon" Symphonies, the man who evolved a form lifted it to its zenith—a phenomenon unique in musical history.

These twelve symphonies owe their supremacy not only to their freedom of expression, but also to the fact that they were written for the best and largest orchestra Haydn ever knew. It would appear pathetically inadequate beside one of the perfectly trained and equipped orchestras of our own day, but it was capable of effects quite beyond the powers of the little household band at Esterház. In short, before composing for London, Haydn had never had a chance to make the most of his newly discovered resources. It is among the more fascinating ifs of musical history to speculate on what he might have done if he had had this vastly superior organization at his command when he was thirty rather than when he was almost sixty. The answer seems to be, on the basis of everything known about the composer, that we would have many more symphonies as fine as the "Oxford" or the "Salomon" No. 5, in C minor—but nothing different in kind. Haydn achieved his ideal of formal perfection, and there is no evidence that, in his symphonies at least, he ever wanted anything more. It took a restless, eternally dissatisfied temperament like Beethoven's to weld the symphony into a tremendous emotional vehicle.*

The truth is that Haydn's symphonies perfectly express his personality and its rather limited outlook. Nobody goes to them for the Aeschylean tragedy of Beethoven or the transcendent, unearthly serenity of Mozart—nor can you wallow with Haydn as you can with Tchaikovsky. Haydn is a prose writer, and as such, unequaled. He is the Addison and Steele of music, with the former's flawless touch and the latter's robust humor and lustiness of outlook. Any one of his great symphonies is the man in small: one and all they breathe his sunny disposition, his wit, his irrepressible high spirits, and his sane and healthy love of life. When his inspiration flagged, his untroubled faith degenerated into smugness, his desire for formal perfection into schoolmasterly finickiness. But his best symphonies are canticles of life enjoyed to the full—works of lively beauty that rank just below the best of Mozart and Beethoven. "Haydn would have been among the greatest," Bernard Shaw once wrote, "had he been driven to that terrible eminence."

When Haydn returned to Vienna he abandoned the symphony, the form with which his name is most popularly connected. He was sixty-three years old, and some of his well-meaning admirers had begun to treat him as though he were dead. They invited him to Rohrau, and showed him a monument to his fame. His reaction is not recorded, but he was properly overcome with emotion when he visited the house where he had been born. He knelt down, solemnly kissed the threshold, and pointing dramatically at the stove, declared that on that very spot his musical career had begun. Despite this premature commemorative service, he returned to Vienna, and continued to be thoroughly alive.

The main reason for Haydn's return from England had been a pressing invitation from a new Prince Esterházy, who wished him to resume his old position. Haydn consented, for the duties were comparatively light, entailing a few months each year at Eisenstadt, and the composition of some perfunctory occasional pieces, notably an annual Mass on the Princess' name day. But now

* The general lines of this argument are not affected by the recent, and loving, exhumation of five typical symphonies of the master's late middle period, ranging from 1779 to 1786. Pieced together by Dr. Alfred Einstein from old manuscripts and early editions, they were performed for the first time in New York during 1939, by the orchestra of the New Friends of Music, under Fritz Stiedry.

Haydn was so famous that it was he who conferred an honor on the Esterházys, rather than they on him. In fact, excepting Francis II and Metternich, he was the most famous living Austrian. It was natural, therefore, that in 1797, when the Imperial authorities wished to combat revolutionary influences that had seeped into Austria from France, they should ask Haydn to help by composing an air that could be used as a national anthem. Basing it on words by the "meritorious poet Haschka," he not only achieved his ambition of equalling *God Save the King*—he far surpassed it. *Gott erhalte Franz den Kaiser*, musically the finest national anthem ever written, served its purpose perfectly until 1938, when it was officially superseded by *Deutschland über Alles* (to the Haydn melody) and the *Horst Wessel Song*. Haydn's hymn was first sung on the Emperor's birthday—February 12, 1797—at the National-theater in Vienna. Francis II himself attended in state, and on the same day it was sung at the principal theaters throughout the Empire. It has always been the most popular of Haydn's songs.

But *God Save the King* was not the only English music Haydn wished to emulate. While in London, he went to a performance of *Messiah*, during which he was heard to sob, "Handel is the master of us all." Later he heard *Joshua*, and was even more moved, saying to a friend that "he had long been acquainted with music, but never knew half its powers before he heard it, as he was perfectly certain that only one inspired author ever did, or ever would, pen so sublime a composition." Just before Haydn left London, Salomon handed him a sacred text originally contrived for Handel partly from *Paradise Lost* and partly from Genesis. A friend of Haydn's made a free translation of it, and the composer set to work. "Never was I so pious as when composing *The Creation*," Haydn declared. "I knelt down every day and prayed God to strengthen me for my task." However, things did not go smoothly. At times the infirmities of age dammed up the flow of his creative genius. Like Di Lasso in his old age, Haydn began to suffer from melancholia and nerves, but he had reserves of peasant energy that the pampered Fleming lacked. So he came through with a masterpiece after eighteen difficult months. On April 29, 1798, *The Creation* was first produced privately at the palace of Prince Schwarzenburg, in Vienna. Little less than a year later, it was performed publicly on Haydn's name day—March 19—at the Nationaltheater. It was an immediate success, and soon was being heard by appreciative audiences throughout Europe. Even Paris, which did not like oratorio, capitulated. More, the French performers had a medal struck in homage to the composer. In England, the work, translated back into execrable English, rapidly became a runner-up to *Messiah*.

Time has not been kind to *The Creation*: it has been all but crowded out of the repertoire. There are various reasons for this, the main one being the advent of Mendelssohn and his catchy oratorios. Under this onslaught, only a consistently effective work could hold its place. *The Creation* is by no means consistently effective. Although "The Heavens are telling" is magnificent choral writing, most of the choruses are feeble—an inexcusable fault in an oratorio. As the musical climax comes in the first third, the rest of *The Creation*, despite scattered beauties, is anticlimactic. The exact truth is that after Haydn has created his two main characters, he does not know how to make them dramatic. The best passages are descriptive—a kind of sublime journalism. They are usually solos, and lose nothing in being performed alone. "With verdure clad" is one of Haydn's most exquisite inspirations: blending simple rapture with a rare contemplative quality, it is one of his infrequent achievements in musical poetry. Unfortunately, the fine things in *The Creation* are scattered too sparingly to prevent a performance of the whole oratorio from being a chore to the listener. He rises from his seat with the paradoxical feeling that he has heard a masterpiece—but a very dull one.

Enormously pleased by the success of *The Creation*, the uninspired translator who had provided its text began to badger Haydn to set another of his adaptations—this time of James Thomson's *The Seasons*. The old man was not too pleased with the prospect of more work: he was in failing health, and doubted his strength to complete another large composition. At last he consented, and *The Seasons* was completed in a remarkably short time. Yet it is a work of great length, requiring two evenings for an uncut performance. Generally, it is not inferior to *The Creation*. Certainly it is far livelier, and the fact that it has had to take a back seat is largely due to its comparatively frivolous (and absurdly adapted) text, which is less congenial to stuffy, single-minded oratorio societies. Haydn himself recognized the absurdity of the

German words, and was inclined to regard *The Seasons* as a step-child. He once remarked petulantly to Francis II that "in *The Creation* angels speak, and their talk is of God; in *The Seasons* no one higher speaks than Farmer Simon."

Haydn's attitude to *The Seasons* was, to say the least, ambiguous. Nowhere did he more successfully transmute his lifelong love of nature into music. Page after page is inspired by the Austrian countryside and the manifold aspects of its life. The vivid descriptiveness of this music is its most immediately engaging quality, and it is no wonder that its early listeners delighted in the literal transcriptions of country sounds in which it is rich. But Haydn was furious when these mimetic passages were singled out for special praise: "This French trash was forced upon me," he stormed. His injustice to this delicious work may be traced to a well-founded conviction that the exertion of composing it had finally made him a feeble old man. At any rate, his creative life was over. After composing *The Seasons*, he dragged out eight years, subsisting on the bitter diet of past accomplishments. He lived in a pleasant house in the Mariahilf suburb of Vienna, which his wife had fondly hoped to inhabit "when I am a widow." Why this woman, who was three years Haydn's senior, expected to outlive him is not clear. She died in 1800, and her widower lived the rest of his life in the Mariahilf house.

The last years are a constant record of mental and physical decline. In December, 1803, Haydn conducted for the last time. After that, he was confined to his house by increasing infirmities. His already enormous fame became gigantic: people of rank and eminence besieged his door; learned organizations and musical societies delighted in honoring him. In 1804, he was made an honorary citizen of Vienna. When Napoleon's armies occupied the city, many French officers called upon him to pay their respects. When he was feeling comparatively well, he received his visitors warmly, often showing them his medals and diplomas, and rambling on about his past. But more often than not callers merely confused and upset him, and his only wish was to be left alone. In 1806 he took steps to discourage visitors by having a card printed, bearing a fragment of one of his vocal quartets, with these words: "Fled forever is my strength; old and weak am I!"

During these last years none were more considerate than the

Esterházys. The Prince increased Haydn's pension to twenty-three hundred florins annually, and paid his doctor. The Princess often called on him. In 1808, four days before his seventy-sixth birthday, his admirers wished to make public acknowledgement of their affection. Prince Esterházy's carriage called to take him to the University, where *The Creation* was to be performed. The venerable old man was carried into the hall, whereupon the entire audience rose. He was very agitated. When Salieri, Mozart's famous enemy, gave the sign to begin, the whole house was stilled. Haydn controlled his emotions until the great fortissimo on the words "And there was light." He then pointed upward, and exclaimed loudly, "It came from on high." His excitement increased, and it was thought prudent to take him home after the first part. As he was carried out of the hall, Beethoven pressed forward and solemnly kissed the master's forehead and hands. On the threshold, Haydn raised his hand in benediction: he was saying farewell to Vienna.

Haydn lingered another year, growing constantly weaker and less and less master of his emotions. On May 26, 1809, he had his servants carry him to the piano, where he thrice played the Austrian national anthem with remarkable strength and expressiveness. It was his last effort: he died five days later. The French, who had again occupied Vienna, gave him a magnificent funeral, and Requiems were sung all over Europe.

Our own time is rediscovering Haydn. He was submerged during the later nineteenth century—admittedly a classic, but usually kept on the shelf. In view of the fact that practically only his "Toy" and "Clock" Symphonies were played, he was in danger of being thought of as a children's composer. The renascence of chamber music has done much to rehabilitate him. His more than eighty string quartets, after decades of neglect, are re-emerging as his most characteristic works. They were little publicized during his lifetime because of the very circumstances of performance. They are much heard now, and a society has been formed to record them. They, as much as the symphonies and the fresh and delightful piano sonatas, give point to the saying, "Haydn thought in sonatas." Possibly we hear Haydn best in the quartets, for they are performed today exactly as he wrote them. By their very nature, they cannot seem thin, as the symphonies sometimes do to ears accustomed to the augmented orchestras of Wagner, Strauss, and Stravinsky. Nor have the instruments of the quartet changed since Haydn's day, as the piano has.

Haydn has been called the father of instrumental music, which is true in spirit if not in entire substance. His almost unique ability to create and perfect musical forms was due largely to his freedom from academic dead letter. "What is the good of such rules?" he once asked. "Art is free, and should be fettered by no such mechanical regulations. The educated ear is the sole authority on all these questions, and I think I have as much right to lay down the law as anyone. Such trifling is absurd; I wish instead that someone would try to compose a really new minuet." This liberalism infuriated some of Haydn's pedantic colleagues, two of whom once denounced him to the Emperor as a charlatan. But he was a profound student, and as careful a craftsman as ever lived. When his strength no longer matched his inspiration, he lamented to the pianist Kalkbrenner, "I have only just learned in my old age how to use the wind instruments, and now that I do understand them, I must leave the world."

This free and living attitude toward music is central in Haydn. It allowed him, for example, to use the rich store of folk melody always available to him, and to use it without scruple—Beethoven's debt to him in this respect has not been sufficiently acknowledged. It allowed him to perpetuate the robust jokes of the period not only in his diary, but also in his music. It allowed him to breathe life into the form that Karl Philipp Emanuel Bach had left quivering on the brink of being, and to stamp it with the three-dimensioned qualities of a generous and glowing personality.

Chapter VI

Wolfgang Amadeus Mozart

(Salzburg, January 27, 1756–December 5, 1791, Vienna)

WHEN Mozart was born, Johann Sebastian Bach had been dead six years, and before he was four years old Handel, too, had vanished from the scene. In his Neapolitan retreat, Domenico Scarlatti was gambling away the last years of his life. The great musicians of the age of Bach and Handel were either dead or, like Rameau, were no longer producing work of any consequence. Nor had most of their successors shown what they could do. Gluck, at forty-two, was diligently imitating the Italians, and had not yet begun his reform. Haydn was still a dark horse: if he was known at all, it was as the accompanist of a popular Italian singing teacher. But the sonatas of Karl Philipp Emanuel Bach had already been published, and these were to be the patterns after which the great instrumental masterpieces of the late eighteenth century were cut.

The age of the baroque was passing, and a more delicate and fantastic style was taking its place. The rococo is merely the baroque seen through the wrong end of a telescope, and with a great deal of superimposed ornamentation. It lay lightly but tenaciously on architecture and decoration for some decades, affecting them profoundly, and also coloring modes and manners and the other arts. Artifice was the keystone of the whole preposterous structure: *chinoiserie*, jewelers' whims, plaster scrollwork, exquisite cabinetmaking, theatrical church fronts, and coloratura roulades were accepted as proofs of civilization. Petty princes feverishly transformed their capitals into monstrous jewelboxes, and none sparkled more brilliantly than the home of the pleasure-loving Archbishops of Salzburg. No more appropriate birthplace could have been found for that new extravagance of the eighteenth century—the child prodigy.

The childhood of Mozart is one of the masterpieces of the rococo. His loving but ambitious father raised him on the principle that he was a performing bear: from his sixth year he was dragged over the map of Europe, and exhibited as a marvel—which, indeed, he was. Great monarchs made much of him, and by the time he was fourteen he had seen the interior of every palace from London to Naples. His amazing virtuosity and facile improvisations made him the wonder of the age. The boy's compositions were so remarkable that skeptics accused his father of having written them.

Mozart's early passion for music cannot, like Bach's, be traced to a long family tradition. Leopold Mozart, his father, was the first of an obscure family of country bookbinders to forsake the ancestral craft. Settling in Salzburg, he had by dogged determination risen to be fourth violinist in the Archbishop's band. Also, being a fine figure of a man, he managed to secure a pretty wife. He was well liked, and the year after Wolfgang Amadeus was born, became court composer to the Archbishop, Sigismund von Schrattenbach. The Mozarts had seven children in all, but five of them died in infancy owing to the dampness and lack of sanitation in their otherwise fine house in the Getreidegasse. Leopold, as ambitious for the two survivors as for himself, could hardly wait until his daughter was old enough to begin her music lessons. Nannerl was eight, and already an accomplished performer on the clavier, when her baby brother began to show an absorbing interest in the musical activities of the household.

Mozart was three when he began to amuse himself at the keyboard, and the next year his formal lessons began. At five, he was improvising little minuets, and his delighted father was writing them down. Like Bach, Leopold Mozart copied into a notebook simple pieces for his children to study, and among them were works by Hasse, Telemann, and—most important—Karl Philipp Emanuel Bach. These were to be, for a while at least, the staples of their concerts. Their travels began in 1762 with a performance before the Elector of Bavaria at Munich. The tremendous furore over the handsome *Wunderkinder* whetted Leopold's appetite, and he was soon busy systematically taking advantage of their childish appeal. Later the same year they proceeded by easy stages to Vienna, concertizing on the way. Everywhere, the children's talent, but even more, Wolfgang's charm, made friends for them, and aroused unprecedented enthusiasm. At Vienna they found the city ready to receive them with open arms: their fame had preceded them. They had scarcely arrived when a command invitation to play at court was presented at their lodgings.

The existence, at Schönbrunn, of the most musical court in

Europe immeasurably helped Leopold Mozart's plans. Every member of Maria Theresa's huge family sang or played a musical instrument, and the Empress had once referred to herself as the first of living virtuosos, because she had sung in a court opera at the age of seven. Of her talented daughters the caustic Dr. Burney said that they sang "very well—for princesses." The self-possessed little Wolfgang more than shared Burney's skepticism about Hapsburg musicianship: before playing, he asked loudly for the Imperial music teacher: "Is Herr Wagenseil here? Let him come. He knows something about it." The court went mad about the children, and the little boy who was forever asking, "Do you love me? Do you really love me?" warmed characteristically to this show of affection, jumping on the Empress' lap and hugging and kissing her. Besides a gift of money, the children each received a court costume from Maria Theresa, and sat for a portrait. Wolfgang, looking very pert and pleased, was painted in his sumptuous suit of stiff lavender brocade and gold lace.

The nobility promptly followed the court's lead, and soon the Mozarts had invitations to the best houses in Vienna. Suddenly the prodigy fell ill of scarlet fever, and before he recovered, interest in him and his sister had somewhat abated. With hopes a little dashed, they were back in Salzburg by the beginning of 1763. Six months elapsed before their next tour. To this period belongs the piously attested, but completely incredible, story of Mozart picking up a violin and playing it with no previous training. Only slightly less suspicious is his alleged mastery of the organ—including the pedals—at first try. His general musical virtuosity, which would have been remarkable in a grown man, was so phenomenal in a seven-year-old that witnesses, and particularly his doting father, hypnotized themselves into an inability to sift the prodigious from the impossible.

Leopold Mozart's plans for the second tour partook of the grandiose: with Paris and London as their goals, they were to progress across Europe like genial musical deities dispensing their favors. As they set out in June, their way led through the summer capitals of the reigning princes, who received them with amazed enthusiasm. At Aix-la-Chapelle one of Frederick the Great's sisters tried to lure them to Berlin. But the royal lady, while lavish with promises, was penniless—and Leopold Mozart was on his way. At Frankfort, the fourteen-year-old Goethe heard the "little man, with his powdered wig and sword." By mid-November they arrived in Paris, where they remained five months. Here, after some delay, their Viennese triumph was repeated and not only the court but the intellectuals took them up. At Versailles, the strict conventions of the court of Louis XV relaxed momentarily—while the Mozarts were there, it was like a family party. Only the haughty Pompadour remained aloof until Mozart innocently put her in her place. "Who is this that does not want to kiss me?" he asked. "The Empress kisses me." What doors remained closed despite court favor were opened through the generous offices of the influential Baron Grimm, a German who had become one of the leaders of French thought. Before leaving Paris, Leopold Mozart had the satisfaction of seeing his children completely capture French society. He signalized their triumph by having four of Wolfgang's sonatas for violin and clavier published, the first two with a dedication to Mme Victoire, one of the King's daughters.

At London they found another musical family on the throne. George III and Queen Charlotte, who were uniformly kind to musicians, not only showered favors on them at court, but also, as Leopold Mozart noted with pride, nodded to them while out driving in St. James' Park. The Queen's music master, Johann Christian Bach, the youngest of Johann Sebastian's sons, and Handel's successor as undisputed arbiter of English music, was entranced by the wonderful boy, and played musical games with him. The affectionate child never forgot Bach. The children's first public concert was such a success that their father confessed himself "terrified" by the size of the box-office receipts. Probably the excitement of a successful and fashionable London season was too much for him, for he took to his bed for seven weeks with a throat ailment. In the interim, Wolfgang composed, and at the next concert all the pieces were his own. In all, the family was in London more than a year, and rather outstayed its welcome.

The Mozarts now turned their steps homeward, but so circuitous was their route, and so indifferent their health (only Frau Mozart was exempt from illness), that they were on the road more than a year. After playing at the court of the Prince of Orange at The Hague, they returned to Versailles, where they were again warmly welcomed. A happy summer in Switzerland followed. From

Geneva they drove out to call on Voltaire at Ferney, but the lion was sick abed, and they were refused admittance. After a triumphal journey up the Rhine, they finally returned to Salzburg in November, 1766, having been away from home three and a half years.

Leopold Mozart did not let any grass grow under his feet. Nannerl, at sixteen, was definitely through as a child prodigy, and he cannily decided to concentrate on the eleven-year-old boy, who had always been the family's stellar attraction. By a lot of well-timed boasting, the wily impresario managed to arouse the skepticism of his master, the Archbishop. His Grace decided to stop his retainer's loud mouth by putting this alleged *Wunderkind* to a stiff test: he divided the text of an oratorio between Wolfgang, the court conductor,* and the cathedral organist, keeping the boy in solitary confinement while he composed his part. The music was evidently satisfactory, for the oratorio was both performed and published the same year. Archbishop von Schrattenbach no longer doubted, and gave proof of his conversion in increased friendliness toward the Mozarts.

Soon the family was off to Vienna again, hoping to play an important role in an impending royal marriage. But a smallpox epidemic frustrated their little scheme: the intended bride succumbed, and the Mozarts fled to Olmütz, where the two children came down with the disease, Wolfgang being blinded for nine days. After being nursed back to health in the home of a humane and fearless nobleman, they returned to the capital, where they found the court plunged in mourning. Nevertheless, Maria Theresa and her son Josef II received them kindly. Although exceedingly stingy, the new Emperor commissioned Wolfgang to write an opera. The boy accordingly composed *La Finta semplice* in record time, but faction ran so high that it was not actually produced until months later, and then in Salzburg by order of the Archbishop, who was so delighted that he gave Wolfgang a high-sounding but unpaid position in his musical household. A second opera, *Bastien und Bastienne*, which was written for Dr. Franz Anton Mesmer, a respectable precursor of Mary Baker Eddy, fared better. Zealots have revived it in late years, but it is in reality a

---

* Josef Haydn's talented brother Michael, of whose roistering ways the tight-lipped Leopold Mozart strongly disapproved.

musical curio faintly adumbrating the mature style of Mozart's other German operas—*Die Entführung aus dem Serail* and *Die Zauberflöte.*

They rested in Salzburg almost a year, for Leopold Mozart was planning nothing less than a conquest of Italy. There was no respite for Wolfgang: he spent these eleven months composing pieces of all descriptions, and practicing, practicing, practicing. Then, after bidding Frau Mozart and Nannerl an affectionate adieu, the travelers set out armed with a battery of gilt-edged introductions. Crossing the Brenner in the dead of winter, they arrived, after a series of spectacular successes, at Milan, where they enjoyed the exalted patronage of the Governor General. Here Wolfgang received the blessing of Gluck's venerable teacher, Sammartini. Parma, Bologna, Florence, Rome, Naples—all capitulated to Wolfgang. He keenly missed his mother and Nannerl, and talked to them through letters that teem with amazingly frank and incisive comments on the music he heard, the famous people he met, and the customs of the country. Like Juvenal, he encountered nothing he did not stuff into his conversational ragbag. Some of these letters are so coarse (to our taste but not to that of the eighteenth century) that their pious editors have scarcely left one unbowdlerized.* Mozart is always in high, and very often in ribald, spirits. In short, it is almost impossible to believe that these are the letters of a thirteen-year-old boy to his mother and sister. But it must be remembered that he was already an old trouper.

At Bologna, the recognized center of Italian musical theory, Mozart was examined by the most eminent of its professors—the old Padre Martini—and passed with flying colors. Much the same tests awaited him at Florence, and from these he emerged even more brilliantly. There, too, he met the omnipresent Dr. Burney, and enjoyed a tender but brief friendship with Thomas Linley,† a talented English lad of exactly his own age—and no doubt a vast relief after the endless catechisms of prying sexagenarians. There were tears at parting, avowals of eternal friendship, and elaborate

* This sentence was written prior to Emily Anderson's superb three-volume annotated translation of the Mozart family correspondence. Miss Anderson—a civil servant in her spare time—is pious, in the best sense of the word. She sticks to the text whatever the consequences.

† He was Richard Brinsley Sheridan's brother-in-law. His death at the age of twenty-two was a serious loss (say pundits) to English music, then starving to death from lack of talent.

plans for another meeting. But their gypsy lives kept them apart, and they never met again.

The Mozarts reached Rome in time to hear the Holy Week music, and there (appropriately enough) Wolfgang performed one of his miracles. A staple of these celebrations was the performance in the Sistine Chapel of Allegri's famed Miserere, a contrapuntal labyrinth in nine voices. After hearing it once, the boy made a copy from memory, a feat that attracted the friendly interest of Clement XIV and brought a shower of invitations from the princely Roman families. Amid all this excitement, Wolfgang took time to send Nannerl a request for some new minuets by Michael Haydn. After less than a month in the Holy City, they set out nervously (their way lay through banditti-infested territory) for Naples. They visited Pompeii, looked at Vesuvius "smoking furiously," and found the right patrons, among them Sir William Hamilton, the English ambassador, now remembered only as the husband of Lord Nelson's Emma.

Returning north to spend the summer near Bologna, father and son stopped in Rome for a fortnight. The Pope (or his deputy) invested Wolfgang with the Golden Spur, which his father described loftily as "a piece of good luck," observing further, "You can imagine how I laugh when I hear people calling him *Signor Cavaliere*." The fact that his son had the same order as Gluck was a great satisfaction to the ambitious Leopold, who for some time insisted that Wolfgang use the title in his signature. The boy was less impressed, and soon dropped the appellation. Signal honors awaited him at Bologna, where the Accademia Filarmonica waived its age limit of twenty years, and elected him to membership after another rigorous test. At Milan he rushed to completion his *Mitridate, Rè di Ponto*, an opera the Governor General had commissioned during the Mozarts' first visit. It was a sure-fire hit, packing the opera house for twenty nights.

At last, after more than two years' wandering in the peninsula, the wayworn troupers were back in Salzburg in March, 1771. In Mozart's pockets were two important commissions—another opera for Milan and an oratorio for Padua, and soon a letter came requesting a dramatic serenata for the nuptials of another of Maria Theresa's numerous progeny. Five months of feverish composing followed, and then another trip to Milan, where Mozart's serenata more than held its own against the last of the aged Hasse's innumerable operas, drawing a typically Pecksniffian comment from his father: "It really distresses me very greatly, but Wolfgang's serenata has completely killed Hasse's opera." But the old man, whose luscious arias had been the consolation of princes, said with true generosity, "This boy will throw us all into the shade."*

The day after the Mozarts returned home, the old Archbishop died. It was a sadder event than they realized: his successor was the forever-to-be-vilified Hieronymus von Colloredo, Bishop of Gurk. His reputation was already so grim that at the news of his election Salzburg all but went into mourning. Of course, his promotion called for special musical services, and though he was an archbishop, opera was particularly specified. As if avenging the future, Mozart, selecting one of Metastasio's most threadbare librettos, proceeded to write, in *Il Sogno di Scipione*, the worst opera he ever composed. Indeed, it was so infernally dull that it might well have roused resentment in a more charitable man than Von Colloredo. After another bout of composing, Mozart went back to Milan for six months. His new opera, *Lucio Silla*, was a triumph, and partly on the strength of it the Governor General tried to wangle a court appointment for him at Florence. But the negotiations came to nothing, and father and son heavyheartedly prepared to brave what difficulties Salzburg under the new dispensation had in store for them. They recrossed the Brenner in March, 1773: Mozart bade farewell to Italy for the last time. Half of his life was over.

The Mozarts soon found their worst fears realized: conditions in Von Colloredo's Salzburg were intolerable. There was no pleasing this martinet of the Church. Obviously, if Wolfgang were to realize his—or his father's—ambitions, it would have to be somewhere else. Remembering the unfailing friendliness of Maria Theresa, the Mozarts decided to try Vienna first. The Empress was just as kind as ever, but that was all: they came away empty-handed, as balked of remunerative employment here as in Italy. But failure did not dam the flow of Wolfgang's pen: both in Vienna

---

* Hasse, who had been a friend of Johann Sebastian Bach without recognizing his genius, could more easily appreciate the Italianate style of the archmimic Mozart.

and after returning home, he continued to pile up work for his future editors.

Before the end of 1774, however, it seemed that if Mozart played his cards well he might soon free himself from the crushing routine of the Salzburg court. Strings were pulled, and a commission for an opera arrived from the Elector of Bavaria. The results were the same as usual: *La Finta giardiniera* delighted its hearers, but Mozart lingered vainly in Munich. There was nothing to do but return dispiritedly once again to Salzburg—and compose, compose, compose. Although he could not know it, his apprenticeship was over: for the first time, he began to produce music that is of as much interest to music lovers as to experts. He got into his stride with a festival play, *Il Rè pastore*, in honor of an archducal visit. As opera, it is lifeless stuff, but among several tasteful arias is one that still gets an occasional airing: "*L'amerò, sarò costante.*" Five brilliant concertos for violin and orchestra followed. Doubtless Mozart wrote them for himself, as his father wanted him to become the foremost violin virtuoso in Europe. So, while the urge was on him, the mercurial youth wrote these five masterpieces of his "gallant" style—and thereafter practically abandoned the violin concerto. Graceful, and brimming over with dash and *brio*, these delectable pieces are as alive today as they were on the day they were written, and violinists like Heifetz, Szigeti, and Menuhin delight in playing them.

Up to 1775, Mozart's compositions were remarkable chiefly because they were written by a boy. Those who take the trouble to work through the volumes of Wyzewa and Saint-Foix's exhaustive treatise on the early Mozart will find this statement amply corroborated by the musical quotations. Aside from the fact that any child composer is something of a phenomenon, Mozart is doubly remarkable for the fecundity of his gift at such an early age. On the other hand, though this stupendous output naturally abounds in hints of his own peculiar genius, it is primarily the work of an extraordinarily facile and sensitive mimic, echoing the styles and forms of everyone from Karl Philipp Emanuel Bach to Hasse. But this early music, which on superficial examination may seem merely clever, is actually more: it is the voice of someone trembling on the brink of greatness, and only awaiting respite from paternal Stakhanovism to realize his genius. And the proof of this is that as soon as his father could no longer exhibit him as a freak, and he was thus allowed a period of comparative leisure, Mozart began to write music that is unmistakably his own. As late as January, 1775, the influential critic, C. F. D. Schubart, was writing with a kind of skeptical faith: "Unless Mozart should prove to be a mere overgrown product of the forcing-house, he will be the greatest composer that ever lived."

The transition from adolescence to manhood, always a difficult phase, is a dramatic crisis in the life of a prodigy. Inevitably, there is danger that his artistic development will not match his physical growth. This was the peril confronting Mozart, his family, and his well-wishers in 1775. There is nothing sadder or more grotesque than a grown man with the mind and talents of the brilliant child he was, and it may be assumed that during these crucial early seventies, while the pretty little boy was changing into a pleasant but not very attractive youth, people were nervously wondering whether this fate was in store for him. They had found it easy to believe that such a delightful little creature was a genius; at nineteen they found him less convincing. This short, slight fellow, with his shock of blond hair and rather too prominent aquiline nose, was really rather commonplace-looking—by no means a good advertisement for his parents, who had been called the handsomest couple in Salzburg. Nor was Mozart insensitive to the change: to compensate for his insignificant appearance, he began to affect embroidered coats and an excessive amount of jewelry, and took special pains with his hair, of which he was very vain.

His well-wishing but apprehensive friends could not know what was happening inside of Mozart, for excepting his changed appearance he seemed much the same as always. His almost morbidly affectionate nature was possibly a bit less intense—the genial Mozart, with his taste for boon companions, billiards, dancing, and good wine, was emerging. As a child he had been precociously aware of women's good looks (and as quick to criticize lack of them), and even before he was out of his teens he began to show evidence of a sexual urge that seems at times to have been excessive. Yet, despite decidedly mature tastes, he remained tied to his father's apron strings. His relationship to this domineering, scheming, and ambitious man is a puzzle to the twentieth-century reader. Until his twenty-fifth year it never entered his head to question, much less to disobey, Leopold Mozart's fiats on every subject under the sun, and he never tired of saying that he considered his father "next to God." Unfortunately, this touching attitude was partly an excuse for his own unwillingness and inability to make decisions for himself. It had served a certain purpose in the past, but was no weapon for the struggles of the future.

In Leopold Mozart's house, religion always held a prominent place. He was a devout and unquestioning Catholic, and assumed that his children would emulate him. And Wolfgang, during his childhood, was certainly as observant of Catholic practices as his father could wish. But his religion was as much a sort of mimicry as was his mastery of every musical style. As he matured, he did not so much rebel against the Church as lose interest in it. The bulk of his religious music was composed early, and though it has found many admirers, it would not of itself have placed Mozart among the immortals. The paradox is that after he had lost his formal Catholic faith, he wrote really great religious music based on a personal, and by no means orthodox, mysticism. His early Masses and smaller church pieces are, at their worst, trivial. Even the best of them—a *Missa brevis* in F major (K. 192)*—is an operatic and often skittish composition. Indeed, its relation to faith and devotion seems remote—the solemn words of the text not infrequently trip to the gayest of Neapolitan dance tunes. The statement has often been made that Mozart's choral technique rivals that of Bach: if true, this is an interesting fact, which may well be pondered as we listen to the empty loveliness of the *Missa brevis* and the even shallower one in D (K. 194).

The year 1776 and most of 1777 are baffling to those who expect to see the promise of the violin concertos immediately fulfilled. Much of the music belonging to this period is perfunctory, and uninspired by any emotion other than a desire to have done with it. Mozart, as we shall see, was capable of turning out a masterpiece at short order, but the business of grinding out salon pieces for a patron whom he thoroughly despised was beginning to sap his strength and impair the freshness of his talent. Feeling the way

* Mozart's hundreds of compositions are identified by their numbers in Dr. Ludwig von Köchel's thematic catalogue, here abbreviated as K. A new edition, with some changes in numbering, was published in 1937, under the editorship of Dr. Alfred Einstein. As this valuable revision is not yet in general use, we have preferred the old numbering.

he did, it is amazing that he managed to produce anything above the mediocre. Yet, to this period belong a really effective clavier concerto (K. 271) and the "Haffner" Serenade, written for the marriage of Burgomaster Haffner's daughter. This Serenade, which incidentally is longer than the average symphony, is in reality a suite of unrelated pieces, themselves very uneven in quality. There are moments, however, when the accents are unmistakably those of the Mozart of the great symphonies.

By September, 1777, Mozart had reached a point at which he could no longer bear the inactivity of Salzburg. All of his desires were to compose operas and symphonies—and Von Colloredo would have none of them. So the birds of passage applied once more for leave of absence. When the Archbishop curtly refused, Leopold Mozart drew up a formal petition. This time, their master's reply was to dismiss them both from his service, though he reconsidered, and allowed the father to remain. As Wolfgang was now twenty-one, he naturally believed that he would be allowed to travel alone. But his hopes were dashed: his father had no intention of unleashing him without a family guardian. As he himself could not go, he delegated Frau Mozart—a bad choice, for she was neither very strong nor very clever. Mother and son set out for Munich on September 23, 1777. Suddenly, Leopold Mozart realized that he had forgotten to give Wolfgang his blessing. He rushed to the window to outstretch a benedictional hand—and saw the carriage vanishing in the distance.

Five weeks later, the Mozarts' carriage rumbled into Mannheim, a bumbling little town, but the seat of the Elector Palatine's profligate and brilliant court. Here they remained more than four months, for Mannheim boasted the finest band in Europe. Under the direction of the renowned Johann Stamitz and his successors, it had so revolutionized ensemble playing that it has been called the father of the modern orchestra. Mozart, who came in at the tail end of this development, missed nothing of it, and lost no opportunity of hearing these famous players. The performances of opera in German interested him even more, and through these, fate (never very kind to Mozart) introduced him to Fridolin Weber, one of those curious personages, mediocre in themselves, but certain of immortality because of their connections with the great. This little man, copyist and prompter at the opera, was to be Carl Maria von

Weber's uncle and Mozart's father-in-law. In 1777, Herr Weber's greatness was all in the future—but he had a family of daughters.

Soon Mozart's letters home palpitated with praise of Aloysia Weber, whom he painted as a Rhenish Venus with a heavenly voice. He was ready to abandon everything, and in the combined role of teacher, impresario, composer, accompanist, and lover, barnstorm through Italy with this paragon, who would, he was sure, captivate Italian hearts forever. But he did not reckon with his father: the awful voice spoke from Salzburg: "Off with you to Paris, and that immediately! Take up your position among those who are really great—*aut Caesar aut nihil*!" Wolfgang obeyed. On March 14, after taking leave of the weeping Webers, Mozart and his mother set out sadly for Paris. Frau Mozart would much rather have gone home.

But Mozart was not destined to be a Caesar in Paris, which was too taken up with the quarrel of the Gluckists and Piccinnists to pay any attention to a former prodigy with no stake in either side. "People pay fine compliments, it is true," he complained to his father, "but there it ends. They arrange for me to come on such and such a day. I play, and hear them exclaim: *Oh, c'est un prodige, c'est inconcevable, c'est étonnant*, and with that good-by." At last, however, Mozart found one noble patron, and for him and his daughter—virtuosos both—he composed a concerto for flute, harp, and orchestra (K. 299) abounding in delightful themes, despite the fact that he abhorred both flute and harp as solo instruments. Marie Antoinette, who had done so much for "*notre cher Gluck*," insulted Mozart by offering him an ill-paid organist's job at Versailles. His mother's mysterious illness added to his worries. In July he had to break the news of her death to his father and sister. Although he did not dissipate his energies in mourning, nevertheless the appearance of his genial old London friend, Johann Christian Bach, must have been welcome to the lonely youth. But Paris obviously had nothing solid to offer him—and the thought of Aloysia Weber was always on his mind.

Accordingly, after reluctantly posting his acceptance of another court appointment his father had wangled for him in Salzburg,* Mozart turned his back on Paris. Evidently he was in no hurry to

---

* Leopold Mozart's sly hint that there might be a job for Aloysia Weber in the choir undoubtedly helped to clinch the matter.

keep his date with Von Colloredo, for he spent four months on the road. Floods detained him in Strasbourg, mere sentimentality in Mannheim (for the Webers had already proceeded to Munich in the Elector's train). In Mannheim, however, he almost wrote two operas, and almost became a conductor. At Munich, where he hoped to dally long, he found that Aloysia Weber had all but forgotten him. Not even a sharp reminder from Leopold Mozart that he was overdue in Salzburg was needed, and by the middle of January, 1779, a very dejected young man had returned home.

For two years, Mozart fretted in captivity. He was court *Konzertmeister* and organist, but despite these exalted titles was no better off than before. Daily the rift between him and the Archbishop grew wider. Worse, he began to realize that his father had tricked him into returning to Salzburg, and though the old affection between them was not materially impaired, they no longer trusted each other. It is not at all strange that so few of the many compositions of these two years show Mozart at his best. The most notable exceptions are the *Sinfonia Concertante* (K. 364), his only Concerto for Two Pianos (K. 365), and the Symphony in C major (K. 338), all of which are still heard occasionally. The first of these is especially fine—a passionate, deeply felt work "not at all suited," as Eric Blom has observed, "to an archiepiscopal court."

Mozart was still lusting after the fleshpots of opera, and probably with the idea of amateur performance in Salzburg, he began to amuse himself with the writing of that curious fragment a later editor christened *Zaïde*. It is a trifling little comedy—a typical Singspiel—with several charming airs that foreshadow Mozart's masterpiece in this genre—*Die Entführung aus dem Serail*. Fortunately for the history of opera, he was interrupted by a long-desired invitation to compose another stage work for Munich, to be given during the carnival of 1781. The result was *Idomeneo, Rè di Creta*, a tragic opera based on a subject from Greek mythology. Mozart had been studying Gluck, but unhappily his librettist had not been studying Calzabigi. It was not a heaven-made collaboration, and the composer overcame the ponderousness of the libretto only by slashing it unmercifully and writing superior music for what remained.

Idomeneo is essentially a compromise—the fusing of Gluck's conception of music as the handmaid of drama and Mozart's far superior gifts as an absolute musician. It shows clearly that Mozart had taken the lessons of *Alceste* to heart, but without being shackled by them. If Gluck ever heard *Idomeneo*, he must have been shocked —and a bit envious—at the way his young rival allows himself to be seized by a purely musical idea, and suspends the drama while he soars aloft. Such goings-on were outside of Gluck's theories— and beyond his powers. The pointedly severe orchestral introduction conforms to the Gluckian canon, but several of the bravura arias might have made the older man wonder if he had lived in vain. And he would have been quite right about the solos in the last act, which are decidedly conventional singers' exhibition pieces.

On the strength of the mild success of *Idomeneo*, which was first performed on January 29, 1781, Mozart decided to remain in Munich to enjoy the carnival, and to haunt the Elector's court— for he still hoped against hope that he would be asked to stay. Then, suddenly in mid-March, he was summoned to join the Archbishop, who had taken his grim face to Vienna for Maria Theresa's funeral, and the following months were among the most critical of his life. It was at once apparent that the brutal churchman was bent on humiliating Mozart in every possible way: he was treated like a menial, made to eat at the servants' table, and addressed in a fashion usually reserved, even under that outlandish caste system, for underscullions and ruffians. Those who have tried to find some slight palliation for Von Colloredo's conduct seem to forget that he was generally detested even by his fellow nobles. Now his treatment of Mozart made him an object of ridicule among those who felt themselves honored by the composer's presence at their table. Agitated letters passed almost daily between Mozart and his father, with the latter playing his usual timeserving role. Mozart was particularly annoyed because the Archbishop forbade him to play elsewhere than at his own palace. Events hurried toward a crisis. On May 9, he had an audience with Von Colloredo, who shouted at him like a fishwife. Mozart rushed to his lodgings, and drafted two letters: the first, to the Archbishop, asked that his resignation be accepted immediately; the second, to his father, asked for moral support. The Archbishop deigned no reply, and Leopold Mozart's letter, after hinting that his son was doomed to perdition, called upon him to submit. This Mozart had no intention of doing. After waiting a full month for Von Colloredo's answer, he once more presented himself at the palace. This time he was kicked out of the room by one of the Archbishop's toadies. This was His Grace's way of accepting the resignation.

Even before finally breaking with the Archbishop, Mozart had enraged his father by moving to an inn where the nomadic Webers were staying. Fridolin was dead, Aloysia had married one Lange, an actor, and now the family was presided over by a slatternly drunken mother. Having failed to carry off Aloysia, Mozart now began to court her younger sister, Constanze. Soon Vienna hummed with gossip of the goings-on at The Eye of God, as the inn was called, and the evil news trickled to Salzburg. A thunderous denunciation came from the tireless old busybody. Mozart denied everything, including any intention of marrying. Evidently referring to alleged irregularities with Constanze, he wrote in July, "If I had to marry every girl I've jested with, I'd have at least two hundred wives by now." But for discretion's sake, he changed his lodgings. Before the year was up, however, Leopold received the bad news that Wolfgang, in the novel role of a Galahad, was determined to rescue poor Constanze from her unappreciative family. "She is not ugly," he wrote, "but at the same time far from beautiful. Her whole beauty consists in two small black eyes, and a handsome figure. She has no wit, but enough sound human sense to be able to fulfill her duties as a wife and mother."

What finally decided Mozart to brave his father's wrath was not only his loneliness (and the insistence of Constanze's guardian that he make an honest woman out of her*), but also an apparent improvement in his worldly position. He had a few pupils, some of his compositions had been published, and once more he was in demand as a virtuoso. Better still, in July, 1781, the managers of the German Opera—Josef II's pet musical project—handed him a libretto to set. With his domestic future so unsettled, Mozart was not prepared to work unremittingly on *Die Entführung aus dem Serail*, however dear to his heart. The routine trivia of a busy musician's life, including an arduous contest with the pianist Muzio Clementi for the amusement of the court, he could take in his stride, but quite as unsettling as Constanze's limited charms was

---

* Constanze's guardian made Mozart sign a promise to marry her within three years or give her a life annuity. To Constanze's credit, be it said that as soon as the guardian was out of sight she tore up the contract.

his meeting with Haydn, which was followed by a more or less complete reorientation of his art. The first act of the opera went fast, but the entire score was not finished for almost a year, some of the delay being due to the clumsiness and absurdities of the pseudo-Oriental libretto. The musical cliques, which in Vienna proliferated like bacteria, were banded against him, and were determined that *Die Entführung* should not be produced. Eventually, Josef II had to intervene, and command its performance. The night of the *première*, July 16, 1782, was an unmarred triumph for Mozart: the house was packed, the court was present, and number after number was encored. During the rest of the season, the management coined money in countless repetitions of the new opera.

Scarcely three weeks after the first performance, with the praise of Vienna ringing in his ears, Mozart led Constanze to the altar at St. Stephen's.

The opera that had made the future seem brighter to Mozart has not worn well. *Die Entführung* belongs to that suspicious group of works that are called great merely, it seems, because they are by great composers. Furthermore, its musical quality has been exaggerated because of its importance as the first complete Singspiel by a major dramatic composer. There are fine things in the opera —the trouble is that they are in all sorts of styles. In the entire piece, Mozart, with his keen nose for drama, developed only one completely convincing character—the richly farcical Osmin. Yet the whole business proceeds in high good spirits, which for the time being reconcile us to a succession of airs in every style from Neapolitan to Viennese Turkish. The bits from *Die Entführung* that recitalists resuscitate are almost as lovely as anything in Mozart, but hearing them out of their context leads one to expect the opera as a whole to be more satisfying than it is.

The success of *Die Entführung* had given Mozart courage to marry Constanze, but when they got home from St. Stephen's they found the cupboard bare. It was, except for short periods, to remain that way for the rest of Mozart's life. He was careless and extravagant; Constanze, though too unimaginative to be a spendthrift, was an even worse manager than he. Even at the height of his fame (which was far more considerable than many sentimentalists have been willing to admit), Mozart never made money in large sums. When, shortly after a special performance of *Die Entführung* arranged by the managers of the German Opera at Gluck's request, the aged autocrat of the music drama asked the Mozarts to his splendid mansion in the suburbs of Vienna, the disparity of their worldly positions must have been painfully apparent. Their own home was in the shabbiest quarter of the city, in a narrow, ill-smelling lane.

The next two years saw Mozart taking what advantage he could of his growing fame. Reading the roster of the phenomenal number of his engagements to play in the homes of the highest Viennese society, it is something of a mystery that he did not accumulate wealth. For instance, in five weeks of 1784, he played nine times at the magnificent Count János Esterházy's, and the same year Haydn invited him to appear several times at Prince Miklós Esterházy's Vienna house. Furthermore, besides taking part in concerts of other artists, including those of his increasingly famous sister-in-law, Aloysia Lange, Mozart began to give subscription concerts of his own, which were attended by the nobility and the diplomatic corps en masse. The Emperor, who was frequently present, always applauded loudly and shouted bravo. As a host, Mozart provided musical fare of indescribable richness. No program was complete without at least one symphony, one or two piano concertos, a *divertimento*, and several small pieces, all topped off with an improvised fantasia. This last always brought down the house.

Some slight conception of Mozart's ability as a keyboard artist may be extracted from the ecstatic eulogy of an early biographer: "If I might have the fulfillment of one wish on earth, it would be to hear Mozart improvise once more on the piano. . . ." The child clavier prodigy had perfectly adapted his maturing technique to the demands of the early piano, which, however, cannot be compared in sonority, volume, or flexibility to the modern concert grand.

The best of Mozart's music for the piano alone, with the exception of the late Fantasia in C minor (K. 475),* was written before

* Bernard Shaw's adventures with this Fantasia in the London of the nineties are worth quoting in full: "Do you know that noble fantasia in C minor, in which Mozart shewed what Beethoven was to do with the pianoforte sonata, just as in *Das Veilchen* he shewed what Schubert was to do with the song? Imagine my feelings when Madame Backer Gröndahl, instead of playing th's fantasia (which she would have done beautifully), set Madame Haas to play it, and then sat down beside her and struck up 'an original part for a second piano,' in which every interpolation was an impertinence and every addition a blemish. Shocked and pained as every one

1779, and therefore does not belong to the high noon of his genius. The sonatas are, with several notable exceptions, rather light-weight works, showing a complete command of the technical resources of the time. Some of them, indeed, show little else, and are full of empty variational passagework. The best, however, are among the permanent delights of music. The most familiar is probably that in A major (K. 331), consisting of a gracious theme and variations, a decorous but almost romantic minuet, and the now hackneyed Rondo alla Turca, which needs the perfect sympathy and flawless touch of a master to rescue it from banality. But the Sonata in A minor (K. 310) has the most body, and is probably the favorite of those whose conception of the sonata is based on the massive structures of Beethoven. It pulses with drama, and is painted with darker colors than are common in the Mozartian palette.

The piano concertos, over twenty in number, are more rewarding to the listener than the sonatas, and are incomparably more important historically. While no one man can accurately be referred to as the inventor of a musical form, Mozart did such a perfect job of fusing and adapting certain elements he found at hand that the classical concerto for piano and orchestra may be regarded as his achievement. In the sonatas, on the other hand, Mozart merely worked out the ideas of Karl Philipp Emanuel Bach and Haydn in his own way. On the piano concertos, which were staples of his musical soirees, he lavished his most exquisite care and unstinted inventiveness.* The best of them belong to the years 1784–86, though he had all but perfected the form by his twentieth year. Picking first-magnitude stars from a galaxy is a

---

who knew and loved the fantasia must have been, there was a certain grim ironic interest in the fact that the man who has had the unspeakable presumption to offer us his improvements on Mozart is the infinitesimal Grieg. The world reproaches Mozart for his inspired variations on Handel's 'The people that walked in darkness.' I do not know what the world will now say to Grieg; but if ever he plays that 'original second part' himself to an audience equipped with adequate musical culture, I sincerely advise him to ascertain beforehand that no brickbats or other loose and suitably heavy articles have been left carelessly about the room."

—London Music in 1888–89 as Heard by Corno di Bassetto

* The piano parts of the concertos are often notoriously bare in outline. When Mozart played a piano concerto in public—he was the first person ever to do so—he enriched the solo part with ornament and other improvisation. It was not until Beethoven's time that it was thought necessary to set down all the notes to be played—and even he once sent the manuscript of his C minor Concerto to the publisher with the piano part missing. He had forgotten to write it down!

fascinating game that anyone can play, and among the Mozart piano concertos there are enough masterpieces to go around. Some stargazers favor the A major (K. 414), small but perfect in design, and full of youthful charm. The B flat major (K. 450) is a Haydn joke in the first movement, typically Mozartian variations in the second, and a premonition of Schumann (in cap and bells, of all things!) in the third. The A major (K. 488) and the C minor (K. 491) were written during March, 1786, while Mozart was finishing *Le Nozze di Figaro*. The slow movement of the former is among the most touching and beautiful music ever written, diffusing the serene melancholy of "magic casements, opening on the foam of perilous seas, in faery lands forlorn." In the C minor, this melancholy has deepened into gloom. Sir Donald Tovey calls the last movement of this Concerto "sublime," and it is known that Beethoven was profoundly affected by it. Anyone who can listen to this C minor Concerto, and still say that Mozart is heartless, simply cannot hear.

What Mozart, pouring out incredible musical riches, was hoping for was not more opportunity for playing in the houses of the great. He wanted the court appointment he knew he deserved. In 1783, tired of waiting, he began to toy with the idea of trying his luck in Paris and London, but his father, who sat sulking in Salzburg, fulminated bitterly against this proposed gypsying. Besides, in June Constanze gave birth to their first child, a boy. At this point, Mozart thought it high time for his father and Nannerl to meet his wife, and so the very next month he and Constanze rushed off to Salzburg, leaving the luckless infant in the care of a wet nurse. It died while they were away.* The Salzburg visit was a failure, and after three months of cool amenities, during which Mozart toiled halfheartedly at two never completed operas, they started for home. At Linz, they found old Count Thun, whose daughter-in-law was one of Mozart's pupils, preparing for a fete. He asked Mozart to write a symphony for the occasion, and with the alacrity and *sang-froid* of a conjuror pulling a rabbit out of a hat, he produced the great C major ("Linz") Symphony (K. 425).

By this time—November, 1783—Mozart had written almost forty symphonies. Most of these are of small account, and show,

---

* In all, this harum-scarum couple had seven children. It is little wonder that only two survived.

for Mozart, a certain slowness in realizing the full possibilities of the symphonic form. Except for the witty but superficial "Paris" Symphony (K. 297), and one or two others, his most characteristic symphonies were composed after his meeting with Haydn in 1781. The effect of this relationship and of a closer knowledge of Haydn's symphonies was, curiously enough, to make Mozart more than ever himself. The first fruit of this stimulus was a second serenade written for the Haffner family, and later recast in the form of a symphony. The "Haffner," in D major (K. 385), is miniature in size—and perfect from beginning to end. The first movement is unique in Mozart for having only one theme, but he rings so many changes on this that the effect is one of infinite variety. The minuet is the formal grace of the rococo in essence; it enfolds a middle section of hushed ecstasy that is one of the tenderest moments in music. The final rondo, which Mozart wanted to be played "as fast as possible," sounds in part like an Ariel's adaptation of *Three Blind Mice*, and brings the "Haffner" to a close in a rush of pell-mell good spirits. The "Linz," though not so flawless, shows Mozart developing. Here, for the first time, he tries a slow introduction—an effect he was to turn into sheer poetry in the E flat Symphony (K. 543). The almost exotic orchestral color, which might be misinterpreted as a deliberate experiment, is really accidental—Count Thun had trumpeters and drummers in his band, but no flautists or clarinetists. The "Linz," unfortunately, is nowadays much neglected: one of the foremost living musicologists had to confess in 1935 that he had heard it but once.

After bidding farewell to Count Thun, Mozart returned to Vienna, and for more than a year nothing broke the monotonous round of his bread-and-butter existence. To compensate for the staleness of life, and to satisfy his yearning for friendship, he became more and more interested in the activities of a Masonic lodge he had joined some years before. Freemasonry in those days was not the stodgy, perfunctory institution it has become—instead of being a haven for backslappers, it was a refuge for liberal thinkers and artists, Catholic as well as Protestant. Mozart took Freemasonry very seriously. He was a militant proselytizer for the order, and even succeeded in converting his bigoted father to its tenets. As the pious Haydn also became a Mason early in 1785, it is possible that Mozart had won him over, too. Unfortunately, the music Mozart composed for his lodge remains buried in Köchel, and so it is impossible to comment on it. A funeral march is said to be particularly fine, but the only musical result we can judge is *Die Zauberflöte*, which has a Masonic libretto.

In February, 1785, Leopold Mozart visited Wolfgang and Constanze, and stayed ten weeks. Sixty-six years had somewhat mellowed his irascible and tyrannical nature, and though he never completely forgave the marriage, his son and daughter-in-law found themselves on easier terms with him. He was much impressed by their affluence—extremely temporary, unhappily—and delighted in watching the enthusiastic response to Wolfgang's musical prowess. His cup of gratification overflowed the night that the great Haydn (with two barons in attendance) called on the Mozarts in state. Later in the evening, Ditters von Dittersdorf and Wanhal dropped in, and then four of the most eminent musicians alive sat down to play Mozart's three new quartets. Before leaving, Haydn drew the elder Mozart aside, and said solemnly to him, "I declare to you before God, and as an honest man, that your son is the greatest composer I know, either personally or by name." Haydn could justly take pride in the quartets they had just played, for they were children of his own quartets. No one realized his indebtedness more than Mozart himself, for in dedicating these and three other quartets to Haydn, he said, "From Haydn I first learned how to compose a quartet."

This memorable evening was the fulfillment of Leopold Mozart's life, which, according to his lights, he had devoted to his children. After returning to Salzburg, he began to fail in health, and died in May, 1787, without having seen his son again.

Those who pause in awe before the vastness of the Köchel catalogue, with its hundreds of listings, will find the string quartets a comparatively easy problem. The key is that they are divided into two groups—those written between 1770 and 1773, and those written in 1782 and after. Unless you are a professional musicologist, you may forget the first group—they are not played often because they contain little but promise, which is an extremely flat diet for a musical evening. That Mozart stopped composing quartets for nine years better to ponder the true esthetics of the form is most unlikely. What happened was, as we know, that he met Haydn in 1781, and during the next four years wrote the set of six quartets dedicated to him. Nowhere, not even in the symphonies, is Haydn's beneficial effect on Mozart so apparent. Indeed, in the first of the "Haydn" Quartets—the G major (K. 387) —the influence forces Mozart's own idiom into the background. Coming upon this quartet unexpectedly would constitute a knotty problem in attribution. Incidentally, this does not mean that it could be mistaken for anything except the best Haydn. But the second of the set, the D minor (K. 421), is pure Mozart, though in an unusually tragic, almost Beethovian, mood. It is classical music with a future—and that future is romanticism, with its glories and mistakes. The sixth of the "Haydn" set, the C major (K. 465), raised a tempest in the critical teapot that has not subsided yet. The introduction contains a discord. The effect on all strata of society was inconceivable: a prince tore up the parts, a printer sent them back with the sharp remark that they contained "obvious misprints," and the professional critics met in solemn conclave, and pronounced Mozart a barbarian. Only Haydn had the sense to say, "If Mozart wrote thus, he must have done so with good reason." We who have eaten of the apples of modern discord can listen to the C major Quartet untroubled by anything except its beauty.

Perhaps the critical barrage left Mozart a sadder man. At any rate, he never again ran foul of the pundits in the same overt way. His four remaining string quartets are well mannered and detached, genius being lavished on technical polish rather than on deep expression. The last three, indeed, are courtly and beautifully surfaced—and correctly so. They were composed to order for Friedrich Wilhelm II of Prussia, who was a cello virtuoso in a small way, which explains why so accomplished a craftsman as Mozart allowed the cello part occasionally to upset the balance of the ensemble. The "King of Prussia" set must yield on all counts to the "Haydn": in these latter, Mozart showed an understanding of the separate personalities of the four strings that no other composer—not even Beethoven—has ever surpassed. Into the "Haydn" Quartets he poured a wealth of musical ideas not inferior in kind to those with which he built his great symphonies and concertos.

When, late in 1785, Mozart turned again to writing for the stage, he was vibrant with a newly perfected command of contrapuntal idiom. *Der Schauspieldirektor*, a humorless parody of theatrical life, is almost too trivial to justify the loving care Mozart gave it. Evidently he was so pleased to be writing in the theater again that he used this dull story as a peg on which to hang numbers worthy of a better idea. Besides, the Emperor had sent him the libretto, and he may have been playing politics, particularly as his formidable rival Salieri was to give an opera of his own at the same court fete. The overture and concluding quartet of *Der Schauspieldirektor* have a richer contrapuntal fabric than Mozart had previously used in opera, and each of the actors is assigned music that cleverly lights up his character. But even with these advantages, the tiny opera has failed to survive except in versions (themselves by no means popular) that Mozart would not recognize.

Der Schauspieldirektor was but an interruption in the creation of one of Mozart's masterpieces, *Le Nozze di Figaro*. Not long after his father's return to Salzburg, he had been approached by Lorenzo da Ponte with a suggestion that he do the music for Beaumarchais' *Le Mariage de Figaro*, one of the twin peaks of French *bouffe* drama. There were all sorts of objections to this scheme, but they were not of the kind to stop this Jewish-born priest, whose rise from the most humble origins to the post of Latin secretary and theater poet to Josef II had given him confidence in his star. The Emperor had forbidden performances of Beaumarchais' play because of its radical political implications, and it was thought that this ban would be extended to an opera based on it. Also, Mozart had reason to fear that Salieri and his other rivals would block the staging of any new opera from his pen. Da Ponte, bold in his role as Metastasio's admitted successor, was equal to his task: he won over the Emperor by sterilizing the play politically, and stymied Mozart's rivals. Incidentally, he produced the best libretto that ever came Mozart's way. The music itself was finished in April, 1786, having been written piecemeal amid a welter of bread-and-butter projects, among them three magnificent piano concertos. *Le Nozze di Figaro* was produced on May 1, and was greeted with an ovation that has rarely been surpassed in the annals of opera. Practically every number was encored, and cries of *"Viva, viva, grande Mozart!"* came from all parts of the house.

While there may be four opinions as to which is the best of Mozart's operas, there can be no doubt that *Figaro* teems with more memorable music than any of the others—indeed, with more than almost any other opera ever written. From beginning to end, the succession of dazzling numbers is bewildering. To hear the opera for the first time is to lose much of its dramatic unity: it sounds too much like a mere anthology of celebrated melodies. It takes long familiarity with *Figaro* to realize fully with what consummate art Mozart has combined musical beauty and dramatic truth. This breathless pageant of beauty begins with the overture (now almost too familiar), which, with its matchless delicacy, liveliness, and wit, sets the atmosphere and pace of what is to follow. And so it proceeds, through Figaro's superb martial aria in the first act, the Contessa's and Cherubino's lovely music in the second, the peerless lament of the Contessa in Act III, and finally to Susanna's tender love song in the last act. To choose a favorite among these is a task—the fact that so many people know "*Voi che sapete*" better than anything else in *Figaro* is due to its excessive whistleability.

The success of this ribald opera did not improve Mozart's financial position. He had received a lump sum for its composition, and this he ran through as fast as possible. He was living way beyond his means, dressing himself and his family in the finest style, and occupying part of a mansion in a good quarter of Vienna. His rather hectic private life was likewise a drain on his resources, physical as well as financial. About this time, he began a series of sordid little affairs with sundry women which add a note of ambiguity to his otherwise constant affection for Constanze. And she, it must be admitted, was not like Caesar's wife, and often had to be reproved for giving gossips something to talk about.

Mozart's extravagant scale of living and his fitful indulgences required some sort of stable income that Vienna seemed unwilling to provide. After *Figaro*, the Emperor was as usual vociferous in his praise—but no official post was forthcoming. In despair, Mozart toyed once more with a fantastic idea of seeking his fortune in England, and it seems that only a warm invitation to see for himself how well *Figaro* was faring in Prague kept him from this venture. He accepted with alacrity, and soon he and Constanze, with the lordly Thun mansion as their own, were receiving a hearty welcome from highborn Praguers. Their reception, in fact, was so gratifying that it must have crossed Mozart's mind that here he might be both understood and recompensed according to his deserts. His presence at a performance of *Figaro* almost started a riot, and when he himself conducted it some days later the plaudits of the audience sounded like one vast claque. Equally successful were his two concerts, at the first of which he conducted a splendid new symphony, the D major, or "Prague" (K. 504), whose proportions suggest a transition from the smaller perfections of the "Haffner" and "Linz" to the more epic structures of the last three symphonies. Mozart was now the darling of Prague society—a state of affairs that must have recalled to him the triumphs of his childhood. He no sooner expressed a wish to write an opera for so sympathetic a public than the delighted impresario who had imported *Figaro* handed him a contract. He had to leave Prague without the elusive appointment, but for once his pockets were stuffed.

Vienna, after the homage of Prague, was cold indeed, and Mozart plunged feverishly into the business of the new opera. Da Ponte suggested Don Juan as a subject, and (doubtless to get the proper atmosphere) sat down with a bottle of Tokay on one hand and a pretty girl on the other. At one stage of the writing, when the crosscurrents of passion and revenge became one too many for him, Da Ponte called in Casanova for expert advice. Mozart, while tossing off the best of his string quintets and the luscious *Eine kleine Nachtmusik*, began to rear the superb structure of *Don Giovanni*. In the midst of all this, he received a visitor who must have seemed as strange to him as the Stone Guest did to Don Juan. This unappetizing young fellow, who looked little more elegant than a Flemish lout, sat down at the piano, and improvised with such originality that Mozart said solemnly to some other guests, "Keep your eyes on him. Some day he will give the world something to talk about." He was right: his caller was Ludwig van Beethoven.

In September, 1787, the Mozarts returned to Prague for two more gala months. The score of *Don Giovanni* was still unfinished, partly because Mozart had been overworked, and partly because he had to consult his singers before putting the final touches on their arias. The overture was the last number composed, and the orchestra had to read it at sight at the final rehearsal.* The *pre-*

---

* Constanze, years later, told her second husband that Mozart had composed the overture the night before the final rehearsal. She said that he was so tired that she had to freshen him with numerous glasses of punch and the reading of fairy tales.

mière, on October 29, surpassed the triumphs of *Figaro,* which was still a prime favorite in Prague. Mozart's appearance in the orchestra was announced by a trumpet fanfare that might have greeted an imperial personage. The performers, especially the singers, seemed to be aware that they were making history, and made the presentation electric with their enthusiasm.

Don Giovanni has drawn to it a host of admirers who think it the greatest opera ever written, and they are just as vociferous as those who noisily claim this honor for *Tristan und Isolde* or *Pelléas et Mélisande.* Certainly, it is a very exciting opera, with its many boldly delineated characters, the rush of events toward inevitable destruction, the shifting from comedy to tragedy with the protean rhythm of life itself, and the *bizarrerie* of the ghoulish finale. *Don Giovanni* was new in 1787—it is still new. The Don is the first of the countless Byronic heroes who were to crowd the operatic stage during the nineteenth century, and his excesses and ruin give us a foretaste of what Weber and Meyerbeer will do with their hellish librettos. All this romantic folderol is expressed in Mozart's highly classical idiom, with a minimum of fustian—until the finale, when the Commendatore's marble statue accepts the Don's invitation to dinner—with dire results. Here we are conscious that the nineteenth century is only thirteen years away, and the Satanic fires that consume the wicked hero's palace lick at the very structure of classicism itself.

But those who hear this romantic note with foreboding have been amply compensated in the earlier scenes. It must be admitted that the overture is not Mozart at his best, and scarcely prepares us for the marvels that are to follow. These begin with Leporello's famous catalogue of his master's infidelities, a masterpiece of *buffa* and bravura. Ten or fifteen minutes later, we hear "*Là ci darem la mano,*" a duet of haunting, tender beauty.* Almost with the profusion of *Figaro,* brilliant arias and dramatic concerted numbers follow. "*Il mio tesoro,*" with its tracery of florid melody, lays claim to being the most beautiful aria in the tenor repertoire. But the

---

* *Re* the connection of *Don Giovanni* with the romantic movement, it is worth noting that the young Chopin was so enchanted with "*Là ci darem*" that he based a set of variations for piano and orchestra (Opus 2) on it. And it was this work, in turn, that fired Schumann to write his first published musical essay, with the celebrated tag line, "Hats off, gentlemen, a genius!" This essay set off the romantic revolt in music criticism.

most celebrated music from *Don Giovanni* is not vocal—it is the instrumental minuet that closes the first act. The boy Mendelssohn gravely informed the venerable Goethe that this minuet was the "most beautiful music in the world." And though we have heard it played on everything from a pipe organ to a hand organ, it would not be difficult to agree with him.

After the *première* of *Don Giovanni*, the Mozarts dallied among the appreciative Praguers, and did not return to Vienna until November 12. Three days later, Gluck died, and a month later, Josef II appointed Mozart his new chamber composer. The post carried considerable prestige, but Mozart described the emolument as "too much for what I do, and too little for what I could do." Gluck had received two thousand gulden a year; the emperor gave Mozart eight hundred, and this paltry sum was, with the exception of a tiny stipend from St. Stephen's that he began to receive in 1791, the only assured income he enjoyed. For a time he squandered his genius turning out trivial music for court functions—charming dances that foreshadow Johann Strauss. Altogether, Mozart was as near to being in a rut as he ever was in all his life. His feeling of neglect was intensified by the cool reception the Viennese accorded *Don Giovanni*. Also, his chronic poverty had become acute, and he now began that series of begging letters to a fellow Mason which is matched in the annals of music only by the more flagrant specimens from Wagner's pen. His improdigality far outstripped his friend's patient generosity, and when the funds came they were mere stopgaps.

Despite indications to the contrary, Mozart was on the edge of the most miraculously fecund period of his life. A few weeks after the chilling Vienna first night of *Don Giovanni*, and while his rival Salieri was crowding him off the boards with a very successful opera, Mozart began a symphony. As if seized by a divine frenzy, he worked for six weeks, and when he laid down his pen, he had completed his three unquestioned symphonic masterpieces. There are two ways of interpreting this phenomenon: either Mozart escaped into music from the sordidness of his life, or his misery put him into the vatic state. Interpreted either way, these three last symphonies are the triple crown of eighteenth-century orchestral music. In deference to Beethoven alone, it is a moot question whether they have ever been surpassed.

The Beethoven symphonies are great as music, but part of their enormous popularity is due to the way they lend themselves to extramusical interpretation. It is easy to read into them the course of Beethoven's—or mankind's—struggles. Mozart's symphonies do not lend themselves to such interpretation, and perhaps for that reason they, like Haydn's, have suffered in the estimation of the more romantic types of concertgoers. They must be approached, and heard, as music alone. Almost all attempts to read vast human or superhuman meanings into Mozart show a violent lapse of mental discipline. They spring from a refusal, or inability, to recognize the intrinsic condition of music as an art, and end, in that final *reductio ad absurdum* of musical determinism, by erecting a certain preconception of Beethoven's symphonies as the only ideal. It was this school of misthinkers who thought they were praising Brahms by calling his First Symphony "Beethoven's Tenth," and who, vaguely realizing that Mozart was a first-rate composer, have read all sorts of strange things into his music, particularly the last three symphonies. But their wrestlings with Mozart's pellucid material produce singularly ludicrous results. For instance, just as they are beginning to revel in the connotations of the vast and mysterious slow introduction to the E flat Symphony, their idea-freighted haze evaporates, and they are left with nothing but music.

Mozart has left no richer or more varied music than these last three symphonies. Each of them abounds in inspired musical ideas, and each has a distinct musical character of its own, truly amazing in view of the circumstances of their composition. After the slow grandeur of the introduction, the E flat (K. 543), which has been called the *locus classicus* of euphony, turns out to be a gay, even impudent, work, with but few notes of pensiveness. The instrumental color is especially rich and full of contrasts, with the wind instruments playing an unusually important role—the E flat was the first major work in which clarinets were prominently used. The lovely minuet, which is almost as famous as that from *Don Giovanni*, is already half a scherzo—Beethoven was to bring the symphonic scherzo to adulthood in his Second Symphony, and perfect it in his Third. The G minor (K. 550) has suffered somewhat from the fact that the first movement is perhaps the most sheerly beautiful music ever written, and thus the last three movements have too often been shoved into the background of the memory like poor relations. Actually, though they lack the inexplicable magic of that wonderful allegro, they do their full share toward making the G minor a perfectly integrated work of art. This symphony, which Eric Blom has called "the work in which classicism and romanticism meet and where once and for all we see a perfect equilibrium between them," is the most troubled of Mozart's symphonies. The pensive note is, for once, tinged with a deeper melancholy and weariness. After it, the C major (K. 551) is untroubled, even resurgent. It happens, under the meaningless pseudonym of the "Jupiter," to be the best known of the symphonies. Also, it is the most patterned and classical of the three: the entire structure is based on a series of inspired musical axioms as neat and spare as propositions from Euclid. The celebrated finale intricately combines five of these themes with a wizardry that gives point to the comparison of this movement to a musical chess game. The whole symphony is a curious, but completely successful, combination of grandeur and high spirits. Altogether, this last of Mozart's symphonies has abounding strength and youthfulness, and is informed throughout by an athleticism that is rare in the rest of his work.

It is not too strange that these three symphonies, the last of which was completed early in August, 1788, seemingly exhausted Mozart's best creative powers, and brought on a fallow period that lasted almost a whole year. Needless to say, he did not completely stop composing: a multitude of dances and minor chamber works flowed from his pen, some of them only hack work. He also began to "fill out" the instrumental accompaniments of certain of Handel's oratorios, notably *Messiah*, on a commission from Baron van Swieten, one of Vienna's most celebrated musical amateurs, who later furnished the libretto for Haydn's *The Creation*. Possibly too much obloquy has been attached to these refurbishings of Handel, but they certainly belong to a very dubious category: it is still a question whether any composer, however great, should try to "complete" another composer's work.

In April, 1789, Mozart set out on a brief tour as the guest of his pupil, Prince Karl Lichnowsky. He played successfully before the Saxon court at Dresden, and at Leipzig performed on the very organ that Johann Sebastian Bach had used. Greatly moved, the

Thomascantor, himself Bach's pupil, had the choir perform *Singet dem Herrn*, one of his teacher's six surviving motets. This so transported the visitor that he asked to see the parts, exclaiming, "Here, for once, is something from which one can learn." The next stop was Potsdam, where Frederick the Great's cultivated nephew gave Mozart the same eager reception his uncle had accorded Bach. Although Mozart criticized the King's band, and heckled the orchestra during a performance of his own *Entführung*, Friedrich Wilhelm tipped him generously, and commissioned him to compose six string quartets and also six easy piano sonatas for the Princess Royal.* The legend that Mozart turned down the munificently paid job of *Kapellmeister* at Potsdam in deference to Josef II is probably sheer fantasy. If he did anything so unlikely, he might have felt himself rewarded on his return to Vienna (with his pockets mysteriously empty), when the Emperor ordered another opera from him and Da Ponte. *Così fan tutte*, their new collaboration, was hurried through for the winter season, and produced on January 2, 1790.

Much has been written about *Così fan tutte*, and most of that much about its libretto, which has been denounced alternately as indecent and shallow. There is a grain of truth in both criticisms, but only because these elements necessarily have their parts in the making of a really comic opera. The libretto is actually quite adequate, with its many absurd contretemps. In general plan it resembles *The Two Gentlemen of Verona*—with extra characters and complications. It is, quite appropriately, the most rococo of Mozart's operas—a carnival of madcap frivolity and fun from start to finish. It is interesting, if irrelevant, to note that *Così fan tutte* had its *première* just when the horrors of the French Revolution were beginning. On this exceedingly flimsy basis, it has been called the swan song of the callous, pleasure-mad aristocracy of the eighteenth century (which in Austria went its own pleasure-mad, callous way for decades after the French Revolution). The opera is a delightful confection, musically like the sugar icing on a cuckold's wedding cake. There are those who think it the best opera Mozart ever wrote.

Così fan tutte delighted the unscrupulous Viennese. Unfortu-

* Mozart composed only three "King of Prussia" Quartets, and but one of the sonatas.

nately, three weeks after the first performance, Josef II died. Again Mozart's hopes were dashed. Leopold II, the new Emperor, was violently lukewarm in his attitude toward music, and indifferent to Mozart, who was not included in the entourage summoned to Frankfort for the coronation. Mozart's actions at this point were hysterical. Constanze was ailing, and required expensive medical care, he himself had only just recovered from a serious illness, and his poverty was becoming unbearable. Yet he pawned the few valuables he had left, and gallivanted off to Frankfort with the idea of giving concerts while the city was crowded with notables. He appeared only once, when he played the so-called "Coronation" Concerto for piano and orchestra (K. 537), which he had really written two years before. As usual, there was much applause but small financial gain, and the sad tale was repeated wherever he stopped to play on his way home. It was a very weary and sick man who reached Vienna in November. The following month, when Haydn came to see him before leaving for London, Mozart wept. He believed, and with reason, that he would not live to see his beloved friend's return.

The early months of 1791 passed uneventfully. In March, Mozart ran into an old acquaintance of his Salzburg days, Emanuel Schikaneder, a sort of theatrical jack-of-all-trades, who at the moment was staging a series of spectacle plays and bawdy farces in a large but flimsy auditorium outside the city walls. As he was a brother Mason, Schikaneder managed to induce Mozart to set a preposterous sheaf of muddled ideas he had gathered from his reading and bound together with ill-digested Masonic symbolism. Yet this potpourri abounded in situations and characters that Mozart could treat effectively. He set to work at once on what was to be his last opera, *Die Zauberflöte*, and as Constanze was away taking treatments at a spa, Schikaneder provided him with a little workhouse near the theater, good cheer, and jolly, loose-living companions. In July, while he was still toiling on the score, a stranger approached him with a commission to write a Requiem by a set date. The remuneration was inordinately generous, and the anonymous visitor made only one stipulation—absolute secrecy. Mozart agreed, but with forebodings: he was far from well, probably running a fever, and the cadaverous stranger may have seemed to him like the Devil ordering him to compose his own funeral music.

No sooner had he started on the Requiem than a third commission arrived, this time a peremptory request to compose an opera for Leopold II's coronation as King of Bohemia at Prague. The libretto of *La Clemenza di Tito*, a humdrum revamping of Metastasio, offered little chance to even so resourceful a composer as Mozart. Also, he was a sick man living on his will power, and had to complete *La Clemenza* in less than two months. To make him even more agitated, just as he was stepping into the Prague coach the cadaverous stranger reappeared, and asked him how the Requiem was progressing. Muttering that he would finish it when he returned, Mozart got inside, and with a strange feeling that all was not well, took up the sketches for *La Clemenza*, the actual writing of which he completed in Prague in eighteen days. He was so rushed that the recitatives had to be entrusted to his friend and pupil, Franz Süssmayr. At its *première*, on September 6, *La Clemenza di Tito* was a failure—and only partly because the court was exhausted after the rigors of the coronation. It is a *pièce d'occasion* in the worst sense of the phrase. Outside of an impressive overture, a brilliant soprano aria, and a couple of duets, it clearly shows the strain under which the composer was working.

Mozart returned to Vienna in bad health and dejected spirits, which did not prevent him from pouring his failing energy into the completion of *Die Zauberflöte*, which was first produced at Schikaneder's Theater auf der Wieden on September 30. At first the work was received coldly, but so rapidly gained in popularity that it was repeated twenty-four times in October alone. Its absurd stage business was probably more responsible for its success than the music—today it is the other way round. With the exception of *Idomeneo*, it is, for all its many lapses into tomfoolery, sustained on loftier heights than Mozart's other operas. The overture, a work of the most solemn beauty despite its rapid tempo, eloquently tells us that we are to hear a work of serious import. And so it is, for even the most farcical passages had originally a symbolic significance, and are couched in Mozart's most sensitive idiom. *Die Zauberflöte* makes use of many musical styles, and yet achieves an effect of unity. The fact that anything can, and does, happen in this Cloud-Cuckoo-Land is matched by the variety of musical exposition. And though the dramatis personae are but symbols, they run the widest gamut of character that Mozart ever exploited in one opera, from the grave, almost unctuous priest, Sarastro, to that delicious eighteenth-century Touchstone, Papageno.

Bernard Shaw has somewhere said that Mozart gave Sarastro the only music that would not sound out of place in the mouth of God. Be that as it may, the smug high priest sings two of the noblest arias ever written for the bass voice—"*O Isis und Osiris*" and "*In diesen heil'gen Hallen*," the first of which has a majesty and foursquareness traceable to Mozart's study of Handel. The Queen of the Night, the very personification of evil, curses her daughter* in a strikingly florid and taxing coloratura aria, "*Der hölle Rache*." Listened to carelessly, this aria sounds much like, and just as empty as, the "Bell Song" from *Lakme*, but under its elegant surfaces a dark and icy fiendishness lies coiled. The Queen's namby-pamby daughter and the birdman, Papageno, have a lusciously tender duet, "*Bei Männern, welche Liebe fühlen*," which might have escaped from the most amorous pages of *Figaro*. As Schikaneder played Papageno in the original production, this personage has more music than the role calls for dramatically, but his songs are farce of such high order that they never fail to bring down the house, particularly in the celebrated "stuttering duet"† with his feather-covered and featherbrained mate, Papagena. Thus, *Die Zauberflöte* has something for every taste. But the final appeal of this fairy opera with a moral is the beauty, range, and aptness of its music.

With this last of his operas off his hands, Mozart collapsed. He was desperately ill (of Bright's disease, it has been conjectured), and not even the news of *Die Zauberflöte*'s growing success could rouse him from despondency. Constanze's absence did not help: in his misery and torture, he needed someone with him constantly. He turned feverishly to the Requiem, and worked on it with desperate concentration. He began to have fainting spells. Fortunately, late in October the still-ailing Constanze returned, bring-

* A strange situation indeed, considering that the Queen of the Night, in the libretto's tortured symbolism, has been identified with the family-loving Maria Theresa.

† The prolonged ovation that greeted this duet, one memorable evening at the Chicago Auditorium, held Marcella Sembrich, as the Queen of the Night, in the wings so long that she refused ever again to sing in that city.

ing her youngest sister to nurse both herself and Mozart. She realized how sick he was, and unsuccessfully tried to make him stop work on the Requiem. A new horror now gripped his mind: being unable to diagnose his disease naturally (it may have been nothing more than overwork and malnutrition combined), he developed a fixed idea that he had been poisoned by Salieri.* Every evening, when theater time came around, he followed in imagination the performance of *Die Zauberflöte*, timing it with a watch. Within a few weeks it was evident that he was fatally ill, and yet so amazing were his recuperative powers that on November 15 he finished a Masonic cantata, and even conducted it a few days later.

Relapse was almost immediate. He continued to work fitfully at the Requiem even when racked with pain. Süssmayr and other friends came in occasionally to sing parts of it with him. On December 4, during one of these gatherings, just as they were beginning the *Lacrymosa*, Mozart began to sob, and they had to stop. Before the day was over, he was partly paralyzed. A priest came to administer the last sacraments, and Mozart said good-by to his family. He then gave some last instructions to Süssmayr about the still-unfinished Requiem, and to the very end seemed preoccupied with it, trying to sing, and even puffing out his cheeks in an attempt to imitate the trumpets. Just after midnight, he died quietly. It was the morning of December 5, 1791.

Constanze, too shattered to think, automatically followed the sensible advice of the penurious Van Swieten to bury her husband as cheaply as possible. On December 6, during a rainstorm that prevented both Constanze and Mozart's friends from going to the potter's field, his body was cast, with the remains of a dozen other paupers, into a common grave. When Constanze tried to find the spot some time later, no one could tell her where it was. Almost seventy years afterward, the city of Vienna erected a fine memorial on the probable site.

The Requiem, Mozart's last musical testament, remained a collection of fragments and sketches until Constanze, who seems to have been injected with a strong dose of good sense as soon as her

* Pushkin used this absurd idea as the basis for a dramatic duologue, which Rimsky-Korsakov later made into an opera. Salieri was so hounded by the rumor that he took the trouble on his deathbed to send for Ignaz Moscheles, and officially deny the story.

husband died, finally entrusted it to Süssmayr, who knew more than anyone else about Mozart's intentions concerning it. Süssmayr filled out the work with sections of his own composition, but doubtless oriented to his master's hints. Thus, the present work is in design not too unlike what it might have been had Mozart lived to complete it—whatever one may think of Süssmayr's own passages. It was delivered to the mysterious stranger, who turned out to be Count Franz von Walsegg's major-domo, as being entirely by Mozart. The Count then had it performed as a composition of his own—which had been his original intention. Thus the Requiem came into the world as a double forgery, which was partly revealed when Constanze allowed it to be performed, and then published, under Mozart's name. The parts that are unquestionably Mozart's, notably the Kyrie, are passionate and tragic, and rise to moments of great beauty. But they are informed by the hectic glow of a sick mind. Let us face the facts squarely: much of the Requiem (when it is not from Süssmayr's earnest but mediocre pen) is tortured in expression and painful to hear. It is easy to believe that Mozart composed this twisted, self-searching, and self-revealing music with his own funeral in mind. It was played thirty-six years later at the solemn High Mass for the repose of the soul of Ludwig van Beethoven.

Myths die hard, and bad myths are just as tenacious of life as good ones. Alexander the Great, Leonardo, and Beethoven have given rise to myths that are constantly renewed by their essential truth. The Mozart myth is another matter: it is a bad myth with just enough truth in it to make it linger on. It presents Mozart as a perpetual child, dowered with an infallible and limitless technique, composing a great variety of delightful but empty music. Now, Mozart wrote a vast deal, much of which—almost all, indeed, of that written before 1780—can accurately be described as delightful but empty. And even some of his finest compositions are marred by uninspired passagework which has about as much significance as a Czerny finger exercise—in this respect, Haydn, who has often been criticized for his abuse of the technical cliché, erred far less than Mozart. Yes, the myth has a core of truth. The amazing thing is that it has persisted whole in the face of the pure gold that it overlooks. The simplest of the many possible refutations of the eternal-child myth is to cite the last three symphonies, which impinge upon almost every conceivable emotion. These are indubitably the expressions of a mature and abounding personality. What has blinded many to Mozart's emotional range and profundity is the fact that its expression is so perfectly disciplined: they have fallen into the fatal error of gauging emotional expression by a preconceived norm—the seeming indiscipline of the best romantic art.

A more serious doubt has been cast on Mozart's place as the peer of Bach and Beethoven. W. J. Turner, who yielded to none in his worship of Mozart, was the most perfectly articulate spokesman of those who find him lacking one essential which, together with his other, unquestioned, qualities, would add up to sublimity. Speaking of the notorious lapse in mood (almost inexplicable on the basis of taste alone) in the finale of the G minor Quintet (K. 516), he said, "That finale is beyond all denial inadequate. Why? Because after the poignant, heart-breaking intensity of the slow movement some affirmation of the soul is inexorably demanded. *Mozart could not make that affirmation.* He could not even attempt to make it . . . he had no faith, he could not lift up his heart and sing from the bottom of that abyss. . . . Therefore, and therefore only, he is not the world's greatest composer."* This argument is based on that ethical approach (more widely held in the nineteenth century of Ruskin and Tolstoi than now) which conceives the greatest artist to be he who struggles most desperately in the waste places of the soul, and emerges singing the song of faith and triumph. Without entering into the validity of this point of view, it is clear that to those who hold it, Mozart must ever seem, in this respect, inadequate.

However, even this criticism might have been obviated had Mozart lived but a few years longer. The last years of his life saw his art deepening, becoming more searching of self and things, turning toward those sources of inspiration that can lead to the hymning of life entire. What these sources were, it is as impossible to know in Mozart's case as in Beethoven's. But everything indicates that this still-young man, who so sorely needed a vacation

---

*Thus Turner in Volume I of *The Heritage of Music* (London, 1927). In *Mozart: the Man and His Works* (New York, 1938), he allowed his hero no limitations at all.

and a little more food, had not yet reached the summit of his genius, and was on the verge of new and tremendous undertakings. There was no sign of abatement in that matchless flood of musical ideas, he was the greatest musical technician of all times, and he died at thirty-six, an age at which Bach and Beethoven were still preparing for their supreme masterpieces. Mozart died in the moment of victory—but *before* he could make his affirmation, as he himself knew:

"I am at the point of death. I have finished before I could enjoy my talent. Yet life is so beautiful, my career opened so auspiciously —but fate is not to be changed. . . . I thus finish my funeral song— I must not leave it uncompleted."

Chapter VII

Ludwig van Beethoven

(Bonn, December 16, 1770–March 26, 1827, Vienna)

THE history of music offers no experience comparable to that sense of an expanding universe afforded by the masterpieces of Ludwig van Beethoven. With the advent of this titanic presence, there is an abrupt break with the past that has few parallels in the entire history of art. The essential Beethoven was completely unprepared for. His great predecessors, from Palestrina to Mozart, were men without whom the musical structure he found, honored, and changed could not have been reared, but only insofar as they gave him his tools was he in their debt. These men, master musicians though they were, had been the creatures of an ordered universe. Their reactions to it had been as various as their characters: they had praised it, accepted it, or disregarded it—but in no case did they question it. Even Haydn, who was Beethoven's contemporary for almost forty years, and who passed the fullness of his maturity during the French Revolution, never questioned the ideas of the times that had molded him. But Beethoven, who came of age at the very high noon of the Terror, passed through the refiner's fire of this crucial chaotic epoch: the flames of liberty, equality, and fraternity blazed hot against his face, and seared him for life.

Beethoven is the first, and in some respects the only, composer who stepped outside the frame of his art, to live wholly and heroically in the world. He could not be content merely to write music: unrest was in his soul, and doubt which in its savage intensity made the polite skepticism of the eighteenth century seem puny. Thought pursued him like a nemesis—he could not get away from it. His wrestling with destiny, not only his own but that of mankind, is one of the great epics of the modern world: he told it in a succession of mighty works which, in their boundless humanity and immediacy of appeal, have never been equaled. By his struggles, Beethoven became one of the heroes of mankind; by his triumphs, he has become one of its prophets.

He was born at one of those strange moments of history when

nature spews forth genius with an inexplicable lavishness. The time was, for better or worse, fateful for the shaping of life and art. Napoleon, whose ambitions created the French Empire and untold misery; Wordsworth, who gave the new age a voice; Beethoven, who lifted music to a new grandeur—these three men, born within seventeen months, were to play great parts in the vast drama that ushered in the nineteenth century. Napoleon, the revolutionary, became the autocrat of Europe, and died shorn of ideals and power alike; the generous-souled Wordsworth ended up a timeserving poet laureate; Beethoven alone had the strength and the integrity to die as he had lived—faithful to the daemon that had moved him. His life has been painted as a tragedy, but he had the only kind of success that could really have mattered to him.

The times, certainly, were propitious for shaping the sort of stormy genius Beethoven was, and his heredity and early environment were equally so. The Beethovens had been musicians for two generations: Ludwig, the grandfather, who rose to be *Kapellmeister* to the Elector of Cologne, also carried on a thriving wine business; his son Johann, a singer in the Elector's choir, was, by the time of his marriage to a young widow, more celebrated for his drinking than for his voice. Thus, at Ludwig's cradle there were as many wicked fairies as good ones: from his Grandfather Beethoven he inherited a certain physical toughness on which he could rely to see him through the energy-burning crises of his life, as well as an earnest consciousness of good and evil. To his Grandmother Beethoven and his father, both of whom became hopeless drunkards, he owed those erratic, fevered qualities which played a salient role in the development of his art, and which always made him a difficult person.

Beethoven first saw the light of day in Bonn, and in this lazy old Rhenish town he passed a miserably unhappy boyhood. The Beethovens were desperately poor: Johann's three hundred florins a year was barely sufficient to support a childless couple, and in twenty years of married life he fathered seven children, of whom three boys reached manhood. Johann, originally a genial fellow, developed swinish habits and a nasty temper. Yet his father believed that this brute had lowered himself by marrying a mere cook's daughter, though to the Elector musicians and cooks were equally servants. Actually, Frau van Beethoven was many cuts above her husband—a sympathetic and intelligent woman whose calm acceptance of a painful *status quo* alone kept a semblance of order in the household. She never complained, but it is little wonder that she was never seen to smile.

There was never any question which parent Beethoven preferred. To him his mother was a beneficent deity—the only gracious thing in his wretched childhood. Johann, whose treatment of his wife was insensitive, was harsh and unimaginative in his dealings with his eldest son. In his frenzied quest for a further source of income, he hit upon the idea of making Ludwig a child prodigy after the pattern of Mozart. Leopold Mozart may justly be accused of putting his son through a forcing-house, but his method was gentle, and he was motivated, at least partly, by a burning love for music. But to Johann van Beethoven music was merely a trade and he set Ludwig to learning it—he evidently thought that Mozarts could be produced at will. He himself undertook the job of turning out the *Wunderkind,* and at first his hopes seemed sure of fulfillment, for at six the boy had learned to perform creditably on the piano and violin. In 1778, Johann gave the public its first chance to hear the prodigy he had been preparing for them, slyly announcing Ludwig as two years younger than he really was. The sole result of what probably was a fiasco (in view of the complete silence as to its effect) was that Ludwig got a new teacher. But this quavering old fellow could teach him nothing, and soon yielded to one of Johann's rowdy pals, a tenor named Pfeiffer who lodged in the same house as the Beethovens. His method of teaching was unique: he would come roaring home in the middle of the night after a round of the taverns with Johann, and get Ludwig out of bed for his lesson. The picture of the small, sleepy lad pestered by his music teacher and his father is absurdly like that of the immortal Dormouse plagued by the Mad Hatter and the March Hare. No wonder Beethoven was an indifferent scholar during the few years he attended common school! Nor was the proud and self-willed lad apt to respond to these repressive methods as his father had hoped.

And yet, develop Beethoven did, though too slowly for a bona fide prodigy. Teachers came and went, none of them very able or inspiring, and a time arrived when these ninth-raters could teach him nothing. He was ten years old before he found a master worthy of his talents—Christian Gottlob Neefe, the newly appointed court organist. Neefe was a conservative, but he worshiped music, and his taste was sure. He immediately set Beethoven to studying a handwritten copy of *The Well-Tempered Clavichord*, then still unpublished, and thus initiated his lifelong interest in Bach. Neefe believed in the urchin: he educated him painstakingly, and stimulated his natural flair for composing by having a juvenile effort published. Beethoven made such rapid progress that in 1783 Neefe said in a magazine article, "If he goes on as he has begun, he will certainly become a second Mozart." After a year's instruction, Beethoven was able to deputize for Neefe at the organ; after Neefe's duties became heavier, he sometimes led the opera orchestra from the clavier. The job was unpaid, the experience invaluable. Beethoven never forgot Neefe's unfailing kindness. In 1792, with a touch of characteristic self-assurance and grandiloquence, he wrote to his old teacher, "I thank you for your counsel very often given me in the course of my progress in my divine art. If ever I become a great man, yours will be some of the credit," and the delighted Neefe published the letter in the *Berliner Musik-Zeitung*.

Beethoven soon got his first big chance. In 1784, the Elector died, and Maria Theresa's youngest son succeeded him. In the shuffling of appointments that ensued, Neefe's thirteen-year-old pupil was appointed assistant court organist at a salary of one hundred and fifty florins a year. Johann van Beethoven's reactions must have mingled relief with chagrin: Ludwig was adding to the family income, but the Elector seemingly did not value Johann's services enough to raise his pay. Young Beethoven did his job so well that for a time there was talk of his taking Neefe's place. He began to lead a full life in a Bonn that was reawakening artistically and intellectually under the enlightened rule of the Elector Maximilian Franz. In the spring of 1787, Beethoven had his first taste of a truly cosmopolitan culture, when he visited Vienna, presumably on funds advanced by a patron. He met Mozart, who spoke flatteringly of his playing, and possibly gave the boy lessons in composition, though in mourning for his father and hard at work on *Don Giovanni*. Beethoven was recalled to Bonn by news of his mother's illness; letters, more and more alarming, reached him on the road, but he found her still alive, though in intense agony.

She was in the last stages of consumption, and died a few weeks later.

The death of his mother, whom Beethoven had adored, brought on the first of those emotional crises that recurred constantly throughout his life. He gave way to gloomy forebodings; he suffered from attacks of asthma—the neurotic's disease par excellence —and feared that it would develop into consumption. Throughout life Beethoven was fortunate in his friends: now he was gradually coaxed back to mental health by the sympathetic interest and patient care of the noble Von Breuning family, the first in that procession of long-suffering Samaritans who, despite his outbursts of arrogance and downright rudeness, ministered untiringly to his difficult needs. Frau von Breuning was a second mother to Beethoven, who was admitted on terms of absolute equality with her children to the cultural freemasonry of their fine home. He passed through its portals as into a friendly university, and there laid the foundation for the obsessing intellectual interests of his life. Scarcely less decisive was his friendship with Count Ferdinand von Waldstein, who gave him his first piano, and generously opened his purse when the finances of the Beethovens were at lowest ebb. With exquisite tact, he pretended that these moneys were gratuities from his friend the Elector.

Beethoven was happy until, after a day of court duty and time with his friends, he turned in at his own door in the Wenzelgasse. There, as like as not, he would find his father in a drunken stupor, and his two younger brothers neglected and unfed. Johann van Beethoven was no longer a responsible person. At his wits' end, in November, 1789, the nineteen-year-old Ludwig successfully petitioned the Elector to divert half of Johann's salary to himself, and make him legal head of the family. This desperate measure worked, and with his domestic affairs on the mend, Beethoven could plunge wholeheartedly into his increasingly engrossing duties. The Elector, after settling the troubled finances of his domains, felt himself justified in indulging his desire for a large musical establishment. Considering his enormous bulk (he eventually became the fattest man in Europe), his energy was astonishing: in a trice, he had organized an operatic troupe and an orchestra of thirty-one pieces that rivaled the famous Mannheim ensemble. Before 1792, when it was dispersed, the opera company achieved a large repertoire, including works by Gluck, Mozart, and Salieri. Beethoven, as viola player in the band, came to know intimately a wide variety of dramatic music. The young bear was well liked by his fellows, and seems to have played a leading part in their off-hours fun.

Toward the end of his life in Bonn, Beethoven achieved a position of local eminence out of proportion to his accomplishments as an instrumentalist. This can only have been due to many of his compositions being circulated in autograph among his friends, including some that were not published until years—in some cases, many years—later in Vienna. Neefe was not the only one in Bonn who thought that Beethoven would one day be the peer of Mozart. It is not surprising, then, that in July, 1792, when Haydn passed through Bonn on his return from London, Beethoven was especially commended to him. Haydn praised a cantata that Beethoven submitted for criticism, and encouraged him to continue his studies. This kind word from music's dictator released a spring in Beethoven: Vienna, with lessons from Haydn practically assured, irresistibly beckoned him. Waldstein and Neefe pled his case with the Elector, who consented to finance the hegira. By November, Beethoven was on his way—and none too soon: just two days before he left Bonn forever, the Elector himself had fled, for the troops of revolutionary France were marching on his capital.

As the Elector's troubles delayed the payment of his official stipend, Beethoven was hard pressed at first. Only a fraction of the special grant ever reached him, and he had to dig into his small savings to make ends meet. Things were complicated by his father's death in December. It seemed momentarily that the pension, which had been earmarked for the support of Beethoven's brothers, would be stopped, but the Elector, after returning to Bonn, continued it until he was chased out again in 1794. Haydn charged Beethoven almost nothing—five sessions with him came to less than a dollar. But Beethoven was dissatisfied: apart from the difficulties arising from their totally divergent temperaments, he was annoyed by Haydn's desultory conduct of the lessons. The student was avid to crowd in as much learning as possible; the master was preoccupied with a new repertoire for his second English tour. Beethoven secretly began to take lessons from a solid pedagogue. Although Haydn invited him to go on the English tour, it nevertheless seems that an open rupture was avoided only by

Haydn's departure. Perhaps the most eloquent comment on this abortive association of two great musicians is Beethoven's refusal to put the phrase "Pupil of Josef Haydn" on some of his early publications when his old teacher requested him to do so. That no simple explanation covers the situation is proved by the fact that though Beethoven inscribed his first three piano sonatas to Haydn, he said in his downright way that he had never learned anything from him.

Beethoven adapted himself to Viennese life with remarkable alacrity. He had come armed with many valuable letters of introduction from Count von Waldstein and the Von Breunings, and within a short time he numbered most of the influential patrons of music among his acquaintances. The doors of Vienna's most splendid palaces swung open to him. Prince Lobkowitz, Baron van Swieten, the Esterházys, and Prince Karl Lichnowsky were proud to call him friend. Within little more than a twelvemonth he was installed in Lichnowsky's fine lodgings in the same house where he had formerly occupied a garret room. He was comparatively affluent: some of his stipend had been restored, pupils were beginning to seek him out, and his already famous improvising made him a favorite society attraction. The seven years after he left Bonn were the most carefree of his life. He was still the same "small, thin, dark-complexioned, pockmarked, dark-eyed, bewigged young musician," who, as his tireless biographer, Thayer, says, "journeyed to the capital to pursue the study of his art. . . ." But the sinewy form was carefully, even elegantly, tricked out in the most fashionable clothes available.

Beethoven was enjoying society, but he never neglected music for a moment. He was taking lessons on three instruments, studying counterpoint with the noted theorist, Johann Georg Albrechtsberger, amplifying sketches made in Bonn, and composing new works. Into the notebooks he had begun to keep before he was out of his teens, he now began to crowd that welter of musical ideas, in all stages of development, which make the notebooks comparable to Leonardo's. To examine them is to be vouchsafed a unique opportunity to see the unfolding—hesitant, baffled, and inspired—of genius. Starting with what may seem an unpromising, even banal, sequence of notes, adding to them, subtracting, emphasizing, finally perfecting, Beethoven worked—sometimes for decades—at these viable fragments. Many a composition which seems like the product of a single mighty inspiration was pieced together from these apparently unrelated sketches. In a very real sense, it may be said that from the very beginning of his creative life, Beethoven was at work on all of his compositions. There is evidence that even the publication of a masterpiece (which may sound well-nigh perfect to us) did not free Beethoven's mind of the problems it presented. His life is one endless quest for the ideal form that would completely express the unity he had envisioned from the beginning.

Anyone watching the progress of Beethoven's career during those first years in Vienna would have been almost sure to assume that he was well on the way to becoming the leading piano virtuoso of his age. He routed all comers who dared measure their powers against his. One of his noted rivals once burst out in semicomic exasperation, "Ah, he's no man—he's a devil. He will play me and all of us to death." His improvisations, which were the sensation of Vienna, have made him the subject of thoughtless and invidious comparisons with Liszt, whose public pianism was as theatrical as Beethoven's was grave and sincerely emotional. In March, 1795, he made his first public appearance at a benefit concert, playing his own B flat Concerto for piano and orchestra, which he had finished two days before. His fame, which had hitherto been confined to the palaces of the nobility, now became public property.

During the next three years, Beethoven was in and out of Vienna, often in Prince Lichnowsky's company, playing at various places in Austria, Germany, and Hungary. Prague took to him as rapturously as it had to Mozart, and there he probably first played his C major Concerto for piano and orchestra. The B flat Concerto, with its elegant pretensions, is a shallow and thankless work, and is rightly neglected. The C major represents a decided advance:* though it does not show Beethoven in full command of his own style, and teems with echoes of Haydn and Mozart, it has just as many touches that show that no one but Beethoven could have written it. The final rondo is a triumph of his most bravura style, with a subtle duality of character: passages of delicate, urbane wit alternate with robust hurly-burly and Papa Haydn cracking

* The C major Concerto, though referred to as the First, was really composed two years after the B flat—the so-called Second.

his most outrageous jokes. Beethoven may have been telling the exact truth when he said that he had learned nothing from Haydn's teaching, but that he learned much from Haydn's music is as evident in the C major Concerto as in the first three piano sonatas (Opus 2). Many of their themes are pure Haydn, but the development is Beethoven in its direction and peculiar unexpectedness: it seems as if he faithfully follows his model up to a certain point, and then begins to reflect, to examine the themes from every angle, and to tell us what he finds in them.

Beethoven, as compared with Mozart, evolved slowly. The second group of piano sonatas (Opus 10), published when he was twenty-seven, show that he was well on the way to achieving his own characteristic treatment of material, but had not yet found the sort of material we now consider typically Beethovian. If Mozart had died at twenty-seven, he would still be regarded as one of the masters; had Beethoven died at the same age, he would now probably be forgotten—an item in a musical dictionary. The story of his life lends weight to the widely held theory that great art flowers out of suffering: happiness did not release his genius— only when he began to suffer was its whole strength unloosed. In 1798, possibly as the result of a severe illness, he began to have trouble with his hearing. At first, it was a mere humming in his ears, and he paid slight attention to it. But it recurred again and again, and he began to brood over it, to consult doctors. Can it be more than coincidence that he composed the Sonata "*Pathétique*" at this time? The famous ten-bar introduction is precisely the sort of material around which the vast dramas of the later Beethoven were to be built. But like so many transitional works, it lacks inevitability of development. Its beauties are isolated, and much is brought forth that may be dismissed as fustian. The tragedy is still on the surface: the general effect is one of attitudinizing, the final result melodrama, which is particularly out of place in a sonata.

The close of the century coincided with the end of Beethoven's apprenticeship, for at that time he first brought forward works indicating beyond question that greatness was in him. Within three years, he was to stake his claim, and carve out a province unmatched in its variety of landscape, from broad and undulating champaigns to alps of most terrific grandeur. On April 2, 1800, at the first of his own public concerts, he inaugurated that unparalleled series of nine symphonies which are still, after more than a century, far and away the most stupendous, and yet familiar, masterpieces in this form. He limited the program to Haydn, Mozart, and two new works of his own—the Septet for strings and wind instruments and the First (C major) Symphony. The Septet, now seldom heard, had such a persistent success that in later years Beethoven, who did not regard it highly, could not bear to hear it praised. It is a pleasant, melodious creation, lovingly enough constructed, but conventional in outline—definitely second-rate Beethoven. Nor can much more be claimed for the C major Symphony, which is light in caliber, eighteenth century in flavor. It is a technically sure first essay, but the problems raised are relatively simple. For all its charm and moments of cheerful noisiness, it is merely hearable, not memorable, music.

The First Symphony, which today strikes us as a Mozartian echo, shocked the Viennese at whatever points the real Beethoven was apparent. He himself was dissatisfied—for different reasons. In 1801, however, he quite captivated the city with an overture and incidental music to a ballet, *Die Geschöpfe des Prometheus*. The cheery little overture, also derivative from Mozart, is still occasionally heard. These lighthearted illustrations of scenes from the life of a suffering demigod are (a few potboilers aside) almost Beethoven's last incursion into the realm of the frivolous. The very next year, he said decisively, "I am not contented with my work so far; henceforth I shall take a new path."

The reasons that prompted Beethoven to make such an aggressive pronunciamento are as simple—and as complex—as those which led him to write, in October, 1802, that tortured, almost hysterical farewell to the world known as the "Heiligenstadt Testament" because it was written while he was rusticating at that village near Vienna:

FOR MY BROTHERS KARL AND [JOHANN] BEETHOVEN

O ye men, who think or say that I am malevolent, stubborn or misanthropic, how greatly do ye wrong me, you do not know the secret causes of my seeming, from childhood my heart and mind were disposed to the gentle feeling of good will, I was even ever eager to accomplish great deeds, but reflect now that for 6 years I have been in a hopeless case, aggravated by senseless physicians, cheated year after year in the hope of improvement, finally compelled to face the prospect of a *lasting malady* (whose cure will take years, or, perhaps, be impossible), born with an ardent and lively temperament, even susceptible to the diversions of society, I was compelled early to isolate myself, to live in loneliness, when I at times tried to forget all this, O how harshly was I repulsed by the doubly sad experience of my bad hearing, and yet it was impossible for me to say to men speak louder, shout, for I am deaf. Ah how could I possibly admit an infirmity in the *one sense* which should have been more perfect in me than in others, a sense which I once possessed in highest perfection, a perfection such as few surely in my profession enjoy or ever have enjoyed—O I cannot do it, therefore forgive me when you see me draw back when I would gladly mingle with you, my misfortune is doubly painful because it must lead to my being misunderstood, for me there can be no recreation in society of my fellows, refined intercourse, mutual exchange of thought, only just as little as the greatest needs command may I mix with society, I must live like an exile, if I approach near to people a hot terror seizes upon me, a fear that I may be subjected to the danger of letting my condition be observed—thus it has been during the last half year which I spent in the country, commanded by my intelligent physician to spare my hearing as much as possible, in this almost meeting my present natural disposition, although I sometimes ran counter to it, yielding to my inclination for society, but what a humiliation when one stood beside me and heard a flute in the distance and *I heard nothing* or someone heard *the shepherd singing* and again I heard nothing, such incidents brought me to the verge of despair, but little more and I would have put an end to my life— only art it was that withheld me, ah it seemed impossible to leave the world until I had produced all that I felt called upon to produce, and so I endured this wretched existence—truly wretched, an excitable body which a sudden change can throw from the best into the worst state— Patience—it is said I must now choose for my guide, I have done so, I hope my determination will remain firm to endure until it pleases the inexorable parcae to break the thread, perhaps I shall get better, perhaps not, I am prepared. Forced already in my 28th year to become a philosopher, O it is not easy, less easy for the artist than for any one else —Divine One thou lookest into my inmost soul, thou knowest it, thou knowest that love of man and desire to do good live therein. O men, when some day you read these words, reflect that ye did me wrong and let the unfortunate one comfort himself and find one of his kind who despite all the obstacles of nature yet did all that was in his power to be accepted among worthy artists and men. You my brothers Karl and [Johann] as soon as I am dead if Dr. Schmid is still alive ask him in my name to describe my malady and attach this document to the history of my illness so that so far as is possible at least the world may become reconciled with me after my death. At the same time I declare you two to be the heirs to my small fortune (if so it can be called), divide it fairly, bear with and help each other, what injury you have done me you know was long ago forgiven. To you brother Karl I give special thanks for the attachment you have displayed toward me of late. It is my wish that your lives may be better and freer from care than I have had, recommend *virtue* to your children, it alone can give happiness, not money, I speak from experience, it was virtue that upheld me in misery, to it next to my art I owe the fact that I did not end my life by suicide— Farewell and love each other—I thank all my friends, particularly *Prince Lichnowsky* and *Professor Schmid*—I desire that the instruments from Prince L. be preserved by one of you but let no quarrel result from this, so soon as they can serve you a better purpose sell them, how glad will I be if I can still be helpful to you in my grave—with joy I hasten toward death—if it comes before I shall have had an opportunity to show all my artistic capacities it will still come too early for me despite my hard fate and I shall probably wish that it had come later—but even then I am satisfied, will it not free me from a state of endless suffering? Come when thou wilt I shall meet thee bravely—Farewell and do not wholly forget me when I am dead. I deserve this of you in having often in life thought of you how to make you happy, be so—

LUDWIG VAN BEETHOVEN

[seal]

Heiglnstadt [*sic*],
October 6th,
    1802

For my brothers Karl and [Johann]
to be read and executed after my death.

Heiglnstadt, October 10th, 1802, thus do I take my farewell of thee— and indeed sadly—yes that beloved hope—which I brought with me when I came here to be cured at least in a degree—I must wholly abandon, as the leaves of autumn fall and are withered so hope has been blighted, almost as I came—I go away—even the high courage—which often inspired me in the beautiful days of summer—has disappeared—O Providence—grant me at last but one day of pure *joy*—it is so long since real joy echoed in my heart—O when—O when, O Divine One—shall I feel it again in the temple of nature and man—Never? no—O that would be too hard.

The most obvious thing about this tragic document (which was never sent, but was found among Beethoven's papers) is his incoherent anguish at the probability that he would go completely deaf. There would come a time, he knew, when he nevermore would hear—except within himself—the music that was his reason for being, a time when he would be cut off from the world. Reason enough, then for such an outpouring! But the "Testament" yields up another, hidden message tending to corroborate outside evidence that Beethoven was suffering from syphilis. It is even possible that he believed his deafness to have resulted from this disease, and though this is by no means certain, the mere supposition, to one of Beethoven's Calvinistic morality, might well have made him feel that he was being judged. That his most valued sense was being taken away from him because of a moral lapse is an Aeschylean concept that would have been peculiarly native to Beethoven.

There are people who still refuse to believe that Beethoven had syphilis. It is true that the evidence against them is overwhelming, but they are armored against evidence by a traditional belief that no great man could have had anything so shameful. The obvious evidence is medical and pharmaceutical; the more subtle is psychological, and can be marshaled under three general considerations. First, Beethoven had a psychopathic abhorrence of women whose morals he considered too free. This was violent enough to make him interfere absurdly and without warrant in his brother Karl's life. Second, he fell in love with a series of highborn, allegedly pure women, whose social position, he knew, automatically made them unavailable to him. Third, though he passionately desired marriage, in part because he believed that it would solve all his emotional problems, he never took a wife. The argument that deafness alone would have seemed to him an insuperable bar to marriage is simply inadmissible.

Beethoven's handicaps served to give his attachments a strained, intense quality. He was desperately seeking something he often found, but could never possess. The women who flicker through his life conform inevitably to one pattern; he who commanded a matchless diversity of style and mood in his art was enthralled by an unvarying, rather limited type of woman. His beloved ones are little more than girls, untouched, fresh, of noble birth—and not too intelligent. It is fruitless to catalogue them, and more fruitless to linger over any of them: they are less individuals than symbols, and not one of them exerted a permanent personal influence on

Beethoven's life. His love, however, was by no means unrequited, and it was said that this massive, rather uncouth man, with his painful awkwardness and social tactlessness, could make conquests beyond the charms of an Adonis.

Countless attempts have been made to connect certain of Beethoven's compositions with one or another of his infatuations. The "Moonlight" Sonata has been called a portrait of his pupil, the Contessa Giulietta Guicciardi, or of Beethoven's feeling for her. Certainly it is dedicated to her. But the rest of the interpretation is a perfect example of putting the cart before the horse. Beethoven's notebooks show that he was working on various ideas used in the "Moonlight" over a period of years. He happened to complete it in the high noon of his passion for the Contessa, and therefore offered it to her as a suitable gage of his love. On one occasion, having dedicated his Rondo in G (let the romantic reader note the key) to this same Giulietta, he rededicated it to Prince Lichnowsky's sister, a lady with whom, as far as we know, he was never in love.

Art unquestionably springs from emotion, and there is no reason to suppose that love has played a less significant part in the engendering of masterpieces than nature worship or religious devotion. Particularization is the mistake, and can go to the length of tacking a *True Story* libretto onto a sublime outpouring of the spirit. The problem of ascribing definite subject matter to music* is very difficult, and had best be left to radio script writers. There can be no question, however, that the man who is perennially—and hopelessly—in love will write quite different music than either he who loves happily or he who loves not at all. Beethoven, who was perennially—and hopelessly—in love, said that his most enduring passion lasted only seven months, and he moved from woman to woman almost as rapidly as Casanova. But to compare Casanova's callous, sense-driven, and insensate tomcat prowling and Beethoven's tortured questing is to see in a flash the exact antithesis between degradation and exaltation. Beethoven's loves were brief because they could never be fulfilled—like Orpheus, he searched the face of every woman, but forever vainly. While he was in love, he was deeply in love. The agony of joy and apprehen-

* In one very real sense, the only subject matter of music is the themes from which it is constructed.

sive fear into which a momentary illusion of having come to the end of his quest threw him, lies revealed in lines almost as painful to read as the "Heiligenstadt Testament"—the famous letter to the "Immortal Beloved":

July 6, in the morning

My angel, my all, my very self—only a few words today and at that with pencil (with yours)—not till tomorrow will my lodgings be definitively determined upon—what a useless waste of time. Why this deep sorrow where necessity speaks—can our love endure except through sacrifices—except through not demanding everything—can you change it that you are not wholly mine, I not wholly thine. Oh, God! look out into the beauties of nature and comfort yourself with that which must be—love demands everything and that very justly—*thus it is with me so far as you are concerned, and you with me.* If we were wholly united you would feel the pain of it as little as I. My journey was a fearful one; I did not reach here until 4 o'clock yesterday morning; lacking horses the post-coach chose another route—but what an awful one. At the stage before the last I was warned not to travel at night—made fearful of a forest, but that only made me the more eager and I was wrong; the coach must needs break down on the wretched road, a bottomless mud road—without such postilions as I had with me I should have stuck in the road. Esterhazy, traveling the usual road hitherward, had the same fate with eight horses that I had with four—yet I got some pleasure out of it, as I always do when I successfully overcome difficulties. Now a quick change to things internal from things external. We shall soon surely see each other; moreover, I cannot communicate to you the observations I have made during the last few days touching my own life—if our hearts were always close together I would make none of the kind. My heart is full of many things to say to you—Ah!—there are moments when I feel that speech is nothing after all—cheer up—remain my true, my only treasure, my all as I am yours; the gods must send us the rest that which shall be best for us.

Your faithful
LUDWIG

Evening, Monday, July 6

You are suffering, my dearest creature—only now have I learned that letters must be posted very early in the morning. Mondays, Thursdays—the only days on which the mail-coach goes from here to K. You are suffering—Ah! wherever I am there you are also. I shall arrange affairs between us so that I shall live and live with you, what a life!!!! thus!!!! thus without you—pursued by the goodness of mankind hither and thither—which I as little try to deserve as I deserve it. Humility of man toward man—it pains me—and when I consider myself in connection with the universe, what am I and what is he whom we call the greatest—and yet—herein lies the divine in man. I weep when I reflect that you will probably not receive the first intelligence from me until Saturday—much as you love me, I love you more—but do not ever conceal your thoughts from me—good-night—as I am taking the baths I must go to bed. Oh, God! so near so far! Is our love not truly a celestial edifice—firm as Heaven's vault.

Good morning, on July 7

Though still in bed my thoughts go out to you, my Immortal Beloved, now and then joyfully, then sadly, waiting to learn whether or not fate will hear us. I can live only wholly with you or not at all—yes, I am resolved to wander so long away from you until I can fly to your arms and say that I am really at home, send my soul enwrapped in you into the land of spirits.—Yes, unhappily it must be so—you will be the more resolved since you know my fidelity—to you, no one can ever again possess my heart—none—never—Oh, God! why is it necessary to part from one whom one so loves and yet my life in W [Vienna] is now a wretched life—your love makes me at once the happiest and the unhappiest of men—at my age, I need a steady, quiet life—can that be under our conditions? My angel, I have just been told that the mail-coach goes every day—and I must close at once so that you may receive the L. at once. Be calm, only by a calm consideration of our existence can we achieve our purpose to live together—be calm—love me—today—yesterday—what tearful longings for you—you—you—my life—my all—farewell—Oh continue to love me—never misjudge the most faithful heart of your beloved L.

ever thine
ever mine
ever for each other.

The fact that the person to whom this letter was directed is not known makes it sound like a cut-and-dried emanation of the romantic *Zeitgeist*. Its writer shows himself a true *enfant de siècle*, but though the letter rightly belongs to the nineteenth century, it was a real heart's cry intended for a real woman, and so escapes the emotional boundaries of a particular era. Hundreds of pages of fine type have been devoted to more or less ingenious guesses as to the identity of this "Immortal Beloved." Was she the Contessa Giulietta? Was she the Contessa's cousin, Therese von Brunswick?

Was she Goethe's admired friend, Bettina Brentano von Arnim? Or was she any one of a dozen others? The answer is still anybody's guess.

Despite the evidence of the "Heiligenstadt Testament" and the letter to the "Immortal Beloved," it is a mistake to think of Beethoven in a constant state of hopeless despair or amorous excitement. Until within a few years of his death, he continued to lead a more or less normal existence, going much into society and passing many happy hours with his ever-widening circle of friends. His eccentricities and frequent boorishness were interpreted as the concomitants of genius, not as the willful posturing of a mountebank. He attained a certain equilibrium through his abounding vitality and broad sense of humor. Without gorging or sousing, he enjoyed the pleasures of the table as much as any man. But his surest way of relief was a ramble in the country, for he loved, almost worshiped, nature. Finally, there was always the magic solace of composition. Beethoven is a perfect textbook exemplar of the modern theory that creation is in part the sublimation of otherwise unrelieved emotion. If this is always kept in mind, it can serve to fill out the seeming eventlessness of his biography, which from early in the century is little more than the story of his creative activity.

But the story of Beethoven's creative activity is not without snares and pitfalls. We are so used to thinking of an artist's development as proceeding at equal pace in all the forms he handles that Beethoven jolts our entire preconceived scheme. And any scheme we have is further complicated by the division of his works into three periods, suggested by early critics and more or less adhered to ever since. The dry but astute Vincent d'Indy aptly labeled these periods "imitation, externalization, and reflection." It would indeed be handy if we could tabulate Beethoven's compositions under these three headings, and then find that column one ended at such and such a date, and so on. Unfortunately, this is impossible. Not only do these divisions merge imperceptibly, but as Beethoven's method was one of trial and error, and as he came to some forms later than others, we often find simultaneously composed works that are in quite different stages of his development. For instance, the Piano Concerto in C minor belongs to the same year (1800) as the C major Symphony. But the concerto was his third, the symphony his first; the symphony, clearly "imitation," is tentative, afraid of the personal. The C minor Concerto, just as clearly "externalization," is assured and self-assertive. The sure vigor of the first movement, the exquisitely made largo, with its hesitant, meditative rhythms, and the rushing, pell-mell rondo, with its abrupt yet artistically satisfying coda—here, at last, is Beethoven *in sua persona*.

When the C minor Concerto was first performed at a public concert on April 5, 1803, a new symphony—the Second, in D major—was also on the program. Here, certainly, were two works on different levels of self-realization, though it may be doubted whether even the many connoisseurs in the audience recognized this fact. They were so shocked by the unbridled vivacity and *brio* of the last two movements of the symphony that they failed to see that it was still essentially a classical product, while the more massive and individual—but somehow quieter—concerto was really much more advanced. Not that the D major is by any means insignificant: the larghetto is among the most exquisite of slow movements, Mozartian in its purity of line, but richer in texture and mellower in color; the coda of the finale is no perfunctory peroration; rather, it is a considered comment on material previously heard in the movement. Judged by the vast architectonics of later codas, it sounds rather stereotyped, and must, in the final analysis, hold its place as a kind of inspired blueprint of things to come.

The Second Symphony, compared with the First, shows exactly the normal development one would expect of a composer who works earnestly at his job. If the distance between these two is fixed at a mile, that between the Second and Third must be fixed at a light-year. The Third Symphony is one of those monumental achievements that at first leave one so bewildered that the immediate impulse is to find some measuring rod that will make them seem more approachable. In the case of Beethoven's Symphony in E flat major, which surpasses all previous symphonies in length, it is somehow comforting to know that it can be performed in forty-six minutes under a conductor with a thorough understanding of the composer's intentions and a nice interpretation of his tempo marks. Further, though the stature of the Third can never be reduced to intimate proportions, it brings it somewhat nearer to realize that its mighty effects are produced by the same orchestra

Beethoven had used previously, augmented by a single additional horn.

It is hard to describe a work on which so many superlatives have been lavished. Bernard Shaw said that the first movement should be played by giants led by a demigod. Which is another way of saying that the grandeur of this allegro makes one involuntarily think of superhuman strength as the only motive power for such an enterprise. The second movement is a march—possibly the most solemn and fitting funeral music ever written—fitting, that is, at the funeral of a genius: it would dwarf a smaller man. In the scherzo, the classical minuet, which in Haydn's hands had begun to outgrow its court clothes, finally comes of age in an outburst of tempestuous joy suddenly and mysteriously deadened in the threatening drumbeats of the coda. The finale is excessively complicated, and abounds in mysteries of form to which no man may boast the key. Briefly, it is a series of free variations on a theme from Beethoven's own *Prometheus* music, interrupted by a fugue and topped off by a very lengthy coda. Rivers of ink have been spilled in the war over its merits. Some of the imputed formlessness of romantic music has entered here: those who like the finale either take the formlessness in their stride or claim to find in it an esoteric design that was never used again; those who dislike the finale say that they do so because it is formless. There can be little doubt, however, that with all its inherent beauties, it falls short of being a perfect culmination to the three preceding movements.

The Third Symphony is evolved out of unpromising and, in many instances, quite un-Beethovian material. But the development is so rich and unexpected that the commonplaceness of the themes is discoverable only by close analysis, and it is in this pre-eminent grasp of the resources and subtleties of elaboration that the E flat marks a tremendous advance not only in Beethoven's career, but in the entire history of music. The result here is something so epic that it would be necessary to call it *"Eroica"* even if no hero had been in Beethoven's mind while he was writing it. But the root inspiration for the *"Eroica"* actually did come from something outside the realm of music: it was originally intended, when Beethoven began sketching it in the late nineties, as a paean to Napoleon, who at that time seemed the very incarnation of the liberal ideals of the French Revolution. He had hardly finished composing it when he learned that the Corsican had crowned himself Emperor of the French. In a rage, he tore the name of the fallen idol from the title page. The symphony now celebrates "the death of a great man," but in 1821, when Beethoven heard of Napoleon's death, he declared, "I have already written the music for that catastrophe."

Beethoven outraged convention by introducing a funeral march into a symphony, but it was not his first offense of the kind. Some years before, in the A flat major Sonata (Opus 26), by all odds the most characteristic he had yet written, the third movement is a somberly grand andante entitled "Funeral March on the Death of a Hero." The A flat major is further remarkable for the theme and variations with which it begins, for in these Beethoven goes far beyond the scope of earlier uses of this device: the variations have a free, improvisatorial quality, though they still grow out of the theme rather than out of one another as Brahms' variations do. But this free, improvisatorial quality should not be misconstrued: it is never haphazard, always planned, always under control. Beethoven had arrived at the point where it was necessary for him to modify and expand already existing forms so they could hold his ideas, rather than compress his ideas to fit the, to him, cramped dimensions of the forms Mozart and Haydn had used so easily and with such brilliant success. Both his next two sonatas (Opus 27, 1 and 2), for example, he marked "*quasi una fantasia*," which is no idle tag: they retain only a few formal essentials of the old classical sonata, and take off into the unknown whenever the composer feels that his material requires it. The second of the pair is the all-too-famous "Moonlight" Sonata, with its unfortunate first movement —an adagio sostenuto which must once have been hauntingly lovely, but has been played dry. It tends to linger in the memory, and numb us to the sprightly charm of the allegretto and the large dimensions and fine architecture of the presto.

Among the three sonatas of Opus 31, composed while Beethoven was hard at work molding the "*Eroica*," the second is one of his most magical evocations. There is not an uninspired note in it, but it needs a Walter Gieseking to reveal its passionate vitality. It is put together like a drama: the first movement, with its agitated and frequently changed tempos, and its passages of almost spoken soliloquy; the meditative, intensely personal monologue of the slow

movement; the fleet, galloping onrush of the denouement (among
the most sheerly clever music Beethoven ever composed)—these
are the perfectly related acts of an inevitable and compelling dramatic sequence. The third of Opus 31 does not communicate itself
so readily as the second—of somewhat mixed character, it has less
structural inevitability. This gives a tentative quality to a work of
much melodic beauty.

In 1804, before abandoning the sonata for some years, Beethoven
composed two of his most brilliant virtuoso pieces. The "Waldstein" and "*Appassionata*" have with reason been favored by concert pianists, and both have sure-fire qualities that recommend
them just as positively to their audiences. The first of these, dedicated to Beethoven's old Bonn friend, is structurally simple: an
energetic allegro (longer than many a complete earlier sonata)
leads through a brief, poignant adagio into what is possibly Beethoven's most celebrated rondo. The three movements are rather like
a storm, calm under a still-lowering sky, and then sunlight. The
last is aerial in its loveliness and bright transparency, and Beethoven never wrote a more memorable melody to project exaltation.
The "*Appassionata*" has been made to carry a lot of pseudophilo-
sophical baggage, Beethoven having begun the mystification by
saying, "Read Shakespeare's *Tempest*," when questioned about its
meaning. This is excellent literary advice, but may be nothing
more than a red herring as far as this sonata is concerned. The first
movement, after some sullen ruminations, bursts out in a wild and
prolonged Byronic fury, and ends in mutterings that leave us with
the ominous feeling that worse is yet to come; the explosion is
delayed by a few pages of exquisite and tragic resignation, which
are suddenly broken into—there is a warning lull, and then a rat-
a-tat-tat of harsh chords fortissimo; the third movement, beginning quietly, gathers anger and speed, rages hysterically, and ends
in an orgy of musical fist-shaking.

The "Waldstein" and the "*Appassionata*" opened up a new world
of sound. They could not have been conceived for the clavier or
the first pianos, and they still tax the resources of the modern
concert grand. In them, Beethoven came to the full realization
that the piano is a percussion instrument.

The year 1804 is even more important as marking the probable
beginning of Beethoven's only opera, *Fidelio*. He had been com-

missioned, possibly as early as 1803, by Mozart's last impresario, Emanuel Schikaneder, to compose an opera for his Theater an der Wien. Before Beethoven delivered any manuscript, Schikaneder failed, and his rival, Baron Braun, director of the Hoftheater, took over the lease, and also renewed Beethoven's contract. Josef Sonnleithner, the secretary of the Hoftheater, a cultivated but uninspired man, supplied a libretto that fulfilled the composer's stringent and stuffy demands as to moral unimpeachability and lofty tone. It is a story of conjugal love triumphant under the most harrowing circumstances of the Terror—evidently, however, nothing was stipulated about literary excellence. Beethoven was so enchanted with the idea of setting its noble message that it was years before he was fully aware of the absurdities of the plot. Meanwhile, he had worked fervently, shuffled and reshuffled thousands of sketches for its original three acts, had probably composed one overture, discarded it, and composed another, and finally produced it, with Vienna full of a French army of occupation who could not understand the German words of its Spanish plot (the scene had been shifted to Spain for reasons of state), on November 20, 1805. It played for three successive nights, and was a complete failure.

Beethoven's friends were in despair: they wanted to save the opera, and finally prevailed on him to authorize certain revisions. Stephan von Breuning, whose intimacy with the composer dated back to Bonn, was entrusted with reducing the three acts to two, and making textual revisions. Equipped with a new overture—the magnificent "Leonora" No. 3—the opera showed signs of a small success, but was withdrawn by Beethoven after a quarrel with the impresario. It lay on the shelf until 1814, when he again radically overhauled the score, and Georg Friedrich Treitschke, the noted dramatist, performed an equally serious operation on the text. This time, *Fidelio* took Vienna by storm, and was selected to open the next season at the Hofoper.

Fidelio (or, as it was called until 1814, *Leonora*) is known by its overtures to millions who have never heard a note of it sung. The four overtures constitute a neat little problem. The least played, and least effective, is the "Leonora" No. 1. It may well have been written first, though there is a theory that it was composed in 1807 for a special performance that never came off; there is no evidence

that it was ever played during Beethoven's lifetime. The "Leonora" No. 2 was used at the actual *première*, "Leonora" No. 3 at
the 1806 performances. The former is superb in many respects,
highly dramatic in effect, but lacking the absolutely perfect proportions of No. 3. Besides, the working out of its middle section is
rather dry and academic. No. 3 uses some themes from No. 2, but
develops them on a grander scale and on an even loftier plane.
The entire overture, and more particularly the new material, is
treated with an unexampled brilliance that has served largely to
make "Leonora" No. 3 the most popular of Beethoven's overtures
—in effect, a kind of symphonic poem or tenth symphony in one
movement. But though No. 3 is an impressive advance over No. 2
from a sheerly musical point of view, it is ruinous as an introduction to the opera. "The trouble with 'Leonora' No. 3," as Tovey
says, "is that, like all great instrumental music from Haydn on-
wards, it is about ten times as dramatic as anything that could
possibly be put on the stage." Beethoven himself undoubtedly
came to realize this, for in 1814 he composed still one more overture—the so-called "Fidelio." This light, generally cheerful piece
is an excellent curtain-raiser for the rather trivial matter of the
first scenes, and is still used to open the opera. As performed at the
Metropolitan, *Fidelio* interposes "Leonora" No. 3 between the first
and second scenes of Act II, for all the world like a gigantic
Mascagni intermezzo. We owe this favor to the dramatic sapience
of Gustav Mahler.

Fidelio is a comic opera with an excessive amount of gloom in
the middle sections. It begins with some broad vaudeville clown-
ing and closes on a conventional happy ending. A more perfunctory story cannot be imagined, and to save the situation
Beethoven expanded the character of Leonora, the heroic wife,
until she bestrides the entire opera like a colossus. Her temporary
sufferings (which have a way of seeming endless) almost persuade
us that the drama is a tragic masterpiece. It is for her that Beethoven wrote the "Leonora" No. 3, and it is for her that he designed the most effective vocal music. The rest of the characters
are so puppetlike and undifferentiated that the best that can be
said of their music is that the villain Pizarro gets passages expressing Beethoven's moral indignation at his character, while the hero
Florestan is made to sing music that just as clearly expresses

sympathy with his patiently borne tribulations. Beside these straw men, Leonora seems as real as Carmen. As far as the opera as a whole is concerned, not much of its dramatic effectiveness would be lost in a truncated performance that would consist of "Leonora" No. 3 followed by the heroine's great *scena*, "*Abscheulicher, wo eilst du hin?*" If the man whom Beethoven transfigured in the "*Eroica*" could only have been Leonora's mate, what an opera this might have been!

All sorts of loyal excuses have been advanced to prove that Beethoven was a great composer for the stage. The truth is that he was a great dramatic musician—one of the greatest of all time, in fact—but he completely lacked a sense of the stage. Drama, in the deepest sense, he fully understood; stage business was beyond, or beneath, him. Treitschke's notes on the 1814 version of *Fidelio* furnish eloquent proof of Beethoven's complete ineptitude in this respect. An age that can afford to neglect *Iphigénie en Tauride* does well to neglect Beethoven's only opera.

Beethoven did not devote 1805 exclusively to working on *Fidelio*. That same year, he began sketching what eventually became the Fifth Symphony, as well as the first of the three quartets dedicated to Count Rasoumovsky, and what is probably the finest of his piano concertos—that in G major. The Fourth Concerto has always been overshadowed by the grandiose effect of the Fifth. It declined in popularity even during Beethoven's lifetime, and was not rescued from oblivion until 1836, when Mendelssohn played it at a concert in Leipzig. It is baffling to explain why it has not always been one of Beethoven's most popular large compositions, for it yields to none of the others in immediacy of appeal. It is ingratiating, intimate as few large works are. Although it does not offer virtuosos such an excellent chance to show off as the Fifth, it is flawlessly constructed, original in detail, and inspired in melody. Beethoven makes history by opening the concerto with a statement of the principal theme by the solo instrument, and then, with the use of a minimum of subsidiary matter, subjects the theme to one of the most subtle and complex developments in the entire course of music. Not one of the least triumphs of this use of the whole armory of technique is that the result does not sound even remotely pedantic. The second movement is a dialogue between the orchestra and the piano. Liszt compared it to Orpheus taming the beasts, probably because the gentle, supplicating solo instrument finally wins over the myriad voices of the orchestra. At which point the rondo begins pianissimo, gradually working into a boisterous rush varied by a transitional theme of broad, singing character, utterly romantic, almost Schumannesque in feeling.

It is particularly interesting to compare the Fourth Concerto with the Fifth, in E flat major. Although written four years later, this last of Beethoven's piano concertos is much less arresting and generally less interesting musically. The name "Emperor" was tacked onto it some years after its composition—but not by Beethoven. It is possible to justify this nickname by the rather pompous, grandiloquent character of the first and third movements—evidently this "Emperor" was a Roman. The first movement, with its beautiful and certainly malleable theme, is developed impressively, but at such great length that it ends by seeming too long—one place where Beethoven's "astronomical punctuality" was not on time. The adagio, however, for all its air of improvisation, ranks high among Beethoven's profound meditations, and is the real glory of the "Emperor." It shades insensibly, and by a stroke of sheer magic, into a triumphant rondo that is a fitting culmination to a virtuoso's holiday. With all deference to this rather breath-taking work, it is to be hoped that a day will come when the phrase "Beethoven piano concerto" will not inevitably mean the "Emperor."

In 1806, the Emperor (and in those days only one Emperor was in everyone's mind) was lowering over Austria and the German states like a great storm, doing a thorough job of unsettling lives. Beethoven's was no exception, though he went right on working at a couple of symphonies and the "Rasoumovsky" Quartets. In October, he visited Prince Lichnowsky at his Silesian estate, and found French officers quartered there. This in itself was enough to upset him, but when the Prince half-jokingly threatened to lock him up if he refused to play for them, Beethoven forced his way out, and returned to Vienna in a rage. Arrived home, the first thing he did was to smash a bust of Lichnowsky. He soon cooled down sufficiently to focus his energies on a piece he had promised to complete before Christmas. Accordingly, on December 23, the new work, unrehearsed because he had just completed it, was presented during a singular program. Its first movement was a feature of the opening half of the entertainment, and the second and third movements were given during the second half. Intervening was, among other compositions, a sonata by Franz Clement, played on one string of a violin held upside down. Clement was also the soloist in the Beethoven, playing his part at sight.

The composition so inauspiciously introduced was the D major Violin Concerto, and it is surely no wonder that, produced under these circumstances, it was a failure. It was at once pronounced insignificant, and went immediately into exile from the concert hall. Its failure may have deterred Beethoven from ever composing another violin concerto. Many years after his death, Joseph Joachim, whose cadenzas have since become an almost integral part of the concerto, resuscitated it, and helped it to a popularity that has never waned, beside the likewise unique essays in this form by Mendelssohn, Tchaikovsky, and Brahms. With that "colossal instinct" which so often moved him when he was pioneering, Beethoven created in a single try music a large part of whose beauty depends on its peculiar fitness for the violin, and its sensitive balancing of the timbres and volumes of solo instrument and orchestra. He expanded the scope of the violin concerto and, without losing sight of the fact that he was writing for a virtuoso, produced something without a trace of empty show.

The Concerto in D is almost deceptively quiet, and its melodies are in themselves close to undistinguished. There is a minimum of ornamentation, except in the seldom fitting cadenzas that virtuosos have written for the second and third movements. The beauty of the Violin Concerto lies deep, and for many performers is not get-at-able: tone, not display, is its secret. It has been said from time's beginning that a performer must bring some profound understanding to his task. Nowhere is this more true than in the Concerto in D. Throughout the first two movements, the soloist is given the rarest opportunities, for in them Beethoven has woven unpromising melodies into an incomparably rich and varied tonal fabric that quite transforms them. Only the rondo thwarts the performer, for even Beethoven's infinite resourcefulness was balked by the essential banality of its principal theme.

In 1806, no less than three symphonies lay in Beethoven's workshop in various stages of development. Of these, the Fourth, in B flat major, was completed toward the end of the year, and was first performed the following spring. The Fifth, in C minor, and the Sixth, in F major, were both finished in 1808, and were performed together on December 22 of that year. This all-Beethoven program also included the *scena* for soprano, "*Ah! perfido*," sections of a Mass composed for the Esterházy family, an extempore fantasy on the piano—and the *premières* of the Choral Fantasy and the C major Piano Concerto! Everything was wretchedly performed (there had been no complete rehearsal of any of the works), the Theater an der Wien was ice-cold, and the program lasted four hours. In addition to being a physical trial to the audience, it became embarrassing when the performers broke down in the middle of the Choral Fantasy because Beethoven had given them a wrong cue. All was calculated to send the audience home in a state of mingled awe and rage. Beethoven, however, insisted that he had merely wanted to give them their money's worth.

Fortunately, the rather delicate Symphony in B flat major had made its debut in a comparatively light program—consisting of the first four symphonies—less than three hours long. Thus it was born in the shadow of the "*Eroica*," where, despite its own sufficing beauties, it has remained ever since. There is a myth that, after the First and Second, Beethoven's even-numbered symphonies are inferior to the odd-numbered. The truth is that the odd-numbered ones are epic, the even-numbered lyric. It is almost as if after each of his cosmic labors, the titan had to play. The Fourth scales no Himalayan peaks, wins no victories, but to conceive of it as made up of inferior stuff is to commit an egregious error of judgment. No symphony has more exquisite proportions, and one would have to go to Mozart to match its sheer deliciousness. The mysterious introduction, with its promise of something important about to happen, has often been invested with a deep significance that makes far too much of what it really is—a prelude to mischief. The cantabile is like an infinitely tender savoring of happiness, and is touched with that slight tinge of melancholy engendered by a realization that of all things happiness is the most evanescent. The minuet is a charming dance, and the finale, which one musical pontiff damned as "too light," is actually just light enough—witty and swift exegesis on the classical allegro of Haydn and Mozart. It is all as easy to listen to as folk melody, and is the product of a technique that commanded the resources of the entire past.

The Fifth is the best known and best loved of Beethoven's nine symphonies—therefore the best known and best loved of all symphonies. The reasons for its outstanding popularity are not far to seek: its comparative simplicity reduces the listener's difficulties to a minimum; the music is never dull, it is spirited and eloquent—and it is Beethoven all the way. In short, it is excellent entertainment, in the best sense of the word. The renowned, almost notorious, and in themselves undistinguished four notes that open the symphony with a defi, lead into four movements of the most eminently whistleable music ever composed. And it is a fact that thousands of people who say that they abhor, or "do not understand," classical music, go about whistling parts of the Fifth Symphony. It is definitely not a work around which a fence can be built: it belongs to the whole world, and this obvious fact has made enemies for it among those musical snobs who delight in fencing off the great masterpieces, and marking them "Private Property."

It is too bad that we cannot share the emotions of those who listened to the C minor Symphony when it was new. It was the *Sacre du printemps* of the early nineteenth century, and seems to have affected its listeners violently. The operatic composer Lesueur told Berlioz, "It has so upset and bewildered me that when I wanted to put on my hat, I couldn't find my head." The years have taken from the Fifth Symphony only one thing—this powerful novelty. But we can still revel in the resilient, athletic rhythms of the first movement, with its brief contrasting moments of melodic questioning. The second movement, an andante with variations, is more studied, yet it sings along freely and with enchanting grace. The third movement is one of the most effective of all scherzos, from the ominous first theme (favored as burglar music by pianists in the days of the silent movies) to the subdued but still-lowering close, which leads without interruption into the finale. This scherzo is notable for a rare bravura passage for suppressed bass-violin virtuosos, wherein Beethoven shows a kinship to Rabelais in an episode of bumbling and sardonic humor. It was undoubtedly in the finale that M. Lesueur lost his head—certainly it was here, after the repeated warnings of the scherzo, that Beethoven broke loose. The symphony ends in a rout of victorious energy, to which the reappearance of parts of the scherzo adds a note of terrible piquancy. The superabundance of ideas and the diabolic pace are still breath-taking, and it is not surprising that Ludwig Spohr, the same pontiff who had found the finale of the Fourth "too light," condemned this finale as "an orgy of vulgar noise."

The Sixth, or "Pastoral," Symphony is, with the piano sonata known as "*Les Adieux*," one of the few extended compositions that, by his own confession, Beethoven built around a program. Now, it is quite true that certain composers, notably Debussy and Richard Strauss, wrote some of their best work under the stimulus of a program. It is equally true that a program, when used merely as a point of departure, rather than slavishly followed, liberated their imaginations: for them it was like a catalytic agent that effected the magic rapport between them and their material. But a program seems actually to have limited Beethoven, and neither of his large program pieces belongs with his best work. We can but wonder at the staying power of the "Pastoral" Symphony, which should long ago, as Edward J. Dent pointed out with his customary brutal frankness, have been retired to the shelf. There are plenty of "good things" in it—but alas! they are technical excellences that would be inevitable in any mature work of Beethoven's. Most of the "Pastoral" is plain dull, and one can only suspect that those who help by their applause to keep it in the repertoire really delight in the birdcalls, the rippling brook, and the storm rather than in the basic themes and their development. Fortunately, it is possible to enjoy Beethoven and the country separately without enjoying them together within the confines of the F major Symphony.

The "Pastoral" was completed and first performed amid the alarums of another onslaught against Austria by Napoleon. Before hostilities were renewed, however, Beethoven (whose efforts to find official employment in Vienna had proved vain) received an attractive offer from Jérôme Bonaparte, King of Westphalia, to become his *Kapellmeister* at Cassel. For a time he entertained seriously the idea of emigrating, and what finally dissuaded him seems to have been, not patriotism, but abhorrence of the reputedly lax morals of Jérôme's court. The rumor that Beethoven might leave Vienna struck consternation into the hearts of his noble patrons. Three of them—the Princes Lobkowitz and Kinsky, and his pupil and newly found friend, the youthful Archduke Rudolf—put their heads together, and decided to offer him a yearly income from their own purses if he would promise to remain. This, with a small annuity he had been receiving from Prince Lichnowsky since 1800, might have added enough to his earnings from the publication of his music to make his life an easy one. Unfortunately, war was declared in April, 1809, and the value of Austrian currency was immediately cut in half.

Beethoven decided to remain in Vienna during the war, but the approach of the French meant that the imperial family had to flee. The composer was sincerely attached to the Archduke Rudolf, and mourned his departure and absence in the first two movements of the second of his extended program pieces—the E flat major Piano Sonata (Opus 81a); he wrote a third movement early in 1810 to celebrate the Archduke's return. By far the most effective part of the Sonata "*Les Adieux*" is the first movement, with its ingenious development of the introductory three notes over which Beethoven wrote the word "*Le-be-wohl!*" which, as he angrily complained, was a far more tender and intimate word than the formal French expression his publishers substituted. It may be said of this sonata that though it was deeply felt, its program inhibited the composer's finest flights of creative imagination. Certainly, it is far inferior to the small but poignant F sharp major Sonata (Opus 78), composed somewhat earlier. Beethoven himself went on record as preferring the F sharp to the even-in-his-time overplayed "Moonlight," which it strongly resembles in mood though not in structure.

There was a seeming lull in Beethoven's activity until late in 1813, when the Seventh Symphony was first performed. The interim was taken up with a number of—for him—relatively small projects. Despite his now almost unbearable deafness, he was going so assiduously into society that he complained of no longer having time to be with himself. After the death of Haydn in 1809, Beethoven was unquestionably the most eminent of living composers, and therefore one of the principal sights of the town. In May, 1810, he met Bettina Brentano, then but twenty-five years old, but already started on her self-chosen career as Goethe's Aspasia. He promptly fell as hopelessly in love with her as she had fallen in love with Goethe. Doubtless, her enthusiasm further stimulated what was to prove his lifelong devotion to the poet. In the same year, he

set several of Goethe's poems and completed an overture and incidental music to *Egmont*, Goethe's drama of the ill-fated champion
of Flemish liberties against the Spaniards. The incidental music
has vanished somewhere behind the gates of horn and ivory, but
the overture has held its own quite as triumphantly as that to
*Coriolanus.** Like the tremendous "Leonora" No. 3, each of these
overtures crystallizes the essence of the drama as Beethoven felt
it. It seems inconceivable that this noble and profoundly realized
music will ever be crowded from the repertoire. Incidentally, the
overture to *Egmont* concludes with an electrifying fanfare for the
brass that actually echoes the trumpet flourishes the Duke of Alva
ordered so as to drown out Egmont's last speech. Here Beethoven
wrote with inflammatory eloquence what might have been a mere
perfunctory effect—the lion of aristocratic Vienna had found a
program that liberated him.

In 1811, Beethoven met a man who was destined to exercise a
mixed influence on his music. This was Johann Nepomuk Mälzel,
the renowned inventor of the metronome, and the contriver of
many curious machines for making music. Beethoven at first took
to him with a kind of innocent fervor. During 1812, while he was
busy writing the Seventh and Eighth Symphonies, he spent much
time with Mälzel, and they even planned to tour England together. Simultaneously, the inventor was perfecting his metronome,
and in July, at what was originally planned as a farewell dinner,
Beethoven and his friends toasted the machine in a round that
parodied its monotonous ticking. This was later used in the allegretto of the Eighth Symphony. But their plans changed: his
brother Karl was so ill that Beethoven was afraid to leave Austria,
and he himself was in such wretched health that he went to take
the waters of various Bohemian spas, where he also hoped to al-
leviate his deafness.

At Töplitz, where the royalty and *haute noblesse* of Europe con-
gregated, Beethoven first met Goethe. They held each other in
high esteem, but got on each other's nerves. Goethe, supreme poet
and philosopher though he was, stood aside, hat in hand, as his
royal friends passed. Beethoven was enraged by such conduct.
Bettina Brentano von Arnim attested that he "with folded arms
walked right through the dukes and only tilted his hat slightly

* By one H. J. von Collin, not Shakespeare.

while the dukes stepped aside to make room for him, and all greeted him pleasantly; on the other side he stopped and waited for Goethe, who had permitted the company to pass by him where he stood with bowed head. 'Well,' he said, 'I've waited for you because I honor and respect you as you deserve, but you did those yonder too much honor.'" As for Goethe, he commented dryly, "His talent amazed me; unfortunately he is an utterly untamed personality, not altogether wrong in holding the world to be detestable, but who does not make it any the more enjoyable either for himself or others by his attitude."

Before leaving for the spas, Beethoven had finished the Seventh Symphony; the Eighth he completed at Linz in the fall while on a visit to his brother Johann. This was by no means a pleasure trip: he had heard that Johann was mixed up with a loose woman, and he spent much time trying to persuade him to mend his morals and his taste. Failing, he had recourse to the religious, civil, and penal authorities, and succeeded in driving Johann into marriage with the disreputable creature. He returned to Vienna in a fury, and seems to have brooded himself into inactivity during the winter. In May, 1813, he went to Baden, near Vienna, and it was there, while making a last despairing attempt to find a cure for his deafness, that news reached him of Wellington's overwhelming defeat of Joseph Bonaparte's troops at Vitoria.

Mälzel had also heard the news, and his shrewd commercial mind was already busy with its possibilities for a musician who was really on his toes. With the English market in view, he asked Beethoven to write a battle piece for one of his musical machines. Mälzel, who seems to have had the mind of a modern advertising man, counted on the popularity of Wellington, the fame of Beethoven, the novelty of his Panharmonicon, and the patronage of the Prince Regent, which was to be secured by an effulgent dedication. Beethoven fell in with the scheme with childish delight. Accordingly, after various false starts and alterations in plan, he produced the notorious composition known as *Wellington's Victory, or the Battle of Vittoria* [sic], also occasionally called the "Battle" Symphony. Meanwhile the Austrians and their allies had defeated Napoleon at Leipzig, and Mälzel saw that his market had thus been shifted to Vienna. The piece was already all set for the Panharmonicon; he now persuaded Beethoven to orchestrate it, and have it performed at one of the many charity concerts being planned for the survivors of the last campaign. He shrewdly foresaw that it would take the town by storm, and that once its popularity was established, it would coin money for the Panharmonicon.

In its appeal, *Wellington's Victory* far surpassed Mälzel's wildest dreams. Vienna responded, not enthusiastically, but deliriously, and Beethoven, already the most famous of living composers, found himself, after its *première* on December 8, 1813, the most popular as well. It seems unlikely that calling the piece the *Battle of Leipzig* would have added a single leaf to his laurels. Besides, the fact that between artillery charges and cannon shots the only music to be heard was *Britannia Rules the Waves, Malbrouck s'en va-t-en guerre*, and *God Save the King* provided three insuperable obstacles to a patriotic change of title. Some faint conception of this atrocious potboiler—unquestionably, as the late Hendrik Willem van Loon said, the worst trash ever signed by a supreme genius—may be achieved by imagining a mixture of the "1812" Overture (with real cannon) and Ernest Schelling's *A Victory Ball* (with rattling bones, offstage bugle, and bagpipes full orchestra *fff*).*

Almost lost amid the tumult and the shouting was the new work that began the concert of December 8—the Seventh Symphony. Yet it was well liked (the allegretto was encored), and its popularity has grown until it rivals that of the Fifth—there are signs that it may soon outstrip its overplayed competitor.† The Seventh is in some respects the most glorious of all symphonies, and is quite as accessible to the lay listener as the Fifth. Its characteristics are even more readily discernible: its rhythms are so varied and emphatic that Wagner called it the "apotheosis of the dance"; it is joyful music made transcendent by a vastness of plan more usually reserved for tragic utterance; finally, it glows with orches-

---

* Battle pieces were inordinately popular during the late eighteenth and early nineteenth centuries. The most famous of them before Beethoven's time was *The Battle of Prague* by Franz Koczwara, whose only other claim to fame is that he hanged himself in a London brothel.

† The 1938 poll of favorite compositions requested by the patrons of WQXR, a New York radio station devoted chiefly to the broadcasting of serious music, showed Beethoven's Fifth Symphony in first place, the Seventh in second. The Fifth was requested in 23.9 per cent of all letters received, the Seventh in 18.3 per cent. Tchaikovsky's Fifth Symphony was in third place, with 16.5 per cent. Beethoven's Ninth, Third, and Sixth were respectively fourth, sixth, and twelfth in the tabulation.

tral color. This does not mean, of course, that color was a new thing in music—Mozart's E flat Symphony boldly experimented with the instrumental palette—but here, for the first time, color became recognizably, undeniably, one of the prime elements of esthetic design, in its way as important as melody, harmony, and rhythm. The subtle, nervous use of varying volume, with an intuitive grasp of the protean thing it can be, provides a chiaroscuro to match the almost Venetian splendor of the instrumental coloration.

The A major Symphony is remarkable in its complete freedom from those perfunctory connective passages and stereotyped devices that even the greatest of composers have indulged in. It starts with supreme confidence, and this endures until the very last bar of the finale. Never was Beethoven's genius more fecund, never more exuberant. The largeness of the introduction sets the stage for a work of heroic proportions, and leads up to an audacious excursion into pure rhythm, which at the verge of monotony is salvaged by one of the most alluring melodies ever written. The second movement is the peerless allegretto—a stately dance whose insistent rhythm carries the curious burthen of alternate melancholy and triumph. Once heard, its melodies can never be forgotten. The scherzo races along to the trio, rests there during moments of supernal peace, and resumes its headlong flight. The finale is a reminder that Beethoven was a Fleming—it is a broad and clamorous kermis (Tovey's description of it as "a triumph of Bacchic fury" is intolerable geography: it is no more Greek than Breughel).

The fate of the Eighth Symphony proves that even the greatest of geniuses cannot stretch and relax with impunity. When it was introduced, on February 27, 1814, it was inevitably compared with the Seventh, which preceded it on the program, and pronounced small, old-fashioned, and unworthy of the master. These strictures merely amused Beethoven, who said dryly that it was not liked as well as the Seventh because it was better. Now, it is possible to interpret this reply as mere perversity, but there is stronger reason to suspect that it was largely serious. In short, Beethoven implied that it was the measure of his greatness that after rearing the mighty structures of the Seventh Symphony he had successfully created something as gay and epigrammatic as the Eighth. But the

public was not interested in his recreations, and his temerity in
introducing the F major on the heels of the Seventh almost resulted
in its complete eclipse. When it was played, the allegretto of the
Seventh was often unfeelingly injected into it as a drawing card.
Even today, though it stands on its own merits, the Eighth is not
one of the most popular of Beethoven's symphonies. The first three
movements are definitely light, but never lightweight, and show
what Beethoven could do as late as 1812 with the classical idiom of
Haydn and Mozart. It is more than a little ironical that the allegretto of the Seventh should have been used to salvage a symphony that already boasted one of the most delightful allegrettos
ever composed. Had Haydn heard the ticking of Mälzel's metronome he might very well have parodied it in this same delightful
fashion. But once the fourth movement begins, all bets are off, and
the "little symphony" (Beethoven's own words) gradually expands
into a spacious essay on the dynamics of pure joy and godlike
laughter. There are those who feel that this increase in scale over-
balances the rest of the symphony. Certainly it lacks the flawless
design of the Fourth, for example, but this should not prevent anyone from taking delight in the beauty of the separate movements
which, moreover, cohere by the pervading joyousness of the
motives.

In the spring of 1814, after the successful revival of *Fidelio*,
Beethoven was at the height of his worldly career, and for a year
and a half he was sustained on a dizzy peak of eminence and popularity. Events conspired to make him for this brief season the object of more adulation from personages of exalted rank than has
ever fallen to the lot of any other composer. On November 1, with
Bonaparte safely immured on Elba, the Congress of Vienna convened to restore the *status quo ante bellum*, and Vienna swarmed
with half the royalty and nobility of Europe. Beethoven received
invitations to all social events of any importance, and everywhere
he was honored as a lion, yielding precedence only to the Allied
sovereigns and Talleyrand. The Austrian government now allowed
him the use of the two halls of the Redoutensaal for a series of concerts, and he himself sent invitations to the sovereigns and other
great dignitaries. Six thousand people were packed into the halls
at the first concert, and more than half that number at the second.
The financial results of these and other concerts were most gratify-

ing, and Beethoven was able to invest considerable sums in bank shares. Yet, even in the midst of his triumphs, he must have been much troubled—and considerably isolated—by his ever-increasing deafness, which that same spring had forced him to abandon ensemble playing forever.

The year 1815 opened promisingly enough, for Beethoven's suits against the heirs of Prince Kinsky, and against Prince Lobkowitz, for defaulting on his pension were finally settled in his favor, and without impairing his relations with those distinguished families. Now the agreement of 1809 was once more substantially in effect: the Archduke Rudolf continued to pay his share, and this, with the other two shares, seemed to assure Beethoven an annual income of 3400 florins until his death. He was going to need that—and more.

From the earliest days of his affluence, Beethoven had become embroiled in complicated money arrangements with his brothers, particularly Karl, who had managed some of his dickerings with music publishers. Certain of Beethoven's friends believed not only that his brothers were taking advantage of him, but that Karl, to whom he had lent large sums, was actually dishonest. Stephan von Breuning took it upon himself to warn him against Karl's weak financial morals. The result was to align Beethoven more than ever on the side of the accused, and to cause a rift of more than ten years in his friendship with Von Breuning. This was a severe blow, for only the year before death had separated him from his beloved patron, Prince Lichnowsky. And now, in November, 1815, an even heavier blow: Karl van Beethoven died, leaving a widow whom the composer thoroughly detested, and a nine-year-old son whose guardianship he shared with the mother.

Beethoven immediately transferred to his nephew Karl all the blind affection he had felt for the father. On the other hand, his dislike of the widow was so violent and neurotic that he made every effort to keep her (whom he extravagantly termed the "Queen of the Night") from taking any part in her son's education. The conflict between these two strong-willed people dragged on for several years, with mother and uncle in alternate possession of the boy. At last, on January 7, 1820, Beethoven was declared sole guardian. The results of this legal war were deleterious to all parties concerned: the widow was permanently embittered; young Karl, after being the ball in this weird game of battledore and shuttlecock, grew up a thoroughly maladjusted young man whose tragic inability to cope with life darkened his uncle's last years; finally, Beethoven, in the full vigor of his creative powers, had the productivity of four years gravely curtailed. Even at this late date, it seems only fair to make a plea for the poor nephew who has been so ridiculously blackened by many of Beethoven's biographers. At an age when he needed a normal family background, he had to live either with a mother who was none too good or with an uncle whose deafness and difficult temperament made him positively an unfit companion for a child. No wonder, then, that Karl, who seems to have been nothing more sinister than a poor booby, made a mess of his life, contracting enormous debts he could not meet, making a feeble attempt at suicide, and finally escaping into the obscurity of a private's berth in the army.

On November 16, 1815, the very day after his brother Karl's death, Beethoven had received the freedom of the City of Vienna, an honor that made him thenceforth tax-exempt. He appeared occasionally in public to conduct various performances of his works, but went less and less into society. His deafness had become all but complete. Late in 1816 he was further cast down by the death of Prince Lobkowitz, though the almost simultaneous arrival of a handsome grand piano—a tribute from the English maker, Broadwood—somewhat buoyed him up. Multitudinous worries and a series of minor ailments served to interrupt the flow of large orchestral pieces that had not only made him the idol of musical Europe, but had placed an ample income at his disposal. The death of Lobkowitz reduced his annual pension by seven hundred florins, and for the first time in years he was hard pressed. It was not until 1823 that he was able to complete two large works that would not only improve his financial position, but would also consummate his fame.

The small works that were the chief fruits of the decade before 1823—five of the most stupendous piano sonatas ever written—were unfortunately not likely to win their audience at once. With them, Beethoven entered his third period, which was characterized by an idiom that for a long time was not only thought difficult to understand, but in certain quarters was actually interpreted as a falling-off of his powers. Some modern critics still resent the fact that Beethoven used so advanced a musical language almost a century before their graphs of musical development show that anyone could arrive at it. Briefly, the most recognizable elements of this new style are a vast increase in size and scope, and the use of elaborate contrapuntal devices. These sonatas are the most truly serious and profoundly thought-out works ever written for the piano—they are symphonies for a solo instrument.

The world had to wait almost ten years after the Eighth Symphony to hear Beethoven's only great orchestral work in his third manner—the "Choral" Symphony. There was no comparable pause between the E minor Sonata (Opus 90) and that in A major (Opus 101), which ushered in the last five sonatas. Opus 90, though mainly an unpretentious work glowing with romantic feeling, contains hints of the new elements Beethoven was preparing to introduce into the sonata. Less than two years later, they showed themselves well abloom. Opus 101 opens with a deceptively lyrical passage, but soon sacrifices the more superficial aspects of its singing style to what can almost be called a commentary thereon, characterized by intense concentration of bar-to-bar development. Here, in this first movement, we can examine at leisure the very articulations of this strange third style which can be analyzed rigorously and yet remain baffling. Possibly the simplest way of explaining it is to say that Beethoven finally evolved an exact musical language for expressing the hidden sources of the emotions. It is a language of ellipses and compressions, and demands unwavering attention if it is to be understood. The evolution of this idiom was no pedantic feat. It grew naturally from an overpowering need: it was the only medium Beethoven could use to convey the most important and complex ideas he ever had.

The five sonatas of this group have as palpable a family resemblance as Mozart's last three symphonies. They are of varying lengths, even (be it admitted) of varying degrees of success. But every one of them—well, not quite every one—has miraculous unity. The exception is that veritable "red giant" of the musical universe—the "*Hammerklavier*" Sonata, in B flat major (Opus 106). The "*Hammerklavier*" is too long, and at some point in every movement its great poetry fades into the listless scientific prose of the experimentalist. In fact, if this were the last of Beethoven's sonatas, its prolixity, its not infrequent dullness, and its almost gaseous diffuseness might justifiably be explained by his deafness. But the

"*Hammerklavier*" was composed in 1818, and was followed by three sonatas that are unquestioned masterpieces. The lyrical E major (Opus 109) found Beethoven more sensible about the exigencies of space, and more realistic about his audiences. The A flat major (Opus 110) is positively genial in its accessibility: it is almost as easy to listen to as the great sonatas of the second period. Every part of it is of "heavenly" length: Beethoven never showed more tact than when he dictated the exquisite proportions of the adagio, and was never more apt in recapturing the vitality of an almost spent form than in the robust fugue. The last sonata, in C minor (Opus 111), is indeed the end that crowns the work—a majestic farewell to a musical form whose full powers he had been the first to call forth. From the first notes of the cosmic defi that introduces the maestoso to the last light-saturated strophes of the arietta Beethoven proves himself music's greatest thaumaturge. In the realm of musical history, it is not easy to be dogmatic, but it may be affirmed positively that Beethoven here set the limits of the piano sonata. No other composer has even remotely approached it in amplitude of conception, perfection of design, vigor of movement, and rightness of detail.

But Opus 111 was not Beethoven's farewell to the piano. He had an even more gigantic work up his sleeve, the circumstances of whose conception were fated to produce a monstrosity. Anton Diabelli, a music publisher, sent a banal waltz of his own composition to fifty different composers (including little Franz Liszt), asking each to contribute a variation on it. Beethoven, in a burst of bravado, himself wrote thirty-three variations on the silly little theme, and exhausted most possibilities of the variation form, the resources of the piano, and the patience of his audience. The "Diabelli" Variations are Beethoven's *Kunst der Fuge*: they are played as infrequently, are as invaluable as textbook examples, and, despite scattered beauties, are supportable in performance only to experts.

While Beethoven was completing his last great sonatas, he was also at work on a solemn High Mass to be used at the installation of his friend Archduke Rudolf as Archbishop of Olmütz. He began the Mass in 1818, and worked feverishly at it through the summer of that year and the next. But it was far from ready when the Archbishop was consecrated early in 1820, and Beethoven did not finish it until almost three years had passed. On February 27, 1823, he was able to announce that he had completed the *Missa Solennis*. It had been intended for Cologne Cathedral, with whose vast interior Beethoven had been familiar as a child; actually it was first heard in St. Petersburg, at a private performance financed by Prince Nikolai Galitzin. The date was April 6, 1824, and Vienna did not hear it until a month later, and then only in an absurdly truncated form, with Beethoven conducting. It was neglected during the few remaining years of his life, and its place in the repertoire dates from its resurrection by Heinrich Dorn, Schumann's teacher, for the Rhenish Music Festival of 1844. Although it has remained a concert favorite on the Continent, it is doubtful that even there it has ever been completely performed as part of a church service.

Like the B minor Mass, the *Missa Solennis* is unthinkable as liturgical accompaniment: it would dwarf rather than enhance the rite. It is ironical that two of the greatest of all composers used the service of the Roman Catholic Church for the creation of works so formidable in size that the Church cannot take advantage of them. Both of these masterpieces require such lavish batteries of performers that even as concert works they can be presented adequately only at festivals or by the most generously endowed of metropolitan orchestras and choral groups. But here the resemblance between these Masses ends: the Lutheran Bach, the simple town cantor, wrote incomparably the more reverential one; Beethoven, the merely perfunctory Catholic, carrying the load of doubt engendered by the intellectual and social turmoil of the late eighteenth century, approached the very words of the Mass in a spirit Anton Rubinstein stigmatized as criticizing and disputatious. Beethoven's ever-immanent faith was in the heroic potentialities of mankind, and that was the faith whose triumph he had hymned in his great secular works. He went right on composing magnificent music when he turned to a sacred text, but his searching point of view was not deflected by the character of the subject matter. It is little wonder, then, that his illustrations of the liturgy fail to carry that conviction of an all-embracing faith in the traditional Trinity which shines forth from the masterpiece of the transparently devout Bach.

Musicians, except for Beethoven's most unquestioning idolaters, find the *Missa Solennis* just as hard a nut to crack as does the orthodox believer. Throughout, it is subtly and nobly conceived, and informed by a musical imagination at its healthiest and most daring. Again and again it rises to climaxes of incredible power and beauty. But it rises, alas! with a forgetfulness of the limitations of the human voice that reduces some of Beethoven's grandest ideas to magnificent might-have-beens. For example, the gigantic fugue, "*Et vitam venturi*," that comes at the end of the Credo is perfect on paper, but never comes fully to life in performance. Paul Bekker has argued that the fault lies with the singers: he says that they are lazy, careless, incompetent. Although singers rarely deserve any defense, here is one place where common sense easily takes the stand in their behalf. Just as Beethoven, finally immured in his tower of deafness precisely when his musical ideas were becoming incomparably elaborate, well-nigh metaphysical, had written for the piano music that became less and less pianistic, so in the *Missa Solennis* he wrote music that is truly unvocal—music whose ideal projection depends not on the singers' intelligence, but on supervoices of inconceivable range and staying power. The discrepancy between conception and practical results arose from the simple fact that Beethoven's deafness cut him off from the realities of performance. For years he had to answer in his head the question of what voices and instruments could do.

In 1812, the year of the Seventh and Eighth Symphonies, Beethoven had already planned one in D minor. This came to nothing at the time, but five years later he began again. Another six years elapsed during which he worked at it in desultory fashion, and it was not until the summer of 1823 that he finally dropped everything else in order to complete it. One section caused him almost insuperable difficulties: in his youth he had been moved by Schiller's *Ode to Joy*, and as early as 1796 he had begun to make sketches for a setting of it. The decision to make this choral setting the last movement of the D minor Symphony came late, and brought with it the knotty problems of how to connect it with the third movement and—even more important—of how to make it seem an integral part of the symphony. As the summer of 1823 deepened, he labored at the vast composition like one possessed. At last, on September 5, he declared the Ninth Symphony complete, though he actually went on perfecting certain details for months.

Beethoven was badly in need of money at this time because of his nephew, and this situation led him to embark on a career of double-dealing. Before the *Missa Solennis* was completed, he had promised it to half a dozen publishers and sold it to a seventh. His manipulation of the Ninth Symphony was even more devious. In 1822, in return for a consideration of £50, he had promised his next symphony in manuscript to the Philharmonic Society of London: the Society took this to mean that they would be the first to perform a work dedicated to them. In the meantime, Beethoven had promised the *première* to Berlin, and so had thoughtfully dedicated the symphony to the King of Prussia. The next episode in the saga of the "Choral" Symphony was his pleased yielding to the demands of a committee of Viennese admirers that the work be first performed in Vienna. Beethoven stuck to the letter of his agreement with the London group, however, and sent them the autograph score. The field was thus narrowed to Vienna when fresh complications arose. "After an amount of bargaining and delay and vacillation which is quite incredible," says Grove, "partly arising from the cupidity of the manager, partly from the extraordinary obstinacy and suspiciousness of Beethoven, from the regulation of the censorship, and from the difficulties of the music," the *première* finally took place May 7, 1824, on the same program with the shamefully abbreviated version of the *Missa Solennis* already mentioned. The "Choral" Symphony aroused frenzied applause, which Beethoven, with his back to the audience, neither heard nor saw. Not until he was turned around to face a riot of appreciation did he know that his Ninth Symphony was a success. But after finding that his profit for the evening was only 450 florins, he went home in a rage and spent the night fully dressed. Thus, amid circumstances quite as comic as tragic, the most controversial of all symphonies was ushered into an unsuspecting world.

To discuss the Ninth Symphony at all, in view of the welter of conflicting opinions—ranging from the truly worshipful ardor of a Paul Bekker through the palaverings of heavy snobs to the cold dislike of any number of sincere people who have their reasons—requires a vast girding-up of the loins. Briefly, the idolaters conceive of the Ninth as a constant and ineffable soaring into the musical empyrean until, at the height of the choral finale, to quote

Bekker, "A giddiness of spiritual intoxication seems to seize the mind, and this greatest of all instrumental songs of life closes with dithyrambic outcry, to echo forever in the hearts of mankind." Sir W. H. Hadow, usually so restrained in his enthusiasms, goes Bekker one better: "When the chorus enters it is as though all the forces of humanity were gathered together: number by number the thought grows and widens until the very means of its expression are shattered and we seem no more to be listening to music but to be standing face to face with the living world." It is not possible to question the sincerity of great students who consummate their listening experience in rhapsodies of this sort, but all too many of us have failed, after anxious listening, to find that "echo" in our hearts. Further, having gone to a concert hall to listen to music, and having heard for three movements some of the best ever written, it is reasonable to complain of having this pleasure suspended, and of "no more . . . listening to music. . . ." Finally, it is impossible not to allow the suspicion to creep across our minds that the reason we are not listening to music is simply that Beethoven, here as little at ease with voices as in the *Missa Solennis*, did not succeed in translating his conception into musical terms. This is the more lamentable because the main theme he wasted on the pompous claptrap of Schiller is of a Bachian severity and magnificence.* The Ninth Symphony rouses and fulfills our highest expectations for three movements and part of a fourth, and ends in a cataclysmic anticlimax.

The story of Beethoven's life after 1824 is simply told: it is marked by anxiety over his nephew's reckless course, an ever-increasing absorption in money matters (so his nephew would be well provided for after his death), and growing ill health. Musically, these years were occupied with the composition of five massive string quartets, the sketching of a tenth symphony, and various smaller projects. Socially, with his deafness complete, Beethoven was just about as difficult as ever, quarreling and making up with his friends in his usual impetuous way. He fell in with one

---

* Some conductors have solved the difficulties of performing the choral movement by omitting it. This may be indefensible by the strictest artistic standards, but at least it assures the first three movements of adequate rehearsal. The traditional procedure is to overrehearse the choral movement (which ends by defeating the singers anyway) and slight the first three movements, with the result that everyone leaves the performance dissatisfied.

Holz, a jolly young violinist of expansive habits, whom Beethoven's older friends jealously suspected of leading the master astray. In a measure, their fears turned out to be reasonable, for conviviality was scarcely the best regime for an aging man probably in an advanced stage of a serious liver complaint. His nephew's attempted suicide in the summer of 1826 all but prostrated him—and left him an old man. Taking Karl with him, he spent an agitated autumn in the country with his prosperous brother Johann. Already, he felt his own end approaching, and the uncertainty of Karl's future haunted him. He pled incessantly with Johann to make Karl his heir, and these discussions, which from first to last were fruitless (as Johann reasonably pointed out, he still had a wife), culminated in a violent quarrel. Dragging Karl along, Beethoven fled precipitately to Vienna in an open carriage, and there he arrived on December 2. He went straight to bed with a raging fever, and never rose again.

Shortly after his fifty-sixth birthday, Beethoven quarreled fiercely with Karl. They were not reconciled when the youth was summoned to join his regiment, and he never saw his uncle again. Now, however, Johann and his despised wife arrived to care for their great relative. In his last days, he was not alone: among his many visitors was Franz Schubert, whose songs he perused, and declared to be works of genius. A set of Handel arrived as a gift from London, and he paged through it in an ecstasy of delight: years before he had declared that "Handel is the greatest of us all." Late in February, 1827, after he had been tapped five times for dropsy, all hope of his recovery was abandoned. He lingered for almost a month. On March 24, the sublime questioner received the last sacrament, and almost immediately the death struggle began. It lasted for more than two whole days, and Beethoven was often in acute agony. On March 26, 1827, a strange storm broke over Vienna—snow and hail followed by thunder and lightning which roused the dying man. He opened his eyes, shook his fist at the sky, and died.

The master who had metamorphosed so many phases of music devoted the last few years of his life to the shaping of five string quartets which not only changed the face of chamber music, but also—with destiny's rare inexorable logic—consummated his own achievement. Dryden nobly said of Shakespeare that "he found not but created first the stage." And, without disparaging Beethoven's great predecessors, it may be truly said that he created modern music. In no department of his thought is this more easily perceptible than in the chamber music, at which he had been working from his prentice years. He wrote a bewildering variety of chamber pieces, among them sonatas for violin and piano and cello and piano, quartets and a quintet for strings and piano, various compositions for wind instruments and strings, and trios, quartets, and a quintet for strings alone. Scarcely any of these are unrewarding, and a few—notably the "Kreutzer" Sonata for violin and piano, with its superb first and second movements and trifling finale—have achieved wide popularity. But the string quartet was the only chamber ensemble he wrote for in every stage of his artistic development, and in his quartets can be traced with wonderful clarity the record of his changing attitude toward the ever more elaborate problems he set himself.

The first six string quartets (Opus 18), composed about 1800, are the children of Haydn and Mozart. They are light and charming works, touched with a fitful melancholy that barely disturbs their eighteenth-century serenity. They sound like the exquisitely polished work of an accomplished musician with no plans of his own for the future. An occasional touch of *brusquerie*, a petulant turn of phrase, alone suggest that their young composer is not so well mannered as he should be. Of the six, only one—the fourth— is in a minor key; it is, beside the lighthearted five, almost a changeling: its loveliness has a remote and archaic quality.

A half dozen years passed, and Beethoven composed the magnificent set of three quartets (Opus 59) for Count Rasoumovsky, Prince Lichnowsky's brother-in-law. They belong to the period of the "*Eroica*" and the "*Appassionata*," and are not unnaturally works of conflict and passion. Still structurally orthodox, they are as romantic in content as the first set of quartets is classical. They are the direct ancestors, in coloration and feeling, of the chamber music of the rest of the century down to Brahms. The first "Rasoumovsky" opens with a lush and alluring melody on the broadest lines: it might easily be the theme song of the romantic movement. The piercingly sweet, introspective adagio is one of the first hints in music of that self-pity which was to echo intolerably through the tragic cadences of Piotr Ilyich Tchaikovsky. Here, if anywhere, is that often described but seldom captured legendary hero—Beethoven, the Emperor of *Sturm und Drang*. Only two years after these three highly personal masterpieces, he wrote, almost simultaneously with the "Emperor" Concerto, the brilliant "Harp" Quartet (Opus 74). It fits in with the old-fashioned virtuoso's idea of the string quartet as a showpiece for a first violinist accompanied by three far less important players. Beethoven closed the quartets of his second period with a transitional work (Opus 95) that Mendelssohn called the most typical thing he ever wrote—a strange judgment. It partakes of the easily projected emotional qualities of the "Rasoumovsky" group and of the more abstract sublimation of emotion characteristic of the last five quartets.

These last five* are considered difficult to understand. The sensuousness and warm emotionalism of the middle period have vanished. Compared with the "Rasoumovsky," for instance, they are cold and severe. The strict four-movement form of the earlier quartets has been abandoned for a freer design whose unity is not at once apparent. The musical thinking is both complex and spare: ornamentation has been excised with Dorian severity, and everything is surrendered to essentials. This, certainly, is abstract music *in excelsis*, and its bareness of effect would at times be insupportable were it not mitigated by contrapuntal weaving that in complexity and effectiveness rivals that of Bach. It is not easy to come away from a first hearing of these quartets with a desire to hear them again. But if we do survive the first shock of this ascetically shaped art, and go back to it again and again, we are almost certain to end up thinking the last five quartets among the most soul-satisfying music ever composed.

So, from the apparently innocent mimicry of Haydn and Mozart, Beethoven had traveled as long a road as any artist ever trod. If today he is the most universally cherished of all musicians, it is because in the course of this heroic pilgrimage he created something enduring for every sort and condition of man. He failed often, but in the one overpowering ambition of his life he succeeded supremely: for the humanity he loved so much he left a testament of beauty with a legacy for every man.

* The opus numbers are 127, 130, 131, 132, and 135. In addition, the *Grosse Fuge*, originally the last movement of Opus 130, is now published separately as Opus 133. Beethoven wrote a new finale for Opus 130 because the fugue was sharply criticized by his friends as too heavy for the rest of the quartet.

Chapter VIII

Carl Maria von Weber

(Eutin, December 18, 1786–June 5, 1826, London)

VERY little is done, nowadays, to disabuse us of the idea that Carl Maria von Weber wrote three overtures, a piano concerto, a notable salon piece—and nothing more. Occasionally a prima donna with the right physique trots out one of his tempestuous arias, or a conductor in an archeologizing frame of mind disinters one of his less-known overtures. Thus Igor Stravinsky, not satisfied with proving that the numbers on Tchaikovsky's symphonies actually mean something, and that a Third preceded the Fourth, began an epochal experiment of keeping a Carnegie Hall audience awake throughout an entire concert by playing a *Turandot* overture by Weber. In general, it was well received, and the subscribers went home content to know that Weber had composed something besides the overtures to *Der Freischütz*, *Euryanthe*, and *Oberon*, the *Concertstück*, and the *Invitation to the Dance*.

Except for a few great arias that are ever fresh, but are heard all too rarely today, time has winnowed wisely in the case of Weber. The best of him is precisely what is most familiar. A tour through his piano works is a depressing excursion: the country at its grandest is little better than undulating, and the romantic tarns and craggy peaks turn out to be mirages. It is no joke to be left high and dry in the midst of a Weber piano sonata. His output was not large, and too much of it consists of patriotic part songs that may have been popular in Hitler's Germany for reasons that would not give them a hearing elsewhere. Nor do his songs for solo voice have any vitality. It may be stated that Weber wrote two Masses, admirable in sentiment and sound in construction, which have been read through with approbation by his biographers—and are never performed. Of his nine operas, only three hold their place, and that precariously. What remains of Weber's once lofty reputation is dwindling rapidly. It is becoming apparent that he was little more than a talented showman who happened, at a strategic moment, to epitomize the *Zeitgeist*, or its trappings, more obviously than any other musician of his time.

Weber came of that same family from which Mozart took his wife—a roving, shiftless, and talented tribe who might well have been the prototypes of Sanger's Circus. His father, having failed to discover a genius among his first brood, remarried at the age of fifty-one, and thus begot Carl Maria, who was born at Eutin, near Lübeck, in 1786. His mother was eighteen at Carl Maria's birth, and a dozen years of her husband's thoughtless and well-nigh brutal treatment sufficed to kill her. Old Franz Anton, on the other hand, was something of a personage, and like Buckingham, "in the course of one revolving moon, was chemist, fiddler, statesman, and buffoon." He dabbled in lithography with its inventor, the eminent Senefelder, sat at ease among the orchestral strings, had the ear of the Elector Palatine in weighty financial matters, and played Tyl Eulenspiegel on the side. Unhappily for his relatives, this self-styled Baron fancied himself most as the impresario of a traveling theatrical company, and more latterly as the father-nursemaid of another Mozart. Nursemaid he was, but scarcely a tender one: the life of the road permanently injured Carl Maria, who had inherited his mother's frailness and nervous instability rather than his father's rugged health and bouncing spirits.

Practically snatched from his swaddling clothes to be rushed over the face of Germany, the intended prodigy, after a makeshift musical education acquired on the run, miraculously achieved his twelfth year. He took a few lessons from Michael Haydn in Salzburg, and there Franz Anton pompously brought out the boy's first published work, six little fugues. These, as well as an opera that has been lost—in fact, all of Weber's juvenile and youthful efforts—were feeble products of the forcing-house. The signs were that Carl Maria was far from a genius, and so his father (who had lately added the unearned title of major to his *von* and other pretensions) claimed all the more loudly that he was. The unadorned facts are that he had become an excellent pianist for his age, had picked up the rudiments of composition without knowing exactly what to do with them, and had already acquired in the theater itself that inexhaustible knowledge of stagecraft that was to be his salient asset as an operatic composer. While other boys were playing at marbles or hopscotch, Carl Maria was sniffing grease paint and powder, dodging sceneshifters, and absorbing the theater's multifarious lore and rule of thumb.

Weber's first performed opera—*Das Waldmädchen*—dates from 1800, and though he himself later dismissed it as immature stuff, it was produced as far afield as St. Petersburg, and actually had considerable success at Vienna. It fell flat at its *première*, however, and the boy had to work hard and wait some years to get a hearing for a second opera, which was even less encouragingly received than *Das Waldmädchen*. Meanwhile, probably realizing that he was trying to make bricks without straw, he began to study theory, at first alone, and then in Vienna under the fashionable and ingratiating Abbé Vogler, whom Browning has immortalized along lines that give no true picture of a man who was little more than a dilettante and quack. The choice of Vogler is typical of old Weber's lavish inattention to matters that required serious thought. But the Abbé, though not a painstaking teacher, had a flair for communicating his catholic tastes. Besides, he had powerful connections, and his boys had a way of getting the plums while the charges of worthier pedagogues went neglected. Thus, before Weber was eighteen years old, he found himself conductor of the opera at Breslau. To serve the Abbé's brash young favorite, many older and more experienced men were passed over, and there were plenty of soreheads.

Weber was not happy in Breslau. While still in Vogler's entourage in Vienna, he had found a friend in one Gänsbacher, a talented wastrel who passed on his frivolous tastes to Weber. Naturally, Carl Maria found a provincial capital tame after the fleshpots of Vienna, and finally, in an excess of boredom, tried to bring those fleshpots to Breslau, dissipated as wildly as the small resources of the town permitted, and ended by smothering himself under a burden of debt. Although he was a delightful companion, and had somehow (certainly not from his noble father), acquired the instinctive good manners of a gentleman, he got off on the wrong foot with the Breslauers. He revealed himself at once as a masterly conductor, but exacted such rigid discipline that his company soon came to resent him. Worse, his innovations ran into money, and he fell foul of the tightfisted business management. Only the *régisseur* saw that Weber was a man of vision, and tried vainly to arbitrate the difficulties. Furthermore, he presented Weber with a fantastic and highly romantic libretto—*Rübezahl*—which he worked at feverishly, but never completed.

Weber spent many pleasant hours with other young musicians, playing the piano and talking shop. These soirees usually ended with his friends sitting back and listening to Weber sing. He had a fine tenor voice, and commonly accompanied himself on the mandolin, to which, strange to relate, he was excessively devoted. These recitals came abruptly to an end. One evening, a friend called at his lodgings to try over the recently completed overture to *Rübezahl*, and found Weber lying unconscious on the floor: he had accidentally swallowed some acid used in his chemical dabblings—he, like his father, was interested in lithographing music. When he recovered, his singing voice was ruined, and he could barely speak above a whisper.

Weber resigned his Breslau position in 1806; and found a temporary stopgap as musical director at Duke Eugen of Württemberg's Silesian residence. Weber moved in with his aging father and an aunt, and spent several delightful months, during which he composed his only two symphonies, both in C major, and a miscellany of other now forgotten music. But the approach of Napoleon broke up this idyl in less than a year, and Eugen went off to the wars, not, however, before securing Weber a snug post in Stuttgart as secretary to his brother Ludwig. From the beginning, this position was fraught with difficulties: his was the thankless task of managing the tangled finances and answering the elaborate correspondence of a debauched and despised younger brother, whose absurd escapades and dizzy extravagances were surpassed only by those of King Friedrich himself. Weber soon found himself swimming with the luxurious tide, and discovered that his income would not adequately support himself and his father. Kingly favor was needed, but kingly favor was denied one whose painful duty it was to be constantly nagging for the wherewithal to stave off Ludwig's creditors. Insensibly the King came to associate Weber with his brother's thriftlessness, and matters were not helped when Weber vented his own spleen at this injustice by playing broad practical jokes on the King. Once he was actually arrested when he maliciously misdirected a washerwoman, who had asked him the way to the laundry, into the King's presence. Friedrich only waited for a pretext to rid himself of this hateful lackey, whose title of baron (which to the end of his days Weber innocently sported) gave him free and constant access to the court. In 1810 the occasion came in a mix-up over some misappropriated funds, the details of which are still unclear. At any rate, old Franz Anton seems to have been guiltily involved. On February 26, father and son were banished perpetually from Friedrich's dominions.

The decree of banishment staggered Weber for more reasons than one. First, he had become entangled with Margarethe Lang, a young singer at the opera, whose accommodating morals had drawn him into a tender alliance. Second, he had found some kindred spirits—dilettantes like himself—who had a great passion for art, and an even greater passion for the bottle.* Finally, after taking his old score of *Das Waldmädchen* from the shelf, and rewriting it almost completely under the name of *Sylvana*, he had it in rehearsal when the blow fell. Now, with so many important issues at stake, this must have seemed like being cast out of paradise, and the effect was to chasten Weber, who suddenly realized that he had been squandering precious time. With a new solemnity, he rededicated himself to his art. He was twenty-three years old.

There now began a confused period in Weber's life, for he had no definite employment, and had to make a living mainly as a concert pianist. After settling his father at Mannheim (the tireless old scamp was threatening a third marriage at the age of seventy-six), he removed to Darmstadt so as to renew relations with the Abbé Vogler, who led the court band there. He saw Gänsbacher again, and struck up a warm friendship with another of Vogler's protégés, one Jakob Liebmann Beer, who was to make a noise— a very loud noise—in the world as Giacomo Meyerbeer. Contact with this talented young trickster, who at seventeen was already more famous than Weber, stimulated him to feverish activity. Musical ideas crowded his mind, many of which did not mature into action until years later, notably the main theme of the *Invitation to the Dance* and some ballet motives eventually used in *Oberon*. More important, he toyed with the idea of using the *Freischütz* legend for an opera. He finally got a hearing for *Sylvana* at Frankfort in Sep-

---

* The friends called their association *Fausts Höllenfahrt*—Faust's Ride to Hell— and addressed each other under fantastic names, thus foreshadowing Schumann and his *Davidsbund* (page 297). They wrote musical criticism for periodicals, discussed literature and folklore, and shared their romantic dreams and fancies. It was all as heavily German as Weber's nickname—Krautsalat. Haydn and Mozart would have been ill at ease in such company, but the romantics down through Wagner would have felt at home among them.

tember, 1810, mainly to empty seats, for only the sternest devotees of music could tear themselves away from a field outside the town, where the generously proportioned Mme Blanchard was making a balloon ascent. The *première* of *Sylvana* turned out to be nothing more than a quiet family affair: Weber conducted; his mistress, Margarethe Lang, was the first soprano; his future wife, Caroline Brandt, sang the title role. Undeterred by the public inattention to his operatic career, he finally completed, after many distractions, a comic Singspiel of lusty vigor, *Abu Hassan*, the frolicsome over- ture to which is still occasionally played. It was first produced at Munich in June, 1811, and the response was such that Weber felt he had not been working in vain. Therefore, it is all the more strange that he did not begin work on another opera for more than six years.

Old Franz Anton died in April, 1812, and left Weber alone in the world. Although his father had caused him endless trouble, and had been a constant drain on his meager resources, Weber sin- cerely missed him. He felt cast adrift without a rudder, though in- deed the externals of his life were sufficiently brilliant. He was acclaimed everywhere as a leading pianist and conductor, moved with ease in the highest society of the day, and was admittedly in the forefront of that astounding galaxy of genius and talent that was striving to create a characteristic German *Kultur* out of the wreckage left by Napoleon. Weber's relations with his famed con- temporaries were not always amicable: for instance, he and Goethe seem never to have hit it off. On the other hand, he had a brief but cordial friendship with the macabre E. T. A. Hoffmann. With Ludwig Spohr, the most renowned German violinist of the day, he became fast friends after the most unpromising beginning.

Weber's wanderings were brought to an unexpected close in January, 1813, while he was stopping in Prague on his way to Italy. He was just preparing for a two-year tour that would take him farther afield than usual, when an extraordinarily attractive offer was made him: the direction of the opera at a salary of two thousand gulden, with an annual benefit guaranteeing him an extra thousand. He was promised a vacation of two or three months every year, and—most important of all—he was to be allowed com- plete freedom of action in running the opera. Weber accepted at once, and set out energetically to get a fine company together. This turned out to be a major job, for his predecessor had let the institution, which in Mozart's day had been one of the finest in Europe, run to rack and ruin, and now almost all new singers had to be engaged—among them, significantly, Caroline Brandt. During his three years' tenure, Weber literally regenerated the Prague opera in all its departments. With his unequaled firsthand knowledge of the stage, he was everywhere, supervising the painting of the scenery, criticizing the cut and color of the costumes, keeping a shrewd eye on the box office, and handling all phases of the publicity, from elegantly worded *feuilletons* for the newspapers to downright ballyhoo in the handbills. His regime, from a musical point of view, was unqualifiedly brilliant: he opened with a splendid reading of *Fernand Cortez*,* a grand opera on a heroic scale, which was then the rage of Europe, and during the season mounted no less than twenty-four newly studied and perfectly coached operas and Singspiels.

To secure these impressive results at Prague, Weber exacted strict discipline—he was always something of a martinet—and squandered his small reserves of physical energy. His precarious hold on good health slackened, and from this time until the day of his death he was never really well. He was probably born tubercular; caravan life weakened the child, dissipation the youth, and overwork the man. Moreover, his health was further impaired by the emotional storms he was weathering with difficulty: after breaking off with Margarethe Lang (a long and painful process), he had begun seriously to woo Caroline Brandt, but found her intractable.

In the summer of 1814, after slowly winning back some of his strength at a Bohemian spa, Weber proceeded to Berlin for the celebration of the King of Prussia's triumphal entry into his capital after the Allies' victorious march on Paris. He was carried along on the mounting wave of patriotism, and, indeed, had some share in the fetes. He gave a gala concert attended by the King and the court, and conducted a well-received revival of *Sylvana*. Some years before, he had summed up the Prussian temperament as "all

---

* Its composer, Gasparo Luigi Pacifico Spontini (1774–1851), is now remembered chiefly, if at all, by *La Vestale*, which rated a Metropolitan performance as recently as 1925. He shared with Cherubini the task of carrying the traditions of classical opera into the nineteenth century.

jaw and no heart," but now glad faces, singing enthusiasm, and infectious patriotic fervor had metamorphosed Berlin into something infinitely attractive. When he left for a hunting trip with the Grand Duke of Gotha, the vision of a victorious people continued to haunt him, and he sat down and wrote choral settings for ten poems from Karl Theodor Körner's *Leyer und Schwert*. These ran through Germany like wildfire, and soon Weber was almost as much a hero as Körner, who had been killed in action against the French at the age of twenty-two. Little more than a year later, after pondering the news of Waterloo, Weber gave vent to another fervid patriotic effusion—the cantata *Kampf und Sieg*, which was first performed at Prague in December, 1815, and almost equaled *Leyer und Schwert* in popularity. These were truly occasional pieces, for they have long since vanished. In 1815, however, it seemed that great ideas could have no more eloquent voice, and when, after the *première* of *Kampf und Sieg*, old General von Nostitz remarked to Weber, "With you I hear nations speaking; with Beethoven only big boys playing with rattles," he was voicing the consensus. Still, it should be noted that the General was but comparing two mediocre compositions, for by "Beethoven" he meant *Wellington's Victory*.

Weber resigned from the direction of the Prague opera in September, 1816: he felt that he had accomplished as much as he could, and besides, the local musicians were so unfriendly to one they considered an upstart foreigner that he had never been happy there. He was idle for only a few months, during which he angled for the post of *Kapellmeister* at Berlin, one of the few juicy plums available. Just when he realized that he was wasting his time in Berlin—the job there was to go begging for three years under an indifferent interim man, and then fall to Spontini—he received notice that Friedrich Augustus, King of Saxony, desired him to organize the performance of German opera at Dresden. After some initial bickering, Weber accepted the onerous duty on condition that he be put on an equal footing, both as to title and salary, with Francesco Morlacchi, director of the flourishing Italian opera. Doubtless confident that he would have his own way, he set energetically to work, and even produced his first opera—Étienne-Nicolas Méhul's *Joseph*—before the King gave way. It must be remembered that Weber's task at Dresden was even more difficult than at Prague, for here he had to create everything from the ground up. But the results were so satisfactory that in September, 1817, less than a year after he arrived, his appointment was confirmed for life.

It all sounds like a success story, but Dresden was no bed of roses for Weber. The King respected him, but he was never on terms of friendly intimacy with the royal family or the court. His position was somewhat ambiguous: his great work as a composer lay ahead of him, and at this period he was known chiefly as the fashioner of epidemically popular choruses, an efficient conductor and master of stagecraft, and a pianist of eminence. Even when the enormous success of *Der Freischütz* made him as well known in Germany as Beethoven, the Dresdeners had difficulty in believing that their German *Kapellmeister* was a really important man. The indifference of the King and the court was more than matched by the hostility of the Italian company and its intriguing and malingering director, bold in his certainty that Friedrich Augustus preferred his kind of music. It is difficult to believe that Weber, with his frail physique and waning energy, could have breasted this tide of opposition alone. He was buoyed up by the assurance that Caroline Brandt would at last become his wife. From a rather frivolous soubrette with a trivial attitude toward music and a hazy notion of Weber's potentialities, she had developed into a woman of strong character and mature understanding, willing to forgo her career in opera in order to fulfill Weber's exacting specifications for a wife. They were married in Prague on November 4, 1817.

More important—at least for posterity—was the fact that on July 2 of that same year, Weber began the composition of *Der Freischütz*. He had been chewing this legend over in the cud of his memory for years, and in February, 1817, had written joyfully to Caroline, "Friedrich Kind is going to begin an opera-book for me this very day. The subject is admirable, interesting, and horribly exciting. . . . This *is* super-extra, for there's the very devil in it. He appears as the Black Huntsman; the bullets are made in a ravine at midnight, with spectral apparitions around. Haven't I made your flesh creep upon your bones?" And yet, after this outburst of enthusiasm, Weber's work on his pet idea was absurdly dilatory: at the end of 1817 he had completed only one aria and sketched a few scenes; in 1818 he devoted exactly three days to *Der Freischütz*; in March, 1819, he took one day off to write the finale of the first act, and then laid the score aside for six months. In September, he resumed work, this time seriously, and on May 13, 1820, blotted the last notes of the overture, which he had left until the end. It is a strange tale, this story of the composition of the germinal master-piece of romantic opera, and in it we may read how the incubus of Weber's dilettantism almost stifled his first major creative effort. His tragedy was that, at a time when he most needed serious train-ing, he was exposed to the pedagogical chicane of the Abbé Vogler, and now he had no appetite for sustained hard work and no un-faltering technique just when his inspiration most cried out for them.

Weber's slow progress with *Der Freischütz* was partly due to the press of his labors at the opera, which were made even heavier by Morlacchi's frequent absences, and the consequent demands on Weber's time at the Italian opera. Then, too, his official position obliged him to write occasional large compositions for court func-tions and national fetes, notably—to celebrate the fiftieth anni-versary of the King's accession—a jubilee cantata whose arias are effective in the Haydn oratorio tradition, and are still occasionally sung. Furthermore, he frittered away what leisure he had in the composition of a number of more or less charming salon pieces, including that hardy perennial, *Invitation to the Dance*, which gave hints to both Chopin and Johann Strauss, and which has, indeed, far more historical than musical significance.

After *Der Freischütz* was completed, more than a year elapsed before it was produced. Forewarned by the cold indifference of the ruling powers at Dresden toward his aspirations as a composer, Weber promised his new opera to Berlin, and Count Brühl, in-tendant of the court theater there, had assured him that it would be used to inaugurate the new Schauspielhaus in the spring of 1820. But the opening of the theater was postponed for a year, and Weber, calm in the conviction that he had written a masterpiece, and that its production would establish his name forever, spent his summer-vacation months in an extended and strenuous tour with his wife. Their route carried them into Denmark, and at Copen-hagen they were feted by the royal family. They did not return to Dresden until November. Meanwhile, Weber was busy composing:

no fewer than three big compositions intervened between the completion of *Der Freischütz* and its *première*. The first of these was an overture and incidental music to *Preciosa*, a gypsy drama based on a novel by Cervantes. The music, charming and atmospheric, is one of the first attempts by a foreigner to imitate Spanish rhythms and color; it is a precursor of an eminent line followed by such men as Rimsky-Korsakov, Bizet, Debussy, and Ravel. The music created a furore in Berlin, and served to pave the way for *Der Freischütz*. Weber next tried his hand at a comic opera, likewise with a Spanish setting, but though he worked at it on and off for two years, *Die drei Pintos* was finally laid aside incomplete.

Weber's third big enterprise was the still-famous *Conzertstück*, one of the most popular piano concertos written in the nineteenth century. Actually composed in his spare hours during the rehearsals of *Der Freischütz*, the *Conzertstück* was finished the very morning of the opera's *première*, when Weber, sitting down to the piano, played the entire concerto for his wife and protégé and pupil, Julius Benedict, meanwhile reciting the highly romantic but stereotyped program on which it is based: a medieval lady is pining to death for her knight, absent in the Holy Land; she sees a vision of him dying, and just as she is sinking back in a deathly swoon, horns are heard, and her hero bursts into the room. "She sinks into his arms"—mark of expression: *con molto fuoco e con leggierezza*. It is all very effective, especially the march of the returning warriors and the swift weaving of triumphant love harmonies on which the curtain falls. Weber, as one of the greatest pianists of the time, knew how to write music that was at once dramatic and pianistic, though certain effects, particularly the glissando octaves when the knight enters the lady's chamber, are difficult to achieve with the heavier action of the modern grand piano. The *Conzertstück*, exciting, showy, and but a step above the superficial, is no longer much played.

When Weber arrived in Berlin to rehearse *Der Freischütz*, he found the whole town given over to the cult of Spontini, who had lately been installed as tsar of all the musical activities there. Moreover, Spontini was preparing to launch the German *première* of his own *Olympie* on a supercolossal scale, doubtless hoping by this Hollywood stroke to make the capital his forever. And its success more than confirmed the worst fears of Weber's friends: *Olympie*, with its huge and expensive scenic display, stupefied the Berliners into submission. With the fate of romantic opera hanging in the balance, Weber alone persisted in believing that all was well, and went calmly and methodically ahead with his preparations. It is, then, all the more remarkable that, badgered by his wife and friends, and about to measure swords with the reigning favorite, he was able to compose the *Conzertstück* between rehearsals. He was right; his friends were wrong. On the evening of June 18, 1821, Berlin heard *Der Freischütz*—and Spontini was dethroned. The decision was never even momentarily in doubt: the overture was encored, and with every succeeding number the temperature of the audience seemed to rise until, at the end, Weber was accorded an ovation unparalleled in the annals of the town. Among the celebrities who witnessed the victory of musical romanticism were Heine, E. T. A. Hoffmann, and Felix Mendelssohn. The apt if embarrassing finale for Weber was being crowned with a laurel wreath, at three o'clock in the morning, by Hoffmann, himself one of the founding fathers of romanticism.

Within six months, *Der Freischütz* was given to shouting audiences all over Germany. On October 3, Vienna set its seal of approval on it quite as decisively as Berlin, and the following January Dresden partly wiped off its indebtedness to Weber by a demonstration that resembled a riot. Romanticism, essentially a great popular movement, had long been awaiting a musical document to match its achievements in the other arts, and here it was. Everything about *Der Freischütz* appealed to the German people: it was emotional to the point of melodrama; it exploited the supernatural and the macabre; it glorified purity (Agathe is the ancestress of Parsifal—and of the Dumb Girl of Portici), and it spun its tale chiefly in the easily understood popular idiom of the day. In short, it was German through and through—or so it seemed to its listeners in 1821, though nowadays not a little of it sounds like snippets of Rossini, whom Weber detested as the archfiend of the meretricious. The still immensely popular overture is practically a potpourri of the best things in the opera, and a truncated version of *Der Freischütz* based on these would slight little of value. Yet, a severe critic, used to the glib craftsmanship of even our least talented composers, might describe this overture as "one damn thing after another," for nowhere is Weber's musical joinery more obvious or less successful. At least two of the arias likewise endure: Max's lyric "*Durch die Wälder*" has a fresh and spontaneous quality and a real infusion of the forest glade; Agathe's dramatic yet meditative "*Leise, leise*" is, with a single exception, Weber's most inspired music for the soprano voice.

The critics had, with few exceptions, received *Der Freischütz* rapturously. Among the dissenters, however, stood the pontifical Ludwig Tieck, an eminent theoretician of the arts, and Weber's friend Spohr. They complained that it was only a Singspiel in a new idiom, and that it lacked both the unity and largeness of effect that bespeak a master. Weber was so nettled that when he received from Domenico Barbaia a commission from the Kärntnerthortheater in Vienna, he sat down cold-bloodedly to write a true grand opera—to prove, in short, that he was not merely a man with a genius for melody, but also a master of his craft. He started off on the wrong foot by accepting a libretto that reads like a hoax by Robert Benchley, actually from the pen of a Dresden poetess, Helmine von Chézy. Weber made her revise the script nine times, and then gave up in despair.* On December 15, 1821, he began to compose *Euryanthe*, which was finished in less than a year, but was not mounted until October 25, 1823. Vienna, then being served Rossini's sparkling champagne by the amiable bottler himself, gave the composer of *Der Freischütz* a respectable welcome at the *première* of his new opera—and turned again to Italian delights. Weber was in despair, and began to doubt himself. He even admitted that some of Rossini's stuff was good. For him, depression could go no farther. He returned to Dresden, and for fifteen months his pen was allowed to gather rust.

In view of the fairly uniform unpopularity of *Euryanthe*, it seems that the Viennese reaction was justified. Performances are rare: the opera has not been produced in the United States since Toscanini made a valiant attempt to force it back into the Metropolitan repertoire after twenty-seven years' neglect, on December 19, 1914, with Frieda Hempel in the name part. It was later revived at Salzburg, when W. J. Turner, after agreeing that "the

---

* The absurdity of the libretto may be judged from the fact that the action hinges on an event that takes place before the opera really begins. To acquaint the audience with these cogent matters, the conscientious Weber hit on the scheme of raising the curtain during the overture, and showing this necessary prologue in a *tableau vivant*.

music never falls below a certain high level of craftsmanship and even of invention," pronounced the opera as a whole "curiously uninspired and unmoving." Mr. Turner's dislike of romantic music is well known. However, Edward J. Dent, with no *parti pris*, says, "*Euryanthe* . . . contains much beautiful music, but it is so badly constructed that it has always been a failure." Mr. Turner and Professor Dent represent the consensus. Sir Donald Tovey, on the other hand, is strongly aligned with the minority. What his arguments amount to is that if the libretto is refashioned completely, and some of the music is deleted or transposed, and some slight additions are made, the result can be highly effective. Even if his contention is correct, it merely confirms the general judgment that Weber failed in *Euryanthe* to show that he was a master of his craft. Its living fragments are fewer than those of *Der Freischütz:* only the overture, a spirited and high-flown pastiche whose moments of lyric beauty and melodic pageantry hint at what we would be missing if Weber's accomplishment had but matched his intentions. Ironically, no one has better summed up the general feeling about *Euryanthe* than Schubert, himself a notorious offender as a craftsman: "This is no music. There is no finale, no concerted piece according to the rules of art. It is all striving after effect. And he finds fault with Rossini! It is utterly dry and dismal."

Weber returned to Dresden with but a single happy memory of his stay in Vienna—the cordial friendliness of Beethoven, whose music he had at last come to appreciate. He had lately staged *Fidelio* with loving care after consulting the master about every difficult point, and had become a leading interpreter of his piano sonatas. Beethoven expressed great admiration for *Der Freischütz*, and assured Weber that he would have attended the first night of *Euryanthe* if he had not been deaf. But it needed more than Beethoven's admiration to bolster up Weber's flagging spirits, his mortally wounded self-esteem. Tuberculosis was gaining on him so rapidly that his horrified friends saw him become an old man in the course of a few months. During 1824 he stuck close to his official duties, and it was at about this time that the young Wagner, "with something akin to religious awe," saw the thin stooped figure going to and from rehearsals at the opera, and occasionally stopping in to talk with Frau Geyer, the boy's mother. That summer, however, Weber received an invitation from Charles

Kemble, that "first-rate actor of second-rate parts," who was then the lessee of Covent Garden, to compose an opera in English for London. After protracted negotiations, the bait was increased—Benedict says to £1000—and Weber could not refuse, even when his doctor warned him that only complete idleness could assure him of living more than a few months: he had to think of the future of his wife and son. Moreover, Caroline was well advanced in her second pregnancy. He wrote Kemble his acceptance, and energetically set about learning English, to such effect that within a year he was speaking it fluently.

Weber began to compose his last opera—*Oberon, or The Elf King's Oath*—on January 23, 1825. The libretto, an adaptation by an English Huguenot, James Robinson Planché, of an English translation of a German version of an old French romance, arrived at Weber's house piecemeal, and so the composer was long left in the dark as to the final direction of the drama he was illustrating. The story of *Oberon* is as complicated as that of *Euryanthe*, and even sillier (after the first performance, Planché said to Weber, "Next time we will show them what we really can do"!). The scene shifts bafflingly from fairyland to Charlemagne's court to Baghdad, while true love remains true in the face of the most preposterous temptations. The setting of this lamentable farrago was pursued throughout 1825, and the following February Weber, with *Oberon* all but complete, left Dresden on his last journey. He stopped off at Paris to visit Cherubini and Auber, and to make his peace with Rossini. The pathetic scene between the two men is vividly described by the generous Italian:

"Immediately the poor man saw me he thought himself obliged to confess . . . that in some of his criticisms he had been too severe on my music. . . . 'Don't let's speak of it,' I interrupted. . . . 'Allow me to embrace you. If my friendship can be of any value to you, I offer it with all my heart. . . .'

"He was in a pitiable state: livid in the face, emaciated, with a terrible, dry cough—a heartrending sight. A few days later, he returned to ask me for a few letters of introduction in London. Aghast at the thought of seeing him undertake such a journey in such a state, I tried to dissuade him, telling him that he was committing suicide, nothing less. In vain, however. 'I know,' he answered,

'I shall die there; but I must go. I have got to produce *Oberon* in accordance with the contract I have signed; I must go.'"

Warmed by Rossini's magnanimity, and inspired by the lavish praises of Cherubini, whom he revered, Weber left Paris on March 2, and was in London three days later, making his headquarters at the house of Sir George Smart, a distinguished conductor. The next day he went to inspect Covent Garden, and was recognized and warmly cheered by the audience—*Der Freischütz* was the rage of London, and at one time had been playing simultaneously at three theaters. A few days later, rehearsals began, and Weber at once realized that he had found his ideal company. Braham and Paton, respectively the Max and the Agathe of the first English *Freischütz*, were secured for the roles of the lovers, and the scarcely less important role of Fatima was entrusted to Mme Vestris—precisely the kind of stellar cast a devotee of opera would give his soul to have heard. Weber appreciated Braham so much that he broke a lifelong rule, and wrote two special tenor numbers for him. The rehearsals went beautifully, and the first performance, on April 12, 1826, was felt by Weber to have approached perfection. The audience thought so too, and he was able to write with deep thanksgiving to his beloved Caroline:

"Thanks to God and to His all-powerful will I obtained this evening the greatest success of my life. The emotion produced by such a triumph is more than I can describe. To God alone belongs the glory. When I entered the orchestra, the house, crammed to the roof, burst into a frenzy of applause. Hats and handkerchiefs were waved in the air. The overture had to be executed twice, as had also several pieces in the opera itself. At the end of the representation, I was called on the stage by the enthusiastic acclamations of the public; an honor which no composer had ever before obtained in England."

Oberon is not really an opera. It is, rather, a drama with incidental music: when the action is going on, the music is stilled, and the music, paradoxically, weaves its atmospheric spells only when the action is suspended. It is therefore not surprising that it has failed to hold the stage. The only vocal number still popular is "Ocean, thou mighty monster," a gigantic soprano *scena* which admirably displays at its best Weber's magnificent if reckless handling of the human voice, and which foreshadows in effect if not in style those epic battles Wagner staged between voice and orchestra. Its melody, too, is the climax of the most popular of Weber's overtures, by far the most nicely constructed of his purely orchestral pieces. Much of the other music in *Oberon* is thoroughly delightful as well as dramatically clever, and there is no reason to believe that a concert version omitting the spoken dialogue would not be popular. Salvaging the libretto itself is quite out of the question.

The dying man became a favorite not only of the populace but also of the Duchess of Kent (who was not fashionable, even though her daughter Victoria was almost certain to become Queen of England), and of certain other minor royalties. Possibly as a result of this, the nobility held aloof, and on the few occasions when Carl Maria von Weber appeared as a pianist at fashionable gatherings, he was used scurvily, made to sit apart from the guests, refused the common politeness of silence while he played, and in every way treated as the inferior of the Italian singers who were the rage of the day. But the pay was good, and to the very end Weber was obsessed by the necessity of leaving his family well provided for. Unfortunately, a concert on the proceeds of which he had relied was scheduled for Derby Day—May 26—and many of the most famous musicians in England performed mainly to empty seats.

This was Weber's last appearance in public. Daily he grew weaker, and though preparations for his return to Germany proceeded apace, it was soon apparent to all but the dying man himself that his own prophecy to Rossini, that he would die in England, was about to come true. On the morning of July 6, 1826, a servant found him dead in bed. He was not yet forty years of age. He was buried in London in the presence of a tremendous crowd, and rested there until 1844, when his wife petitioned to have his remains brought back to the family vault in Dresden.* Wagner, who had been one of the leaders in the movement to get Weber's body for Germany, arranged from *Euryanthe* the special music for the reinterment, and delivered a stirring oration at the tomb.

Today we hear so little of Weber's music that it is easy to forget how strongly he influenced other composers. With a literary bent

---

* The intendant of the opera was against the whole idea on the grounds that it might furnish a precedent for exhuming the body of any Dresden *Kapellmeister* who happened to die out of town.

as marked as Schumann's, he gave to his operas—the most characteristic, and certainly the most important, products of his genius —a definitely extramusical quality that asserted itself in innovations of varying degrees of merit, but all broadly suggestive to rebels and questioners of the past. His interest in folklore, particularly in its more violent and macabre aspects, his excessive nationalism, and his hankering after the overwrought had, together and separately, a vast progeny. Schumann, Berlioz, Chopin, and Liszt marched, at one time or another, under his flamboyant banner. He poured new color into the orchestra. Looking at every field of composition through exaggeratedly theatrical eyes, he composed acres of now unplayed virtuoso pieces, themselves too essentially febrile, too dependent on mere surface effects, to last, but which gave strong hints to Liszt and others of his stripe. Weber's final epitaph must be, however, that he made German opera respectable. With a bold gesture, he turned his back on the past, and on the ridiculous fallacy that German opera must be Italian or it could not be good. Weber's stand gave courage to Wagner when he needed it, and nothing more fitting can be conceived than the forger of *Der Ring des Nibelungen* pronouncing the panegyric on the composer of *Euryanthe*.

Chapter IX

Gioacchino Antonio Rossini

(Pesaro, February 29, 1792–November 13, 1868, Paris)

IN MARCH, 1860, a young composer who was desperately trying to win the battle of musical Paris, made a respectful call on a portly old gentleman who, having won that battle many years before, now sat godlike above the strife and storm. Later, the creator of *Der Ring des Nibelungen*, recollecting this meeting, declared that his host was "the only person I had so far met in the artistic world who was really great and worthy of reverence." Nowadays we would think twice before speaking in such terms of the composer of *The Barber of Seville*—for Wagner's host was Rossini—and the very fact that Weber's greatest successor as champion of German opera so emphatically expressed his esteem for one whom his master had regarded as a fabricator of tawdry and frivolous tunes makes us feel that the current low opinion of Rossini (precisely Weber's) needs revising. As that opinion is based largely on performances of the overtures to *William Tell* and *Semiramide* by brass bands, for which they were not written, and overenthusiastic renditions of the "*Largo al factotum*," it has not unnaturally overlooked the excellent musical ideas in which those pieces abound. Wagner's opinion, on the other hand, grew out of an acquaintance with many of Rossini's operas sung by the greatest singers of the time. Wagner's opinions were seldom haphazard, and though he was equally well acquainted with the operas of Donizetti, there is no record that he ever expressed any admiration for the composer of *Lucia di Lammermoor*.

Whether Weber or Wagner was nearer the truth about Rossini's music, the man himself is one of the most fascinating figures in the history of the arts. He began his unusual career by being born on the last day of a leap-year February. His father combined the offices of town trumpeter and inspector of slaughterhouses at Pesaro, a little Adriatic seaport; his mother, a baker's daughter, was extremely pretty, and from her Gioacchino inherited his good looks. The Rossinis quite equaled the Webers in nomadic habits, and while they wandered from theater to theater, Giuseppe playing the horn and Anna singing, the boy was left with relatives in Pesaro. He grew up like a weed, had practically no schooling, and was nothing more than a street arab. His first music teacher played the piano with only two fingers, and went to sleep during lessons. Item: not much progress was made, and there seemed to be method to his father's apprenticing him to a blacksmith after the family was reunited in the village of Lugo. But Gioacchino showed a new tractability, also a vast yearning for more musical instruction. So he was turned over to a priest, who taught him to sing and inspired him with such a love of Haydn and Mozart that he became known, later on, as "the little German."

Removal to Bologna meant better teachers, though not always more congenial ones. Rossini learned several instruments, and his fresh soprano voice was in much demand, mainly in churches. It is recorded, too, that in 1805 he played a child's role in an opera. The next year, the Accademia Filarmonica elected him a fellow, just as they had his idol Mozart, thirty-six years before, at precisely the same age. Gratified, he enrolled at the Liceo, and entered the counterpoint class of Padre Mattei, a redoubtable pedant whose method was to treat his pupils as so many peas in a pod, and who almost killed Rossini's enthusiasm. Not quite, however, for he began to compose, and even won a medal in counterpoint. But he did not finish his course, as his family's growing destitution made it necessary for him to skip fugue in order to help support them by various musical odd jobs.

Rossini was eighteen when he left the Liceo, and fairly ill equipped to hang out his shingle as a professional composer. That did not hinder him from accepting a commission to do a one-act opera for the Teatro San Mosè at Venice. American subjects seem to be too exotic for Italian composers: the Canadian villain of *La Cambiale di matrimonio* is about as credible as the cowpunchers of Puccini's *The Girl of the Golden West*, and the music cannot be very much worse. The tiny opera was a success, and so Rossini, with coins jingling in his pockets and his head in the clouds, returned to Bologna. Never was so popular and prolific a talent launched with so little fanfare. San Mosè was not one of the really big houses, but the applause, that November night in 1810, gave Rossini the idea that opera could be a profitable business. As with George Sand and her novels, composing operas was as easy for him as turning on a faucet: during the next nineteen years he composed almost forty of them, sometimes at the rate of five a year. Within six years of his debut at Venice, he had achieved performances at both of Italy's leading theaters—the San Carlo at Naples and La Scala at Milan—and had written the most popular opera of the nineteenth century.

After a false start in 1811, Rossini produced, the next year, three successes and three failures—all equally forgotten, though Toscanini has a fondness for the overture to *La Scala di seta*—a brightly colored puppy chasing its tail. Another of them—*La Pietra del paragone*—was mounted at La Scala in the autumn, and was Rossini's first important success. In the overture occurs the earliest of those long crescendos which eventually degenerated into a mere mannerism, but which created a great furore at the time. The device was not original with this master of musical trickery: he had lifted it from others who did not know its strength, but it helped largely in securing fifty performances for *La Pietra del paragone* the first season. With Napoleon's recruiting sergeants active throughout Lombardy, it was lucky for Rossini that the general commanding in Milan was a devotee of *La Pietra*: he exempted its composer from service—a lucky break for the French army, Rossini said. A rich crop of false stories has grown up about many of those early operas, but the truth of one story that sounds like a myth is attested by the score itself. Finding that a certain contralto had only one good note in her voice—middle B flat—he wrote for her an aria in which the orchestra carries the melody while she repeats B flat ad infinitum. The audience (who customarily chattered and ate sherbet at that given point in the second act when the poor *seconda donna* stepped forward to do her stint) applauded in a rapture, the singer was transported at being noticed at all, and the composer patted himself on the back.

Rossini wrote only four operas in 1813, the first of which—*Il Signor Bruschino*—was first produced in the United States in December, 1932, at the Metropolitan, as a curtain raiser to Richard Strauss' *Elektra*—a clever stroke of musical contrast that left the conservatives in the audience with an uneasy feeling that they had won a famous victory. The libretto is a wearisome comedy of errors based on willfully mistaken identities, which Rossini has honored with a delicious and lighthearted score. As it abounds in outrageously *buffa* effects, the Venetians suspected that he was poking fun at them, and would have none of Mr. Bruschino and his son. Offenbach revised it for the frivolous Parisians of the Second Empire; they took it to their hearts, and today it is the earliest of Rossini's operas likely to remain in the roster. Far different was the effect on the Venetians of *Tancredi*, a serious opera cut on rather grandiose lines, and based on Voltaire out of Tasso. The overture, though borrowed from an earlier opera, smote the first-nighters with an impact of spurious freshness, and one of the arias—"*Di tanti palpiti*"—caught like wildfire, and overnight became a public nuisance. In *Tancredi*, Rossini took a hint from Mozart, and began to give the orchestra a more important and expressive role than Italian composers usually did. His next offering to Venice, which he now held completely in thrall, was a comedy—*L'Italiana in Algeri*. Pitts Sanborn has called this delicious entertainment, with its echoes of Haydn, Mozart, and Cimarosa, "one of the glories of Rossini's youthful years, when melodies bubbled as birds sing, when his slyness and his incomparable wit had all of their joyous recklessness." The overture has survived precisely because it crystallizes those qualities.

At twenty-one the Swan of Pesaro (for such was the nickname of this stout, floridly handsome young man with a pleasing tenor voice) was the most successful composer in Italy, and though he never made a fortune until he left the country, he was already supporting himself and his parents in comfort. And now, with two tremendous hits, he felt established. His next three operas were flops, more or less deservedly. About the third of these Rossini himself had no illusions: he always had a tender spot in his heart for the Venetians for listening to it in silent martyrdom rather than throwing brickbats at him. Possibly because of a feeling that he might be going stale, he retired to Bologna for several months to be with his parents (his devotion to his mother was always morbidly intense) and to think things out. This last was a difficult job, considering that as a result of Bonaparte's escape from Elba the town was soon swarming with Murat's insolent troopers. Rossini's solitude was rudely but welcomely invaded by Domenico Barbaia, a preposterous fellow who had risen from the scullery to the direction of Italy's most important opera houses. He now bestrode the musical life of Naples like a colossus, and had come to offer Rossini

—nay, to dictate that he take—a position as his chief of staff. The terms were fair enough, and by the middle of 1815 Rossini was established in his new home.

Never did Rossini play his cards better. Realizing that Barbaia's Spanish mistress, Isabella Colbran, was the real power at the San Carlo, he soon was on such a footing with her that supplanting the impresario in her affections was merely a matter of waiting for the strategic moment. He set out cold-bloodedly to compose an opera —*Elisabetta, regina d'Inghilterra*—that would display the special qualities of her voice and acting ability. The sumptuously costumed role, teeming with situations that ill befit a virgin queen, gave her a wonderful chance to show off her statuesque beauty. Colbran played the part to the hilt: her acting rather than his music captured Naples for Rossini. Probably the most signal proof of the diva's affection for him was that she allowed him to write out the vocal ornaments in her arias. This simple action, which today is taken for granted, seemed revolutionary to singers accustomed to embellish their melodic line with improvised ornaments that sometimes completely distorted it.

With Venice, Milan, and Naples in his pocket, Rossini took a leave of absence, and laid siege to Rome. But for a siege one needs siege guns—and he had provided himself with birdshot. The Romans hissed his insultingly careless offering, and the perpetrator of the outrage sent his mother a drawing of a large, straw-covered bottle known throughout Italy as a *fiasco*. Fortunately for him, he had signed the contract for his second Roman opera before this rashly ventured *première*. This time he himself selected the libretto—a version of Beaumarchais' *Le Barbier de Séville*—and worked on it with such ardor that within a fortnight he had produced a complete opera. One of the reasons that he finished it so expeditiously was that he borrowed numbers from five of his earlier operas. However, the new material is so fresh, so apparently eternal, that, even with his wholesale plagiarizings from himself, his accomplishment remains a miracle. Verdi, himself an occasional high-speed artist, only partly explained it away by saying that Rossini must have been revolving the music in his mind long before he began to write it down.

First produced at the Teatro di Torre Argentina on February 20, 1816, *The Barber of Seville* was a resounding failure. Out of deference to the aged Giovanni Paisiello, who for almost half a century had held musical sway over Naples, and whose setting of the same Beaumarchais libretto had once been popular, and was still well known in Italy, Rossini introduced his own version under the title of *Almaviva, ossia l'inutile precauzione*. Useless precaution it was, indeed, for Paisiello from his very deathbed—he died early the following June—seems to have posted a claque in the house in order to strangle the opera in its cradle. With the help of several ludicrous accidents, Paisiello's plotting ruined the first night. Rossini rushed home sure that all was lost, though when some friends came to console him he was asleep—or pretending to be. The next night he absented himself on a plea of illness. This time his friends roused him with better news: the Romans had shown a measured but definite liking for *The Barber*. Other cities made up for Rome's reticence. Within a season or two, it became the rage of Italy, and then—in a space of but few years—of Europe. On November 29, 1825, less than ten years after its *première*, it reached New York*—the first opera to be sung there in Italian—brought thither by Manuel García, the original Almaviva of the Rome cast. It became the most popular opera of the nineteenth century, and though newer operas have forced it from first place, it shows no signs of being shelved. Today Rossini's *Barber* is more than a century and a quarter old, and still in the best of health.

As one of the two signal triumphs of the pure *buffa* spirit in music, *The Barber of Seville* ranks with *Le Nozze di Figaro*. Both are based on Beaumarchais—they are, in fact, Books I and II of the same great story—but there, in the deepest sense, the resemblance ends. Where Mozart is delicate and witty, Rossini is deft and comic. Both the Austrian and the Italian are sophisticated, but of Rossini's of-the-world worldliness there is no trace in Mozart. *Le Nozze* rises to ineffable tenderness in its love scenes; *The Barber* is supremely the music of gallantry—gay, mocking, knowing, of unflawed superficiality. Best to sum up the difference between these two masterpieces, one must call in the aid of metaphysics: *The Barber* is a great *opera buffa*; *Le Nozze* is a great opera in the *buffa* style.

The Barber abounds in music which for sheer gaiety, *brio*, and irreverence has never been surpassed. Hardened operagoers will

---

* An abridged version had been presented there as early as 1819.

not be inclined to dispute the statement that it is one of a pitiably meager number of operas that are long but seem short. The pace is breathless, from the brilliant overture* to the hearty finale where all loose ends are tied together in the tidiest way possible. That immortal piece of nose-thumbing, the "*Largo al factotum,*" comes dangerously early in the first act, but what follows is so good that there is no sense of anticlimax. A half hour later comes "*Una voce poco fa,*" an extravagant but singularly apt outburst of vocal bravura. A fine bass aria (Rossini was one of the first to use this voice importantly in opera) known as the "Calumny Song" was made the focal point of a remarkable—possibly (since it tended to upset the equilibrium of the opera as a whole) a too remarkable— performance by the late Feodor Chaliapin. To list the good things in *The Barber* would be to name substantially every number in it. However, some absurdities have crept in, notably in the "Lesson Scene." Rossini had written some very effective music for the con- tralto who created the role of Rosina, but when it was transposed for coloratura soprano (then, as now, wanting to outdo the flute), the original music was discarded, and the Rosina of the occasion allowed to choose her own, her own usually being anything suffi- ciently gymnastic and unmusical. That superb showwoman, Adelina Patti, considered by oldsters as the greatest of Rosinas, first discovered that she could actually interpolate such an anach- ronistic, and voice-resting, ditty as *Home, Sweet Home*, and get away with it. She had, in fact, nothing quite so sure-fire in her bag of tricks.

Back in Naples after *The Barber*, Rossini rested. In September, he brought out a flop, and then, toward the end of the year, burst forth like a nova, composing—in the six-month period from De- cember, 1816, to May, 1817—three of his finest scores. Colbran was by now his obsession, and he strove to find a role that would display the more pathetic side of her histrionic ability. That of Desdemona, in Shakespeare's *Othello*, seemed promising. So far, so good. But next, as if bent upon proving that his choice of an effec- tive libretto for *The Barber* had been utterly fortuitous, he allowed a highborn hack to tinker with the story. The resulting ravages, briefly, were these: the Moor was reduced to a bundle of nerves,

---

* Not the original one, which was lost soon after the first Rome season. What we hear had done service for two earlier operas before being attached to *The Barber*.

Iago became a Relentless Rudolph, and Desdemona became even more feeble-minded than she is in Shakespeare.* Rossini lavished on this pitiable makeshift some of his most beautiful music, particularly in the third act (which the librettist had tampered with least), and everything about *Otello* bespeaks his earnest devotion to the task of creating a serious opera. Here, for the first time, Italian opera caught up with the up-to-date productions of the French and German composers: the piano-supported recitative was abandoned for continuous orchestral background, thus permitting whole scenes to be conceived as uninterrupted musical units. *Otello* was for more than half a century one of the most popular operas of the standard repertoire, and might still be sung today if it had not been superseded by one of the masterpieces of Verdi's old age, which, moreover, had the advantage of a superb libretto by Arrigo Boïto.

In *La Cenerentola*, produced at Rome on January 25, 1817, Rossini recoiled from seriousness as far as possible, reverting to *buffa*. As he had a lifelong aversion to representing the supernatural on the stage (in sharp contradistinction to Weber), he instructed his tame librettist to excise the fairy element from this version of the Cinderella legend, and so left the heroine little more than a poor slavey who outwits her flashy, scheming sisters and dishonest father at their own game. *La Cenerentola* is definitely something not to take the children to. The score is second only to that of *The Barber* in gaiety and glitter, and though the libretto leaves much to be desired, the opera is good entertainment from beginning to end. Unfortunately, Cinderella needs a florid mezzo voice of a sort that is all but extinct, and since the death of Conchita Supervia no one has attempted to sing the role. Another reason for the opera's disappearance from the stage is that it belongs, as one of Rossini's early biographers said, "to the composite order of operatic architecture": that is, much of it, including the overture, is borrowed indiscriminately from his earlier operas, and therefore does not fit the spirit of *La Cenerentola*. He even called in another composer to supply two arias.

In May, 1817, Rossini made a triumphal return to La Scala

---

* The modern dislike of unhappy endings is not modern. At many performances of *Otello*, it was found necessary to close with a reconciliation scene between the Moor and his bride. When the tragedy was allowed to run its course, the audience turned the action into farce by audibly warning Desdemona that Othello was coming to strangle her.

with the third opera of this notable group—*La Gazza ladra*, a picaresque tale of a thieving magpie. As he was in disgrace with the Milanese as the result of two consecutive failures in their city, he took special pains with all details of this new work. He found a story with wide variety of appeal—it contains almost all type dramatic situations except pure tragedy—and set it not only with inspired intuition but also with an intelligent grasp of the subtle relationships of character, incident, and music. He gave such unprecedented importance to the orchestra that Stendhal, his first biographer, complained of the heaviness of the scoring: up to this point he had yielded to none in his worship of Rossini, but from now on he insisted on regarding him (with qualifications) as an angel who had been tempted by the Germans, and had fallen. But surrendering to the Germans was not a mortal sin in 1817, and soon *La Gazza* was being sung from one end of Europe to another. In 1833 this ubiquitous magpie came ashore at New York, and warbled under the aegis of no less a personage than Mozart's erstwhile librettist, Lorenzo da Ponte, and was used to inaugurate the city's first Italian opera house, at Church and Leonard Streets. Given an adequate cast, *La Gazza* could be successfully revived today: the overture (which really has a bearing on what follows) has a symphonic solidity and a distinction of contour that place it alongside that to *William Tell*, while many of the arias and concerted numbers are among the best Rossini ever contrived. *La Gazza* might well have passed the tests of so severe a critic as Gluck, so sensitively does the music further the action.

Little in the next five years of Rossini's life need detain anyone except the professional student of musical history. He wrote a dozen operas, most of which were successful. Their titles mean about as much to us now as those of Irving Berlin's musical comedies will mean to our great-grandchildren. The music is, in most cases, as dead as the librettos, though Rossini later transformed two of the scores into extraordinarily successful French operas. Many of these productions he devised as stellar vehicles for Isabella Colbran, who by this time was openly his mistress, apparently with Barbaia complaisant. As Colbran's voice and beauty were both fading, and as, on the other hand, Rossini was the darling of Italy, it will be understood why Barbaia had so little difficulty in seeing everything and saying nothing. Probably he was as tired of

Colbran as Naples was. On more than one occasion, the excitable Neapolitans flared out against the aging Spanish passion flower whose tiresome singing out of tune they could more easily forgive than her, and Barbaia's, espousal of the unpopular royalist cause. Her sultry wiles as the Lady of the Lake, in a curious version that poor Walter Scott would never have recognized, merely aroused a derisive demonstration Rossini thought was directed against himself. A stagehand appeared with a request that he take a bow. Rossini knocked the fellow down, and left at once for Milan, where he told everyone that *La Donna del lago* had been a bang-up success. This was (he thought) a lie. Meanwhile, however, news of the acclamation that greeted *La Donna*'s second night had reached Milan, and Rossini's bitter jest at himself missed fire.

On July 20, 1820, the Neapolitans revolted, and drove Ferdinand I from his capital, also eventually affecting the fortunes of Barbaia, Colbran, and Rossini. Barbaia, as an avowed favorite of the King, was temporarily ruined, and began to lay plans for emigrating; Colbran, whose fortunes still depended on his, suffered further eclipse; finally, Rossini, tired of Naples anyway, was only waiting for his contract to run out, and used the crowd's hostility to his friends as a good excuse for leaving. The trio lingered in Naples until February, 1822, when Rossini took farewell of the San Carlo with *Zelmira*, a score with which he had taken particular pains.* It was a triumph even Colbran seems to have shared, and she and Rossini left in a blaze of glory. The very day after *Zelmira* closed, they started for Vienna, where Barbaia had found a new and lucrative berth for himself. They broke their journey at Bologna, and there, on March 16, 1822, Gioacchino Antonio Rossini made Isabella Angela Colbran a married woman. Whether he married her out of deference to his mother's prejudice in favor of legitimacy, or because she had a tidy annual income, remains an open question: doubtless both factors swayed Rossini in his decision. What is certain is that by the time he got around to marrying Colbran, the great days of their romance were past. He was thirty, she thirty-seven.

A week after their wedding, the Rossinis were in Vienna. The dashing *maestro*'s fame was already at the boiling point there, and

---

* Not, however, out of love for the Neapolitans. *Zelmira* had been devised especially for Vienna, and he was using the San Carlo merely as a tryout house.

he had only to make his entry into the city to carry all before him. There were, of course, anti-Rossinians, but they soon found that the most exasperating thing about Rossini was that it was impossible to fight him: he disarmed his enemies with a smile. Several of his operas were produced with such success that the sick and nervous Weber, struggling with the score of *Euryanthe*, was seized with alarm—it boded ill that German opera was being betrayed in its very citadel. Vienna was soon in the throes of Rossiniosis: everyone from emperor to artisan had the symptoms—a feverish rum-tum-tum in the head and a tripping tongue. Austria's most notable musicians were not immune. Schubert succumbed, and even Beethoven, who was seeing no one, allowed the charmer to wait upon him. The titan warned Rossini to stay away from serious opera, and advised him to "give us plenty of *Barber*s." Rossini, literally under the spell of the "*Eroica*," which he had just heard for the first time, and outraged by the sordidness of Beethoven's surroundings and his apparent neglect, tried vainly to persuade his own rich admirers to join him in providing handsomely for the greatest of living composers. Rossini's Viennese visit ended with a testimonial banquet at which he was presented with a silver vase containing thirty-five hundred ducats.

Rossini was now so famous that Metternich invited him to attend that extraordinary gathering of high society known to history as the Congress of Verona, pointing out that naturally the God of Harmony was needed for its success. Here, then, while the Holy Alliance dawdled over the Greek Question and the Spanish Question and the Italian Question, Rossini served up a series of completely uninspired cantatas fitting to the occasion. He met Alexander I, sang at a party at the Duke of Wellington's, and received a large collection of snuffboxes. The Congress of Verona was not a success, musically or politically.

The hero's next destination was Venice, the scene of his debut. His return was inglorious. The Venetians hissed the indifferent vehicle he had chosen for his reappearance, though it appears that their real venom was aimed at Signora Rossini, whose now mediocre voice was not improved by a throat ailment. Rossini retired sulking to his *palazzo*, and in thirty days composed one of his longest, most carefully constructed, and impressive works. This was his last Italian opera, *Semiramide*, the pompous but workable libretto of which was furnished by that same Gaetano Rossi who had perpetrated the flimsy nothing on which he had first tried his hand thirteen years before. On the gore and incest of Rossi's monumental chronicle of Babylon's sensational queen and her lover-son, Rossini turned his full battery of tricks: a large patchwork overture in quasi-Weberian style, vocal *fioriture* of the most shameless sort, a monstrous example of his own peculiar crescendo. These did not suffice for the shattering effect at which he was aiming, so he put a brass band on the stage. It may not sound so, but all this was calculated to a nicety: after its *première* on February 3, 1823, *Semiramide* ran solidly for a month at the Fenice, and for several decades was everywhere considered Rossini's *chef-d'oeuvre*. There was something in it that got in people's blood; it went capitally, it seems, with deep draughts of after-dinner port, three-decker romances, the Exposition of 1851, and the opening of the Crystal Palace. But all things pass—even the Crystal Palace—and *Semiramide* passed with the follies of our grandparents. With quite amazing good taste, the Metropolitan has refrained from reviving it since 1895, when the combined talents of Melba, Scalchi, and Édouard de Reszke failed to re-establish it. Paging through its yellowed score is like ransacking a what-not: there are some pretty and affecting odds and ends, but an awful lot of trash. As to the famous overture, it is almost as popular as that to *William Tell*, and is possibly one tenth as good. But even it is losing concert status, and is fast becoming a mere brass-band fixture.

Composing *Semiramide* silenced Rossini for more than two years, and the rest of Europe's professional operatic composers breathed a sigh of relief. He was by all odds the most talked-of musician in the world,* and was besieged by bids for his—and, tactfully, Signora Rossini's—services. He accepted one from the King's Theater in London, probably intending to settle permanently in England. On his way, however, he saw Paris, and glimpsed something better. The charm of Parisian life and the possibility of be-coming the arbiter of French music were uppermost in his mind

---

* In 1823, Rossini could boast that twenty-three of his operas were running in various parts of the world. The Sultan of Turkey instructed his brass band to play selections from them, and in far-off, chaotic Mexico one of them was given at Vera Cruz. They were the favorite music of Italy, Russia, Portugal, Spain, and South America.

during the extremely uncomfortable Channel crossing and on his arrival in London—it was a hellishly cold December day, and he had caught a chill. During the season he made 175,000 francs, was repeatedly honored by George IV, and was lavishly entertained by everyone that mattered. The King made a special trip up from Brighton to hear his fat friend sing at the Duke of Wellington's house. Some of the more serious Londoners were annoyed at this expensive dawdling: though his operas were running (he even sometimes deigned to conduct), and he pretended to be writing a new opera for them (which never materialized), as far as they could see he had become just another Italian singer. The only new work he actually gave London was a vocal octet called *The Plaint of the Muses on the Death of Lord Byron*. While he was getting rich on the English, and philosophically doing nothing about the shambles which was English music in the year 1824, he was negotiating with the French ambassador to return to Paris and assume direction of the Théâtre Italien.

During Rossini's brief tenure of office at the Italien, he devoted most of his time to learning French and studying Parisian taste in music. He showed Paris how his own music should be performed, successfully introducing several operas not heard there before, and winning his audience over to others they had disliked under earlier conductors. He launched Meyerbeer on his career as the eventual idol of Paris by producing the best of that parvenu's Rossinian operas in 1825. But as a composer he himself seems to have been in a period of slothfulness. While at the Italien his sole new offering was a one-act opera-cantata—*Il Viaggio a Reims*—which, moreover, was nothing but a pastiche of much old material, a few new numbers, and arrangements of seven national anthems. First produced on June 19, 1825, *Il Viaggio*, which died after its third performance, celebrated Charles X's coronation progress to Rheims, and is notable for two departures from Rossini's usual tact: he set an event in French history to Italian words, and its single act lasted three hours.

Not unnaturally, Rossini was criticized as a trifler, and was compared unfavorably with serious people like Spontini and Weber, who disdained pastiches. But in Paris, at least, he had reasons for idleness. He was ill and unnerved by the insecurity of his position, for his contract at the Italien was for but eighteen months. He was wheedled into something like his old activity only by a brevet from Charles X as *premier compositeur du roi et inspecteur général du chant en France,* a reward for his rehabilitating labors at the Italien. Digging down into his luggage, Rossini extracted the manuscript of *Maometto II,* a second-rate opera that had persistently failed. This he all but rewrote to the words of a new French libretto, and introduced it at the Opéra on October 9, 1826, under the title of *Le Siège de Corinthe.* Three factors assured its success: the dramatic intensity of the music, a superb cast, and a French libretto illustrating an incident in the Greek struggle for independence from the Turks. As the Greek cause was very fashionable in Paris at the time, and Rossini was well aware that most of the enthusiasm at the *première* was inspired by the cause and not the music, he tactfully refrained from taking a bow. Soon, however, *Le Siège* established itself on its musical merits, and Rossini became a successful French composer.

The exacting standards of his French confreres and audiences were salient in shaping the unusually solid construction of *Le Siège,* and may have been partly responsible for his delay in writing a large work for the French stage. He realized, no doubt, that he could no longer get by with his careless Italian formulas. For the first time he boldly abandoned his elaborate vocal ornamentation and superficial tricks for a larger architecture and a simpler melodic line. His next effort, a resetting of *Mosè in Egitto,* which in its Italian form had already won favor in Paris, showed even more clearly that Rossini had been converted to careful workmanship. Here, with a libretto completely lacking in fad appeal, he triumphed more signally. Called simply *Moïse,* it opened at the Opéra on March 26, 1827. In effect partly opera, partly cantata, *Moïse* is yet a work of quite notable unity. Its choral writing is often magnificent, the culminating point being the prayer of the Jews for safe passage through the Red Sea. These choruses were its fortune in England when, because of the prudishness that forbade Biblical personages being depicted on the stage, *Moïse* was adapted there as an oratorio. It put the final stamp of unqualified official and popular approval on Rossini. The venerable and austere Cherubini, from his throne at the Conservatoire, declared magisterially that he was pleasantly surprised. And Balzac looked up from the composition of *La Comédie humaine* to pronounce *Moïse* "a tremendous poem in music."

Rossini should have been supremely happy—but he was not. During the final rehearsals of *Moïse*, he heard that his mother had died. He was still tenderly devoted to her, and recovered slowly and painfully from the shock. He was lonely, and now, desperately seeking some living tie with his mother, invited his father to come and live with him in Paris. From Isabella he asked no solace: a coldness had grown up between them, and for years she had been living at her villa near Bologna. His father's presence gradually produced the desired effect: Rossini roused himself from his stupor of grief, and admitted to himself that as the ruler of musical Paris he owed something to his subjects. He called in Eugène Scribe, the most famous of French librettists, and together they concocted a comic opera, *Le Comte Ory*. No new work had been heard from Rossini's pen for seventeen months, and the first-night audience gave *Le Comte* an ovation on August 20, 1828. It betrays the composer's growing Frenchification: it is elegant rather than brilliant, graceful rather than brisk. It contains much delightful, and some really fine, music, notably the orchestral prelude to the second act, which is decidedly Beethovian in quality. But the *Comte* lacks *The Barber*'s peculiar magic. It has never been popular outside France, and today if it is ever revived elsewhere (which seems unlikely), it will be as a mere historical curiosity—an ancestor of the still-popular light operas of Offenbach.

Having now successfully produced three French operas of his own, and fortified with a bank account that allowed him to indulge any whim, Rossini decided that he wanted to devote all his energies to the writing of opera. He petitioned Charles X for the cancellation of his contract, and the granting of a new one along the following lines: he promised to compose five operas over a ten-year period, for each of which he was to receive fifteen thousand francs and a benefit performance; upon the expiration, lapsing, or voiding of this contract he was to receive a life pension of six thousand francs per annum. With the King and his ministers mulling over these memoranda, Rossini retired to the palatial country seat of his friend, the banker Aguado, and began work on the first of these proposed operas. Fondly recalling how the fashionable interest in the rights of small nations had clinched the success of *Le Siège de Corinthe*, he selected Schiller's *Wilhelm Tell* for dissection by a trio of French librettists. They did a singularly ugly piece of work, excelling in vast deserts of inactivity and flat, unrealized characterization. To this listless fabrication Rossini blithely attached some of his most expressive, and certainly his most somber, music. This time he firmly disdained to use any old material. He labored over his script for at least six months, and then put it into rehearsal at the Opéra. A series of delays, more or less accurately explained in the press, raised anticipation to fever pitch. The truth was that Rossini was himself postponing the *première*: he was using *William Tell* as a lever to force the signing of the contract, and even threatened to withdraw the work unless he had his way. Charles X acceded in April, 1829, and so, on August 3, Paris heard Rossini's monstrous five-acter for the first time.

From the very beginning, the response to *William Tell* must have been unique in Rossini's experience: the people listened with cold respect; the critics raved. And such, with minor exceptions, has been its history ever since. In its original form it was insupportable to the audience, and after a few performances drastic cuts were made. One by one the acts were sheared off, until finally only Act II was given. This process of erosion got under Rossini's skin. Years later, he met the director of the Opéra on the street. "We're giving the second act of *Tell* tonight," the director said brightly. "What! the whole act?" Rossini replied. The bitterness of this jest was too keen to be relieved by the praises of Bellini, Mendelssohn, Wagner, Verdi, and even Berlioz, bitterest of anti-Rossinians.

The low level of expressiveness in the operas of the time accounts for much of the critical enthusiasm. *Tell* has solid virtues—earnestness, some psychological verisimilitude, a certain understanding of the architecture of large musical forms. Wagner told Rossini that in it he had previsioned—"accidentally," Wagner explained —some Wagnerian theories of music drama. Whether or not *Tell* is indeed a spiritual ancestor of *Der Ring des Nibelungen*, it certainly foreshadows Wagner's symphonic conception of opera. When he was composing *Tell*, Rossini was profoundly influenced by the music of Beethoven. Unfortunately, this led him to make many of the same mistakes his idol had made in *Fidelio*. There are passages in *Tell* that sound like excerpts from a symphony with an irrelevant vocal obbligato tacked on. And yet the score is not without moments of singular beauty. The second act, besides being the least offensive in the libretto, contains the largest proportion of these, and Rossini always felt sure that it would survive, along with the third act of *Otello* and *The Barber of Seville* in its entirety. *Tell*, even cut down to three acts, is too unwieldy for modern taste, but there is no reason why a concert condensation made up of Act II, with a few other such expressive numbers as Tell's prayer from Act III and Arnold's lovely air from Act IV, "*Asile hérédi-taire*," would not be perennially fresh and popular. Now, however, with performances of *Tell* so few and far between, what we have to judge it by is the overture, a work of great charm and attractiveness. It is beyond question the most popular music Rossini ever composed. It shows that Beethoven could really benefit him when taken lightly.

Rossini was thirty-seven years old. At the height of his creative powers, and in adequate, if not hearty, health, he had thirty-nine more years to live. The acknowledged autocrat of opera, he now went into self-imposed retirement, and never again wrote for the operatic stage. Except for inconsequential chirpings, he broke his silence only twice, with the *Stabat Mater* and the *Petite Messe solennelle*, two religious works in his early *buffa* style.

There is no simple, adequate explanation for this strangest of all abdications. Our natural impulse is to take Rossini's own words about the matter. The trouble is that he told different things to different people on the few occasions when he deigned to explain, and thus contrived effectually to throw dust in the eyes of posterity—a sport at which he was singularly adept. Sometimes he seems shamelessly to have pulled his questioner's leg, as when he said that he would have gone on writing if he had had a son. He told Wagner that composing forty operas in twenty years had exhausted him, and besides, there were no singers capable of performing even them. Again, he explained that he quit when melodies no longer sought him, and he had to seek them—which sounds absurd in view of the fertile melodiousness of the *Stabat Mater*. So we are forced to piece together our own reasons for Rossini's retirement. What superficially started it was the Revolution of 1830, which overthrew Charles X, seemingly invalidated Rossini's contract, and placed on the throne Louis-Philippe, who, the composer complained, cared only for the operas of Grétry.* His agitation over the (to him) black political situation was increased by his realization that he might have to share his throne with Meyerbeer, whose star was then rapidly rising in the musical firmament. Rossini would not compete, or—what seems more likely—he could not.

For shortly after the production of *William Tell*, Rossini's neurosis caught up with him: it had revealed itself shyly as early as 1816, after the cold reception of *The Barber of Seville*; political disturbances and musical rivalry brought it to a head, and he became more and more touchy, increasingly hysterical. In 1836 he first boarded a train, collapsed with fright during the brief ride from Antwerp to Brussels, and was carried from the coach in a faint. By 1848 he was practically bedridden, sometimes on the verge of insanity, and so he stayed for eight years. Some attempt has been made to suggest that his neurasthenia and physical depression had a venereal origin, but advanced *vénériens* do not rise from their beds, at the age of sixty-four, to spend the last twelve years of their lives making dignified carnival. Which is exactly what Rossini did.

In 1832, Rossini met Olympe Pélissier, a fascinating French courtesan, and began the *Stabat Mater*—by far the most important events of the last thirty-six years of his life. Olympe had come to him with unimpeachable references, having been the mistress of a French peer, an Anglo-American magnate, and the painter Vernet. Soon she was indispensable to him, and in 1847, two years after Isabella had died with Rossini's name on her lips, they were married. For twenty-one years Olympe was Rossini's faithful and much-appreciated wife, and their domestic bliss was so unclouded as to be positively uninteresting to read about.

The story of the composition of the *Stabat Mater* leads one to believe that with the right kind of wheedling Rossini might have continued to write operas. In 1831 he visited Madrid as Aguado's guest, and was requested by one of his host's clerical friends to compose a *Stabat Mater*. He was so indebted to the banker that he

* He was in good company. Henry Adams tells how the sixth president, who was devoted to Grétry's music, used, after he failed of re-election, to go about muttering "O, Richard! o mon roy! l'univers t'abandonne," from the great baritone aria in *Richard Coeur-de-lion*. But then, John Quincy Adams was always an eccentric.

could not refuse. Accordingly, as soon as he returned to Paris, he composed the first six sections; then, feeling indisposed, he asked Tadolini, conductor at the Théâtre Italien, to complete the task. The manuscript was thereupon turned over to the Spanish priest on the understanding that it would never leave his hands. But the priest died, and his heirs sold the Rossini-Tadolini script to a French publisher, who informed Rossini of his intention to market and produce it. The composer was furious, and at once sold all rights to the work to his own publisher for six thousand francs. Meanwhile, he began to replace Tadolini's efforts with his own, and finally, on January 7, 1842, Paris heard another Rossini *première*, after almost thirteen years of silence. The soloists included the incomparable Giulia Grisi, the romantic Mario, and Tamburini, the greatest bass-baritone of the period. Paris again bowed to the old wizard: Heine pronounced Rossini's liturgical style superior to Mendelssohn's, and one of the critics reached back to the first performance of Haydn's *Creation* for a comparison. All contemporary sources except one indicate that Paris went wild over the *Stabat Mater*: three days after the *première*, Mme d'Agoult wrote to Liszt that it was not much of a success.

The *Stabat Mater* is a fine theatrical composition which is by no means out of place when performed in a gay baroque church. Sir W. H. Hadow (who was no prude) flatly called it "immoral," but so, too, by Protestant standards are some of the Masses of Haydn and Mozart. So, too, pre-eminently is Pergolesi's great *Stabat*, which Rossini admired so inordinately that he hesitated to court comparison with it by writing one himself. It is partly a matter of geography, partly a matter of time. We have come to recognize a standard of expressiveness which may be interpreted as unimaginatively as the letter that killeth, but which has the virtue of demanding at least a minimum relationship between words and music. By this standard Rossini's *Stabat Mater* is tasteless. It is best listened to as fragments of a serious opera, for as illustrations of the feelings of Mary as she stood at the foot of the cross it is ridiculous—almost a travesty of the touching thirteenth-century poem on which it is based.

Rossini was not on hand for the *première* of the *Stabat Mater*. After the Revolution of 1830, he loitered in Paris for six years, doing little except watch with troubled eyes the Meyerbeer comet sweeping the heavens. After February 29, 1836, the date of the first performance of *Les Huguenots*, and Rossini's forty-fourth birthday as well, the upstart's following equaled his own, and he had little wish to remain in Paris. Moreover, he had won a lawsuit: his contract with the deposed Charles X was adjudged valid for the rather silly reason that the King had signed it in person, and his pension of six thousand francs was reapproved. By October, 1836, Rossini was in Italy, and there he remained for almost twenty years. For the first twelve of these he lived chiefly in Bologna, taking an active part in local musical politics, and presiding like a benevolent despot over the Liceo Musicale, to which he made lavish grants. He might have vegetated there until his death if in 1848 some town radicals had not staged a demonstration against him, on the grounds that he was a bloated conservative. This so intimidated Rossini and Olympe, who were both ill at the time, that they fled to Florence the next day. Rossini soon took to his bed, and there for the next eight years, physically and mentally wretched, he remained. And then, another flight, this time from the Tuscan climate and the bungling methods of Italian doctors.

Rossini and Olympe drove into Paris on a May day in 1855. He was an apparently broken man, and for more than a year those who were eager to do him homage wondered whether he had returned to Paris only to die. In the summer of 1856, he was transported—somehow—to Germany, to see whether taking the waters would ease his last days. His friends had gloomily witnessed his departure, and thought that was the last they would ever see of him. The next thing they knew he was back, and had opened a large apartment at 2, rue de la Chaussée d'Antin—a memorable address in the history of Parisian society. For twelve years—in the winter in town, in the summer at his suburban villa at Passy—he settled down to the business of enjoying himself and making Olympe happy. His Saturday nights became a Paris institution, and to be seen there gave a cachet that attendance at the court of Napoleon the Little could not. The story of Rossini's life became that of musical and artistic Paris. Only the salon of the Princess Mathilde, with Taine and Sainte-Beuve as twin deities, compared with Saturday night at the Rossinis'. A list of his courtiers becomes plethoric: Wagner, Liszt, Verdi, Patti, Clara Schumann, Saint-

Saëns. . . . Properly to celebrate his own follies, the shameless old gentleman settled his wig on his bald pate, and composed a box of musical bonbons, mostly for piano solo, which he called *Péchés de vieillesse*. One of them is *Miscarriage of a Polish Mazurka*, another *A Hygienic Prelude for Morning Use*, titles that call to mind the amusing nonsense of Erik Satie. Naturally, the *Petite Messe solennelle*, written in the summer of 1863, is more dignified stuff. It lasts two hours, and has some ravishing moments, notably a touching duet for soprano and mezzo that would melt the heart of the stoniest operagoer.

In 1868, it being a leap year, Rossini was able to celebrate his seventy-sixth* birthday on February 29. It was his last. He was beginning to fail. On September 26 he gave his last Saturday soiree. In October he was dying of old age and a complication of ills—catarrh, a weak heart, a painful fistula. The fistula was attacked vainly, septic poisoning set in, and hope was abandoned. He had been a lax communicant, and Pius IX (with all his own troubles) was so worried for the repose of Rossini's soul that he sent the papal nuncio to Passy to administer extreme unction. This annoyed and frightened Rossini, though he submitted. So, with accounts squared, he passed away on November 13, 1868—a Friday. Olympe fell across the body, sobbing hysterically, "Rossini, I shall always be worthy of you."

Much has happened to tarnish the glory of Rossini's name since the day when Marietta Alboni and Adelina Patti lifted their voices at his funeral in the "*Quis est homo*" from the *Stabat Mater*. What Chorley said as early as 1862—"*Il Tancredi* is already old, without being ancient"—now applies emphatically to almost all of Rossini's operas. Alone *The Barber of Seville* remains preternaturally young and supple, miraculously unwithered by the years. Beethoven hit the nail on the head when he advised Rossini to write "more *Barbers*." His failure to follow this advice led him eventually to found modern French grand opera—and so we are occasionally treated to at least a three-act view of that wondrous historical curiosity, *William Tell*. But today opera means mainly Wagner

---

* Purists, allowing for the fact that 1800 was not a leap year, will relish the final absurdity of Rossini's career—dying more than three years before his nineteenth birthday.

and Verdi, both of whom learned something from Rossini. Much wider might be Rossini's province if his taste had been surer, his intelligence more disciplined, his disregard of the intellect less profound. He would have composed less, and the quality of what he composed would have been higher. And, who knows?—he might even have written a serious opera as good as *The Barber of Seville*.

Chapter X

Franz Peter Schubert

(Vienna, January 31, 1797–November 19, 1828, Vienna)

A FTER enjoying the excellent theater of Rossini's life, with its incomparable and surprising last act, it is shocking to turn to the sordid little playlet in which Franz Peter Schubert acted the pathetic stellar role. At first blush, Stendhal's savage epitome of man's fate—"He lived, he suffered, he died"—seems to fit Schubert perfectly. But unlike Rossini, who for all his success spent twenty years commiserating himself, Schubert apparently never even realized that he was suffering. In those rare moments when he was not composing, and had a chance to think things over, he sensed that life was hard. But by and large his life, which seems a tragedy to us, did not seem one to him. The fact that a richly endowed natural genius should have been a pauper, humiliating himself constantly to earn less than a living, is so unbearable that addicts of the peculiar sort of magic Schubert alone was able to weave, refusing to face the harsh reality of his life, have romanticized him into the hero of *Blossom Time*. But there is no evidence that Schubert himself ever felt his penury more acutely than when he was casting around vainly for the insignificant trifle he needed for a walking tour. Even his death at the age of thirty-one, possibly before his powers had reached their full—even his death, which to us seems so tragic, so wasteful, was robbed of its terror for him, for he had no premonition of it, and until the very end was living in the moment as he always had.

Schubert had no thought but music. Furthermore, he had no time for anything else. The place of friends in Schubert's life has been much emphasized by biographers, and yet his attitude to them was affectionately wayward, a shade this side of perfunctory. As enthusiasts for his music, they impinged upon, but never entered, his private universe. And this private universe—what was it? It was nothing less than a reservoir of the imagination fed from a thousand freshets, constantly welling over, constantly tapped, constantly renewed. Within, there was seldom room for anything except melody and the need to use it poetically. At this point, the contrast with Beethoven is instructive: no such freshets poured into the dark tarn of his imagination, and his notebooks prove that his store of the raw matter of music was, compared with Schubert's, meager. But in the tortured process of shaping his ideas, Beethoven's spacious intellect, focused savagely and indomitably on the material, was quickened by the ideal of perfection. Beethoven had his vast failures, but when he succeeded, the conscious creative labor had been gauged perfectly to the highest potency of the musical ideas. This sort of creative labor was foreign to Schubert, though not necessarily beyond his capabilities. He "whelmed"— his own word—his ideas down on paper, and then tossed the paper into a drawer. The pressure of new musical ideas left him no peace for the perfecting of those he had already noted down.

It is no accident that this man, to whom melody came more easily than speech, to whom, indeed, it was literally as natural as singing is to birds, should have excelled in the writing of songs. For a song, more than any other musical form, can be set down in one lyrical inspiration. Schubert looked at any poem, good, bad, or indifferent, and instantly a melody came into his head. And nothing could stop a melody when it was on its way. Take, for example, the almost incredible story of the composition of *Hark, Hark, the Lark!* On a summer afternoon in 1826, Schubert was sitting in a noisy beer garden, and idly turning over the pages of a German translation of Shakespeare. All of a sudden he exclaimed, "The loveliest melody has just come into my head! If I only had some music paper with me! . . ." One of his friends drew a few staves on the back of a menu, and there and then Schubert wrote this perfect song. After a song was written—and in seventeen years he wrote over six hundred lieder in just about this way—it was to all intents and purposes done with. An occasional tidying up of purely mechanical details, and that was all. Even when he produced several settings of the same poem, he was not trying to perfect the original setting. A new tune, and not necessarily an intrinsically better or more appropriate one, had come into his head.

The fact that more than a tenth of his songs are set to poems by Goethe is apt to lead the unwary into believing that Schubert had a taste for only the best in poetry. Actually he was so indiscriminate in his choice of lyrics that he might almost have said with Rossini, "Give me a laundry list, and I will set it to music." Some of his

best songs are set to doggerel. Ninety poets or versifiers are represented in the collected edition of his songs, and of these a scant two
dozen have achieved some measure of immortality in their own
right. Schubert did not need good verse, nor is there much evidence that he recognized it when he saw it. The spineless plati-
tudes of Rellstab's *Ständchen*, which he selected in the last year of his
life, served him just as effectively as Goethe's moving dramatic
ballad, *Der Erlkönig*, which he discovered at the age of eighteen.
What he needed was a mere peg on which to hang a melody. His
adoring friends knew this, and were not above exploiting it with
brutal good humor, locking him up in a room with any volume of
verse that happened to be at hand. The number of songs he set
down under these strange conditions was limited only by the
length of his imprisonment. And as he himself was wont to say,
"To complete one song is to begin another."

Wilhelm Müller, to whose verses Schubert wrote his two major
song cycles, was a sentimentalist of small talent. Schubert merely
happened on a copy of the *Müllerlieder* in 1823, and there is no evidence to show that he realized the twenty poems of his first cycle—
Die Schöne Müllerin—were drivel. Indeed, four years later, he set
two dozen more of Müller's lyrics in a cycle called *Die Winterreise.*
Yet, in some respects, these cycles are among Schubert's most
remarkable achievements, and though separate songs in them may
be judged on their own merits, the effect of hearing the cycles in
totality is cumulative, and distinctly heightens their impressiveness. Another collection of fourteen songs was published posthumously under the title of *Schwanengesang*, but it has no real unity.
It includes such dramatic pieces as *Der Atlas* and *Die Stadt*, as well
as the haunting *Doppelgänger*, which has been called the finest of
Schubert's songs.

But most of Schubert's six hundred-odd lieder were written
separately. Almost a quarter of them are still often sung. *The
Gramophone Shop Encyclopedia of Recorded Music* lists no fewer than 127
separate songs, some of them in a baffling number of recordings of
both the original and various arrangements and transcriptions.
Ständchen and *Ave Maria*, to cite the most flagrant examples of over-
supply, have been recorded more than fifty times apiece, including
a carillon version and one for the Hawaiian guitar. To millions of
otherwise unmusical people, the very name of Schubert signifies

song. The reasons are simple, at least as regards the most popular of his lieder: they run a comparatively small gamut of emotions in easily apprehensible terms; they sing of love, nature, religious devotion, death; their melodies have a way of staying in the memory, and without being in the least catchy or vulgar, have an intimacy of appeal that one can match only in folk melody.

In the *Ave Maria*, in which the Queen of Heaven descends from her pedestal, and becomes the sympathetic confidante of the poor peasant maiden, Schubert never once makes a misstep in a situation so susceptible of vulgarization and mawkish overstatement. The musical means are amazingly simple: the long flowing melody ranges but an octave, and the accompaniment—an insistent, repetitive figure—depends for its magical effect on subtle harmonic shifts. The joyful celebration of *Hark, Hark, the Lark!*, the elegant precision of *Who Is Sylvia?* (an exquisite hybrid all around, being neither typical Schubert nor typical Shakespeare), the somber hopelessness of *Am Meer*, the serene peace of *Du bist die Ruh'*—all testify to his sureness as a poet of the lyrical or contemplative. And Schubert could be a great storyteller. The *Erlkönig* is in effect a tiny opera; it has, at least, the best qualities of a magnificent operatic *scena*, so well has it caught the spirit of Goethe's melodramatic ballad. It needs a thoughtful artist to interpret the *Erlkönig*, to differentiate the various personages of the story without caricaturing them. Ernestine Schumann-Heink made it one of the great dramatic songs of the world.

For fathering the lied, Schubert was perfectly endowed, and the ancestral, tentative efforts of Mozart and Beethoven do not detract from, but rather emphasize, the bold and effortless originality of his creation. The great lieder composers—Schumann, Robert Franz, Brahms, Hugo Wolf, Richard Strauss—have all been deeply influenced by his songs, and even in evolving the idiosyncrasies of their own mastery have by no means rejected all Schubertian touches. No one has ever denied that Schubert breathed life into the song. But the matchless natural gifts that were adequate for that act of creation were not in themselves enough to deal with the less tractable elements of the larger musical forms. He needed also an intellectual grasp of complex materials, a willingness to wrestle with the knotty problems arising from them, and a thorough training in musical theory. In varying degrees, he lacked these requisites, and so was grounded incontinently on his most daring and promising flights. What a thorough training would have given him can only be guessed at, particularly since there are reasons for suspecting that he would not have been amenable to such a discipline. It might have been a sturdier understanding of big musical ideas and a taste for wringing the most from them.

What is certain is that Schubert, for various reasons, did not have that training. Born in 1797 in Vienna, then the musical capital of Europe, he was the son of a desperately poor schoolmaster. At the age of seven, after he had picked out a few tunes on the piano without instruction, his father and his brother Ignaz, amateurs both, began respectively to teach him the ABC's of the violin and piano. His aptitude and eagerness soon outstripped their lessons, and he was turned over to the *Kapellmeister* of the parish church, who trained his piping voice, but largely let the boy's musical education run itself. In 1808, he became a chorister in the court chapel, and was accepted as a student at the training school attached to it. Although Salieri, its director, had raised the school's prestige, it actually provided only the sketchiest musical education. Schubert left it with a certain grasp of orchestral playing and directing, and some familiarity with the music of Haydn and Mozart, and possibly that of Beethoven. Except for a few private consultations with Salieri, who warned him not to set the verses of Goethe and Schiller, and personally excised any stray echoes of Haydn and Mozart he detected in the boy's compositions, this ends the tale of Franz Peter Schubert's musical education. Just before his death in 1828 he was planning to begin lessons in counterpoint.

Schubert's years at the chapel school failed to give him a solid foundation in theory, but it was there that he found the nucleus of that circle of adoring friends who not only gained for his music what currency it had during his lifetime, but also were largely responsible for his being able to keep body and soul together as long as he did. It was by the happiest chance that, wretched urchin though he was—shy, awkward, shabbily dressed, almost ugly— he drew to himself the sympathetic regard of a few of the older boys, chief among whom was Josef von Spaun. When he was about **twelve or thirteen,** Schubert first felt the urge to compose, and at this critical time Von Spaun generously pressed upon him the music paper he could not afford to buy. Among his prentice pieces were several string quartets, which he composed for performance by a little chamber group consisting of his father, two of his brothers, and himself. They met regularly Sundays and holidays. Such gatherings delighted the elder Schubert, who did not even mind being brought to book by Franz for his technical lapses. For some time, the old schoolmaster regarded his son's talent as pleasant and harmless, but when it began to interfere with the boy's studies, and he began to fear that Franz was not the stuff of which schoolmasters are made, he blew up. Franz refused to abandon his ruling passion, and his father forbade him the house. In 1812, however, Frau Schubert died, and in the course of the family mourning there was a good deal of weeping on shoulders, and the erring son was quite naturally forgiven—without promises on either side. Schubert seems to have been only mildly fond of his mother, and when his father remarried, he transferred his affection easily to his stepmother.

In 1813, Schubert's voice broke, and like Haydn, sixty-four years earlier, he became useless to the choir. While Haydn had been turned brutally into the streets of Vienna, Schubert had two courses open to him: to accept a foundation scholarship or to take a teaching job in his father's school. As the former involved going on with studies that bored this bespectacled, studious-looking, but thoroughly unintellectual youth, he chose to teach. He must have known the drudgery that awaited him, but schoolteachers were exempt from military service, he would not have to study any more, and he would have plenty of leisure for composition. For three years he served as his father's assistant, and be it said that this period, when he doubtless was getting three square meals a day as well as a certain stipend, was the most miserable of his life. Against all his natural instincts, he went about his petty daily tasks with a stolid persistence, and only rarely gave vent to the rage that was consuming him. He hated the school and everything about it—the damp urchins, the ill-smelling classroom, the maddening rote of elementary teaching.

Deficient Schubert may have been in intellect, but certainly not in courage and persistence. In this most unpromising milieu, from 1813 to 1816, he attempted almost every form of composition, setting down string quartets, five symphonies, sonatas for piano and violin, Masses and other church music, eight stage works of varying lengths and intentions (but all dismal), and more than two hundred and fifty songs. Much of this output is unimportant judged by the standards of anyone not writing an exhaustive treatise on the works of Schubert. But many of the songs are fresh and perfectly realized, and several are masterpieces: a boy of seventeen composed *Gretchen am Spinnrade*, a boy of eighteen *Der Erlkönig*. The miracle of Schubert's creation of the lied becomes all the more miraculous when it is considered that though he went on to compose many other kinds of song, he never composed any finer than these, and for a very simple reason: these are perfect. Among the other work is one of the most fragrant and guileless tributes ever paid by a young composer to his great predecessors— the Fifth Symphony, in B flat major. Only a very sophisticated pair of ears, hearing it for the first time, could distinguish it from Mozart when he is most like Haydn. There is nothing in it that would have surprised Mozart: it is thoroughly classical in structure, and for the most part in feeling. Its originality—just enough to give piquancy—is the songlike quality of some of the themes and the romantic tints in the andante. As a passing phase, ancestor worship that produces symphonies like Schubert's B flat major is all right.

After three years' teaching in his father's school, Schubert applied for the post of musical director at Laibach, a provincial capital about two hundred and fifty miles from Vienna. He was refused, and as there seemed no relief imminent, he took the revolutionary step of quitting, and so began a Bohemian, happy-go-lucky kind of life that, except for two brief attempts at conventionality, he never abandoned. First to take the innocent under his wing was the gay and temperamental Franz von Schober, an Austro-Swedish law student of good family. Von Schober not only provided lodgings and food for Schubert, but also began to show him the town. He had an apt pupil in the short, stocky youth, and within a few years Schubert was seeing more of the town than was good for him. Of much more moment was Von Schober's bringing into the jealously exclusive clique of young artists who called themselves Schubertians the eminent baritone, Johann Michael Vogl, who was more than a generation older than the rest of them. It was this strong-willed and widely admired artist, known for the severity of his taste, who brought Schubert's songs their first fame, introducing them, on every possible occasion, at the most fashionable parties in Vienna. Nor was this all: he persuaded the Kärntnerthortheater to risk ordering an opera from Schubert.*

Vogl's wirepulling at the Kärntnerthor was typical of the solicitude of the Schubertians for the pygmy god around whom they revolved. They were, in their way, as remarkable as Beethoven's patrons. Without an Archduke Rudolf or rich socialites like the Princes Lobkowitz and Kinsky, the Schubertians made up in energy and devotion what they lacked in prestige and wealth. The affluent and courted Vogl was in every way an exception among them. The others were young men trying to get along in the world —even the dilettante Von Schober toyed with various careers. During his short life Schubert lodged with various of them, and somehow, some way, they saw to it that he was usually fed and usually supplied with a piano, music paper, and plenty of verses by themselves or better poets. With them, the shy and awkward composer let himself go, and rather fancied himself strolling through the streets of Vienna at the head of these devoted henchmen, whom he treated with a kind of rough affection.

Most of the Schubertians are now mere names, even the once famous Moritz von Schwind, who painted a *Schubertiade*, one of the get-togethers at which a few guests were permitted to share with the Schubertians the pleasure of hearing some new works by their idol. There was Beethoven's friend Anselm Hüttenbrenner, and his brother Josef, who for a time literally waited on Schubert hand and foot. There was Johann Mayrhofer, a poetaster of antique cast whose immortality is secure only because Schubert made songs of forty-seven of his melancholy verses. There was Von Spaun, Schubert's first benefactor and lifelong friend, and finally the courtly Eduard von Bauernfeld, who came late into the circle. Of all these, Schubert seems to have cared most for the carefree and sparkling Von Schober and the gloomy and neurotic Mayrhofer, who ended his unhappy life by jumping out of a window for the extremely surrealist reason that he was afraid of getting cholera. Becoming a Schubertian was something of an honor, and

* This opera, *Die Zwillingsbrüder*, was duly performed for six nights, and then, like the rest of Schubert's listless stage pieces, fell into deserved desuetude.

rather more of a task, for not only did the initiates guard the circle jealously, but Schubert himself was punctilious about the qualifications of would-be joiners. "What can he do?" was his invariable question when a new name was mentioned.

In the summer of 1818, Schubert gave up his freedom for a brief period of bond servitude as music teacher at Zelész, a Hungarian seat of Count János Esterházy. At first, the novelty of life in a well-ordered and lavishly appointed establishment appealed to him, and he was enraptured by the beauty of the countryside. Unhappily, he was treated like a servant, ate apart from the family with the maids and scullions, and had to associate with people whose musical standards were low. Shortly he was sending self-commiserating notes to the Schubertians, and picturing himself as an exile from the Eden that was Vienna. But even when Zelész was becoming really hateful, life had compensations: ". . . the chambermaid very pretty, and often in my company . . ."

When Schubert returned to Vienna, his only prospect of earning a few coppers was that of giving lessons to the Esterházys, who lived in the city during the winter. His father, who had always regarded Franz' Bohemianism as a prolonged vacation, now thought it high time for him to return to schoolteaching. When Schubert flatly refused, they quarreled violently, and for three years were not on speaking terms. Franz' stepmother, with great common sense, refused to recognize this silly business, and whenever he was really in desperate straits, reached down into her money stocking to help him out. Meanwhile he skirted the abyss of pauperism with his friends clutching at his coattails. Again he lived wherever he could work and sleep; again the manuscripts piled up; again his little affairs were in a chaos, to which Anselm Hüttenbrenner vainly tried to impart some order. There were signs, however, that the Schubertians might not have him long as their private property. On February 28, 1819, on the program of a public concert, there was, for the first time, a Schubert song—the plaintive *Schäfers Klagelied*, which received a benevolent pat on the back from the formidable *Allgemeine musikalische Zeitung* of Leipzig. Vogl, too, continued his yeoman work, and that summer went on a walking tour through Upper Austria with Schubert. They made their headquarters at the old rococo town of Steyr, where they were entertained by a local musical enthusiast who suggested that

Schubert use the theme of *Die Forelle*—that vivacious apostrophe to a flashing brook trout which is still a favorite Schubert lied—in a chamber work. In a twinkling, Schubert sat down, and wrote out the four string parts of a piano quintet. Then, without making a complete score, he had it performed for his host, himself playing the piano part, which he had not yet had time to write down.

This was the incomparable Piano Quintet in A major. The earliest of Schubert's chamber works still played, it outranks in popularity even the piano quintets of Schumann and Brahms. The *"Forellen"* Quintet is a rarity of its kind, for people who insist loudly that they "can't stand" chamber music yield at once to its ingratiating charms. Although the gay and guileless melody of the song is used only in the theme and variations of the fourth movement, its darting rhythms pervade the entire five movements. It is impossible to conceive of more easily accessible music. It is picturesque in the exact sense of the word, and in many places the idea of rippling water and gleaming fish occurs voluntarily to the mind. It is romantic music, too, and its moments of poignancy are something absolutely new in music, so intimate and personal are they. It is, of course, the music of youth. These qualities rather than any masterly design give it a kind of unity, and tend to conceal the diffuseness from which the *"Forellen,"* like almost every other extended work of Schubert's, suffers.

The *"Forellen"* Quintet is easily the best known of Schubert's numerous chamber works, and few of the others can be mentioned alongside it. These few, except for a lovely fragment—the *Quartettsatz*, in C minor—belong to the last years of his life. Two piano trios, lovely in every particular, emphasize how effective the piano was in helping Schubert successfully to overcome miscalculations in design and instrumentation that often baffled him when composing for strings alone. The last three of his fourteen string quartets are quite likely to survive as delightful and easily understood examples of a genre that is still considered somewhat esoteric. Possibly the reason they are so readily got at is that Schubert either misunderstood or never gave a thought to the problems of design and balance involved in writing for four strings. His quartets are really more of his songs, with two violins, viola, and cello substituted for voice and piano. He was haunted by song in and out of season, and had the greatest difficulty in relinquishing the song

quality and coming to grips with the special demands of instrumental media. Only the captious can stand out against the sheer
melodic beauty of the A minor Quartet or the more somber, more
reflective one in D minor, part of which is based on his own song,
Tod und das Mädchen. The trouble with these beautiful collections of
melody is that they are not string-quartetistic, as, for example,
those of Mozart and Beethoven pre-eminently are. The same lack
of insight into the personality of his medium, and the same failure
to exploit its potentialities to the full, mar even the fine String
Quintet in C major, which shows, however, that in the year of his
death Schubert was beginning seriously to tackle the special
problems of string ensembles. This is no happy, feckless effusion,
no mere outpouring of song set down for five strings: it is richly
various, thoughtful, bold in harmonic combinations, and shows
that the instruments had some say in dictating texture and melody.

In 1820, two of Schubert's ill-fated operas reached the stage.
The first was a failure, and just when the second was showing signs
of mild success, the management of the Theater an der Wien,
where it was running, went bankrupt. Vienna was at the feet of
Rossini, and both the Italian and his theatrical manager were
minting money from his operas. It was in the vain hope of divert-
ing some of this golden stream into his own pockets that Schubert,
himself an ardent Rossinian, wrote operas. Nor was he easily discouraged: his pathetic attempts to interest the Viennese in his
operatic talents extended over a ten-year period, and as late as
1823 he was doggedly writing these often grandiose stage pieces—
one of them, *Fierrabras*, runs to a thousand pages of manuscript.
When Weber was in Vienna in 1822, he discussed with Schubert,
who so greatly admired *Der Freischütz* that he went around humming snatches of it, the possibility of mounting one of his operas.
The following year, however, Schubert told Weber exactly what
he thought of *Euryanthe*—"not enough melody, Herr von Weber"—
and that avenue was closed. Apparently the absurdities of Helmine
von Chézy's libretto for *Euryanthe* did not feaze Schubert, for that
same year he agreed to furnish an overture and incidental music
for another of her high-flown plays—*Rosamunde, Fürstin von Cypern*,
which made its debut at the Theater an der Wien on December 20,
1823. It ran two nights, and was discontinued forever. Much of the
music is delicious, and the piquant G major ballet, a sort of cousin-

german to the equally famous F minor *Moment musical*, trips along with inimitable delicacy.*

Schubert made little or no money from the stage, and while he toiled for it, carelessly threw away a small fortune. On March 7, 1821, at a charity concert at the Kärntnerthortheater sponsored by Ignaz Sonnleithner, a noted musical patron, *Der Erlkönig* was sung in public for the first time. Vogl's superinterpretation had to be repeated, and thereupon Leopold Sonnleithner, Ignaz' son, believing that the song could be published with profit for Schubert, approached several music publishers with the idea. He was turned down, and accordingly induced three of his friends to help him underwrite a private edition of one hundred copies. They were put on display at a musical soiree, and by the end of the evening were all sold. During the course of the year, six more folios containing nineteen songs were issued by this private publishing group. Out of the profits not only were Schubert's debts paid, but he was also presented with a considerable sum of money. Had he held on to the copyright, he might have had a comfortable income for life. But he was without a trace of business acumen, and in 1823— seemingly because he no longer wished to be bothered with periodic settlings of account with Anton Diabelli, who had engraved and printed the seven folios—he sold the plates and copyrights to the publisher for the equivalent of $350. He had thoughtlessly thrown away the best chance he ever had to earn a decent livelihood.

As some palliation for this act of sheer stupidity, it can be urged that when Schubert wrote away his rights in February, 1823, he was desperate. During the preceding year he had begun to ail, and by New Year's the illness declared itself so violently that he was taken to a hospital. He was suffering from syphilis, evidently in an advanced stage, for in a brief time he lost much of his hair, and had to wear a wig. He was thereafter from time to time under the care of venereal specialists. As long as he pursued the proper treatment, he seemed well enough, but the careless fellow was quite as incapable of adhering to a strict health regimen as he was of applying himself to a stiff problem in the esthetics of composition. He would dissipate, overdrink, neglect his medicine, and the dis-

* The *Rosamunde* music, long forgotten, was unearthed in Vienna in 1867 by Sir Arthur Sullivan and Sir George Grove.

ease would prostrate him. Eventually his hitherto sunny disposition succumbed to the strain: he had moods of irritability, of moroseness and gloom, alternating with outbursts of bravado. Occasionally he vented his despair in his music, so much so indeed that a Vienna musical organization wrote him a polite note, begging him to make his compositions less gloomy.

Schubert had a right to be gloomy. With the autumn of 1822, bad luck came to hound him: his health was on the downgrade, the managers consistently refused to stage his operas, and the Gesellschaft der Musikfreunde blackballed him for membership. Yet it was about this time that he was offered the post of organist at the imperial chapel, and refused it for no more apparent reason than that he did not want to tie himself down in any way. His election as honorary member of the musical societies of Graz and Linz was some compensation for the slight from Vienna. It is not known how he showed his appreciation to Linz, but to Graz he decided to present a symphony. He set to work in October, 1822, wrote two movements, sketched a third and fourth, orchestrated nine bars of the third movement—a scherzo—and then suddenly tired of the whole thing and sent it to Graz. There it eventually passed into the hands of Anselm Hüttenbrenner, who tucked it away in his desk for forty-three years. Hüttenbrenner was an ancient when Johann Franz von Herbeck, the conductor of the Vienna Gesellschaft concerts, looked him up in Graz in 1865, hinting that he would like to present a new work by Schubert. "I have many of his manuscripts," was Hüttenbrenner's reply, which, in view of the fact that the whereabouts of many Schubert works is still unknown, may be deemed significant. Hüttenbrenner handed Von Herbeck the manuscript of the 1822 symphony, and it was first performed on December 17, 1865, at a Gesellschaft concert.

The "Unfinished" Symphony, thus happily unearthed, is the noblest fragment in music. It is certainly the most popular of Schubert's orchestral works. Only six years had elapsed since the B flat Symphony, that beautiful and perfectly behaved bow to the past, and in the interval he had composed a transitional symphony of no great distinction. The "Unfinished," actually Schubert's seventh, shows a development of his own characteristic symphonic idiom that is as baffling to uncritical Schubert devotees as to textbook critics. While the Fifth Symphony was but a classical recreation, the "Unfinished" is undilute Schubert—romantic music from beginning to end. The first movement opens gloomily and agitatedly (a sort of spiritual pacing the floor), and then moves by an inspired *coup de théâtre* into one of his most opulent and poignant melodies.* It is possibly the most famous single movement in symphonic literature, for reasons by no means disgraceful to the popular taste: no amount of hackneying has been able to destroy its fresh and wistful charm. The second movement is not so indisputably eternal—a happy inspiration, yes, but wanting the breath-taking white magic of the first. Critics have stood on their heads trying to prove that these two movements in themselves constitute a musical whole, but without derogation to what Schubert found enthusiasm to compose, it can be stated dogmatically that they do no such thing. They are as clearly part of a larger design as the choir of Beauvais is part of a great cathedral church that was never built. The "Unfinished" Symphony is indeed the noblest fragment in music.

After the final wrecking of his operatic career, Schubert went again, in May, 1824, to stay with the Esterházys at Zelész. Here he seems to have occupied the same servile position he had six years before. This did not prevent him, legend has it, from raising his eyes to a daughter of the house, the seventeen-year-old Countess Karolin. Never has a larger bubble been blown from a smaller pipe, for the story that Schubert was deeply enamored of this high-born adolescent rests flimsily on two statements, only one of which can be authenticated. It is said that the Countess once asked him why he had never dedicated anything to her, and he replied, "Why, because everything *is* dedicated to you." Certain it is that he wrote to Moritz von Schwind: "In spite of the attraction of a certain star, I am longing most terribly for Vienna." The first remark, if it was ever made, is a piece of stereotyped gallantry; the expression in the letter is hardly that of a lovelorn man. In the meager tale of Schubert's loves, there is far more likelihood that he was deeply attached to Therese Grob, who as little more than a child had sung in one of his early Masses. He continued to walk out with her for some years, but in 1820 she married a rich middle-

---

* By torturing the rhythm of this melody into waltz time, and setting it to moronic words, the perpetrators of *Blossom Time* evolved one of the great smash-hit ballads of all time.

aged baker, presumably after realizing that Schubert would never be able to support her. He himself once remarked that he would have married Therese if his finances had permitted. After 1822, when his disease manifested itself, Schubert never again spoke of marrying. There is no evidence that being denied the joys of domesticity ever bothered him very much: here, as in his relations with his friends, he was too absorbed in music to have any strong desire to divide his allegiance.

The year 1825 was, after all the troubles of the past few years, one of singular happiness for Schubert. His health was much improved, he managed to sell some of his songs for a fair price—Artaria paid him the equivalent of $100 for his settings of Walter Scott, including the famous *Ave Maria**—and in the summer he again tramped through Upper Austria and the Tirol with Vogl. Sir George Grove, the music lexicographer, firmly believed that while at Gastein Schubert completed a "Grand Symphony" in C major. If he did, it is lost. But among the music he certainly composed on this trip was the Piano Sonata in A minor (Opus 42).

Schubert's piano music is a microcosm of his virtues and vices as a composer. The larger works—the two fantasias and the sonatas—are much less often heard than the smaller ones, and not merely because they offer more technical problems. They are far less successful. In the sonatas, Schubert stuck manfully to classical form, adorned it with lovely melodies, and just when a Mozart or a Beethoven would have been most absorbed in the possibilities of development and recapitulation, succumbed to boredom. His regrettable procedure was to lengthen the movement without adding anything; for instance, he seems often to have conceived of recapitulation as nothing but slavish repetition in another key. Such maundering is ruinous to the design, and no amount of inspired melody can triumph over it. Of his more than twenty sonatas, not one lacks moments of poignant lyricism—and not one lacks desert wastes. Of special loveliness are one in A major (Opus 120) and one in A minor, both belonging to 1825; on a more majestic scale are the three so-called "Grand Sonatas," all written in the year of Schubert's death, more intellectual in their contours, richer in texture, and altogether more profound in material. They, too, have their moments of high enchantment: the rondo of the A major and

---

* The words are a German translation of Ellen's prayer from *The Lady of the Lake.*

the andante sostenuto of the B flat major come immediately to mind. Of the two fantasias, the "Wanderer" is the more often discussed and the less played: it is an interminable, dreary piece of music with a certain grandiosity that often enough degenerates into meaningless and apparently automatic shuttling. The G major Fantasia, a far superior piece, has a minimum of padding and many exquisite pages, including a minuet as lovely in its way as that from *Don Giovanni*.

The smaller piano works—impromptus, *moments musicaux*, waltzes, and other dances—are another matter. Just as, despite the songs of his predecessors, Schubert may be said without exaggeration to have created the lied, so, too, he may be said to have created the kind of short piano piece on which Schumann, Chopin, and Brahms lavished some of their loveliest inspirations. Freed from the bondage of classical forms, Schubert abandoned himself completely to his melodies. These pieces are almost never too long, for their length was truly dictated by the requirements of the material. They are uncomplicated, transparent, easy to listen to, and a delight to play. Some of them are as lyric as the little pieces Mendelssohr. called *Lieder ohne Worte*; others are pure dance, ancestors of the waltzes of Chopin and Brahms; finally, certain of the impromptus have a dramatic character that Schubert did not often attain. The repertoire will never be too crowded for these small but perfect compositions, some of which are already locked enduringly in the hearts of mankind.

Many of these delectable trifles were among the flood of compositions that issued without stint from Schubert's pen during the otherwise almost completely uneventful last three years of his life. Two fine string quartets belong to 1826, during which, on a single day, he tossed off *Hark, Hark, the Lark!* and *Who is Sylvia?* The great song cycle *Die Winterreise* came in 1827, the string quintet, the "Grand Sonatas," and the songs later collected as *Schwanengesang* in 1828. Schubert's finances were again all but nonexistent, and his health was bad. He had fallen once more into a careless way of living, drinking freely, keeping late hours, and neglecting his treatments, and so had frequent relapses. He tried halfheartedly to better his position, but in vain. The post of vice-*Hofkapellmeister* slipped through his fingers: he was not a favorite at court. The conductorship of the Kärntnerthortheater, which was almost in the bag, went to another because Schubert refused to play local politics. And so on—an increasingly depressing chronicle. Early in March, 1827, Anselm Hüttenbrenner showed the dying Beethoven a large number of Schubert's songs, which so filled him with generous admiration that he burst out excitedly: "Certainly Schubert has the divine spark!" At Beethoven's request, Schubert went twice to see him, the first time with Hüttenbrenner. Then it was that Beethoven is reputed to have said to them: "You, Anselm, have my mind, but Franz has my soul." On Schubert's second visit, Beethoven was too weak to talk, and the motions he made were pathetically futile. Schubert was overcome with emotion, and rushed from the house. Three weeks later he was a torchbearer at Beethoven's funeral.

The year 1828 began propitiously. Schubert's health was definitely better, he sold a few compositions at a tithe of their value, and, besides, he seems to have been planning an unusually long-range, large-scale program of work. He began with a cantata along Handelian lines (he appears to have fallen heir to Beethoven's Handel scores, and to have been studying them), and in March, on the anniversary of Beethoven's death, gave his first and only public concert, the program being made up exclusively of his own works. He was so well received that it is a wonder he never tried the experiment again. With the proceeds—rather more than $150 —he lived high for a while, and it is characteristic of his careless generosity that he went a second time to hear Paganini merely for the pleasure of treating a friend even poorer than himself.

March, 1828, was doubly remarkable, for it was also then that Schubert began the composition of the C major Symphony, which many consider his masterpiece. It was written at breakneck speed, put into rehearsal by the Gesellschaft der Musikfreunde, and then shelved as too long and too difficult. It lay among his brother Ferdinand's papers until 1838, when it was rescued by Robert Schumann, and handed over to Mendelssohn, who first performed it at Leipzig the same year. In rejecting the C major Symphony, the Gesellschaft was right in one respect: no amount of referring to it as "the symphony of heavenly length" can alter the fact that it is far too long. Yet there is ample evidence that Schubert, doubtless because his friends constantly urged him to study Beethoven's methods of work, labored over this symphony. The 218-page manuscript is by no means the miraculously fair copy he usually provided: it is starred with erasures and penknife marks—second and third thoughts, corrections.

The C major Symphony is Schubert's masterpiece, but not a Schubertian masterpiece. It is a big, impressive work, often restless and impassioned, dark and tragic in its harmonies, and altogether planned on a vastness of scale that the impatient Schubert must have needed a new stamina to handle. It is orchestrated with unusual care and boldness, and shows an exquisite sensitivity to the color range of the instruments separately and in combination. Schubert aimed at new effects, and achieved them with ease and a minimum of miscalculation—the "digression" for trombones pianissimo in the first movement is a peculiarly magical example. The main themes throughout, particularly the first subjects of the andante and the andante con moto, are the stuff of which great music can be made, utterly beautiful in themselves and susceptible of infinite development. But alas! it was again on the rock of development that Schubert foundered. After proving conclusively that he could write page after page of great symphonic music, he seems to have unfocused his attention on the extremely difficult business at hand, and to have lapsed into a vein of irrelevant garrulousness. Thus, the C major concludes on a maundering, inconsequential note after a beginning as promising as any symphony ever had.

As we have seen, the C major Symphony was but one great work in a year of great works. Poverty and adversity seemed to spur Schubert on. By the summer of 1828, he realized sadly that he would have to forgo his vacation in the country: "Money and weather are both against me," he wrote with bitter humor. In September, however, he was so run down that his physician insisted on more fresh air and exercise. Accordingly, he took a brief walking tour in the Viennese countryside, lived abstemiously, and felt a new access of animal spirits. Nevertheless, on his return home, he was at once stricken by his old complaint, this time accompanied by dire mental concomitants: he thought that he was being poisoned; he walked around for hours in a complete daze. Amid this agony of mind and body, the passion for his art burned undamped. Only a fortnight before the end, he arranged to take lessons in counterpoint from Simon Sechter, an eminent theorist who,

twenty-seven years later, was to become the teacher of Anton
Bruckner. On November 11, he wrote a pathetic letter to Von
Schober, telling him of violent nausea and asking for some novels
by James Fenimore Cooper. Three days later, he was able to discuss a new libretto, but by evening was delirious. The next day
this new turn for the worse was diagnosed as typhus, the type disease of city slums. In his feverish ravings he uttered the name of
Beethoven: apparently, to Schubert's poor tortured mind, the fact
that Beethoven was not with him meant that he had been buried
alive. The agony finally ended on Wednesday, November 19, 1828.

They buried him the following Friday. He who had in his lifetime of genius earned less than the equivalent of $3000, left an
"estate"—old clothes and old music, mostly—too small to pay for
even the poorest funeral. His father and his brother Ferdinand
strapped themselves to bury him where they were convinced he
would have preferred to be—as near Beethoven's grave as possible. Early in 1829, from the proceeds of some special concerts, a
monument was erected back of the grave, with the following epitaph from the pen of Schubert's friend the poet Grillparzer:

MUSIC HAS HERE ENTOMBED A RICH TREASURE
BUT STILL FAIRER HOPES

The epitaph caused violent controversies at the time, but in the
main it was eminently fair. Today no one denies that much of
Schubert's music is "a rich treasure," and those who are realistic
even about their idols will admit that "still fairer hopes" is equally
just—and not merely in the way Grillparzer meant it. He was
mourning for this Keats of music, cut off thus untimely. We mourn,
too, that (unlike Keats) Schubert, with perhaps the richest natural
endowment ever vouchsafed a musical artist, used it with complete
success only in the realm of the song. He was, as Liszt said of him,
"the most poetic of all musicians." Had he but been the most
musicianly as well, he might indeed be where he would most want
to be—next to Beethoven.

Chapter XI

Felix Mendelssohn-Bartholdy

(Hamburg, February 3, 1809–November 4, 1847, Leipzig)

THE story of Felix Mendelssohn is that of a Prince Charming. When he was born, amid the rejoicings and *Gemüthlichkeit* attending the birth of an heir to a prosperous Jewish family, the good fairies were ranged around his cradle. One of them gave him riches, another beauty, another charm. Their sisters on the other side of the cradle were not to be outdone, and from them the baby received genius, a capacity for hard work, a noble character, and a strong constitution. The conclave of fairy godmothers was about to break up in complacent jollification when a silvery but unfamiliar voice was heard: it belonged, alas! to a fairy whom they had thoughtlessly forgotten to invite. In the most dulcet of tones, she declared that she, too, had a gift for the child. "Throughout his life," she purred, "I shall see to it that he does everything easily and without effort." Her more dull-witted sisters thought this the best gift of all. The brighter ones merely pursed their lips.

Mendelssohn's is the happiest life in musical history. He was brought up in a cultivated household by sympathetic parents who from the very beginning fostered his musical ambitions. At a tender age he enjoyed the intimate friendship of the undisputed literary dictator of Europe, and all his life he had many warm—and influential—friends whose principal object in life seems to have been to serve him. Success came to him in the fullest measure at an absurdly early age, and at twenty-six he occupied the most important post in musical Germany. He married, without the slightest opposition, the woman of his choice—a pretty, intelligent, and talented girl with whom he led a life of unblemished happiness, heightened, moreover, by five delightful children. Before reaching young middle age, he was the most revered composer in Europe, and just when the first real clouds appeared on the horizon of his happiness, he died speedily and without pain.

Mendelssohn's ancestry was distinguished. His grandfather, Moses Mendelssohn, was called "the modern Plato": one of his philosophical books had been translated into at least eight languages, and Mirabeau, in the midst of stage-managing the French Revolution, found time to praise it. His lifelong battle to effect a sympathetic understanding between Jews and Christians was waged so eloquently that his son Abraham, Felix' father, became a Lutheran, appending Bartholdy to his surname to distinguish himself from Mendelssohns still adhering to the Jewish faith. This estimable man, a successful banker and connoisseur of ideas, had a lively sense of his own sterling mediocrity: after Felix had become famous he once gently complained, "I used to be the son of my father, and now I'm the father of my son."

Abraham Mendelssohn married a rich, amiable, and intelligent girl, and they set up housekeeping at Hamburg. Their first child was a girl, Fanny, who became a talented pianist and a composer of sorts. Felix appeared next on the scene. When he was three years old, the family fled to Berlin in the path of Napoleon's Russiabound legions, and there it was that the tiny lad began his studies. There was nothing provincial or restricted about the curriculum laid down by the doting but thoughtful parents for their wonderful children. Their days were crowded with lessons of all sorts—piano, violin, harmony, drawing, languages—so crowded, in fact, that Felix later said that he lived in anticipation of Sunday, for that meant he would not have to get up at five o'clock in the morning to work. Nevertheless, he responded to this cramming system as a duck does to water, and in a very short time was sitting easily among the adults, discussing the most learned questions with the gravity of the young Jesus disputing with the rabbis of the Temple. Nor was his moral education likely to be neglected in so comprehensive a schooling: here, too, he seems to have had a natural adaptability—he never had to struggle to be good. A work schedule that would drive a modern child berserk produced only the happiest results in him, doubtless because the family also knew how to have a good time. There is testimony galore—the Mendelssohns entertained lavishly and often—that the house resounded with gaiety and fun. There were plenty of games, plenty of good talk, plenty of good things to eat. Plenty, indeed, was the keynote of the Mendelssohn home, and the center of all its activity was the boy Felix—a slender, high-strung child, with great dark eyes and a mop of curly brown hair, mercurial, sensitive, bubbling over with high spirits.

Felix quickly established himself as Mozart's only rival as far as musical precocity was concerned. On October 28, 1818, he made his first public appearance, as a pianist in a concerto for two horns and piano. For some time he had been taking harmony and composition lessons from Carl Friedrich Zelter, the director of the Singakademie, which he entered in 1819 as an alto. By the end of the next year, when he was eleven years old, he had composed more than sixty separate pieces, among them a cantata and a little *Lustspiel* in three scenes. The next five years teem with incredible musical productivity, and even before this period reached its term, Mendelssohn had achieved a facility and finish of technique beyond which progress was impossible. The difference between his now unplayed *juvenilia* and the best works of his maturity is that the former spin out prosy commonplaces with uncanny adroitness while the latter have real distinction of musical idea. A C minor Symphony, actually the thirteenth he had composed, but the first he was willing to own up to, is very occasionally revived: it is pleasant, uneventful stuff, with, however, a minuet of considerable verve and grace. Meanwhile, the lad developed rapidly as a pianist, and in 1824 Ignaz Moscheles, at thirty already a most distinguished virtuoso and pedagogue, was persuaded to give him a few lessons. Moscheles agreed with extreme diffidence, saying, "If he wishes to take a hint from me as to anything new to him, he can easily do so; but he stands in no need of lessons." Already Felix was a poised and competent conductor. For some years, it was the Mendelssohns' custom to give musical parties on alternate Sundays, when the children* joined a small group of professional musicians in programs that always included at least one of Felix' compositions. Even while still too short to be seen above the instruments without standing on a stool, the boy always took the baton on these occasions.

In May, 1821, Mendelssohn met Weber, who was in Berlin superintending the rehearsals of *Der Freischütz*, and was present at the memorable *première* that ushered in a new era in German music. Responding excitedly to the novel style, with its glowing color and romantic atmosphere, he conceived a lifelong admiration for Weber, whose idiom he adapted lavishly, particularly in his overtures.

* There were two children younger than Fanny and Felix: Rebecka, who sang, and Paul, who played the cello.

After meeting Weber, Mendelssohn within a very few years was on friendly terms with many of the most famous personages in Europe. In November, 1821, he visited Weimar for the first time, and spent more than a fortnight as Goethe's guest. When they first met, Goethe asked the boy to play something for him. "Shall it be the most beautiful music in the world?" Felix asked, as he sat down to the piano and played the minuet from *Don Giovanni*. The relationship between the seventy-two-year-old philosopher-poet and the twelve-year-old composer was neither artificial nor perfunctory: it was a real friendship that lasted until Goethe's death in 1832. Several years later, Mendelssohn accompanied his father to Paris, where he made many new acquaintances, among them Rossini and Meyerbeer. The formidable Cherubini, after astounding his confreres by approving of the lad, with austerely pedantic condescension invited him to set a Kyrie for five voices and orchestra. Mendelssohn, who was a polite child, did so, and contented himself with saying of the old Italian that he was an "extinct volcano, still throwing out occasional flashes and sparks, but quite covered with ashes and stones." For French music in general he felt nothing but the most profound scorn.

Only one magnifico stood out against Mendelssohn's overwhelming charm and precocious gifts: Spontini, still smarting from his defeat at Weber's hands, used his all-powerful position in Berlin to prevent *Die Hochzeit des Camacho*, a two-act opera Felix had completed on his return from Paris, from being given at the Hofoper. Spontini, who was mortally afraid of new talent, tried to discourage him with pompous criticism. "My friend," he said, pointing to the dome of a church, "you lack big ideas—big like that dome." Maybe Spontini was right: Mendelssohn himself was disappointed in the opera when it finally reached the stage in 1827, and was not noticeably crushed when, despite popular acclaim, it was withdrawn after the *première*. Even the overture, still heard now and then, is a jejune bit.

Up to 1826 Mendelssohn's compositions had not unnaturally been distinguished by little more than facility and earnestness. *Wunderkinder* have a disheartening way of petering out, and even though no composer except Mozart did much of importance before he was twenty, Mendelssohn's admirers must already have been wondering whether the seventeen-year-old was to develop into something more than a surpassingly competent third-rater. They had not long to wait, for even then he was working on a masterpiece. He and his sisters had been reading Shakespeare, and a whole new world of magic had been opened up to him. Nothing fired his imagination more than the lightness and elfin fantasy of *A Midsummer Night's Dream*. He set down his musical impressions in a piano duet, which sounded so promising that he decided to orchestrate it as an overture. It was first performed privately in the *Gartenhaus* of the Mendelssohns' new home at 3, Leipziger-strasse, for many years a rendezvous of musicians and artists from all over Europe. Six months later, in February, 1827, Felix drove more than eighty miles through a blinding snowstorm to conduct the public *première* at Stettin.

The overture to *A Midsummer Night's Dream* became during Mendelssohn's life, and has ever since remained, the best loved of his purely orchestral compositions. After a few evocative chords, it opens with a rippling staccato figure that instantly sets the scene in Fairyland, and for the most obvious of reasons—no mortal could dance to this aerial rhythm. Momentarily the dance is interrupted by a sweetly dissonant chord, there is a hint of hurly-burly, and we hear the horns of Duke Theseus. He and his train pass by; the dancers resume, only to be crowded from the scene by the mortal lovers. With nice calculation, Mendelssohn has given these young people a more earthbound theme, a broadly romantic melody of Weberian character that not only affords a telling musical contrast, but also beautifully points up their muddled loves. What can be more natural at this point than to introduce a reference to Bottom and the other clownish actors by a rustic dance with the veriest hint of peasant buskins? The rest of the overture is made up of recapitulation and development of these themes. All is exquisitely designed, thought out with flawless logic, and reverently adapted to the spirit of Shakespeare's play. The harmonies throughout are bold without being obtrusive. They were revolutionary in Mendelssohn's time, and have only now become commonplaces. The orchestration is equally original. Of this overture, Bernard Shaw, in 1892, wrote with evident surprise: "One can actually feel the novelty now, after sixty-six years." And today, after almost sixty years more, though we can no longer experience it as a novelty, its true originality keeps it fresh. Altogether, it is an amazing composition for a boy of seventeen.

It is all the more amazing when considered as merely one of the coruscations of a life abnormal only in its extreme activity. Before the overture was finished, Mendelssohn had matriculated at the University of Berlin, where he listened with relish to Hegel's lectures on the esthetics of music. Moreover, he went about building his physique as conscientiously as his mind, and became a fine swimmer and rider. He danced elegantly, played a stiff game of billiards, and bowled on the green. In short, he had the accomplishments of a gentleman, and the graces as well. The world of art and fashion came to 3, Leipzigerstrasse, and as Mendelssohn reached young manhood, he assumed with ease a leading role in these gatherings, and bore with equanimity the penalty of being the cynosure of all eyes. With his great musical future almost upon him, he became a better than mediocre water-colorist, and developed his linguistic aptitude (he was the first to translate Terence into German in the original meter). If in these early years he was not the most famous person at the parties, he was the most precocious in genius, the most varied in talent. The conversation must have been worth listening to: Heine's alone would have made any soiree memorable, and the presence of Alexander von Humboldt, scientist and world traveler, Bettina von Arnim, Wilhelm Müller, Hegel, and the macabre Paganini, trailing clouds of spurious glory, guaranteed variety.

As if this were not enough, Mendelssohn, in the last months of 1827, formed a choir of sixteen picked voices to meet weekly at his home and practice the *Matthew Passion*. Even as a child, he had been passionately devoted to the neglected masterpieces of the old Thomascantor, and now was stung into action by the casual remark of another musician that "Bach is a mere arithmetical exercise." Mendelssohn knew the *Passion* by heart, and soon his own enthusiasm was communicated to the little group. By the end of 1828, they were determined that the work should be given by the Singakademie, where his old teacher, Zelter, still reigned as director. Despite Mendelssohn's own feeling that the work's huge physical requirements and the indifference of the public were cogent arguments for not pushing production plans, in which opinion he was supported by his family and several of his friends, he allowed

his own devotion to the music and the crusading zeal of the versatile actor-singer, Eduard Devrient, to propel his reluctant feet to
the Singakademie, where he hesitatingly stammered out the proposal. At first, Zelter was opposed, but when Devrient joined his
own pleas to Mendelssohn's, the day was won. Zelter, having given
his word, threw the whole force of the Singakademie behind the
production. The public was so curious about the novel doings that
it flocked to the rehearsals. For the performance itself, on March
11, 1829, with Mendelssohn conducting, more than a thousand
were turned away. It was the first performance of the *Matthew
Passion* outside Leipzig since Bach's death almost eighty years
before.

From these casual beginnings sprang the dissemination of what
has proved the most fruitful musical influence of modern times.
Others, including Schumann, soon joined the cause of Bach—it
really was a cause in those days—and within a century Bach has
changed in the public mind from "a mere arithmetical exercise"
to a position where he is acclaimed, with pardonable inaccuracy,
as the Father of Music. We who take our Bach for granted as one
of the staples of popular musical entertainment can scarcely realize that Mendelssohn and his scant cohorts were in the most real
sense pioneers: the first steps in this revival took courage, and often
aroused antagonism. There was even some display of hostility
against Mendelssohn over the first performance of the *Passion*. Fortunately, he was fully aware of the importance of the task he was
undertaking, and was resolved to brook no opposition in preaching
his new gospel. He was proud of his part in the business, and once
pointed out that "it was an actor and a Jew who restored this
great Christian work to the people." This seems to have been the
only time he ever referred to his race, for having been baptized a
Lutheran, he always thought of himself as a Christian.

After conducting a second performance of the *Matthew Passion*
on Bach's birthday, Mendelssohn took ship for England, embark-
ing at Hamburg and reaching London four days later. He arrived
at the height of the opera season, and for a time did nothing but
frequent Covent Garden and the theaters. He heard Malibran as
Desdemona in Rossini's *Otello*; he saw Kemble as Hamlet, and
deplored the performance—too many cuts for such a strict Shakespearean. It was not until late in May that he got around to making

his English debut, conducting his own C minor Symphony from the piano at a Philharmonic concert. It was a heart-warming occasion, especially after the recent hostility of a bloc of Berlin musicians—act one, in fact, of that long-drawn-out love affair between Mendelssohn and the English public that is still going strong. A few days later, dressed in "very long white trousers, brown silk waistcoat, black necktie, and blue dress coat," he played Weber's *Conzertstück* "with no music before him," as *The Times* put it. Everywhere the crowds succumbed to his charm, and soon he was writing home, "London life suits me exactly": the English did not know much about music, but they knew what they liked, and they liked Mendelssohn. As the trip to England was originally planned by his father as but the first stage in a grand tour, in the summer Mendelssohn toured Scotland and Wales, whose wild scenery and ruined abbeys gave him ideas that he later used in such musical landscapes as those in the "Scotch" Symphony and *Fingal's Cave*. Toward the end of the year, he was back in the cooler atmosphere of Berlin, with his reputation completely established in the British Isles. He was not yet twenty-one years old.

Nursing a lame knee sustained in a carriage accident in London, Mendelssohn improved the shining hours by composing the "Reformation" Symphony to commemorate the tercentenary of the Augsburg Confession. It turned out to be solid, pompous music with a setting of *Ein feste Burg* imbedded in the last movement. Political and religious disturbances prevented its performance in Germany in 1830; the good sense of a Paris orchestra let it get no farther than rehearsal in 1832; today a revival of this windy tract is rightly resented.

Early in 1830, Mendelssohn was offered a specially created professorship of music at the University of Berlin, but refused it: Switzerland and Italy remained to be done, and the last thing in the world he wanted was to be tied down. An undignified case of measles delayed his departure, but in May he was at last ready. Halting at Weimar for what proved to be his last visit with Goethe, and stopping en route at the best houses and consorting with the best people, he proceeded by such easy stages that he did not arrive in Rome until November. Here he visited the art museums, haunted the Sistine Chapel, and duly astonished the Roman musicians with his fluid musicianship. He could not get the Gregorian chant through his Lutheran head—in fact, the subtleties of the Roman service were incomprehensible to his irascibly Protestant temper. He managed to unearth a few fine things in Palestrina, as he admitted to Baini, the most erudite of latter-day Palestrinians. In general, however, Rome wore as alien an aspect to Mendelssohn as it had to an Augustinian monk named Martin Luther, three hundred years before. Appropriately, it was in this winter city that he completed the first version of the somber *Fingal's Cave*.

Naples appealed to him more—though even there he longed for London—and its lightness and unthinking gaiety echo through some of his later compositions. After six weeks' delicious dawdling, Mendelssohn remembered that he was a German, and started north. In Milan he played Mozart to the composer's son Karl. In Switzerland he amazed some monks by introducing them to the organ fugues of Bach, a composer previously unknown to them. September found him hobnobbing with the King of Bavaria in Munich, where he composed, and played for the first time, his second-rate G minor Piano Concerto. Before Christmas he was in Paris, which proved less susceptible to his charms than London. The Société des Concerts du Conservatoire did the overture to *A Midsummer Night's Dream*, balked at the "Reformation" Symphony —and left Mendelssohn severely alone for eleven years. The coolness of Paris was disheartening enough, but here, too, he received news that Goethe had died at Weimar. Around Mendelssohn in Paris shone the glitter of mid-nineteenth-century music: Liszt, himself to rule at Weimar before many years had passed, Chopin, Meyerbeer, and Ole Bull, half genius, half charlatan, heir to Paganini's crown. Mendelssohn lingered in Paris for four months, living the life of a well-behaved society butterfly, but completely failing to establish himself musically.

In April, 1832, Mendelssohn reached London again. The "smoky nest" he had pined for in Naples now showed its fairest face, and one he had not previously seen: the weather was balmy, the lilacs were in blossom—and he fell more than ever in love with the city. He was received with open arms, and responded by a fine burst of musical activity, playing both piano and organ in public, arranging various of his pieces (notably Book I of the *Lieder ohne Worte*) for publication, and composing the *Capriccio brillant*, a clever bravura piece for piano and orchestra. Most important, on May 14,

the Philharmonic performed the "Hebrides" Overture. Mendelssohn was not satisfied with it: he at once revised it radically, and
by the end of June had finished what was essentially a new work.
Known under a variety of titles, among them *Fingal's Cave*, the
"Hebrides" Overture disputes place with that to *A Midsummer
Night's Dream* in quality. We have the composer's own testimony
that the lapping figure with which it opens came into his mind
during his visit to Fingal's Cave in the remote Hebrides. Wagner,
with his genius for trivializing the truth, sneeringly called the overture an aquarelle. Actually, it is one of the great seascapes of music.
The severity and aptness of the themes, unquestionably among
Mendelssohn's happiest inspirations, the utter sufficiency of the development, and the uncanny balancing of the instruments—all
contribute to a formal perfection that has, as Tovey says, "the vital
and inevitable unexpectedness of the classics." In the "Hebrides"
Mendelssohn wins the right to be called a great composer, for
starting with material of surpassing beauty and originality, he lovingly molds it into a form exactly suited to its requirements.

Mendelssohn was still in London when news reached him of
Zelter's death: this meant that the directorship of the Singakademie, a post of great prestige, was open. On returning to Berlin, he
indicated that he would accept the position if elected, but refused
to push his candidacy against that of Carl Friedrich Rungenhagen,
long Zelter's first aide. It turned out that assuming this passive
role was the most tactful thing Mendelssohn could have done: he
was not liked among the petty, spiteful musicians of the Prussian
capital, and Rungenhagen's election was all but certain from the
beginning. Mendelssohn accepted his overwhelming defeat calmly,
but it clouded his temper, and made him eager to leave Berlin for a
more congenial arena. An offer to conduct the important Lower
Rhine Festival at Düsseldorf the following spring assuaged his
vexed spirit. Close on its heels came a most flattering bid from the
London Philharmonic, accompanied by a hundred-guinea order
for a new symphony and other pieces. He at once began completing an A major symphony he had begun in Italy in 1831. Oddly
enough for so facile a composer, the process caused him acute
agony of mind. He literally wrestled with the materials, and did
not lay his pen aside until March 13, 1833.

The "Italian" Symphony, produced in (for Mendelssohn) such

long-drawn-out travail, shows no sign of effort. Its inspired spontaneity never flags, and in a certain sense the pace never falters. It begins with an allegro and ends with a presto, and though the middle movements are in slower tempos, the information is subtly conveyed that the rapid pace will shortly be resumed. This sense of a pervasive motion germane to the character of the symphony as a whole is not unique with Mendelssohn, but as one element of unity he has used it here with a complete success that has often eluded more profound musical thinkers. Yet the "Italian" Symphony does not lack variety: the first movement rushes along with gay and assertive impetuosity; the andante is a processional, dignified but not solemn, with a staccato suggestion that the marchers are impatient to get on to the lighter business of the day; they do so via a lyrical but practical moderato—and go into their dance. It is one of the enigmas of musical history that Mendelssohn was never satisfied with this saltarello, and until his death nursed hopes of revising it. Fortunately, he never touched it, for it is perfect as it stands—the most lighthearted and swift-footed of all symphonic dances. In hearing it, one thinks immediately of that other great symphonic dance of a more robust people—the gigantic kermis that closes the A major Symphony of Ludwig van Beethoven. Mendelssohn's is a supremely fitting conclusion to an "Italian" symphony.

First produced under the composer's baton on May 13, 1833, the "Italian" delighted the Londoners, and when three days later he left to keep his date at Düsseldorf, it was with a promise to return immediately the Rhine Festival was over. Exalted by the triumph of a work of which he had entertained the darkest misgivings, he carried all before him at Düsseldorf. It has been said that Mendelssohn was the first conductor to play upon the orchestra as upon a single instrument, and his Rhenish debut was indeed impressive. The programs included Beethoven's "Pastoral" Symphony, his own noisy "Trumpet" Overture, and a complete performance of *Israel in Egypt* in its original form—something of a slap at the Berlin Singakademie, which had lately felt called upon to reorchestrate Handel. Mendelssohn's pleasure over the warm recognition of his talents was intensified by the fact that his father, who had begun to lose his sight, was able to be present. It knew no bounds when that recognition took the form of an invitation to become musical director at Düsseldorf for three years. Mendelssohn accepted at once, and after several weeks in London with his father—a frank vacation they both enjoyed—returned to the scene of his new activities.

With his accustomed energy, Mendelssohn rolled up his sleeves, and began to reorganize Düsseldorf music from top to bottom. First came the church music: "Not one tolerable solemn mass, and not a single one of the old Italian masters; nothing but modern dross" was to be found in the town, so he drove to Elberfeld, Bonn, and Cologne, and within a few days was back with a carriageload of Palestrina, Di Lasso, Pergolesi, and Leonardo Leo. After that, there were—at least during Mendelssohn's incumbency—no more "scandalous" Masses heard in Düsseldorf. He was successful in raising the standard of music heard in the concert rooms, but at the opera house he struck a snag. He mounted *Don Giovanni* and *Le Nozze di Figaro*, Cherubini's *Deux Journées*, and *Egmont* with Beethoven's incidental music. But the opera audiences objected to the severity of his taste, and also to the scaling-up of the prices. There was a little revolution in Düsseldorf, and Mendelssohn resigned from active direction of the opera before he was deposed. Opera had never been his métier: his own tentative experiments had been failures, and like Beethoven, he objected to the loose tone of most librettos. This new rebuff steeled him in a resolve to turn to the more genial atmosphere of the oratorio. The very month he resigned from the opera he began working in this, to him, new field, sketching the outlines of an ambitious work to be known as *St. Paul*, which took two years to complete.

In general, Mendelssohn's life at Düsseldorf was extremely happy, with only the pettiest of difficulties to surmount: the greatest crisis was at the opera, and its seemingly disappointing outcome came actually as a relief to him. As a composer, however, he was rather disposed to rest on his laurels. When one is twenty-five, and already world-famous, there can seem little reason for hurry. A bland but unimportant overture—*Die schöne Melusine*—a *Rondo brillant* for piano and orchestra, and some pleasant songs are the outstanding productions of his Düsseldorf years. One of the songs is the luscious and ever-popular setting of Heine's *Auf Flügeln des Gesanges*, now heard more often in Liszt's piano transcription than in the original. Its treacly effusiveness and the almost embarrassing sentimentality of its melodic line make one thankful that Mendelssohn did not waste much time on lieder.

Early in 1835 there came to Mendelssohn, in his pleasant provincial backwater, an invitation that he could not refuse: Leipzig wanted him for the Gewandhaus concerts. The negotiations leading to his acceptance of this offer show him, on one hand, as a close, even a hard, bargainer, and on the other, as almost neurotically anxious lest he injure someone's position and sensibilities. Once the deal was closed, he took it easy until June, when he conducted the Lower Rhine Festival at Cologne with great acclamation, coming away with a fat fee and a complete edition of Handel, presented to him by the festival committee. In August, he took up his new duties at Leipzig, and explored the social possibilities of the town. Chopin came to visit him, and together the pair found their way to the home of Friedrich Wieck, a noted music teacher whose sixteen-year-old daughter Clara was already one of the most famous pianists in Europe. There, too, they met a moody and silent young man named Robert Schumann, the editor of a radical musical sheet, and composer of a piano suite called *Carnaval*. At the Gewandhaus Mendelssohn found more than a satisfactory band, and his Leipzig debut as a conductor passed without mishap. The audience was more than polite to his own early "*Meeresstille*" Overture—rather a trifle for opening so important a concert—and shouted its bravos after each movement of Beethoven's Fourth Symphony. While there were varying opinions as to Mendelssohn's ability as a conductor, there is no doubt that he whipped up the Gewandhaus orchestra into the most efficient in Europe. He was persevering, earnest, and reverent toward the intentions of the composers he conducted. Furthermore, he was on friendly terms with his men, and always got their enthusiastic co-operation. The most serious charge leveled at him was that he tended to rush certain tempos. Berlioz, Schumann, and Wagner complained bitterly of his treatment of Beethoven, whose works appeared constantly on his programs. Chorley, who was devoted to Mendelssohn, said that on the podium he was "lively rather than certain," and there seems no doubt that this liveliness contributed largely to his tremendous popularity as a conductor.

In October, shortly after his debut at the Gewandhaus, Mendelssohn went off for a two-day holiday in Berlin with his friend

Moscheles. Never had the Leipzigerstrasse house been gayer, despite the fact that its host was now quite blind. It was the last time Mendelssohn ever saw his father, for little more than a month later, he received news that the old man had died in his sleep. This was a heavy blow, for he had been deeply attached to him. It did not, however, materially affect his life. "The only thing that now remains is to do one's duty," he wrote solemnly. "I shall now work with double zeal at the completion of *St. Paul*, for my father urged me to in the very last letter he wrote me."

Mendelssohn had originally contracted to give Frankfort the first hearing of *St. Paul* in November, 1835. But his father's death had naturally slowed down his work all along the line, and the oratorio was not finished until spring. He used it, instead, to lead off at the Lower Rhine Festival at Düsseldorf that May. The soloists were professionals, but most of the 172 men in the orchestra and of the chorus of 364 voices were amateurs. The performance was rough: the professionals, like an embattled minority, tried to do their best, but at the end Mendelssohn was not wholly satisfied with either the day's work or *St. Paul* itself. "Many parts caused me much pleasure," he wrote, "others not so; but I learned a lesson from it all, and hope to succeed better the next time I write an oratorio." If *St. Paul* did not please its own composer, there seems little reason to linger over this unsatisfactory incense offering to Bach. It was tremendously popular throughout the nineteenth century, particularly in England, but it is now more often scornfully talked about (by persons who can never have heard a note of it) than performed. There are certain solemn works so foreign to modern taste, and because of their length so boring, so absurdly amusing, or so infuriating, that it is now impossible to do them justice. Among these, like one of the prosy heroes of *The Dunciad*, *St. Paul* stands well in the forefront. It was a fine experience to hear Schumann-Heink proclaim "But the Lord is mindful of His own," which is but one of several effective numbers buried in the score, but only a now unforeseeable revolution in taste could revive the oratorio in its entirety.

After the festival was over, Mendelssohn went to Frankfort to do some substitute conducting. He was coddled in the charming home atmosphere of the versatile Ferdinand Hiller, whose house was as much a rendezvous of artists as that of the Mendelssohns in Berlin.

Among those he met was Rossini, "sitting there—as large as life, in his best and most amiable mood." Now it was the charmer's turn to be charmed. He wrote to his mother that anyone who did not think Rossini a genius had but to listen to his conversation. But it was at the home of a Mme Jeanrenaud that Mendelssohn was most often seen, and at first there were whispers that he was courting this attractive young widow. A troubled Mendelssohn then left for a month at the seashore to think things out, after which, with his mind completely made up, he returned to Frankfort, and requested the hand, not of Mme Jeanrenaud, but of her seventeen-year-old daughter, Cécile Charlotte Sophie. The betrothal was announced in September, and six months later, on March 28, 1837, they were married at the Walloon French Reformed church, of which the deceased M. Jeanrenaud had been pastor.

Mendelssohn's married life was one of idyllic happiness, though his wife seems to have been a woman of rather trivial tastes. Five children, all of whom outlived their father—one of the daughters, indeed, into the twentieth century—literally blessed their union, for Mendelssohn was a doting parent who delighted in the guileless ways of small children. The Mendelssohns, in short, were an exact pattern of everything expected of the Victorian gentleman and his family.

In August, Mendelssohn had to tear himself away from his wife. England was clamoring for him, and he had promised to conduct the Birmingham Festival that year. While staying in London, he played the organ several times, and once at St. Paul's drew such huge crowds that the verger took the drastic step of disconnecting the bellows in the middle of a Bach fugue: it was the only way the church could be emptied. Many of Mendelssohn's contemporaries believed that this slight, elegant man was the greatest organist of the time. At Birmingham, *St. Paul* was acclaimed by enthusiastic thousands: Handel's rival—in popularity—had appeared. Scarcely less frenzied was the applause that greeted Mendelssohn's own playing of the D minor Piano Concerto he had composed especially for the occasion. If it seems inconceivable to us that any audience could go wild over this merely perfect and well-mannered music, it must be remembered that it was, on this occasion, being played by a magician. For this incredible man was also in the very front rank of the pianists of his day—we have as witnesses not merely the indiscriminate, pious English press, but his best-qualified contemporaries: Clara Schumann, Joachim, Hiller, and many others. Berlioz declared that Mendelssohn was even able to convey "an accurate idea" of instrumental color by playing an orchestral score on the piano—an amazing tribute from one who detested the piano, and was himself an unrivaled master of the orchestral palette.

The next few years were uneventfully prosperous for Mendelssohn. The Gewandhaus concerts were soon known throughout the length and breadth of Europe, for not only was the orchestra itself first-rate, but Mendelssohn was pronouncedly hospitable to new compositions of merit or striking originality. When Berlioz visited Leipzig, early in 1843, Mendelssohn devoted an extra concert to the Frenchman's music, which he thoroughly detested. All the leading virtuosos of the time performed under his baton: Bach's Triple Concerto, for instance, was heard once with Hiller, Liszt, and Mendelssohn, while another time Clara Schumann and Moscheles joined him in playing it. His fine taste was revealed in the selection of his programs, his rare musical scholarship in the resurrection of the classics of the past.

Most of the compositions Mendelssohn wrote during the first few years after his marriage need detain no one. Although amply supplied with the familiar finish and gloss, they were too bloodless to survive into this century. The overture to Victor Hugo's *Ruy Blas* is very much an exception. Describing the play's rodomontade as "detestable and more utterly beneath contempt than you could believe," Mendelssohn softly acceded to the solicitations of the Theatrical Pension Fund of Leipzig that he provide curtain music for their production of it in 1839. In three days, he turned out in a fit of annoyance at both himself and the Fund one of the most bang-up overtures of his career. It has absolutely no relation to Hugo's tragic villains and victims. It is, in fact, little short of rollicking, except for a few sinister chords that seem to have been injected into the score for the joke of the thing. It has outlasted many of Mendelssohn's attempts at grander and more profound effects. In 1840, the quatercentenary of the invention of printing drew from him one of his most solemn and self-conscious flights— the vast symphony-cantata known in Germany as the *Lobgesang*, to English festival audiences as the *Hymn of Praise*. The use of a battery of soloists, chorus, orchestra, and organ could not cover up the fact that here Mendelssohn was out of his depth. What w. intended to be solemn sounds pompous; what was meant to be moving too often sounds like schoolgirl rhetoric; and when the forces mass in a bid for overwhelming grandeur, the result is a cavernous grandiloquence. If Mendelssohn had to be judged solely on the merits of his imitations of the greatest designs of Bach and Handel, he would be written down as a second-rater.

After a sixth visit to England, during which the *Hymn of Praise* was triumphantly presented at the Birmingham Festival, Mendelssohn returned to Leipzig in full anticipation of continuing his happy life there. It was not to be. Within a few months, his brother Paul appeared on the scene as an emissary from Friedrich Wilhelm IV, King of Prussia. Having just ascended the throne, and being desirous of raising the cultural level of Berlin, the monarch had drawn up plans for a mammoth academy of the arts. It was to be divided into four sections—painting, sculpture, architecture, and music—a commanding figure was to direct each division, and Friedrich Wilhelm was determined to have Mendelssohn among his directors. The salary offered was, even to a man of Mendelssohn's more than comfortable means, attractive. But he was highly dubious about the great scheme, and very reluctant to leave Leipzig. Negotiations dragged along interminably, but by May, 1841, he was settled in Berlin, where he had promised to remain for a year. He came on his own terms, with no feeling that the arrangement was final. He was allowed to retain the formal direction of the Gewandhaus, though for practical reasons his friend Ferdinand David was appointed temporary conductor.

Once in Berlin, Mendelssohn found the King an autocrat whose mind teemed with a thousand abortive ideas, and who wanted him at his beck and call every minute. Mendelssohn's misgivings about the proposed academy were justified at once: it simply failed to materialize, and the composer found himself metamorphosed into the King's *Kapellmeister*, a position he held concurrently with the Gewandhaus directorate for the rest of his life. Friedrich Wilhelm's grandiose schemes involved, among other things, the resuscitation of great dramas, and for the production of several of them Mendelssohn was commissioned to write incidental music. Of that to *Antigone* and to *Oedipus Coloneus* not a note is now to be

that to Racine's *Athalie* has fared somewhat better: a
ar March of the Priests" is still played.

ction of Mendelssohn's next masterpiece was reserved
ed Leipzig. At the Gewandhaus, on March 3, 1842,
a companion piece to the "Italian" Symphony—the
"Scotch" Symphony, in A minor, which he had begun in Italy
eleven years before. Like the "Hebrides" Overture, it was a result
of his artistically fruitful trip to Scotland in 1829. More varied in
mood, and technically more showy than the earlier of the two
"national" symphonies, it lacks the bright spontaneity and effort-
lessness of the "Italian." Whereas the earlier of the symphonies had
been Italian only by courtesy, its Latin flavor residing mainly in
its lightheartedness and the use of a Neapolitan dance rhythm in
the last movement, the "Scotch" is clearly programmatic. Not
only are the harmonic intervals suggestive of those in Scotch folk
music, but the melodies themselves are so reminiscent of Highland
folk tunes that the chief theme of the second movement has been
described as an echo of *Charlie Is My Darling*. The symphony opens
with a broad landscape painting in Mendelssohn's best style: this
passage, little more than sixty bars long, serves to set the scene,
after which we at once hear a minor melody as Scotch as heather.
There is a sudden thundershower—Mendelssohn's attempt at realism, though clever, sounds a bit amusing nowadays—the storm
dies down, and the movement closes with a brief return to the
peaceful landscape of the opening. The second movement is a
dancing vivace, the third a rather unexpected return to Germany*
—a wishy-washy affair withal, with deplorable excursions into
pseudo grandeur. The fourth movement is quite as effective as the
marvelous saltarello of the "Italian" Symphony—a wild dance of
rude Highlanders who stamp furiously into a smug coda that closes
the symphony. A marred masterpiece.

In May, 1842, Mendelssohn, accompanied by his wife, crossed
over to England. He conducted the "Scotch" Symphony at a Philharmonic concert to such wild applause that the grateful directors
tendered him a fish dinner at Greenwich. Summoned to Buckingham Palace, he was requested by Queen Victoria and Prince Albert
to play a miscellany of German trifles. Mendelssohn was a man
after their own hearts, and soon was asked back. This time the

* Though it is said to have been inspired by his meditations at Holyrood Castle.

Queen graciously granted him permission to dedicate the "Scotch" Symphony to her. He could not have been wholly indifferent to this mark of royal favor, but he was in general disinclined to put much stock in the condescension of kings.

From the King of Saxony, however, Mendelssohn obtained something he really did want: a decree founding a conservatory of music at Leipzig. Almost simultaneously, he received notice that he had been appointed general music director to the King of Prussia, and was on the point of leaving for Berlin to settle all details when the news came that his mother had died. He spent a cheerless holiday season at 3, Leipzigerstrasse, which had now become his property, and returned to Leipzig to immerse himself in the details incident to the establishment of the conservatory. He persuaded Schumann to share the piano and composition classes with him; David was selected to teach violin and orchestral ensemble, while, as a graceful gesture to his predecessor at the Gewandhaus, he insisted that Pohlenz (who, however, died before the conservatory opened) head the department of singing. On April 3, 1843, the new institution, temporarily located in the Gewandhaus, was formally inaugurated, and under Mendelssohn's energetic supervision became within a few years a fine music school.

But Mendelssohn's hold on these scenes of congenial activity was becoming all too tenuous. In August, he was commanded to speed up incidental music for three of the dramas involved in the King of Prussia's apotheosis of the stage. This entailed a tremendous spending of energy, for not only did Mendelssohn have to complete a large amount of music, but he had to arrange and rearrange plans for the actual productions according to the sequence of the King's whims. Finally, after unprecedented stewing and fretting, the first of them—*Antigone*—took place in September. A month later, on October 14, *A Midsummer Night's Dream* was given at the Neue Palais, Potsdam. Shakespeare was at once voted to be in bad taste (though some believed that he had merely translated a German play into English), but the music enchanted everyone, as it has continued to, down to this day.* Using the overture he had composed seventeen years before, Mendelssohn added to it thir-

---

* Except, of course, in Nazi Germany, where pure Aryan music was supplied by one Theo Knobel after Richard Strauss admitted his inability to improve on Mendelssohn.

teen new numbers of almost uniform effectiveness, the result being a pattern of what incidental music should be. Several of the pieces, wrenched from their context—where their aptness adds immeasurably to their charm—are among the most familiar music ever written. The triumphant, delightfully trashy Wedding March—for the Victorias and Alberts of all eternity—has been played literally millions of times, usually as a pendant to the more solemnly mawkish Bridal Chorus from *Lohengrin*. But it is more than unlikely that the Funeral March, with its mock-tragic strains, will ever accompany a single corse to its sepulture. The Intermezzo and the Nocturne have their devotees. Quite as spontaneous and inspired as the Overture itself is the Scherzo—an aerial *moto perpetuo* of gossamer texture, the sprightliest of all possible illustrations of the word "Mendelssohnian."

Forced against his wishes into a position of musical dictatorship in Berlin, Mendelssohn found that he would have temporarily to resign the Gewandhaus direction to Hiller. In November, he moved, lock, stock, and barrel, to Berlin, and set up his household at 3, Leipzigerstrasse. A most unpleasant winter followed, during which the composer was harassed by piddling official duties that vexed his spirit and depleted his strength. By spring things had come to such a pass that he decided to give up his house. The city had become hateful to him. In May, leaving his family in Frankfort, he went to London for an eighth visit, and conducted the last six concerts of the Philharmonic season. One unfortunate incident marred this visit: among the novelties he intended to introduce were Schubert's C major Symphony and his own *Ruy Blas* Overture. At rehearsals the orchestra responded so coldly to the Schubert that he withdrew not only it, but also the overture. In general, however, he was idolized. The Philharmonic had never ended their season so happily: they were able to put £400 away in a reserve fund, and Mendelssohn himself rejoined his family with his pockets bulging with money he did not need. He idled away the rest of the summer in the country, and in September grudgingly returned to Berlin. He was not well, and sensing that his malaise was due to the combination of duties that bored him and a city he had come to detest, he finally persuaded the King to release him from any except an honorary tenure of his official posts. He was back in Frankfort before the holidays, and there he re-

mained in stubborn isolation until September, 1845, ev
to budge for the first performance of his Violin Con
Gewandhaus on March 13.

The E minor is the most popular of all violin concertos, and u
Mendelssohn, who had an innocent, almost childlike love of applause, was not at its highly successful *première* is ironical. Yet he
himself, five years before it was finished—it was begun in 1838—
had been assured by Ferdinand David that it would stand with
Beethoven's as one of the two big concertos for violin. And, allowing for its smaller proportions, for its suaver and more feminine
contours, that is exactly where it stands. The E minor is as slick as
a whistle with a lyric note, and the mere expertness of its fashioning is not the least part of its perennial attractiveness. Here, in
truth, is a work of "heavenly length": the themes have a beautiful
punctuality of statement and development; there is not a moment
of malingering in the concerto, not a bar of padding. No better
lightweight music has ever been written: it is ineffably sweet, tender, lyrical—and heartless. In some undefinable, but unmistakable,
way it just escapes real greatness. It is a masterpiece of a musician
of genius but not of a great man.

In September, 1845, the Mendelssohns returned to Leipzig,
Felix apparently much the better for his months of rest. The Gewandhaus concerts began in October. The season was an especially
brilliant one, during which Jenny Lind, to whom Mendelssohn
was devoted, made her first Leipzig appearance. He threw himself
with a new energy into his teaching at the conservatory. He was
worshiped by his students as by his audiences, and stood in happy
contrast to the shy and self-absorbed Schumann, who in one year
had proved a complete failure as a teacher. Except for occasional
bursts of temperament, Mendelssohn's way with his students was
affable, easygoing, chatty, and thorough. He kept up a running
fire of comment, often of a witty nature. One of his favorite methods of teaching was to write a musical theme on a blackboard, and
then have each of the pupils add a counterpoint to it. On one
occasion, when the last man up was unable to add anything more
to the theme, Mendelssohn asked sharply, "Can't you tell where
to put the next note?" The student shook his head, and Mendelssohn said in a relieved voice, "That's good! Neither can I."

Mendelssohn's resumption of his Leipzig duties was coincident

with the last stages of the largest-scale creative effort of his career
—the composition of the oratorio *Elijah*, which he had begun to
think about as early as 1837. Now, with but the finishing touches
lacking, it was promised to the Birmingham Festival. Putting on a
work of such vast proportions required—ideally, at least—many
rehearsals, but unfortunately he was detained in Leipzig until
about ten days before the *première*. Conducting the Lower Rhine
Festival at Aachen, and a German-Flemish celebration at Cologne,
the arrangement of an all-Spohr program at the Gewandhaus,
with the vain old violinist quartered on him and the already formidable and sharply critical Wagner on the scene—all this, and
much more, Mendelssohn had to edge in before he could leave for
his ninth visit to England. It was an unusually hot summer, and
it was a very tired Mendelssohn who arrived at Birmingham, only
three days before the *première*. Fortunately, Moscheles had been
invaluable in rehearsing the soloists. And in the scant seventy-two
hours allotted to him, Mendelssohn worked miracles. He had his
reward: the world *première* of *Elijah*, on the morning of August 26,
1846, was the crowning success of his life. He was able to write to
his brother Paul with pardonable exultation: "During the whole
two hours and a half that it lasted, the two thousand people in
the large hall, and the large orchestra, were all so fully intent on
the one object in question, that not the slightest sound was to be
heard among the whole audience, so that I could sway at pleasure
the enormous orchestra and choir and also the organ accompaniments. . . . No work of mine ever went so admirably the first time
of execution, or was received with such enthusiasm, by both the
musicians and the audience, as this oratorio."

The roar of acclamation that greeted *Elijah* that sultry August
morning almost a century ago has been equaled, if not outdone, a
hundred times since, particularly in England, where the oratorio
stands next to *Messiah* in the popular affection and as a festival
staple. The British Empire would not be the British Empire if a
year's suns went by without shining down on a performance of
Elijah. America is not so oratorio-loving, and in recent years, at
least, the B minor Mass and the *Matthew Passion* have been performed here more often than *Elijah*, which is unknown to thousands of our music lovers. Of the many recordings of excerpts of
the work, more than ninety-five per cent (including, of course, the

complete recording) are by British artists. Nor is it probable that more performances of *Elijah* would win many new friends for it here. It is long and windy, with interminable passages of false eloquence, highfalutin rectitude, and bloody Jehovistic dogma. The many fine lyric pages tend to get lost amid this turgidity. *Elijah* lasts two hours and a half: during the first half it sounds like a tolerably good imitation of Bach and Handel, but by the end of the second half it is likely to sound like an intolerably bad imitation. Why the English like not only *Elijah*, but tenth-rate imitations of it by their own composers as well, is a problem that for years engaged the attention of George Bernard Shaw, without his being able to find an answer to it. To own recordings of "If with all your hearts," the solemn "It is enough," and "O rest in the Lord," one of the most moving of all contralto arias, and to abstain strictly from complete performances of the oratorio, is man's whole duty toward *Elijah*.

Mendelssohn, in his hour of greatest triumph, returned exhausted to Leipzig. Niels W. Gade, as his deputy at the Gewandhaus, henceforth conducted most of the concerts. At the conservatory, Mendelssohn resumed his teaching conscientiously but without his old enthusiasm. He revised parts of *Elijah*, and began an opera on the Lorelei legend for Jenny Lind, which, however, was left a fragment. In the spring of 1847, he returned to England for his tenth, and last, visit, Joachim accompanying him in the role of sympathetic special nurse. He was foolhardily wasteful of his strength, and within a fortnight conducted a command symphonic program in London and six performances of *Elijah*—four in London alone. At Buckingham Palace, Victoria and Albert kept the ailing man at the piano for two hours. Furthermore, he fulfilled many social obligations, and was among those who heard Lind win London at a single performance at Her Majesty's. After a farewell call on the Queen, Mendelssohn crossed over to the Continent the next morning. At the Prussian border he was mistakenly detained as a Dr. Mendelssohn wanted for political underground activity, and was subjected to several hours of wearisome questioning before he was allowed to proceed to Frankfort. He felt intense vexation, but this soon gave place to tragic depression. Being told abruptly that his sister Fanny had died, he shrieked, and fell unconscious to the floor. He had ruptured a blood vessel in his head, and from that moment he was a dying man.

By June Mendelssohn had rallied enough to take a vacation in Switzerland, where he did no composing, but filled his water-color sketchbooks with the scenery around Interlaken. Lingering there, he did not return to Leipzig until September. Great plans filled his head—a production of *Elijah* in Vienna with Jenny Lind, vast new compositions, the coming season of the Gewandhaus. But an insidious depression mastered him, and he was forced to give up his duties and settle down where he had ruled as king, in the unfamiliar role of private citizen. Early in October, he paid a call on his friend Livia Frege, one of the most eminent of German lieder singers, to request her to sing over the last set of songs he had composed. She left the room for candles, and returned to find Mendelssohn in agony. He was borne back to his own house, where leeches were applied. Within a few days he seemed better, and before the month was over was even able to take a walk with his wife. But the will to live was gone, the recovery but apparent. Two apoplectic strokes left him unconscious, and on Thursday night, November 4, 1847, he died in the presence of his grief-stricken relatives and friends, including Moscheles and David. He was not yet thirty-nine years old.

When the Wagner-Liszt regime came into power, Mendelssohn's was one of the first reputations to be put to the ax. Liszt was at least well disposed toward Mendelssohn, but Wagner, though he never came to blows with him during his lifetime, vilified him and his music unmercifully. The Wagnerians, quick to take a cue from their master, belittled his memory on every possible occasion— and this campaign of denigration is still being carried on by that large and faithful band who judge music by its degree of Wagnerishness. It is a campaign conducted actually without rules, but with a fine show of reasonableness. They declare that Mendelssohn is trivial, and prove it—by pointing to the most inane and vapid effusions of his pen. By judging him on the basis of such *Lieder ohne Worte* as those known as the "Spring Song" and "Consolation," by the Wedding March from *A Midsummer Night's Dream*, and by *Auf Flügeln des Gesanges*, they do as grave disservice to truth as if they were to evaluate Schumann by *Träumerei*, Sibelius by the *Valse triste*—or Wagner by the "Evening Star."

Now, there is no doubt that Mendelssohn wrote a great deal of either merely adequate or plainly bad music. His chamber works belong mainly to the former category, though the piano trios particularly are deft, amiable, and even endearing. Most of his piano music belongs to the second category, though there are notable exceptions: the scherzolike *Rondo capriccioso*; the E minor Prelude and Fugue, with its Bachian dynamics; the ingeniously devised and hauntingly lovely *Variations sérieuses*, and a very few of the *Lieder ohne Worte*. The piano did not often evoke Mendelssohn's happiest inspirations, nor did he treat it with the sure mastery he possessed over the orchestra. It seems that in writing most of the *Lieder ohne Worte* he was enslaved by sentimental moods that dulled his critical sense. Their indisputable originality as brief statements of mood is apt to be overlooked nowadays, mainly because as sheer music they are overshadowed by so many later romantic piano pieces of similarly intimate character.

It is fair, however, to judge Mendelssohn on the basis of his best orchestral works. The man who wrote the "Italian" and "Scotch" Symphonies, the Violin Concerto, the overture and incidental music to *A Midsummer Night's Dream*, and the "Hebrides" and *Ruy Blas* Overtures need have no fear for his laurels. He was not, like Mozart or Schubert, a composer of the happiest inspirations, or like Beethoven, a musical thinker of the most profound order. Nor did he, for all his understanding love of Bach and Handel, scale the heavens. No, Mendelssohn was of a smaller order all around, but with enough discipline and scope to escape being a *petit maître*. A flawless master of the technique of his art, he succeeded in pouring the new wine of romanticism into the old classical bottles. And though his vintage is never quite heady enough, it sparkles, warms without intoxicating, and exhales a rare bouquet.

Chapter XII

Robert Schumann

(Zwickau, June 8, 1810–July 29, 1856, Endenich)

*We all have a deep regard for Schumann; but it is really not in
human nature to refrain from occasionally making it clear that
he was greater as a musical enthusiast than as a constructive
musician.*—George Bernard Shaw: *Music in London.*

ROBERT SCHUMANN is the central figure in the musical romanticism of the nineteenth century. He first attracted the attention
of Europe as a revolutionary critic. Long before he was able to get
a hearing for his own radical compositions, he had published a
rhapsodic welcome to Chopin—he called the article "Hats Off,
Gentlemen, a Genius!" Almost a quarter of a century later, in his
last published utterance, he saluted a struggling nobody by the
name of Johannes Brahms. He was the untiring prophet of the
romantic ideal in music.

Heredity accounts for much in Schumann's life; its pattern was
set before he was born. His father's health was chronically bad
before marriage, and became progressively worse after it. His
mother was gloomy and morose, sparing of affection, and morbidly
conventional. His sister Emilie, whom his first biographer, Von
Wasielewski, described with unconscious humor as the victim "of
an uncurable melancholy, which gave unmistakable signs of quiet
madness," drowned herself at the age of twenty. His three brothers
died young. His own mental instability manifested itself as early
as his twenty-third year.

Schumann's heredity was bad enough; growing up in the unhealthy jungles of German romanticism made its tragic outcome
inevitable. Brought into the world during the *Sturm und Drang* of
Napoleon's struggle for world dominion—his birthplace was near
the principal theater of the war—Schumann grew up under the
influence of a gifted but immoderate father. August Schumann
was cultivated, fervid, and obscure—a publisher, journalist, and
novelist, and a translator of Byron. In short, a stock romantic
figure. He lived in a kind of creative rage, and once confessed that

reading Young's *Night Thoughts* had brought him "near madness" in his youth, though this was obviously literary affectation: his reason was not affected.

Schumann's first eighteen years were passed in Zwickau, where he received a conventional schooling and was graduated creditably from the *Gymnasium*. He began to play the piano and to compose in his sixth year, and in his eleventh was directing the school band. Throughout Europe everyone was earnestly playing piano duets, and he was no exception. With the local bandmaster's son, he raced through arrangements of Beethoven's symphonies and pieces by Haydn, Mozart, Weber, Hummel, and Czerny to such effect that August Schumann presented his twelve-year-old son with a grand piano. Now the lad reveled more than ever in the piano music available in a stodgy provincial town, while at the home of the prosperous Carus family he heard the best chamber music. His father did not doubt Robert's ability, and solicited the powerful but still accessible Weber to superintend the boy's musical education. Although Weber was amiable, for some reason the plan fell through.

August Schumann's death in 1826 was doubly unfortunate, for it occurred just as he was planning to send Robert to better teachers than Zwickau afforded, and it left the boy in the hands of his unimaginative and straitlaced mother. Under her chilling influence his musical ambitions temporarily waned. At this time he did everything carelessly, vaguely, without plan: he wrote fugitive verses, took long walks, and read Jean Paul Friedrich Richter, the most overwrought of German littérateurs. He acted, that is, like a typical adolescent of this improbable pre-1830 period.

It was this moonstruck dreamer whom Johanna Schumann now decided to force into the legal profession. Accordingly, in March, 1828, he matriculated, *studiosus juris*, at the University of Leipzig. Henceforth his life was to be devoted to music.

For, with scarcely a perfunctory bow to the study of law, Schumann returned to his versifying and piano playing. Professor Carus had also removed to Leipzig; at his home Schumann met, among other celebrities, Friedrich Wieck, whose knowledge of music and musical technique was boundless. Contact with this gifted pedagogue revived the lad's musical ambitions. He formally enrolled as Wieck's pupil. This association was, from the beginning, not entirely happy. Schumann could have little fault to find with the teaching that had produced, in Wieck's nine-year-old daughter Clara, the most noted child prodigy in Europe, and there is no doubt that he struggled to master the difficulties of pianism. But he infuriated his farsighted teacher by neglecting theory. Also, he practiced when he wished, therefore unsystematically, and, as a substitute for more formal studies, read the scores of the best music of all periods. He also took part in chamber ensembles, and began to study the music of Schubert, at the news of whose death, on November 19, 1828, he burst into tears.

The favorite reading of this despiser of theory was *The Well-Tempered Clavichord*. He admired Bach intensely, and was among the first to recognize the "mysterious depth of sentiment" behind the contrapuntal miracles. But unfortunately, Bach and Jean Paul happened to have been born on March 21, and the coincidence was to place Schumann in an absurd position. On that day, in 1850, in a public speech, he invoked them together as "the immortal rulers of music and poetry." When someone objected to this grotesque bracketing, he left the hall in a rage.

Wieck suddenly dismissed Schumann, ostensibly because he had no time for teaching, but more probably because the boy's sporadic enthusiasms irritated him. Schumann decided to leave Leipzig for Heidelberg. In that most romantic of Rhenish towns, his life was easy and attractive, but he soon missed Wieck's instruction, and began a three-cornered negotiation with his mother and his teacher, begging to be allowed to return to Wieck. Although he had glimpsed some of the "majesty of jurisprudence" at Heidelberg, he longed for music as some men long for a mistress, and now decided to abandon the law forever. Fortunately, Wieck had faith in his potentialities as a pianist, and eventually told the skeptical mother that in three years he would make her son a great virtuoso, the peer of Moscheles and Hummel. Johanna Schumann consented.

Schumann interrupted his stay in Heidelberg with a trip to Italy in the autumn of 1829. He spoke enthusiastically of Pasta, the soprano for whom Bellini wrote *Norma* and *La Sonnambula*, but this was almost his only reference to the artistic opulence of the South, though his letters palpitate with the business of passing sentimental attachments. He did not return empty-handed to Leipzig, for in

Heidelberg he had composed parts of the *Papillons*, still, undeservedly, among the most popular of his compositions. The
quality of these rather banal pieces recalls some of Schubert's
waltzes, though they are much less graceful. Their basic unity,
despite much that has been said and written about it, may still be
considered the composer's secret; relating them to a masked ball in
Jean Paul's *Flegeljahre*, as Schumann did, is now a task for the
musical archeologist. Nor was he successful in his last-minute attempt to unify the *Papillons* by ending it with two of the pieces
combined contrapuntally.

Back in Leipzig, Schumann took up his residence in the house
where Wieck lodged. The prospect of becoming as brilliant as
Moscheles, whose playing had dazzled him as a small boy,
spurred him on to fantastic efforts. He even invented a device for
keeping the fourth finger of his right hand inactive while he practiced, evidently hoping that this curious procedure would overcome the laws of nature, and make the fourth finger as strong as
the others. To his horror, the favored finger tended to retain this
artificial position when free. Despite the most elaborate and expensive treatment, the disability persisted, and he was forced to
renounce the alluring career of a concert artist.

Schumann turned to composition and theory as a solace, finding
in Heinrich Dorn—later famous for his supposed antagonism to
Wagner—a welcome successor to the sometimes irascible Wieck.
Late in 1832, he conducted part of a G minor symphony at
Zwickau. His townspeople received the fragment coldly, though
Schumann said that the same piece won him "many friends among
the greatest musical connoisseurs" when repeated at Leipzig the
following June. He was not discouraged by the public's reaction,
and worked unceasingly at various compositions, especially the
Studien nach Capricen von Paganini, which he erroneously believed to
prove his command of theory. In the midst of this activity, he lost
his sister-in-law Rosalie, whom he loved deeply, and this shock
precipitated the first overt symptoms of his mental instability. It is
even said that during the night of October 17, 1833, the distracted
man tried to throw himself from the fourth floor of his lodgings.
We know for a certainty that from this time on he always insisted
on ground-floor rooms.

Then suddenly, abruptly, everything was changed. Schumann

began to become conscious of another side of his own romantic nature. He fell in love—not once, but twice. Clara Wieck was growing up, and noticing this, he began, almost insensibly, to feel toward her something more than the easy affection of an elder brother. Of course, she was only fifteen, and yet, when she left Leipzig to study, he felt lost. The habit of love was upon him, and he could not shake it off. Among Wieck's pupils was Ernestine von Fricken, "physically luxuriant, emotionally strongly developed, and intellectually insignificant." A girl with these qualifications might well appeal to any man, but Schumann had to romanticize her into a sort of Madonna with a milk-white soul. He even thought for a time of marrying her.

But this hectic interlude was a substitution gesture. Clara's image persisted, and Schumann learned that Ernestine had deceived him about her social status. She was not the rich daughter of Baron von Fricken, but his bastard, and poor. The double drawback was too much. Instead of his daughter, Schumann took from the baron a theme in C sharp minor, on which he wrote his variations known as the *Études symphoniques*.

Artistically, too, 1834 was one of great activity for Schumann: he composed the *Études symphoniques* and began the *Carnaval*. With a group of friends, he founded the *Neue Zeitschrift für Musik*, and overnight became the most advanced music critic in Europe.

Twenty years later, when the night of madness was closing in on Schumann, his last accomplished work was the preface to a selection from his critical writings, many of which had appeared in the *Zeitschrift*. In this salute to the past, the tiring mind was momentarily refreshed, and less than two months before the doors of a madhouse shut behind him, he re-created with unsullied freshness the ardent youth of the idealistic thirties.

"At the close of the year 1833," he wrote, "a number of musicians, mostly young men, went together every evening in Leipzig, apparently by mere chance and for social intercourse, but no less for an exchange of ideas in regard to the art which was their meat and drink—music. It cannot be said that the musical condition of Germany at that time was very satisfactory. On the stage Rossini still flourished, while Herz and Hünten held almost exclusive sway on the piano. And yet but a few years had passed since Beethoven, Carl Maria von Weber, and Franz Schubert were in our midst. Mendelssohn's star was indeed in the ascendant, and wonderful things were rumored of a Pole named Chopin, but the latter excited no lasting influence till later. One day the thought flashed upon the young hotheads: let us not stand idly by; let us set to work, and strive to improve matters, so that the poetry of Art may once more be held in honor. Thus arose the first pages of a new journal."

The *Zeitschrift* confirmed the growing fame of Schubert and Mendelssohn, helped to found that of Chopin and Robert Franz, and introduced the names of Berlioz and Brahms. Its contributors included, besides Schumann himself, Wieck, Wagner, Dorn, and many others whose names were hidden under the fantastic *noms de guerre* Schumann invented for them. The publication of the *Zeitschrift*, important though it was, constituted in Schumann's eyes only one of the activities of the *Davidsbündler*, "an association," he said, "existing only in the imagination, whose members are recognizable less by outward signs than by inward resemblance. It will be their endeavor, by word and by deed, to dam up the tide of mediocrity."

The *Carnaval*, completed in 1835, was the most comprehensive musical expression of the *Davidsbündler*. It is based on four notes: A, S (E flat in German notation), C, and H (B natural). These notes had a double significance for the composer: they represent the only musical letters in SCHumAnn, and ASCH, the Bohemian home of Ernestine von Fricken. In sending a copy of the *Carnaval* to Moscheles after its publication in 1837, Schumann wrote, "To figure out the Masked Ball will be child's play to you; and I need hardly assure you that the putting together of the pieces and the superscriptions came about *after* the composition."

Apart from its alleged literary program, the *Carnaval* has no unity, and we may interpret the letter to Moscheles as a kind of elaborate fake invented by Schumann to quiet his own artistic conscience. Like the *Papillons*, the *Carnaval* suffers from a lack of organic integration. Contemporary opinion divided sharply over its merits: Liszt proclaimed it one of the greatest works he knew; Chopin declared that it was not music. It is the most popular of Schumann's piano compositions despite its flaws. When all deductions have been made, the rewards to the listener are incalculably rich. The pieces are tone portraits and moods limned by a sympathetic and generous musical intelligence. They range from the tender sentiment of *Eusebius* through the frenzied enthusiasm of *Paganini* to the booming heroics of the *Marche des Davidsbündler*, and include such high pastiche as *Chopin*, and a waltz—*Lettres dansantes* —worthy to be placed with the finest of Schubert and Chopin. The Schumannesque quality persists throughout—a note of personal idiosyncrasy colors the *Carnaval* from the *Préambule* to the *Marche*, all exuberant, warm, and boldly rhythmic.

The *Études symphoniques* are altogether less successful, and Schumann himself was rightly skeptical of their appeal to the public. Audiences received them coldly, and they had to wait for Anton Rubinstein, fifty years after their composition, to establish them. These frequently overrobust pieces are dedicated to the pallid William Sterndale Bennett, the Caspar Milquetoast of English music, and one of Schumann's mistaken enthusiasms. The most successful part of the *Études symphoniques* is the grandiosely conceived finale, for which Schumann wisely added to Von Fricken's theme one from an opera by the popular romantic Heinrich Marschner. Although this suffers as much as the other parts from "too, too solid blocks of chords," it is, in effect, an amazingly sustained flight.

In 1835 the musical life of Leipzig was quickened by the arrival of Mendelssohn to become director of the Gewandhaus concerts. All succumbed to his genius and charm, but the heart of Schumann went out to him ever more unreservedly. A friendship sprang up between them that endured, with minor frictions, until Mendelssohn's death. While Schumann considered Mendelssohn godlike both as man and artist, his hero was more reserved: he judged Schumann a musical dilettante, and, worse, one who wrote about music. He nevertheless performed many of Schumann's orchestral works brilliantly, and so did him an invaluable service.

Schumann's love for Clara Wieck was growing constantly (as was hers for him), and about the beginning of 1836 he determined to marry her. Four years earlier, Johanna Schumann had been won by the girl's charming manner, and had said, "Some day you must marry Robert," but at that time neither Robert nor Clara had taken his mother's words seriously. His final break with Ernestine von Fricken occurred in January, 1836, and his mother's death the following month may have recalled her prophetic words. In any event, these happenings made his need for companionship peremptory. When Wieck saw that Clara reciprocated Schumann's love, he reacted violently, spitefully adducing Schumann's poverty and intemperance (he had spent too much money on beer and champagne), though, oddly enough, ignoring what would have been a reasonable objection—his mental instability. Behind Wieck's attitude looms his real fear that Clara, whom he regarded as his creation and chattel, would be diverted from her career. He shuddered to think of her "with the perambulator."

At first, Wieck's opposition was not wholly unjust, but in time Schumann's conduct and prospects improved so as to make the ostensible objections absurd. Although Clara had been packed off to Dresden to make her forget Schumann, that miracle did not happen. The lovers met during one of Wieck's absences, and Wieck, hearing of this, forbade Schumann all access to his house. Further, he told Clara that he would shoot her suitor if he persisted. There actually followed an eighteen-month interval during which the lovers were both in Leipzig, yet completely cut off from each other. Clara had to hold her faith in Schumann against the mendacity and malice of both her father and her stepmother, and the intolerable situation was further complicated by the ambiguous friendship of Carl Banck, once one of the *Davidsbündler*. He seems to have misrepresented Clara to Schumann, and to have described her as a frivolous girl with no capacity for true love.

On August 13, 1837, Clara gave a concert at Leipzig, and on the program was an F minor sonata that Schumann had dedicated to her the year before. He described it as his heart's cry for her, and Clara caught the message, for she wrote, "Did you not think that I played it because I knew no other way of showing something of my inmost heart? I could not do it in secret, so I did it in public." The lovers managed to communicate with each other, and on the following day became formally betrothed. They agreed that on Clara's eighteenth birthday Schumann should again write to her father. The letter, with its dignified statement of the composer's position and prospects, evoked an unsatisfactory reply, and Schumann's interview with Wieck some days later was violent in tone and discouraging in outlook. Schumann and Clara decided to resort to law if, at the end of two years more, her father still withheld his consent.

Wieck's next move was to take Clara on a highly successful concert tour to Prague and Vienna, which kept her away until the following May. She met her great rivals, Liszt and Thalberg, in Vienna, and was feted in a manner that might have turned a less level head. But not Clara's—even though Liszt, in his eagerness to meet her, threw his calling card in at the window. Her letters to Schumann continued, and though both these and his answers reflected passing doubts, their love endured, and on her return to Leipzig they were able to meet with considerable freedom despite Wieck's obduracy. They decided to marry in 1840, come what might.

One thing was certain: Clara would come to Schumann without a dowry. This situation, then very unusual, was so heightened by Wieck's contempt for Schumann as a man of affairs (only a go-getter like himself would have pleased him) that the composer concluded that he himself must provide a dowry. His modest income suited a bachelor who knew where to borrow money, but not the husband of Clara Wieck. His only asset with possibilities of rapid increase was the *Zeitschrift*, but he felt that its location in Leipzig was against it. He had always wanted to visit Vienna, which he believed to be a city of music lovers, and the idea of moving the *Zeitschrift* there gave him a good excuse.

And when he saw Vienna in the autumn of 1838, he was inclined to like it. His spirits soared when he found a pen on Beethoven's grave and received the great C major Symphony from the hands of Schubert's brother. He met Liszt and Thalberg, and saw Taglioni dance, but soon realized that Vienna, under crazy Ferdinand I, was not the place for the *Zeitschrift*. Far from worshiping at the shrines of Mozart, Beethoven, and Schubert, the Viennese were concerned with the politics of petty cliques. The strict censorship would have made the liberal *Zeitschrift* unwelcome there, while the lack of a central musical authority like Mendelssohn's at Leipzig seemed to Schumann an even more serious drawback.

Early in 1839, news of his brother Eduard's serious illness recalled Schumann to Leipzig. While he was en route, according to a letter he wrote Clara, "I heard a whole choral of trumpets—he died just at that time. . . ." Clara, of course, could not see (as we can) that this "choral of trumpets" was the first of the auditory hallucinations that were to attend the disintegration of Schumann's mind.

Clara was not in Leipzig to comfort him, for in January she had set out for Paris. Wieck, for the first time, did not accompany her: he wanted her to realize the discomforts involved in securing concerts without his help. If he expected, in this tortuous way, to prove his indispensability, he had misjudged his daughter. Vexation there was, but more for him than for Clara: the French tour was a measured success. She met Heine, dined with Meyerbeer, and founded many lasting friendships. Yet she was far from happy, for her father's letters were persecutional, her lover's often reproachful and doubting. Back in Leipzig, she united with Schumann in one more friendly attempt to gain Wieck's consent to their marriage—she was still not yet of age. They finally had to go to law. Wieck barred his doors to his famous daughter, and went so far as to endanger her career and Schumann's by slander. The case dragged on until his objections were reduced to one—intemperance—and that had to be proved within six weeks. Schumann was vindicated, Mendelssohn, among others, being ready to testify for him. Almost simultaneously, the University of Jena gave him an honorary doctorate. Wieck then withdrew his formal opposition.

Robert Schumann and Clara Wieck were married on September 12, 1840.

"Truly, from the contests Clara cost me, much music has been caused and conceived," Schumann wrote to Dorn. And even though it seems likely that these "contests" hastened the progress of Schumann's mental trouble, the fact remains that the stormy years of the courtship did bring forth his most ambitious contributions to piano literature, including *Die Davidsbündlertänze*, the *Fantasiestücke*, the *Kinderscenen*, the *Kreisleriana*, and the C major Fantasie. Of his best works for piano alone, only one—the *Album für die Jugend*—was composed after his marriage, and that because he had become a family man, and wrote these pieces for his own children.

Despite the popularity of the *Papillons* and the *Carnaval*, the essence of Schumann as a composer for the piano is in the best pages of the *Fantasiestücke* and the *Kreisleriana*. With what James Huneker preached as "the greater Chopin," they are romantic piano music at its finest—until the advent of Brahms. Chopin has intense Slavic passion, Gallic edge, poignant—if sometimes saccharine—lyricism; Schumann is drenched with Teutonic qualities: broad sentiment,

lively humor, domestic charm. He translates the "poetry of everyday life" into music. To the transparent sweetness and naïveté of
Schubert he adds an intense psychological preoccupation.

Few people nowadays care to listen to the *Fantasiestücke* or the
Kinderscenen in their entirety. Schumann himself thought them too
long for public performance, and often spoke of individual pieces
as complete in themselves. Furthermore, he favored some against
others. Even the most prejudiced classicist or modernist must surrender to the passionate sweep of *In der Nacht* or the warm humor
of *Grillen*: in these, as in other short pieces and in sections of the
Kreisleriana, Schumann speaks to us most intimately and persua-
sively. In the faded pages of the *Kinderscenen*, the intimate note
persists, but the unrelieved *Gemüthlichkeit* is unbearable, rising to
irritating pitch in the hackneyed *Träumerei*. The trouble with the
Träumerei is not that it is hackneyed (so are Beethoven's Fifth and
"Handel's Largo"), but that it is spineless and cloying.

Schumann intended the C major Fantasie as his contribution
toward the raising of funds for a Beethoven memorial, which may
explain its unusually large proportions. It contains many fine pages,
but lacks architecture. It is full of typically Schumannesque epigrams, delightful in themselves, but out of place in so extended a
composition. But Schumann's lasting fame as a composer depends
neither on the Fantasie nor on the sonatas, which are resurrected
rarely—and even then too often.

Just as his courtship of Clara evoked Schumann's finest piano
works, so, in the year of his marriage, it brought forth almost all
his great songs. It was as though he suddenly needed a more personal idiom than the piano, and so went to the poetry of Heine,
Von Chamisso, and other poets and poetasters for the sentiments
germane to his love. Among these verses he found much drivel,
some of which he set as fastidiously as the real poetry. However,
the emotional range of these magnificent song sequences makes
them a glorious epithalamium for Clara.

In Schumann's hands, the accompaniment of the lied achieves
equal—sometimes more than equal—status with the voice, and the
meaning of the lyric dictates the entire shaping of the music. But
he often approached the lied too pianistically, treating the human
voice as though it possessed the flexibility and range of a keyboard.
For this reason, some of his songs are best sung by a phenomenal

mezzo-soprano or baritone. The accompaniments are always rich and varied, frequently of great harmonic interest. The excellent English musicologist, Francis Toye, has even said that "a little gem like the piano-epilogue to the *Dichterliebe*, so satisfying, so exactly right, remains, perhaps, the most striking attribute of Schumann's as a song-writer!"

The songs range from a great dramatic narrative like *Die beiden Grenadiere* to *Erstes Grün*, a trifle packed with almost insupportable poignancy, and include such radiations of pure genius as *Der Nussbaum*, *Ich grolle nicht*, *Die Lotusblume*, *Widmung*, and others less familiar but no less masterly. In his greatest lieder, Schumann achieved a melodic line which, if not so spontaneous as Schubert's, has a deeper and more intellectual configuration. In them, as in the *Carnaval* and the *Fantasiestücke*, the psychological closeness is startling. Not only does the music match the words with exquisite sensitivity, but it has profound overtones not to be echoed until the days of Hugo Wolf and Richard Strauss.

Schumann's life as a composer was divided into periods by abrupt changes of interest. He had abandoned the piano for the lied; now he began to write for orchestra. As early as 1839 he had written to Dorn: "I often feel tempted to crush my piano; it's too narrow for my thoughts. I really have very little practice in orchestral music now; still I hope to master it." In his past was the fragment of a G minor symphony that had met with such meager success that he never completed it. During the nine years between its performance and the writing of the B flat major ("Spring") Symphony in 1841, he had probably yearned more than once to compose in this larger form. The "Spring" Symphony not unnaturally exhibits traces of a fine frenzy (at least for two movements, after which it collapses). It was outlined at the piano in four days, the orchestration followed at once, and it was performed less than two months later at a Gewandhaus concert, with Mendelssohn conducting. The parts baffled the musicians, who were hostile to the work—and not without reason, for Schumann often wrote awkwardly for instruments other than the piano.

Nevertheless, this ambitious flight established Schumann as a "serious" composer. Mendelssohn had lavished great care on the performance, and Schumann could write with pardonable exaggeration that it had been "received as no other since Beethoven."

Its respectable success spurred him on, and shortly afterward he composed the D minor Symphony. This prematurely Tchaikov-skyan work failed to catch the public, and was completely revised ten years later. Wagner heard Liszt and an accomplice play a four-hand arrangement of this revision, and pronounced it banal—to the distress of Liszt, who was trying to promote cordial relations between Wagner and Schumann.

Musicographers have justifiably called 1842 Schumann's cham-ber-music year, for the best of his chamber works belong to it. The Piano Quintet, one of the happiest of his inspirations, was greeted effusively by Mendelssohn, usually positively stingy with praise. It is, indeed, the most sustainedly great chamber writing between Beethoven and Brahms, and remains a favorite with audiences. Lush in harmony and richly varied in theme, this romantic mas-terpiece has a remarkable immediacy of appeal. Here, as in only one other extended composition, Schumann's touch is mysteri-ously sure: he had found the form his material demanded. The string quartets were much less successful, and only the Piano Quar-tet shows something of the genius that shaped the Quintet.

It is little wonder that this debauch of composition in new forms brought on what Schumann called "nerve exhaustion": in three years he had composed thirty of the 148 works published with opus numbers. His appointment, the following year, to teach piano and composition at the newly founded Leipzig conservatory brought distraction from his labors, as well as needed source of income. (His family was growing; the second of his eight children was born in 1843.) Mendelssohn had been named head of the conservatory, and Schumann looked forward eagerly to his work there. But he was an impossible teacher—shy, taciturn, and erratic; his failure to create a rapport with his students sprang from the same cause as his failure as a conductor: his obliviousness to everything except what was going on in his own head. He remained on the staff little more than a year, and then suffered a complete nervous break-down.

Schumann's teaching was interrupted when he went with Clara on a tour through Russia, and by the composition of *Die Paradies und die Peri*, an intolerably dull and sugary business for chorus and orchestra based on the second part of Thomas Moore's fake-Ori-ental epic, *Lalla Rookh*—according to Schumann "one of the sweetest flowers of English verse." This work had some scant success in Germany, but nowhere else, for it exemplifies most of Schumann's faults and his uncertain taste. The Russian tour was a financial success for Clara, and Schumann was welcomed as the champion of romanticism. But he did not improve in health, and reacted petulantly to Clara's enormous fame and popularity.

There has been a conspiracy among the Schumanns' right-thinking biographers to agree uniformly that their marriage was an unqualified success. Such, however, was by no means the case. Clara frequently suffered from not being able to practice for fear of disturbing Schumann in the throes of creation, and from not being able to tour because he disliked her being away. He never reconciled himself to the anomaly of the composer being less popular than the performer. His wife stood with Liszt and Thalberg on the dizziest heights of pianistic fame, and it quite naturally irked him to be referred to as "Clara Schumann's husband." Clara saw it as her duty to act as a buffer between Schumann and the outside world, and there is no doubt that she did that duty with high-minded—and deadly—efficiency. But Schumann, instead of a buffer, needed a bridge to reality. Already, for lack of free contact with outsiders, he was peopling his own private world with phantasms which, as time went on, became increasingly evil.

There can be no doubt that from an exclusively romantic point of view Schumann's marriage was successful. The idea that it was conducive to either his artistic or mental well-being belongs to the world of fable.

On his return from Russia, Schumann gave way to the most ominous melancholy, and for a time wavered perilously near to insanity. He gave up all connection with the *Zeitschrift*, and resigned from the conservatory. His despair when Mendelssohn entrusted the Gewandhaus directorship to Gade was not relaxed by his exaggerated respect for the Dane (he called one of Gade's cantatas "the most important composition of our modern times"). His moroseness over this slight may well have been aggravated by some realization of his own inadequacy as a conductor. Clara says that "he gave himself up for lost." The waters of Carlsbad did not, and could not, help him: he was suffering from an osseous growth that exerted increasing pressure on his brain, though this fact was not revealed until a post-mortem examination. It was agreed that only a complete change of scene could save him. Accordingly, in October, 1844, the Schumanns removed to Dresden.

At first, Schumann lived in complete seclusion, but gradually the ease and gaiety of Dresden life drew him from his solitude, and he began to meet many artists and musicians. Wagner, then *Kapell-meister* at the court theater, had not yet achieved his characteristic style, and Schumann therefore found something good to say of his work. However, he was not carried away by Wagner at any time, and years later wrote of him: "He is, to express myself briefly, not a good musician; he has no understanding for form and euphony. . . . The music apart from the representation is poor, often quite amateurish, empty, and repellent. . . ." Much more uniformly genial was Schumann's association with Ferdinand Hiller, until he went to Düsseldorf a leader of Dresden musical society. Hiller, a musical handyman in the noblest tradition, proved a loyal and admiring friend, always ready to use his strategic position to help his unworldly friend.

Schumann's health varied, but generally it seemed improved. Not so the state of his mind. By this time even a semblance of calm on his part depended on the course of his life running without a single hitch. Unfortunately, he lost an infant son in 1847, and two years later his last remaining brother died. Mendelssohn's death, also in 1847, affected him even more intensely, for Schumann's admiration of him had been tinged with an almost religious awe. His old torments now returned increased. He suffered from lapses of memory; he heard premonitory voices; he fell easily into melancholy and despair, and his temporary recoveries became more and more laborious. Yet he kept on composing indomitably, though many of the works completed in Dresden show evident signs of waning power and growing mental confusion. The most important compositions of this period are *Genoveva*, the *Album für die Jugend*, the Piano Concerto, and *Manfred*.

Genoveva is a musical curiosity, important only as Schumann's single opera. "Do you know what is my morning and evening prayer as an artist?" he had asked. "*German opera*." Yet he selected the legend of Genevieve, the patron saint of Paris, for his libretto. Unfortunately, Genevieve had none of those loose moments that made St. Thaïs a suitable operatic subject. Furthermore, Schumann, in rewriting the libretto, took away from her the few dramatic qualities she possessed. Wagner, with real friendliness, tried vainly to point out what was wrong. When the opera was first performed at Leipzig, with the composer conducting, the consensus was that he had no dramatic gift. The single important dissenter seems to have been Spohr, who mistakenly supposed that *Genoveva* carried out his own operatic theories. Schumann, however, was heartened by the polite applause of critics and audience. He did not realize that opera was decidedly outside the range of his gifts, and that of *Genoveva* only the overture, which has some good moments, would survive.

The much finer *Manfred* music has likewise vanished from the stage, largely because Byron had neglected to make his poem stageable. The overture, however, is sure to last: the music, though unrelievedly somber, is passionate and dramatic; the harmonies are gorgeous and yet subtle, and the whole atmosphere is quintessentially romantic. It is, beyond question, the most successful of Schumann's works for orchestra alone. With superb tactlessness, he planned to dedicate his setting of Byron to Queen Victoria. Fortunately for both parties, this plan fell through.

The Piano Concerto, dedicated to Hiller, and possibly the best known in the standard repertoire, was first performed by Clara. It was for her an occasion of the greatest rejoicing: she had always wanted a "large bravura piece" from her husband. When the Concerto was performed in Leipzig, the Gewandhaus patrons (then the most enlightened on the Continent) were already thoroughly acquainted with Schumann's ideas, but it took this definitive expression of them to evoke the Leipzigers' unqualified enthusiasm. The Piano Concerto offered them an experience for whose equal they had to reach back to Beethoven. The opening allegro, which had had an independent existence since 1841 as a fantasia for piano and orchestra, is unstintedly opulent in melody, and rises to moments of sheer rhapsody. Its cadenza, far from interrupting the mood of the whole movement, sustains it—which makes it a rarity among piano cadenzas. The intermezzo is more restrained and comtemplative, and the marvelously varied rhythms of the finale mount and mingle in a paean of unrestrained joy. These elements combine to produce, in the A minor Concerto, the sovereign gesture of musical romanticism.

The *Album für die Jugend*, a collection of forty-three brief pieces, is often misleadingly bracketed with the *Kinderscenen*, on the grounds that both are music of childhood. The *Kinderscenen*, composed ten years earlier, is a grown man's reverie of his own childhood; the *Album* is actually for children—sharp little pictures that might appeal to any child. In view of Schumann's mental torments, their marked clarity of outline is baffling. They are no more than charming trifles, but are important as the ancestors of thousands of repulsive little pieces—those "Dolly's Lullabies" and "Birdie's Boatsongs" that are the staples of the musical kindergarten.

Schumann continued to compose for the piano, but without his name on them those earnest marches, fugues, and *Albumblätter* would never have found homes even in music libraries. But once more, and inexplicably, he produced a masterpiece for the piano—one unlike anything he had done before. *Vogel als Prophet*, from the *Waldscenen*, is an enigma, with all the magical quality and strange beauties of a changeling. Years later, Claude Debussy heard the same faery note, and musical impressionism was born.

By the middle of 1850 the Schumanns were thoroughly dissatisfied with Dresden, where the composer's talents went unrecognized by court, artists, and public at large. When Wagner lost his post as *Kapellmeister* because of his part in the revolutionary outbreaks of 1848-9, Schumann was passed over in choosing his successor. He abandoned all hope of securing a good musical position in Dresden. Happily, however, the directorship of the Düsseldorf Gesangverein fell vacant when Hiller left to become town musician at Cologne. Before leaving Düsseldorf, he recommended Schumann for this honorable enough post, which carried an annual stipend of seven hundred thaler. Schumann hesitated (he still hoped for bigger things at Vienna or Berlin), but by August it was clear that Düsseldorf was the best he could expect, and he accepted Hiller's proposal.

After a rosy beginning, Schumann got on badly with the Düsseldorfers. His conducting rapidly became notorious. He was incompetent, so lost in a dreamworld of his own that he could not even beat time accurately. Of course, the subtleties of conducting —those attributes of a truly great conductor—were entirely beyond him. On one occasion he went on automatically waving his baton after a composition was finished. Another time, a member of the Gesangverein complained to Clara of Schumann's apathetic gentleness. The more intelligent Düsseldorfers, who had expected a bold and valiant *Davidsbundler*, were overtly disappointed in the taciturn and antisocial composer, whose actions at the conductor's desk seemed to insult their musical sophistication. The bickering between Schumann and his committeemen is at once tragic and comic, and is given a satiric twist by the good burghers' natural desire to get their money's worth. Although most of the time only so in name, Schumann remained director of the Gesangverein until the autumn of 1853.

Of almost fifty works composed during the Düsseldorf period, only one, the E flat major ("Rhenish") Symphony, is still much played. What charm it has reflects Schumann's very warm feeling toward his new home. But its interminable length—it is five movements long—is too sparsely populated with good things, and its windy transitions show Schumann's self-criticism working less than ever. It is hard to judge the *Faust* music, written over a period of years, and completed in Düsseldorf, for it is never performed. As it is possible to hear any number of respectable but uninspired cantatas every few years, the complete silence of Schumann's *Faust* tells an eloquent tale in a novelty-hungry world. Not a bar of this music is available in recordings. And though the learned Dr. Philipp Spitta avers that "up to the latter half of the last chorus it is a chain of musical gems, a perfectly unique contribution to concert literature," the elaborate score looks far from promising.

The Düsseldorf compositions reveal one thing all too clearly: the drying up of Schumann's inspiration. They show, instead of profound conviction, a pedantic, classicizing tendency and a technical facility not at all characteristic of his best efforts. Many of them are choral, and are as empty and sentimental as the verses to which they were written.

Meanwhile, shadows were falling more deeply on Schumann's mind. Years before, he had heard ghostly voices, but only at rare intervals. Now these auditory sensations multiplied and became painful, though it was not until the beginning of 1854 that the process of disintegration became so manifest that Clara, who had been very reluctant to admit that her husband was anything more than moody, became alarmed for his sanity. Fortunately for her, Brahms had appeared in September, 1853, and both the Schumanns were won over by the young viking with his massive blond

mane and awkward, unaffected manner. Schumann roused himself long enough to greet Brahms with the ardor of youth. And
now, in his desire to help this young man, whose genius he at once
recognized, and whom he rather pathetically saw as someone "sent
by God" to carry on his own work, be bethought himself of the
Zeitschrift. It had passed into the hands of Franz Brendel, who was
wholeheartedly devoted to the Neo-German school of Wagner and
Liszt, and therefore unalterably opposed to Schumann. However,
he sent Brendel a high-flown but prophetic article on Brahms, and
the editor felt obliged to print this last message from the magazine's
illustrious founder.

Respite from final darkness was granted until February, 1854,
and these last months in Düsseldorf were gladdened for Schumann
by the warm friendship of Brahms and Joseph Joachim, the latter
of whom the Schumanns had met as a child more than ten years
before. Schumann amused himself with table tapping, a frightening symptom in one whose intelligence and understanding had, up
to this time, been sane and firm despite his growing melancholy.
Strangely enough, Clara did not see the significance of the new
toy. In fact, she treated the whole situation rather lightly. And
possibly she cannot be blamed, for Schumann after his arrival at
Düsseldorf had been ostensibly "cured." And so he stayed, with
some lapses, until the final stage of his malady. As late as the last
months of 1853, he was able to accompany Clara on a Dutch tour,
during which he enjoyed himself. They were back in Düsseldorf
by Christmas, and the January of 1854 passed uneventfully.

On February 6, Schumann wrote to Joachim: "I have often
written you with sympathetic ink, and between these lines, too,
there is a secret writing which will afterwards be revealed. . . .
Music is silent at present, externally at least. . . . And now I
must close. Night is beginning to fall." And darkness was indeed
closing in upon him. The auditory hallucinations developed with
alarming rapidity. He heard choirs of angels, cries of demons. The
spirits of Schubert and Mendelssohn appeared, and gave him a
theme, which he noted down. Voices whispered. He could not
sleep. On the twenty-fourth, he disposed of his fortune and works,
and bade a touching farewell to Clara, now heavy with their eighth
child. On the twenty-sixth, he left the house, walked to the Rhine,
and threw himself in. He was brought home still alive some hours

later by strangers who had managed to get him to shore, and the facts were carefully hidden from Clara in view of her pregnancy.

On March 4, Schumann was removed at his own request to a sanatorium at Endenich, near Bonn. He was never to return home. At times a ray of light penetrated his clouded mind. He did some musical arrangements, and noted down quotations for his projected *Dichtergarten*, which he intended to be a compendium of the best remarks on music from all the greatest writers. He had lucid intervals, during some of which Brahms was with him. But in less than two years all hope of his recovery was abandoned. He lingered, often in acute pain and anguish, until July 29, 1856, when he died in the arms of Clara, who had previously refrained from seeing him for fear of aggravating his condition.

"I saw him in the evening, between six and seven," she wrote. "He smiled at me and put his arms around me with great difficulty, for he had almost lost control of his limbs. Never shall I forget that moment. I would not give that embrace for all the treasures on earth." The next day he was buried in the cemetery at Bonn, and Clara, Hiller, Brahms, and Joachim were present at the ceremony.

Schumann has been called a great music critic so often that it is annoying to discover that he was nothing of the sort. When, in 1831, he penned his first critical effusion, he was a young man with a small literary gift and an overwhelming enthusiasm. His critical method was certainly the strangest ever used: it was based exclusively on impulse. An examination of his so-called critical writings discloses a depressing mixture of praise for the best, the good, the mediocre, and the positively bad. His fame as a critic rests on the happy chance that he began his career by gushing over the young Chopin, and closed it by doing the same service for Brahms.

Schumann was ever betrayed by his uncertain taste. Most of his enthusiasms were for men whose names are today as deservedly dead as the Herzes and Hüntens he himself reprobated in the prologue to his collected writings. Even Meyerbeer, one of his few hatreds, deserved better at his hands than such mediocrities as Gade and Sterndale Bennett. Wagner baffled him completely, even though he heard nothing later than *Tannhäuser*. Hero worship impelled him to overpraise not only the less inspired works of Mendelssohn, but also the trifling imitations of Mendelssohn's satellites.

But Schumann's worst fault as a critic is that he does not criticize. He effuses, he palavers, he strikes a pose, occasionally he vituperates; he almost never describes or analyzes. Even when he is talking about a composition like Mendelssohn's *St. Paul*, his discourse is lyric rather than critical. If by some chance every score of this oratorio were to be destroyed, nothing Schumann said about it would help us to recapture its quality. He always says, "I like" or "I do not like"—rarely does he say anything more.

Schumann was not a true critic of other men's music, and he was not a true critic of his own. He understood the piano, and his happiest and most characteristic pages were composed for that instrument. He did not understand the special character of the chamber ensemble and the orchestra, and in writing for them too often treated them as expanded pianos. Even in the field of the lied, where he has few peers, he did not unfailingly give the human voice music best adapted to its peculiar genius. Schumann was fecund in musical ideas, but his way of expressing them seems often to have been determined by nothing more cogent than the genre that was his passion at the moment.

Everything points to Schumann's inability to cope with this problem of musical choice. Closely allied to it is the failure of his attempts to project his ideas on a large scale. His material is intensely subjective, and is suited just to those short pieces and passages which, in fact, represent him at his best. He lacked that sense of large design which would have enabled him successfully to relate several of these fragments in a symphony or sonata. There is much sound wisdom in Bernard Shaw's wisecrack about the desirability of boiling down all the Schumann symphonies into a potpourri called "Gems from Schumann." There are many moments of great harmonic, rhythmic, and melodic beauty in his larger compositions, but his way of stringing unrelated fragments together does not make for that feeling of inevitability that is the hallmark of the greatest music. But, of course, Schumann was not one of the greatest composers.

Schumann's position is, rather, a high one among masters of the second rank. A few of his works are sure to survive—the Quintet, the Piano Concerto, the overture to *Manfred*, the best of his songs and piano pieces. In them his peculiar genius is at its flood—in the daring rhythms, the somber-textured harmonies, the melodies that distill their essence in bittersweet epigrams. These are not the utterances of a god. Schumann's special magic is his disturbing nearness to us. And he is most disturbing because, once heard, he can never be forgotten. He is the voice of romance.

Chapter XIII

Frédéric-François Chopin

(Zelazowa-Wola, February 22, 1810—
October 17, 1849, Paris)

THERE are still many people who persist in thinking of Chopin as a more or less inspired dilettante and evoker of small musical moods. Yet, he was the most truly original of all composers.* He arrived almost immediately at a personal idiom that is absolutely unmistakable—an original style so pervasive that a fragmentary bar or two will serve to identify a composition as his. With a rare sense of what kingdom he could make his own, he chose to write music for the piano. He never composed an opera or an oratorio, never a symphony, never even a string quartet. These large forms he left to others, and cultivated his own garden. He worked in a dozen or more forms, several of them of his own creation. He is the composer par excellence of inexhaustible variety in infinite detail. Nor, except when he tried to force his idiosyncratic poetry into some larger classical form, did his Flaubertian feeling for the musical *mot juste* interfere with his respect for the architecture of a composition as an entity.

Chopin has never lacked champions, but there is no doubt that his intelligent self-limitation has acted adversely on his fame. The very pervasiveness of his idiom has acted no less adversely. In a certain limited sense, all of his music sounds alike: in their peculiar melodic line and rhythms, their acid-sweet harmonic sequences, their persistent trend to the minor, and their lavish use of ornamentation, the *oeuvres complètes* of Frédéric-François Chopin are a singular phenomenon whose component parts have a deceptive— and, to some, a monotonous—similarity. The elements that shaped his musical language are easy to isolate. Partly Polish, he was the first to introduce a Slavic note into Western music—the experiments of earlier composers, who cast Slavic folk melodies into the absorbent, neutralizing classical mold, do not affect the argument.

* This chapter is written on the assumption that Chopin was a great composer— this as a warning to any violent dissenters from this opinion. The writers know that no argument, however good, would make these dissenters change their minds.

314

He was a neurotic, and his music often expresses a hypersensitive, decadent, and rather feminine personality. Further, he lived in a time and place overfriendly to the flowering of such a personality, and therefore it is no accident that this pampered Pole who spent most of his creative life in Paris wrote the most characteristic musical illustrations of French romanticism.

Chopin is always spoken of as a Polish composer. With more justice, he could be called a French composer. His mother was Polish, he spent the first twenty years of his life in Poland, and he was always violently patriotic—from a safe distance. On the other hand, his father was French, and it was in France, under French influences, that he wrote most of the music by which he is today remembered. Nicolas Chopin, his father, was an *émigré* who had been stranded in Warsaw by the failure of the French snuff manufacturers for whom he had worked. Becoming a tutor in the home of Count Skarbek, he had married the Countess' lady in waiting, Justina Krzyzanowska, herself of noble birth. Frédéric-François, their second child and only son, was born on February 22, 1810, at Zelazowa-Wola, a small village near Warsaw, where the Skarbeks had a country place. The Chopins shortly removed to Warsaw, Nicolas began teaching in several schools (he soon opened a successful tutoring academy of his own), and their home became a favorite resort of artists and intellectuals. They were neither poor nor rich—always comfortable, with money enough for an occasional small luxury. Nicolas was a flautist, Justina a singer of pleasing voice, and the eldest child, Ludwika, played the piano. We must conceive of music, then, as always going on in this pleasant household, and of the fond parents violently distressed when they saw that their infant son reacted with floods of tears to the sound of music. They thought he hated it, and it was only when he began to pick out tunes on the piano that they realized he had been crying for joy. They had a hysteric on their hands, not a music hater.

And so, at the age of six Frédéric began to take lessons from a solid and withal sympathetic Czech piano teacher, Adalbert Zywny, for whom he always entertained a lively feeling of gratitude. Zywny was a devotee of Bach, and trained the boy on *The Well-Tempered Clavichord*, thus giving a firm foundation to his pianism. Not the most brilliant of virtuoso prodigies, Frédéric nevertheless publicly played a concerto on his eighth birthday. The noblemen, and even more the noblewomen, who made up the audience were enchanted by the tiny, winsome child, and from that day until his death Chopin was the darling of the Polish *haute noblesse*—an excellent buffer against the cruel world. He took to his noble admirers as much as they to him. One of his childish pleasures was being taken in Grand Duke Constantine's carriage to a party at the palace. He not unnaturally became a snob, and instead of his snobbishness leaving him, it throve as he matured, and remained one of his less pleasant traits. It must be admitted, however, that Polish society at that time was, with all its absurd prejudices, among the most highly cultivated in Europe, having a genuine interest in the arts, particularly music and poetry.

Frédéric began to dabble with little compositions of his own almost as soon as he could play the piano. His father, without any demur, sent him to Joseph Elsner, the best composition teacher in Warsaw, and a widely known and all too prolific composer. This was the happiest of choices, for one of Elsner's favorite maxims (which should be emblazoned over the door of every music school) was: "It is not enough for a student to equal or surpass his master; he should create an individuality of his own." He instantly recognized that Chopin's were no usual gifts, and allowed him what certain austere critics have considered too much leeway in developing them. Chopin realized his debt to Elsner, and the bond between them lasted throughout his life. These lessons with Zywny and Elsner constituted his entire formal education, with the exception of three years at the Warsaw Lycée, where he took no interest in his courses. He passed them by the skin of his teeth, and was graduated at the age of seventeen—a slender, dandified, effeminate boy, whose pallor and feeble physique told of a hothouse life divided between the music room and the salons of high society.

Chopin craved adventure, adventure to him meaning life as it was lived in the cosmopolitan centers of Europe. In 1828, he got a glimpse of Berlin as the guest of a family friend who went there to attend a scientific congress presided over by the eternal Alexander von Humboldt. He stared wistfully at Spontini and Mendelssohn, but was too timid to introduce himself. He reveled in the sumptuous stagings of several operas, and wrote home that Handel's *Ode for St. Cecilia's Day* "most nearly approaches my ideal of

sublime music." After this tactful and far from intoxicating four-
week introduction to the great world beyond the Polish frontier,
Chopin was back in Warsaw absorbed in musical study and composition. The advent of Johann Nepomuk Hummel, that phenomenal ambassador of the eighteenth century to the nineteenth,*
aroused the lad's restlessness; that of Paganini made it intolerable.
Furthermore, he was racked by all the torments of calf love: the
object of his passion was a pretty soprano, but Chopin had not
the courage to declare himself, and merely suffered and talked
about his "ideal."

Nicolas Chopin decided that such agony and nostalgia should
be indulged, and accordingly, in the summer of 1829, the money
for a Viennese trip was somehow found. In Vienna, Frédéric succumbed gracefully to a slender success. He found, to start with,
that a publisher was on the verge of issuing his variations for piano
and orchestra on "Là ci darem" from Don Giovanni. Then he was
persuaded, almost against his will, to give a concert "in a city
which can boast of having heard a Haydn, a Mozart, and a Beethoven." He was needlessly nervous, for the concert was so successful that, a week later, he had to give another. The critics were
extremely friendly, and there was a flurry in the female dovecotes.
There were a few dissenters: Moscheles said his tone was "too
small," and one woman was heard to say, "It's a pity he's so
insignificant-looking."

Chopin returned home sighing more woefully than ever for his
soprano and bored to death with the attractions of Warsaw. His
letters to Titus Wojciechowski, the confidant of his maidenly hopes
and fears, quiver with self-pity and verbal breast-beating. This no
doubt thoroughly masculine young man seems to have been for
some years a surrogate for the girls Chopin lacked the boldness to
speak out to. There is something decidedly ambiguous about these
letters, with their kisses, embraces, and wheedling sentimentality,
gently chiding "my dearest life"—Titus!—for his unresponsive-
ness. There is no suggestion of the overtly abnormal anywhere in
Chopin's life, and indeed he outgrew his effusive outpourings to
men friends, but without developing into an aggressive male. It is

---

* The pupil of Haydn, Mozart, and Salieri, and the friend of Beethoven, he
taught, among other *notabili*, Czerny, Hiller, and Thalberg.

impossible fully to understand his music unless we recognize the generous feminine component in his nature.

Warsaw held Chopin for little more than a year, during which time he fretfully and vaguely made and unmade plans for the future. He thrice played successfully in public, the third time with his pretty soprano as assisting artist—which may well have been the climax of his intimacy with her. At last he made up his wavering mind: on November 1, 1830, he left Warsaw. He was still vague about his plans, his itinerary was "parts unknown," but for the time being he was going to Vienna with Titus Wojciechowski. As he passed through his birthplace, Elsner had a cantata sung in his honor, and did not (despite a legend to the contrary) present him with an urnful of Polish earth—an appropriate gift, it would have been for Chopin never returned home.

Vienna amazed and annoyed Chopin by turning an exceedingly cold shoulder. The publisher who had been so nice to him on the previous trip still wished to sponsor certain of his compositions— if he could get them for nothing. His former friends were either bankrupt or sick or out of town. And scarcely had Chopin and Titus settled down before they heard that the Poles had rebelled against the Russian tyranny. Titus was off at once to fight for Poland, and Frédéric, after weeping for a day, decided to follow him. En route he changed his mind, and within a few days was back in his comfortable lodgings. It seems more than odd that the bereft youth remained for over six months in a city that was not only indifferent to him, but which, after the rebellion broke out, became violently anti-Polish. In July, 1831, Chopin was again on the road, with no destination except a vague feeling that he might end up in London. At Stuttgart he heard that the Russians had retaken Warsaw, which seems to have surprised as well as agitated him, though fortunately he received letters from his family that banished his more horrific visions. Late in September, he arrived in Paris, intending merely to see the sights and meet the important musicians. Instead, he stayed for the rest of his life.

The slight, blond-haired young Pole with the prominent aquiline nose, who arrived on the Parisian scene in the second year of Louis-Philippe's reign, already had a small fame. He was known in his homeland and in a few cities outside as a pianist whose delicate style and exquisite nuances made overhearing him in a large hall something of a problem. He was by now the composer of several ambitious piano works with orchestral accompaniment, not to speak of a number of smaller pieces for piano alone. The history of Chopin's development as a composer indicates that these orchestral works—all written before he was twenty-one—were little more than shrewd bids for recognition in a musical world whose snobbish arbiters were inclined to look askance at anyone who had not a symphony or an opera, or at least a concerto, to his credit. A composer of mere piano pieces had no chance to enter this charmed circle. Chopin knew this, got the required big works off his chest, and, with his reputation established, turned exclusively to the solo pieces in which he knew his strength lay.

No man ever made a wiser decision. Chopin had no talent for orchestration, no real understanding of the deeper issues involved in composing a work in several movements: he lacked the long breath needed for such an enterprise. Schumann's mistaken choriambics over the "*Là ci darem*" Variations come under the heading of clairvoyance rather than of criticism. The two piano concertos are both played, but no one has ever been satisfied with them. Numerous musical mechanics have tried their hands at virilizing the orchestration, once so successfully that the piano part itself had to be reinforced. No amount of tinkering, however, could ever give either of them more than a surface unity. It is true, but by no means complimentary, to say that the concertos are at their best when they most nearly resemble Chopin's solo pieces, when, in short, he forgets the orchestra (which he often does), and writes a sprightly waltz or rondo. Separate movements of these concertos could easily be made into solo pieces without loss of effectiveness— and possibly with gain in the allegro vivace of the F minor or the rondo of the E minor. Among the many reasonable criticisms leveled at the Chopin concertos, no one has impugned their melodic charm, insinuating adornments, or persuasive rhythms. They are not great music, but they are very pleasant to listen to.

So we may gather that Chopin at once stepped into a respectable if not distinguished niche in Parisian musical life. Paris, in the early thirties of the nineteenth century, was the capital of artistic Europe. Cherubini was still, despite his Italian name, the grand old man of French music, and the popular composers were, after Rossini, who led the field by a long stretch, Meyerbeer,

Auber, and Louis Hérold, whose *Zampa*, produced just after Chopin's arrival, gave him a phenomenal popularity that was cut short by his premature death two years later. Vincenzo Bellini, the composer of *Norma*, though already a great name, was not to arrive on the scene until 1833, when he and Chopin, so alike in melodic style, and sharing a passion for Mozart, formed a friendship that lasted until the young Sicilian's death in 1835. Berlioz was shaking his fierce red locks at the dried-up elders of classicism. Franz Liszt, youthful and dreamy as in Ingres' poetic drawing, divided honors at the keyboard with Friedrich Kalkbrenner, a massively correct pedant who once told Chopin that he might do something for his playing if Chopin would but study with him for three years. At the Opéra the galaxy included such luminaries as Malibran and Pasta, Rubini and Lablache. No less brilliant was the literary scene, where the already aged Chateaubriand, with many years of literary doddering before him, was yielding to the ultraromanticists led by Victor Hugo, the colossus of the future, whose hectic *Hernani* was the defi of the young fanatics. Balzac was established, Stendhal was at the height of his powers, and Gautier, Dumas, and Mérimée were on the ascent. Heine, with his puny, ailing body and flashing mind, was in Paris squeezing out the utmost rapture from the pseudo revolution of 1830. Over painting, the coldly disciplined genius of Ingres exercised a chilling dictatorship; the youthful opposition was rallying around Delacroix, whose tumultuous canvases scandalized the official salons.

Everywhere classicism was in retreat. Music alone awaited its first out-and-out romantic masters: two of them—Chopin and Liszt—were at hand.

To make his name weigh in such a splendid artistic society was, at first, no easy task. Chopin was next to penniless, but there seemed no doubt that among the many publics Paris could offer, there must be one for him. A debut concert, arranged for December, 1831, was postponed until late January. Then the critic Fétis, who had a strong aversion to praising anyone, shouted his approval, and Mendelssohn, though he was wont to speak condescendingly of the composer as "Chopinetto," warmly applauded the pianist. The concert enhanced Chopin's reputation among musicians, but only a few Polish *émigrés* had bought tickets, and his pockets remained empty. Three months later, he played with

equally depressing financial results at a fashionable charity concert, and was so dejected that he decided to move to America. Unfortunately for the muse of comic history, Chopin never had a
chance to add another by no means needed note of color to Andrew Jackson's United States. Fortunately for him, he accidentally
met Prince Valentin Radziwill, who was aghast at the idea of
Chopin departing for such savage shores. He persuaded him to try
his luck at Baron Jacques de Rothschild's. There, amid some of the
best names in the *Almanach de Gotha*, he conquered Parisian society,
and came away with a prince, a princess, a duchess, and a count as
his sponsors. As a result, with engagements to play, and with plenty
of lessons at twenty francs a head, his financial problems were
solved for over a decade.

Chopin never deplored the inroads of society on his time: he had
a well-developed frivolous side, adored the company of beautiful
women of rank, and unfolded all his petals in a really select
gathering. Once he had entree, he gave much attention to the
business of cutting a fine figure in Parisian high society. He kept his
own carriage, was something of a clotheshorse, and in many respects was quite like one of the young swells of the Jockey Club.
His social vices were characteristic of the highborn Pole domiciled
in Paris: he was snobbish to the point of stupidity, and often
treated those he considered his inferiors with brusque discourtesy.
Of a part with this was his fanatical contempt for Jews—unless
they happened to be Rothschilds, a Mendelssohn, or a Heine.
He used the epithets "Jew" and "pig" interchangeably for anyone who incurred, even unwittingly, his disfavor. Ever a sensitive
plant, imbibing his impressions, and most of his nonmusical ideas,
from his immediate ambience, Chopin did not think out these
absurd attitudes, but accepted them as unthinkingly as he did the
fashion of wearing yellow gloves.

The Chopin of the overheated ballrooms with countless countesses moving in the candlelight was the composer of the valses—
less than a score spaced over almost twenty years. There are
valses in all moods—gay, insouciant, disdainful, *dolce far niente*,
somber, languorous, pensive—all evoking the ballroom and the
spirit of the dance. Only rarely, however, are they truly dance
music, and never are they valses in the good, forthright Johann
Strauss tradition. They have rhythm, and when this rhythm is not

too vagrant, parts of them could be used in a ballroom. As it is, several of them have been orchestrated for ballet—witness those in that appalling choreographic museum called *Les Sylphides*. It takes a ballet dancer, disciplined to cope with all manner of musical surprise, to follow the subtle retards and accelerations of Chopin's perplexing conception of unchanging three-four time. The valses are really just what Chopin intended them to be—piano pieces, salon pieces to be played intimately. They are all charming, many of them enjoy world-wide popularity,* some of them have moments of exquisite tenderness and meditation. Yet, with the possible exception of the C sharp minor, they are without the special tang and color of Chopin, the revolutionary of the pianoforte. The valses are Chopin's trivia.

The truth is that the valses, having their source in no deep emotions, but bubbling off the surface of Chopin's life, could never rise above charm. Yet, he could make other dance forms the vehicles of eloquent emotion. Such were the polonaise and the mazurka, where the fact that they were Polish dances touched off a complex of personal feelings—patriotism, homesickness, pride of race, a realization of exile—that make them spiritually sincere, artistically creative as the valses almost never are.

The polonaise, which in Liszt's deft but insensitive hands became an omnibus of piano effects, in Chopin's was a magnificent catch at lofty and poetic moods. In this superb dozen of epic dances—great vigorous dances for noble men—it is hard to find the Chopin whom John Field (himself a minor poet at the keyboard) described as "a sickroom talent." With the exception of the clangorous *"Militaire,"* the polonaises have seldom won the great popular favor they deserve: they are too difficult for any except the strongest and most agile virtuoso; they are entirely beyond the reach of the amateur who can manage a valse or a prelude. Yet, even a long-neglected polonaise can be dusted off, and used by a great pianist to bring down the house. In capable hands they are absolutely sure-fire. The main reason for this is that, apart from their specific musical beauties, they are amazingly exciting. Three of them tower above the rest, and belong definitely to the greater Chopin. These big works require such a wide range of dynamics,

* In one case, at least, unfortunately. Of the so-called "Minute" Valse, in D flat, James Huneker said that "like the rich, it is always with us."

and teem with so many fortissimos and sforzandos, that it is impossible to imagine their own composer, with his feeble attack, doing them justice. Chopin often said that he "heard" certain of his compositions only when Liszt played them for him, and these three giants must have been among them. The F sharp minor Polonaise is a tortured, stormy introspection divided into two parts by a whispering aside in mazurka style—an enigmatic pause that, in addition to supplying vivid dramatic contrast, suggests nostalgia and bittersweet musings. The A flat Polonaise is a triumphant composition; occasionally called the "Heroic," it almost equals the *"Militaire"* in popularity. It is as outward-turned as the F sharp minor is inward-searching. It represents the joy, completely impersonal, of great issues happily decided. There remains the Polonaise-Fantaisie, likewise in A flat, vast, ambiguous, and less structurally well knit than most of Chopin's piano pieces. After some difficulty in getting started—it makes three false starts (a Lisztian trick)—it vaporizes beautifully for several pages, which are studded with quasi-Schumannesque epigrams, achieves a satisfactory climax, collapses, and inconsequentially sets off on another tack and works up into one of the most effective climaxes in all of Chopin.

For expressing more intimate and evanescent moods than seem native to the polonaise, Chopin turned to another Polish dance— the mazurka. He wrote fifty-six mazurkas of amazing variety, but almost all intensely Slavic in feeling. Many have recourse to the most exotic harmonies and melodic intervals. The way they break the rules, sometimes to produce an authentic Slavic effect, sometimes out of sheer disdain, infuriated the theorists of the day. Even the much freer rules of modern harmony might not admit some of these strange progressions, but the ear—music's best arbiter— allows them because they seem to arise inevitably out of the whole design and context of the music. Lovely, haunting, eerily seductive though they are, the mazurkas have never been concert hits, not because audiences would not like them, but because they offer few big chances to heroic virtuosos. This is perhaps just as well: the mazurkas would lose some of their bloom at the hands of keyboard giants in the wide spaces of the concert hall. They need, far more than the valses, and quite as much as the preludes, the small room, the right time, the personal touch. Among the fifty-six, you are bound to find at least one that will fit your mood (unless you long to overturn a dictator or improve your game of golf), and the technical difficulties are not formidable enough to keep you from expressing yourself adequately. There are, as Huneker said, Chopin mazurkas that are "ironical, sad, sweet, joyous, morbid, sour, sane and dreamy"—moods for any man.

It is not easy to picture this master of moods as a piano teacher, however fashionable. Yet, from 1832 on, much of his everyday life was a pedagogue's, and the strange thing is that he seems to have relished teaching. It led him to the best houses. Oddly enough, not one of his known pupils became a great pianist, though there is a legend that Louis Moreau Gottschalk, that Creole Don Juan of the keyboard, studied with him. This story is supported by the fact that Gottschalk introduced Chopin's music in America. The most promising pupil Chopin ever had was a child prodigy who died at the age of fifteen, and of whom Liszt said, "When he starts playing, I'll shut up shop." But most of Chopin's pupils were dilettante aristocrats of both sexes, female predominating.

It was left for Chopin the composer, through two sets of twelve etudes,* to become, after Bach, the most inspired of keyboard pedagogues. Bach, in seeking to establish the perfect relationships of the tempered scales, produced forty-eight preludes and fugues that, besides being inherently beautiful, are still the classic touchstone of piano pedagogy. Chopin, who always limbered up for his own concerts by playing from *The Well-Tempered Clavichord*, made, in the etudes, a series of field maps of the territories he had had to explore in order to enlarge the range of piano technique. In almost every one of them he dealt with a problem, or related problems, incidental to the new kind of music he was composing, and there is plenty of internal evidence, despite the multifarious programs that have been suggested for various etudes, that they were deliberately designed as exercises for overcoming specific difficulties. The study in thirds (Opus 25, No. 6) and the tremendous one in octaves (Opus 25, No. 10) reveal their teaching purposes at a glance. But even such a demoniac outburst as the "Revolutionary" (Opus 10, No. 12) is easily analyzed as "a bravura study of the

---

* For the three supplementary etudes, published in 1840 as part of Fétis and Moscheles' *Méthode des méthodes pour le piano*, there have been many apologists, though they are the least strong of Chopin's studies.

very highest order for the left hand." In a few, the specific problem is not so easily isolated, but it is always there. Yet Edward Dannreuther absent-mindedly stated that Chopin's etudes "have no didactic purpose": he seems to have been duped by their musical quality into believing that they could not have had a practical inception. But that is the miracle of the etudes: in setting forth the technical problems, Chopin invariably created music that could stand on its own merits. The best of the etudes, indeed, are among the finest compositions for the piano. It has been truly said that he who can play the Chopin etudes can play anything in modern piano literature. Nor does this refer merely to technique.

When Chopin was not teaching or composing or attitudinizing gracefully in candlelit salons, he was competing with other famous pianists of the day. Early in 1833, he appeared with Liszt on a benefit program for Harriet Smithson, the mediocre Irish actress who had kindled a forest fire of passion in Berlioz' heart. The next year he played at a concert given by Berlioz himself, though he once said maliciously of the mad Hector's music that anyone was fully justified in breaking off with the man who wrote it. Meanwhile, other pianists were bringing certain of his own compositions (precisely those that are more or less forgotten today) before the public, not only in Paris, but in Germany. Clara Wieck and Liszt were among his early interpreters.

Little more than two years after he was prepared to stake everything on a melodramatic expedition to America, Chopin had become one of the most famous men in Paris. His compositions were eagerly sought after by publishers, and yet it is curious that one of his most popular pieces, the Fantaisie-Impromptu, though composed at this time, was not published until six years after his death. As most of his posthumous compositions were those he considered unworthy of publication, can it be that he had small use for this favorite? The sloppy cantabile (which, almost unchanged, was to become the epidemic *I'm Always Chasing Rainbows*) lends color to this supposition, though the sheer rhythmical inspiration of the allegro agitato and presto more than compensates for it. The whole piece has a brilliant improvisational quality that makes it a true impromptu: the word "Fantaisie" was a meddlesome afterthought by the publisher.

In May, 1834, with money secured hastily by selling a valse be-

hind his regular publisher's back, Chopin went with Hiller to the
Lower Rhine Festival at Aix-la-Chapelle. Mendelssohn was there
in high spirits, and after the festival was over bore them off to
Düsseldorf. He was enthusiastic if ambiguous about Chopin's
playing: "As a pianoforte player he is now one of the very first—
quite a second Paganini. . . ." But the classicist in Mendelssohn
added that Chopin often lost sight "of time and calmness and real
musical feeling": in those days the Pole's "leaning about within
the measure"—his notorious rubato—was a revolutionary novelty
not yet dulled by volumes of discussion. Evidently Mendelssohn
never understood its real function.* And, indeed, he was of two
minds about Chopin the composer, finding him "discordant"
and too mannered, though admitting his soulfulness—a dubious
compliment that Chopin returned by damning Mendelssohn's
works *in toto*. Nor was Chopin more appreciative of Schumann,
whom he met during his last visits to Germany in 1835 and 1836.
In view of Schumann's continuing service to Chopin's reputation,
the unhappy fellow might have hoped for something better at his
hands than the cold remark that "*Carnaval* is not music at all."

The year 1835 was one of the stormiest in Chopin's life. In the
first place, he became deeply depressed by the public's tepid reaction to his playing—he foolishly matched his salon touch against
Liszt's thunderous pianism in large halls, and naturally cut a poor
figure. In early April, the two of them played at a charity concert,
and the applause for Chopin was almost as delicate as his playing.
He concluded gloomily that he had better stick to composing, and
said unhappily to Liszt: "I am not fitted to give concerts. The
crowd intimidates me; I feel asphyxiated by its breath, paralyzed
by its curious look, dumb before the strange faces; but you, you
are destined for the crowd, because when you do not captivate
your public, you have the wherewithal to overpower it." A spiteful remark. Was he implying that what Liszt could not do legiti-
mately, he accomplished with sex appeal and piano-pounding?
After this, Chopin rarely played in public. His reputation as a keyboard sorcerer depends almost exclusively on the reports of friends
and fellow musicians who heard him play his own compositions at
private musicales.

* It remained for Berlioz, the unflinching breaker of rules, to castigate Chopin
primly for his rubato, saying: "Chopin *could* not play in strict time."

The figure Chopin cut at these aristocratic gatherings healed whatever wounds his vanity suffered at the hands of the larger public. He was a male coquette—there are abundant traces of coquetry in his lighter pieces—and many of his usually inconclusive romances began as he poured out his ardent Slavic soul at the keyboard and swept his susceptible audience with his lustrous eyes. There was something about this slight, poetic-looking exquisite that would have made conquests easy for him if he had had more sheer male drive. But so shrinking was he that the woman had to be the aggressor, and there is good reason for believing that he did not have his first sexual experience until 1834 or 1835, when he was seduced by a misunderstood wife, the talented and glamorous Countess Delphine Potocka. There was real affection between them, but the liaison was cut short when her jealous husband, by stopping her allowance, forced her to return to Warsaw.

Apparently while suffering from this deprivation, Chopin went to Carlsbad to visit his parents. After two happy months, not realizing that they would never meet again, he left them and went on to Dresden to see the Wodziński family, friends of his childhood. There, or the following year at Marienbad, he seems to have offered marriage to the youthful Countess Marja Wodzińska, though evidently without being passionately in love with her. The details of the affair, about which so many doleful conjectural pages have been printed, remain extremely obscure. Certain it is that Count Wodziński objected to a musician son-in-law, but just as certainly Chopin for two years looked forward to marrying Marja. He was longing for a wife and home—the specific Marja was a secondary consideration. In 1837, while he still considered himself plighted to her, she made it clear, by the cold tone of her letters, that marriage was out of the question.

If these abortive relationships, these yearnings for romance, these searchings for lasting love, have a musical gloss, it is preeminently in the nocturnes. Unlike the mazurka or polonaise, the nocturne is a fluid mood piece, not a distinct musical form. What gives Chopin's nocturnes their family resemblance is precisely their yearning, searching, often darkling mood. In the hands of Haydn and Mozart, a *notturno* had been an orchestral serenade. John Field, the Irish virtuoso who was St. Petersburg's most fashionable piano teacher in the early nineteenth century, published the first piano pieces to be called nocturnes, by which he meant evocations of night moods, and Chopin, who knew Field, appropriated the idea. Field, to judge by his sane, pellucid nocturnes, felt the same by night as by day. Not so Chopin, whose moods deepened as the shades of night fell. His nocturnes are the music of exacerbated nerves. Their sickly phosphorescence illumines the jungle places, the tropical miasmas of his psyche. They express not only Chopin the thwarted lover, but Chopin the neurotic, the ambivalent, the decadent. The most flagrant ones would be appropriately heard in a hothouse. Almost all of them are harmonically lush—"fruity," Huneker called one of them. At least two are Chopin in the grand manner—the C sharp minor (Opus 27, No. 1) and the C minor, the latter one of his finest inspirations, if the least nocturnelike, with its sonorous Mendelssohn-*cum*-Wagner triumphal march and the magical *doppio movimento* with its strangely Brahmsian motion. In some respects, the nocturnes, which so often exaggerate his idiosyncrasies to the point of caricature, are the most Chopinesque of all his works. They have ended by doing a disservice to his reputation, for it is upon oversentimentalized interpretations of them by oversentimental pianists that the conception of Chopin as "the Polish tuberose" chiefly rests.

An excellent corrective for this one-sided conception of Chopin is furnished by the four scherzos, the most human and variable of which—that in B flat minor—was published the very year his hope of settling down with the Wodzińska was dashed. The scherzos are stalwarts, and the first three are works of impassioned vigor. Like the three giant polonaises, they demand great strength, a bravura technique, and an understanding of musical Byronics. They have little if any likeness to earlier scherzos, which developed out of the minuet, and which, in the hands of Beethoven, became pieces of titanic playfulness. They are almost equally distant from Mendelssohn's gossamer adaptation of the classical scherzo. Indeed, it is difficult to understand why Chopin called these four moody pieces scherzos at all. The first one, for example, might just as well be called *War and Peace*. But instead of criticizing his arbitrary naming, we ought rather to enjoy them as prime examples of musical energy at high speed (they are all marked presto), and be thankful that their creator did not shackle them together with unnatural bonds, and call the whole a sonata—a thing he was quite capable of doing.

In composition Chopin could find release for ordinary emotional pressures, but in the case of Marja Wodzińska he could not thus exorcise the specter of his shattered hopes. His health suffered, and he sank into ominous lethargy. When he did not rally, two of his friends coaxed him into going with them to London. They were gone less than a fortnight—but long enough, it has been said, for the combination of English weather and his lowered vitality to impair Chopin's congenitally weak lungs. He returned home suffering in body and mind, and might well have surrendered himself completely to despair and disease if the entire course of his life had not been changed by one of the most remarkable women of the nineteenth century—George Sand. They had met in the winter of 1836 at the home of Liszt's mistress, the Countess d'Agoult, and were on friendly terms even before his ill-advised English journey. Almost immediately after his return, they were seen everywhere together. By the summer of 1838, they were so intimate that they spent their vacation together at Nohant, her château in the Loire country. Thus began the most publicized love affair in musical history.

In the game of love, the febrile Frédéric was no match for this Semiramis of letters. Mme Sand came of a line of great lovers: Augustus the Strong of Saxony was her paternal great-great-grandfather. Her mother's father sold turtledoves in the streets of Paris. She herself was illegitimate—by a month. Although she married a baron and bore him two children, her present fame rests largely on her affairs with a singular cavalcade of distinguished men, which in no way interfered with her frightening productivity as a writer. She was at least as famous in her day as George Eliot, but whereas the Englishwoman had to content herself with the author of an indifferent book on Aristotle, Sand tried and discarded, besides a few anonymities, Mérimée, De Musset, and Chopin. Among those who literally worshiped her not only as a priestess of letters but also as a humanitarian, feminist, and nature cultist were such diverse personages as Heine, Balzac, Sainte-Beuve, Flaubert, Arnold, George Eliot, and Elizabeth Barrett Browning—who knelt to kiss her hand when they were introduced. Six years Chopin's senior, she was, at the time of their meeting, at the height of her fame, a woman of wide sympathies, powerfully male in intelligence, but devouringly maternal in her attitude toward her lovers.

At first Chopin had found Mme Sand repellent, but before he knew precisely what was happening to him, her enveloping sympathy had lapped him in the mother love he yearned for. He became enslaved. Nothing else explains a man so prim about moral appearances (he broke off friendly relations with Liszt because he had used Chopin's rooms for an assignation) going off to spend the summer with this dumpy sibyl, for it was as much as a young man's reputation was worth to be seen in her company in those days. He then threw discretion farther to the winds, and spent a wet, miserable winter with her on the island of Majorca. Chopin was desperately ill during this nightmarish honeymoon: he and Mme Sand and her children were objects of vengeful suspicion by the superstitious natives (primarily because they did not go to church), and were starved into seeking refuge at an abandoned monastery, where they put up for several wretched months. His ill-heated, damp cell and the vile food again wrecked his health, and when finally they made their escape from the island, Chopin, suffering constantly from hemorrhages, was carried aboard the stinking freighter in an advanced stage of phthisis. Eventually the weary travelers put in at Marseilles, and there Chopin recuperated slowly before returning to Nohant for the summer.

A novelist, faced with the problem of solving the fate of so wrecked a hero as Chopin was when he landed at Marseilles, might be excused for incontinently killing him off. Not being a fictionist's puppet, Chopin chose to live ten years more. Not only that, he brought back with him from Majorca, besides two polonaises and a ballade, the twenty-four preludes of Opus 28. It is not known how many of these were actually composed there—probably but a very few—but certainly most of the business of "selecting, filing, and polishing" them was done on the island. It was, in fact, by promising to deliver a book of preludes that Chopin had received the wherewithal for the Majorca trip. Like the nocturnes, the preludes do not have a formal character of their own. They are, again, mood pieces, but there is good reason to play them as a group, for they are arranged, like the preludes and fugues of *The Well-Tempered Clavichord*, in key sequence, one in every possible major and minor key. They range in length from that sketch for "the funeral march of nations" in C minor to the turbulent, rampaging B flat minor, in mood from the truly happy D major to the Caliban's face in A minor. The preludes, if they have any family resemblance at all, lie between the improvisatory nocturnes and the etudes with their masterly free working-out of technical problems. Several of them are extremely popular, notably the brooding, sunless E minor, the yearningly sad B minor, the tiny mazurkalike A major, the so-called "Raindrop" Prelude, with its muffled march of dead monks (George Sand's idea), the solemn C minor, and the rippling, open-air F major. The nineteenth, in E flat major, is one of the most light-shot pages Chopin ever composed—its swirling rhythms are as graceful as those of a Botticelli drapery.

The refining of these preludes had been somehow accomplished in the sordid misery of the Majorca winter. Now, after the healing months in Marseilles and Nohant, Chopin returned to Paris and entered upon one of the most productive periods of his life. He was unquestionably much in love with Mme Sand, and through her achieved a kind of emotional stability he had craved and needed. His work benefited: "His melodies are purer, his rhythms more virile, his harmonies richer," William Murdoch has noted. "Something has happened that has broadened every idea, made nobler every inspiration and given greater shape to every conception." Settled down in Paris in the same house with Mme Sand, Chopin worked at his art with a passion, a concentrated fervor that, in the brief space of two years, produced a spate of splendid new pieces, many of them on an unwontedly large scale. The first to see the light of day after the preludes was that amazing suite of pieces Chopin chose to call the B flat minor Sonata.* Hearing it for the first time, Schumann declared, "To have called this a sonata must be reckoned a freak, if not a piece of pride; for he has simply yoked together four of his maddest children. . . ." The first two movements are Beethovian in scope, though scarcely in character, the first breathless and disturbed, with musing episodes quickening finally into a gigantic crescendo; the second a vigorous, stormy, impassioned scherzo that demands muscles of steel for an eloquent

---

* Chopin had already made one desperate attempt to write a true classical sonata —in C minor—and failed.

reading. These two movements glow and give off sparks. What, however, can be said of the next part—the famed *Marche funèbre*, with its sudden and irrelevant heavy-footedness? Some pianists play it with such magic (though even they cannot relate it to the rest of the sonata) that we momentarily forget that it is Chopin at his worst. Self-conscious mourners plod along in their secondhand mourning, bells toll, somewhere a voice is calling. . . . A trio in D flat major that cuts the march in two is pure sugar. The fourth movement is a whirring toccata, classic in shape but not in harmony. Played pianissimo and in one color, it brushes the ears like the ghost of music.

The second and best of Chopin's three* impromptus came hard on the heels of the B flat minor Sonata. Not as carefree or as truly improvisational as the previously published one in A flat, and free of the overexoticism of the nocturnelike G flat major published later, the F sharp major Impromptu seems to be telling a story— but a musical story that needs no program. It is difficult to think of this as an impromptu: it is more like a lovingly planned ballade, various in mood, bafflingly unified in design, dramatic in build-up and impact. In the four ballades, the middle two of which were also published in this same period of renascence, Chopin actually wrote program music. The specific story of each matters not at all, for though they have a storylike quality they are persuasive and sufficient as absolute music. The G minor, endowed with one of the most insinuating of melodies, explores in many directions, has its moments of victory, soars aloft on an ethereal valse tune, and seems about to end as it began when the irruption of some vast and indomitable force, tragic in effect and blind in fury, wreaks its havoc in some of music's grandest and most powerful dynamics. The second ballade, in F major, which has been called "mysterious," is, after this, a poor thing. The A flat is elegant, suave, a society dandy—the favorite of all the ballades. It is beautiful, ingratiating, slight. The last ballade—the F minor—is a nocturne *in excelsis,* storied in some fabulous south. Its emotional climate shifts from calm to a threat of storm. The calms of its Eden seduce but cloy, yet the storm is magnificent when it breaks. Altogether a superb if enigmatic composition.

Finally, the very keystone of Chopin's greater art belongs to this

* Four, if the Fantaisie-Impromptu is counted.

remarkable period of unstinted creativeness. The F minor Fantaisie has been called "a Titan in commotion," and all sorts of programs have been suggested for it, one more absurd than the other, as if Chopin could not have reared this vast fabric without binding it together with trivial anecdotage. Even he himself had a program for it—according to Liszt, whose biography of Chopin must be taken as a floral tribute rather than a source of information.* The Fantaisie is a big composition in every sense: the themes are not only very beautiful but also extremely malleable and susceptible to development; the large design is carried out with complete success, sustained by passionate and unfaltering intellectual attention. This masterly composition finally refutes Sir W. H. Hadow's careless statement that "in structure Chopin is a child playing with a few simple types, and almost helpless as soon as he advances beyond them." Woe to the brash pianist who attacks the Fantaisie as if it were what its name might imply—a piece with only vague formal unity! He must realize that the Fantaisie has an architecture of its own as discoverable and as cogent to its interpretation as that of a classical sonata. When played by an artist who thinks as well as moves his fingers, the Fantaisie emerges in all its three-dimensional grandeur as one of the most dramatic, impressive, and satisfying works ever written for the solo piano.

The creative effort that had produced within two years such a ponderable and splendid part of Chopin's lifework was superhuman in a man who was slowly dying. It could not be kept up. The story of his life after 1841 is one of decline, and for six years its pattern was unvarying. Every summer he went to Mme Sand's château at Nohant, where her sensible nursing helped him gather strength for the autumn and winter season in Paris. Every winter he had a few pieces ready for his publishers, and he always had strength enough to quarrel with them over terms. Otherwise these years passed almost without incident, unless they be judged in terms of a day-by-day history of the Parisian salon. Twice Chopin came out of his retirement. Like Achilles sulking in his tent, he had for years held aloof from the concert stage of his beloved Paris.

* A floral tribute, however, with some malodorous and poisonous blooms. Part of this book is said to come from the pen of one of Liszt's last mistresses, Princess Carolyne Sayn-Wittgenstein.

Suddenly, on April 26, 1841, he appeared in a semipublic concert with the great soprano, Laure Cinti-Damoreau, who had created Mathilde in *William Tell*. The privileged, selected audience—mostly his aristocratic friends and pupils—received him rapturously. The next year, on February 21, he gave another concert, this time with his friend Pauline Viardot-García, one of the most intelligent singers of the age.

In 1844, his father died, and news of this, together with the growing tension between him and Mme Sand, prostrated Chopin. Every year he submitted himself to the now painful ordeal of Nohant, seeing in her less and less the mistress, more and more the nurse and strong-willed mother. Her son and daughter were growing up, and Chopin often disagreed with Mme Sand over household politics, even taking the children's part against her. Troubled and increasingly weakened by his disease, he turned over fewer and fewer compositions to his publishers each year. Yet, as late as 1845, he signed the fine B minor Sonata. Here, the vigor and passion of the "four maddest children" of the B flat minor Sonata have all but vanished. In their place is a mastery of form that is eminently satisfying, real adequacy in the art of deploying materials over the skeleton of a design. The scene is varied. The turbulent introduction, lyrical, dewy, exquisitely modulated episodes, a light yet dynamic scherzo, a pensive elegiac largo, and a sweeping finale that is a first-rate bravura number in its own right—these are the interrelated components of the best of Chopin's three sonatas. The B minor Sonata was the last of Chopin's great works, for neither the rather Debussyan Berceuse nor that perfect music for the full flood of love—the Barcarolle—can be called great. Henceforth Chopin was to be submerged by his personal tragedy.

In 1847, after signs that it might drag on wearily until one of them died, his romance with George Sand came to an abrupt end. Those who choose to regard her as the villain of the piece say that Chopin took umbrage at the publication of her novel *Lucrezia Floriani*, in which he was caricatured under the guise of the epicene Prince Karol. This is not so. He read *Lucrezia* as Sand wrote it, and took no offense. Rather, she maneuvered herself into the position of the injured party, using as a pretext Chopin's siding with her daughter, Solange, in a complicated family quarrel. Unfortunately for sentimental historians, the final battles of the war were waged by mail, Chopin having left Nohant for Paris. The separation meant little to the woman: she was strong, at the height of her powers, very much absorbed in the liberal causes she had espoused—and she was, anyway, tired of Chopin. To him it was quite literally a deathblow: she had preserved a certain pattern in his life, provided him with a home. He saw her but once again, and then by accident, on which occasion he had the honor to tell Sand that she had become a grandmother.* When he was on his deathbed, she tried to see him, but was refused admittance by his friends.

For some years Sand had been addressing him playfully as "my dear corpse": now he truly looked like one—an ailing wisp of a man who weighed less than a hundred pounds. His purse, too, was almost empty, and though every added exertion meant agony, he had to do something to fill it. His friends and publishers persuaded him to give a concert. On February 16, 1848, he made his first public appearance in six years, playing a long and taxing program, including the piano part in his Cello Sonata, the last extended work he composed. The concert was a great social and financial success. Chopin played exquisitely, but almost fainted after the last number. It was his farewell to the Paris public, which in this case consisted of royal dukes, members of the peerage, and Chopin's pupils.

That brilliant gathering in the Salle Pleyel was one of the last great social events of the Orléanist monarchy: eight days later, the bourgeois Louis-Philippe and his dowdy Queen were no longer rulers of France. Chopin viewed the revolution with spiteful disfavor: he feared that a republican France meant that the nobles would emigrate, and his sources of income would be further reduced. At this juncture, his devoted friend and pupil, Jane Wilhelmina Stirling, a Scotswoman of ample means, induced him to go to England. She took care of all details of the trip, and hired rooms for him in London, where he arrived late in April, 1848. He played privately at several fine houses, refused an invitation from the Philharmonic—"I would rather not—they want classical things there," he wrote—and met shoals of celebrities, including Carlyle

* Solange had quarreled with her mother, but not with Chopin, who thus was often favored with the first news of intimate family matters—in this case, the birth of Solange's first child.

and Dickens. At first, the critics and musicians were inclined to welcome Chopin, but as he evinced such a decided preference for playing privately, their enthusiasm cooled, and he was set down as a society snob. He grew more and more unhappy. Critical unfriendliness, bad weather, and ever-waning health added to his depression. He longed for the lost peace of Nohant.

The well-intentioned Miss Stirling, who seems to have been in love with Chopin, now prescribed a visit to Scotland. This was not so bad during the summer, but he lingered there until well into the harsh northern autumn, giving mildly successful concerts in Manchester, Glasgow, and Edinburgh, and expending what little strength he had left in a round of calls on titled friends. At the end of October, convinced that he was dying, he returned to London. A flicker of humor remained: "I have not yet played to any Englishwoman without her saying to me, '*Leik water*,'* They all look at their hands, and play the wrong notes with much feeling. Eccentric folk. God help them." Humor remained, yes, but will power was gone. He was wheedled into playing at a Polish ball. It was a three-ring circus, and nobody paid the slightest attention to him. Even the press completely ignored this last unfortunate public appearance. It was November 16, 1848.

In January, Chopin returned painfully to France. As his train neared Paris, he mused bitterly on that ill-advised hegira from which he was returning. "Do you see the cattle in that meadow?" he asked his valet. "They've more intelligence than the English." When he arrived, he took it as a last evil omen that the only doctor in whom he had confidence had died in his absence. No longer able to teach, much of the time unable even to sit up, Chopin had no way of earning a living. Income he had none, for he had always sold his compositions outright—on a royalty basis he would have been assured of a handsome living. He was well-nigh destitute when two of his wealthy women friends came forward, one of them, the Countess Obreskov, secretly paying half his rent. The other was the pathetically faithful Miss Stirling, who sent him 25,000 francs, of which he seems to have kept about half, and returned the rest. His hosts of friends were unceasingly attentive. Delacroix, though stiff and unbending with most, showed Chopin a brother's affection. His own sister Ludwika and her husband

---

* The italicized words represent Chopin's phonetic attempt at English.

came from Poland to attend him. Daily, the princesses and countesses whose company he so adored came to pay homage to the dying man.

Out of the past, almost as if the last act of the drama of Chopin's life demanded her presence, came Delphine Potocka. When they had met, many years before, she had enchanted him with the thrilling quality of her voice, and now one of his few pleasures was to hear her sing. A few days before he died, she came to his bedside, and sang an aria by his beloved friend Bellini. Chopin was fully aware that his days were numbered. With perfect composure, he asked his sister to burn his unpublished manuscripts. "I owe it to the public and myself to publish only my best works," he explained. "I have kept to this resolution all my life—I wish to keep to it now." As the end approached, he was tormented by the fear of being buried alive, and one of his last acts was to scrawl a note asking that his body be cut open before burial. On the night of October 16, 1849, a Polish priest gave him extreme unction. His doctor then asked him whether he was suffering, and he whispered, "*Plus*"—no longer. He died early the following morning.

At Chopin's request part of the Mozart Requiem was sung at his funeral in the Madeleine. Lablache, who had sung the bass part at Beethoven's funeral, now sang it at Chopin's. The great world of society and art attended reverently, and among those who followed the hearse to Père Lachaise were Meyerbeer and Delacroix. A year later, at Jane Stirling's request, Polish earth was sprinkled over the grave.

Chapter XIV

Louis-Hector Berlioz

(La Côte-Saint-André, December 11, 1803–March 8, 1869, Paris)

> *He is not, perhaps, as great as Cervantes, but he is as great as Don Quixote. Only very silly people will take him seriously, but they are not as silly as the people who don't.*
> —Sir Donald F. Tovey: *Essays in Musical Analysis*, VI.

SYMBOLIC of the slowness of widespread appreciation for the music of Hector Berlioz is the fact that the first considerable English book about him was published in 1934, sixty-five years after his death. This is even more significant when compared with the posthumous fate of those four of his most distinguished contemporaries who died after him: Wagner, Liszt, Brahms, and Verdi. Almost before they had breathed their last breath, the presses had begun to groan under the vast load of commentaries and biographies. Their music was being played everywhere (as it still is), as was Tchaikovsky's. Yet each of these five men outlived Berlioz by many years, Wagner by fourteen, Verdi by thirty-two. Each was securely established in recognized greatness, while Berlioz maintained a precarious fame during his lifetime only by his persistence in pushing his own compositions. To this day he remains the least played and the least understood of the great composers of the past two hundred and fifty years.

In about equal parts, Berlioz suffered from his position in time and from his artistic idiosyncrasies. During the artistically pinched days of the Bourbon restoration he early developed into a full-blown romantic—and came into unequal conflict with the chilly musical autocracy headed by the austere, classicizing Cherubini. As a French romantic he had no predecessors, and in France he found no disciples to translate for a wider public his admittedly difficult idiom. It was an idiom difficult both to grasp and to convey. The melodic line so protracted as to require concentrated listening, the highly personal harmonic concept, and that nervous, dramatic movement from idea to idea which at first hearing seems fragmentary: these have proved a stumbling-block to an easy acceptance of what, on acquaintance, turns out to be some of the most beautiful music ever written. Thus did Berlioz hold off audiences. And to musical organizations of all sorts he offered quite as effective excuses for resistance: he early acquired a reputation—only occasionally deserved—of composing huge compositions calling for equally huge forces. Impresarios and conductors, faced with what seemed to them unreasonable and overexpensive demands, were blind to that perfect choice and balance of instruments and voices which justified those demands. Nor was Berlioz a Richard Wagner, able by sheer force of character, scheming, and mystical egotism to impose his art upon a reluctant world.

Berlioz was born on Sunday, the nineteenth day of Frimaire, in the twelfth year of the French Republic—five months before Napoleon Bonaparte decreed the creation of the First Empire; he lived almost long enough to see the extinction of the Second. During his lifetime, France suffered from an unparalleled series of political vicissitudes, from the splendors of Napoleon I through the jitters of Louis XVIII and Charles X and the doldrums of Louis-Philippe to the transparent glories of Louis-Napoleon. Yet Berlioz fought on no barricades, wrote no political pamphlets. In a political world politics moved him not at all. From his early adolescence he existed in two dimensions: as artist and as lover.

It was in a small village near Grenoble, in Dauphiny, that Berlioz was born to Louis Berlioz, physician, and his wife, Marie-Antoinette-Joséphine Marmion. He was the first of six children, three boys and three girls; only Hector and two of his sisters grew to maturity, and he outlived them all. Dr. Berlioz, who provided a moderately comfortable living for his family, was a man of some intellectual attainments, which meant that he was a revolutionary and a freethinker. He once served as mayor of the village, where he was known for his affable disposition and even temper. Mme Berlioz was a devout Catholic who tried earnestly to pass on her faith to her children. With Hector, at least, she succeeded only temporarily, and he instinctively disagreed with her bigoted opinion of poets, theatrical people, and musicians. With both parents he quarreled early over his independent decision to take up music as a career, though his father had not objected to his learning the rudiments of the art as an amateur.

Dr. Berlioz had high-handedly decided that his eldest son was to become a physician, but so rapid had been Hector's progress as an amateur composer that shortly after his sixteenth birthday he had put together a potpourri on Italian airs and sent it to a publisher in Paris. And indeed he had already a rather impressive musical equipment: he could, as W. J. Turner summarized it, "sing well at sight . . . play the flute, the flageolet, the guitar, the drum. . . ." A quintet for flute and strings composed about a year later could not make the elder Berlioz relent: Hector was entered in the École de Médicine in Paris in 1821. He could not face the ghastliness of the dissecting room. "When I entered that fearful human charnel house, littered with fragments of limbs, and saw the ghastly faces and cloven heads, the bloody cesspool in which we stood, with its reeking atmosphere, the swarms of sparrows fighting for scraps, and the rats in the corners gnawing bleeding vertebrae, such a feeling of horror possessed me that I leaped out of the window, and fled home as though Death and all his hideous crew were at my heels." The inevitable happened, and soon he was skipping classes to study scores and haunt the Opéra.

From this period dated Berlioz's passion for Gluck, founded upon the tremendous impression produced by a performance of *Iphigénie en Tauride*. "I vowed as I left the Opéra that I would be a musician come what might, despite father, mother, uncles, aunts, grandparents, and friends." Indeed, some time before 1823 he urgently informed his father of his decision, and a few months later was accepted as a private pupil in theory and composition by Jean-François Lesueur. For this amiable traditionalist Berlioz never lost his appreciative devotion. Although he worked doggedly at music, composing and studying the compositions of the great masters of the past, it was not until 1826 that the Conservatoire opened its doors to this fractious innovator whose music was not at all to the taste of its director, the stiffnecked Cherubini. Meanwhile, Berlioz did everything to convince his father that he was a dutiful son (did he not secure his *bachelier ès sciences physiques* in 1824?) and deserved to get his big chance. In 1825, by going heavily into debt, he managed to secure the first public performance of one of his compositions—a Mass, most of which he later destroyed.

Living on an allowance that could be stopped at his father's whim, Berlioz looked around frantically for ways of supplementing this meager sum. For instance, he began to write those reviews which eventually were to make him one of the great forces in Continental music criticism. He took an occasional pupil in voice, flute, or guitar. But his one real hope was the hope of any young French composer: winning the Prix de Rome, with its *réclame*, its guarantee of performance—and its four years of freedom from financial worry. He was to make five attempts before winning it. The first time, in 1826, he was cast out at the preliminary examination. Dr. Berlioz could not understand his failure, and Hector had to rush back to La Côte-Saint-André to argue his case through a series of stormy sessions. Finally he won a grudging permission to return to Paris for a restricted period, during which he might become a pupil at the Conservatoire. The fiat was: no success, no allowance. Oddly, Cherubini surpassed himself in unbending—he actually broke a rule by allowing Berlioz to enter the class in theory and Lesueur's in composition simultaneously instead of seriatim. In view of Berlioz's later adoration of Beethoven, it is interesting that his fugue and counterpoint professor was Anton Reicha, Beethoven's exact contemporary and his colleague in the electoral orchestra at Bonn.

Just as life seemed a little less stormy, several blows fell at once. Hector's chief creditor, out of sheer kindness of heart, wrote to Dr. Berlioz, saying that the repayment of the money advanced for the performance of the Mass was proving a terrible strain on his son. The righteous doctor repaid it in full and temporarily cut off his son's allowance. Not hesitating at all, Berlioz decided to live on the scraps from teaching and music-reviewing, and right up to 1828, when he won second place in the Prix de Rome competition, he lived precisely this way. But his life was further complicated by his passion for the Anglo-Irish actress, Harriet Constance Smithson.* Just after his

---

* Berlioz always referred to her as Henriette; she is familiar to readers of the English program notes of the *Symphonie fantastique* as Henrietta of the *idée fixe*.

second rejection for the Prix (the committee declared his cantata *La Mort d'Orphée* unplayable, a decision confounded by the success of later performances), he went to the Paris first night of Charles Kemble's production of *Hamlet*. While this new revelation of Shakespeare (as a source of romanticism) had a traceable effect on many personages who are known to have been in the audience, including Dumas *père*, Victor Hugo, Sainte-Beuve, Vigny, Gérard de Nerval, and Delacroix, it shattered Berlioz.

Just as, a dozen years before, a boy of twelve, he had become hopelessly infatuated at first sight with Estelle Duboeuf, a girl six years his elder, and had idealized her beyond recognition, to the point at which even her symbolic value to him is blurred, so now he transformed Henriette from a mediocre, rather plain-looking woman of twenty-seven into a fantastic paragon of age-less delight. Part of Estelle's hold on his imagination had been derived (he long believed) from her having worn pink shoes, a glamorous fact to which Berlioz clung throughout the years as to a fetish. Now he undoubtedly confused Henriette with the heroine she played, investing her somewhat colorless personality with the poetry of Ophelia. From that moment he acted like one demented, casting himself in the role of Hamlet. Until October, 1833, when he finally persuaded Henriette to become Mme Berlioz, he alternately raged, moped—and forgot to do either. The incredible part of Berlioz's mania was that it was not until less than one year before their marriage that he met his Ophelia in the flesh. Long before Dowson, he had discovered the art of being faithful to Cynara in his fashion. He pretended that he had written the history of his tempestuous emotions about Henriette in the pages of the *Symphonie fantastique*, though the timetable of its composition partly contradicts him.

In May, 1828, Berlioz gave a concert of his own music at the Conservatoire, Cherubini muttering monumentally to the last. The program consisted of the *Waverley* Overture, extracts from the opera *Les Francs-Juges*, the cantata *Scène heroïque: La révolution grecque*, and—replacing *La Mort d'Orphée*, withdrawn at the last minute so as not to insult the sensibilities of Cherubini and his colleagues—the *Resurrexit* from the Mass. Schumann, who thought *Waverley* delightful, professed to find in it reminiscences of Mendelssohn, which to Berlioz would have been a dubious compliment. All that survives of *Les Francs-Juges* in its original form is the familiar overture. Ringing with the fanfares Berlioz loved, it is touched with Weberian romanticism, though its rhythms and orchestration are characteristic of Berlioz himself. The success of the concert was sufficient to lift his spirits a little, and he was sustained on a lofty plain by his first reading of Goethe's *Faust* in Gérard de Nerval's translation. His enthusiasm led him at once to begin sketching the series of musical incidents that he was to publish, as his Opus 1, the following year as *Huit Scènes de Faust*. This Ernest Newman once called "the most marvelous Opus 1 that any composer . . . ever produced. . . ." On the other hand, Berlioz was dispirited by his third failure to gain the Prix de Rome, though this time his effort, a cantata called *Herminie* and based on episodes from Tasso's *Gerusalemme liberata*, gained him the second prize, a gold medal whose value he so deprecated that he later pawned it. Perhaps even more infuriating were the results of the 1829 competition, when still another Berlioz cantata—*La Mort de Cléopâtre*—so baffled the jury by its intransigent originality that no prize was awarded.

Meanwhile, Berlioz's passion for Henriette waxed and waned —and waxed again. As no response to his epistolary protestations of fiery longing came from her, it became essential for him to exorcise her image. This he did by the best of all methods: early in 1830 he burned out his passion in a masterpiece of musical confession, the *Symphonie fantastique*, which, with the later autobiographical *mélologue*, *Lélio*, is subtitled "*Episode de la vie d'un artiste.*" Although this gigantic five-movement work was put together within four months, parts of it were composed earlier, being transferred to it with little change from *Les Francs-Juges* and a never completed Faust ballet; the melody of the *idée fixe* itself was adapted from *Herminie*.

As his best-known composition, the *Symphonie fantastique* has tended to crystallize the legend of a Berlioz who bears small relation to the mature artist who created such restrained works of genius as *Roméo et Juliette* and *Les Troyens*. For this, Berlioz himself was largely responsible, for few were able to resist the extravagant self-advertisement that is his printed program for this work. As a document comparable in importance to Beethoven's letter to the "Immortal Beloved," this program must be quoted in full:

A young musician of morbid sensibility and ardent imagination is in love, and has poisoned himself with opium in a fit of desperation. Not having taken a lethal dose, he falls into a long sleep in which he has the strangest dreams, wherein his feelings, sentiments, and memories are translated by his sick brain into musical ideas and figures. The beloved woman herself has become a melody that he finds and hears everywhere as an *idée fixe*.

First Movement. Reveries, Passions.

First he remembers the uneasiness of mind, the aimless passions, the baseless depressions and elations that he felt before he saw the object of his adoration, then the volcanic love that she instantly inspired in him, his delirious agonies, his jealous rages, his recovered love, his consolations of religion.

Second Movement. A Ball.

He meets his beloved at a ball in the midst of the tumult of a brilliant festival.

Third Movement. Pastoral Scene.

On a summer evening in the country he hears two shepherds playing a *Ranz des Vaches* in dialogue. This pastoral duet, the place, the gentle sound of wind in the trees, a few recently conceived grounds of hope, all tend to give a new calm to his heart and a brighter color to his thoughts. But She appears again. His heart misses a beat; he is troubled by grievous forebodings. What if she should deceive him? . . .

One of the shepherds resumes his simple lay; the other does not answer. The sun sets. Distant thunder. Solitude. Silence.

Fourth Movement. March to the Scaffold.

He dreams that he has killed his beloved; that he is condemned to death and led to the place of execution. The procession moves to a march, now gloomy and wild, now brilliant and grand, during which the dull sound of heavy footsteps follows abruptly upon the noisiest outbursts.

At last the *idée fixe* reappears for a moment, as a last thought of love, cut short by the stroke of death.

Fifth Movement. Dream of a Witches' Sabbath.

He finds himself in a witches' sabbath, in the midst of a frightful crowd of ghosts, sorcerers, and all manner of monsters assisting at his entombment. Weird noises, groans, bursts of laughter, distant cries echoed by others. The Beloved Melody enters again, but it has lost its noble modesty; it has become a vulgar dance-tune, trivial and grotesque. SHE has come to the witches' sabbath.

Roars of joy at her arrival. She joins in the devilish orgies. Funeral bells, parody of the *Dies Irae*. Round dance of the witches. The round dance and the *Dies Irae* are heard together.

Psychologically, the most significant permutation of the *idée fixe* (Henriette-Ophelia's motive) is its vulgarization in the last movement: this meant that Berlioz had released himself temporarily from the actress's spell. Musically, the *idée fixe* serves to bind together the five movements, which could not easily be related in any other manner. This use of a label motive, though not original with Berlioz (it had been used in the earliest operas, and Mozart had notably exploited it in *Don Giovanni*), was to have a sensible influence on his contemporaries and successors. Liszt, Wagner, Tchaikovsky, César Franck, and Richard Strauss all seized upon this device. Not only did Berlioz, by the power of his creative vision, naturalize it in instrumental music, but he also rescued it from its perfunctory role as a mere ticket,* making it a malleable, protean agent of the musical imagination.

In judging the *Symphonie fantastique*, it is wise not to confuse the music with its somewhat overwrought program. Like all great creations, it must be judged in terms of the art to which it belongs. As music, then, the *Symphonie*, if not quite transcendent in the hierarchy of Berlioz's work, would alone entitle him to a place far above that of the merely accomplished technicians with whom he competed, and near that of the masters he revered. The first movement, though thoughtfully conceived, does not presage the many remarkable, moving, and novel effects of what follows; the second, based largely on one of Berlioz's long-breathed, enchanting melodies, has a rhythmic

* The label motive has, of course, now become the debased commonplace of every screen composer.

interest quite surpassing that of any earlier waltz and equaling the later complexities of Ravel and Richard Strauss; the third movement, which pays its respects to Beethoven's "Pastoral," could be cited as the *locus classicus* of romantic melancholy; the "March to the Scaffold" is, of course, one of the most exciting of Berlioz's inspirations—here the program could almost be written from the music, and nothing could better the description of its pace than Berlioz's own "now gloomy and wild, now brilliant and grand"; the finale apotheosizes the Berlioz of the flaming locks, the extravagant emotionalist he pretended to believe himself to be—only here and in *Harold en Italie* can be found the macabre figure that so many believe falsely to be the essential Berlioz. How the echoes of this last movement went ringing down the century can best be detected in such a work as Mussorgsky's *A Night on Bald Mountain*.

One result of the catharsis effected in Berlioz by composing the *Symphonie fantastique* was that of his finding an Henriette-substitute. She turned out to be the cacophonously named Marie Moke, an eighteen-year-old pianist with whom Ferdinand Hiller was in love. Marie, even at this tender age, was something of a loose woman, and was willing to listen to Berlioz. In later years, as Mme Camille Pleyel, she became a most eminent pianist, and it is at least possible that Berlioz, more romantic than carnal, was enraptured less by the girl than by the artist. He found a Shakespearean label for her too, and among his intimates was wont to refer to her as Ariel, a long remove from Ophelia, but quite as sexless. At first Mlle Moke's mother looked with extreme disfavor on the penniless suitor, but when his cantata *La Mort de Sardanapale* finally won for him the Prix de Rome she quickly changed her mind. By the end of 1830 Hector and Marie were engaged to be married, though it was cautiously stipulated that the marriage should not occur until Marie was twenty-one.

And indeed, momentarily fortune seemed to smile on the newly crowned prize-winner. *Sardanapale* was successfully performed at its dress rehearsal,* as was, somewhat later, Berlioz's fantasy for orchestra, chorus, and two pianos, on Shakespeare's

---

* At the performance on October 30, the final section was not played because the wind instruments missed their cue—a characteristically Berliozian mishap.

Tempest. It is symbolic of the close association of much of Berlioz's early music with his personal life that the *Tempest* fantasy was inspired by Mlle Moke (her former love, Hiller, was one of the pianists when it was performed), and was later incorporated into *Lélio*, a farrago that commented on his affair with her much as the *Symphonie fantastique* had commented on that with Henriette. Then, on December 5, the *Symphonie fantastique* was given with great success, under the baton of François Habeneck, at the Conservatoire. The audience included Fétis, Spontini, Meyerbeer, and Liszt. The *"Marche au supplice"* was encored, and Liszt, wrote Berlioz, "carried me off, as it were by force, to dine with him, overwhelming me with the most vigorous enthusiasm." Even more gratifying to Berlioz's starved vanity was Spontini's friendliness: not content with declaring that Beethoven alone could have equaled the *"Marche au supplice,"* this reigning god of music signalized his young friend's twenty-seventh birthday by presenting him with an inscribed score of *Olympie*, worth, the recipient carefully noted, 125 francs.

Although Italy was next on the schedule for a Prix de Rome winner, it scarcely beckoned. Berlioz had no desire to leave his Ariel, who might well flit as readily to another as she had flitted to him from Hiller. But in order to keep the prize pension, a year's residence in Italy was necessary. He tore himself away, paid a farewell visit to his family, and arrived in Rome early in March, 1831. He was prepared to dislike Rome, and he did. He called Italy "a garden peopled by monkeys." The truth is that his emotional state did not permit him to appreciate anything except the luxuries of introspection. Staying at the Villa Medici, where the Académie de France was located, scarcely long enough to meet its director, the painter Horace Vernet,* and his fellow-students—who ribaldly nicknamed him Father Joy because of his lugubrious expression—he rushed back toward France after spending several pleasant days with Mendelssohn. There had been no word from Marie, and his intention was to return to Paris. Fortunately for him, bad news caught up with him at Florence: a letter from Mme Moke an-

---

* Vernet's portrait of Mendelssohn, painted at this time, is reproduced facing page 255.

nounced her daughter's marriage to Camille Pleyel, the piano-manufacturer.

At this juncture, Berlioz behaved like the hero of a farce-melodrama. In his *Mémoires* he wrote that his decision was made instantly: "It was to go to Paris, where I must kill without mercy two guilty women and one innocent man [the female Mokes and himself]." His weapons were two pistols, laudanum, and strychnine. But he had no intention of being recognized, and purchased also the costume of a lady's maid as a disguise. At Genoa he found that he had lost the disguise, and promptly replaced it. Apparently he tried to do away with himself, an action that in a measure dispelled the black humors. At Nice, then still Italian territory, he had a change of heart. He wrote Vernet to retain his name on the list of *pensionnaires* of the Villa Medici. Vernet sent a friendly reply, and Berlioz settled down to a vacation in Nice, where he composed the overture *Le Roi Lear*. Before returning to Rome in June he had also begun the sketches for *Lélio, ou Le retour à la vie*, which as its subtitle indicates, he conceived as a pendant to the *Symphonie fantastique*. Before leaving Italy in May, 1832—he somehow evaded the stipulation that he remain in Rome for two years—he had completed *Lélio* and composed *Rob Roy*, an overture. It is significant that during his eighteen months in Italy he laid at least some of the plans for all of his important future works.

After spending some months with his family, Berlioz returned to Paris armed to battle once again for fame and fortune. December 9, 1832, turned out to be one of the most important days of his life: that afternoon he gave a concert that included the *Fantastique* and *Lélio*. The presence of Harriet Smithson in the audience made the choice of works truly symbolic, for the first of them dramatized Berlioz's unrequited passion for her, and the second, signifying his "return to life" after a vain attempt to secure a substitute, implied that the return had been to her. Unfortunately for him, her recent attempt to recapture the favor of Paris had been a failure, and she was consequently all too ready to listen to his renewed advances. At this point the extravagant, romantic Berlioz of legend became a slave to duty. It is quite obvious that now his protestations were inspired less by passion than by pity, and indeed he seems like a man acting the role of a knight errant. They met, he proposed, their families objected (her sister even going so far as to tear up a marriage contract). During this prolonged tempest, Berlioz for the second time tried suicide, this time by poison, but had the forethought to provide himself with an emetic. But, domestic results apart, the concert of December 9 brought him great *réclame*. Dumas *père*, Hugo, and Paganini were in the audience, and the concert had to be repeated three weeks later. This recognition, under ordinary circumstances, might have inspired Berlioz to passionate creative activity, but he was so taken up with Henriette's welfare that he concentrated during 1833 on planning to rescue her from fate. In his spare time he planned an assault on the Opéra by sketching *Béatrice et Benedict*—which he completed thirty years later.

Some of these plans were not without interest. Early in 1833, after Henriette had added a broken leg to her disabilities, Berlioz organized a benefit concert for her. He besought the help of his old friend Liszt and of Chopin, whom he had just met.* The profits of this concert were scarcely a stopgap. The financial picture stayed bleak, but perversely Berlioz insisted on marriage. Earlier in the year he had steadfastly refused to carry out another Prix de Rome stipulation, a stay in Germany; now he threatened Henriette with imminent departure thither unless she married him at once. She capitulated, and finally, after he had borrowed three hundred francs on which to marry, he made her keep her promise on October 3.† His obligations to this flighty, unintelligent, and rather unpleasant woman, formerly sentimental, were now legal. Thenceforth, but for a brief interval, their life together was to be scarcely mitigated torture.

Berlioz's plans for Henriette did not cease with their marriage. He next tried to reintroduce her to theatergoers, but so poor was her performance that he was forced to realize that their ménage (swelled in August, 1834, by the birth of a son, Louis)

* At first it seemed that Berlioz and Chopin were to become friends. But Chopin soon cooled—Berlioz was too radical for him musically and too flamboyant for him personally. In January, 1836, however, they were on sufficiently amicable terms for Chopin to assist Berlioz in making a piano-duet arrangement of the overture to *Les Francs-Juges*.

† Eight days after the wedding, Berlioz wrote his friend Humbert Ferrand that, to his gratification, he had discovered Henriette to be "as virginal as possible"— *aussi vierge qu'il soit possible de l'être.*

had to be supported by his efforts alone—a blessing in disguise, for now followed another period of feverish concert-giving, review-writing, and composing on a large scale. It may have been after the very successful concert of December 22, 1833 (or it may have been on December 9, 1832), that Paganini made his first public obeisance to Berlioz. Then he suggested that Berlioz provide him with a piece to display his talents as a virtuoso on a newly acquired Stradivarius viola. But Berlioz was not the man to compose virtuoso pieces to order: the project—tentatively entitled *Les Derniers Instans** de Marie Stuart*—gradually evaporated, though the solo viola in *Harold en Italie*, begun shortly afterward, was undoubtedly its indirect result. Reminiscences of Berlioz's travels in Italy soon fused with his ramblings in Byron to produce one of his most spectacular concert works, which was completed in June, 1834. Before the year was out, *Harold* had been performed three times with great success, and Berlioz had begun an opera based on episodes from the life of Benvenuto Cellini.

In *Lélio*, Berlioz had exhibited himself in his most fantastic phase; with *Harold en Italie*, after a final Byronic fling, he bade farewell to attitudinizing. He was never one to do things by halves, and *Lélio* is, formally speaking, a monstrosity, a jerry-built structure of shreds and patches. Because it is designed for a non-singing actor, as well as for mostly invisible soloists, chorus, and orchestra, *Lélio* should be produced in a theater. It requires theatrical properties, among them a couch where Lélio can recline while reading a book, pistols, and a skull. Lélio is not only Hamlet, he is also Berlioz, and he is even Berlioz's imaginary self—a combination of personalities that needs a juggler's rather than an actor's ability. *Lélio* is a protracted monologue—a "*monodrame lyrique*," as Berlioz also called it —interrupted, usually without cause, by dramatic trumpery set to various unrelated pieces of music from his files. These latter include snippets of the *Fantastique*, a setting for tenor solo of Goethe's poem "*Der Fischer*," and the fantasia on Shakespeare's *Tempest*. For a chorus of shades he reached back to *Cléopatre*, one of his unsuccessful Prix de Rome submissions.

* This curious word reflected a momentary trend toward simplified spelling.

From the critical consensus that little of *Lélio* is memorable, at least the *Tempest* fantasia must be excepted: not only did Berlioz describe it as "new, tender, sweet, and surprising," but those who have been fortunate enough to hear one of its rare performances have remarked upon its charm.

Whereas *Lélio* was destined for almost instant oblivion (it is notable that Liszt, who alone seems to have had an interest in keeping it alive, made stringent cuts when he staged it at Weimar in 1855), *Harold en Italie* needs only a first-rate violist to keep it perennial in the repertoire. Seldom does one of its four movements descend from a high level of unceasing musical inventiveness. Its materials are both attractive and beautifully calculated as parts of a large composition. Indeed, *Harold*, which came so close after *Lélio*, is as perfectly designed as *Lélio* is chaotically strung together. Materials and design alike are made luminous by the subtle balance and justness of the instrumentation. The solo viola is so discreetly blended with the orchestra as to give *Harold* more the character of a symphony than that of a concerto—Chopin, who vehemently denigrated the formal structures of Berlioz, might have found a lesson in it.

Harold en Italie is one of the central romantic masterpieces, a judgment easily bolstered by examining each of its four movements in turn. The first, "Harold in the Mountains, Scenes of Melancholy, Happiness, and Joy," is precisely a classical statement of romantic melancholy. The theme given out by the solo viola, hauntingly wistful and unmistakably Berlioz, is used as a signature in all the movements. In the second, "March of Pilgrims Singing Their Evening Hymns," there are a sobriety and a solemnity that portend a new dimension in their composer. It is an unmonotonous monotony, achieving variety by the slightest of shifts. Part three, the "Serenade of an Abruzzi Mountaineer to His Mistress," exploits the wind choirs in producing effects that are both tender and exciting. Quite as remarkable are the supple use of innately naïve rhythmic patterns in triple time and the never-ceasing harmonic surprises, which are at no time vulgarly shocking. The finale, "Orgy of Brigands, Recollections of the Preceding Scenes," is not in quality up to the other parts, and undeniably has its moments of the kind of fustian and bombast that do not fit even an orgy of brigands. During these the solo viola, which otherwise in this movement is used only in startling and touchingly lovely reminiscences of the earlier movements, is silent. The actual orgy is merely effective theater music. Because of its thematic relation to the earlier movements, the fourth movement has been compared, doubtless as a compliment, to the choral movement of Beethoven's Ninth—like it, the least integrated portion of the symphony of which it is a part. Fortunately, the somewhat shoddy concluding pages of *Harold* do not affect retroactively the earlier beauties of this splendid creation.

Now, and for some years to come, the Berlioz family, which had moved to a small house in Montmartre, was in sore straits. The way ahead was not clear. Knowing full well that musical Paris would not take seriously a composer who had not had an operatic success, Berlioz worked hard on the score of *Benvenuto Cellini*, even though the libretto had been declined by the Opéra-Comique. To support his wife and son, he slaved at journalism, which he loathed, and continued to give his artistically rewarding, but financially unsuccessful, concerts. It was during this period that he finished, from sketches begun some years earlier, *Le Cinq mai*, a cantata on the death of Napoleon. This was set to a poem of Pierre-Jean de Béranger, and for the most part Berlioz experienced no difficulty in its composition. These banal lines, however, proved a stumbling-block:

> *Poor soldier, I shall see France again,*
> *My son's hand shall close my eyes.*

Before leaving Rome in 1832, Berlioz had been wandering absentmindedly along the Tiber one day and slipped into the river. At first he was alarmed, but soon realized that getting wet was the worst that could happen to him. At this juncture, the musical theme for the difficult lines came to his mind, again exemplifying the tragicomic element that often accompanied his creative activity. Yet the copious lyrical outpouring of this period is seemingly devoid of that autobiographical dimension which adds piquancy to a view of his large orchestral works. Such luscious songs as *La Captive*, *Villanelle*, *Absence*, and *Le Spectre de la rose** have no program beyond their own texts. They are immediately communicative.

At the beginning of 1836, Berlioz scarcely knew which way to turn, for he had now received the final installments of his Prix de Rome pension. More than ever did he feel the necessity of finishing *Benvenuto Cellini*, and his income as critic for the *Journal des débats* was insufficient. But in the spring his friend the dramatist Ernest Legouvé lent him two thousand francs, and even Dr. Berlioz (whose wrath at the Smithson *mésalliance* had been mitigated by the arrival of a grandson named after himself) sent him a small sum. And he was getting a foothold at the Opéra through his association with the powerful Bertin family, which controlled the *Journal des débats*, the official newspaper of the Orléanist regime. He helped Louise-Angélique Bertin to professionalize her opera *Esmeralda*, for which Victor Hugo—taking episodes from his own *Notre-Dame de Paris*—had provided the libretto. *Esmeralda* failed, but Berlioz had succeeded in two of his objectives; he had put the Bertins further in his debt (needless to say, his review of *Esmeralda* in the *Journal* was not unfavorable), and he now had a foot inside the Opéra. In March, 1837, that debt began to be paid off, when the minister of the interior commissioned Berlioz to compose a requiem for the commemoration of the victims of the infernal machine used in 1835 by the Italian anarchist Fieschi in his unsuccessful attempt on the life of Louis-Philippe. The Commission was valued at four thousand francs, and the only stipulation the composer made was that he be guaranteed five hundred performers. The minister demurred, and they finally compromised at four hundred and fifty.

Writing to Liszt on May 22, 1837, Berlioz said that he had completed the Requiem, but the autograph score is dated June 29. Even if the latter is the true date of completion, the period of time is astonishingly short for the achievement of so vast and so magnificent a work. Berlioz said that ideas for it crowded on

---

* The last three of these belong to the fine song-cycle *Nuits d'Été*, set to poems by Théophile Gautier, and composed in 1834. The others in the cycle are *Sur les lagunes*, *Au cimitière*, and *L'Ile inconnue*. All six were rearranged in 1841, and later orchestrated.

him so fast that he was obliged to invent a musical shorthand. However, the Requiem, or *Grande Messe des morts* as it is sometimes called, contains ideas from earlier works. For instance, the renowned *Tuba Mirum* borrows from Berlioz's earlier *Resurrexit*, and there must be imbedded in the fabric of the Requiem material from one of his most fantastic aborts, *Le Dernier Jour du monde.** No doubt Berlioz was hurrying toward a deadline that would allow sufficient rehearsal time for the Requiem to be performed on the second anniversary (July 28, 1837) of the Fieschi attempt. His haste was wasted: official procrastination staved off performance until Bertin took a hand in the proceedings. But even he might not have succeeded had not the death of a popular general necessitated a government memorial. Eager to stop Bertin's cries of rage, the ministry of the interior scheduled the Requiem for performance at the Invalides on December 4. When the last echo of the tympani had died, Berlioz began actively to wait for the promised four thousand francs. He had to wait an unreasonably long time, but, as W. J. Turner wrote, ". . . he was probably paid quicker than anybody else would have been, as his capacity for making a fuss and his physical endurance in making it were alike more than normal."

Even with the modification of forces imposed by the ministry, the *Messe des morts* calls for a stupendous number of performers if it is to be given as Berlioz conceived it—surely the only way to give it. It demands eighty sopranos, eighty altos, sixty tenors, seventy basses, fifty violins, twenty violas, twenty cellos, eighteen doublebasses, four flutes, two oboes, two English horns, eight bassoons, four clarinets, twelve horns, four cornets, twelve trumpets, sixteen trombones, six ophicleides (now replaced by tubas), sixteen tympani, two side drums, four gongs, and five pairs of cymbals. The contention that Berlioz might have achieved his effects with smaller means is irrelevant: the point

* Conceived first as an oratorio and then as a three-act grand opera, this apocalyptic conception concerned the machinations of an antichrist finally discomfited by the coming of the true Christ, after which, as Berlioz wrote: "The piece should not, nor can it, be carried further." It was to have soloists, choruses, and two orchestras totaling more than two hundred and sixty instrumentalists. When the director of the Opéra finally rejected the proposed work, Berlioz's comment was: *"He dare not accept it."*

is that he achieved them with these, achieved them, too, without a touch of vulgarity or blatancy. It is merely unfortunate that the size of these forces will always prevent the Requiem from becoming familiar in full dress. Those who have heard it in actual performance—a tiny group—count it among the superlative musical experiences of their lives. For instance, Schumann said of one section: "This Offertory surpasses all!" And W. J. Turner, admitting that the single performance he had heard was "good without being adequate," said of another section: "There is nothing even in Verdi's magnificent Requiem to compare with this *Tuba mirum*. It is an apocalyptic vision unparalleled, unimagined before or since in music."

The *première* of the Requiem was so successful that, for the first time in his life, Berlioz tasted true fame. His various projects were pushed ahead by this new *réclame*, and soon he learned that *Benvenuto Cellini* had been accepted by the Opéra, though unhappily it could not be scheduled until new operas by Auber and Halévy could be staged. There was some organized opposition, largely because of Berlioz's connection with the government paper. Anyhow, it was not until September 10, 1838, that his music was heard for the first time at the Opéra. The overture was applauded; the rest of *Benvenuto Cellini* was hissed. Grimly, Berlioz pretended that the reaction to the second and third performances was better, but even if this was true the cause of the opera was hopeless after Gilbert Duprez, the leading tenor, dropped out. The opera was sung once more four months later, and that was all.

Be it said that it would have taken a mature Mozart who had already threaded his way through the mazes of *Die Zauber-flöte* to make anything of the complex libretto provided by Léon de Wailly and Auguste Barbier. By 1844, Berlioz, perhaps convinced that *Cellini* would never be given again, worked up some of its most attractive melodies and fused them together into the dashing and ever-popular overture, *Carnaval romain*. In 1851, however, Liszt, then musical director at Weimar, expressed a desire to stage the opera there. Originally *Cellini* had been a two-acter; to Weimar, Berlioz delivered a three-act version for which Peter Cornelius provided a German text.

Liszt made the opera successful, and he frequently repeated it. Germany, indeed, continued to appreciate *Cellini*, though it has never been naturalized elsewhere. Outside Germany, *Benvenuto Cellini* is not likely to be heard (except for a pious, patriotic French revival now and then), and except for *Le Carnaval romain* only the original overture to the opera itself can be known to a large audience.

Berlioz's despair over the reception of *Cellini* was aggravated by a further disappointment, this time from an official quarter: he had applied for the professorship in harmony at the Conservatoire, and had been turned down. The reason given was that he could not play the piano.* The blow was softened, somewhat later, by his appointment as assistant librarian of the Conservatoire. But what really lifted him from his despondency resulted from Paganini's presence at a performance of *Harold en Italie*. The satanic violinist was hearing for the first time music he had indirectly inspired. He knelt at Berlioz's feet, an act followed, two days later, by a more substantial gesture: by his young son he sent Berlioz a draft on the Rothschild bank for 20,000 francs, accompanying it with the following letter:

My dear Friend,—Beethoven is dead, and Berlioz alone can revive him. I have heard your divine compositions, so worthy of your genius, and beg you to accept, in token of my homage, twenty thousand francs, which will be handed to you by the Baron de Rothschild on presentation of the enclosed.—Your most affectionate friend, Nicolò Paganini.

While it is not beyond the bounds of credibility that Paganini was giving away his own money, it has been said that the real source of the gift was the Bertin family, who had tactfully used Paganini as their agent in order to spare Berlioz's sensibilities.

Freed for a time from journalistic hackwork and the specter of penury, Berlioz used the first nine months of 1839 to compose the richest of his tributes to Shakespeare. This was the "dramatic symphony," *Roméo et Juliette*, which he gratefully, if inappropriately, dedicated to Paganini. When, with Berlioz

---

* Berlioz was entirely free of the increasing nineteenth-century tendency to think in terms of the piano. He thought directly in orchestral terms, and he suffers more than most in piano transcription.

conducting, it was performed by two hundred instrumentalists and singers at the Conservatoire on November 24, 1839, it was so enthusiastically received that he repeated it twice during December, each time in slightly revised form. While success elated his spirits, his finances were not substantially improved: the three concerts netted him only eleven hundred francs.

Because *Roméo et Juliette* is still rarely performed, a legend persists that it is a formless and extremely uneven collection of *scènes*. Familiarity with this music teaches that, despite the modicum of truth in this legend, this delicately strung necklace of beautifully fashioned musical effects has quite as much formal unity as certain of Berlioz's works that have achieved—one almost wonders how—the canon of respectability. The totality of *Roméo* is much more than a matrix in which are imbedded the scintillant Queen Mab scherzo, the ecstatic Love Scene, the gaily tumultuous Grand Fete at the Capulets', and other sections of varying quality. Rather, it is the dramatic succession of the episodes and their final congruity (not necessarily Shakespeare's), reverently achieved. The element that inimical critics have sneeringly castigated as fragmentariness is really an exquisite use of music's unique ability to be all suggestiveness and evocation. It had been enough for a Bellini to have set the feuds of the Capulets and the Montagues: Berlioz's music is about quite another thing—Shakespeare's poetry. This is the secret of his grand isolation as a program composer. He neglected the events and concerned himself with what music can best complement, atmosphere and essence. If *Roméo et Juliette* has flaws, they come precisely at those moments when Berlioz deserts atmosphere and essence for other dimensions. Thus, the long moral tract intoned by Friar Laurence has a Meyerbeerian orotundity that is true to the words sung, but momentarily blighting to the overall spirit. Fortunately, the effect of this curiously inept official laying of the funeral wreaths is soon obliterated by the memory of the sweet and grave intensity of the earlier sections of this unquestionable masterpiece.

Although no government position opened up for Berlioz, it seemed, in 1839 and 1840, as though France had begun to consider him a national asset. First he was made a Chevalier

of the Legion of Honor, and then he received another big
commission, this time to supply music to accompany the reinterment of patriots who had fallen during the July revolution ten years before. His various ideas quickly cohered into
the largest composition ever written for military band, the
Symphonie funèbre et triomphale. Berlioz, who feared the usual mis-
haps attendant on public ceremonies, took the precaution of
asking a large assembly of notables to the final rehearsal.
Fortunately so, for he reports that, as played during the parade
on July 28, the *Symphonie* was all but drowned out by the clamor
of the crowd and finally by the beating of fifty drums as a bored
corps of the Garde National marched off. And all this despite
the enormous forces collected to give full weight to the *Symphonie*
—augmented military band and a chorus of two hundred voices.

The *Symphonie funèbre et triomphale* is truly a carefully executed
pièce d'occasion. Gone from it are the subtleties and niceties of
Berlioz's orchestral writing, and gone too are those delicately
related episodes which are at the core of his dramatic idiom.
Here he submerged himself and dedicated his unparalleled
instrumental technique strictly to the business at hand—to a
rhythmically dignified *Marche funèbre*, an appropriate *Oraison
funèbre* with an extensive and telling trombone solo, and a
jubilant *Apothéose*. Wagner, who heard a somewhat revised
version of the *Symphonie*, thought it the best of Berlioz's works up
to that time, and wrote of the *Apothéose*, with its mighty fanfares: "Berlioz has a gift for popular writing of the best kind.
I felt that every urchin with a blue blouse and a red bonnet
would understand this music thoroughly." It is amusing that
Wagner had been content to dismiss the Berlioz of *Roméo et
Juliette* as "devilishly smart."*

After the *Symphonie funèbre et triomphale*, Berlioz did not complete a major work for six years. This artistic inactivity reflected
the sad state of his domestic affairs, giving point to the oft-
repeated idea that he was dogged by ill luck a large part of
his life. Just when he was beginning to receive substantial

* The first complete American performance of the *Symphonie funèbre et triomphale*
was given on the Mall in Central Park, New York, by the Goldman Band, on June
23, 1947.

worldly recognition, his marriage to the Henriette of his dreams went to pieces. In eight years she had become a fat, blowsy, and shrewish woman whose sole virtue was loyalty to him, but a loyalty perverted by jealousy into a vice. Her tantrums left Berlioz limp and drove their seven-year-old son into hysterics. Sentimentality alone held Berlioz to her, but finally increasing separation became essential to his peace of mind—and he foolishly fled to the arms of another woman with whom he was to repeat, with little change, the cycle of Henriette. This woman was Marie-Geneviève Martin, who for the operatic stage had adopted the name of Marie Recio. Berlioz first heard her in the role of Ines in Donizetti's *La Favorita*, and was more impressed by her fine figure than by her middling voice. By 1842, when he set out for Brussels, she accompanied him as his mistress. Now his financial difficulties were complicated by the necessity of keeping up two households. He soon came to realize that he had exchanged one shrew for another, but so inextricably was he held in Marie's toils that within seven months of Henriette's death, in 1854, he married her.

Now succeeded a long period of wanderings throughout Europe, possibly calculated as much to escape his domestic troubles as to enhance his fame and fill his pockets. Also, two failures wounded him deeply: first, he did not succeed to the Institut chair left vacant by the death of Cherubini; second, he was passed over for the inspectorship of singing in the primary schools. Unless he was to devote his time to journalism, it seemed to Berlioz that the only hope lay outside France. After two concerts in Brussels in December, 1842, he made what was largely a triumphal tour through Germany, not returning to Paris for five months. He was rightly acclaimed, for as a conductor he was without a peer. En route, he met, or renewed acquaintance with, Schumann, Meyerbeer, Wagner, and Mendelssohn. With the last, who disliked Berlioz's music violently, he exchanged batons. He was delighted to learn that some of his compositions had found great favor in Germany, notably the overture to *Les Francs-Juges*, parts of the *Fantastique*, and the cantata *Le Cinq mai*.

From May, 1843, Berlioz remained in France for over two

years, during which time he composed the *Carnaval romain* and the first version of the *Corsaire* overture (*La Tour de Nice*), published his *Traité de l'instrumentation et d'orchestration* (which he listed among his musical works as Opus 10) and *Voyage musical en Allemagne et en Italie,* the first installments of his pungent musical reminiscences.* He was often outside Paris, no doubt recuperating from too much of Henriette (the generously provided-for invalid never ceased to throw out martyr's tentacles) and from too much of Marie and her Spanish mother. By August, 1845, Berlioz was sufficiently calm to represent the *Journal des débats* at the unveiling of the Beethoven monument at Bonn. There, again, he was warmly greeted by Liszt, who had enlisted his help, some years before, to raise a part of the miserly sum that France contributed to the memorial. There, too, he witnessed the tumultuous scenes that succeeded on Liszt's calling attention to the regrettable phenomenon of French parsimony.

Thus far, Berlioz's nomad years had borne small fruit. Now, during 1846, a year marked by the adulation of crowds in Austria, Bohemia, Germany, and Hungary, and by the gift of a purse of eleven hundred francs from the mad Emperor Ferdinand (who confessed himself "amused"), he found time to work out the revision of that remarkable Opus 1, *Huit Scènes de Faust* (1828-29). At inns along the way, in jolting *postchaises,* wherever he could snatch a few minutes alone, he thought and sketched, transforming that cantata with solo numbers into the "dramatic legend" he called *La Damnation de Faust.* Some disparate elements went into its fabrication. For instance, he took the liberty of transporting Faust to the plains of Hungary in order to include his orchestral version of the traditional Hungarian *Rákóczy March,* written in one night at Vienna for use

---

* Berlioz salvaged other considerable portions of his journalistic work in three enchanting miscellanies of criticism and gossip: *Les Soirées de l'orchestre* (1853), *Les Grotesques de la musique* (1859), and *À travers Chants* (1862). Parts of the *Voyage musical* were mosaicked into the *Mémoires.* Witty and acute, and abounding in memorable phrases and prophetic judgments, these writings, in a century, have lost none of their vitality. They have the fascination of fiction (and, indeed, Berlioz was not averse to creating a legend so as to point a moral) and the solidity of great criticism. In the use of the printed word, he is not the peer of Schumann and Wagner, but their master.

at Budapest some days later. Finished in October, *La Damnation*, at its first performance, in Paris on December 6, only half filled the Opéra-Comique, and was received coldly. Two weeks later, its second performance was an utter failure. At this point Berlioz, again let down by the Paris he so loved, may have wished that he had not prevented his name from being placed in nomination for the directorship of the Imperial Chapel in Vienna.

Time was when it was relatively easy to hear *La Damnation de Faust* even outside France, but now, paradoxically, with the vogue for Berlioz increasing, it has dropped outside the plans of our musical dictators, in this apparently sharing the fate of all but a few works that partake of the nature of oratorio. Nor is it any longer heard adapted as an opera. Few losses to the variety and vitality of the repertoire are greater, for it contains some of Berlioz's most dramatic pages. If in *Roméo et Juliette* Berlioz's music is about the poetry of Shakespeare, in *La Damnation de Faust* it is as little as possible about Goethe's philosophico-poetic mélange. In its best sections, Berlioz has, in fact, Shakespeareanized Goethe. World-famous, in addition to the *Rákóczy March*, and always to be heard, are the Minuet of the Will-o'-the-Wisps and the Dance of the Sylphs, but equally alluring is much of the vocal music, especially Marguerite's wistful soliloquy, *Le Roi de Thulé*, Faust's sumptuous invocation, "*Immense nature*," and Méphistophélès' lush and seductive "*Voici des roses*." *La Damnation de Faust* is an album of wonderfully poetic, economically composed scenes, almost always—not usually a Berliozian merit—of heavenly length. Of all these composers, great or otherwise—Liszt, Wagner, Gounod, and Boïto included—who have gone to the Faust story for inspiration (or puzzlement), Berlioz, at least in returning richly laden, is *facile princeps*.

In 1847, Berlioz tried his luck in Russia, conducting in St. Petersburg, Moscow, and Riga. Throughout this tour, his artistic success was monumental, his profits satisfactory. A piquant note was added by a passing and innocent romance with a young Russian corset-maker (his taste in women was never to gain in relevance): this was probably a necessary respite from the complaints of the now-paralyzed Henriette and the tirades of the shrewish Marie. Returning toward France, Berlioz lingered at Berlin to conduct a performance of *La Damnation de Faust* under the double patronage of Friedrich Wilhelm IV and Meyerbeer. The Prussian king complimented him, but the higher critics were incensed by what they considered his cavalier treatment of Goethe, and sulked loftily. He returned to Paris with one tenth of the 150,000-franc profit Balzac had prophesied for the tour, commenting dryly: "This great mind had the weakness of seeing fortunes everywhere . . ." A summer visit to La Côte-Saint-André prepared him for the disasters of the coming season.

By November Berlioz was in England for the first time, having been engaged by Louis-Antoine Jullien, one of the prime fantastics of the age,* to conduct four concerts and a season of opera at Drury Lane, including the world *première* of a three-act opera composed especially for this English season. Although Jullien's plans were on an unrealistically vast scale, his arrangement with Berlioz, apparently generous, was, on analysis, on the cautious side: £400 for the opera-conducting, £400 for the concerts, and £800 for the new opera—if it reached a seventieth performance. As it worked out, Berlioz touched only the first of these moneys, for shortly Jullien was suffering from one of his numerous bankruptcies. The opera season had opened auspiciously with the triumphant success of *Lucia di Lammermoor*, but the profits were quickly eaten up by fees to the expensive official window-dressing (Sir Henry Bishop and others, whom Jullien had ostentatiously engaged to advise him). By January, 1848, the season could be chalked up as a failure. But Berlioz remained stubbornly in London: he liked the English, and was dismayed at the idea of returning to a revolution-torn France (Louis-Philippe was overthrown in February, and not until December were conditions somewhat stabilized by the election

---

* This madman was a strange compound of the best and the worst. He had such a reverence for Beethoven that he would conduct his works only with a jeweled baton and wearing a pair of white kid gloves handed to him on a silver salver just before the performance. He was once barely dissuaded from publishing a setting of the Lord's Prayer with this legend engraved on the title page: "Words by Jesus Christ; Music by Jullien."

of Louis-Napoléon as president). He was not inactive, and between two successful concerts he began to put together those *Mémoires* which give him pre-eminence as a musical littérateur. When he finally returned to Paris in July, *The Musical Times*, anticipating the fame Berlioz was later to enjoy in England, commented: "We feel that a great and original mind has gone from among us."

The Paris to which Berlioz returned was in its doldrums, and it was difficult to give concerts or work as a musical journalist. Fortunately, his financial prospects brightened. In July his father died, and he could hope eventually to receive a legacy of 130,000 francs. In the meanwhile, he could borrow against this. In November, too, any fears he may have entertained about his relations to the new regime were quieted when the National Assembly, which had cut off his salary at the Conservatoire, voted him five hundred francs to encourage his efforts as a composer, and his position in the Conservatoire library was continued. By 1849, he was again hard at work as critic for the *Journal des débats* and the *Gazette musicale*. The composition of a *Te Deum* was proceeding simultaneously: possibly the waxing of Louis-Napoléon's star gave Berlioz the not unnatural hope that mighty events might soon be commemorated by mighty music. But the third Bonaparte was apathetic to art, and this enormous work for three choirs, orchestra, and organ had to wait six years for a performance, when, in the Church of Saint-Eustache, Berlioz conducted it, on April 30, as a prelude to the opening of the Exposition Universelle of 1855. As a comment on Berlioz's shrewd and economic borrowings from himself, it is amusing to note that parts of the *Te Deum* date back to sketches for an apotheosis of Napoleon I, which had been pondered in Italy in 1832.

The *Te Deum* is one of those too-numerous compositions of Berlioz's about which, as a listening experience, it is all but impossible to write at first hand. Examination of the score and the testimony of musical observers of the past easily persuade us that the *Te Deum* should be resurrected. Berlioz himself called the *Judex crederis*, its seventh section, "my most grandiose creation," and Tom S. Wotton, one of the most sapient of Berliozians, pronounced it "amongst the greatest movements in music," adding that "it alone should place Berlioz amongst the supreme masters of the art." Apparently it is a high spot in the music of terror, the opposite number to Michelangelo's *Last Judgment*. Not all of the eight sections of the *Te Deum* are of this oppressive mightiness; several of them are of persuasive lyrical beauty. Throughout, Berlioz makes the most discreet use of his big choral batteries, reserving them for the true climaxes. And the use of the organ, too, marks Berlioz's supremacy in the understanding of instruments: not merely does it add its diapasons to the most tremendous cascades of sound, but it is also used tenderly as a solo performer, notably in the prelude to the second section, *Tibi omnes*. As any *Te Deum* is in a real sense a *pièce d'occasion*, Berlioz's might lose some of its effectiveness if given apart from a large celebration of a jubilant nature.*

While in England, Berlioz had been impressed by the Philharmonic Society, the conduct of whose instrumentalists he excepted from his condemnation of the casualness of English musicians. In 1850, he attempted to establish its counterpart in Paris. The first concert of the Société Philharmonique was given on February 19, with the nineteen-year-old Joachim as soloist; little more than a year later, on March 25, 1851, the Société, soon to breathe its last, presented Berlioz's new choral work, ominously entitled *La Menace des Francs*. More important, during this period Berlioz was working on *La Fuite en Égypte*, eventually to become the second part of *L'Enfance du Christ*. He tried out part of *La Fuite* late in 1850, incidentally perpetrating a malicious practical joke on the critical pundits of the French capital. He announced this little chorus of shepherds as the work of "Pierre Ducré, music-master of the Sainte-Chapelle in Paris in the seventeenth century"—and only one critic seemed to imply that Ducré was a figment of Berlioz's imagination: Léon Kreutzer, probably tipped off by the joker himself, remarked in the *Gazette musicale* that this music "was

---

* The *Te Deum*, conducted by Walter Damrosch, was sung at the opening of Music (later Carnegie) Hall, New York, on May 5, 1891.

very happily modulated for a period when they scarcely modulated at all."

After the failure of the Société Philharmonique, Berlioz was sent, as the official representative of French music, to the Great Exhibition of 1851, held in London's new Crystal Palace. While in England, he completed negotiations to become for six years the conductor of the New Philharmonic Society, a post he assumed the following year. He must have gone to London that time with some reluctance, for on March 20, 1852, Liszt staged, at Weimar, the first performance of *Benvenuto Cellini* since its original failure thirteen years before. Four days later, at Exeter Hall, Berlioz led the orchestra of the New Philharmonic Society in its first concert, presenting the first four parts of *Roméo et Juliette* in English translation. Another concert was a more dramatic occasion: he conducted excerpts from *La Vestale* with a baton brought to London by Spontini's widow, and which the great classicist had used in directing the operas of Gluck and Mozart. On April 28, Berlioz's program included Weber's *Conzertstück*, with the piano solo confided to his former inamorata, Mme Camille Pleyel. Things went badly during the Weber, but after this lapse of years it is impossible to tell whether her charge that the conductor had bungled the accompaniment was true or catty. No doubt, however, about Berlioz's stature as a conductor was left after two magnificent readings of Beethoven's Ninth Symphony. Yet, though the press was wildly laudatory and the glories of these concerts lingered in the minds of musical London for years, the season ended with a deficit, and Berlioz's contract lapsed.

Fortunately, the disappointment of the London venture was mitigated by Liszt's decision to set aside a week in November, 1852, for a Berlioz festival. At Weimar, Berlioz was lionized wherever he went, and *Benvenuto Cellini*, *Roméo et Juliette*, and the first two parts of *La Damnation de Faust* (*Cellini* under Liszt's baton, the others led by the composer) were received with the applause that his music was eliciting throughout Germany. At a banquet, the Grand Duke of Saxe-Weimar bestowed upon him the Order of the Falcon. This uninterrupted ovation was the beginning of a series of visits to Germany that lasted until

September, 1856. In the midst of his triumphs, Berlioz's cool-headed wit did not desert him: he noted that when Bettina von Arnim, the now-decrepit lady who had been Beethoven's friend and Goethe's Egeria, called on him, she said that she had come "not to see me, but to look at me." His German canonization may be said to have taken place when he conducted two Gewand-haus concerts in December, 1853: Liszt, Brahms, Cornelius, Joachim, Raff, and Eduard Reményi were in the audience. This unreserved acclaim must have intensified Berlioz's mortification when, at the height of his German triumph, the news came to him that he had again been passed over for a seat in the Institut, for a nonentity as usual.

On March 3, 1854, the official Mme Berlioz finally died. Three days later, Berlioz wrote to his son, now an apprentice seaman: "You will never know what we have suffered from one another, your mother and I . . ." Considering the circumstances, it is not at all strange that he was able, less than a month later, to conduct a concert at Hanover with vigor and success. All in all, Henriette's death was a great release, and after a decent interval he married Marie Recio. Again he wrote to Louis: "This liaison, as you will readily understand, had become indissoluble from the mere facts of its duration; I could neither live alone nor abandon the person who had been living with me for fourteen years." This sounds like a conscientious man's excuse for a bad habit he could not relinquish, and Marie is never mentioned by name in the *Mémoires*. In the meantime, another official post had eluded his grasp when Liszt and Hans von Bülow failed to get him appointed to the Hoftheater at Dresden—and this despite the superb series of concerts Berlioz had just conducted there. Yet 1854 was important to him for more than the death of Henriette and his marriage to Marie: before it was over he had completed the *Mémoires* (except for a few later additions) and *L'Enfance du Christ*.

At the Salle Herz, Paris, on December 10, 1854, Berlioz conducted the *première* of this oratorio or "sacred trilogy," the first of his works for which he wrote the entire text. Its success was so immediate and unmixed (five performances in Paris and three in Brussels in four and a half months) that Berlioz was almost embittered by it, as he felt that it tended to cast doubt retroactively on the quality of earlier works composed in quite different spirit. For *L'Enfance du Christ* is primarily meditative and pastoral, and is often lighted by a sort of antique, lyrical grace. The scoring is delicate, the orchestra small. The first section, *Le Songe d'Hérode*, centers on the obsessive fears of the neurasthenic King of Judaea, and ends, with a dramatic change of scene, in the manger at Bethlehem, where a choir of angels warns Mary and Joseph to flee. Part two, *La Fuite en Égypte*, consists of a brief overture followed by two sections of extraordinary beauty: *L'Adieu des bergers*, a piercingly sweet vocal melodic line exquisitely caressed by the oboe, and *Le Repos de la Sainte-Famille*, the tenor-narrator's simple comment on a poignantly touching situation. The third section of *L'Enfance* is called *L'Arrivée à Saïs*. Here Mary and Joseph seek lodging, knocking vainly at doors until at the home of the Ishmaelites they are finally admitted. This pitiable situation is made the most of, and the section ends in a choral epilogue about which Berlioz himself wrote ecstatically: "It seems to me to contain a feeling of infinite, of divine love."

Berlioz's friendship with Liszt reached its height during 1855 and 1856. He made three visits to Weimar, the first time to attend another Berlioz week, for which Raff had written a Latin cantata in his honor. He found a new intimate in Liszt's mistress, Princess Carolyne Sayn-Wittgenstein, a woman with a vigorous cast of mind, a busy pen, and a quenchless box of black cigars—a true original for whom Berlioz felt a kinship. It was in April, 1855, that she forthrightly directed him to compose an opera based on the *Aeneid*, thereby pulling together various ideas that had been floating around in his mind. These concerned the composition of a big opera, a project that he himself had at times vaguely connected with his childhood worship of Virgil. For one month short of three years he was to be intermittently at work on the libretto and score of what turned out to be a five-act opera, *Les Troyens*. Before it was finished, Berlioz had again conducted in London, had composed

L'Impériale, * a cantata for the closing of the Paris Exposition (which the *Te Deum* had ushered in), and had received a gold medal from Napoleon III. Intellectually, he was refreshed by several meetings with Wagner, who at this period reciprocated his feelings. Finally, his ego was elated by that prize after which he had so long yearned, election to the Institut, in which he succeeded to the *fauteuil* left vacant by the death of Adolphe Adam.

Although Berlioz by this time enjoyed some financial security, this was outweighed by increasing torture from what his physicians called "neuralgia of the stomach," a vague term that precise modern medical nomenclature does not recognize. Doubtless this was a neurasthenic condition brought on by thwarted ambition and exacerbated by hopes delayed. Nevertheless, *Les Troyens* progressed. He discussed the finest points with Princess Sayn-Wittgenstein by letter, but the final text was as completely his own as the music. The entire five-act opera lay complete on his desk by March, 1858. Then began the grim, disheartening fight to have it produced. At first it seemed that the Opéra would mount it, perhaps even—like *Tannhäuser*—at Napoleon III's behest.

Suddenly, and rather paradoxically, after the failure of *Tannhäuser* (which must have seemed to the directorate a most radical work), the Opéra decided, in June, 1861, to stage *Les Troyens*. Then for almost two years the directors kept Berlioz dangling, and at one time definitely scheduled the staging for March, 1863. While he alternately hoped and despaired, tragedy and success were his in equal portions. In 1860, partly to relieve his nerves, he had accepted a commission to compose a comic opera, and had elected to write his own libretto to Shakespeare's *Much Ado About Nothing*, calling it *Béatrice et Benedict*. This was for Baden-Baden, the cosmopolitan spa whose music festivals, sponsored by the proprietor of the casino, Berlioz had been conducting since 1856. *Béatrice et Benedict*, completed in the spring of 1862, was presented successfully at the festival the following August, but in June, Berlioz's second wife had

---

* Perhaps "dusted off" is a better phrase, for *L'Impériale* appears to have been identical with *Le Dix décembre*, presented earlier that year.

died suddenly, and he conducted in physical pain and mental anguish. As the crucial month of March, 1863, came and went, and the Opéra failed to stage *Les Troyens*, the weary composer began to listen to the entreaties of Léon Carvalho, who wished to stage a section of the long opera at his Théâtre-Lyrique. Berlioz, who above all wished to hear his opera performed before he died, agreed with misgivings. Then he went to Weimar, where *Béatrice et Benedict* was sung in German translation. In June he conducted *L'Enfance du Christ* at the Lower Rhine Festival at Strasbourg. Finally, on November 4, the last three acts of *Les Troyens*—rearranged as five acts, and provided with a prologue especially written to acquaint the audience with the preceding two acts—reached the stage as *Les Troyens à Carthage.*[*] It had a dress rehearsal and twenty-one performances. This was the only part of his great opera that Berlioz ever heard, and it was not until twenty-one years after his death that Felix Mottl, Wagnerian extraordinary, nobly staged *Les Troyens* whole, though in German, at Karlsruhe.

The spirit of *Les Troyens* is as far removed from that of the *Symphonie fantastique* and *Lélio* as music could well be and still be recognizably the same composer's. Here at last is Berlioz's *éloge* to Gluck, the more glorious because so long meditated. This is not, in any sense that Weber, Schumann, or the young Berlioz himself would have admitted, romantic music: it is a classical work with romantic touches derived faithfully from Virgil—or it is a romantic work in classical leading-strings. At all events, it exists to confound those who would rigorously parcel off areas with little signs marked "classical" and "romantic."

This tremendous tale of the taking of Troy, the loves of Dido and Aeneas, and Aeneas's departure to keep his date with destiny (as the opera closes, the chorus chants, *"Rome! Rome!"* and the Capitol looms in the background like a Mediterranean Valhalla) runs for four hours and a half, not counting intermissions. Opera managers, willing to subject their patrons to *Parsifal* at least once a year, can find reasons for depriving these same patrons of Berlioz's masterpiece. Therefore, it is possible

---

[*] The first part, given alone, is known as *La Prise de Troie.*

to judge the quality of *Les Troyens* only from the printed score, from excerpts, whether recorded or heard in the concert hall, and from the reports of those fortunate musical observers who heard the Karlsruhe performance of 1890 or the Glasgow revival of 1935, the latter disclosing it, as Sir Donald Tovey testified, "as one of the most gigantic and convincing masterpieces of music-drama." Even a knowledge of *Les Troyens* confined to Hylas's "*Vallon sonore,*" Aeneas's "*Inutiles regrets,*" the *Marche troyenne*, and the *Chasse royale et orage* would persuade us to echo this pronouncement. *Les Troyens*, quite as much as *Roméo et Juliette*, leads inevitably to the conclusion that Berlioz was the greatest French composer between Rameau and Debussy.

Les Troyens would have been a fitting capstone to Berlioz's career. In it, as Cecil Gray wrote, ". . . he is a classical master in the pure Latin tradition; the volcanic, tempestuous energy of the early works gives place to a majestic dignity and restraint worthy of Sophocles himself, and to a serenity and sweetness that can only be called Virgilian." But though it was the last of his major works to reach performance, *Béatrice et Benedict* was the last of them to be composed. This two-acter is both an *opéra-comique* in the French sense (it has spoken dialogue) and a comic opera in the English sense (it is amusing and has a happy ending). Again, though *Béatrice et Benedict* has been compared by W. J. Turner to such masterpieces of the comic spirit as *Le Nozze di Figaro*, *The Barber of Seville*, and *Falstaff*, it has been almost utterly neglected, and must be judged, as we are forced to judge *Les Troyens*, chiefly at second hand. Its overture is light and deft, a pleasant concert number, but by no means so ingeniously conceived and executed as many of the scenes in the opera. It would be pleasant to record that this light, witty music reflected an eventide serenity like that reflected in Verdi's *Falstaff*: that it was written in the depths of spiritual malaise makes it almost a miracle. One of its most charming scenes is built around an idea added to the story by Berlioz—the rehearsal of a fugal epithalamium by inept singers and instrumentalists. In part reminiscent of the drolleries of the "Lesson Scene" in *The Barber*, this also recalls the Beckmesser episodes in *Die Meistersinger*, for it can be interpreted as Berlioz's way of getting back at the petty pedantries of academic music professors and critics.

Berlioz's creative life ended with *Béatrice et Benedict*, but his emotional struggles were still not resolved. Publicly, he proceeded slowly to an apotheosis, refuting in advance the legend, manufactured by sentimental biographers, that he was without honor in his lifetime. In private he was a lonely and tortured man. His wants tended by Marie's mother, he focused his unquenchable hopes momentarily on a young girl whom he met some time in 1863. But Amélie—no more is known of her than her first name—died too, and Berlioz was again left alone. He poured out his moods in letters to his son Louis, who, despite his unstable temperament, was rising in the merchant marine. In the autumn of 1864 his melancholy drew him to revisit the scenes of his childhood—to, in fact, the Estelle country. He was seized by an urge to see his early ideal again (the *idée fixe* of the *Fantastique* was as much her signature as Henriette-Ophelia's), and somehow sought her out at Lyons. The grandmotherly Mme Fornier was polite and sympathetic, but obviously mystified. When he mentioned the well-remembered pink shoes, she denied ever having owned any—perhaps they seemed improper to her. Anyhow, with due caution, she allowed Berlioz to correspond with her, and even sent him her portrait. Here was no answer to his loneliness. There was no answer.

The young Berlioz had felt himself separated from his fellows by his fiery romanticism; now, at the end of his career he must have appeared as austerely classical as Cherubini himself. Thus the inevitable sum at the end of every equation was loneliness. For instance, though Liszt visited him in Paris, and their relations were superficially friendly, they had really split on the problem of Wagner. Little broke the monotony of Berlioz's life. He had ample time to suffer and think. In 1866, he conducted *La Damnation de Faust* at Vienna. In 1867, no doubt as an antidote to the anguish caused by the death, in Havana, of his son (a victim of yellow fever), he consented, though a dying man, to undertake an onerous conducting tour in Russia. His success in St. Petersburg and Moscow was clamorous, and both the nationalists and the Rubinstein-Tchaikovsky group paid him all honor. By February, 1868, he was back in Paris, but restlessness and increasing ill health drove him south. At Monte Carlo he suffered a serious fall from the effects of which he never recovered. The year left to him is chiefly a record of physical and mental disintegration. In August he dragged himself to Grenoble to attend the unveiling of a statue of Napoleon. There, during a festival in his honor, he was presented with a silver-gilt wreath, the immemorial tribute to a conqueror. It was his last journey. He died at Paris on March 8, 1869.

Camille Saint-Saëns once complained that "Berlioz's miseries were the result of his hankering after the impossible," and some of his well-wishers and apologists have inherited that tendency. They not only wish him to receive his very considerable dues—they also wish, by scarce-veiled implication, to elevate him to the rank of Bach, Mozart, and Beethoven. Mussorgsky, who looked at music through a special lens, spoke of "Beethoven the thinker and Berlioz the superthinker." This can be a double-edged truth, and some of Berlioz's frustrations (and those of his admirers) can be attributed to diseased thinking. He was indeed "sicklied o'er by the pale cast of thought," at least as far as his hopes and ambitions were concerned. As a result, the absurd claims of such an idolater as W. J. Turner (willing to tear down all but Mozart in order to build up his hero) are counterbalanced by the grudging, niggling admissions of critics and biographers who are apparently attracted to Berlioz only by his outré qualities. In fact, some of his critics loathe him almost as much as many Boswellians loathe their subject.

What is the truth? Admitting that Berlioz was a supreme orchestrator, a melodist of surpassing originality, and a harmonic inventor worthy to follow in the line of Rameau, he nevertheless suffers from having to be labeled as one of the great originals of music. What to some extent negated the effectiveness of these great gifts was megalomania, producing vast, impressive—but too often inchoate and distended—structures. A formal sense of humility (which in relation to music itself he never denied) would have salvaged a thousand brilliant musical ideas by putting them in a framework of proper relations. Then Lélio,

L'Enfance du Christ, Les Troyens, Roméo et Juliette even, would not continue to exist merely as fabulously stocked museums from which individual jewels are abstracted for temporary display. Berlioz, the supreme critic, the hard worker, the galley-slave of the *Journal des débats*, was not consistently severe enough with himself in the final phase of composition—the fusing of a work as an artistic entity. The *mot unique et juste* is always found—but not always its use.

Chapter XV

Franz Liszt

(Raiding, October 22, 1811–July 31, 1886, Bayreuth)

LISZT, more than any other major figure of the romantic movement, is a creature of legend. Born while Halley's comet was
coursing through the heavens, he came out of the almost fabled
land of Hungary, the home of gypsies and werewolves and Esterházys, a pianist of such dazzling powers that there seemed to be
something supernatural about him. He was subject to cataleptic
fits and religious ecstasies. He had been kissed by Beethoven. The
Parisians called him the ninth wonder of the world—who or what
the eighth was does not develop. He was beautiful beyond the
ordinary manner of man, and at a tender age began his career as
the great lover of the century. Noblewomen were his specialty: by
a countess he had three illegitimate children; he all but married a
partly divorced princess by special decree of the Vatican, and
when he was over sixty a Polish-Cossack countess—his castoff
mistress—threatened to put poison in his soup. Having made a
large fortune as a virtuoso, at the height of his fame he decided
to play only for charity, and to teach for nothing. At the point
where his loves became too complicated and an old persistent
yearning for the spiritual life reappeared, he took minor orders in
the Church. He turned his collar around, became the Abbé Liszt,
and thenceforth divided his time between Rome and Budapest
and Weimar, between the Church and a court of pupils thronging
from every quarter of the globe. He taught half the great pianists
of the nineteenth century, one of whom is scheduled, as this
chapter is written, to give a New York recital. He lived seventy-
five years, and died in the shadow of his son-in-law.

Liszt was also a composer. His separate works number between
thirteen and fourteen hundred. Of these, a staggering percentage is
made up of transcriptions and arrangements of other composers'
works. Of his wholly original pieces, some are among the most
popular music ever composed. These, almost without exception,
are not of high musical quality. But there is a legend about Liszt's
music, too. It is based on the supposititious high musical quality of

various large works, mostly orchestral or choral, that are seldom if ever performed. Those who sustain this legend ask us to believe that time has, in the case of Liszt, winnowed maliciously, saving the chaff and throwing away the good grain. Time might conceivably cut such capers among the compositions of one long dead and all but forgotten. But Liszt has been dead little more than sixty years, and since the middle of his life has been as famous as Beethoven. It seems incredible, then, that if these neglected works were indeed masterpieces, they would be suffered to remain on the shelf. We are forced, at any rate, to judge Liszt on the basis of what music of his is played or recorded.

The truth is that Liszt was first a performer, and only later, and secondarily, a composer. At the age of nine, he was shown off as a virtuoso by his father, a disappointed musician serving as land steward to the Esterházys. Some rich Hungarian nobles thereupon guaranteed six years of study in Vienna. Adam Liszt and his mainly German wife were glad to leave the dull hamlet of Raiding, and accompany Franz. After studying with Czerny and the aged Salieri, he made a sensational debut in Vienna shortly after his eleventh birthday, and was among those invited to contribute to the books of variations on a theme by Diabelli. This was his first published composition. Solidly endowed by Czerny with the essentials of what was to become a unique piano style, Liszt was taken on his first extended tour. The venture turned out well, and it was decided that the boy was now ready for Paris. A letter from Metternich was calculated to unbar for this prodigious little foreigner the jealously guarded doors of the Conservatoire, but Cherubini stuck by the letter of the rule against admitting foreigners. The boy had to content himself with private masters.

For four years Liszt continued his musical studies, keeping himself and his family in funds with Paris concerts and modest forays abroad. During three brief visits to England, he was made much of and, of course, was received several times by George IV. A few days before his fourteenth birthday, his operetta, *Don Sanche*, was presented in Paris. But he was no Rossini: after two repetitions, the paltry business was withdrawn, and his career as an opera composer was over. The fiasco did not mar his fame as a virtuoso, which by 1827 had become so considerable that he could face the future without economic fears. The same year, his father died with the prophetic words on his lips that women would mess up Franz' life.

The necessity of paying his father's debts and of supporting his mother forced Liszt, at sixteen, to add to his income by giving lessons. He promptly fell in love with almost his first pupil, the young daughter of one of Charles X's ministers. She returned his love, but her father did not, and soon he was shown the door. He reacted like a good little romantic, fell into a decline, and was even reported dead. He moped in his rooms, reading Byron and books on religion, and toying with the Socialistic ideas of Saint-Simon. For the first time in his dizzying career, he began to think, not always too successfully: there were so many conflicting currents of thought that reconciling them was a most difficult matter. Confusion was in the air, and ended in the absurd revolution of 1830, whereby the young Parisian bolshevists replaced a dictator-king, who at least had a certain antique arrogance, with a silly, mule-headed bourgeois. But Liszt needed something more exciting than the July revolution to wake him from his musings. He met, in rapid succession, three men who changed the whole tenor of his life and gave new impetus to his musical urge. The first was the student Berlioz, already a musical anarch experimenting with new, bold orchestral effects that Liszt quietly annexed when he needed them, and whose ideas on program music also influenced him profoundly. In Chopin he glimpsed the power of a lyricism surcharged with intense and fluctuating emotions. Berlioz and Chopin gave wings to his yearning: they opened vistas into a musical never-never land. But it was the diabolical fiddler, Nicolò Paganini, who showed Liszt, already aspiring to be the virtuoso of virtuosos, that technique itself could be sorcery. In this unsavory Italian, he found exactly the elements he was to use in becoming the most phenomenal pianist of the century—absolute command of his instrument, a battery of outlandish technical tricks, a dash of diablerie, and an elaborately built-up professional personality.

Liszt the composer was slow in emerging: many years were to pass before he addressed his audience with his first large original compositions. After meeting and hearing Paganini, for two years he lived the life of an ascetic: with his decision made to become the unrivaled pianist, he practiced as no one had practiced before, and as few have practiced since. The fruits of this painful self-denial were not slow in appearing: he had always, it seemed, been an accomplished performer, but now, emerging from his retirement in 1832, became almost at once what he had intended to become—the Paganini of the keyboard. Paris lay at his feet, and among those who succumbed to his newly found greatness was "Monsieur Lits" himself. Just as Chopin wafted himself and his adoring countesses into a dreamworld of his making as his fingers whispered over the ivory keys in darkened salons, so Liszt, as he walked onto the stage and saw the whole great world of Paris as a blur of expectant faces, was intoxicated by his power.

Mme Liszt, who shared her son's modest rooms, could not have been an effective duenna, for it was during this time that he embarked seriously on his amours. He made a few trial flights, and scandalized the old gossips of the Faubourg Saint-Germain by going off to Switzerland with a countess and her husband. They were in for worse floutings of their conventions. In 1833, Liszt's extraordinary beauty and Byronic manner attracted the attention of a great lady, Countess Marie d'Agoult. Although she was six years his senior, married, and the mother of three children, Liszt responded so ardently that they were both carried off their feet and, before they were fully aware of the possible consequences of their actions, were immersed in a passionate love affair. Liszt had no qualms, and Mme d'Agoult had few: her husband was twenty years older than she—a cold, boring court official from whom she was estranged. As early as March, 1835, they were so inextricably involved with each other that they could not have turned back, even if they had wished. They decided to elope, and by August, after a distracted search for the most congenial retreat, were settled at Geneva. There their first child, Blandine, was born in December, and their rejoicings over her birth seemed a guarantee of eternal happiness.

And at first the lovers were happy, idyllically so. Liszt was trying to compose—the first sketches for the *Années de pèlerinage* were published in 1835—and was teaching at a music school in Geneva. As for the Countess, she was content to be cut off from the world with Franz and her children. She did not reckon with Liszt's love of adulation or with the fact that the scandal they had caused had made them objects of interest to prurient sightseers. Soon their solitude was invaded, first by a madcap boy of fifteen,

Liszt's favorite pupil. Then George Sand, disguised as an army officer, burst in on them, and it may well be that this sudden intrusion gave the Countess the impulse that later transformed her into the writer Daniel Stern. The idyl was over. From this time on they were wanderers, slowly drifting apart, though for some years apparently wholly devoted to each other. They had two more children: Cosima, born on Christmas, 1837, and Daniel, born two years later.

The Countess mistrusted the world, but the need for money made going back to it a necessity. Liszt had settled most of his earnings on his mother, the Countess had but a small income, and a fortune lay at the tips of Liszt's fingers. They decided to face the censorious eyes of the *faubourgs*, and so returned with Mme Sand. Liszt re-entered Paris in what must have seemed to him an evil hour: the city was ringing with praise of the pianist Thalberg, the beautifully mannered illegitimate son of an Austrian prince, and momentarily he found himself in second place. He accepted the situation as a challenge. When Thalberg came back early in 1837, they entered on a protracted keyboard duel that culminated in an epochal bout at the home of Princess Cristina Belgiojoso, a noted musical philanthropist. Both of them played works that would hardly be tolerated on concert programs today, Thalberg his own fantasia on Rossini's *Moïse*, Liszt his fantasia on the *Niobe* of Giovanni Pacini, a Rossini imitator. Briefly, Thalberg played more suavely, Liszt more excitedly—and Liszt was judged the winner. It was a famous victory. Thalberg retired discomfited, but not so discomfited as the Lisztians would have us believe, and both victor and vanquished went on to make a great deal of money playing the piano for many years thereafter.

His defeat of Thalberg made Liszt the most sought-after pianist alive. Up to 1847, his life is the story of his concert tours. For several years, while his love for the Countess d'Agoult still exercised a strong restraining influence, he remained a musician who gave a few concerts, though it is probable that at this very time he was already conceiving of the virtuoso's career in revolutionary terms. But in 1840, when it was obvious that, despite the common responsibilities entailed by three children, the bonds were loosening, Liszt abandoned himself completely to its allures. Had not his virtuosity already raised him to a pinnacle of glory attained by few of even the greatest composers? In November, 1839, leaving the Countess with five children on her hands (two D'Agoult, three nameless), he went off to Vienna to give a series of six piano recitals, having agreed to raise singlehanded all the money for the Beethoven memorial at Bonn. This was the first series of real piano recitals ever given, though earlier that year he had experimented with a Roman audience in giving an entire program of piano solos. Moreover, he had revolutionized the art of piano showmanship: in order to advertise his striking profile (which became more and more Dantesque with the years), he turned the side of the piano to the audience. (Previously even the handsomest of keyboard Adonises had either presented their backs to the public or faced it over the instrument.) The Vienna recitals fully justified his innovations: three thousand people were in the hall for the first recital, and the series ended in a fanfare of triumph. A Hungarian delegation came to invite him home, and after stopping at Pressburg, where his arrival forced the Prince Palatine of Hungary to postpone his levee rather than be ignored, Liszt made a royal progress into Budapest. There, in a hysteria of national fervor, attired in a magnificent thousand-franc Magyar costume bought for the occasion, Liszt was presented with a jeweled saber. There was talk at the time of his being ennobled, but it came to nothing except as material for persiflage among the Parisian wits. His vanity had become so monstrous that the Countess wrote him not to make an ass of himself.

But the Countess' words carried little weight with him now. He was wedded to his gilded wayfaring. He lived for the applause, the adulation of the Lisztians whom he created as he played, the flattery of kings and their jeweled orders—and the complaisant noblewomen, with a peasant girl or two thrown in to add tang, who waited along his route. Within seven years his tours took him to Berlin, Copenhagen, Constantinople, Leipzig, Lisbon, London, Madrid, Moscow, St. Petersburg, and Warsaw, as well as scores of smaller towns, some of them jerkwaters in remote Moldavia and Russia. England alone greeted him coldly: though Queen Victoria received him at Buckingham Palace (this indiscretion may be laid to her youth), her subjects judged him a libertine and poseur, and stayed away from his recitals. Everywhere else he went, the honor of entertaining Liszt was fought for by the local nobility, much to his delight. He dearly loved a title, and while he was still corresponding with Mme d'Agoult, though neglecting to speak of his amorous conquests, rarely missed a chance to boast of the princes and counts he bagged. And yet, Liszt stopped short of being a toady, and even ruling monarchs were not exempt from his wrath when his, or music's, dignity was impugned. He once reprimanded the Iron Tsar himself for talking while he was playing. He refused to play for Isabella II of Spain because court etiquette would not allow him to be presented to her personally. And he was snobbish even about kings. He snubbed poor old Louis-Philippe repeatedly for not belonging to the elder branch of the Bourbon family.

Today, when the vast majority of piano recitals are given for the purpose of re-creating the best music in that repertoire, it is a harsh comment on the taste of Liszt's age that he climbed to the zenith of musical fame largely by playing his own compositions at public recitals. In private, he played everything, inventing, in fact, the repertoire that has been standard ever since. Nothing available for the piano escaped his omnivorous attention, and he was equally at home with Bach and Scarlatti, Mozart and Beethoven, Chopin and Schumann. Had his public programs represented this catholicity of interest, the subsequent history of the piano recital might have been different. He had an opportunity given to few: that of creating simultaneously an audience and its taste. He chose the showman's way,* and whipped up a passion for virtuoso exhibitionism for its own sake from which pianists suffered for more than half a century. He played mainly his own transcriptions of everything from a Donizetti march to a Beethoven symphony, from the national anthem of whatever country he happened to be visiting to a Schubert lied; he played the showiest and noisiest of his *Études transcendantes*, and almost inevitably closed with his *Grand Galop chromatique*, an absurd collection of scales and difficulties that even the idolatrous Sacheverell Sitwell cannot stomach.

* In more ways than one. His appearance was deliberately theatrical: his style of dress was exaggeratedly rich, his coiffure absurd. At his Russian debut he was covered with clanking orders, and we read that he "mounted the platform, and, pulling his dogskin gloves from his shapely white hands, tossed them carelessly on the floor." Part of his act was to lead a deeply emotional life at the piano, and he cleverly used his disheveled locks as excitants. "Constantly tossing back his long hair, with lips quivering, his nostrils palpitating, he swept the auditorium with the glance of a smiling master": such was the impression of the dramatist Legouvé, who was writing in an entirely friendly spirit.

It took a Paderewski and a De Pachmann and a few others to free the punch-drunk audiences from that unnatural conception of the recital as an athletic bout of piano-pounding and sensationalism, of which Liszt himself may not have approved, but for which he was unquestionably to blame. For the saddest part of Liszt's public perversion of his unparalleled pianistic gifts is that he was aware of it. He had a certain contempt for much of what he was playing—and, by implication, for his audiences. Once, when he was reproached for his trashy operatic fantasias, he said, "Ah, if I had written only *Faust* and *Dante* Symphonies, I shouldn't be able to give my friends trout with iced champagne."

Mme d'Agoult shared Liszt's triumphs, but only from a distance, and with increasing displeasure. She disliked the charlatan in him, and was affronted by his affairs, particularly when the names coupled with his began to include such women about town as the Princess Belgiojoso and George Sand, and such out-and-out courtesans as Lola Montez and the lovely Marie Duplessis, whom the younger Dumas immortalized in *La Dame aux camélias*. By 1844, they had come to the final parting of their ways, though they corresponded well into the fifties. After that, except for a chance encounter or so and one coldly formal letter from Liszt, dated 1864, there was silence between them. Liszt did not even send her a formal condolence when two of their children—Daniel and Blandine—died, and when the Countess herself died in 1876, he spoke of her in the most perfunctory and stilted phrases.

In 1843, Liszt was invited to spend a few months each year as musical director of the grand ducal court at Weimar. Although he did not realize it at the time, his acceptance brought about a complete change in the direction of his life. He had begun to grow weary of constantly gallivanting around Europe and, as he already had all the money he needed, he wanted to settle down and devote most of his time to composing. Slowly he came to the decision to retire from the concert stage, and in 1847 made his last tour. This took him finally to Russia, where at Kiev he was captured by the second woman who played a salient role in his life. This was Her Serene Highness the Princess Carolyne Sayn-Wittgenstein, a highly connected Polish matron of twenty-eight. To her vast estate at Woronince, where she lived in feudal state, surrounded by the thirty thousand serfs she had inherited from her father, he was carried off in triumph. The Princess was, of course, a misunderstood wife, and soon they were lovers. There, on the edge of the Russian steppes, while she lay on a bearskin rug smoking a cigar, Liszt played to her, and exposed his plan of abandoning the tinsel and glitter of the world. The Princess, who was of a religious and mystical nature, clung to the master, and agreed to retire with him to Weimar. With their plan of renunciation complete, Liszt went off to play his last paid recital—at Elisavetgrad, of all places! The Princess, on her part, got in touch with a good house agent in Weimar, and leased a commodious residence there. Within a year they were comfortably settled in the Altenburg, which was to be their joint home for ten years.*

Having renounced the world, Liszt now entered upon three major careers. Henceforth he was to become the most sought-after of piano teachers. For more than a dozen years he was to be the most hospitable of conductors, with especial warmth toward young composers. And finally, until within four years of his death, he was to unloose the floodgates of one of the most original, daring, and tasteless talents in the history of musical composition. The Altenburg, far from being a retreat, became an active center of European culture, a development that horrified the right-thinking burghers of Weimar. The little town, whose picture of an artist was still based on the portly, respectable figure of the aged Goethe, took a long time to get used to Liszt's long hair and his cigar-smoking Polish mistress.

But it was at stuffy little Weimar that Liszt first won the regard of all his serious confreres. He received about a thousand dollars a year as general director, and his budgets were similarly pinched. Yet, with them he wrought miracles. Having raised his band to something approximating concert pitch, he began a series of concerts remarkable alike for their range and discrimination. In addition to the best works of dead composers—Handel, Haydn, Mozart, Beethoven, and Mendelssohn were liberally represented—he gave many novelties by his contemporaries. In choosing these compositions, Liszt was above any petty spites. He was notably generous in his attitude toward Schumann, who treated him with

---

* The court maintained the polite fiction that Liszt was not living at the Altenburg, and for twelve years addressed official communications to him at a hotel where he had stopped briefly on his first arrival in Weimar, and where he apparently kept a room.

rude animosity. He gave enthusiastic performances of Schumann's symphonies. He was even more lavish toward the difficult and generally misunderstood Berlioz, performing within a week not only the *Symphonie fantastique*, but also several of his overtures and the long-neglected *Harold en Italie*.

At the opera house, Liszt undertook a small revolution of his own, revolutions being in style about the year 1848. It was not that he neglected Gluck and Mozart or Rossini and Meyerbeer, the gods of the epoch, but that he challenged their operas with the most frightful inventions of newcomers. Most brazenly, in February, 1849, he staged an opera by Richard Wagner—a doubly bold act, for the composer was a banished political agitator. *Tannhäuser* was as outrageous for its musical radicalism as for Wagner's politics. And perhaps the fare was too rich for the people of Weimar. Within a few years, they were asked to accept three operas by this bold, bad radical, not to speak of *Fidelio*, Berlioz' *Benvenuto Cellini* and rather cheerless *La Damnation de Faust*, two stage pieces by a young Italian named Verdi, and Schumann's *Genoveva*, which was generally esteemed sad stuff, but of which Liszt said, "I prefer certain faults to certain virtues—the mistakes of clever people to the effects of mediocrity. In this sense there are failures which are better than many a success." All these the Weimarers took, though grumblingly. When they finally balked, it was unexpectedly at the jovial *Barbier von Bagdad* by Peter Cornelius, with its timid traces of Wagnerism.

Opinions of Liszt as a conductor differ, though they are at one today as to his intelligence as a musical host. Ferdinand Hiller accused him bluntly of beating time inaccurately and of confusing his men. But Liszt's friends pointed out that Hiller had heard him at the Karlsruhe Festival conducting an orchestra to which he was a stranger. Chorley, who heard him conduct a Berlioz opera in Weimar, said that "the real beauties . . . of this perplexed and provoking work were brought as near to the comprehension and sympathy of those who heard it as they will probably be ever brought." It seems reasonable that Liszt, who assumed the baton unexpectedly and rather later than usual, was never a really good conductor. In all probability, he carried over into conducting the theatricality and unpredictable personal effects of his pianism— not the best equipment for inspiring an orchestral ensemble with the necessary confidence: the unpremeditated flashes of inspiration that had done much to make him an exciting virtuoso would merely throw orchestral players off the track. Liszt, in short, was an occasionally brilliant but not reliable conductor. Wagner, who had much to thank Liszt for, in writing of the first Weimar performance of *Tannhäuser*, evades, in a moment of forbearance, the touchy question of Liszt's actual conducting by saying that he had a perfect *musical* grasp of the opera.

Liszt's enthusiasm for Wagner was the indirect cause of his leaving Weimar. For some years, he had been trying to force a performance of the entire *Ring* on Grand Duke Karl Alexander, who had neither the funds nor the taste for such a production. An anti-Liszt party gradually gained the upper hand at court, moralistic tongues wagged faster than ever, and Liszt chose this inopportune time to state that if he could not give the *Ring*, he would at least give *Tristan und Isolde*. The sovereign responded to this challenge by cutting his budgets to the bone. Liszt was infuriated and, despite warning that he would have to soft-pedal anything newfangled, went ahead with plans for producing his pupil Cornelius' mildly advanced opera. At its *première*, on December 15, 1858, *Der Barbier von Bagdad* was hissed off the boards. Liszt promptly resigned his post.

As a matter of fact, Liszt's position in Weimar had been getting daily less and less tenable. At first, the Princess had been received at court, and the gossips had had to restrain their tongues. But when she ignored the Tsar's command to return to Russia, and was forthwith banished from his realms, she was no longer received. Liszt viewed with anguish the growing isolation of the woman who had already sacrificed position and a large part of her possessions to be with him. Her efforts to have her marriage annulled so that she could marry him dragged fruitlessly on, for even after the Russian ecclesiastical authorities no longer stood in the way, there remained Rome. The Princess, a devout Roman Catholic, hoped to convince the Curia that she had been forced to marry a heretic—that is, a Greek Orthodox Catholic. But on this plea the local bishop turned a fishy eye, and in May, 1860, she left for Rome, realizing that her only hope lay in appealing to Pius IX himself. Left behind, Liszt looked forward gloomily to his fiftieth birthday. Unhappy memories and dire misgivings crowded his mind. He felt lonely. Both of his daughters, whom he had come to know well during their frequent visits to Weimar, had been married in 1857: Blandine to Émile Ollivier, the fond and foolish minister of Napoleon III; Cosima to Hans von Bülow, one of Liszt's pupils and an eminent pianist-conductor. His only son, Daniel, a brilliant law student, had died two years later, and that same year the Princess' only daughter, Marie, married Prince Konstantin von Hohenlohe-Schillingfürst, and went off to live in Vienna. And finally, Wagner, whom he greatly admired and liked, was acting up: he plainly showed his resentment at Liszt's inability to have more of his operas produced, and beleaguered him with requests for loans of a size beyond Liszt's means.

Liszt grew more and more restless at Weimar. In September, 1860, he poured his discontent into a last will and testament—a melodramatic and high-flown document that leaves the Princess ("whom I have so ardently desired to call by the dear name of wife") the bulk of his fortune. Wagner ("my friendship with him has had all the character of a noble passion") is remembered. But the name of the Countess d'Agoult is conspicuously absent. Nevertheless, early the next year, when Liszt visited Paris for a bit of distraction, he could not avoid seeing his old mistress, now fully transformed into Daniel Stern, the prolific but ineffectual rival of George Sand. Their meetings were frigidly formal, and left both of them unmoved. He was received by Napoleon III, and dined with the first Napoleon's son, Count Walewski. "Plon-Plon," the brilliant son of Jérôme Bonaparte, entertained him in princely style. He talked with Berlioz, Gounod, Meyerbeer, and a chastened Wagner, who had just seen his hopes for easily conquering Europe dashed by the Parisian failure of *Tannhäuser*. More relaxing was a dinner with Rossini, who ran his fingers through Liszt's hair, and asked him whether it was really his own. Liszt returned to Weimar in somewhat better spirits, which improved even more when he received definite word that the Holy Father had reviewed the Princess' case favorably. After hearing Von Bülow conduct the first performance of the "Faust" Symphony as the culmination of the Weimar Festival, Liszt set out for Rome by a strangely tortuous route. He knew in advance that the date for his wedding to the Princess had been set for that very fiftieth birthday he had so dreaded—October 22, 1861—and yet he did not arrive in Rome until two days before that momentous anniversary.

On the night of October 21, a messenger from the Vatican delivered a letter to Her Serene Highness. Her husband's powerful relatives had demanded another review of her case, and the marriage had perforce to be postponed. Other reasons for this sudden change of face on the part of the Curia have been adduced, among them that Liszt himself no longer really wanted to marry, and had, through his own influential friends, induced the Roman authorities to reconsider their reconsideration. As for the Princess, she was stupefied, and interpreted this new obstacle as proof that Heaven itself frowned on their banns. Both she and Liszt began to take an exaggerated interest in religion, though for some years they continued to lead in Rome much the same sort of life they had led in Weimar. In 1864, Prince Sayn-Wittgenstein died, and at last the Princess was free to marry the man she idolized. By that time, however, she was well on the way to becoming an eccentric recluse, and was already wedded to those ambitious literary schemes that ended by giving birth to *The Interior Causes of the Exterior Weakness of the Church*, a twenty-four-volume book designed to save the world.

In 1862, his daughter Blandine died, and Liszt, stricken by the news, began to spend more and more time withdrawn from the world and discussing religious matters with clerical friends, including Monsignor von Hohenlohe, Marie Sayn-Wittgenstein's brother-in-law. He wanted to become a priest, but had to be content with minor orders. His reckless past and lack of training militated against his complete ordination. The reasons for his taking this overt step at all are complicated and by no means clear. Possibly, it was nothing more than a desire for internal peace. Possibly the Hohenlohes feared that he might still be induced to marry the Princess, and took this means of making it difficult for him to do so. Finally, it was whispered that both the Princess and the Hohenlohes were afraid that Liszt, in whom the fires of youth had not died out, might contract a misalliance with an adventuress. What is certain is that on April 25, 1865, Liszt entered the Third Order of St. Francis of Assisi. By receiving the tonsure, he was allowed to perform the functions of doorkeeper, reader, exorcist, and acolyte. Thenceforth he was known as the Abbé Liszt. When in Italy, he divided his time between Rome—at first he lived in the Vatican itself—and the Villa d'Este at Tivoli. There was never a time in his career when Liszt was not well accommodated. He hoped for many years to become music director to the Pope, but in vain, and the honorary canonry of Albano, which he received in 1879, may be construed as a slight sop to his wounded feelings.

Until 1869, Liszt's official residence was Rome, but he made various trips to Germany and Hungary to superintend the productions of his larger orchestral and choral works. In 1867, for instance, he went to Budapest to hear his "Coronation" Mass performed when Franz Josef was crowned Apostolic King of Hungary. Two years later the comparative peace he had achieved in Rome was shattered by a bold indiscretion on the part of his daughter Cosima. She had for some years been under the spell of Richard Wagner, and in 1869 she openly left Von Bülow to live with him. As Wagner was already one of the most talked-of men alive, the news caused reverberations in every European capital, and not least in Rome. To the Abbé Liszt the news had the sound of a tocsin: his old adventurous spirit flared up—that old worldly bent which Carolyne Sayn-Wittgenstein knew so well and combated so violently. Now began what Liszt called his *vie trifurquée*, when Rome had to share him with Weimar and Budapest, and for four years seemed to be less attractive to the Abbé than they.

Away from the Princess' critical eye, Liszt doffed his cassock and was soon indulging his taste for charmers. In packed drama, one of these affairs outshone his liaison with the Princess herself. For once, even with his love of theatricality, Liszt might well have hesitated before dallying with the Countess Olga Janina. He had accepted this semibarbaric Polish girl as a pupil in Rome, and soon she was traveling with him as his mistress. In 1870, she lost her large fortune and Liszt's interest simultaneously. He repudiated her, and she reacted like a madwoman, running off to America in a fruitless attempt to become a concert pianist. When she spurned P. T. Barnum as a lover, her chances were gone. She began to send hysterical and threatening cables to Liszt. Returning to Europe, she caught up with him in Budapest. There ensued a lurid scene during which she tried to end both her own life and his. When this failed, she retired sputtering to Paris, and there published a scandalous and mocking book about him. Liszt never forgave her. He rushed for consolation into the arms of another noble-woman, but when this new affair tapered off into dignified friend-ship, his amorous tendencies began to die their natural death, though as late as 1883, when he was seventy-two, his name was linked scandalously with that of one of his young pupils.

When Liszt returned to Weimar in 1869, he was once more on good terms with the Grand Duke, who placed at his disposal the royal gardener's house—the *Hofgärtnerei* of his pupils' memoirs. It was there, during the rest of his life, that the apotheosis of Liszt the teacher was accomplished. This process had been taking place ever since he first settled at Weimar in 1848, and some of his early pupils, including Von Bülow and the ill-fated Carl Tausig (he died at the age of twenty-nine), were already world-famous. His method, stated simply, was that of criticism and example: he listened to a pupil play a piece, made suggestions, and might even show how a particular passage was to be executed. In his early teaching days, Liszt restricted his classes, accepting only those students who obviously had real talent. After 1869, however, and notoriously as the years passed, he relaxed his standards until he virtually kept open house. He was surrounded by a crowd of adoring disciples of all ages and stations, some of them out-and-out impostors, some mere parasites, a small fraction really gifted. For Liszt not only taught without pay, but also lent money to needy pupils. Von Bülow tried vainly, time and again, to weed out this rank garden, but was always blocked by the master, with whom uncritical generosity had become an affectation. Nevertheless, those capable of getting something from his instruction and conversation did so. Some of them became noted pianists, others conductors, violinists, and even composers. For not only piano students flocked in droves to the *Hofgärtnerei*. A roster of those who were, in one sense or another, Liszt's pupils takes up pages of fine type. The amazing thing is that, despite the ever more relaxed conditions of his classes, it includes the names of many distinguished musicians, such as Eugène d'Albert, Isaac Albéniz, Georges Bizet, Arthur Friedheim, Joseph Joachim, Rafael Joseffy, Sophie Menter, Moritz Moszkowski, Arthur Nikisch, Moriz Rosenthal, Camille Saint-Saëns, Giovanni Sgambati, Alexander Siloti, Bedřich Smetana, and Felix Weingartner.

After leaving his religious ambitions behind him, and after his last passional flare-up, Liszt entered a period of intense, wide-spread, and rather monotonous activity. He taught in both Wei-mar and Budapest, where the Hungarian government appointed him president of a nascent music academy that eventually became a flourishing institution. Honors were showered upon him from all sides. In 1873 two particularly affecting events brightened the old man's life: he went to Budapest to take part in fetes celebrating (a year late, it would seem) his golden jubilee as a pianist; he was reconciled to his daughter Cosima and her new husband, Wagner. Thenceforth the bonds between him and Bayreuth, the capital of his son-in-law's empire, were strengthened yearly. Wherever and whenever he could, he spread the gospel of Wagner. Now, too, he began to return to Rome each year, staying at Tivoli, but visiting the Princess in her all but hermetically sealed room. As he gravi-tated toward the Wagners, his Carolyne complained more and more: there was no room for Wagner in her world. In 1874, Liszt turned down an American concert tour for which he would have been guaranteed 600,000 francs. He rarely played in public, and then only for some specific charity. Besides, the machinery was running down: at sixty-three he was a prematurely aged man. Two years later, when both Daniel Stern and George Sand died, it was a reminder to him that the *siècle de Liszt* was itself expiring. These deaths in themselves affected him little, but in 1883 he re-ceived a blow from which he could not recover—Wagner's sudden death at Venice. Of the major figures of Liszt's life, only the Prin-cess was to outlive him, and she but a year. Early in 1886, he bade her a solemn farewell, but, as Sacheverell Sitwell observes, they had in reality parted long before.

Yet, in 1886, the very year of his death, feeble, with failing eye-sight, this relict of a past age, deprived of most of his friends and great associates, had the energy to undertake, after forty-five years, a trip to the one country that had not received him well—England. His English pupils smoothed the way, and the paunchy old man, with his long snow-white hair, his warts, his veritable ugliness, was greeted as he had never been when he was young, almost godlike in appearance, and had real magic at his fingertips. Most of the public celebrations centered around performances of his *St. Elisa-beth*, and his playing was confined to semiprivate functions. One day he went out to Windsor, and there played to an imperious lady whom he had met as a bride almost half a century before. He left England on April 22, a good week later than he had planned, so gratified was he by the unparalleled homage he had received. He proceeded by slow stages to Bayreuth, stopping to rest at various places en route. The English trip had cost him too much strength. He reached his daughter's home in a pitiably weakened condition. Even then he roused himself to attend performances of *Parsifal* and *Tristan und Isolde* at the Festspielhaus, the second superlatively fine, for the singers had been inspired by the presence of the greatest of Wagnerians. But before the performance had ended, Liszt was carried home and put to bed. He never rallied. A week later, on July 31, 1886, he died painlessly, less than two months before his seventy-fifth birthday. His last word was "Tristan."

Thus died, histrionic to the last, the most tremendous musical failure of the nineteenth century. The more one hears of his music and the more one reads about him, the more ambiguous his position as a composer becomes. The most notable fact about Liszt is that today only a fraction of his vast output is to be heard either in actual performance or in recordings. Whole classes of his compositions are completely ignored. This is an insuperable bar to knowing him *in toto*, not only to the layman but also to the trained expert to whom a complicated musical score is no mystery. For Liszt, perhaps more than any other composer, depends upon a virtuoso performance to be brought to life at all. In years of concertgoing, it is possible to hear a fairly large percentage of his piano pieces brilliantly played, but the same is far from true of his orchestral and choral compositions, most of which are beyond the interest and competence of the average orchestra or choral society. It seems unlikely that this situation will change: interest in Liszt is constantly lessening, and his apologists grow fewer and more frantic. It is obvious, then, that only by evaluating what Liszt is still played can we decide whether we should sorrow or rejoice that we do not hear more.

The truth is that Liszt's historical importance as an innovator and adapter has given him a position that his compositions, judged as music, do not justify. He diverted the attention of composers toward program music by preachment and example. In 1854, referring to his own *Tasso*, he invented the term "symphonic poem," by which he meant an extended orchestral piece, sometimes with chorus, transcribing in musical terms the general significance or, sometimes, the actual contents of a specific poem, painting, or story. In this new free genre, he exploited the leitmotiv—a theme representing a person or idea, and repeated whenever the composer wants to recall that person or idea to his listeners. Liszt did not invent this device, which was already old when Berlioz startled the musical world with the *idée fixe* that recurs throughout his *Symphonie fantastique*, but it was Liszt who made it one of the standard resources of orchestral music. His chief heir, aside from Wagner, who borrowed lavishly from him, was Richard Strauss. Liszt consciously evolved so-called "cyclical form," in which unity is achieved by the repetition and transformation of germinal themes throughout an entire composition. He was untiring in experiments with new harmonic combinations, and made discoveries of which others besides Wagner have taken advantage. Finally, though he learned orchestration after he was forty, and even allowed others to score so pretentious a creation as *Tasso*, Liszt eventually added new and scintillant color to the orchestra's resources. While this by no means makes it reasonable to call him, as Cecil Gray does, "the most potent germinative force in modern music," it explains why he would still have a place in the history of music even if not a single note of his were ever played.

Liszt's compositions fall easily into categories distinct from those in which their instrumentation and form place them. The most familiar group is that composed by the virtuoso, and consists of the Hungarian Rhapsodies, the B minor Piano Sonata, etudes, concertos, and certain of the *Années de pèlerinage*. They also include such of his arrangements, transcriptions, and paraphrases of other composers' works as, to name but a representative pianoful, the *Soirées de Vienne* (after Schubert), the *Rigoletto* Paraphrase, the waltz from Gounod's *Faust*, the *Don Juan* Fantaisie (after Mozart), and that muzzy and magniloquent organ fantaisie and fugue on a theme from Meyerbeer's *Le Prophète*, "*Ad nos ad salutarem undam.*" The most widely played of these virtuoso pieces are certain of the Hungarian Rhapsodies (they are really gypsy rather than Hungarian), particularly the second, which strikes a typical average— showy, clever, effective, even stirring music, built up of sharp dramatic contrasts of mood, color, and rhythm. Doubtless the best of Liszt's virtuoso music, even if not the best known, is the B minor Sonata—a one-movement giant pieced together with diabolical finesse out of meretricious scraps. It is one of the most successful scissors-and-paste jobs in music, and at the hands of a master pianist sounds much better than it really is. The two piano concertos are still played. One can only wonder why: they are windy, sentimental, invertebrate, and as dated as plush. The transcriptions, paraphrases, and arrangements constitute a ragbag of good and bad odds and ends, chosen for the ease with which they could be used for Liszt's nefarious purposes. Admitting the ends at which he aimed, his choice was not far from infallible. When the original had quality, the result is sometimes pleasing enough; if the original was trash, Liszt compounded its vacuities. In general, this entire class of Liszt's music, composed mainly for his own use in recitals and concerts, is worse than third-rate, and art would suffer no appreciable loss if it were all to be destroyed overnight in a great cleansing conflagration.

Another ponderable group of compositions effused from the lover's pen. One of these is possibly more popular than even the Second Hungarian Rhapsody—the A flat major *Liebestraum*, written originally as a song, but now familiar as everything from a piano solo to an orchestral prelude.* Love's dream to Liszt (at least in A flat major) comes as close to the odor of tuberoses as anything in music. The lover must have been in a cruel mood when he wrote it, for every time this melodic sugar comes to a boil, the morbid repetition of a single note is like the probing of a wound. But not all of Liszt's love music is so sickening. *Au Lac de Wallenstadt*, for instance, has a kind of pellucid charm; so, too, has *Au Bord d'une source*, which, however, is nothing more than earnest watering down of Chopin. In the second of the *Tre Sonetti di Petrarca*, Liszt surpassed himself: having found a musical idea of distinction, he treated it in the main poetically and perceptively.

When we come to the compositions of the tonsured Abbé, it is time to turn back. For here is *terra incognita* indeed, and heaven knows what monsters may lurk there. For the average music lover, nay! for all except the most widely traveled critic and collector of curiosa, *St. Elisabeth*, *Christus*, Psalm XIII, and the Masses are

* The rare recording by the J. H. Squire Celeste Octet is recommended.

closet music. In view of the theatricality of Liszt's religious attitude, it is hardly conceivable that religion would have fertilized him, in these vast choral works, with the large musical ideas that are so conspicuously lacking from the rest of his work. An examination of these scores bears out this suspicion, and shows merely that his usual faults and lapses were here proliferated, and in a more pompous voice. Nor was the Abbé more convincing in his attempts to express or inspire religious emotion via the keyboard. In the fulsome *Bénédiction de Dieu dans la solitude,* the sock and buskin stick out brazenly from under the cassock. The *Deux Légendes— Saint-François d'Assise prédicant aux oiseaux* and *Saint-François de Paule marchant sur les flots*—are, on the other hand, charming impressionistic aquarelles from which Debussy may have taken a hint. Of genuine religious emotion they are scrupulously free.

There remains one more category—the multifarious efforts of the thinker. These are Liszt's translations into music of literary and artistic conceptions. The most familiar of them is the symphonic poem *Les Préludes,* inspired by Lamartine's *Méditations poétiques,* which asks the rhetorical question: "What is our life but a series of preludes to that unknown song of which death strikes the first solemn note?" In it a series of themselves unpretentious musical ideas is by means of resplendent orchestration given a full Max Reinhardt production. The music is vigorous, and has great surface attractiveness. In addition to the almost diurnal *Préludes,* conductors occasionally exhibit that musical rodeo known as *Mazeppa,* and the sugary *Orpheus.* Or, taking their courage and their budgets in their hands, they stage a revival of *Tasso,* the "Dante" Symphony, or the "Faust" Symphony. Getting the "Faust" up to production pitch must be like assembling the giant mastodon for museum display. The end result is much the same: a thing that inspires awe—and bewilderment—but, alas! no love. The "Faust" Symphony is a wondrous hash that contains every aspect of Liszt's personality: thinker, lover, virtuoso—all are here, uncomfortably associated in a final ad lib choral ending, written at the request of the Princess, in which the figure of the Abbé climbs laboriously to the clouds.

Of these various categories, which, of course, overlap, one is tempted to ask which expresses the real Liszt. The answer is none —or all. The real Liszt is the expert handler of musical tools, the bold, if often tasteless and clumsy, experimenter with new forms and combinations of sound. But in the sense that Chopin is Chopin, whether composing a polonaise, a prelude, or a bad concerto, or Mozart is Mozart, whether writing *Die Zauberflöte*, a German dance, or a clarinet quintet, Liszt is never Liszt. He is a series of poses, some of them quite sincere. He grew up the sport of every passing impulse, and swept along on every current of thought: these he never integrated, never resolved. Instead, he followed them all. Thus, instead of being one person, he became a collection of self-delusions, trances, half-conscious impersonations, struck attitudes. He is a circus rider, a Don Juan, an oracle, a priest, a peasant praying at a wayside shrine, an emperor too large for the world, a stage Mephisto. He is never all these things at once (a Beethoven might have been), but only seriatim. Here, possibly, is a clue to the deplorable paltriness, the occasional downright cheapness, of most of his music. In each of these aspects, Liszt had an abiding desire to be a great composer. He was, in fact, obsessed by the conception of greatness in all departments of his life. But, as Bernard Shaw has said, "He was rich in every quality of a great composer except musical fertility," and it is a lamentable fact that a careful scrutiny of all his compositions would hardly disclose a single first-class musical idea.

Chapter XVI

Richard Wagner

(Leipzig, May 22, 1813–February 13, 1883, Venice)

WITH Richard Wagner, the musical artist's process of social emancipation is finally completed. With him, in fact, the musical artist is not only emancipated, he is apotheosized. Wagner is at the opposite pole from the all but anonymous Church musician of the Middle Ages, whose sole aim, seemingly, was to serve God and earn his bread, and who expressed his own personality only fortuitously. That many of those dim figures burned to "whelm" their very selves into the music they made is not impossible, but neither the social demand for their output nor the technical means at hand allowed them this comparatively modern luxury. These men had emotions just like us moderns, but they were forced to express them tangentially, as when Josquin Des Prés projected his vexed spirit, rebuking Louis XII by means of an artfully chosen text. We cannot conceive of so complex a man as Orlando di Lasso not wanting to express his ego, if only to abate emotional storms. Yet, he was perforce obliged to find the larger part of such expression outside his art. Gradually, as music's technical resources grew richer, the opportunities for self-expression increased. By the time of Beethoven they were so considerable that a shrewd analyst can guess his emotional biography from the shifting character of his music. Fortunately for Wagner's impatient and explosive psyche, by the time he reached creative maturity he found at hand opportunities as far in advance of Beethoven's as Beethoven's were in advance of Di Lasso's. A Wagner of the Middle Ages is unthinkable: he would simply have burst. He was the most self-absorbed egotist of all times, and every note of music he put down was part of a lifelong drive to externalize his ego.

Of course, a Wagner is possible only after certain social barriers have been passed. Not only did he insist upon social equality with everyone, including king and emperor, but he went even further, and showed that he actually considered himself their superior. In short, he insisted upon the prerogatives of genius. To a Bach, the very expression "prerogatives of genius" would have been meaningless, and even a Handel, living in the more socially sophisticated England of the eighteenth century, could have had only an inkling of its meaning. Haydn unquestionably accepted his position as a household servant, and did not even realize that he was pinioned. Only when a fortunate chance freed him did he really find wings. Mozart literally died of debilitation because his peculiarly modern personality could not come to terms with the patron system. Leopold Mozart had been content to be a prince's servant: his son quivered with rage at the idea, but did not have strength to break the system. Beethoven did break it, though it must not be supposed that he did so singlehanded: the times were ripe, and there were plenty who were breaking through the frame in every field. Once the frame was broken through, the task was not only to assure the musician's autonomy, but also to guarantee his livelihood and, finally, to invest him with a halo. Wagner assumed that he was a great man, with a message for mankind, and that the world owed him a living—a luxurious living. It was fatal to his disposition that it took him so long to convince the world of these facts. The fascinating thing about Wagner is that, starting out with these monstrous assumptions, he sold himself to the world at precisely his own value, and lived to see his own apotheosis.

There is something odd about the biographies of people who become demigods in their own lifetimes: fact becomes indistinguishable from legend, as we have seen in recent years in the case of T. E. Lawrence. What we have to deal with is an alloy. Large elements of mystification always creep in from various sources. Partisans exaggerate, enemies distort; both are powerless to resist the storytelling impulse invariably awakened by a glamorous figure of this sort. In the case of Wagner, by nature a maker of legends, the mystification is further complicated by the fact that his own glamour awakened this impulse in himself. He constantly talked and wrote about himself, and when the picture did not square with his own ideal conception, he wove a mesh of truth, half-truth, and sheer falsehood that cannot be wholly disentangled even now. The result is that Ernest Newman's masterly life of Wagner, which was over fifteen years in the writing, and which occupies four bulky volumes, is one of the most absorbing detective stories of all times.*

The mystery begins with Wagner's parents: no one will ever be quite certain who either his mother or his father was. Frau Wagner was generally credited with having been Johanna Pätz, the daughter of a Weissenfels baker. But the lady herself was secretive about her antecedents. In her youth, she had been befriended by the ducal family of Weimar, and gradually the idea gained ground that she was the natural daughter of Prince Friedrich Ferdinand Constantin, the younger brother of Goethe's patron, Grand Duke Karl August. Color is lent to this theory by the fact that on the death of Prince Constantin (whose turbulent life and refined musical taste made him a likely grandsire for Wagner), Johanna was summarily removed from the academy for highborn girls she—ostensibly a baker's daughter—had been attending. She married Carl Friedrich Wagner, a Leipzig police official, and by him had several children whose paternity has never been doubted. But whether this good functionary was the composer's father is a hotly disputed question. Many people, including Wagner himself, have thought it more than possible that he was the son of the actor Ludwig Geyer, a close friend of Carl Friedrich's, who is supposed to have taken too seriously the time-honored role of consoling the wife while the husband is occupied elsewhere. Geyer's intimacy with Johanna Wagner is evidenced by the following sequence of events. Carl Friedrich died on November 2, 1813. Geyer, who was on tour at the time, returned to Leipzig, and took charge of the widow's affairs. They were married on August 28, 1814, and their daughter Cäcilie was born less than six months later. The facts speak for themselves, and also suggest that Geyer, who for years had had the freedom of the Wagner home, may very well have been the father of the boy born in May, 1813, and christened Wilhelm Richard Wagner. When Wagner was in his late fifties, Cäcilie sent him a packet of her parents' letters. These he destroyed, but not before he found in them what he must have con-

---

* No one realizes this better than Mr. Newman himself. As a lesson to those brash enough to take Wagnerian source materials at face value, he has examined a few small facets of the Wagner legend in what can be called a true detective story. His *Fact and Fiction about Wagner*, a key to the methods of source-sifting he used in the biography itself, deserves space on the same shelf with Sherlock Holmes, *Trent's Last Case*, and *The Road to Xanadu*.

sidered decisive evidence that he was Geyer's son. The entire question is further complicated by the fact that resemblances can be found between Wagner and both his paternal uncle, Adolf Wagner, and Geyer—and that no portrait of Carl Friedrich has survived.*

Probably the controversy over Wagner's paternity would not have raged so long and so violently had it not been suggested that Geyer was partly Jewish. There are unquestionably German Jews of that name, but the most painstaking research of the birth entries of both sides of the actor's family has failed to disclose a single Jewish ancestor. The remote possibility that Geyer came of Christianized Jewish stock has led many who would enjoy believing that Wagner was partly Jewish into stating that he was. As Wagner was a ferocious anti-Semite, and as he posthumously became the official composer of the Nazi regime, finding proof of a Semitic strain in him would be a real pleasure. But the sober fact is that he may well have been the legitimate son of the good "Aryans," Carl Friedrich Wagner and Johanna Pätz, the baker's daughter, and the stepson of the equally good "Aryan," Ludwig Geyer.

Richard was little more than a year old when his mother married Geyer and removed the family to Dresden. As Geyer continued his acting, and as Wagner's eldest brother and sister were already on the stage, his mother was afraid that the rest of her children might also take to this not too highly esteemed profession. At first, it looked to her as if her youngest son was to be free of any hankering for the stage. He was a lively, impish boy, whom Geyer nicknamed "the Cossack." He was in no sense a child prodigy,

* These are the bare essentials of the Wagner paternity case, whose complexities proliferate with the years. For instance, there is the story that Nietzsche said he saw the words "I am the son of Ludwig Geyer" at the beginning of the manuscript from which the Basel printers were to set up the privately printed original edition of Wagner's autobiography, *Mein Leben*. While Wagner almost certainly told Nietzsche that he was Geyer's son, these words do not appear in the manuscript. In 1869, the philosopher gave Wagner as a Christmas present a portrait of Schopenhauer, the frame of which bore as a crest a carved vulture, the original design for which he had obtained from Wagner. As the German for vulture is *Geier*, the implication is obvious. More significant is the presence of the vulture crest on the title page of the privately printed edition of *Mein Leben*. Finally, the title page bears no other indication of the author's identity, unless the reader looks very closely indeed. Then he can see the seven stars of the Big Dipper on a shield covering the bird's belly. Ernest Newman has guessed that this is a reference to the name Wagner, which means wagoner. *Wagen* (wagon) is the German for an English nickname (Charles' Wain) for the seven stars of this constellation.

and showed no special aptitude for any kind of artistic expression. Geyer, whose dilettante tastes including painting and playwriting, tried to teach Richard how to paint, but when the boy found that it took more than a day to equal his master, he quit in disgust. In 1821, the beloved stepfather died, and for a while Richard had to live with relatives in a small Saxon village. There he began his schooling, which he continued when he returned, the following year, to live with his mother in Dresden. He was an indifferent if naturally apt student. When his imagination took fire, as it did from the Homeric world of gods, demigods, and heroes, he responded brilliantly. To amplify his knowledge, he read Greek dramas, and pored over the epics.

Of all the great composers, Tchaikovsky excepted, Wagner came latest to the study of music. True, as a small boy he had learned to read notes, and drum on the piano—he never mastered any instrument. His musical awakening came when he heard *Der Freischütz*, the overwhelming hit by his mother's friend Weber. Shortly, the piano score of this opera became his Bible, for which everything was put aside. Evidently Wagner's mother thought her duties as chaperon to her daughters more pressing than those to the unruly boy, for in 1826 she packed up and went to Prague, where her eldest daughter had found a good job in the theater. Left behind in the charge of family friends, Wagner dawdled away at the piano, neglected his studies, and became aware of the girls in the household. Also, he read everything in sight—with distressing results, for he embarked on the writing of a vast tragedy of revenge, love, insanity, and death, which is something like a cross between *Hamlet* and a Kentucky mountain feud. *Leubald* is nothing but the dregs of Wagner's deep draughts of the Greeks, Shakespeare, Goethe, and E. T. A. Hoffmann. Absurd though *Leubald* is, it contains dramatic elements that reappeared as late as *Tristan und Isolde*.

At Christmas, 1827, Wagner heard that his mother had moved back to his birthplace. Fired with a vision of himself as a swashbuckling Leipzig student, he informed his schoolteachers in Dresden that his family had sent for him (which was not true), and was given his release. When he turned up in Leipzig, his mother sent him to the Nikolaischule. But school was dull: Wagner had discovered the Gewandhaus, and at the Gewandhaus had discovered Beethoven. The symphonies, misunderstood and wretchedly performed, yet gave him a glimpse of how great music could be; the incidental music to *Egmont* filled him with an overpowering desire to compose something appropriate for *Leubald*. There was only one hitch: he knew nothing about composition. He borrowed a treatise on the subject from Friedrich Wieck's lending library, and within a few months had composed, not music for *Leubald*, indeed, but a piano sonata, a quartet, and an aria, as well as a tiny pastoral more indicative of the future librettist-composer, for he wrote both play and music. It was his first shot at orchestration, the technique of which he had cribbed from a score of *Don Giovanni*. It would appear, on the strength of Wagner's own testimony, that hearing the passionate Wilhelmine Schröder-Devrient sing Leonora in *Fidelio* was an illuminating experience comparable only to his first realization of Beethoven. For, though he had heard the operas of Weber, Marschner, and other composers, he here first glimpsed the possibilities of music drama. In one blinding apocalyptic flash, the main course of his destiny was revealed to him. It was years before the full implications of this vision became clear, but from this time on, Wagner's constant struggle was to write operas, not like *Fidelio*, which he soon regarded rightly as a failure, but like those unwritten music dramas toward which, according to him, Beethoven was striving during his last years. From this time on, Wagner was consumed by a single passion. One of its effects, specifically in the year 1829, was that he simply forgot to go to school. His family had no choice: they had to let him become a musician.

Frau Geyer's reluctant permission carried a stern proviso: Richard was first to enter the Thomasschule, and then move on to the University. But he flunked out at the Thomasschule, and so had to matriculate at the University as a second-class student. As if to make up for his languid interest in his studies, he entered enthusiastically into the rowdiest extracurricular activities. He was still at the Thomasschule when he made his debut as a revolutionary in the riots with which his schoolfellows greeted news of the Paris uprisings of 1830. At the University, he concentrated on the corps life of the students—chiefly drinking and gambling. He would have dueled, too, but fate intervened in his behalf by disabling his opponents before they reached the dueling field.

But nothing kept Wagner away from music. Early in the fall of

1830, he made a piano arrangement of the "Choral" Symphony, and sent it to a music publisher. They did not issue it, but to Wagner's delight sent him a score of the *Missa solennis*. The immediate results of his fervid study of these vast Beethoven works were two overtures, one of which was in several respects an astounding composition. The young composer thought of this B flat major Overture as compounded of different "elements," each of which was to be printed in ink of an appropriate color. Already the mystical side of his nature was having its say: these mysterious "elements" were nothing more esoteric than the separate instrument families of the orchestra. But the most amazing part of the work was its allegro, in every fourth measure of which the kettledrummer was to give a tremendous thud on what normally would have been a weak beat. Heinrich Dorn, then *Kapellmeister* of the Leipzig theater, surprisingly accepted the overture, and thus had the honor (which he lived to regret) of being the first to play publicly a work by the most controversial of all composers. Fortunately for Wagner, that Christmas Eve of 1830, it was listed on the program without his name: the insistent drumbeats roused the audience to rage, and then to laughter. Wagner said that the reproachful look in the eyes of the doorman haunted him for years.

In 1831, Wagner took his first formal lessons in theory and composition from Weinlig, one of Bach's most obscure successors as Thomascantor. In exactly six months he learned all this man had to teach him. Compositions now began to pour out of him: within a year he had completed three more overtures, seven scenes from *Faust*, a symphony, and various piano pieces. Family influence in theatrical and musical circles enabled him to have several of these performed. The C major Symphony—the only one Wagner ever completed—achieved some success in its three performances, one in Prague and two in Leipzig, the second on January 10, 1833, when the fourteen-year-old Clara Wieck appeared on the same program. Wagner also began an opera, himself writing the text— a custom he never abandoned. But *Die Hochzeit* was summarily laid aside when his sister Rosalie pronounced the libretto too blood-curdling. Wagner then started on *Die Feen*, a new opera of less horrifying nature, and might have finished it in record time had not an opening for a chorusmaster turned up at Würzburg, where his brother Albert was stage manager and leading tenor. Not the least of his motives for going to this small Bavarian town was to get out of the Kingdom of Saxony, where he was liable for military service. The job lasted less than a year.

Just before returning to Leipzig early in January, 1834, Wagner finished the scoring of *Die Feen*. He never heard his first completed opera: not until five years after his death, or fifty-four years after its composition, was this not unmelodious mélange of Beethoven, Marschner, and Weber presented for the first time, under the baton of the master's friend Hermann Levi, at Munich, on June 29, 1888. Within seven years, it achieved more than fifty performances in Munich alone, and Ernest Newman, whose detailed acquaintance with even Wagner's now unplayed scores is unexcelled, says that *Die Feen* would today be at least as grateful in performance as *Rienzi*. The sometimes played overture might pass as a minor effort of Weber: it has romantic charm, even occasionally a certain vigor. An unexpected recurrent quotation from Haydn's "Drum Roll" Symphony is explained by the fact that in 1831 Wagner had arranged one Haydn symphony for piano, and had looked over others with an eye to arranging them too. The one thing that cannot be heard in the overture to *Die Feen* is a hint of the essential Wagner.

To please Wagner's sister Rosalie, the director of the Leipzig opera promised halfheartedly to stage *Die Feen*, but fulfillment of the promise was postponed so often that Wagner saw that he was being politely staved off. He was plunged into profound gloom, and saw his situation as desperate. He was on the outs with his family: his seemingly incurable passion for gambling and his cavalier refusal of a conductor's job at a Zurich theater had overtaxed his mother's patience. A series of love affairs had ended in disillusionment and disgust—a critical state for so highly sexed a man. Already the creditors were at his door, and he had embarked on a lifetime of borrowing that is unmatched in history or fiction except in the careers of professional swindlers. These cumulating troubles brought on the first of those crises that occur with grim persistence until overwhelming success served to make him shockproof. He now began to doubt those artistic ideals which a romantic young man, particularly in the Germany of the thirties, would give up only when pressed to the wall. Circumstances juxtaposed themselves absurdly to give him a new orientation: he heard an execrable performance of Beethoven's Ninth, and straightway began to doubt his idol; he heard a memorable performance of a Bellini opera, and was just as easily convinced that the Italians had the real secret of operatic technique. Illogically assuming that *Die Feen* was getting nowhere because it emulated Weber and Marschner rather than the Italians with their set forms and light and facile melody, he sat down and wrote an article repudiating all his high-flown views about the sacred mission of German opera. This effusion, dated June 10, 1834, marked Wagner's debut as one of the most tireless polemicists of the nineteenth century.

In late July, Wagner made a trip to Lauchstädt, summer headquarters of a Magdeburg theatrical troupe of which he had been offered the musical direction. He took one look at the mangy outfit and its eccentric old director, and refused the job. Wearily he sought lodging, but there his plan for a good night's rest and immediate return to Leipzig was shattered. He met another member of the troupe—a young woman named Minna Planer—fell in love with her at first sight, and promptly changed his mind about the Magdeburg job. Return to Leipzig the next day he did, but only to get his few belongings and hurry back to Lauchstädt. The next Sunday he broke himself in as conductor with *Don Giovanni*—an ambitious trial flight for a novice with a fifth-rate company. He plunged feverishly into the rather heavy duties of his office, but devoted even more energy to wooing Minna Planer. He had discovered almost at once that she was no easy mark: it would have to be marriage or nothing. The most perplexing thing about Minna was that though she evidently liked him, the idea of marriage did not seem to interest her. Reluctantly, Wagner concluded that siege tactics were essential, and it was during the course of these that he learned the chief reasons for Minna's apparent indifference to his urgings.

It was an old, old story: Minna had listened to a deceiver, and when little more than a girl herself, had borne a fatherless child, whom she now passed off as her sister.* Once bitten, she was twice shy. After years of bitter struggle, this basically respectable woman had, at the age of twenty-four, reached a position of promise in the theater. She had no desire to marry a penniless nobody whose

---

* In pleasing contrast to Wagner's general maltreatment of Minna in later years was his scrupulous concealment of her secret. Only when he began to dictate *Mein Leben*, years after Minna's death, did he reveal it, and then only to his second wife.

professional standing was precarious, and whose wild ways made him suspect to one whose main objective in life was stability. Had Minna known as much about Richard Wagner as we do, she would have married him at once, realizing that he could not be thwarted when he really had his heart set on something. As it was, it took him two years to wear down her resistance. Paradoxically, it was those very wild ways she so condemned (and which he slyly exaggerated as soon as he realized how they could be used to play upon her) that finally brought them together at the altar of the church of Tragheim, a village near Königsberg, on November 24, 1836. If Wagner's own testimony is to be believed, it was not until the marriage was being performed that he realized that he was taking a rash step. Then it flashed through his mind that, with all her physical attractiveness and admirable human qualities, Minna was not likely to prove the ideal sharer of his mental and artistic life.

The period of Wagner's courtship saw the composition, production, and failure of his second opera, *Das Liebesverbot*, the text of which he based on *Measure for Measure*. In twisting the plot to make it express his new theories and fevered state of mind, he changed it with a highhandedness that would otherwise have been strange in one who regarded Shakespeare as a god. He conceived of *Das Liebesverbot* as a hymn to sensuality, in contrast to the pseudo-philosophical mystical claptrap and high moral tone of German opera. This, as well as his new Italian bias, led him to move the locale from Vienna to Sicily, and to change the nationality of the hypocritical Angelo to German. The composition of the opera proceeded slowly: Wagner was doing an uphill job to raise the standards of the Magdeburg company; Minna's unwillingness to say yes was driving him to distraction; his creditors were becoming importunate, and he was already plagued by the erysipelas that troubled him all his life. But on March 28, 1836, *Das Liebesverbot* was finally produced, and Wagner selected its second night as his own benefit. The first night was a fiasco of epic proportions: the orchestra was not ready and the singers forgot their parts—one of them filled in with fragments from French operas. Without a libretto synopsis, the infuriated audience could not make head or tail out of the action. On Wagner's benefit night, the theater was empty. As Ernest Newman says, "The Magdeburg fiasco . . . may or may not have been a catastrophe for German art, but it certainly sounded the knell of the hopes of Wagner's creditors." *Das Liebesverbot* was shelved for almost a century, and rightly so, for if it can be judged by hearing its bustling, empty overture and by glancing at the rest of the score, its only interest is historical. Wagner used leitmotivs here for the first time, but in the crudest way—as unchanging tags mechanically repeated.

Das Liebesverbot proved a deathblow not only to Wagner's immediate plans, but also to the Magdeburg company. He was out of a job, penniless, and in imminent danger of arrest for debt. Minna went to Königsberg to look for work, and within a couple of months Wagner, warily eluding the police, joined her there. He found Minna well established—too well established, it seemed to Wagner, whose jealousy misinterpreted the favors to other men she felt necessary for the furtherance of her career—and his. For her needy suitor she wangled a conducting job in the Königsberg company, but he was in abject misery. As we have seen, Minna capitulated in November, 1836, and for a time Wagner's spirits soared. But domestic quarrels began almost immediately: Wagner could not stand Minna's familiarity with other men, and she loathed his financial irresponsibility and resented the threats that hung over them. But he had hopes: a new opera was gestating in his mind, and he was emboldened to send the text to Scribe, *doyen* of librettists, with the modest suggestion that he would be willing to set a French version for the Opéra. Scribe did not answer. Then Wagner attacked him with a score of *Das Liebesverbot*, this time suggesting that, after having it favorably passed upon by Meyerbeer and Auber, he translate the text and produce it at the Opéra-Comique. Meanwhile, things were moving in Königsberg. The conductor resigned, and Wagner got his post. The change was fatal to the Königsberg company, which immediately collapsed, thereby precipitating the first of the many major crises in Wagner's married life.

Hedged in by Richard's creditors, Minna determined to dissociate herself forever from his Bohemian existence. She chose to emancipate herself from unconventionality by fleeing with another man. Wagner was beside himself with grief and rage. Finding that Minna's destination was her parents' in Dresden, he set out in pursuit of her. They now played a cat-and-mouse game for some months, with no decision reached. He then landed a job as opera conductor at out-of-the-way Riga. Minna refused to accompany him, so he set out on the long journey alone. One of Wagner's tactics, which evidently had no effect on her, was a threat of divorce. Less than two months later, Minna showed up in Riga with her sister Amalie, to whom he promised work at the theater. He threw himself wholeheartedly into his job, and though he thoroughly despised most of what he had to stage, in two years he put on thirty-nine operas. Conditions in Riga were a shade better than in Magdeburg or Königsberg, but the politics were more devious. Soon Wagner was at swords' points with the impresario, who resented his conductor's lofty attitude toward the trash in the repertoire. Early in 1839, the break came: Wagner literally awoke one morning to find that he had been replaced by Heinrich Dorn. Thereafter, he never tired of vilifying both Dorn (who seems to have been guiltless of complicity in the intrigue) and the impresario, though the latter was somewhat justified in not wishing to keep an aide who might be clapped into debtors' prison at any moment.

As the time for his departure from Riga drew near, Wagner desperately turned over various plans of action. Getting out of Russia was hard enough for the jobless, debt-harassed fellow, but the choice of a new place to try his luck was even more difficult. At last he hit upon Paris, chiefly in the thin hope that Scribe and Meyerbeer would be interested enough to help him. Minna, who had given up her stage career, resigned herself to a move of which she had the gloomiest forebodings. On July 10, eluding frontier guards, they crossed into Prussia. They had decided to make the westward journey by water, partly because it was cheaper, and even more because their Newfoundland dog, Robber, was too large and obstreperous for coach travel. Accordingly, they sailed for London from Pillau, near Königsberg, on July 18. The voyage should normally have taken about a week, but they encountered storms so violent that it was almost a month later that the little one-hundred-ton sailing vessel weighed anchor in the Thames. Minna was terrified as the ship approached England: screaming about danger whenever a buoy or signal light was sighted in the fog, she added to the sailors' misery. But to Wagner, the perils of these troubled waters were exhilarating. It was during this hideous crossing that he first conceived the idea of writing an opera about the Flying Dutchman—the Wandering Jew of the sea.

After an uneventful week in London, the Wagners crossed to Boulogne, where they chanced to meet Meyerbeer, then by all odds the most influential musician in France. Bearing friendly letters of introduction from the man he was sure he would soon supplant in public favor, Wagner arrived in Paris in a bumptious mood. Disillusionment came fast. For more than two and a half years, he struggled against mounting woes, lured by deceptive hopes and empty promises. At times only a mystical faith in his star kept him going at all. Never did troubles bear richer fruit, for it was by this tragic *via crucis* that Wagner returned to those ideals of German opera that he had incontinently abandoned for the fashion of the hour. Beethoven's Ninth again played a salient role in orienting him: shortly after his arrival in Paris, he heard it magnificently played under François Habeneck, and at once his acceptance of music as mere entertainment fled before the renewed revelation of its boundless emotional possibilities as a means of expression. His immediate reaction was to begin a symphony based on *Faust*. This never progressed beyond one movement, but was revised in 1855 as *Eine Faust Ouvertüre*. Wagner could not afford such serious essays: he needed money, and he made it—in pitiable handouts—by composing mediocre French songs, translating, writing articles, and making transcriptions.

As soon as Wagner knew anything at all about Paris, he realized that he could hope for nothing from Scribe, who was primarily a high-powered businessman. Nor did much come from his letters of introduction until the Théâtre de la Renaissance, urged on by Meyerbeer, accepted *Das Liebesverbot*. It was to be produced in French as *La Novice de Palerme*. With this supposed sure thing a matter of days, Richard and Minna moved to fine quarters in the fashionable Opéra section, and prepared to enjoy themselves at last. Then the Théâtre de la Renaissance failed, Minna had to take in boarders, and Wagner seems actually to have spent some time in debtors' prison. In these darkest hours, Minna stood stanchly by him: was he not trying to live according to her lights? He returned to the dull grind of translations, articles, and transcriptions. In some of the articles the cry of his struggling spirit breaks through, and a few of them are more truly Wagnerian than much of the music he was to compose in the next five years.

In the summer of 1840, the idea of the Flying Dutchman haunted Wagner so ferociously that he had to find time to write a one-act French libretto about it. Again Meyerbeer helped him by inducing the Opéra to consider *Le Vaisseau fantôme*. The director liked it, but enraged Wagner by offering to buy it for the use of another composer. Nothing is more eloquent of Wagner's grim poverty than that, after several scenes with himself, he agreed to sell. He received five hundred francs. This meant a little leisure, which he used to expand the libretto into a three-act German text. Meanwhile, he had completed *Rienzi*, an opera begun in Dresden more than two years earlier, and had sent the score to the King of Saxony in the hope that he would recommend it to the Dresden opera. Alleviation seemed to come all at once. *Le Vaisseau fantôme* was sold in May, 1841, and a few weeks later word came that Dresden had taken *Rienzi* for production the following year. Wagner turned with new gusto to the Flying Dutchman libretto, and by December had composed *Der fliegende Holländer*, which he promptly submitted to Berlin. This, too, was accepted in March, 1842, and the next month the Wagners set out from the now-hated French city toward what seemed a glowing future in Germany.

Rienzi was produced at the Dresden Hoftheater on October 20, 1842. The cast was chosen to assure success: Schröder-Devrient created the role of Adriano, the great Joseph Aloys Tichatschek that of Rienzi. With them, despite Schröder-Devrient's being too burgeoningly female to make a convincing man, Wagner was unfeignedly delighted. But the skimping on the sets and costumes vexed him. He need not have worried: an enraptured audience sat through more than five hours of *Rienzi*, and Wagner left the theater a famous man. Before Christmas, Dresden demanded six repeats of this excessively long and noisy opera, which for years was to remain his only success. Some of its original popularity can be credited to the grandiose libretto Wagner had evolved from Bulwer-Lytton's novel, with its chances for heroics and sumptuous mass effects. "From the wretchedness of modern and domestic existence," Wagner wrote, ". . . I was carried away by this picture of a great political and historical event. . . . Rienzi, with great ideas in his brain and strong feelings in his heart, dwelling in gross and vulgar surroundings, set all my nerves thrilling with sympathy and affection." Can there be any doubt that Wagner, disgusted with sordid poverty and lack of recognition, and already resentful of Minna's suburban personality, identified himself with the hero?

Rienzi, composed in cold-blooded imitation of Spontini and Meyerbeer, is a true grand opera in the French style—the only one Wagner ever composed. The whole work, and particularly the first two acts, is full of sensationalism—heroic displays for the tenor, brassy outbursts for the orchestra, and tremendous, ear-splitting choruses. The predominance of march rhythms produces a triumphant, martial, but finally monotonous effect. *Rienzi* is a first cousin to *Les Huguenots*, but without Meyerbeer's beautifully calculated variety and infinite command of musicodramatic device. One of the few signs in *Rienzi* of the Wagner of the future is a more subtle use of leitmotivs. He has now begun to understand that they can be altered to express shifting moods, and combined contrapuntally. The opera may be fairly judged by the overture, which, contrary to all of Wagner's later theories, is little more than a potpourri of high spots. It is by turns brilliant and exciting, noble and smug—the music of a Von Suppe who happened to be a genius. As much a favorite with brass bands as the *William Tell* overture, it is the only part of the opera we hear today. *Rienzi* has not been mounted in New York since 1923.

The success of *Rienzi* improved Wagner's fortunes in some ways, but increased his financial difficulties. Friedrich August of Saxony was much impressed by the opera, and wanted Wagner in his service. The *Kapellmeister*, Weber's *bête noire* Morlacchi, conveniently died just at this time, and Wagner succeeded him early in 1843. A life income of fifteen hundred thalers—five times as much as he had been paid for *Rienzi*—seemed momentarily very handsome after years of privation. Unfortunately, news of his affluence came to the ears of Wagner's creditors, and in an amazingly short time peremptory demands for payment began to pour in from Leipzig, Magdeburg, Königsberg, Riga, and Paris. He was so frantic that he had to pour out his woes to Schröder-Devrient. As rash as himself, she lent him more than a thousand thalers—actually a negligible stopgap, for by this time the *Kapellmeister* owed many times that amount. Nor did the production of *Der fliegende Hol-*

länder, on January 2, 1843, help much. Rather the contrary, in fact, for its failure made Wagner's creditors tighten the screws, fearing that *Rienzi* might prove only a flash in the pan.

Berlin had originally accepted *Der fliegende Holländer*, but its *première* took place in Dresden because Wagner, vexed by many postponements, angrily demanded it back for the city that had received *Rienzi* so enthusiastically. It had no part for Tichatschek, but Schröder-Devrient, who was luxuriating in the storms of a new love affair, made up for his absence by a romantically vibrant portrayal of the overwrought Senta that might have carried the opera to success if the other singers had had even a slight understanding of their roles. Ordinarily the audience would not have had much trouble with the music itself, but the patent bewilderment of the actors and their inability to project the drama wrapped the entire occasion in a pall of gloom. The listeners missed the pageantry and glittering meretriciousness of *Rienzi*. Wagner's new opera was a failure, and after four nights was taken off, not to be heard in Saxony's capital for twenty-two years. Nor was Berlin much kinder a year later. *Der fliegende Holländer* was shown to increasingly enthusiastic audiences there, but the critics treated it with such calculated savagery that after four performances it was withdrawn, and did not reappear for a quarter of a century. And though the self-centered Spohr broke all precedents by not only giving it at Cassel, but also sending the composer a warm letter of praise and encouragement, Wagner was forced to realize that *Der fliegende Holländer* would not help his fortunes.

When, on November 5, 1841, Wagner had completed the overture to *Der fliegende Holländer*, he had written on the title page, "In night and wretchedness. *Per aspera ad astra*. God grant it!" Through deprivation, pain, and hardship he had achieved his star—the creation of the first music drama. It was drawn out of his own deep need for a woman's understanding and unquestioning love. It is significant, as a sidelight on Wagner's restless search for this kind of complete love, that in the first draft of the opera, the woman whose faith in the Dutchman redeems him was called Minna, and was changed to Senta only when he realized definitely that Minna could never redeem him. From the moment he had first read in Heine the legend of the accursed Vanderdecken, it seized his imagination. His passage of the North Sea served to bring it forcibly to his mind again, and there is no doubt that by this time he had identified himself with the wanderer. This is reason enough for the music of *Der fliegende Holländer* registering so striking an advance over *Rienzi*: it is deeply felt. Also, Wagner had returned to his ideals, and was writing a German opera, though one still within the limits of the Weber tradition. The score is reminiscent of *Der Freischütz*, but is more consistently dramatic, less shackled by that creaking set-number scheme which, inherited from the classicists, had proved the curse of romantic opera, making it seem jumbled and spasmodic. A few set numbers remain, but Wagner has gone an amazingly long way toward continuous action and melody. The somber overture, surcharged with catastrophe and the sea, is no mere potpourri, but rather a cunningly woven prophecy of conflict and salvation. It, Vanderdecken's *"Die Frist ist um,"* the Spinning Chorus, and Senta's Ballad have by constant repetition come to seem autonomous, but in the opera they are merely high points on a fairly continuous line. Much of the music darkles and lowers: it throbs with the vast impersonal energy of the sea and the sky. No more here than in *The Ancient Mariner* do we expect to meet ordinary people. Nor do we: Vanderdecken and Senta are the timeless symbols of Wagner's spiritual strife.

With *Der fliegende Holländer* Wagner performed the inevitable homage to Weber that had been implicit in his whole musical development. He had to write it in order to discover what could, and could not, be done with Weber's tools. In 1844, with a completely new-type opera in all but final shape, he paused to arrange special music to be given at the reburial of Weber's body in Dresden. During the ceremony he was so overcome with emotion that while delivering his carefully prepared eulogy he fell into a kind of cataleptic trance, but managed to speak his piece to the end. In it he dedicated himself once more to the creation of a national opera for Germany. Be it said that in forty years of unparalleled ups and downs he never deviated even slightly from this ideal.

Wagner was eventually to decide that purely mythical subjects best fitted his conception of music drama, but until reaching that decision he combined history and myth. *Tannhäuser* is a triumph of this mixed marriage: the story combines details from an actual singing contest held at the Wartburg in the thirteenth century with the legend of a minnesinger who fell under the spell of Venus, and lived with her in a mountain not far from the Wartburg. Wagner transformed this material into a dramatic conflict between sensual and spiritual love. Even in the libretto, however, Venus is a more vivid figure than the goody-goody Elisabeth because Wagner, here again identifying himself with the hero, had a passionate *parti pris* in favor of Venus. He had finished writing the poem in April, 1843, worked at the music off and on for two years, and finally completed it in April, 1845. On October 19 of that year, it was produced at the Dresden Hoftheater, with the composer's niece, Johanna Wagner, as Elisabeth, Schröder-Devrient as Venus, and Tichatschek as Tannhäuser. Makeshift scenery had to be used, as that ordered from Paris did not arrive on time. Only the Venus had any conception of her role, but even she protested to Wagner: "You are a man of genius, but you write such eccentric stuff, it is impossible to sing it." The others merely walked through their parts, and Tichatschek had so rudimentary an understanding of the plot that in the singing contest he horrified Wagner by addressing the impassioned Hymn to Venus directly to the virginal Elisabeth. It is no wonder, then, that an opera which, even in a flawless production, might have seemed a daring novelty, failed at its *première*. Stories began to circulate: that Wagner was a Catholic propagandist, that he wrote music that could not be sung—singers rash enough to attempt it would certainly ruin their voices—and that *Tannhäuser* was, moreover, a morbid, pornographic concoction. Eight days later it was given again, this time with the Paris scenery. There was only a scattering of people in the house, but these few carried such glowing tales to their friends that the opera began to catch on, and soon was a popular success. A popular success, yes, but not a critical one. *Tannhäuser* emphasized that division between Wagner's audiences and his critics that endured, with minor exceptions, the rest of his life.

Tannhäuser as we know it today is not the opera Dresden heard in 1845. Not only did Wagner revise the libretto and score in 1860, but he expanded the Venusberg scene into one conceived in the advanced style of *Tristan und Isolde*. Even so, this new version has no hearer difficulties today. On the contrary, it has begun to sound old-fashioned, almost pre-Wagnerian. A whole library of exegesis, partly by Wagner, partly by his commentators, has prepared us— and the singers—for a full understanding of *Tannhäuser*'s meaning.

Now, at any rate, it is no misunderstanding on our part, but the failure of Wagner's musical achievement that makes the opera as an entity seem flat. At thirty-two, he was not yet in sufficient command of his new resources—leitmotivs woven into a continuous thread of narrative melody, the orchestra used as a means of dramatic expression—to make *Tannhäuser* the music drama of his most ambitious dreams. There are prosy, explanatory sections in the libretto that are faithfully set to threadbare, dull-useful music. The result is a work very little different from a classical opera: it seems to have the same set numbers, the same high spots, the same relapses. *Tannhäuser* lives today by the orgiastic Bacchanale, the catchy *Festmarsch*, Elisabeth's Prayer, and the intolerably sentimental "Evening Star." The Pilgrims' Chorus, even amid this collection of musical Bartlett's Quotations, is in a class by itself. In popularity among Wagner "gems" it runs a close second to the so-called "Wedding March" from *Lohengrin*: it is the musical apotheosis of unleavened smugness. Several of these high spots are quoted and adapted to make up the shoddy splendors of the long, rhetorical overture. Much of the *Tannhäuser* music is excellent theater in itself, wonderfully calculated to help out the action— but anything but first-class Wagner.

The tepid first reactions to *Tannhäuser* dejected Wagner, but his recoil was a resolve to continue uncompromisingly along the path he had chosen, and to educate a public to follow it with him. Within a few months, he saw that he already had a nucleus for this public, but realized simultaneously that his task was no easy one. The libretto of *Lohengrin*, which (as he visioned it) would demand even more understanding from the audience, was already finished. He had sketched out the stories for two more operas—one about Parsifal and the Holy Grail, the other about Nuremberg in the time of Hans Sachs, the cobbler poet—which would inevitably carry him farther from the traditions that the bulk of his Dresden audience found palatable. At this juncture, the reinstallation of *Rienzi* in the Hoftheater repertoire, instead of cheering Wagner, made him all the more depressed: he had already gone so far beyond what Meyerbeer and Spontini had to offer that he considered *Rienzi* a youthful mistake. Bitterly he reflected that it had been his sole success, and that a series of *Rienzi*s might easily make him rich and famous. From an official critical point of view, the composer of

Rienzi was indeed famous. The composer of *Der fliegende Holländer* and *Tannhäuser* was merely notorious.

It was the composer of *Rienzi*, too, who occupied the post of royal *Kapellmeister*. Those above Wagner were not interested in his efforts to reform opera. Donizetti was favored by the court, and *Martha* was looked upon as a sum of delights. Slowly it was borne in upon Wagner that few—certainly not Minna, the King, the critics, or most of his colleagues—realized what he was trying to do. On the other hand, a few gifted musicians began to rally to him. Schumann, who had come to live in Dresden in 1844, at first wrote enthusiastically, though with reservations, about *Tannhäuser*. Liszt, whom Wagner had met in Paris in 1840, lent him consistent and—after taking up his residence at Weimar—powerful support. In 1846, Von Bülow, then an impressionable youth of sixteen, summoned up courage to present himself to Wagner, whose music was already a religion to him. And Wagner felt positive that if he could get his music before "the common man," an abstraction to which he became more and more devoted with the years, success would be assured. Red tape and conservatism were in his way when he wanted to produce Beethoven's Ninth in 1847; the next year, they were in his way when, after recasting *Iphigénie en Aulide* to conform with his own conceptions of Gluck's publicly proclaimed ideals, he staged a German version. Disaster was predicted for both: both were tremendous popular successes. Wagner drew from these events a parable of his own predicament.

In the late forties, Wagner had to manufacture optimism: coldbloodedly surveying his present, he had to admit that everything was dark. His marriage was failing. Minna's intellectual deficiencies grated on him more and more, and the only bond that held him to her was sexual. The most tactless of men deplored his wife's gaucherie. As an aid to his ambitions, he found her hopeless. In Minna's place, a Clara Schumann might have smoothed out Wagner's increasing difficulties with the higher-ups. But Minna was not even a good hostess—a grave failing in the wife of a man who held a not unexalted official position. If Wagner was in a deadening rut at home, at the Hoftheater his situation was rapidly becoming untenable. He saw, down to the finest practical detail, what was wrong with music in Dresden, and twice submitted elaborate, lengthy memorials to the King, suggesting complete overhauling of facilities, personnel, repertoire, and aims. Had these memorials been acted upon, Dresden might within a short time have become the real musical capital of Germany. In the process, of course, Wagner would have emerged as the dictator of Saxon artistic life, and several of his superiors would have been dethroned. Not unnaturally, a tension sprang up between him and those he was in effect trying to supplant. If for no other reason than self-preservation, they struck back by restricting his activities, and consistently ignoring his plans for his future as a composer. Wagner added to the nasty business by showing his lack of interest in his job as he was forced to do it. He construed his life appointment not as a privilege, but as a term of perpetual imprisonment.

His debts were, as usual, driving Wagner mad. He had no appreciable income aside from his salary, for throughout Germany, except in Berlin, there prevailed the nefarious system of buying an opera outright for a pittance, and thereafter paying no performance royalties. And all Wagner's elaborate scheming failed to establish one of his works in the Berlin repertoire. His financial troubles assumed colossal proportions after Breitkopf and Härtel had made him what he considered an insulting offer, and he rashly began to publish his operas at his own expense. Not only did he have to borrow still more money to float this scheme, but the scores he issued—*Rienzi*, *Der fliegende Holländer*, and *Tannhäuser*—were returned, sometimes unopened, by the opera houses to which they were offered. The project was an unmitigated disaster for Wagner and for the poor, unsuspecting music printer he had involved in it. At the crucial moment, Schröder-Devrient, aggrieved because she thought Wagner had ungratefully imported his niece in order to supplant her at the opera, gave Wagner's notes for a total of three thousand thalers to her lawyer, who immediately began to threaten suit. To save his *Kapellmeister* from ignominy, the long-suffering intendant of the Hoftheater, Baron von Lüttichau, had five thousand thalers advanced to him from the theater pension fund, and later used his good offices in getting him a further small loan and a slight increase in salary. It is no wonder that Wagner, distracted by creditors, and suffering from recurrent attacks of erysipelas, had his nerves shattered, and had to spend still more money taking expensive cures.

Wagner's last hope was that his new opera, *Lohengrin*, would save him. But, as he truly saw in his heart of hearts, this was a slim hope. *Lohengrin* contained more shockers for the critics than his previous operas. The shockers began with the libretto: those to whom Wagner read it were horrified by its unhappy ending, and many said that it could not be made into an opera. Momentarily Wagner seriously considered changing the ending, but the intendant's wife dissuaded him. To assure himself that the original ending could indeed be set, he composed the last act first. Early in 1848, *Lohengrin* was finished, but unbought. Several years earlier, he had tried to interest the King of Prussia in the libretto, but Tieck, in the most friendly spirit, warned him not to waste his time—for this was the monarch who had nearly driven Mendelssohn to distraction with his grandiose shilly-shallying. So, with the only remunerative house in Germany closed to him, Wagner offered *Lohengrin* to Dresden. In December, 1848, it was turned down. This refusal to stage *Lohengrin*, coming as a final touch to years of tragedy, precipitated Wagner into overt revolutionary activity that was not germane to his real character.

Wagner had no interest in politics as politics, but like many people with long-standing personal grievances, felt that only a thoroughgoing social change, beginning with a political house cleaning, could help his situation. There was rancor aplenty in Wagner, but he did not consciously become a revolutionary for petty, spiteful reasons: he merely, as was his lifelong formula, identified his own need with the world's. Once his mind was made up, he acted fearlessly, indeed rashly. The news that trickled in from Paris of the February Revolution thrilled him, and when the German liberals began to organize, Wagner joined a revolutionary group. By the spring of 1849, he was contributing articles to a radical paper, and tried to proselytize among the members of his orchestra. He became an object of interest to the chief of police. In May, rioting began in Dresden, and Wagner was in the thick of it. High in the confidence of the radical leaders, among whom was Mikhail Bakunin, he passed out inflammatory literature. He spent parts of the sixth and seventh of May in an observer's eyrie signaling to the rebels.

The revolution was put down by Prussian troops. After seeing Minna to a place of safety, Wagner fled, escaping capture by the skin of his teeth. Deciding to take advantage of Liszt's many protestations of friendship, he reached Weimar several days later. Liszt, who was at that moment preparing to stage *Tannhäuser*, received him warmly, and shortly Wagner was writing to his brother-in-law that he would establish himself permanently in Weimar "should I lose my post in Dresden." He was rudely awakened by word from Minna that a warrant had been issued for his arrest. As extradition treaties existed between the various sovereign states of Germany, this meant that Wagner would have to flee to a foreign country. He stayed just long enough to hear a rehearsal of *Tannhäuser* and to arrange a farewell meeting with Minna. On May 28, traveling on a borrowed passport and on funds lent him by Liszt, Wagner crossed into Switzerland. He was not to see Germany again for twelve years.

Wagner the expatriate, exactly thirty-six years old, was by no means a prepossessing man, to judge by his picture in the Dresden police archives. On his Swiss passport, he is described as five feet, five and a half inches tall, with brown hair, blue eyes, round chin, and medium nose—this last a polite understatement. At the instigation of some friends in Zurich, his first place of exile, he went to see how things were shaping up in Paris. Everything he saw there disgusted him: Meyerbeer reigned supreme at the Opéra, the Revolution was dead, and no one was interested in the plans of a Saxon refugee. He then returned to Zurich, where Minna soon joined him. For the time being, he shelved his musical plans, and began a voluminous literary activity, much of it based on social revolution as inextricably connected with a decent future for art. Some livelihood was to be gained from the sale of his books and articles, and it is certainly true that Minna did not disapprove of his writing. Only after discovering that his time was being spent largely on the libretto of an opera she was sure would bring him no *réclame* did she insist on his again seeking his fortune in Paris. All his friends backed Minna up on this stand. Even Liszt, who for all his friendliness, did not, at least at this time, understand what Wagner was trying to do, added his voice to theirs, and lent Wagner the money for the trip. In January, 1850, Wagner dragged himself back in a third attempt to woo Paris.

Wagner had promised Minna to try to compose an opera for Paris, but a few days there convinced him that he could not bring himself to do it. He was too wedded to far-reaching, artistically ambitious plans to be diverted into the fashionable stream of French opera. Both of the projects he had under way—librettos built around Wayland the Smith and the death of Siegfried—were uncompromisingly serious, intensely Teutonic. He felt that remaining in Paris would only emphasize his mood of despair. Happily, he met a rich Bordeaux couple—Eugène and Jessie Laussot, friends of his devoted Dresden admirer, Julie Ritter. The young wife, an attractive and intelligent English girl with marked musical talent, went to Wagner's head. Had everything panned out as he was soon envisioning it, *Tristan und Isolde*, his great lyric of guilty love, might have been started in 1850 instead of seven years later. He soon made his financial plight clear to his new friends, and after a three-cornered correspondence between Frau Ritter, the Laussots, and himself, Dresden and Bordeaux offered to contribute three thousand francs annually to his and Minna's support. The idea of becoming a pensioner was distasteful enough to Minna, but when rumors reached her that Wagner, who had gone to Bordeaux, was enamored of Jessie, she set out angrily for Paris. Meanwhile, Wagner was planning to escape to Greece with his inamorata, and to live there on money from Jessie's husband and Julie Ritter. His plan included supporting Minna, but he had clearly made up his mind to leave her, had, indeed, convinced himself that she would be better off without him. Jessie spoiled it all by telling her mother, who told Laussot, who threatened to kill Wagner, but contented himself with separating the lovers. Frau Ritter, undisturbed by her protégé's bad faith, showed a deep understanding of his soul-torturing problems by coming to France to console him. He avoided meeting Minna, who was frantically searching Paris for him. She finally had to return to Zurich without him. By July, however, the Laussot episode had petered out completely, and Wagner was back with her.

After the Laussot affair was over, and Julie Ritter had told him that she could not afford singlehanded to pay the pension, Wagner wrote to Liszt, telling him in what desperate straits he was, and beseeching him to stage *Lohengrin* immediately. Liszt had begun by saying that the "superideal tone" of the opera would make it unpopular, but now he generously put his doubts aside, and agreed to produce it at the Hoftheater in Weimar. His promise was made in June, 1850, and on August 28 it was carried out. Wagner, of course, could not go into Germany, and waited anxiously for news of the opera's reception. It was not wholly encouraging: its excessive length (Wagner had permitted only one brief cut), the terror the music inspired in certain of the singers, and the handicaps of time and limited resources Liszt had to contend with conspired to create a far from perfect production. *Lohengrin* was tepidly received, and at first, certainly, Wagner could not guess that this opera would gradually win him a vast public.

Lohengrin is one of the two or three most artistically successful operas Wagner ever wrote. It is impossible not to agree with Ernest Newman when he says that if Wagner had "died after *Lohengrin* he would still have been the greatest operatic composer of his time." Except for *Die Meistersinger*, he never wrote an opera that equals *Lohengrin* in sheer entertainment value from beginning to end. Listening to this shimmering lyrical score, it is likewise impossible not to share Mr. Newman's passing "regret that the daemon within him drove him on so relentlessly to another style." The libretto is a good story, dramatically told, and its only weakness today is that we cannot take seriously the ethical and philosophical implications Wagner intended. Again he projected himself as the hero betrayed by a woman's lack of unquestioning faith, but our common-sense generation is apt to laugh at a man who leaves the woman he loves merely because she asks him who he is.

To enjoy *Lohengrin* fully, we must accept the conventions of the story. The music itself presents no barriers. Wagner's orchestration is already mature, showing that he is ripe for the revolutionary idiom of *Tristan und Isolde* and the *Ring*. In *Lohengrin*, it has a light-shot, ethereal texture that is unique even in Wagner. It attains a supreme height in the Prelude, which Bernard Shaw called "the first work of Wagner's that really conquered the world and changed the face of music for us. . . ." But *Lohengrin* is still primarily a singers' opera—the most consistently lyrical of Wagner's stage works—and the orchestra, though it plays an unflagging role, is usually only a background for the voices. Because of the increased continuity of the musical web, separate excerpts do not stand out so sharply as they do in *Tannhäuser*. The Bridal Chorus is an exception only because of its international use as a wedding march.

With the instrument of his art as well forged as it was in *Lohengrin*, Wagner nevertheless waited until 1853 to do any further composing. There were many reasons for his apparent inactivity, the chief one being the constantly expanding proportions of the vast mythological music drama he had at first seen as a single opera, *Siegfrieds Tod*, the libretto of which had been completed before he left Dresden, in 1848. He kept working at this material for three years. In May, 1851, partly as a result of a growing interest in *Tannhäuser* and *Lohengrin*, Liszt persuaded the Weimar Hoftheater to commission *Siegfrieds Tod*. Instead of setting to work on the music, Wagner re-examined the libretto with a coldly critical eye, and realized that what he had was really the culmination of a series of events, with a great mass of prefatory material jumbled together. His first step was to write an introductory book called *Der Junge Siegfried*. Still he was not satisfied, and for the first time the cyclic plan of his undertaking dawned upon him. During the first half of 1852, he finished Books I and II—*Das Rheingold* and *Die Walküre*—of what he now saw as the four-part saga of the Nibelungs. By the end of that year, he had reworked *Der Junge Siegfried*, and called it simply *Siegfried*. Similarly, *Siegfrieds Tod* had become *Die Götterdämmerung*. He now had the books of four full-length music dramas, none of which, he admitted to himself, could be staged before the others were completed. The *Ring*, to produce its effect, would ideally have to be performed on four consecutive days. As an artist of unwavering integrity, Wagner had checkmated himself by a project that could not bear fruit for years. The decision to proceed with the *Ring* was indeed a courageous one for a man whose wife and friends had their eyes on the immediate thing, and not at all on the long chance. Further, even were the *Ring* to be finished, there was small hope that it would ever be produced. For in 1853, when he began to compose the first part of this utterly revolutionary operatic cycle, Wagner was still relatively obscure, an exile, an eccentric hopelessly outside the main current of operatic fashion. But he was really the man who did not know the meaning of "impossible." He survived to see the first complete performance of the *Ring*, twenty-three years later, in a theater he had himself designed for it.

Simultaneously with the formulation of the *Ring* books, Wagner led two other lives, either of which would have sufficed for an

ordinary man. He took a commanding position in the musical
world of Zurich, conducting both operas and concerts. At the
theater, Von Bülow was at first associated with him, but the
audiences so obviously preferred Wagner that his young disciple
was forced out. Wagner then severed his own connection in protest, and devoted himself to the symphonic concerts. Meanwhile,
he was writing prolifically. Books, pamphlets, and articles streamed
effortlessly from a pen guided by many diverse motives. Least
important to this vehement-willed pensioner was the need for
money. Somewhat more urgent was the need to work off a few
old grudges. Paramount was the drive to explain himself and his
aims—a job that involved destroying the bases of the old opera
and creating a public that would necessarily demand the music
dramas of Richard Wagner. Considering the obstacles, it was an
unprecedentedly bold scheme of propaganda. Also, in view of
Wagner's trifling talents as a literary artist, it is truly amazing
that his writings were so effective in doing approximately what he
intended them to do. They seem like anything but the writings of a
genius: they betray a muddled mind that has ill-digested large
chunks of philosophy, religion, and esthetics. They are a mélange
of Schopenhauer, Buddhism, Aryanism (fully recognizable,
though traveling incognito), unvarnished Wagner, and sheer
nonsense of varied provenance. Diffuse, incoherent, and chaotic
they often are, but there is a unifying thread: Wagner is always
busy projecting his own personal prejudices into a world scheme.

The most curious of these writings of the fifties is *Das Judenthum
in die Musik*, apparently a violent anti-Semitic tract, but in reality
not much more than an immature explosion of resentment against
specific Jewish musicians. It sprang from a dislike of Mendelssohn,
who not only had been lukewarm toward Wagner's music, but also
had carelessly mislaid the manuscript of a symphony Wagner had
sent him. It sprang more savagely from a hatred of Meyerbeer,
whose operas Wagner sincerely detested. He mistrusted the reality
of Meyerbeer's early kindness, and suspected this music millionaire
of jealously blocking his career. It is probable that the facts in
these matters will never see the light,* but there can be no doubt
that Wagner viewed the scandalously successful Jakob Liebmann

* It has been suggested that the forthcoming publication of Meyerbeer's diaries, if
unexpurgated, may serve to solve the mystery of their relationship.

Beer with a jaundiced eye and a forgetful memory. Out of these and other personal dislikes, Wagner fabricated a case against the Jew in art, insisting that he not only contributed nothing, but also was poisoning public taste. It must be said that Wagner's anti-Semitism was an erratic and inconsistent phenomenon, quite as intermittent as a common cold, and allowing him, finally, to marry the granddaughter of a Jewess. And though he republished *Das Judenthum* in 1869, he chose a Jew, thirteen years later, to conduct the first performances of his sacrosanct masterpiece, *Parsifal*. The saddest aspect of Wagner's anti-Semitism is that it furnished extra ammunition for the Aryan polemics of his future son-in-law, Houston Stewart Chamberlain, one of the founding fathers of Nazism.

Das Judenthum is scarcely more difficult to accept than Wagner's most ambitious esthetic treatise, *Oper und Drama*. After proving that Gluck and Beethoven had been trying to create Wagnerian music drama, and had been defeated because of insufficient intellectual grasp of their materials, he goes on to show that music for music's sake is a colossal mistake. Beethoven, for example, had been striving toward the light in the choral movement of the Ninth Symphony, but had erred by making the poet serve the musician. What is needed if we are to have *the* one great human art, instead of separated, and therefore unsatisfying, arts, is that painter, sculptor, and musician shall serve the poet. Music is nothing in itself, but only achieves its destiny when it contributes its part to the common enterprise—the music drama. Thus Wagner, who had almost no appreciation or understanding of painting and sculpture, and who alone of all the great composers had been attracted to music not for its own sake, but as a means of making drama more dramatic.

The books of the *Ring* lay untouched for several months, and then, in August, 1853, during a trip to Italy for his health, Wagner conceived the orchestral prelude to *Das Rheingold*. He returned to his "melancholy home"—probably a subtle dig at its mistress—and composed the entire opera in nine months. After a four-week rest, he began on *Die Walküre*. Working at fever heat, he might well have gone right on and finished the cycle if Minna had not chosen this time, when her husband was in constant need of female solace after hours with his score, to traipse off to Germany in a valiant

attempt to get him an amnesty. Almost automatically, Wagner
turned to the attractive young wife of his principal Zurich benefactor, the wealthy silk merchant, Otto Wesendonck. He had
known the Wesendoncks since 1852, and their admiration for him
was so lively that in May, 1853, Otto had subsidized a series of all-
Wagner concerts in Zurich. All the proceeds were generously
given to Wagner, who accepted this as an entering wedge into a
bottomless purse that was to supply him money for necessities—
and extravagances—for many a year. To make a long *cause célèbre*
short, Wagner repaid his kindhearted banker by playing fast and
loose with Frau Mathilde's affections. As composing made him
more than ever susceptible to erotic influence, he was soon in the
throes of a violent passion. By the end of 1854, he was seeing himself as the hero of a heavy drama of renunciation, and simultaneously—perhaps as compensation for thwarted desire—began to
consider the tragic medieval love story of Tristan and Isolde as
fitting artistic material for a new music drama.

In January, 1855, an emissary of the London Philharmonic
Society, a gentleman known to history only as Mr. Anderson, appeared at Zurich in a borrowed fur coat, and bearing Wagner an
invitation to conduct a season of that renowned organization.
Their regular conductor had just resigned, and Berlioz was conducting the rival New Philharmonic concerts. They had applied
vainly to Spohr. Then one of the orchestra suggested Wagner, then
only a vague name in England, on the ground that "a man who has
been so much abused must have something in him." Mr. Anderson
was dispatched to fetch him. Wagner did not want to look up from
the *Ring*, but £200 was too large a sum for him to refuse. He went
over to London, and between March 12 and June 25 conducted
eight concerts, approximately one every fortnight. His beautifully
balanced programs included all the Beethoven symphonies except
the first two, five Weber overtures, and (despite *Das Judenthum*)
five compositions by Mendelssohn. The English people rather
liked Wagner than not, but the critics lashed out furiously at him.
They were prejudiced by his writings, and were not inclined to
excuse dogmatic self-advertisement, even in so skilled a conductor.
Victoria and Albert, taking time off from the headaches of the
Crimean War, appeared in the royal box for the seventh concert,
at which the *Tannhäuser* overture was played by command. The

Queen was graciously pleased to tell Herr Wagner that she would be happy to hear his operas sung in London—in Italian.* Altogether, except for a few pleasant meetings with Berlioz, the guest conductor of the Philharmonic did not enjoy England, and was delighted to return to Mathilde and the score of *Die Walküre*.

During 1856 and 1857, Wagner worked intermittently at the *Ring*, finishing *Die Walküre*, and completing a little more than two acts of *Siegfried*. Early in 1857, Wesendonck gave Wagner and Minna, who was now suffering from heart disease, the summer-house on his new estate, rent-free. The Asyl, as Wagner romantically christened it, was next door to the main house, into which the Wesendoncks moved in August. Contiguity to Mathilde, coupled with the strong temptation to compare her with his rapidly aging wife, precipitated the inevitable. As soon as Mathilde moved next door, Wagner dropped *Siegfried* in the midst of Act III, and wrote the book of *Tristan und Isolde* in four weeks. Amid all this portentous activity, the Wagners had guests—Hans von Bülow and his bride, Cosima Liszt. As if to bid defiance to the already electric atmosphere of the Asyl, Wagner read separate acts of *Tristan* to an audience consisting of his wife, his mistress, his mistress' husband, and his future wife and her husband. On everyone except Mathilde, however, the significance of this literature seems to have been lost. The Von Bülows left, and Wagner plunged into the music of *Tristan*. The tension grew. The patient Wesendonck played his role with dignity and submissiveness to fate. The others were not so philosophical: Wagner could not conceal his passion; Mathilde was unsure and wavering; Minna was in a pitiable state, hopelessly ill and torn by uncontrollable jealousy. The five songs Wagner composed at this time to Mathilde's lyrics, notably the poignant *Träume*, are so many proofs of his invincible callousness to all feelings except his own. This volcanic seething persisted until August, 1858, when Wagner suddenly decided that he could not stand the strain any longer, and went off to Venice in the company of Julie Ritter's son Karl. Minna went to friends in Germany, and the Wesendoncks were given a breathing spell in which to readjust their lives.

Cut off from Mathilde, Wagner poured his passionate yearning

* As usual, Victoria had her way. The first Wagner opera to be sung in London (July, 1870) was the Holländer, traveling on an Italian visa as *L'Ollandese dannato*.

for her into the score of *Tristan*, the second act of which he completed at Venice in March, 1859, just before the Austrian authorities, acting on a request from Dresden, ordered him to move on. He was again corresponding with the Wesendoncks, though at first they had returned his letters unopened. It was partly in the hope of seeing Mathilde again that he returned to Switzerland, though not to Zurich. He went, instead, to Lucerne, and there completed *Tristan*, which during the next few years he tried vainly to have produced. With *Tristan* finished, a seal had been set upon his Swiss interlude, and Wagner was at loose ends. He longed for cosmopolitan life, opportunities to hear music, a chance to hear one of his own operas performed. At this juncture, Liszt suggested Paris, where Léon Carvalho, who had a real interest in having *Tannhäuser* performed, had a theater of his own. Accordingly, in September, 1859, Wagner set out on his last—and most disastrous —trip to Paris. On the way, he stopped at the Wesendoncks', both to see Mathilde and to help Otto quell the gossip that he had been forbidden the house. While there, he did a fine stroke of business, selling Otto the publishing rights to *Das Rheingold* and *Die Walküre* for six thousand francs apiece, and getting his promise that *Siegfried* and *Die Götterdämmerung* would be purchased at the same rate when finished.

The forty-six-year-old Wagner had left far behind him the unsure and callow little man, the composer of *Die Feen* and *Das Liebesverbot*, who had arrived in Paris twenty years before with a conservative young wife and the half-completed score of *Rienzi* in his bag. Still an exile, still a bad risk for moneylenders, still unknown to Paris audiences, he nevertheless was to be reckoned with —and knew it. *Rienzi*, *Tannhäuser*, and *Lohengrin* were already managerial favorites in Germany. The pontifical Liszt was devoted to him, as was a scattered but solidly loyal coterie of less famous musicians, notably some zealous youngsters who had selected him as a war cry for their advanced ideas. Liszt's support was not an unmixed blessing. His own cheap and flashy compositions were suspect to a large bloc of respectable musicians, who unfairly damned Wagner for being associated with the greathearted charlatan. Liszt and other Wagnerians began, about 1850, to be called—usually in derision—*Zukunftsmusiker*, or "musicians of the future"—a term Wagner had invented in one of his Zurich polemics. A few rulers of petty German states were strongly tempted to defy the Saxon ban, and invite him to court. More than half of his big music epic of the Nibelungs (that was to revolutionize the arts) had been achieved. And *Tristan und Isolde*, which Wagner himself thought the perfect flowering of his theories, was also finished. Now he was a master in full command of his art—and again he knew it.

Whether or not *Tristan und Isolde* really represents the perfect working out of Wagner's theories, it is music of such exciting beauty that it makes everything else he wrote seem anticlimactic. (It has, of course, a peer in *Die Meistersinger*, but its beauty is of a different order, of a different world.) Among Wagner's manifold gifts, and the very keystone of his art, was that of imminent communication of actual experience, and naturally it is most powerfully used in an opera that is autobiographically motivated from beginning to end. *Tristan* is the music of passion: it is almost as beautiful as passion itself. True, the necessity of telling a coherent story prevented Wagner from keeping his inspiration at white heat: music and audience become listless at precisely those times when the love interest is sacrificed to the exigencies of the narrative. But whenever the lovers are on the stage together, the music glows, flames, burns with an intolerable heat. The great second-act duet is unique in music: nowhere else is passion's fulfillment the very stuff of music itself. This *Liebesnacht* is prolonged orgasm, not, indeed, as viewed by the *voyeur*'s eye (for that would disgust, which the *Liebesnacht* never does), but experienced as the culmination of a great yearning. Quite as overwhelming is the tremendous scene of Isolde's apostrophe to the dead Tristan. Far from being a tragic outburst, her *Liebestod* is a song of hope triumphant. To Wagner's Isolde, death is not the end of love, but another beginning: her song has the inevitability and splendor of a natural force. Wagner's mystical drive in this scene rends the veil of individuality: Isolde is not a woman—she is woman.

A fine performance of *Tristan* is apt to produce one of two effects, depending upon the listener's point of view and state of mind. Either it is a wholly absorbing experience, a sublime catharsis of the emotions, or it is an irritant, a prolonged excursion through the rank jungles of the psyche. In either case, *Tristan* is an excitant, and we are naturally curious as to how it exerts its spell.

The chief musical tool used to shape the peculiar magic of *Tristan* is a harmony based principally upon the chromatic scale. An effect of restless yearning, of exacerbated nerves, is achieved by a melodic line that moves by half-tones. Seldom does this music come to rest: the very nature of the half-tone scale made it easy for Wagner to avoid the resolution of chords—that is, bringing the musical phrase to a close. The *Liebesnacht* climbs up and up, begins on a higher step, and climbs farther, and finally, when we can no longer stand the tension, bursts the dike in a series of chords recognizably in the same key. The timing is perfect—and salutary. With sheer sadistic genius, Wagner sets the harmonic and melodic patterns of *Tristan* in the prelude: in short, on page one he poses a torturing question, and defers the answer until the strain can no longer be endured. That is why the end of the *Liebesnacht* is the most inevitable moment in music, and, in one specific sense, the most satisfying. In working out the fundamental harmonic and melodic fabric of *Tristan*, Wagner creates en route some of his greatest pages, beginning with the prelude itself, ending with the *Liebestod*, and including the magical solo-horn incantation after the prelude to Act III. Following the orchestral richness of the prelude, this slender line of chromatic melody effects a singularly exquisite contrast. Here, for a moment, Wagner tenderly recalls that his flesh-and-blood Tristan and Isolde are figures out of medieval romance.

With good grounds for believing that Karlsruhe would take *Tristan*, Wagner now concentrated on getting a Paris hearing for *Tannhäuser*. At first, things looked hopeless. Carvalho was interested, but his theater had been destroyed under his feet in the course of Baron Haussmann's wholesale rebuilding of the city. Wagner tried the Opéra, but there Meyerbeer's friends reigned supreme, and he got nowhere. The court remained: some of his powerful admirers, led by Princess Pauline Metternich, wife of the Austrian ambassador, drew Napoleon III to his side. Accordingly, the Emperor highhandedly ordered the Opéra managers to put *Tannhäuser* into rehearsal. Meanwhile, negotiations with Karlsruhe collapsed, but this disaster was partly compensated for by the sale of the copyright of *Das Rheingold* to the Mainz publishing firm of B. Schott for ten thousand francs. The fact that he had already sold the same copyright to Wesendonck did not worry Wagner, especially as he planned to use the Schott money to stage several of his operas in Paris. After renting a fine house for three years, hiring a companion for Minna (who had finally agreed to rejoin him), and getting a liveried servant for himself, Wagner decided to buy some advance publicity. He leased a theater for three nights at four thousand francs a night, and gave three concerts of excerpts from his own operas. Although they were warmly received, the theater was not thronged any night. Wagner was left with important new adherents among the Parisian intellectuals—and a deficit of eleven thousand francs. When his finances were at their lowest ebb, Minna went to make a last desperate attempt to have the decree of banishment lifted. This time she was successful: in June, 1860, Wagner went to Baden-Baden to thank Princess Augusta of Prussia, who had been largely instrumental in getting permission for him to live anywhere in Germany except Saxony. In March, 1862, Saxony too declared his exile at an end.

Tannhäuser began to encounter difficulties as soon as the French text was ready. Immemorial tradition at the Opéra required an elaborate ballet as the climax of the second act of any opera, and the management demanded that Wagner meet this requirement. He refused, but consented to change the Venusberg scene in Act I. This solution, though not entirely satisfactory to the managers, was agreed to, and Wagner sat down and wrote what is by far the best music in the opera. Although the Opéra was the stronghold of Meyerbeerism, the Emperor's favor secured Tannhäuser one of the costliest performances ever given there: the bill ran to about forty thousand dollars, and there were 164 rehearsals. The conductor was Pierre-Louis-Philippe Dietsch, for whom, twenty years before, the Opéra had bought the libretto of Le Vaisseau fantôme The première, on March 13, 1861, was turned into a shambles by the rioting of the aristocratic bloods of the Jockey Club, who objected to the upstart Emperor, to the Austrian Princess Metternich, and, naturally, to their protégé, Wagner. When they looked in on the second act, hoping to see their idolized coryphées, they were told that they had missed the ballet. The singers were scarcely able to proceed: the music was mingled with derisive shouts and imprecations. After a third disastrous performance, the brokenhearted composer withdrew Tannhäuser.

The Paris debacle made Wagner a wanderer again. For three

years he was like an Ishmael dogged by failure. All attempts to have *Tristan* produced came to nothing. In Vienna, it reached fifty-seven rehearsals, and then was withdrawn. Other houses refused to glance at it. Yet, it was at Vienna that Wagner had the satisfaction of hearing *Lohengrin* at last—eleven years after its Weimar *première*. These *Wanderjahre* also saw the practical dissolution of Wagner's marriage: after a harassing series of domestic quarrels, he and Minna parted, though with the perverse hope in their minds that they would someday be reunited. Minna was mortally ill. She settled in Dresden, and there Wagner saw her for the last time in November, 1862.* His wanderings continued: he roamed fruitlessly through Russia, Italy, Austria, Hungary, Switzerland, France, and Germany, giving concerts that were always failures, and indulging in cynically empty liaisons. He happened on the Wesendoncks in Venice, and Mathilde suggested, as a panacea for his depressed spirits, that he take up again an old project of a comic opera about Hans Sachs and the *Meistersinger* of Nuremberg. He succeeded in completing the book, but found no spirit for composing much more than the overture, which he conducted at a Gewandhaus concert in November, 1862. He worked at the score painfully, wearily, and by the spring of 1864 things were so bad with him that he was on the verge of giving up the whole struggle. The most telling symptom of his advanced spiritual malaise was that never once in these three years did he add a note to the *Ring*. His once invincible egotism was at its nadir: he wanted only to rest.

Richard Wagner, a beaten man, was in Stuttgart, and headed toward Switzerland, when the private secretary of the eighteen-year-old Ludwig II, King of Bavaria, waited upon him. When Wagner saw Herr Pfistermeister's card, he tremblingly thought of his debts, and believed that this dignitary had come to arrest him. Instead, the man handed him the King's signet ring and portrait, with an invitation to become His Majesty's permanent and honored guest at the royal palace at Munich. Wagner was stunned. He could not know that this seemingly quixotic gesture was but a

---

* Death came to her in January, 1866. Wagner was stupefied. "She is to be envied for the painless cessation of her struggles," he wrote. "Peace, peace to the tormented heart of this most pitiable woman!"

step in a carefully planned campaign on the part of a powerful and psychopathic boy, consumed by a passion for Wagner's music, to have his idol by his side. The first meeting with the mad young Wittelsbach should have warned Wagner that he was dealing with a strange and dangerous personality. At first, however, joy banned thought and judgment. When he recovered, Wagner began without delay to plan a glorious musical future for Munich.

For the first time since leaving the Asyl, Wagner was comfortably situated. The openhanded Ludwig paid his most pressing debts, gave him a generous pension (that was soon increased), and established him in a commodious house near the palace. Lapped in the luxury he craved, and with resurgent ego, Wagner energetically set about getting his music performed. As Ludwig's fervor for Wagnerism, first roused by *Lohengrin*, had boiled over after he read the *Ring* poems the year before, it was only natural that he should commission the whole opera cycle. Wagner received the formal contract in the autumn of 1864, and an architect was summoned to design a fit temple for the performance of the masterpiece. The first Munich presentation under Wagner's supervision was *Der fliegende Holländer* on December 4, 1868. For *Tannhäuser*, Wagner secured the services of Ludwig Schnorr von Carolsfeld, a young tenor whose intelligence and glorious voice had impressed him in *Lohengrin* some years before. Schnorr acquitted himself so well as Tannhäuser that Wagner invited him to create the role of Tristan. As Schnorr's wife, Malwine, was an excellent soprano, the arrangement was perfect. The Schnorrs were largely responsible for the magnificent *première* of *Tristan und Isolde* at the Hof-und-Nationaltheater on June 10, 1865, under the baton of Von Bülow. The audience, including many foreign music lovers who had traveled far just to hear the opera, listened attentively, but showed little enthusiasm. The King made up for their lukewarm applause by ordering three more performances by July 1.* Later that month, acting on a memorandum from Wagner, Ludwig ordered the Akademie der Tonkunst closed, and appointed a royal commission to ponder its reopening along Wagnerian lines, with Von Bülow as director. Wagner's hold on the King was now so strong

---

* Three weeks after this last performance, Schnorr was dead. *Tristan* was not revived for four years, as Wagner could not find a worthy successor to this first of the "heroic tenors."

that he began to interfere in affairs of state, and was instrumental in ministerial appointments.

Meanwhile, Wagner was embroiling himself in an emotional tangle that was to have far-reaching consequences for all concerned. In June, 1864, only a month after his rescue by Ludwig, he was sending out wild SOS calls to Von Bülow and Cosima to come and live with him. "We simply must have each other," he wrote, "and the moment for it is now, now!" He addressed the letter to Hans: he meant it for Cosima. He had fallen in love with her* in Berlin the preceding year, and despite the formidable difference in their ages—he was fifty, she twenty-six—Cosima had returned his love. This was not unnatural, seeing that the energetic, strong-minded daughter of Franz Liszt and Daniel Stern was not only unhappy with her vacillating, fuddy-duddy husband, but was determined to be the inspiration of genius. She went about it in the time-honored fashion. Von Bülow unwittingly connived by sending her and their two daughters to stay at Wagner's before he himself could go. So well did Cosima play her role that within five years she bore Wagner two daughters and a son, though Von Bülow was still her husband. Von Bülow, for whom Wagner had wangled a court appointment, evidently did not see how things were going, even when, on April 12, 1865, Cosima bore a third daughter, and named her Isolde. Wagner, of course, kept up the deception by standing godfather to his own child.

In Munich resentment was growing against Wagner. A musicians' cabal gathered against the King's increasingly powerful favorite. It was led by the ex-general music director, Franz Lachner, whom Wagner had replaced with a Wagnerian, and its ranks were swelled by the disgruntled pedants who had been thrown out of work by the closing of the Akademie. At court, a whispering campaign was whipped up into an outcry against the alien who was meddling in Bavarian state matters, and flouting Ludwig's rightful counselors. Even at this early date, the newspapers began to carry attacks on Wagner and Cosima for their loose living, and on Von Bülow for his complaisance—insinuations that neither Von Bülow nor the King believed. It began to

---

* Evidently while his anti-Semitism was in abeyance. Cosima's mother, the Countess d'Agoult, was the granddaughter of Johann Philipp Bethmann, a Jewish banker in Frankfort.

be said that Wagner's influence over the King was hypnotic: he had but to wave his hand for Ludwig to do his bidding. Others went further: they said that the Saxon upstart was to Ludwig II what Lola Montez had been to Ludwig I. The general public paid little attention to all this, but the anti-Wagnerian bloc managed to convince the King that he faced a national uprising. Sadly, reluctantly, Ludwig bowed to the storm, and told his hero that he must leave Bavaria for a time. He wrote Wagner a touching letter, with the plea, "Believe me, I had to do it. Never doubt the loyalty of your best friend." Wagner, for his part, could not understand why a king should give in to his ministers, but he accepted Ludwig's fiat, and prepared to go once more to Switzerland.

For the unhappy man who was to outlive him and die in a madhouse, Wagner had nothing but thanks and love. In 1877, summing up what Ludwig had done for him, he wrote, "My creditors were quieted, I could go on with my work—and this noble young man's trust made me happy. There have been many troubles since—not of my making or of his—but in spite of them I am free to this day—and by his grace." Wagner's consistently grateful respect for Ludwig is almost unique in his career of pettifogging, chicanery, and abuse of benefactors who had, in some way, annoyed him.

At first, Wagner was alone in Switzerland. Wasting little time on sad repinings, he resumed work on Act I of *Die Meistersinger*. In March, 1866, Cosima joined him for a while, and together they went on a leisurely jaunt through German Switzerland, on the lookout for a likely house where Wagner could settle down permanently. They found the ideal spot at Triebschen, on the Lake of Lucerne, and there, after going back to Munich for the children, Cosima rejoined Wagner. At the same time, Von Bülow accidentally discovered the whole truth about his wife's relations with his best friend. He went to Triebschen, and more or less calmly accepted the *fait accompli*. Knowing his own shortcomings as a husband, he agreed to an eventual divorce, but implored the lovers to part for two years so as to save face for all concerned. He pled in vain: Cosima remained with Wagner, and Von Bülow had to return to Munich to face ridicule and calumny alone. While Wagner, lapped in luxury and Cosima's love, progressed rapidly with the composition of *Die Meistersinger*, and began to dictate parts of

Mein Leben to her (he had begun it at Ludwig's request the preceding year), Von Bülow took up his duties as director of the Akademie. Newspaper attacks on him and his absent wife and friend multiplied, and in a last-minute attempt to quash the scandal and prevent her husband's fall, Cosima persuaded the credulous monarch to write an open letter to Von Bülow, certifying the purity of all parties. But she left Triebschen—where she bore Wagner a second daughter, Eva, in February, 1867—only when political changes in Bavaria made Wagner's return to Munich practicable. Again, to quiet public rumor, she returned to her husband's house, where Wagner was their guest whenever he was in town assisting Von Bülow and Hans Richter in staging *Die Meistersinger*, the score of which was finished on October 24, 1867.

In creating this masterpiece, Wagner momentarily receded from his most cherished theories, and wrote an old-fashioned opera. Having chosen for comic treatment much the same sort of song contest as plays a salient role in *Tannhäuser*, he was perforce driven back on a variant of the traditional set-number scheme, which involved, also, sacrificing the elaborate sign language of leitmotivs he was using in the *Ring*. Yet, *Die Meistersinger* rejoices in everything that makes for perfection. Its libretto, besides having an authentic flavor of poetry, abounds in good situations, and writing and mime that are funny to this day. A warm and homely wisdom pervades it, finding its mouthpiece in one of the few truly full-bodied characters in opera—Hans Sachs. *Die Meistersinger* is full of shafts that found their intended lodging places in the vulnerable spots of Wagner's hated enemies, the critics. But this element of rancor never once usurps an undue importance, and is finally submerged in the general good fun and all-pervasive kindly glow created by the humane philosophy of Sachs, the loves of Walther and Eva, David and Magdalene, and the bustle and hurly-burly of the townspeople. The physically misshapen and mentally twisted Beckmesser is a cruel caricature of the chief of the anti-Wagnerian critics, Eduard Hanslick of the powerful Vienna *Neue freie Presse*.*. But the pedantic Beckmesser merely serves to heighten the broad humanity of Sachs and the enterprising boldness of Walther.

With an unrivaled gift for translating every element of a libretto into music, Wagner achieved in *Die Meistersinger* a score superior

* In the first draft of the *Meistersinger* libretto, Beckmesser was called Hans Lick.

to *Tristan* in every respect except intensity. It has more dimension, greater variety, richer invention, and (what *Tristan* conspicuously has not) uninterrupted vitality. The action is so unflaggingly translated into an inspired melodic stream that *Die Meistersinger* can be called a truly popular opera—exactly what Wagner intended it to be. In *Tristan*, the master magician Wagner, with his personal experience of the power of love, had the stuff of passion to work with, and could not fail. In *Die Meistersinger*, he had no such earth-shaking stuff to deal with: the elements of the drama are drawn from the everyday life of Nuremberg in the sixteenth century, and even the central love conflict is on a human, more easily comprehensible scale. Wagner's triumph with this less intense material is, therefore, all the more remarkable—is, indeed, the triumph of Wagner as pure musician. The sensation of burgeoning life and irrepressible vitality imparted by the conventional potpourri prelude carries right through to the exciting choral apostrophe to Sachs on the banks of the Pegnitz, where the Mastersingers are assembled for their competition. No other Wagnerian opera abounds so liberally in great moments, some of them as familiar, without being as notorious, as "Evening Star" and the Bridal Chorus. The orchestra has for itself, apart from the prelude, the lighthearted, cleverly gawky Dance of the Apprentices—the only true waltz Wagner ever composed. The music given to Sachs is of a reflective and philosophic cast, yet robust and of great movement, including the magnificent character piece on the world's madness, "*Wahn! Wahn!*" For Walther, of course, the composer reserved his most lyrical inspirations, culminating in that cantilena of sheer poetry, the *Preislied*. The quintet uses the same lyricism, adding to it an unbridled ecstasy, a kind of communal joy that is unmatched in music. *Die Meistersinger* is one of Wagner's longest operas: it seems his shortest. It soars on a rush of musical wings that carry us to the final curtain all too quickly.

The audience for the first performance of *Die Meistersinger*, on June 21, 1868, was more brilliant, and more international in character, than that which had assembled for the *première* of *Tristan*. The King broke all laws of etiquette by inviting Wagner to share the royal loge—an action that furnished more ammunition to the composer's enemies. The response at the close was a wild ovation, and rightly so. Von Bülow had drilled the orchestra to perfection, and Richter had not been behind in training the chorus. Edward Dannreuther, writing in 1889, said categorically that the Munich *Meistersinger* had been matched among Wagnerian performances only by the Bayreuth *Parsifal*. The critics, incensed by the implications of the libretto, and regarding Beckmesser as a lampoon on the entire critical fraternity, subjected Wagner to the most poisonous, and certainly the most unfair, attacks of his career. By this time, he had successfully sold his music to the public. The critics still lagged behind. The popular misconception of Wagner as a misunderstood genius, too advanced for his public, arose from the attitude of bigoted brothers of the press—and there were eminent exceptions among them. After *Die Meistersinger*, the attacks on Wagner's character and influence grew in frequency and violence. Disgusted, he left for Triebschen, vowing never to set foot in Munich again. There was no longer any reason to keep up appearances, and Cosima joined Wagner permanently. Ludwig, finding too late that she had been playing him for a fool, was enraged. He never forgave her, and even when the festal atmosphere of the Bayreuth opening in 1876 might have made for a gentler attitude, refused to receive her.

For over three years, Wagner enjoyed with Cosima a life of almost flawless happiness, devoting most of his time to completing the *Ring*. Early in June, 1869, she presented him with a son, who was called Siegfried, after the hero of the music drama he was then at work on. Three months later, *Siegfried* was finished, except for scoring, and in October Wagner began *Die Götterdämmerung*. The first two acts were completed in 1870, the last in 1872. *Siegfried* was scored in 1871, and the most ambitious of all operatic projects stood complete when the scoring of *Die Götterdämmerung* was finished in November, 1874. Interruptions in this vast program of work were few, and they mainly incidental to straightening out Cosima's status. On July 18, 1870, Von Bülow, who had filed papers in Berlin, charging his wife with infidelity, won his divorce. On August 25, after the once devoutly Catholic Cosima had become a Protestant, she was married to Wagner at Lucerne. Liszt, who had been inclined to side with Von Bülow, could not forgive her for renouncing her religion, and it was years before he was reconciled to the Wagners. This estrangement from a man of whom he was genuinely fond preyed on Wagner's mind, and he made all manner of vain overtures to the Abbé. But in general, life at Triebschen was so peaceful and full that the outside world intruded very little.* As a tribute to this domestic bliss, Wagner composed the *Siegfried Idyl*, and had it played in the hallway of their home on the morning of Cosima's thirty-third birthday, Christmas, 1870. It is far and away the loveliest of his occasional pieces for orchestra. Combining themes from the last act of *Siegfried* with an old cradle song, it glows with the intense tenderness of young love—it is eternal springtime set to music. The orchestration is shot with light and color: the whole piece exhales a delicate flowery magic that is rare even in this poet of the subtle gradations of love.

Wagner had never relinquished the idea of a special theater dedicated solely to performances of his own music. Now that the *Ring* was nearing completion, he began to think that it was high time to make his dream a reality. Munich was still anathema, but his gratitude to Ludwig, as well as the hope of enlisting him as one of the bankers of the projected Festspielhaus, limited Wagner's choice of a site to Bavaria. To Bayreuth, a little town about sixty miles northeast of Nuremberg, the honor finally fell, mainly, it seems, because Cosima was attracted to it by a description in an encyclopedia. In April, 1871, she and Wagner visited the town, and were enchanted by the reality. The idea of him establishing the seat of his cult at Bayreuth appealed strongly to the local authorities, for Wagner was now the greatest name in German music, and they rightly foresaw, drawn there by the festivals, throngs of tourists jamming their hotels and filling their coffers. They therefore granted him land both for the theater and for a residence. All that remained was to get the huge sum of money that would have to be spent before the Festspielhaus could open its doors. Except for the time devoted to completing the *Ring*, for the next five years

---

* There were occasional guests, of course, the most frequent and most welcome of whom was the youthful Friedrich Nietzsche. Stupefied by Wagner's music and his Schopenhauerian mouthings, Nietzsche was only too glad to sit at the feet of the master—and the master was just as glad to have him. He used the ardent young thinker as a sounding board for his theories, and was pleased to entrust him with the task of seeing a privately printed edition of *Mein Leben* through the press. The friendship endured until 1878, when Nietzsche began to regard Wagnerism as a kind of spiritual opium with dangerous degenerative power. He attacked his erstwhile teacher in a violent pamphlet, which Wagner answered. But Nietzsche had the last word: five years after his enemy's death, he wrote *Der Fall Wagner*, a withering but overwrought book that still supplies fuel to the anti-Wagnerians.

Wagner worked at raising it. On May 22, 1872, the cornerstone of the theater was laid at an impressive birthday ceremony—Wagner was fifty-nine that day—marked by the playing of Beethoven's Ninth Symphony and his own *Kaisermarsch*.

With characteristic audacity, the ex-barricade fighter of Dresden carried his problem to the Iron Chancellor himself. But Bismarck turned him down, commenting that Wagner was the most conceited man he had ever met. After that rebuff, the scramble for funds began in earnest, with Richter acting as generalissimo. Various plans were made, only to be discarded as impractical, until finally one of the master's friends hit upon the ingenious scheme of starting a Wagner Society. This organization worked so zealously for the project that similar societies were formed throughout Germany and even in foreign countries, often in the most unlikely places—Cairo, for instance. For he whom the critics still reviled as a musical anarch and maker of unpleasant noises had a huge popular following. Benefit concerts were given in many towns, often with Wagner himself conducting. A reconciliation with Liszt proved most opportune: having drawn away somewhat from the influence of the Princess Sayn-Wittgenstein (who ever loathed Bayreuth and all its works), he campaigned vigorously for his son-in-law. The King of Bavaria blew alternately hot and cold. Already half mad, one day he would be ready to drop the whole scheme, and the next would send a hundred thousand thalers. Time and again, everyone except Wagner grew numb with discouragement. In 1876, with the theater all but ready to open, it was thought for a while that the often postponed festival would have to be abandoned altogether. Five thousand dollars came in the nick of time, and helped to revive a drooping morale. It was payment for the last hack job Wagner ever did—the *American Centennial March* for the Philadelphia Exposition. Rehearsals began in June, and everybody breathed a sigh of relief.

Wagner had moved from Triebschen to Bayreuth in April, 1872. At first he lived in a rented house, but two years later his own luxurious Villa Wahnfried was ready. By this time, the eyes of the world were focused on the little Franconian town. By the summer of 1876, it was so crowded with curiosity seekers that the police had difficulty keeping order at the public rehearsals in the Festspielhaus. The first complete performance of *Der Ring des Nibelungen*,

from August 13 to 17, 1876, was an event without precedent or
parallel in the history of music and high society. The theater was
provided with a "princes' gallery," and this was crowded with the
elite, from Kaiser Wilhelm I, Dom Pedro II of Brazil, Ludwig II
of Bavaria, and so on, down to petty princelets and dukes. Liszt,
Tchaikovsky, and Saint-Saëns attended. Wagner's friends and enemies mingled excitedly, among them the Wesendoncks and Hans
von Bülow's mother. Von Bülow himself, one of the chief instruments of Wagner's success and happiness, was conspicuously absent. He had been invited, but was too ill to attend. Of all the
cruel blows dealt by fate to Minna Wagner, the cruelest was that
she did not live to see her Richard's apotheosis as the foremost
operatic composer in the world. Three complete productions of
the *Ring* cycle were given to clamorously enthusiastic, completely
subscribed, houses. Perhaps the only notable dissenters in the chorus
of praise were the critics who had come, literally, from the four
corners of the earth. But now even their ranks (never solid) were
breaking. The foreign critics, a few German ones too, were beginning to realize that they had a genius to evaluate.

Even the most sophisticated of operagoers among those first
eager *Ring* audiences could not have been prepared for what they
saw and heard during the twelve hours and forty minutes of that
weighty musicodramatic epic. Nothing in the works of other composers, nothing in the works of Wagner himself, could have made
them ready for digesting the incredibly complex machinery of this
audaciously long work of art. First, they were asked to follow a
series of interrelated poems that required a guidebook for their
perfect comprehension. Second, they were asked to hold in their
memories for four days a set of ninety leitmotivs, one third of
which make their appearance in *Das Rheingold*, the first of the
cycle. Nor was this second demand a mere empty convention: to
forget even one of the motives was to lose a part of the essential
dramatic significance of the *Ring*, which depends for development
of character and the carrying forward of the action on the reappearance, mingling, and transmutation of these leitmotivs. Finally, they were asked to sit through four consecutive performances
of unrelieved seriousness: there is not a single comic touch in the
Ring, as is perhaps only correct in a work that purports to have a
high philosophical message.

Now that the smoke of battle has cleared, and even the timidest critic in the most backward land has accepted Wagner's music, we see the *Ring* as a glorious failure. Wagner intended it as a synthesis of the arts, defining their roles with the naïveté of a man obsessed by a fixed idea. Poetry—the essential vehicle of the drama, that is —was to take pre-eminence. Music, far from being independent, was merely to amplify and illuminate the poet's meaning. Painting and sculpture had their parts in *décor* and costumes; the dance was to be content with miming. The final result was to be the unified art work—the music drama. It is precisely this that Wagner failed to achieve—or even to approximate. The only reason thousands still stand in the ticket line in the coldest winter weather whenever the *Ring* cycle is announced is that it contains some of the most absorbing music ever written. The libretto is a bore—windy, flatulent, repetitious, and frequently absurd. No one less cocksure than the builder of Bayreuth would have dared these excessive *longueurs* or have mistaken chunks of undilute Schopenhauer for relevant musical text. These show a basic misconception of the very nature of drama. Even worse, because they are egregious interruptions that might easily have been excised by a careful editorial pen, are those moments when one or more of the characters says, in effect, "Hold everything!" and proceeds at great length to narrate what has already been better presented in the action of earlier scenes. It is a matter for legitimate amazement that Wagner, who proved again and again that he knew how to shape a truly dramatic libretto, imposed on himself the Procrustean scheme of the four *Ring* poems essentially unchanged. They had been written in reverse order, and therefore involved the inclusion of synopses of the scenes still to be written. Oddly enough, though Wagner composed the actual operas in correct order, he left these synopses in. What might possibly be tolerable to read is intolerable to listen to. The most telling indictment of the *Ring* librettos is that they contain hours of talk that even Wagner could not translate into living music.

Once it is freely admitted that the *Ring* is a spotty, generally unsuccessful work of art, its many pages of surpassingly beautiful music can be appreciated for what they are. The appeal of the *Ring* at its best is effected by magnificent texture and a most eloquent musical speech. The first of these is achieved by the most varied and subtle use of orchestral and vocal color, and by the rich weaving together of leitmotivs, many of which, though as terse as can be, are extraordinarily viable. The last twenty minutes of *Die Götterdämmerung*, for example, when all the musical elements that have been gathering throughout the four operas culminate and are resolved, shape one of the most sheerly splendid climaxes in all music. Here is Wagner at his supreme greatest, with all the vast amplitude and scope of his style perfectly displayed. It has an enduring quality that the clever and (at first hearing) exciting Ride of the Valkyries lacks. Quite as memorable, however, are the Magic Fire Spell, Siegfried's Rhine Journey, and Siegfried's funeral music. And the tantalizingly lingering *Waldweben* discloses an unfamiliar Wagner, a precursor of Debussy—delicate, shimmering, impressionistic. Strangely out of place in this sophisticated texture is Siegmund's limpid, moronically lovely *Liebeslied*, which might easily have come out of *Tannhäuser*. More in the style and tone of their great orchestral surroundings are Wotan's Farewell and Brünnhilde's immolation aria. But these only serve to prove that the mature Wagner of the *Ring* was essentially a symphonic composer, who used the voice most adroitly, most effectively, as but another instrument in his superb orchestra. By a monumental irony, Wagner, who faithfully believed that Beethoven had introduced voices into his last symphony because he had discovered that the orchestra alone could not express all that he had to say, seems, in this most considered, theory-filled product of his maturity, to be striving to free himself of the impositions of the human voice.

The three cycles of the *Ring*, thronged though they were, left the Festspielhaus with a deficit of close to 120,000 marks, for which Wagner himself had to shoulder the chief responsibility. At first he was too tired to think of ways of paying it off, and went to Italy for a much-needed rest. On his return to Bayreuth, he fell in with a scheme suggested by the violinist Wilhelmj, apparently a man of childlike faith, that he raise funds by conducting concerts of his own in London. These were organized on a ridiculously lavish scale that ate perilously into future profits before they were even sighted. The six concerts of excerpts from his own works that Wagner conducted in Albert Hall in May, 1877, suffered from a double handicap: the tickets had to be priced too high, and the composer was too ill and fatigued to do himself justice—an artistic tragedy, for Wagner at his best was a great conductor. Attendance was good, but by no means capacity. To save the venture, two additional concerts were given at much reduced prices, and these were so crowded that not only were the costs defrayed, but he was able to send back to Bayreuth almost £7000. This was a mere drop in the bucket, but Wagner had neither means nor energy to do anything more about Bayreuth's muddled finances. His heart now began to trouble him, and so, after taking a cure, he returned to Wahnfried.

In August, 1877, Wagner began to compose the first-act music of *Parsifal*, the libretto of which was published separately a few months later. By April, 1879, *Parsifal* was complete but for the orchestration, which was not finished until January 13, 1882. The years of its composition were by no means happy ones for Wagner. Tragically, just as he achieved unblemished domestic serenity, he began to die of a complication of diseases. Erysipelas, the scourge of his youth, returned with special violence toward the end of 1879. Gastric troubles and rheumatism of a peculiarly stubborn nature further weakened his heart. The specter of debts, laid during his Munich and Triebschen periods, stalked again in a more than ever fearsome aspect. For Wagner's personal lavishness now assumed truly Babylonian proportions. His cherished plan of repeating the Bayreuth festival every year had to be abandoned, but in 1878 a way of financial rehabilitation was suggested by the still-enthusiastic Ludwig of Bavaria. He owned the rights to the *Ring* (the long-suffering Wesendonck having greatheartedly ceded his interest), and had before its completion flouted Wagner's well-known wishes that it never be given except as a cycle. He had had *Das Rheingold* and *Die Walküre* performed separately at Munich. Now he wanted to stage the entire cycle there, but ran up against Wagner's insistence that the *Ring* be given only in the specially designed Festspielhaus. He could, of course, simply have given the *Ring*, but did not wish to annoy his revered friend. Instead, he offered, in return for Wagner's blessing, to turn the proceeds of the Munich performances into a fund for lifting the Bayreuth debt. Further help came from the farsighted and courageous impresario, Angelo Neumann, who organized a Richard Wagner Touring Company, and carried cyclic performances of the *Ring* to many a European town. Wagner salved his artistic conscience by saying that he himself had at least given the *Ring* three times under perfect conditions.

At last, in 1882, a second Bayreuth festival became possible—and, indeed, imperative, if Wagner was to live to see *Parsifal*. The year before, parts of it had been rehearsed under the direction of the last of Wagner's famous disciples. This was Engelbert Humperdinck, who was to achieve an un-Bayreuthian immortality with a by no means un-Wagnerian opera, *Hänsel und Gretel*. Full rehearsals began early in July, 1882, and on the twenty-sixth of that month a picked audience of subscribers heard the *première* of the longest single opera ever composed. Not the least strange episode in the strange life of Richard Wagner is that though an unrepentant anti-Semite, he chose, to conduct this "consecrational festival stage play," a Jew by the name of Hermann Levi, who, moreover, remained chief director at Bayreuth for many years. Not quite so strange—in fact, well in keeping with the odd mélange of Christianity and Buddhism that had brought *Parsifal* into being—were Wagner's mystical reasons for refusing to allow Neumann to add it to the repertory of his operatic stock company. Everything Wagner said about *Parsifal* makes one suspect that he conceived of it as a new kind of religious ceremony.

And perhaps *Parsifal* is appreciated best by those who like new kinds of religious ceremonies. Those who like it least call it a combination of megalomania and senility—the devotional maunderings of an elderly ex-genius. Of all the Wagnerian music dramas, *Parsifal* cries out most for concert-excerpt treatment. Given as an opera, it is intolerable. It never comes to life except for a few minutes at a time. Its length is no sin, but that it seems sluggishly, incredibly long, is. Far from having learned the dead-weight effect of long, uninterrupted narrative (as he should have by listening to a single cycle of the *Ring*), Wagner has peopled *Parsifal* with talking textbooks of religious doctrine and ethical theory. And for all its technical virtuosity, most of the music is not measurably better than the libretto. The transformations to which the leitmotivs are subjected show unimpaired intellectual ingenuity, but the motives themselves seem to be of an inferior species. The orchestration, as rich as ever, is not often resplendent or glowing. The musical weather of *Parsifal* may be described as a persistent rosy fog, with extremely low visibility. The garden of Klingsor—what corresponds in this long-drawn-out drama of salvation to the *Tannhäuser* Venusberg scene—is sensualism of a very second-rate order. Its effect is like that of going into a garishly lighted burlesque theater between church services. Amid all this folderol, this mixture of jeweled pother and muggy sanctimoniousness, there are but few passages that show the hand of the old magician. The prelude, for example (which Wagner had played for Cosima as a birthday surprise on Christmas Day, 1878), exhales a radiance and fragrance that are worthy of the Holy Grail they symbolize. As for the piously static Good Friday Spell, one can only surmise that its persistent popularity is due to the spurious atmosphere of unctiousness that is whipped up with clocklike regularity every Eastertide.

Wagner's enfeebled constitution barely stood the strain of sixteen performances of his last opera. On the closing night, however, he was strong enough to take the baton when Levi suddenly fell ill during the third act. But with the festival finally over, he decided that he could not endure the rigors of a German winter. In September, he and Cosima headed south: their destination was Venice, where Wagner had leased a luxurious palace on the Grand Canal. Liszt soon arrived, and stayed with them for two happy months. Meanwhile, Wagner's health, instead of responding to the mildness of the south, deteriorated further, and he had an alarming series of heart attacks. In his agony, he did not forget the wife who had given him full measure of happiness. Making a superhuman effort, he managed to rehearse his fifty-one-year-old C major Symphony, and conduct it at the Liceo Marcello on the eve of her birthday. The choice was not fortuitous: his interest in purely orchestral music had been gaining on him. At this time, he even projected another symphony. It is a cliché of Wagnerians to deplore that this was never composed. Considering the decline from *Die Götterdämmerung* to *Parsifal*, it is impossible to agree with them. What is sad is that Wagner did not compose such a symphony when his powers were at their full. In any event, by January, 1883, it was too late to do more than dream of new compositions. Life was ebbing painfully away. Early in February, he suffered an unusually sharp attack of angina pectoris, and on the thirteenth died in Cosima's arms.

When the news of his son-in-law's death reached Liszt in Budapest, he at first refused to believe it. "Why not?" was his casual comment as he turned back to his work. But soon confirmation came. This time he received it as an omen, remarking, "He today, I tomorrow." The first wreath to arrive at Wahnfried, whither the body had been removed for solemn interment in the garden, was from Johannes Brahms. Cosima, who had sacrificially cut off her hair and placed it on her dead husband's breast, received Brahms' tribute with cold disdain. "We shall not acknowledge it," she said. "He did not love the master's music." Soon there converged on Wahnfried messages and wreaths from a world that knew a great man had died.

After the funeral, the widow Wagner pulled herself together, and took into her strong hands a trust to preserve unchanged the empire her lord had carved out. For forty-seven years she stood jealous guard over "the Bayreuth tradition," which ended up by being more Wagnerian than Wagner. Not only was she the all-powerful priestess of what became a real cult, but she managed to extend the influence of Wagnerism into the most remote corners of the musical world. Huneker called her, satirically, but not without a trace of respect, Cosima I of Bayreuth. Her rule was stern and unflinching, unmitigated by a trace of humor. It was only when old age relaxed her grip, and she saw with grim certainty that the heir apparent—the incongruously named Siegfried—was a weak man, that the boundaries of the empire began to shrink. Those who either owed nothing to Wagner, or refused to acknowledge their debt, now began to lead music away from the cult of Bayreuth. When Cosima died in 1930, at the age of ninety-three, it had been whispered for many years that Wagner was old-fashioned.

Chapter XVII

Giuseppe Verdi

(Le Roncole, October 10, 1813–January 27, 1901, Milan)

THE story of Richard Wagner is one of the most complex in art: it is full of mysteries, philosophical and literary detours, posturings in the limelight. It is a crowded canvas, fuller of extramusical episode than the life of any other composer. Verdi's story is simplicity itself—a straightforward career piece, with a minimum of applied ornament and a maximum of common sense. First, second, and third, he was a practicing composer of opera, and only fourth and thereafter was he anything else. The complexities of his character were expressed in his music and in his private life, which he kept eminently private. He was an intelligent but intellectually unpretentious man whose concentration on his métier was unaccompanied by esthetic flag-flying. He left no collected prose works. Aside from his music, he was, in comparison with Wagner, a mute.

Giuseppe Fortunino Francesco Verdi was born about a half year later than his great German rival, at a tiny village in the grand duchy of Parma, then part of Napoleon's empire. The names on the birth certificate of this only son of Carlo Verdi, grocer and innkeeper, and Luigia Uttini are "Joseph Fortunin François." When the French were driven out in 1814, and Austrian troops, suspecting the natives of being pro-French, pillaged Le Roncole, killing many of its inhabitants, Luigia Verdi saved her baby's life and her own by hiding in the church belfry. The tales of the Austrian terror that Giuseppe heard as he was growing up helped to make him a stalwart patriot. When he showed more than the average childish interest in music, he was sent to the village organist for instruction. At the age of twelve, he was voted a salary of ten dollars a year as his teacher's successor, and his father decided that such phenomenal talents deserved wider fields. Accordingly, Giuseppe went to live at Busseto, the district metropolis, three full miles away, lodging with a family friend, cultivating the three R's at the town school, and walking to his native village on Sundays to perform his official duties.

News of the boy's considerable musical talents aroused the interest of the local Maecenas—Antonio Barezzi, a well-to-do grocer whose house was the meeting place of the Società Filarmonica di Busseto. He took Giuseppe under his wing, into his home and into his business, and sent him for further musical study to the cathedral organist. This venerable fellow, several of whose comic operas had actually been produced, taught the boy what he could—in short, prepared him for the big-city hegira that was bound to come. Under his tutelage, Giuseppe began to compose, and some of the fifteen-year-old's efforts, including marches and an overture, were found good enough for performance by the Busseto band. More important, it turned out, were the numerous piano duets he devised for himself and Barezzi's pretty daughter, Margherita.

By 1832, it was clear that young Verdi could learn nothing more in Busseto. His thoughts and his hopes turned automatically to Milan, then as now the nerve center of Italian opera. But he had no money. When things looked blackest, his tireless patron not only persuaded a local charity to double a scholarship grant within its gift, but also added an appreciable sum to it. Thus provided with funds for two years' study, Verdi set out for Milan. The directors of the conservatory turned him down. While admitting his phenomenal gifts and even predicting a brilliant career for him, they mentioned his weakness in musical theory and the fact that he was beyond the usual age for admission. This was a severe setback to the naturally reserved and pessimistic young man. Pride and hope were alike salvaged when the influential Vincenzo Lavigna accepted him as a private pupil. For the first time in his life, Verdi was exposed to really thorough methods of training, and he forged ahead at a great rate. At Busseto the music had not been wholly bad: the Filarmonica did its best for Rossini, Haydn, and other popular composers of the day. Under Lavigna, Verdi came to know Bach, Mozart, Beethoven, and, above all, Palestrina, for whom he conceived a lifelong passion.

In 1833, Verdi's old master in Busseto died, and Barezzi and a clique of his friends invited their protégé to return as cathedral organist. The invitation put Verdi on the spot. On the one hand, a strong sense of duty and gratitude as well as Margherita Barezzi's charms argued Busseto's claims; on the other hand, his strongest ambition urged him to remain in Milan. Through a series of fortunate accidents which had brought him into contact with Milanese high society, he was becoming something of a personage in musical circles, and indeed had just been asked earnestly to write an opera. Busseto won. Verdi returned for six years' vegetation. It turned out that Barezzi and the pro-Verdi group in Busseto had not been entitled to speak for the cathedral authorities, who peremptorily appointed a nonentity as organist. The Filarmonica responded by appointing Verdi as its conductor, and the town itself voted him a stipend as organist of a rival church. A tiny civil war threatened: the clerics tried to have the Filarmonica outlawed, and the musicians retaliated by "stealing" music they had themselves lent to the cathedral.

Verdi's six years at Busseto did little to further his career: he marked time, and was happy. In 1835, he asked Barezzi for Margherita's hand, and was delighted to find that his poverty was not held against him. The marriage took place in May of the next year. By the time Verdi returned to Milan in 1839, he was the father of two children. Meanwhile, he had completed the score of *Oberto, conte di Bonifacio*, the libretto his Milanese friends had asked him to set some years before. But whatever high hopes he had for easy success were dashed when he reached Milan: friends on whom he had counted most were no longer in high places. At last, however, *Oberto* was taken by La Scala, put into rehearsal, and then withdrawn indefinitely when the tenor fell sick. When Verdi's funds were at the utmost ebb, the impresario Merelli happened to hear two members of the cast—one of them the soprano Giuseppina Strepponi—talking aggrievedly of the abandonment of an opera with so many excellences as *Oberto*. He looked at the score with new eyes, sent for the young composer, and made him an unusually attractive offer, considering that in those days unknowns were expected to pay for staging their first efforts. In this case, Merelli agreed to shoulder all expenses and share the profits with Verdi, whose cup of happiness must have overflowed when the enterprising publisher, Giovanni Ricordi, bought the rights to *Oberto*. The opera had its *première* on November 17, 1839. It was a measured success, and as its defects were charitably attributed to the inhibiting effects of a bad libretto, Verdi was immediately signed up to write three operas in two years.

More than a year later, Verdi had done nothing with the first libretto Merelli had given him. Therefore, he was asked to compose, instead, a comic piece for the fall season. He was scoring *Il Finto Stanislao* when there occurred the last of a series of tragedies that might well have deprived of his senses a man less master of himself: he had already lost his two children in two years, and now Margherita died. Verdi, who had himself been very ill, laboriously finished what had become a galling task, and the opera, renamed *Un Giorno di regno*, naturally fell flat at its *première*. Seventeen years later, securely established as the foremost composer of Italian opera, Verdi had not forgotten the discourtesy of that cruel Milanese audience. "If the public then had, I will not say applauded, but just received the work in silence," he wrote, "I should not have had words enough to express my thanks," and frigidly added: "I accept severity and hisses only on condition that I am not asked to be grateful for applause."

Verdi abandoned composition. He retreated to Busseto, found it intolerable, and returned to Milan, hoping to live by coaching singers. One evening he met Merelli, who was hot on his trail, and who then and there forced on the obstinate ex-composer a Babylonian libretto that had been turned down by Otto Nicolai, the adroit deviser of a number of now-forgotten scores and the perennially favored overture to *Die lustigen Weiber von Windsor*. Verdi read it, and returned it to Merelli, saying in a listless voice that it was very fine, but that he would not score it. Merelli thereupon called him an ass, stuffed the manuscript in his pocket, and locked him out. This was just the sort of medicine Verdi needed. He began to compose *Nabucodnosor* right away, and was soon fretting the librettist with plans for extensive revisions. Merelli was convinced that Verdi was cured, and staged the Biblical extravaganza on March 9, 1842, at the height of the carnival season.

In *Nabucodnosor*, Verdi was compensated for years of defeat. The Milanese received it with riotous enthusiasm, and the critics praised it for the qualities he had intended it to have. After the third crowded performance, he was invited to write the chief novelty for the coming season. He literally became the rage: new food creations and articles of dress were named after him. But the best proof of his success was that he was to receive for his next opera the same fee Bellini had received for *Norma*—eight thousand lire.* In *Nabucco* (as it is usually called), Verdi found his way to the heart of the masses, and the overture and a chorus are still prime favorites in Italy. The opera was revived with great success for the Verdi centenary in 1913, and Francis Toye, most brilliant of recent Verdi biographers, considers it the most effective of his pre-*Rigoletto* operas. Like practically all his early librettos, that of *Nabucco* could be twisted into a patriotic message of courage and hope to his audiences, who were dreaming of a free and united Italy. Although this feature was played down at the *première*, it contributed to *Nabucco*'s early success. A surging vitality in the music itself accounts for its occasional revival nowadays.

Verdi, though an ardent patriot and decided anticlerical, had hitherto held himself aloof from overt expression of his allegiances. But beginning with *I Lombardi alla prima crociata* in 1843, he found himself constantly embroiled with the police and the censors, both civil and ecclesiastical, over the political implications of the librettos he chose. *I Lombardi* was ready for production when the police interfered: they discovered not only that it represented certain holy sites (fairly inevitable in any stage work about the First Crusade), but that it might be interpreted as a plea to the Pope—the violently reactionary Gregory XVI—to undertake the unification of Italy. Verdi contemptuously refused to listen to the suggestions for changing the story. At last the official demands were reduced to substituting the words "*Salve Maria*" for "*Ave Maria*," and he gave in. *I Lombardi* fired the Milanese, but left the Venetians, quite rightly, cold. Verdi had become such a box-office attraction throughout Italy, however, that Venice immediately ordered a new opera from him. Now he rode roughshod over the police, the manager of the Teatro Fenice, and his leading lady: he foisted a garbled but still inflammatory version of Hugo's *Hernani* on the *gendarmería*, a stage horn call on a shocked *régisseur* who thought it lowered the dignity of the Fenice, and a last act without solo fireworks on the soprano. Although the Venetians responded less warmly to *Ernani* than the Milanese had to *Nabucco*, it was this opera that finally made Verdi an international figure, introducing him to both London and New York. *Ernani* is notable for two reasons: it contains, in "*Ernani, involami*," the earliest Verdi

* He was advised to ask exactly this amount by Giuseppina Strepponi, whose shrewd business sense was invaluable to Verdi in this stage of his career.

aria still (for no discernible reason) frequently sung, and makes use of something closely resembling the leitmotiv, thus by its date disposing of the often repeated charge that Verdi took this device from Wagner. Oddly enough, this crude effort was revived at the Metropolitan as late as 1921.

Against the *réclame* that Verdi almost universally enjoyed after *Ernani*, he paid a price for the feverish demand for more and more operas from his pen. Seven years elapsed between its production and that of *Rigoletto* in 1851, during which time he composed ten new works and completely rewrote another. Several of these were very successful, and one of them, *Macbeth*, is interesting as an experiment that bore rich fruit in his last period. None of them, however, maintains a high level of musical interest: for all their fertile melody-making, their raw vigor, their easy translation of action into obvious musical speech, they are hopelessly flawed by their composer's lack of taste, chiefly in accepting the librettos his playwrights offered him. True, he did not accept them without demur: no one troubled himself more than Verdi in the matter of text, but until fairly late in life he was betrayed by faltering literary judgment. Passion for the universal geniuses he had, but not until he came under the sure guidance of Arrigo Boïto did he have a libretto worthy of his abounding musical gifts. Otherwise, unless he accidentally got hold of a credible, workmanlike, and stageworthy text, he set absurd makeshifts—with gusto but with little else. This situation was particularly disastrous for Verdi, who responded to the character of his book with bold truthfulness.

Although his gifts were generously recognized, Verdi was not worshiped blindly, and he had his percentage of failures. When he gave his audiences indifferent stuff, they generally refused their approval, and on occasion showed their annoyance in forthright Italian fashion. But when he gave them a *Luisa Miller*, quite the best of this transitional group of operas, they did not spare their applause. His first attempts to write expressly for the foreign stage were none too happy. *I Masnadieri*, composed for London in 1847, was received tepidly, despite the efforts of Jenny Lind to make something effective of the heroine's role. "Her Amalia," Chorley commented coldly," . . . could not have pleased had it been given by Saint Cecilia and Melpomene in one, so utterly worthless was the music." A revision of *I Lombardi*, fitted with a French text, fared scarcely better in Paris.

Verdi, to whom there always clung something of the robust common-sense Italian peasant, was nevertheless becoming a man of the world. He adapted himself easily to foreign life, and found much to admire in London and Paris. In his late thirties, he seemed cosmopolitan, but was only superficially so, and he remained Italian to the core. In 1848 he acquired a farm outside Busseto, which as the Villa Sant' Agata was to play the same role in his life that Horace's Sabine villa did in his. Doubtless he planned from the beginning to fix it up for himself and his future wife. Within a few years the house was ready to be lived in, but he did not marry for the second time until 1859. This did not mean that love was missing from his life. He had never lost track of Giuseppina Strepponi, who had done so much to salvage *Oberto* in his salad days, and in Paris, in the late forties, it seems that she became his mistress. For some inexplicable reason, they shrank from formalizing their union. Could it have been that Verdi's anticlericalism had something to do with it? Everything here is conjecture: nothing is known.

There is no mystery attaching to Verdi's close friendship with the Contessa Clara Maffei, a sensitive and intellectual woman who was, probably more than any other person until he met Boïto, the confidante of his ideas about art and life. Between the two women, each distinguished in her own way, there was no conflict as there was between Minna Wagner and Mathilde Wesendonck. Clara Maffei was Giuseppina's friend, too. The letters the Contessa received from the *maestro* and his companion contain most of what is known about Verdi's intimate life. These documents, always lively and often humorous, are open and candid. Unlike the Wagner correspondence, they do not have to be deciphered with the aid of special knowledge.

In 1850, Verdi's gestational period came abruptly to an end. That year, having been commissioned to write an opera for Venice, he was feverishly casting about for new material, turning over and rejecting such diverse plots as *King Lear*, *Hamlet*, Schiller's *Don Carlos*, and the elder Dumas' *Kean*. What he really wanted was a Spanish play called *El Trovador*, but at the moment his librettist could find no copy of it. As a last choice, he took up a second Hugo play, no doubt musing that *Ernani* had been the vehicle to spread his fame outside the peninsula. This time he invited censor trouble: *Le Roi s'amuse* had been banned in Paris after only one performance, partly for political reasons and partly because it read like a paean to vice. Verdi, undaunted by the past history of the play, and sensible only of its operatic adaptability, had his own tame librettist, Francesco Maria Piave, make an Italian text, which was christened *La Maledizione*, and submitted to the Venetian censor. This functionary tossed it back as though it were indeed an accursed thing, with "profound regret that the poet Piave and the celebrated Maestro Verdi should have found no better field for their talents than the revolting immorality and obscene triviality of . . . *La Maledizione*. . . ." After a series of tragicofarcical episodes that would in themselves make a good libretto, Verdi won the battle merely by changing the names of the characters, and *La Maledizione*, renamed *Rigoletto* after its jester-villain-hero, finally reached La Fenice on March 11, 1851.

When these vicissitudes culminated in *Rigoletto*'s overwhelming success, Verdi must have felt repaid for his obstinate persistence in getting past the censor. Perhaps he had even felt doubt about the public's reception of what he considered a revolutionary work. It may come as a shock to the modern operagoer, but Verdi actually conceived of *Rigoletto* as being free of those arias and tableaux that had for so long been the chief stock in trade of the musical stage. In composing *Rigoletto*, he made the dramatic appropriateness of the music his paramount consideration, and if we are to believe him, there is not a single haphazard bar in the entire work. Like Gluck, like Rossini, like Wagner, who fought the same battle with varying degrees of success, Verdi was trying to get away from the old, hard-dying idea that an opera is a parade of set numbers held together by an often exceedingly tenuous thread of story. This is borne out by his reaction to the censor's proposal that he adapt the music of *Rigoletto* to an altered libretto. "If I am told that my music will fit this version as well as the other," he wrote, "I reply that such an argument is utterly beyond me; my music—good or bad as it may be—is written in no casual manner. I invariably try to give it a character of its own. . . ." If some soprano dared to sing such a stock piece as "*Caro nome*" as Verdi, in the score, plainly asks that it be sung, it might then emerge as a moving revelation of character, a soliloquy contributing to the drama, and not merely as just another bravura aria. Even the quartet, now (because of its popularity and the way it is sung to the gallery) calculated to interrupt the action, flows inevitably from the action. Although the sins of generations of singers have established a bad tradition that makes it impossible to hope for a presentation of *Rigoletto* following the composer's intentions, the opera itself is deathless. For even if the caprices of fashion were to banish it from the stage, it would be kept alive, until its inevitable resuscitation on the boards, by renditions of "*Caro nome,*" the quartet, and the wanton Duke's "*La donna è mobile*" on the barrel organs and tinny pianos of the world. No one can claim that this is great music; equally, no one can deny that it is universal music.

From *Nabucco* to *Rigoletto*, Verdi had produced anywhere from one to three operas a year, but now he refused to be hurried. A librettist had been found to adapt *El Trovador*, and Verdi retired to the Villa Sant' Agata with Giuseppina to wait for the Italian text to be delivered. Meanwhile, in June, 1851, his mother died— an event, it has been conjectured, that influenced his conception of the gypsy mother, Azucena, in his new opera, the text of which was in his hands by the end of the year. Although *Il Trovatore* had not been commissioned, he completed the score in twenty-eight days. With many opera houses clamoring for something new from him, Verdi calmly locked it away, and went to Paris on an extended business trip. The management of the Opéra wanted a Verdi *première*, but had to be content with a contract allowing him two full years for completing the work. News that his father was seriously ill sent him rushing back home. Only when the old man was fully recovered—he survived fifteen years more into ripe old age— did Verdi set about deciding what opera house he would prefer for *Il Trovatore*. This time there was no trouble with the censors. Perhaps they had as much difficulty figuring out the plot as we do today. At any rate, the coveted honor fell to Rome, and there, despite the Tiber being in flood, it was presented to a cheering audience on January 19, 1853.

"To this day many persons have not found out the right and wrong betwixt the false child roasted by the gipsy and mistaken vengeance and the true one, spared, and mistaken, and flung into all manner of miserable dilemmas, and at last beheaded, in order to give the avenging Fury an opportunity of saying to her noble persecutor, '*He was thy brother!*'" This sentence, written in 1855 by Henry Fothergill Chorley, is as clear an exposition, as sharp a criticism, as we are ever likely to have of the exasperating libretto of *Il Trovatore*. To this frenzied puzzle, Verdi fitted some of the baldest, most vigorous, and most blatantly melodramatic tunes ever written. In it, he taps his least golden, if most prodigal and glittering, vein without let or surcease. The melodies of *Il Trovatore* are, indeed, the fool's gold of song. Here, without losing sight of his dramatic aims altogether, he swamps them in catchy tunes. Not even the best-intentioned artists (for there must be some) could prevent an opera containing "*Stride la vampa*," "*Il balen*," the *Miserere*, and "*Ai nostri monti*" from becoming a singers' carnival. The "Anvil" Chorus, once an interesting sound novelty, is no longer even that—it is merely ludicrous. To hear *Il Trovatore* today is like hearing a collection of overscored folk songs sung with unnecessary energy. It follows, then, that this opera, though inferior to *Rigoletto* in almost every respect, enjoys precisely the same sort of immortality.

For clinching his fame, 1853 was Verdi's banner year. In February, 1852, it seems that he was present at the Paris *première* of the younger Dumas' scandal-provoking drama of a consumptive courtesan—*La Dame aux camélias*. He was deeply impressed by it, and little less than a year later, about the time *Il Trovatore* was being produced, selected it as the subject of an opera he had promised to the Fenice. He retired at once to Sant' Agata, and though he described the work of composing it as "real penance," finished *La Traviata* in less than a month. Exactly six weeks after the triumphant presentation of *Il Trovatore*, he saw his version of *Camille* jeered off the boards of the Fenice. That the critics attributed its failure to Venice's keen sense of the ridiculous did not assuage Verdi's wounded feelings: the soprano was too bouncingly healthy for a credible consumptive, the tenor was hoarse, and the baritone —with a strange lack of historical foresight—did not realize that he had been given the biggest plum in the opera. With unruffled dignity, Verdi took the score back to Sant' Agata, and rewrote five of the weaker numbers. On May 6, 1854, the Venetians had a chance to reverse their judgment. At the first production of *La Traviata*, the use of contemporary costumes had upset the audience, so at the revival the costumes were set back to the time of Louis

XIII, though the heroine was incongruously permitted to retain her fashionable Parisian gowns. An excellent cast was found to fit the new costumes, and the refurbished version won great and immediate approval. Within two years it was the rage of London, Paris, New York, and St. Petersburg; in 1857, a version in English was successful in London.

Both *La Dame aux camélias* and *La Traviata* were considered pornographic in the days of their youth: aged, they have become delicate period pieces to which no moral stigma can be attached. It is clear, however, that part of the original success of *Traviata* was due to its being seized upon as a symbol of moral rebellion. After the social hubbub had died down, the music quietly asserted itself as a sufficient reason for endurance. In *Traviata*, Verdi wrote what has been called a "chamber opera": in contrast to the booming heroics of *Rigoletto* and *Trovatore*, it is gauged to a credible human scale. *La Traviata* is not melodrama—it is real tragedy, even if not of the most profound sort. It needs no special self-hypnosis, no suspension of disbelief, to be enjoyed as a real drama in musical terms. Artistically, too, *Traviata* was a new departure for Verdi. The melody, bubbling up as profusely as ever, is more subtle and thoughtful, less blatantly catchy than that of his earlier successes. Not that there are no epidemic numbers in the score. But even the giddy "*Sempre libera*" and the folksy "*Di Provenza il mar*" are free of the indisputable cheapness that mars some of his most effective early tunes, while the soprano aria "*Ah! fors è lui*" has a wistful, meditative note that Verdi rarely achieves. Even the bustling drinking song in Act I is gay, sparkling music without the slightest trace of vulgarity. In *Traviata*, Verdi seemed at last to have learned the powerful uses of understatement.

With the revision of *Traviata* off his hands, Verdi spent most of 1853 at his country place, devoting his artistic leisure wholly to plans for an opera based on *King Lear*, a project he played with until his death, actually composing some music for it.* But with the coming of autumn, he bethought himself of his contract with the Opéra. The promised libretto by Scribe had not materialized, so he went to Paris to see what all the delay was about. In the first place, he found that the date for the opera had been moved ahead

* These fragments were unfortunately destroyed after Verdi's death, by his expressed wish.

so that it would be first performed at the Exposition Universelle of 1855. Scribe was both dilatory and insulting: the long overdue libretto did not reach Verdi's hands until December 31, and thereafter Scribe refused to make any changes in it, however needed. Verdi, who smarted under such treatment, and who was annoyed at the cold response of the Opéra management to his legitimate requests, eventually pieced together, in *Les Vêpres siciliennes*, something that satisfied neither himself nor, in the long run, his public. The libretto, built around a Sicilian St. Bartholomew's that, after six hundred years, still rankled in the French memory, also tactlessly insulted Italy (and Verdi, the Italian nationalist) by making the hero a run-of-the-mill melodramatic conspirator. Yet, despite hurt feelings all around and the caustic comments of a powerful bloc of French musicians who thought that one of themselves should have had the honor of composing the opera for the Exposition, *Les Vêpres* was a resounding success. Presented on June 13, 1855, it ran through fifty consecutive performances at the Opéra. Translated into Italian, it failed in Italy. *I Vespri siciliani*, though it boasts the most effective overture Verdi ever composed, a couple of fine arias and duets, and some very attractive ballet music, is in the main a distressing medley, and has passed almost completely from popular favor. There was something more than mere Teutonic contempt in Wagner's lofty reference to "*I Vespri siciliani* and other nights of carnage."

After the *première* of *Les Vêpres*, Verdi waited a year before signing a contract for a new opera. Then, with a strange blindness to true dramatic credibility and effectiveness, he chose another melancholy and completely absurd play by the same Spaniard who had concocted *El Trovador*. Neither Piave's nor his own doctoring was able to make a good libretto out of the vicissitudes of a Genoese Oliver Cromwell. First produced at the Fenice on March 12, 1857, *Simone Boccanegra* was a flat failure in spite of several "strong" numbers that Verdi, with his usual canniness, had placed at strategic points in the opera. As he himself had a special fondness for *Simone*, he tried time and again to force it on the public, but unsuccessfully. At last, more than twenty years after its first production, he and his friend Boïto put their heads together over the problem, but solving it was beyond them. Indeed, as Boïto had feared, they made "confusion worse confounded." But Verdi revised the music drastically and, as he was then at the height of his matured powers, produced a beautifully workmanlike score. In addition, he introduced into Act II a whole new scene, which, though it slows up the action intolerably, is musically the most powerful in the opera. This gloomy hodgepodge was again tried out on the public in 1881, and won moderate success. Although it is occasionally revived— Lawrence Tibbett was a superb Simone in a modern Metropolitan staging—it will never win a place among the Verdi perennials.

Five months after the original *Simone* fiasco, Verdi drained the cup of humiliation to its dregs when the audience of the little provincial town of Rimini turned a completely cold shoulder to something he had pieced together especially for the opening of its new opera house. *Aroldo* is a tasteless patchwork rewriting of a tasteless early effort called *Stiffelio*: both are now rightly forgotten. Rejected by these bumpkins, Verdi may well have felt, at least temporarily, that he had lost the golden touch. Therefore, he was doubly cautious in selecting the libretto for an opera he had promised the San Carlo at Naples, finally choosing one by Scribe that had already proved its stageworthiness, having been successfully set by Auber. As soon as he received its Italian text, he set to work, and by the end of 1857 completed what must have been an unusually well-integrated dramatic work. Even before he set sail for Naples, however, he had stepped down the august victim of *Un Ballo in maschera* from a king to a duke on advice from the censors. But it was when he arrived there that his troubles really began. There had been an attempt to assassinate Napoleon III, and though *Un Ballo* was to be given in a capital of the Bourbons (who had every reason to loathe a Bonaparte), monarchical solidarity clamped down on anything that might be interpreted as an attack on established authority. The censors demanded a thorough pasteurizing of the libretto, and as this would have meant rewriting all the music, Verdi refused. News of his stand percolated through the town, and made him a hero of the revolutionary cause. "*Viva* Verdi" became a war cry, more particularly when the Neapolitans figured out that the letters of the composer's surname were the initials of *V*ittorio *E*mmanuele *rè* *d'I*talia, and that when they were shouting for Verdi they were secretly shouting for a united Italy under the popular Sardinian monarch. The inflexible attitude of the Neapolitan censors forced the composer to turn to

Rome, where he was told the authorities were more lenient.* He had been misinformed. The same agonizing trouble began all over again. This time he gave in: the duke became an English count, and the locale was transferred to the wilds of seventeenth-century Massachusetts—changes that undid much of Verdi's careful work in selecting a good story and making his music fit just that. However, the emasculated version of *Un Ballo in maschera* was duly produced at the Teatro Apollo on February 17, 1859, and voted a tremendous hit.

Un Ballo will never be a loved opera: it is too long and unwieldy, and the music is by no means constantly engrossing. Some of its characters are strongly delineated, Oscar, the gay and foppish page, being a particularly brilliant and original creation. Indeed, the entire score is strewn with masterstrokes of technique, the harmonic texture is more subtle than is usual with Verdi in this stage of his career, and there are individual numbers, especially the great baritone aria of accusation, "*Eri tu*," that stand beside the best he ever composed. The trouble with *Un Ballo*, which is not without a certain grandeur of total effect, is that it is constantly foundering in the manifest absurdities of the stage action. It is, of course, not uncommon for an opera to triumph over a muddled and preposterous libretto, but to do so it must make amends with a wealth of engaging melody that *Un Ballo* lacks.

Little more than two months after the *première* of *Un Ballo*, Verdi finally led Giuseppina Strepponi to the altar. The reasons for his taking this step at all are as much guesswork as his reasons for not having taken it long before. They were getting along in years— Verdi was forty-five, Giuseppina two years younger—and it seems possible that she, as a devout Catholic, wished to square her accounts. Also, there was malicious gossip in Busseto and the surrounding countryside about Verdi and his woman, though it is hardly probable that such pettiness would have moved a man of Verdi's Yankee individualism had not Barezzi, the father of his first wife, been foremost among the indignant expostulators. Verdi was not only in Barezzi's debt, but was also extremely fond of him, and had him as a permanent guest at Sant' Agata. A desire to

---

* To do so, he had to repudiate his contract with the San Carlo, which promptly sued him for not giving them a satisfactory opera. He replied in a countersuit, suing them for not staging the opera he had provided.

smooth things all around must have prompted Verdi and Giuseppina to slip away like elopers, and regularize their relationship. The ceremony took place at Collonge, a little Swiss village on the shore of the Lake of Geneva, on April 29, 1859—a historic day in more ways than one, for while the marriage was taking place, the Austrians were crossing the Ticino, thus setting the stage for the penultimate scenes in the struggle for Italian unity. For several years, the peninsula was in a turmoil, and among those who found their plans interrupted was Verdi, who temporarily suspended his usual activities, and enjoyed, despite some alarums, the pleasant life of a country squire.

One of the few heroes of the prosperous lord of Sant' Agata was Cavour, the architect of that united Italy of which Garibaldi (a figure out of Verdian melodrama) was the master mason. When Cavour, summoning the first Italian parliament to meet in Turin in 1861, asked his friend Verdi to stand for Busseto, the composer protested, but the patriot could not refuse. He was elected, and served faithfully if without distinction—a stanch middle-of-the-roader—for four years. His sole recorded* act of statecraft was to lay before Cavour, who unhappily died shortly afterward, an elaborate plan for free musical education. Until April, 1861, this was the only outward sign that Verdi was still actively interested in music. He seemed absorbed in his squire's duties, his broad acres, his blooded livestock, the large staff of farm workers for whom he entertained a warm affection. But those who think these years lost are mistaken: this once pale and rather sickly man was laying by (as it turned out) a store of health and vigor for the forty years that remained to him. It was, at least in part, due to the peace and fresh air of Sant' Agata that Verdi was able, at the age of eighty, to electrify the world with one of the supreme masterpieces of opera.

In April, 1861, the managers of the Imperial Theater at St. Petersburg asked Verdi to write an opera for them. He had a story—unfortunately, another of his Spanish massacres—in mind, and accepted eagerly. By January of the following year, he was able to leave for Russia with a complete sketch for *La Forza del destino*. The long trip to St. Petersburg was in vain, for the illness

---

* Data for the period 1859–67 are scanty, for during those years Verdi neglected to make those copies of his correspondence which are the chief source of personal information about him.

of one of the principal singers forced a postponement of the *premiere* until autumn. Agreeing to return, Verdi went to Paris on no apparent mission except, perhaps, to see whether, as he once said, the Parisians were madder than ever. He went often to Rossini's famous Saturday nights, meeting there an erudite youngster of twenty by the name of Arrigo Boïto, who was interested both in composing opera and in the improvement of librettos. So impressed was he with Boïto that when an invitation came from London to compose something for the Universal Exhibition of 1862, Verdi asked him to write the words for a hymn of the nations that he finally decided upon as his offering. He heard this successfully sung in London, and then hurried to Sant' Agata to complete the scoring of *La Forza del destino*. With this heavy job done, the tireless man, with his equally tireless wife, returned to St. Petersburg, where the reception accorded to *La Forza* on November 10, 1862, was as chilly as the weather. The Russian nationalist composers had plotted against this foreign work with considerable success, and Verdi had to be content with a decoration from Alexander II rather than popular applause. Undaunted, he packed up and took his opera to Madrid, where it had a much warmer welcome.

La Forza del destino, like *Don Carlos*, which followed it five years later, is a transitional opera, and as such lacks the dramatic forcefulness of certain earlier works, though it has moments of great expressiveness and concentration. Unlike *Don Carlos* it is lavish in ready lyric appeal, but to judge from these operas, it would seem that Verdi's sure-fire theatricality was ebbing. Verdi has begun to husband his resources with the care of a man uncertain of his wealth. The harmonies are more carefully considered, less stereotyped; the orchestration is more varied and imaginative. Yet, because Verdi is not completely at home in these new surroundings, both works are a trifle stilted. Less and less often revived, *La Forza* and *Don Carlos* are now known chiefly by a few stock numbers that without too much incongruity might fit into such operas as *Rigoletto* and *Il Trovatore*. Such are "*Solenne in quest' ora*," the richly emotional duet from *La Forza* that Caruso and Antonio Scotti, a generation ago, sang on every gramophone in the land, and "*Pace, pace*," the big soprano *scena* from the same opera. These are matched in *Don Carlos* by such numbers as the mezzo-soprano's powerful "*O don fatale*" and the baritone's gloomy and impressive "*O Carlo, ascolta.*"

The years between the production of *La Forza del destino* in 1862 and that of *Aïda*, almost a decade later, were not happy ones for Verdi. The public, possibly puzzled by the experimental element in his new stage works, gave them but qualified approval, while a revision of *Macbeth* on which he had counted heavily was a failure after two weeks. The story of the production of *Don Carlos* makes sad reading. It was ordered by the Opéra, and a pompous, highly rhetorical libretto supplied by two French librettists. Verdi, with the best will in the world, set out to write a true French grand opera in the highfalutin style Meyerbeer had made so popular. It was produced in 1867, just when events in Italy had made Italians unpopular in France. Verdi, who was sensible of this animus, tried to withdraw from his contract, but the management would not agree. When *Don Carlos* was given on March 11, the Empress Eugénie, said to have been annoyed by the libertarian ideas propounded by one of the characters in the opera, turned her back on the stage. Society took the hint. The critics, though accusing Verdi of imitating Meyerbeer and Wagner, were on the whole fair to the opera. But Verdi was in no mood to have his disappointment assuaged by their praise. He was grief-stricken by his father's death early that year, and in July was stunned by Barezzi's. His own health had been none too good, and finally, as if to submerge his personal woes, the outcome of the war of 1867 had left him disillusioned and numb. Italy's payment had been half a loaf—to Verdi, a cheap reward after so much bloodshed and strife.

In 1868, Rossini died, and Verdi, who had done much to destroy the conventions of the Rossinian stage, saw the event as a national tragedy. He observed gloomily that Manzoni—who on the basis of the excellent novel *I Promessi sposi* was then considered Italy's greatest man of letters—was his country's sole remaining glory. He at once bestirred himself to honor the dead man fittingly. Oddly enough, he projected the idea of a Mass, to be sung only once and then deposited in the archives of the Liceo at Bologna. It was to be a community affair, the production of the pious pens of thirteen leading Italian composers: we should describe them nowadays as twelve nonentities and Verdi. Naturally, the scheme fell through, and Rossini rested in peace.

In 1869, Verdi received the oddest request of his life. Ismail Pasha, Khedive of Egypt, had decided to signalize the passing of the first ship through the Suez Canal by staging a specially written grand opera at Cairo. Ignoring Wagner, who might conceivably have fabricated a vast epic of the twilight of Isis, Osiris, and Ptah, he set his royal mind on Verdi, who twice refused, saying that he had no appetite for further composition. The French librettist Du Locle, who represented the Khedive's intermediary, thereupon sent Verdi an outline of a possible Egyptian plot. Verdi took one look at it, and agreed to negotiate. His terms for coming out of retirement were stiff: 150,000 francs and the rights for all countries except Egypt. Ismail, who was a spendthrift, blithely told all concerned to go ahead. As the *première* was scheduled for January, 1871, there was no time to lose. The opera was well under way when the Franco-Prussian War broke out. As one of the important collaborators in the concoction of the libretto was detained in Paris for the duration of the war, *Aïda* was not staged until December 24, 1871.

Verdi did not go to Cairo for *Aïda*'s turbulently successful opening, but six weeks later, at La Scala, he witnessed the enthusiasm it could evoke. Within a few years it had achieved that universal popularity it has never relinquished. It is too bad that Verdi's delight in this acclaim was somewhat spoiled by the absurd accusation that *Aïda* consciously imitates Wagner. In cold fact, it grew directly out of Verdi's own past, and might be note for note what it is if Wagner had never lived. Traces of Meyerbeer at his most sumptuous grand it undoubtedly has, but by 1872 the music critics smelled Wagner in the most unlikely places. Some of them have never got over the habit.

Aïda is not only a synonym for "grand" opera, but is very probably the most popular opera ever composed. Although, as a wit has said, "You can't judge Egypt by *Aïda*," you can judge the essential Verdi by it. It does not contain his best music, but is by far the cleverest evening's entertainment he ever devised. Once more the melodies flow untrammeled, and a simple and sufficiently credible story is told in broad dramatic idiom. It has the appeal of a pageant: the triumph of a general, the solemn march of the priests of Ptah, the moonlit banks of the Nile, a subterranean crypt—the very scenes themselves contribute mightily to *Aïda*'s tremendous drawing power. The music may not be psychologically searching, but it has a relevance to the shifting character of the stage action that would be difficult to better. There is not a dull moment in the entire opera. It is by turns exciting, moving, and simply absorbing as a spectacle. "Big" arias and concerted numbers are scattered through the score with the prodigality of youth controlled by the firm judgment of mature experience. There is nothing experimental in *Aïda*; it has none of the questing, groping quality of a transitional work. Far from being opera in a new genre, it is merely the quintessential product of the tradition Verdi was exploiting in *Rigoletto* and *Trovatore*. The simple, sure-fire "*Celeste Aïda*," coming early in the first act, is a superbly effective stock aria of obvious ancestry that wins any audience right away. Nor are there any violent shocks in store. The music says what it has to say with real mastery of harmony and orchestration, but the melodic element predominates throughout. In *Aïda*, the human voice is still king. A thousand subtle touches give the score a slightly Oriental tang—one shudders to think what the composer of *Trovatore* might have done with this coloring. If Verdi had written nothing after *Aïda*, it would have been impossible not to say that he had fully realized his potentialities.

Verdi was now almost sixty years old, and there must have been many, possibly even including the composer himself, who felt that he had crowned a long, useful, and brilliant career with the creation of so stupendous a work as *Aïda*. In 1873, however, while loitering in Naples, he surprised his intimates by tossing off a delightful and craftsmanlike string quartet. A few months later, the death of Manzoni stirred him as deeply as had Rossini's. This time he had learned his lesson: instead of delegating parts of a Requiem Mass to various composers, he sat down and wrote a complete one himself, working in part from the sketches he had made for the abortive Rossini commemoration. He himself conducted the first performance of the "Manzoni" Requiem at San Marco's, Milan, on May 22, 1874. It was as successful throughout Italy as *Aïda*—and for much the same reasons. It is theatrical, full-bodied, noisy, sweepingly melodic, more like a sincere and impulsive paean than anything else. Some sections are catchy and even alluring, but only professional Protestants could deplore the high spirits of this Requiem Mass. In judging it, we must enter into the Latin temper, and forget Bach and all such solemn fellows. We can then admit that the "Manzoni" Requiem is magnificent.

After the Requiem, for thirteen years no new work came from Verdi's pen. During this time, he did not immure himself at Sant' Agata. He traveled widely, at first to conduct the Requiem, and later to supervise new stagings of his operas. Once he went as far afield as England, and Paris saw him often. After several years of silence, it was generally believed that he would never again compose for the stage, nor was Verdi disposed to contradict this assumption, most probably because he shared it himself. But in 1879, his publisher, his favorite conductor, and the Contessa Maffei conspired to rouse him from the lethargy of a prosperous old age. Not for a moment did they admit that he had written himself out: their job was to get him started again. Boïto was their man, despite the fact that he had once thoughtlessly belittled Verdi. With the best resources of his early radicalism assimilated, and with an unrivaled sense of the libretto, Boïto seemed to them the spark that would surely ignite Verdi. Three days after the two were brought together, Boïto handed him the sketch for a libretto based on Shakespeare's *Othello*. Verdi hesitated, but by the end of the year it seems certain that he had decided to compose his second Shakespearean opera. Its composition occupied him, off and on, for seven years, during which time Boïto practically became a permanent house guest at Sant' Agata. The revised version of *Simone Boccanegra*, produced in 1881, was the first public earnest of one of the most fruitful collaborations in the history of music.

Verdi, always a conscientious artisan, outdid himself in *Otello*—no detail of costuming and scenery was too insignificant for his attention. The collaboration ran smoothly except when Boïto was quoted in the newspapers as saying that he regretted not being able to set the libretto of *Iago* (as it was then called) himself. Verdi at once offered to give Boïto back his libretto, and they were not reconciled until it was made clear that Boïto had been misquoted. Meanwhile, public interest in Verdi's rebirth was nearing fever pitch, and all sorts of wild guesses were being hazarded as to the nature of his new opera. Some people were annoyed because he had chosen a subject that, they claimed, Rossini had already immortalized. Others merely said that he was too old to write a good opera. On November 1, 1886, Verdi wrote to his collaborator: "Dear Boïto— It is finished. Here's a health to us . . . (and also to Him . . .) Good-by. G. Verdi." On February 5, 1887, all doubts as to the youthful creative vigor of the seventy-four-year-old composer were dispersed when *Otello* was given at La Scala. Its success was tremendous and instantaneous, and for once critics and public vied with each other in acclaiming the composer.

He who goes to *Otello* and listens only to the music misses half the opera's greatness. Here is a perfect fusion of music and libretto, and we must think of it as the creation of two miraculously coalesced talents. It is as plainly by Boïto-Verdi as *The Mikado* is by Gilbert-Sullivan. As Shaw once pointed out, *Othello* as Shakespeare wrote it is already very like an Italian opera book, so Boïto's task was not so difficult as it might have been if Verdi had set him to adapting *King Lear*. With a superb sense of what was usable on the operatic stage—he had himself composed to his own libretto the beautiful but now rarely performed* *Mefistofele*—he took just those relevant parts of *Othello* and really adapted, not merely translated, them for Verdi's use. Magnificent in his good sense, he sacrificed the first act. From various Shakespearean plays he pieced together a villainous credo for Iago—a departure that infuriated academic literary critics, but which remains one of the most effective moments in opera. Verdi accepted the challenge of a masterly libretto by mating it to a score luminous with precisely those qualities that many of his otherwise fine early scores conspicuously lack—unfaltering good taste, melodic subtlety, expressive harmonic texture. *Otello* moves on as a relentless continuum: it comes close to the Wagnerian ideal of an opera without arias, though rising to moments of arresting poignancy in Desdemona's pathetic "*Salce, salce*" and tremulous "*Ave Maria*." It has no barrel-organ tunes, but is instinct with melody of true dramatic pertinence. Lacking the obvious appeal of *Aïda* or several of Puccini's tear jerkers, it nevertheless gives proof of an ageless vitality. In 1938, for the second time in its history, the Metropolitan Opera House opened its season with a most successful performance of *Otello*.

The extraordinary success of *Otello* momentarily pulled Verdi from a slough of despond in which he was foundering. In July,

---

* In the United States. In Italy, after failing at first, it achieved, and has maintained, tremendous popularity.

1886, the Contessa Maffei, for forty-four years his most intimate friend, had died. It was not strange that the old man's friends were dying off, but it was more than a little odd that Verdi, who was so renowned for his sturdy common sense, reacted anything but stoically to these losses. He indulged his grief, and became edgy and morose. In 1889, he squelched a plan to celebrate the fiftieth anniversary of his first opera, though the same year he lent his name to a Beethoven festival at Bonn, remarking that he disliked festivals and such, and was agreeing only because Beethoven was involved. In 1892, however, the centenary of Rossini's birth enlisted his active co-operation: he led the famous prayer from *Mosè in Egitto*. It was his last public appearance as a conductor.

And yet, Verdi was not through. As early as the week following the *première* of *Otello*, there was talk of his considering a comic opera, possibly based on *Don Quixote*. Within the next couple of years, Shakespeare's conception of Falstaff was chosen as the focal point of Boïto's libretto and, it was hoped, Verdi's new opera. By 1890, Verdi had begun to work at the music, but was strangely coy about both his progress and his ultimate intentions. When he finally admitted that he would finish *Falstaff*, he indicated that he might have it performed only privately at Sant' Agata. When at last he was wheedled into giving the new work to La Scala, he kept the right of withdrawing it from production if he chose. His own illness and Giuseppina's delayed the completion, but finally, just before his seventy-ninth birthday, it was finished. A public largely unaware that Verdi, more than fifty years earlier, had, under the most tragic circumstances, produced a *buffa* work waited in breathless anticipation of the master's "first" comic opera. It was produced at La Scala on February 9, 1893. Verdi and Giuseppina were in the audience: more than half a century before, she had sung in his first opera.

Richard Strauss called *Falstaff* "one of the greatest masterpieces of all time." Most musicians agree with him about this comic complement of *Otello*. In many respects, it is a far more remarkable creation than its tragic predecessor, which, after all, was but the last and best of a long line of serious operas. It is one of the wonders of music that a tired old man, with grief in his heart, struck the most mellow of comic notes in a work that stands shoulder to shoulder with *The Barber of Seville*, the epitome of youth's conception of comedy, and *Die Meistersinger*, the great character-istic comedy of middle age. In *Falstaff*, the extreme frivolity of the one and the rancorous satire of the other are alike missing: in it, we meet, instead, the deep, ripe humor that rises from a seasoned understanding of life. A glowing wit, rare as an orient pearl in music, matches the exquisite patterning of Boïto's libretto—for here again the collaboration is perfect. *Falstaff* is, as is quite proper, slighter than *Otello*, but it is even more erudite musically: to its fashioning Verdi brought an encyclopedic understanding of tech-nical device, and used it with the sensitive taste born of more than half a century of experience. For example, the perfectly correct eight-voice fugue sung by the principals at the end of the last act uses this so-called dryest of musical forms to distil the very essence of gaiety. The perfection of *Falstaff* gives point to Verdi's statement that he had been waiting twenty years for a comic-opera libretto. The delicious score ranges from the broad humorous passages of Falstaff himself through the exquisitely felt music of the lovers, and includes such a delightfully bold departure as the almost De-bussyan pages given to the masquerade in Windsor Forest. But, for reasons that are by no means easy to fathom, *Falstaff* has never become a popular opera. Possibly its skimming over of mere plot interest is against it. Possibly it is just too subtle for the big spaces of a great opera house. It is worth noting that Verdi himself feared that *Falstaff* was too intimate for La Scala. At any rate, it is an obligation to keep this masterpiece in the living repertoire.

Although Verdi lived eight years after completing *Falstaff*, his career was practically over. For a few years he led an active if uncreative life. In 1894, for example, he attended the Paris *pre-mière* of *Falstaff*. He wintered in either Milan or Genoa, in July going to Montecatini for the cure. For the most part, however, he remained at Sant' Agata, busying himself with the trivia of man-aging an estate, playing with his dogs, working out plans for his pet philanthropy—a home for aged musicians in Milan—and talk-ing over old times with Giuseppina. On November 14, 1897, the last of these distractions was denied him: his faithful and loving companion died. After that, though he still had the strength to arrange for performance a few religious compositions,* it was evi-

* To the thirty-one-year-old Arturo Toscanini fell the honor of conducting their first Italian performance in 1898.

dent that he was failing. Outwardly his health seemed rugged: loneliness was his disease. In July, 1900, King Humbert was assassinated, and Queen Margherita wrote a simple little prayer in his memory that for a moment warmed the chilled embers of Verdi's artistic imagination. He sketched a setting of it—the last music he ever wrote. In January, 1901, he suffered a stroke of apoplexy in Milan, and lingered in some agony until the twenty-seventh day of that month. Boïto is authority for the statement that he fought death until the very moment he ceased to breathe.

Chapter XVIII

Johannes Brahms

(Hamburg, May 7, 1833–April 3, 1897, Vienna)

Less than half a century after the death of Johannes Brahms, the phrase "the three B's"—Bach, Beethoven, and Brahms—has such wide currency that it no longer evokes surprise or protest. When Hans von Bülow first sprang the phrase, he drew a double wrath upon himself: there were those who thought that he was taking a belated revenge on Wagner for a personal injury, and there were those who thought that he was violating the loftiest canons of his profession (as well as ordinary common sense) by raising a parvenu to the supreme fellowship of the greatest masters. A third party dryly concluded that he was merely giving a friend a hand up. Few—and least of all, Brahms himself—took the bracketing seriously. Today the only comment it causes is, among dissenters, a pursing of the lips or a shrug of the shoulders, but though they may consider it fantastic, they cannot laugh it off. For Brahms' reputation has grown vast, and his cohorts have waxed numerous and vociferous. In point of fact, Von Bülow's words contain, if interpreted sanely, an indisputable truth: that is, if they are taken to mean that Brahms' conscious artistic genealogy was predominantly classical, no one can refute them. In his persistent and masterly use of counterpoint, Brahms was among Bach's fairest children; in his conception of the larger musical forms he stemmed from, and added little to, Beethoven. These are facts, and not in the realm of controversy. But only the most perfervid Brahmsian can accept without question the other implication of "the three B's": that Brahms is one of the three greatest composers who ever lived.

One of the best antidotes to an overestimate of Brahms that can end only by doing him a grave disservice is to read what he had to say about himself. "I know very well," he remarked in his old age, "the place I shall one day have in musical history: the place that Cherubini once had, and has today." Brahms' modesty was excessive. He declared that he and his contemporaries made a living out of composing only because the public had forgotten so much of the music of the past. Once, after playing Bach's Violin Sonata in C major with Joachim, he threw to the floor his own sonata in the same key, exclaiming, "After that, how could anyone play such stuff as this?" Possibly few great composers have not had these moments of feeling small beside Bach, but Brahms also had a perhaps exaggerated reverence for masters whose genius did not, at best, exceed his own. Witness his almost servile remark about Mendelssohn: "I'd give all my compositions if I could have written such a piece as the 'Hebrides' Overture!" He thought of himself as a good composer whose duty it was to work as hard as possible on what ideas came to him, and to publish only what dissatisfied him least. He was pre-eminently an artisan, with an almost medieval feeling for his craft, and quite content to let the products of his workshop speak for themselves. Such a man with such stern ideals could only be embarrassed by Von Bülow's ballyhoo. Everything that was deepest in his character revolted against claiming too fair a kingdom for himself or aiming at too easy a success.

Although born in the crowded slums of a vast commercial city, Brahms was a peasant of the peasants, and so he remained all his life. This does much to explain the temperance of his ambitions, the obstinacy of his ideals, and the rather static quality of his genius. Even when his fame made him the intimate of royalty, he never by a single action showed that he had "gone up in the world." He remained true to his own past and his family's. His father had come to Hamburg from the barren and sparsely populated marshlands of the Elbe estuary; his mother was a proletarian of the same great city. Johann Jakob Brahms, a stupid musical Jack-of-all-trades who eventually attained the eminence of first double-bass at the municipal theater, at the age of twenty-four married Johanna Nissen, a woman of some superiority, but seventeen years his senior, ugly, crippled, of irascible and dominating temper. This inevitably mismated pair had three children, of whom the composer was the second. Separation was the foreordained end of such a marriage, but Brahms, who was deeply devoted to his mother, managed to stave it off until 1864, when the jealousy of the seventy-five-year-old woman drove her husband from the house.

We do not know whether it was Johann Jakob's undoubted passion for music, or merely a desire to add to the family income, that made him decide upon music as a career for Johannes. It does not seem that he had any grandiose plans for the boy: he envisioned him, almost certainly, as walking approximately in his own footsteps. He undertook his son's musical education himself, soon exhausting his own limited knowledge. As the Brahmses could not afford a piano, at the age of eight Johannes was sent to a modest little pedagogue to learn that useful instrument. He was so apt that within a year or so he was much in demand in what his cautious biographers gloss over as "humble places of entertainment" or "sailors' taverns." These were brothels, and according to Brahms himself, he was the darling of the prostitutes, who thought it fun to try to arouse his immature emotions. It is impossible to overestimate the influence of these odd experiences on Brahms' sexual make-up: he depended all his life on prostitutes for physical release, and withdrew from a relationship with a decent woman as soon as an overt amorous element showed itself. The "women in Brahms' life" are anonymous.

Little Johannes was not exclusively a redlight-district virtuoso. He attended the local schools, such as they were, and continued his musical studies. In 1843, his teacher pled with Eduard Marxsen, Hamburg's leading music master, to take the boy. Marxsen consented reluctantly to give him an occasional lesson, and Brahms made his public debut at a concert arranged to defray the costs of this more expensive instruction. He played, besides a few solos, the piano part in chamber works by Mozart and Beethoven. Marxsen, finding him a willing slave to music, gradually undertook not only to perfect his piano technique, but to teach him composition. Shortly, Brahms was grinding out an interminable series of potboilers—mostly arrangements of popular tunes of the day. His ambition was to become a fine composer, but before he succeeded in writing anything he cared to publish under his own name he had published 151 ephemera under the pseudonym of G. W. Marks, as well as a few he considered somewhat better, attributing these latter to the cacophonously named Karl Würth. Music lessons and composition, combined with schoolwork and night jobs, wore him out. He was rescued by a family friend who treated him to two summers in the country, but even then he worked, making the hundred-and-twenty-mile round trip every week to take his lesson, and conducting a rural chorus. Rest and fresh air did wonders, and when he returned to Hamburg in the fall of 1848, he was glowing with that rugged good health that scarcely varied for half a century.

On September 21, Johannes Brahms gave his first public recital, showing the classical rectitude of his taste by venturing a Bach fugue—an unheard-of feat of daring in those days. At another recital the following April, he gave Hamburg its first taste of Brahms the composer, with a fantasy that has not survived. On the whole, these first attempts at a serious career were disappointing, and he had to resume his hack labors. But these could not hold him long, for he had been fired by two experiences: he had heard the already famous Joachim, only two years his senior, play Beethoven's Violin Concerto, and had met the brilliant Hungarian-Jewish violinist, Eduard Reményi. Joachim stirred him more deeply than he realized at the time. Reményi, with his extravagant collection of travelers' tales, captivated him with a vision of that great world Brahms in later years came, if not to detest, at least to disregard. He fretted more than ever under a hateful routine, but found precisely the solace his artist's soul needed in composing the two piano sonatas, scherzo, and songs that now constitute his first four opus numbers.

Just about the time of Brahms' twentieth birthday, Reményi again appeared on the scene with a tempting offer to take him as accompanist on a vagabond concert tour. At Hanover, they fell in with Joachim, who enraptured Brahms by expressing an understanding admiration for his compositions. After arranging a court concert for Reményi and Brahms, Joachim, who at that time was still warmly espousing the cause of the *Zukunftsmusiker*, sent them off to Weimar with a generous letter. Although Liszt was lavish with his praise, Brahms was so disgusted by the trumpery court politics of the Altenburg that he disdained to give its master his meed of flattery. This was fatal to any real *rapprochement* between them, particularly as Brahms found little to admire in the "music of the future." He decided to move on, leaving Reményi swooning under the spell of Kundry Liszt. He did not miss the young Hungarian: musically, Reményi gave Brahms little that he could use except a smattering knowledge of gypsy folk tunes.

On September 30, 1853, Robert Schumann wrote in his diary, "Brahms to see me (a genius)." For after the disheartening visit to Liszt, Joachim had persuaded his friend to go to Düsseldorf. The Schumanns received the handsome young fellow with open arms. As a bosom friend of Joachim's, he was welcome, and when he played his music for them, they treated him at once as an equal. Brahms, still vexed by the artificial ways of the Altenburg, gave his heart immediately to his new friends, who (he could not but remind himself) were, for all their simplicity and forthrightness, two of Europe's leading musicians. Clara was to become his friend for life. Robert, with but three years before him, and those clouded, at once translated enthusiasm into action. He successfully urged a publisher to issue some of Brahms' early compositions, but almost more effective in establishing his protégé's name was the farewell article he wrote for the *Neue Zeitschrift für Musik*. Called "New Paths," this high-flown panegyric hailed Brahms as "vouchsafed to give the highest and most ideal expression to the tendencies of the times, one who would not show us his mastery in a gradual development, but like Minerva spring full-armed from the head of Zeus." The article aroused wide interest in the newcomer, but there were plenty, particularly among the adherents of the Neo-Germans, who felt that the Elijah of romanticism was casting his mantle over the wrong man. Worse, they whispered that this violently enthusiastic manifesto was proof of the rumors that Schumann was losing his mind. The fact was that he had written "New Paths" in one of those dazzlingly lucid intervals that preceded his collapse: less than six months after his meeting with Brahms, he was incarcerated in a madhouse. During the period of Schumann's insanity, Brahms visited him as often as he could, and was to the unhappy wife and mother a tower of strength.

What was the music that had stirred the weary Schumann to his swan song? Appropriately enough, it was as romantic music as Brahms ever composed. It consisted of three piano sonatas, a scherzo, and some songs, besides certain compositions that Brahms, tempering Schumann's enthusiasm, refused to publish because they did not come up to his own standards. The Scherzo—the first piece he played for both Liszt and Schumann—is a bright youthful display, rather empty, rather dazzling, and altogether as near to pure virtuoso music as any he ever contrived. The C major

Sonata is not entirely successful: Brahms here uses the sonata form awkwardly, academically rather than spontaneously, and much of the result is so unpianistic as to seem an extended sketch for an orchestral work. Yet, it is vigorous, confident, always provocative in thematic material, manfully reverent in its obvious Beethoven worship. In short, possibly the most satisfactory Opus 1 ever composed. The F sharp minor Sonata is a cold and rather dour work that pianists rightly consider thankless. The F minor Sonata—the last Brahms ever wrote for the piano—is important. Though far too long, and in a medley of styles, it yet contains many consecutive pages of beautiful music. There are still Beethovian echoes, especially in the development of the first movement, but here already are Brahms' widely spaced harmonies, broken chords, and perilous modulations, as well as the trick of carrying a melody on the inner notes of chords.* The scherzo reads like a Brahms rewriting of parts of the *Carnaval*, but the andante is the kind of music fully matured Brahms was to turn into sheer magic.

The total effect of these early piano works suggests a composer of genius who has not yet found his métier. The extravagance of the romantic material in them tends to obscure what on analysis appears equally obvious—that Brahms was faithfully, if not always happily, devoted to the sonata form as Beethoven left it. Those who can bear to study a work like the C major or F minor Sonata as a laboratory specimen can uncover the whole catalogue of Brahms' artistic virtues and vices. Their proportion may vary, but the dichotomy remains. It is less noticeable in the four ballades composed little later than the pieces that inspired Schumann's eulogy: Brahms never carried out his intentions more successfully than in the archaic and severely pared "Edward" Ballade, based on an old Scots poem. All the ballades hint that Brahms' genius as a composer for the piano would find its happiest outlet when freed from the conventions of the sonata.

It is probable that the four ballades were the last of Brahms' music that Schumann ever heard. Certain it is that Brahms played them to the dying master during one of his sane interludes in the madhouse. About the same time, Brahms delighted Schumann with a set of "Short Variations on a Theme by Him. Dedicated to

---

* One of Brahms' last-published piano pieces—the C major Intermezzo (Opus 119)—is a superb example of the use of this device.

Her." This not very inspired composition is interesting for two reasons: it is a trial flight in a form that Brahms was to infuse with new meaning, and it is dedicated to Clara. During the last two years of Schumann's life, Brahms had become warmly devoted to her, so warmly, indeed, that there was gossip about them. There were some who went so far as to whisper that he was the father of Clara's last child, and now, almost half a century after their deaths, people are still guessing and theorizing about the status of their relationship. In the absence of any documents except their increasingly ardent letters, it is possible to belong to one of two camps. One holds that it was a high-minded, purely platonic friendship based on a common grief and common sympathies and interests. The other, referring to them as Johannes and Clara (the analogue of Richard and Cosima), takes a Freudian point of view.

Robert Haven Schauffler, without committing himself to what actually took place between them, summed up the case for the prosecution. It is, briefly, that Brahms (clearly the victim of a mother fixation) chose Clara, fourteen years his senior, as a mother surrogate. It is significant, perhaps, that he occasionally addressed her as "*meine liebe Frau Mama.*" Grief and mutual admiration brought them together under highly emotional circumstances, and it may be that Brahms persuaded the distraught woman to become his mistress. This school of thought makes much of the fact that Brahms and Clara, less than a year after Schumann was incarcerated, went on a five-day pleasure trip with only her maid to chaperon them. This sounds incriminating, but certain physiological and psychological peculiarities in Brahms' development as a functioning male suggest that, whatever their impulses may have been, they could not have been lovers at this time. In the first place, Brahms' voice did not change until 1857, at which time also his beard began to grow. Secondly (and Mr. Schauffler is authority for this astute conjecture), it seems likely that Brahms' mother fixation and infantile erotic experiences in brothels made him incapable of consummating a physical relationship with a decent woman. His whole life bears out this contention.

No specifically sexual foundation was required, however, to make Brahms and Clara friends for life. She came to regard him as the greatest composer of the age—after Schumann—and his reverence for her as artist and critic never abated. Even as an old man, he continued to submit his compositions to her before publishing them. For almost forty years they carried on, with few interruptions, a spirited correspondence, and were together whenever possible. Clara's letters make somewhat more interesting reading than Brahms': her interests were wider, her culture was deeper, her many triumphal tours gave her more contact with the great world. So powerful was her influence on him that in time he inherited her quarrels (some of them dating from her life with Schumann) and absorbed her prejudices. For example, his dislike of Wagner, which has been much exaggerated, in part reflected Clara's own reflection of Schumann's misunderstanding of the scant fraction of Wagner's music he knew, as well as her own Victorian abomination of the sensual content of many of the later operas. At heart, Brahms was too good a musician not to recognize Wagner's genius.

At first, Clara's friendship for Brahms asserted itself in a helpful and practical way. Then, as always, she had more pupils than she could handle, and she turned several of them over to Brahms. Some of them happened to be well-born ladies from Detmold, and they, with the help of a good word from Clara (who had fine connections everywhere), wangled a semiofficial appointment for him at this sleepy little town, where the Prince of Lippe held his court. There, from 1857 to 1859, Brahms spent a portion of each year, giving lessons to the Prince's sister, conducting a chorus of doting *Fräulein*, and presiding over the court orchestra. Here was an ideal place for thinking things out. The decisions Brahms came to musically he expressed only in music, and they are not easy to express in words. Briefly, he went to Detmold saturated with the type of romanticism summed up in Schumann, and, after much vigorous self-criticism and experimentation, emerged as a Brahmsian, which is the only accurate description of a man who is variously called a neoclassicist, an eclectic, or a classical romanticist, depending on what measuring stick is used. Certainly, those who think exclusively of the contour and emotional atmosphere of the overwhelming majority of his themes are justified in calling him a romanticist; those who focus their attention on the way he handles his musical material are equally justified in calling him a classicist. Between them they have a complete judgment of one who, starting with classical sympathies, ran the gauntlet of romanticism, and came out with an eclectic style that eventually became as idiosyncratic as Chopin's.

To the Detmold period belong Brahms' first three compositions for orchestra. Two of these—extended serenades or *divertimenti*—are of little more than historical interest. Both are excessively long and excessively dull, though the second of them, in A major, is suave enough in its instrumentation, chiefly because Brahms re-orchestrated it many years later. Their discursiveness and blurred outlines suggest that he was wise in never again venturing to use the classical-suite form. Yet, composing them was of incalculable value in putting him at ease among the instruments of the orchestra. The scoring of the D minor Piano Concerto, effected at about the same time, is still not of the happiest, but clearly shows not only the solid results of working on the serenades, but also the fruits of directing his own band. Its immense advance over the serenades is as much psychological as technical: he has gained confidence in handling the orchestra. The themes have more distinction, more clarity of contour. Altogether, the First Piano Concerto has surprisingly little tentativeness for a work that began as a symphony sketched for two pianos, and was written as a concerto only as an afterthought. In spite of many virtuoso passages, Brahms subordinated the soloist's role to a degree previously unknown in the piano concerto.

The D minor opens with a titanlike theme that promises more than is actually achieved, for here he falls victim to his incurable tendency to ramble. The edifice, though constructed of fine materials, is constantly on the verge of toppling over, and in the end we are left with a feeling of having been cheated of what we were promised. If this tendency to formal decadence were not so persistent, it might be possible to interpret its presence in the D minor Concerto as merely a device to point up the parable of Schumann's decline, to which Brahms is known to have referred in at least the first two movements.

On January 22, 1859, Brahms played the D minor Concerto in Hanover. It was a failure. Five days later he played it at a Gewandhaus concert in Leipzig. It was roundly hissed, and he himself, as a pianist, with it—a fact that was instrumental in causing him to abandon a possible virtuoso career. Hamburg was kind to the concerto, but only the first time, for when it was repeated there a

year later, it was received with icy silence. While Brahms was inclined to view all this merely as a temporary setback, enough
rancor simmered in his mind to lead him to the only foolhardy act
recorded of him. The *Neue Zeitschrift für Musik*, then an organ of
the Neo-Germans, published an article stating that almost every
good composer in Germany belonged to the Liszt camp. The idea
was certainly a silly one, if for no other reason than that it made a
Hungarian cosmopolitan the arbiter of German music. Brahms
and Joachim fell into a rage and, with two less-known musicians,
signed a manifesto attacking the article. Then they began collect-
ing other signatures, but it was accidentally published without
these. The reverberations were far-reaching, particularly as
Wagner, too, had been tacitly aspersed in the manifesto. Brahms
was unwittingly jockeyed into being a paladin of the anti-Wagnerians, and worse, the incensed Wagner was moved to discharge
the vials of his wrath on the imprudent Brahms. Without wishing
to, he had created overnight a powerful bloc of vituperative enemies who for years delayed the full appreciation of his music.

In 1860, Brahms gave up his connection with Detmold, and for
three years made his headquarters in or near Hamburg. Here he
organized a women's choir, for whom he drew up a quaintly medieval charter and wrote much of his smaller choral work. Often he
took his ladies into the country, and practiced out of doors; as he
was a stubby little man, he often chose the branch of a tree as his
podium. Anyone who glances at a chronological list of Brahms'
compositions will notice that this period is one of his least productive, but its barrenness is more apparent than real. He was either
actually at work on several major compositions or thinking them
out. One of them—*Ein deutsches Requiem*, his most pretentious choral
work—was not completed until 1866; the First Symphony took
more than twice that long. The spate of song continued unabated,
and he also wrote a considerable amount of chamber music.

The most impressive earnest of Brahms' genius in the early sixties was the set of piano variations on a theme by Handel, the
undertaking of which involved some temerity on his part, for Handel himself had written five exquisite variations on the same theme.
The result justified what Brahms' enemies no doubt considered
sacrilege: his twenty-five variations and the mighty concluding
fugue constitute a veritable milestone not only in the history of

the form, but in the entire realm of piano music. Cut-and-dried academics still find them offensive. Certainly, Brahms had a curiously nonclassical conception of the variation form, regarding it not so much as a series of comments or disguised elaborations on the original theme as a series of comments on ideas engendered by the organism—the original theme and its variations up to that point—as it unfolded. The result is that the connection between the theme and particularly the later variations is extremely tenuous. It is paradoxical, and not a little ironical, that this work of the so-called neoclassicist Brahms presents, despite its great freeness of structure, an effect of much more unity than most of his large works in strict forms. Brahms made the variation a perfect vehicle for his native discursiveness: in the "Handel" Variations, Brahms is like a subtle storyteller who is constantly reminded of some new tale, but who, at the end, leaves us with the perfect satisfaction of having heard a complete story. The variations are of singular beauty, shifting in mood, shading, and rhythm, and unobtrusively making use of every technical device to achieve a dazzling variety. On the basis of the gigantic fugue, it is possible to understand the oft-repeated statement that Brahms is the greatest contrapuntist since Bach. Even Wagner was moved to praise his official enemy after hearing him play this masterpiece.

Much less interesting musically are the variations on a Paganini theme which Brahms completed in 1863. Paganini himself would have adored them: they are the most difficult virtuoso music ever written. "Practically nothing new in virtuoso technique has been thought of since" is the considered opinion of William Murdoch, English pianist and devoted Brahmsian. Volcanic, daemonic, explosively energetic, their vast gigantic ways too often seem much ado about nothing.

In 1862, the directorship of the Hamburg Philharmonic fell vacant, and Brahms was among the handful considered for the post. While waiting for his fate to be decided, he visited Vienna for the first time, remaining for several months and giving a number of concerts, perhaps believing that a success there would tip the scales in his favor at Hamburg. Success he had in lavish measure, but the careful conservative Hamburgers brushed aside the claims of their young townsman—be it remembered that Brahms was only twenty-nine—and chose his considerably older friend,

Julius Stockhausen. It was a strange choice, for Stockhausen had previously been known only as a lieder singer. Brahms, naturally disgruntled, had his indignation fed by Joachim who, though a friend of Stockhausen's, was infuriated by the election. Brahms' return to Hamburg was almost funereal, for besides having his hopes dashed, he found his family at sixes and sevens. He just managed to patch up the quarrel between his parents for a year, when they finally separated. Altogether, Hamburg had become ashes in his mouth, and he desperately desired to go elsewhere. On his thirtieth birthday, when the decrepit Vienna Singakademie invited him to become its director, he accepted with joy this opportunity to settle permanently in the city that had seemed so pleasant to him on his single visit. Although within a year he gave up the Singakademie post as a bad job, Vienna remained his headquarters for the rest of his life.

The first major work completed by Brahms after settling in Vienna had a curious history. In 1862, he had written it as a string quintet, but had been much dissatisfied when the Joachim Quartet and an extra cellist played it over for him. He then revised it as a sonata for two pianos, and was even more dissatisfied. Late in 1864, he again rescored it, this time for piano, two violins, viola, and cello, and so, after these almost unexampled labor pains, the famous F minor Piano Quintet came into the world. It is possibly the best of a large group of baffling pieces that some have not hesitated to call the crown of Brahms' achievement. In speaking of his chamber music, Edwin Evans, the English musicologist, says that in it "Homer never nods," but omits the pertinent fact that Brahms is never Homer. It is perfectly true that the chamber works, from the B major Piano Trio (1853) to the clarinet sonatas (1894), maintain a uniformly high level. But that high level is nevertheless far from epic grandeur. If you are a really devout Brahmsian—if the things Brahms says inevitably hit an answering chord in your psyche—then there is hardly one of his chamber pieces that will not be a favorite of yours. But if your criteria of enjoyment emphasize the way things are said, then much of Brahms' chamber music may well rub you the wrong way. It is not that Brahms did not know the native speech of his instruments. But he was not infallible. The chamber works are one and all spotted with thick, muddy passages that suggest not so much lack of taste as actual insensitivity to effect. It seems as if Brahms could not always hear in his mind how the lines of the separate instruments would sound when played together. The stone-deaf Beethoven was infinitely his superior in this respect.

A careful analysis of the chamber music will show that Bernard Shaw's irate blasting of Brahms as the Leviathan Maunderer is often justified. No matter how vigorously he starts out, he soon enough settles back in his chair and rambles on, often like an old man telling some already twice-told tale to his cronies. Too many times the voice becomes a drone, and it is we, the listeners, who nod. Of course, Brahms wakes us up frequently with a fine comment made with a master's finesse. But then, as like as not, he goes on reminiscing, forgetful of the hourglass. For Brahms' sense of timing when writing in large forms was as deficient as Beethoven's was perfect. The F minor Piano Quintet is an exemplar of the best and worst in Brahms' chamber music. It opens with a broad and eloquent declamation that seems to promise a movement of spacious architectural solidity. This really develops. The movement is half over, in fact, before it slowly but surely collapses. A countertheme would have saved it (supposing it had to be as long as it is), but nothing deserving that name ever appears. The second movement also has a beautiful opening theme, rather like a lullaby, which Brahms treats with embarrassing sugariness. The scherzo is the weakest section of the quintet: for all its brevity, it is monotonous. The finale is diffuse, allusive, and thoroughly inept for ending a work of large proportions. The F minor Quintet has many noble moments, but they, in the final analysis, only emphasize defects that far outweigh them.

In all, Brahms composed two dozen chamber works, seven of them duet sonatas and the rest for three or more instruments. A sextet in G major written about the same time as the Piano Quintet is of peculiar biographical interest. Of it Brahms said earnestly to a friend: "In this I have freed myself of my last love." One of the themes is built on the sequence A-G-A-D-E, and so refers to a certain Agathe von Siebold, who had a small slice of Brahms' heart for rather more than a year. He had come across her in Göttingen in 1858. It is not clear why he was attracted to her: Agathe was a plain-featured young woman of slight charm. Perhaps he merely fell in love with the way she sang his songs. At any rate, he was soon writing more of them just for her, and what Clara Schumann saw of their relationship was enough to make her jealous. Despite this, they exchanged rings, and the girl seems to have considered herself betrothed to Brahms. When a common friend chided him for keeping Agathe dangling, Brahms wrote her a passionate love letter with the news that he longed to hold her in his arms, but could not consider marriage. This paradox was too much for Agathe, who, moreover, was thoroughly respectable. Five years later, as a final salving of his conscience, Brahms composed a tribute to her in the G major Sextet. This tepid romance was probably the closest he ever came to marrying, but it was by no means the last of his heart flutterings. One of his most famous songs—the *Wiegenlied*—was dedicated to a former inamorata on the birth of her second child.

With all his friends, Brahms suffered from loneliness, which he combated by frequent travel. Besides professional touring as far afield as Budapest, he roamed the resort towns of Germany, Austria, and Switzerland, and in later life often visited Italy, which he came to love. An innate dislike of all things French and English made the Rhine the barrier of his westward wanderings, and he took no pains to conceal his ungracious attitude toward those nations. From about 1857 on, Brahms was free of financial worry, for his music was selling well, and he could easily afford to indulge his taste for summer rambling, particularly as his scale of living was simple. After resigning the direction of the Singakademie in 1864, he went to Baden-Baden to spend the season with Clara Schumann and her family. There he met Turgeniev, with whom he discussed plans for an opera, which fortunately (for Brahms was anything but a dramatic composer) remained at the discussion stage. His mother died the following year, and he had the tough assignment of getting his father to the funeral. Although profoundly affected by this loss, he accepted his father's remarriage, a few months later, with cheerful equanimity, and even grew very fond of his stepmother and her crippled son.

It has often been carelessly said that the death of his mother led Brahms to compose *Ein deutsches Requiem*. The facts are actually these: he had begun it years earlier, while still affected by Schumann's death, and had worked at it sporadically. By 1867, the six sections of the work as originally projected were finished, and the first three were given at Vienna on December 1. The performance was rowdy rather than reverent, the audience hissed, and for a time Brahms was in eclipse. On Good Friday of 1868, all six sections were produced so well at Bremen that the *Requiem* was immediately established as an important work. It was not until this year that Brahms wrote a new section for soprano solo to commemorate his mother; this is now the fifth part of the *Requiem*. The whole work was finally sung under the happiest auspices at the Gewandhaus on February 18, 1869, under the baton of the careful Karl Reinecke, a friend of Schumann and Mendelssohn. It was soon popular throughout Germany, and was the first large composition by Brahms to achieve world-wide fame.

Ein deutsches Requiem is scored for chorus, soloists, and orchestra, with organ ad libitum. It is not a Requiem in the traditional sense: that is, it does not follow the specific liturgical text of a Requiem Mass. It is a Protestant work built on words chosen by Brahms himself from the German Bible, which he knew intimately from cover to cover. The outstanding musical feature of this vast work is that it is a veritable compendium of technical effects. Every contrapuntal resource is laid under contribution, often to excess, chiefly in certain fugal passages, which though marvels on paper are confusing in performance. Here, again, Brahms draws out some of his best effects to the point of boredom. The result is a general amorphousness that is not sufficiently compensated for by many passages of real beauty. The whole *Requiem* is instinct with earnestness, with a genuine reverence for the sacred texts that makes one wish the results were better. Yet the total effect is one of noble dreariness. There are factors quite independent of Brahms' musical limitations that had their part in flawing the *Requiem*. No soul-lifting faith in the transcendental aspects of religion shines from it. Brahms had no such faith. At best, he had a homely respect for the Good Book. He repeatedly stated, for instance, that he had no belief in life after death. Without absolutely echoing the brash Shaw of the early nineties, who said that listening to the *Requiem* was a sacrifice that should be asked of a man only once in his life, it may be said that the reputation of this interminable work is, among critics, justifiably waning—with no especial loss to Brahms' position. Perhaps quite the contrary.

During the very years Brahms was toiling over the completion of this solemn monument, he tossed off several groups of small pieces that have done more service to his reputation among music lovers than a dozen *Requiems* would have. The sixteen waltzes for piano duet, now more familiar as solos, are among the most sure-fire encore music ever composed. They are delicious little master-pieces, deceptively simple and engagingly unpretentious, yet made with exquisite care and subtlety. The A flat major Waltz shares with the *Wiegenlied* top popularity among Brahms' original com-positions. His arrangements of twenty-one Hungarian Dances, the first two books of which were issued as piano duets in 1869, were, however, the earliest of his compositions to gain a large popular audience. He was the first composer who ever became comfortably well off from the sale of his music alone, and the widespread de-mand for certain of the Hungarian Dances was the foundation of his not inconsiderable fortune. Three years later, he published piano-solo arrangements of the first two books, and these, with Joachim's versions for violin and piano, added still further to their popularity. In 1880, Brahms issued the third and fourth books for piano duet. Although these pieces are also heard as solos, they are not his own arrangements. Nor are the many orchestral transcrip-tions usually Brahms' own: he orchestrated only three of them—the first, third, and tenth. No matter how he issued them, he was careful to say that the Hungarian Dances were merely "arranged by Johannes Brahms," though a few of the melodies were his own. This scrupulousness did not avert charges of plagiarism by Reményi and others. Brahms' publisher issued a pamphlet containing the facts in the case, but the composer himself held aloof from the unsavory mess. He was content to have enriched the repertoire with these clever, vibrant, and rhythmically vigorous dances, whose popularity to this day is undiminished.

Despite his increasingly comfortable circumstances, Brahms con-tinued to take a few pupils. In 1863, a beautiful young girl had come to study with him, and soon a warm sympathy had sprung up between him and the engaging and talented Elisabeth von Stockhausen, who was clever and understanding beyond her years. Brahms was so taken with her that he eventually had to dismiss her as a pupil, but this discreet step did not end their friendship. Even when she married Baron Heinrich von Herzogenberg, an Austrian pianist-composer, she and Brahms continued to correspond, and were often together. Until her death in 1892, she was something like an Aspasia to him, dividing with Clara Schumann the role of chief critic and trusted confidante. Had Brahms been the marrying sort, there seems little doubt that he would have chosen Elisabeth von Stockhausen, and that she would have accepted him.

Less happy in its outcome was Brahms' sudden and intense infatuation for Julie Schumann, Clara's daughter. This flared up in 1869, and was crushingly squelched by unanticipated news of her engagement to an Italian nobleman. What we know of Julie Schumann suggests a less sympathetic personality than Elisabeth von Herzogenberg, and it may well be that the basis of Brahms' passion was her strong physical resemblance to her mother. That he was easily resigned to losing her is evident from his remark when he first heard of her betrothal: "Now it merely remains to compose a bridal song." That it was indeed passion he felt toward her is just as evident from the note to his publisher that accompanied the score of the "Alto" Rhapsody: "Here I have written a bridal song for the Schumann Countess—but I do this sort of thing with concealed wrath—with rage!"

There is no bitterness in the "Alto" Rhapsody, though the lines from Goethe's *Harzreise im Winter* would justify it. There is, rather, a serenity, a deep hopefulness tinged with melancholy, that is exquisitely appropriate for a young woman's epithalamium. The unusual scoring—alto voice, male chorus, and orchestra—has kept this simple, heartfelt, and altogether engaging music from being easily accessible to a public that would almost certainly be attracted to it. Much the same factor has kept the gay and brightly colored *Liebesliederwalzer*—scored for piano duet and mixed vocal quartet—from being heard often in their original form. Composed about the same time as the restrained, almost monochromatic "Alto" Rhapsody, the *Liebesliederwalzer* are the most truly "Viennese" of all Brahms' compositions, and seem to pay tribute to Johann Strauss, whom he greatly admired, and whose excellent band he often went to hear.

Brahms, though domiciled in the Austrian capital, was never a true Viennese. He remained, to all intents and purposes, a north German, and his deep, abiding, but rather uncritical patriotism was German to the core. Because of his youth and Hamburg's isolation from the centers of discontent, he had been unaffected by the revolutionary upheaval of 1848–9. But the Franco-Prussian War stirred him profoundly. He was resolved to volunteer immediately if the Prussians suffered a major setback, and he followed the daily course of the war with avid interest. A portrait of Bismarck long remained the only nonmusical decoration of his rooms —he worshiped the Iron Chancellor, and execrated Napoleon III as an archfiend. Fortunately for music, if not for humanity, the Prussians won the war, and even as early as Sedan, Brahms was moved to compose a pompous *Triumphlied* for eight-part chorus and orchestra, with organ ad libitum. Dedicated to Kaiser Wilhelm I, it is a worthless piece of jingoism that is best forgotten.

In the summer of 1871, Brahms was again at Baden-Baden, where he first became friendly with Von Bülow, though he had actually known him for many years. Von Bülow was among those who had sneered at the *Zeitschrift* article about Brahms, whom he was at first inclined to regard as just another of Schumann's Sterndale Bennetts. In 1871, despite all he had suffered at Wagner's hands, Von Bülow was still in bondage to the Wagner-Liszt group. But he was favorably impressed by Brahms, and within a decade was, as pianist and conductor, to become the official chief of the Brahmsians.

In February, 1872, Johann Jakob Brahms died, leaving his wife and stepson in Johannes' care. This duty he interpreted generously. His father's death drew him more closely to the widow, and he remained on the most intimate terms with her for the rest of his life—far more intimate, indeed, than with his own brother and sister, neither of whom he liked. Fortunately, money was no problem to him, and in the fall, his circumstances improved still further, when he was appointed to succeed Anton Rubinstein as director of the Gesellschaft der Musikfreunde, far and away the best of Vienna's choral organizations. The Gesellschaft found their new chief a strict and rather terrifying taskmaster, and it is evident that his severity of taste was not altogether palatable to the members of the chorus. As Roman Catholics, they were a little bewildered by the Protestant music of Bach and Handel, but Brahms' three years' tenure of office was in the main beneficial to their morale and standard of taste.

More than fifteen years had passed since Brahms had completed a purely orchestral composition. In 1873, while summering at the beautiful lakeside resort of Tutzing in the Bavarian Alps, he began and finished what some have pronounced his most consistently successful orchestral work—the *Variations on a Theme by Josef Haydn.* Brahms had found the theme in some recently unearthed manuscript material—incidentally, it is by no means certain that it was Haydn's to begin with. The fact that the theme was labeled *Chorale St. Antoni* [*sic*] led Brahms' first biographer to interpret the "Haydn" Variations as something so Lisztian as scenes from St. Anthony's temptations. Whether or not Brahms had a struggle between good and evil in mind when he wrote them (which, to say the least, seems unlike him), they stand in no need of a program. The theme is an attractive one, square and vigorous, and quite as well suited for comment as that of the "Handel" Variations. In the eight variations and finale, Brahms sets the orchestra ablaze in a manner quite unusual for him, with masterly efficiency using every color resource of his enlarged band, with its extra horns, trumpets, and kettledrums.

The "Haydn" Variations are almost as compendious in their musical erudition as the "Paganini" set for piano, but are utterly free from any pedantic or artificial feeling. Again Brahms interprets the variation in the freest way, and again it sets his imagination free. Yet, the total effect is one of almost incredible unity, of absolutely satisfying form. The music is joyful and (what is even rarer in Brahms) frankly sensuous. The whole composition is irradiated by a kind of luminous sanity. This does not mean that the coloring and mood are always bright: they are actually sometimes dark and somber. But when the wind choir reiterates the theme triumphantly at the close of the finale, it is with no mere unimaginative smugness. If the "Haydn" Variations can be made to symbolize anything, it is Brahms the man accepting all human experience as his province. It is a rare view, and may not be entirely welcome to those who prefer their Brahms dispensing an unleavened brand of thick Teutonic philosophy. Yet there is no doubt that the "Haydn" Variations brought him his first triumph as an orchestral composer, and that even the critics who had snubbed his D minor Piano Concerto echoed the enthusiasm with which Vienna greeted the Variations when they were first played on November 2, 1873. Today they stand in the shadow of the more pretentious symphonies, but they are played often enough to give

us a chance to realize how great Brahms could be when his creative powers were unhindered by a hankering after a traditional
formalism he was destined never to master.

The salutary effects on Brahms of not having to conform to the
restrictions of the sonata form are illustrated most clearly in his
more than two hundred songs, written over practically the entire
span of his creative life. The best of these are exceedingly fine,
and it may seem strange that only one—the flawless *Wiegenlied*
(1868)—has attained that thoroughly universal popularity which so
many of Schubert's songs, and not a few of Schumann's, enjoy.
But a moment's reflection will reveal the reason. They are without
the feckless spontaneity, the effortless melody of Schubert, and
also lack that profoundly sympathetic understanding of the poetic
line that informs the best of Schumann's songs. Brahms is often
positively insensitive to the precise rhythmic demands of his text,
to such an extent that singers are sometimes forced to mispronounce
words in order to do justice to the musical beat. In this he affords
an instructive contrast to Hugo Wolf, who at times went to the
opposite extreme of sacrificing purity of musical contour to an
ironclad reverence for the poetic meter. Although most of Brahms'
songs are love songs, they sing of, or comment upon, what seems a
rather passionless love—they are reflective, nostalgic, pessimistic,
even aloof. Almost without exception, they lack drama. One of the
most dramatic—*Vergebliches Ständchen*—is cast in an innocuously
light mood. We are left to gather that for the most part Brahms was
afraid to touch the heavier emotions. The intensely passionate *Von
ewiger Liebe* is not Brahms at his most characteristic, but it is his
greatest song.

Most of Brahms' songs are of high musical interest quite apart
from their relation to their texts. Looked at merely as a fusion of
melody, harmony, and rhythm, such a song as the *Sapphische Ode*
is a beautiful and moving piece of music. It would be just as effective written to another set of words. Not a few of Brahms' happiest
melodic inspirations are to be found in his songs, and invariably
they are handled with tact and finesse. Even when the results are
not very good as songs, they are still good Brahms—fine music-
making. The songs point up a salient peculiarity in his creative
gift: it is as though he had at his command a splendid treasury of
the raw materials of music, and apportioned it more or less indis-

criminately among his compositions in various media. In short, he seems rarely to have performed the only inevitable marriage between medium and material, and to have used whatever was bubbling up at the moment in whatever sort of composition he was working on. Constant Lambert has well said of Brahms that with him "the creation of musical material and its subsequent treatment appear to be two separate mental processes." This discrepancy prevents all but a handful of Brahms' songs from being the total successes they might have been had he asked himself constantly what the nature of song actually is.

Except for songs and choral pieces, Brahms published little during his years as director of the Gesellschaft der Musikfreunde. This is the best evidence that he took his job seriously and performed his duties conscientiously. It is impossible to guess what a prolonged tenure of this exacting position would have done to his career as a composer, but the nature of most of his compositions completed during these years does suggest that he might have been permanently sidetracked. The ostensible reason for his resignation in 1875 was that he was annoyed by the machinations of one of his predecessors, who was plotting to get the directorship back. Actually, Brahms must have left official life with relief, for great projects were pressing for completion, and he needed leisure to carry them out. For years he had been at work on a symphony. He was now forty-two years old, and it was still incomplete. Within little more than a year after leaving the Gesellschaft, he had finished the First Symphony and sketched the Second. He was feverishly at work when, in 1876, he was invited by Cambridge University to visit England to receive an honorary doctorate of music. Brahms refused to go. He said that he disliked "concerts and other disturbances"; his friends said that he hated the English and feared the sea. The most likely explanation of his rather churlish refusal (which he repeated in 1892) was that he was too pressed to take time off. At any rate, that same summer saw the completion of the First Symphony. Within a decade he had put the finishing touches to his Fourth and last.

Brahms' four symphonies are the most eloquent and decisive commentary on the prophecy contained in Schumann's *Zeitschrift* article, assuming that in hailing Brahms as the "Messiah of music . . . he who was to come," Schumann meant the successor of the great classical masters, specifically Beethoven. Color is lent to this interpretation by Schumann's own growing classical bent in the last years of his life. There is no doubt that Brahms took Schumann's incautious words with grave seriousness, and throughout his career endeavored to fill the role in which Schumann (rather than his own innate tendencies) had cast him. Although he never postured as a great master, Brahms felt his mission confirmed when Von Bülow pronounced his First Symphony "Beethoven's Tenth." Von Bülow set a style: devoted Brahmsians almost inevitably refer to the four symphonies as "the greatest since Beethoven." Anti-Brahmsians and middle-of-the-road admirers unite in pointing out that it is precisely in the symphonies that Brahms failed most signally to measure up to the demands of the larger classical forms.

That Brahms viewed the writing of a symphony with more than ordinary apprehension is indicated by the chronology of his orchestral work. He had published two serenades of quasi-symphonic scope, a large piano concerto, and the "Haydn" Variations before completing a symphony on which he had been at work for almost twenty years. Begun in Brahms' early twenties, the C minor Symphony is nevertheless by no means a youthful work. It represents a considered whipping into shape by a fully matured man. It is unfortunate that we have no revealing notebooks to show us the early ideas out of which, twenty years later, Brahms evolved this symphony. Certainly, as it stands, the C minor has had any young quality taken out of it. It is predominantly a dour work and, except for the introduction to the first movement and the finale, could be interpreted as the last composition of an embittered old man. The introduction is an effective swirl of nebula—music of enchanting loveliness in itself. Its presence needs no excuse, but its function is problematical. If out of it rose the vigorous germinative themes essential to the construction of a recognizable symphony, it might seem as much a stroke of architectural genius as the sublime adagio introduction to Mozart's E flat Symphony. But nothing of this sort takes place. Instead, the invertebrate nature of the introduction pervades the first three movements. Suddenly, in the finale, Brahms hits upon a truly energizing first theme, about which it might be carping to say that it is in part lifted from the choral finale to Beethoven's Ninth Symphony were it not for the fact that zealots of the Brahms cult make such a point of repeating the master's famous growl when someone mentioned this resemblance: "Any fool can see that!" The point is that this strong Beethovian theme, whether hit upon by accident or purposely, is just the right sort of material on which to erect a soundly constructed symphonic movement. This Brahms proceeds to do with complete success. But it must be said that a triumphant conclusion —almost a swift victory march—after three vast movements of transitional music produces an odd effect.

The Second Symphony, the most cheerful of Brahms' larger compositions, is attractively bucolic in nature. It has often been called his "Pastoral" Symphony, but the implied comparison must not be strained. The D major contains, in fact, better music than Beethoven's Sixth, but is not so well constructed. Also, programmatic effects were foreign to Brahms' Dorian conception of symphonic dignity. The scoring is light and clear. The instrumentation is, for Brahms, unusually transparent—free of the sluggish turgidity that so often clogs the machinery in his other symphonies, and sometimes makes them difficult to follow. The circumstances of the composition of the D major Symphony—it was composed during the summer of 1877, on the shores of the Wörthersee, a beautiful Austrian lake—doubtless have much to do with its spontaneous quality. Two of Brahms' most seductive melodies appear in the first and third movements respectively, and the whole is liberally sprinkled with delights. The entire allegretto enjoys a popularity of its own: it is, after all, much like a theme and variations, and naturally Brahms is at his happiest in it. As a suite of attractive symphonic effects, the D major is not surpassed by Brahms' other symphonies, but even more than the others, it lacks the perfectly achieved cohesiveness that is the hallmark of a true symphony.

In 1883, Brahms composed a third symphony, and began to sketch a fourth. The first of these, in F major, is the shortest of all his symphonies, but often seems the longest because of its heroic cast and grandiosity. A few attentive listenings to it should dispel forever the notion that Brahms is essentially a classical composer. It begins with a burst of romantic virtuosity, and is steeped throughout in an almost Schumannesque romanticism. In the first two movements, Brahms seems to be speaking *in propria persona*, a persuasive romantic poet uninhibited by any sense of duty to the great classical dead. The breathless flow of melodic beauty is nothing short of intoxicating, and momentarily, at least, we scarcely care that we are listening to a free fantasia rather than to a symphony. After these heroic draughts, the third and fourth movements are tepid and unadventurous. The skeleton in Brahms' closet is indeed neoclassicism—a very self-conscious neoclassicism—and its bones rattle throughout the andante and the allegro. In no other large work is the descent from mountain to plain made so rapidly. The idiom suddenly becomes harsh and monotonous, the melodic line studied. The whole symphony sags, and in trying to find distinction for this industrious classicizing Brahms descends to real ugliness in his orchestration. Had Richard Strauss concocted some of this, we should say that he was orchestrating a sandbank, and compliment him for doing it perfectly. The last half of the F major Symphony has given those critics who make a specialty of judging a composer by his lapses something to hold on to: from it, more than from anything else, has come Brahms' reputation as a harsh melodist and a muddy orchestrator.

Brahms lived to be almost sixty-four years old, but he finished his last symphony when he was only fifty-two. In many respects, the E minor is the most remarkable of the four, just as it is the least conventional. In movement sequence it violates some of the most time-honored canons of the symphonic form: it begins with an allegro, moves on to an andante, then to another allegro, and ends with a third allegro, *energico e passionato*, that is actually a passacaglia—a theme and variations in triple time. It begins and ends tragically, violating another supposed rule that even a tragic symphony must close on a yea. Be it said that Brahms' innovations are, in themselves, completely successful, and that none of his other symphonies so consistently holds the attention as the Fourth. It is unquestionably one of the sovereign works for orchestra, never for a moment devoid of great melodic inspiration, and orchestrated sensitively, sometimes brilliantly. Coming after the spacious but mysterious and darkly questioning first movement, the melancholy, tender andante, and the robust good-humored allegro giocoso, the majestic passacaglia, with the mind-dazzling variety of its thirty variations and finale, is as inspired a conception as the grand fugue of the "Handel" Variations.

The First Symphony, which had its *première* at Karlsruhe on November 4, 1876, under the listless baton of Felix Dessoff, was received indifferently, even by some of Brahms' stanchest partisans. Nor did Brahms' own conducting of it later help matters much. Hanslick, who was rapidly assuming leadership of the pro-Brahms bloc of critics, found it "difficult." That Brahms took Hanslick's attitude to heart may be gathered from a letter he wrote him the following year: "In the course of the winter I will let you hear a symphony which sounds so cheerful and delightful that you will think I wrote it specially for you, or rather for your young wife." This time the mighty Hans Richter was entrusted with the conducting, and the band was the Vienna Philharmonic. The response to the first hearing, on December 30, 1877, cheered Brahms immensely, particularly as the D major was always one of his favorites. Not only Hanslick, but a wide public, was won over, and Brahms' reputation as a promising symphonist dates from the *première* of the Second Symphony.

With two symphonies for the critics and the public to ponder, Brahms felt that he was entitled to a real vacation. With his Zurich friend, Dr. Theodor Billroth, and the composer Goldmark, he set out, in April, 1878, for the first of his eight Italian tours. Although he had a much-needed rest from composing, and conceived a deep and lasting love for Italy, the trip was, in some respects, unsatisfactory. It lasted but a few weeks and was conducted in rush tempo: evidently the friends "did" the sights all the way to Sicily in the most approved tourist fashion. This sort of mad scramble got on Brahms' nerves, and he was further depressed by a meeting with his godchild, Felix Schumann, who was dying a consumptive's death in Palermo. Under the circumstances, he was glad to get back home, though with the resolve to resume his Italian travels as soon as possible.

For some years Brahms had intended to compose a violin concerto for Joachim, and during the summer of 1878, having returned to the Wörthersee, did so. Joachim naturally introduced it, at the Gewandhaus, on New Year's Day, 1879. The public reaction was cold, and it took years of proselytizing on Joachim's part to get it accepted widely. That it is today solidly established is a tribute to the great violinist's conviction that he was advertising a masterpiece. Again Hanslick was a dissenter and a powerful deterrent to immediate acceptance. Many still agree with him. The D major Violin Concerto is as uneven as the Third Symphony. It has an absorbingly beautiful, if rather errant, first movement, a hopelessly inadequate second, and a sometimes exciting, but far from perfectly achieved, finale. Except for the cadenza, which Brahms leaves to the soloist's taste (Joachim's or Fritz Kreisler's is ordinarily used today), it is not a display piece for the soloist, whose role, indeed, is sometimes worse than secondary. Von Bülow, in one of his acidulous and bitter-truthful moods, once said that Max Bruch had written a concerto *for* the violin, Brahms a concerto *against* the violin. The roles of solo instrument and orchestra are best balanced in the first movement—an emotional, nobly speaking allegro. The andante is ruined by flagrantly inept orchestration: the thin note of the oboe carrying the main theme is swamped by too massive accompaniment, and the solo violin's comments are insignificant and weak. In the finale, there is much fine gypsy music of bravura cast, but here Brahms, halfway to success, swamps the solo instrument itself.

Late in 1879, the University of Breslau informed Brahms that it intended to honor him with a Ph.D. Possibly to the surprise of the University authorities, he accepted graciously, and bethought himself of some music fitting to the occasion. Let us, under the guidance of Sir Henry Hadow, follow his ruminations at the lovely summer resort of Ischl: "A ceremonial of so solemn and academic a character naturally demanded an unusual display of learning. Symphonies were too trivial, oratorios were too slight, even an eight-part *a cappella* chorus in octuple counterpoint was hardly adequate to the dignity of the occasion. Something must be done to mark the doctorate with all the awe and reverence due to the Philosophic Chair. So Brahms selected a handful of the more convivial student-songs and worked them into a concert overture which remains one of the most amusing pieces of pure comedy in the whole range of music." This rollicking piece was the still immensely popular *Academic Festival Overture*. Oddly enough, when performed under Brahms' direction at Breslau, on January 4, 1881, it was received with less enthusiasm than its perfect gauging to the occasion deserved. It may be that the presence on the program of the *Tragic Overture*, also completed at Ischl the preceding year, explains the audience's low spirits. This is a gloomy, not to say dull, work. Although Brahms insisted that he had no specific tragedy in mind, it has been guessed that the overture was meant as a prelude to *Medea, Hamlet, Macbeth*, or *Faust*.

For many years, Brahms was accustomed to go on concert tours, performing either as conductor of, or pianist in, his own works. In neither role was he superlative: there is no evidence that he was ever regarded as a first-rate conductor, and as he grew older, his pianism, which at times had approached brilliancy, became slipshod. Yet there is no doubt that he naturally was influential in establishing a tradition for the performance of his compositions. As time passed, and the memory of the unpleasant reception of the First Piano Concerto dimmed, Brahms concluded that he needed another concerto to vary his programs. He played with the idea for several years, and after spending the spring of 1881 in Italy and Sicily, completed it during the summer, announcing the news to Elisabeth von Herzogenberg in a typical letter: "I don't mind telling you that I have written a tiny, tiny pianoforte concerto with a tiny, tiny wisp of a scherzo. It is in B flat, and I have reason to fear that I have worked this udder, which has yielded good milk before, too often and too vigorously." This was Brahms' backhand manner of telling his confidante that he had composed one of the longest piano concertos in existence. He also characterized it in another letter as "a few little piano pieces."

On November 22, 1881, the B flat Concerto was brought out at Stuttgart, with Brahms as soloist. The critical reaction almost matched the coldness with which the D minor had been greeted twenty-two years before. Because it has four movements instead of the concerto's conventional three, and because the solo instrument is so closely woven into the orchestration, Hanslick called it a "symphony with piano obbligato." It has caught on more slowly than most of Brahms' large works for orchestra. The fact that its extreme complexity requires a surpassing executant has not helped the B flat, for it is all too often attempted by pianists who find it quite beyond their competence. Even that greatest of ensemble players, Artur Schnabel, though none of it is beyond him, cannot give interest to this unwieldy work throughout its entire length. The opening allegro constitutes a serious stumbling block: it is a tortuous maze that may well puzzle even the most loyal Brahmsian. The main theme, pleasant in itself, is transitional in character, and scarcely suffices to launch a mammoth concerto. The "extra" movement follows: it is another allegro, vigorous and passionate, yet ominous and lowering. It seems incredible that Brahms' explanation of its presence—that the first movement was so "harmless"—could ever have been taken seriously. The charmingly songlike andante, not precisely happy in its surroundings, is followed by a finale of generous proportions—unquestionably, in its vitality and firmness of structure, the best thing in the concerto.

It was not until the summer of 1881 that Brahms physically became the familiar bearded figure of most of his portraits. He began the composition of the B flat Concerto smooth-shaven, and emerged with a heavy beard. The growing of this famous ornament, which became more and more luxuriant with the years, has been interpreted by Freudian critics as a compensatory gesture for "the smooth cheeks of his early twenties." In view of the fact that the hoarseness of Brahms' voice from middle age on was due to his having artificially lowered its pitch, this explanation has some slight plausibility, though it is almost negated by the fact that he grew his beard in the very heyday of excessive hirsuteness. The most likely reason is that Brahms grew tired of shaving and of wearing a tie. His careless dress became proverbial, his old brown overcoat and battered hat one of the sights of Vienna. About this stubby, rather paunchy little man there was small glamour. The ashes of interminable cigars fell unheeded on his waistcoat, and were smudged in. He was a heroic beer drinker, withal a connoisseur, and his taste in food was heavily German. As he aged, his hosts of friends regarded Brahms with affection, his appearance and habits with delighted amusement, though his wide acquaintance with ladies of easy virtue, who often greeted him brightly on the street, embarrassed them. Until the very end of his life, people remarked on his piercing, extremely blue eyes, fair skin, and magnificently domed forehead, and it was these characteristics that, much to Brahms' amused gratification, led a geographer to include his portrait in a textbook as a typical representative of the Caucasian race.

As Brahms neared fifty, his life settled more and more into a routine of summer composing and winter touring. He kept his quarters in Vienna, but as soon as the weather warmed, he was to be found at one of his favorite mountain resorts—Thun, Mürzzuschlag, or Ischl—and there he did most of his creative work. In the winter, his tours often served to introduce his latest compositions to a growing public. Whenever possible, he spent a part of each year in Italy. The Third Symphony, for example, was begun at Ischl during the summer of 1882, and finished at Wiesbaden the following year. On December 2, Richter led the Vienna Philharmonic in a successful *première*, following which Brahms introduced the symphony at various places, notably at Berlin early in 1884.

For some years, Von Bülow had been established at Meiningen as leader of the orchestra, and through his unswerving devotion, backed by the friendly sympathy of Grand Duke Georg of Saxe-Meiningen and his wife, soon made it one of the principal centers of the Brahms cult. Therefore, it was no surprise when Meiningen was chosen for the first performance of the Fourth Symphony— the chief product of two delightful holidays in Styria—on October 25, 1885, with Brahms himself conducting. The youthful Richard Strauss, who had just become Von Bülow's assistant, recalled Brahms as a less polished and subtle, but more warmly human, conductor than his chief. After the *première*, the Meiningen band took the work on tour through parts of Germany and Holland. It was arranged that Brahms was to conduct all performances of the new symphony. At Frankfort, Von Bülow, who truly felt that the composer slighted the full beauty of the work, dared to announce that he himself would conduct it during a return engagement. Brahms was annoyed, and insisted that the letter of the original arrangement be strictly observed. When Von Bülow, delicately balanced man that he was, and suffering from ill health, quite reasonably took this in bad part, and resigned, they quarreled. Two years were to elapse before Brahms tacitly acknowledged his fault by seeking Von Bülow out for a reconciliation.

Brahms had treated his selfless champion with that brusque insensitivity even Clara Schumann had often complained of, and which once led to a temporary cooling in their relationship. But this gruffness, this apparent callousness, was only a façade that Brahms' wisest friends learned in time to discount. Actually, he was so tenderhearted and kind that it may merely have been self-protection. In 1888, for instance, when Clara, almost seventy years old, found that she could no longer support herself and her family on the proceeds from concerts alone, Brahms stepped in, and in the most roundabout and thoughtful manner contributed a large

piece of what he called "my superfluous pelf" to easing the financial burden of her last years. Furthermore, he could be tactful in
a quite unusual degree when the delicacy of a situation forced itself
upon him. Once, in the late eighties, he made a special trip to
Hamburg to hear Tchaikovsky conduct his Fifth Symphony. He
honestly disliked it, but invited his Russian colleague to dinner,
and confessed with such diffidence and warmth that the hypersensitive Tchaikovsky plucked up courage to make a similar admission about Brahms' music.

The lovable side of Brahms' nature is nowhere better illustrated
than in the circumstances surrounding the composition of the Concerto for Violin and Violoncello, which he finished in 1887. For
six years he had been on the outs with Joachim because he had
sided with the violinist's wife in the series of quarrels preceding
their divorce. This was even worse than being estranged from Von
Bülow, for Joachim was Brahms' oldest friend, as well as the first
enthusiast for his music. Too shy or too awkward to approach
Joachim directly, Brahms slaved at the "Double" Concerto during
the summer of 1887, and sent it to his sulking friend with the dis-
arming inscription: "To him for whom it was written." Joachim
was deeply touched, and though he had his doubts about the
musical worth of the concerto, the reconciliation took place. He
and Robert Hausmann, a member of Joachim's world-renowned
quartet, appeared as the soloists at the *première* in Cologne, but
Brahms was not slow in noting that the work was anything but a
favorite with his friend. He had started a second concerto for violin
and cello, but shelved it with the wry observation that no one cared
to listen to the first one. This was an exaggeration, of course, for
there is a certain public for any Brahms work, even one as unleavened as the "Double" Concerto. This last of Brahms' larger compositions is the least spontaneous of them all. A revival of the old
concerto grosso, it clearly bears out the evidence that it is partly composed of discarded symphonic material. It is of appalling difficulty
both for soloists and audience: playing it may give the pleasure of
obstacles overcome, but there is no such reward for most listeners.

Almost ten years more of life remained to Brahms—years of
meager outward eventfulness, but sweetened, on one hand, by
lavish official and public recognition, and on the other, saddened
by the loss of beloved friends of long standing. In 1889, Franz

Josef, Emperor of Brahms' adopted country, bestowed the coveted Order of Leopold on him, and the same year, his birthplace pleased him even more by giving him the freedom of the city. Brahms ordinarily refused to wear his numerous decorations, but relaxed during solemn state dinners at the Meiningen ducal *Schloss*, and amused himself by wearing the whole lot. Generally speaking, pleasures outweighed sorrows. In 1892, however, the still young Elisabeth von Herzogenberg died, and for months Brahms was inconsolable. He was growing old, and could not lose himself so completely in composition as had been his wont earlier in life. Fortunately, at Christmastime, he was reconciled to Clara, whose growing touchiness had caused a break between them in 1891. He managed to see her at least once a year for the next three years, perhaps feeling that each time might be the last. And in May, 1896, when Clara was almost seventy-seven, the dreaded news came in a telegram from her daughter Marie: "Our mother fell gently asleep today." Brahms was at Ischl, and the telegraph people had had difficulty in finding him. He set off at once for Frankfort, read in a newspaper that the funeral was to be at Bonn, and reached there just in time. A few months less than forty years before, he and Clara had walked beside the bier of Robert Schumann.

At Clara's funeral, weakened by fatigue and grief, Brahms caught a chill from which, in a sense, he never recovered. By September, it was obvious to his doctor at Carlsbad that he was dying of a liver complaint. When he returned to Vienna the next month, his altered appearance shocked all his friends. It seemed that he had grown old and feeble overnight. He grew steadily worse, and when 1897 came around, knew that he would not get better. On March 7, he attended a Philharmonic concert, and heard the great Richter do a superb job of his Fourth Symphony. It turned out to be an intensely emotional occasion for all concerned: after each movement, the music was wildly cheered, and at the end of the finale, when Richter indicated Brahms' presence, the audience rose as a man, and saluted him. Almost sobbing out his emotion, the old man bowed, and then stepped back into the shadow of the box. Less than a month later, on April 3, 1897, he died of cancer of the liver. He died with tears in his eyes—he had loved life, and hated to give it up.

A chronology of Brahms' life that listed only works in large forms would show his last decade as singularly barren of achievement. After 1887, he wrote nothing more pretentious than a few chamber works, songs, some minor choral music, and short piano pieces. But it is precisely these last—the four collections of piano pieces that make up Opuses 116, 117, 118, and 119—that, in the opinion of many, constitute his most certain claim to immortality. After the magnificent "Handel" Variations of 1861, for ten years Brahms wrote little for piano alone until he began that series of intermezzos and capriccios that he eventually collected as Opus 76. These, together with the two rhapsodies of Opus 79, represent a return to his earliest love, but would not, in themselves, place Brahms among the foremost piano composers. The earlier set, which contains the light and humorous B minor Capriccio, one of Brahms' most popular pieces, shows the strong influence of Chopin* and Schumann— not the late, classicizing Schumann of the *Zeitschrift* salute to Brahms, but he who had composed the *Fantasiestücke* and the *Kreisleriana*. They are not quite certain of themselves, and oversentimentalize in spots. Of Opus 79, poor Dr. Billroth, with whom Brahms imperiously broke for being civil to Massenet in face of Brahms' known contempt for the Frenchman's music, said: "In these two rhapsodies there remains more of the young, heaven-storming Johannes than in the last works of the mature man."

But even the charms of these middle-period pieces do not wholly prepare us for the unique quality of the twenty pieces of the last four sets—the finest solo piano music between that of Chopin and Schumann and that of Debussy. Here, untrammeled by his nemesis, the duty of classicizing, Brahms is an out-and-out romanticist, but a romanticist who has found perfect forms for his material. The brevity of these pieces has deceived more than one otherwise shrewd critic into dismissing them as "slight," but to do this in the case of a piece like the E flat minor Intermezzo is to misunderstand completely the nature of lyric poetry in music and, indeed, lay oneself open to the charge of not recognizing it when it appears. Here, if anywhere, is most apparent Brahms' gift of expressive melody, his harmonic originality, his ability to evoke a mood in a few bars. Not all the pieces are uniformly good. Here and there a tendency to the lachrymose creeps in, notably in the E flat Rhap-

* The Intermezzo in A minor opens like a parody of Chopin's F minor Nocturne.

sody, where a tasteless middle section all but ruins an exciting beginning and end. Nor does the composer consistently overcome
one of his most flagrant defects—a certain rhythmic listlessness and
lack of variety. But the best of these pieces—for instance, the G
minor Capriccio, the G minor Ballade, and the Scarlattilike C
major Intermezzo—are music of a very high order. They would
not, it is true, put Brahms in the company of Bach and Beethoven.
It will be a macabre joke on the thirty-third degree Brahmsians,
but hardly on Brahms, if, as seems likely, his last piano pieces place
him among the great romantic masters of the small, intensely personal forms.

Chapter XIX

Piotr Ilyich Tchaikovsky

(Votkinsk, May 7, 1840–November 6, 1893, St. Petersburg)

T HE greatest symphonist of the nineteenth century—after Beethoven, of course—was born of totally unmusical parents at
Votkinsk, a small town almost equidistant from Kazan and Perm.
Of his mother we know only that she was the granddaughter of
an epileptic Frenchman who may have been a straggler from the
Grande Armée. Ilya Tchaikovsky, a pleasant man of modest men-
tality and means, was an inspector of mines, and later director of a
technological school in St. Petersburg. The few facts known of Piotr
Ilyich's childhood are more fruitful for the Freudian analyst than
for the hopeful musicologist looking for precocity. His first governess described him, after his death, as having been "a porcelain
child." In less literary language, he was high-strung, oversensitive,
morbid, but extraordinarily charming.

For those who profess to find a French accent in much of
Tchaikovsky's music, one early anecdote is illuminating. The same
governess—a Frenchwoman—found him poring over a map of Europe, kissing Russia and spitting at the rest of the continent. When
Mlle Fanny reminded him that he was metaphorically insulting
her, he answered, "Didn't you see that I covered France with my
hand?" It was impossible to be angry at so docile and quick-witted
a child, which was a good thing, for the least talking-to or threat of
punishment would make him hysterical. He was more attached to
his mother than is usual with even so sensitive a child. Once, when
he was ten, Mme Tchaikovskaya took him to St. Petersburg to
leave him in boarding school. As her carriage drove off, he ran
after it, trying to cling to the wheels. He brooded over this first
separation until his dying day. When his mother died of cholera in
1854, he was for a long time inconsolable, but gradually found an
outlet for his welling love by mothering his younger twin brothers.

Tchaikovsky's first recorded reactions to music were quite as
neurotic as Chopin's. He adored the pathetic melodies of Donizetti
and Bellini, but would often scream for his governess after being
tucked into bed, insisting that they were still in his head, and

would not let him sleep. He had the musical attainments of an ordinary child of good family. He began to take piano lessons at the age of five, learned to sight-read fairly well before he was eight, and could improvise a pretty valse at fourteen. He was, on the whole, indifferently taught by teachers unable to rouse his latent abilities. The truth is that there is nothing in Tchaikovsky's life of either human or musical interest to detain us until 1859, when, after leaving the School of Jurisprudence, he became a clerk in the Ministry of Justice in St. Petersburg. At this time, he seems like a stock figure out of Turgeniev: elegant, superficial, foppish, and diffuse. He was a very bad civil servant even in that paradise of bad civil servants. He hung around the Ministry for three years, so listless in attending to his duties that when he left he promptly forgot what they had been. He did not forget music: he obliged at the piano at dances, improvised nicely, and haunted the opera and ballet. He finally consummated this frivolous period of his career by composing and publishing, apparently at his own expense, an operatic song with Italian words, *Mezza notte*. This sugary bunkum was the sole artistic fruit of a passing friendship with one Piccioli, an antique Italian singing teacher with painted cheeks and artificially raven locks.

In the summer of 1861, Tchaikovsky traveled through Germany, Belgium, and England with a family friend. One of his letters to his beloved sister Alexandra shows him precisely on the verge of a new life, and poignantly foreshadows the triumphs and tragedy of his later years. After berating himself for his extravagance, he asks, "What can I expect from the future? It's terrible to think of it. I know that sooner or later I shall no longer be able to battle with life's difficulties. Till then, however, I intend to enjoy it and to sacrifice everything to that enjoyment. I have been pursued by misfortune during the last fortnight; official work—very bad. . . ." And then, a significant postscript: "I've been studying thorough-bass and am making good progress. Who knows? Perhaps in three years' time you'll be hearing my operas and singing my arias." Earlier that year, Tchaikovsky's father (could he have been impressed by the sight of the printed *Mezza notte*?) remarked casually that if Piotr Ilyich wished to become an artist, there was still time. Tchaikovsky did not need a second hint: he was already sick to death of petty officialdom. He did not immediately relinquish his job, but went at once to sign up with Nikolai Ivanovich Zaremba, a thorough pedant who had the reputation of working his pupils to the bone. Not unnaturally, the still-dilettante Tchaikovsky was at first a lax student, but nevertheless, when Zaremba joined the staff of the newly created Conservatory of Music in 1862, Piotr Ilyich followed him faithfully.

Fate favored Tchaikovsky's determination to change his life by giving him a not undeserved blow in the face. At the Ministry, he was passed over in the promotions, and the slight rankled. In April, 1863, despite the fact that his father had lately lost most of his small fortune, and could offer his son only shelter and food, Tchaikovsky resigned his post. Music had by now become his absorbing passion, and he could not bear to give time elsewhere. He entered Zaremba's advanced classes, and worked hard at the dry husks of his new profession. Now, just when he needed it, came inspiration in the person of the Conservatory's director—Anton Rubinstein, only ten years Tchaikovsky's senior but already one of the key figures in Russian music. In the great pianist's class in orchestration, Tchaikovsky suddenly found wings. Rubinstein's method was to set his pupils problems involving the most expanded modern orchestra—a medium for which Tchaikovsky had a phenomenal natural flair. It is no wonder that the impressionable youth, who changed within a brief year from a silly fop into a hardworking, fever-eyed, and threadbare student, conceived a pathetically sincere schoolboy crush on the brittle, subtle, and empty cosmopolitan. Even later, as one of the most famous composers alive, he hungered for a word of praise from Rubinstein. But his old teacher was Tchaikovsky-deaf to the end of his days.

Tchaikovsky was graduated from the Conservatory in January, 1866. He was too nervous to appear at the required *viva voce* examination, and for a time Rubinstein threatened to withhold his diploma. He relented, however, and even suggested to his brother Nikolai that Tchaikovsky be attached to the staff of the new Moscow Conservatory of Music. Nikolai, its director, not only accepted the young graduate—at a salary the equivalent of about twenty-five dollars a month—but also gave him a room in his own house. As the house served temporarily as Conservatory headquarters, there was method in Nikolai Rubinstein's altruism. Until his school became a going concern, he could overwork his guest and still keep his conscience clear. A capable, bustling, domineering man, for many years Nikolai shared his brother's low opinion of Tchaikovsky's music. Tchaikovsky arrived in Moscow eager to have some of his compositions performed. He was even a little puffed up, for had not the most famous bandmaster in Europe, Johann Strauss, thought a dance of his worthy of being included in a program at the Imperial palace at Pavlovsk? Nikolai, however, deflated his tiny conceit by scornfully turning down the first thing Tchaikovsky submitted to him. He gingerly, condescendingly, agreed to conduct a second overture, which was moderately successful in introducing Tchaikovsky's name in Moscow. Thereafter, he faithfully, but without conviction, brought out his protégé's work.

In March, 1866, the young professor began to struggle with his first symphony. In the creative throes he worked himself into a nervous breakdown. On his enforced vacation, he took the unfinished score to Anton Rubinstein, who pronounced it poor stuff. This increased Tchaikovsky's despair, but though firmly convinced that he would die before doing so, he managed to complete this lengthy romantic effusion that he called "Winter Daydreams." Oddly enough, Anton now accepted two movements of the symphony, but they were coldly received in St. Petersburg. In February, 1868, Moscow heard "Winter Daydreams" entire with more enthusiasm than it deserved, and Tchaikovsky took his first curtain call. Success did not quiet his nerves. Nor did Moscow night life, tasted gluttonously with the convivial Nikolai, put him in a better frame of mind. His debut as a conductor in a dance from his forthcoming opera, *The Voyevoda*, threatened to be disastrous, but the well-drilled performers saved the day. On the podium he had the hallucination that his head was coming off, and actually held on to it with one hand during the entire performance. This experience so terrified him that ten years elapsed before he had courage to repeat the experiment. *The Voyevoda* itself enjoyed a brief spurt of success, but soon this first opera fell into desuetude, and he destroyed the score.

Late in 1868, Tchaikovsky came as close to conventional romance as was possible for him. The enchantress, Désirée Artôt, was a French opera singer, five years his senior. The train of events makes it clear that she thought of him only as a possible *affaire*, but he evidently believed that her intentions were serious. Early in 1869, he wrote to his father, saying in effect: this woman is pursuing me—what shall I do? Old Ilya answered yes and no, and Mlle Artôt solved the problem by going off to Warsaw and marrying a Spanish baritone. It is certain that Tchaikovsky greatly admired her, and so was naturally cast down. He recovered quickly. Twenty years later, when she had doubled in size, and he was internationally famous, they chanced to meet, and she seems to have exercised her old spell over him. Obviously a real Platonic love affair.

Of far more importance than his harmless intrigue with Désirée Artôt was Tchaikovsky's introduction into the charmed circle of The Five, nationalist musicians who revolved around the saturnine, Tartar-faced Mili Balakirev. As the pupil, protégé, and friend of the Rubinsteins, who were conventional Occidentals in music, Tchaikovsky was at first looked upon with suspicion by the nationalists. But when they discovered that he was ready to take them at their own valuation, was eager for their praise, and admitted the greatness of their spiritual ancestor, Mikhail Ivanovich Glinka, they welcomed him with open arms. He never knew Borodin or Mussorgsky well, and he resented the Pecksniffian acidity of César Cui, the least important of The Five. But Rimsky-Korsakov became his friend, looked up to him, and was even influenced toward traditionalism by reading a little harmony textbook Tchaikovsky wrote. As for Balakirev, he was soon subjecting the strayed Rubinsteinian to that overweening supervision which made his companions of The Five think of him as a martinet. He began his lessons by suggesting that Tchaikovsky compose a symphonic poem about Romeo and Juliet, accompanying this suggestion with a detailed prescription for the writing. But when he went so far as to sketch some of the music, Tchaikovsky called a halt, scrapped Balakirev's themes, and went ahead on his own to compose one of his most successful orchestral works. It must have been with mixed feelings that Nikolai Rubinstein conducted the *première* of this result of his friend's fraternizing with the enemy. As it failed, Tchaikovsky doctored it up during the summer of 1870, six months after the first performance, and presented it again.

The overture-fantasia *Romeo and Juliet* is the first composition

Tchaikovsky wrote that is still played today.* Except for Berlioz's
Roméo et Juliette, this is the best music ever to illustrate some of
Shakespeare's most luscious lines, far superior to Gounod's trivial, long-winded lucubrations, and more relevant than, and at
least as lovely as, Bellini's now forgotten opera. Already Tchaikovsky is writing music that bears his unmistakable sign manual.
The vigorous and varied rhythms, the lush, ripe harmonies, the
pull toward the minor, the melodic spontaneity, the feeling for
large climaxes—already all are here. Although sections, notably
the haunting love melody, are Tchaikovsky at his best, *Romeo and
Juliet* as a whole seems thin and shallow. As a true and original
master of orchestration, Tchaikovsky has certainly arrived, but he
is still using material that in later years he might have cast aside.

Considering how late Tchaikovsky came to the serious study of
music, the quickness of his technical development is amazing. In
half a dozen years he acquired all the subtleties and nuances of
the musical language, all the tricks of its rhetoric. *Romeo and Juliet*
shows that at thirty he had a vast vocabulary, a large and engaging
fluency of speech, but very little to say. Had everything gone as
smoothly as he wished, this facility might have been fatal, at least
as far as shaping a great composer is concerned. But life treated
Tchaikovsky savagely, his sensitive little-boy soul did not get the
meed of praise it craved, and so he went on composing, composing,
composing, both to express and to stanch his grief and to create
something that would satisfy him so fully that it must satisfy others.

In view of the generally high level and surface attractiveness of
much Tchaikovsky did before completing his Fourth Symphony in
1878, it is more than a little strange that he was not flattered to
his heart's content, especially considering his elaborate and sometimes insensitive connivings to give his music the spotlight. One
instance suffices to show that his desperate need for recognition
could anesthetize him to the most obvious points of honor. In
1874, he began to compose an opera for a competition under the
auspices of the Russian Musical Society. First, though anonymity
was naturally the essence of such a contest, he went around ascer-
taining that no formidable rival was entering. Then, having com-

---

* Except, unfortunately, the third part of the *Souvenir de Hapsal*—the endemic
Chant sans paroles, which, composed originally for solo piano, has since appeared in
various noisome arrangements. This dates from 1867.

pleted *Vakula the Smith* ahead of time, he discussed it all over Moscow, and contrived to have Nikolai Rubinstein, one of the judges, play the overture publicly. Finally, he sent in the manuscript in an envelope bearing a motto in his unmistakable handwriting. Having violated all the rules, he then won the competition. It was an unsavory business all around, and Rimsky-Korsakov, also one of the judges, put his conscience to rest by reflecting that Tchaikovsky's was far and away the most deserving entry, anyhow. The public did not agree with the judges: *Vakula* had been announced as a comic opera, but Moscow did not laugh. In fact, even when Tchaikovsky had achieved great popularity, he was never the rage among operagoers. None of his ten operas has secured—except in Russia—a permanent place in the repertoire. This was a source of keen disappointment to him. Not only was his artist's vanity piqued, but his hopes of easy financial success were blasted. Musicians have ever yearned to write a successful opera, just as writers yearn to write a successful play.

It was need of money that led Tchaikovsky to compose his first string quartet. At Nikolai Rubinstein's suggestion, he announced an all-Tchaikovsky program. He needed a large work for the occasion, and as he could not afford an orchestra, compromised on music that required only four players. Who today knows the D major Quartet? Not one to the thousands who know its second movement as "the *Andante cantabile*." Wrenched (with ease, one must admit) from its context, this suave setting of a folk melody Tchaikovsky had heard on his sister's estate has played an exaggerated part in ensuring his popular fame and in damaging his reputation with serious musicians. Neither very good nor very bad music, it is one of those unassuming little pieces that have, through constant playing, acquired connotations that smother whatever musical value they may originally have had. Decidedly, the present repute of much of Tchaikovsky's music is absurdly fortuitous. There is little reason, for example, why the last movement of his Second Symphony (1872)—an extraordinarily catchy allegro—has not been picked up and adapted for dinnertime ensembles. Finally, is it not odd that this perfectly respectable C minor Symphony, so well tricked out with charmingly adapted folk melodies, is never played at all? Most emphatically, it is odd. Tchaikovsky composed three of the world's most popular symphonies, and it is

high time that some conductor, instead of dragging out Franck's
D minor or Dvořák's "From the New World" for the *n*th time,
try his hand at popularizing the Tchaikovsky Second. "Winter
Daydreams" is probably embalmed forever, but now that the Third
has reacted so encouragingly to Stravinsky's attentions, there is
every chance that the C minor might prove just as much of a find.

In November, 1874, Tchaikovsky began the composition of what
is indubitably his first masterpiece—the B flat minor Piano Concerto. He intended it for Nikolai Rubinstein, and when it was
complete except for the orchestration, rushed to play it to his chief.
For a moment Rubinstein, who was vexed because Tchaikovsky
had not asked his advice on technical matters, was silent, and then
subjected the music to a blasting fire of criticism. A bit later, he
returned to the attack, suggesting changes tantamount to complete rewriting. At this, Tchaikovsky became as furious as Rubinstein. Muttering, "I'll not change a note of it," he erased his
master's name from the score, and rededicated it to Hans von
Bülow, who had once made some pleasant comments about his
music. Rubinstein lived to change his mind about the concerto so
thoroughly that it became one of the prime staples of his repertoire.
Tchaikovsky, older and wiser, also changed his mind, and in 1889,
after pondering Rubinstein's excoriating criticism for fourteen
years, completely revised the piano part. At the time of its composition, however, he felt nothing but resentment toward his over-
critical friend, and there is no doubt that this difficult scene had
much to do with his moving from Rubinstein's house and taking
a three-room apartment of his own, with a manservant to see to
his needs.

While it is too strong to say that the B flat minor Concerto is in
eclipse, it is certainly far less played than it was ten or fifteen years
ago, when a veritable epidemic of it threatened to obscure its more
solid musical qualities, especially as many pianists of less than
virtuoso stature dared to attempt it. The B flat minor is definitely
for the virtuoso: the piano part is both showy and extremely difficult. Today, in reaction, the concerto is glibly dismissed as morbid, trivial, and sentimental. Possibly there is something in our
hard-boiled mores to account for this unthinking contempt—certainly that something is not in the concerto itself. Possibly, too,
this hoity-toity attitude is simply more of the sort of criticism that

abuses B for not being A. Thus, Handel is not great because he is not Bach,* Verdi because he is not Wagner, and Tchaikovsky because he is not Beethoven and Brahms.

The B flat minor Concerto of Tchaikovsky (who, incidentally, wrote some excellent criticisms of Brahms) is a far more successful and a better-integrated piano concerto than Brahms ever wrote. No attempts at dark philosophical meanings and no tortuous musical pedantries interpose themselves between the listener and this mightily attractive, unabashedly romantic music. On the score of torrential spontaneity disciplined by an entirely adequate technique, the B flat minor is assured of immortality. It is at times flighty, at times tasteless, but if even the very greatest compositions were to be judged by their lapses, only a handful would survive. The perfectionists would soon tire of them if they had nothing else to listen to. There is some sugar in the andante of the B flat minor, but far from being morbid, the work as a whole is informed by gusto, manliness, and high spirits. Those who listen to it thoughtfully and without *a priori* notions will agree with Von Bülow, who found it "lofty, strong, and original," its form "perfect, mature, and full of style—in the sense that effort and craftsmanship are everywhere concealed."

Although Von Bülow had gratefully accepted the dedication of the B flat minor Concerto, and had enthusiastically decided to make it one of the mainstays of his forthcoming American tour, Tchaikovsky was depressed because it was not immediately played in Moscow. He was momentarily cheered by a cable from Von Bülow announcing a magnificent ovation at the world *première* in Boston, but was again plunged into gloom because his finances were so low that to send an answering cable meant spending his last ruble. This condition was the result, not of personal extravagance, but of an almost foolish willingness to place his meager resources at the disposal of every Tom, Dick, and Harry. In view of his steadily growing fame, the salary he received from Nikolai Rubinstein was, despite grudging increases, ridiculously inadequate. He made something from journalism after having broken into print with a spirited defense of a piece by Rimsky-Korsakov,

---

* The latest lunacy of this school of criticism is to take Bach severely to task for not being Buxtehude.

but as he wrote with painful slowness, eventually gave it up with a sigh of relief.

Actually, however, in the middle of 1875, when Tchaikovsky was so agitated by his lack of larger success and of financial ease, he was at least on the verge of the former. With a commission in his pocket for a ballet, he retired to the country for the summer, and wrote his Third Symphony. That November, it was given at Moscow with considerable success, and rapidly made its way in St. Petersburg, Paris, and New York. At St. Petersburg, even the vinegarish Cui admitted that the Third Symphony "must be taken seriously"—high praise from him. Only Vienna turned it down, on the ground that it was "too Russian." This was a singularly obtuse comment on a symphony that is often called the "Polish,"* and is in reality among the least Slavic of Tchaikovsky's major works. Except for the introduction—a businesslike, neatly-constructed, and sturdy moderato that, possibly with humorous intent, is marked *Tempo di marcia funebre*—the Third Symphony is light music. Most of it is merely gracious and superficial. The breezy scherzo is more exhilarating: a kind of *moto perpetuo* with jolly, jolting halts, it is a fine *jeu d'esprit*. In the finale, Tchaikovsky's love for vast volumes of sound gets the better of him, and produces an effect as funny as a Rossini crescendo that has outstayed its welcome. The second half of this movement is nothing but the composer playing around with various earsplitting endings. The worst that can be said of the D major Symphony is that it is scatterbrained. With all its good things, it shows no improvement over the Second, and nothing to indicate that its successor is to be one of the most impressive symphonies ever composed.

A rousing reception for the B flat minor Piano Concerto at its first Moscow performance followed close on the successful *première* of the Third Symphony. These events, coupled with his lucky finaglings in the opera competition, put Tchaikovsky in high good humor. Taking his brother Modest, he went off to Paris, and fell in love with a new opera called *Carmen* and with the fashionable ballet music of Léo Delibes—a taste that has, for some reason, been adduced as a final proof of shallowness. The first half of 1876 was

---

* It was called this because the fifth movement is marked *Tempo di Polacca*. As the second one is marked *Alla Tedesca*, there is no good reason why the Symphony should not as well have been called the "German."

comparatively uneventful. By summer, Tchaikovsky was in holiday mood again: he looked in at Vichy, and then, in company with the rest of fashionable Europe, migrated to Bayreuth, where he observed the first *Ring* cycle as a reporter for *The Russian Gazette*. Some of his critiques were decidedly frivolous; some had more than a grain of truth; all tried to be scrupulously fair to Wagner—then a rather unusual procedure for a music critic. But when it was all over, Tchaikovsky had Festspielhaus claustrophobia: "After the last chords of *Götterdämmerung*, I felt as if I'd been let out of prison." In short, he admired Wagner without liking the *Ring* as a whole. The only Wagner opera he thoroughly enjoyed was *Lohengrin*.

Now, for the first time since the episode of Désirée Artôt, thoughts of women began to play some part in Tchaikovsky's life. After Bayreuth, he had returned to Russia unaccountably depressed, and settled down for the rest of the summer at Verbovka, an estate belonging to his brother-in-law, Lev Davidov, Alexandra Tchaikovskaya's husband. From there he sent Modest the news that "I've decided to marry. This is irrevocable." This must have flabbergasted Modest, who was himself homosexual, and knew that Piotr Ilyich was, too. Actually, the key to this rash decision was simple: Tchaikovsky lived in mortal terror of having his private life exposed,* and longed for someone to take care of him—a second mother, in fact. But even though he wrote, "This is irrevocable," he had no specific woman in mind. One of his confidants later said that Tchaikovsky was looking for a middle-aged woman who would make no sexual demands on him. That very autumn, when Nikolai Rubinstein established a contact between him and the music-loving Mme von Meck, he may momentarily have felt that he had found the woman.

Nadejda Filaretovna was a respectable widow with grown children, like himself shy and retiring, and ten years his senior. And, though Tchaikovsky was no fortune hunter in any vulgar sense, he could not have been averse to the fact that Mme von Meck was one of the richest women in Russia. Rubinstein, who knew his friend's dire financial situation, had suggested that she commission some

---

* Even in his letters to Modest, he veiled all references to their common homosexuality by using the code word, *This*. Nevertheless, Modest's twin, Anatol, knew their secret, and so, probably, did Alexandra Davidova. And all Tchaikovsky's elaborate precautions did not keep fashionable Moscow from whispering.

music from him, and she had fallen in love with the rather inferior samples of Tchaikovsky's art Rubinstein had shown her. Not only did she accede to Rubinstein's suggestion, but she also began to correspond with the man whose music so poignantly touched her recluse's heart. It soon developed that though she was eager for Tchaikovsky's friendship, she had no wish to meet him. He wrote her that he quite understood this point of view, nay, felt closer to her because of it. Did he not suffer from this selfsame misanthropy—this fear of disillusionment? So began, in perfect understanding, one of the most extraordinary friendships in history.

Fate had dealt kindly with Tchaikovsky in giving him Nadejda von Meck at the time when he most needed a sympathetic woman friend. But he still wanted a wife-housekeeper-nursemaid. Early in 1877, fate, this time in a vindictive mood, supplied him with one. She was Antonina Ivanovna Miliukova, a slightly unbalanced woman of twenty-eight who had become violently enamored of Tchaikovsky while a pupil at the Conservatory. She wrote her professor a mash note, and he foolishly answered it. He tried to fend off her attentions, telling her everything that might serve to cool her ardor—except the dark secret. It was no use. On May 18, 1877, she sent him a letter containing a suicide threat, whereupon he went to see her, told her all the truth—and ended by asking her if she still wanted to marry him. Of course, her answer was yes, for she firmly believed that she could change his nature. One of the reasons for Tchaikovsky's quixotic and naïve conduct was that he was at work on a setting of Pushkin's *Eugen Oniegin*, in which the callous, Bryonic hero receives a love letter from the unsophisticated Tatiana. Tchaikovsky, who had been enraged by Oniegin's heartless treatment of the girl, identified Mlle Miliukova with Tatiana, and determined not to repeat Oniegin's cruelty. And so, from the most kindhearted of motives, he brought stark tragedy into his own and this foolish girl's life. On July 18, 1877, they were married.

At first, Tchaikovsky strove manfully, despite his horror, to be a husband to this strange woman. But after a fortnight, he was like a man trying to escape from a nightmare. Pretending that he was going away for a cure, he fled to one of the Davidov estates. There, by convincing himself that his marriage was only a bad dream, he so recovered himself that he was able to resume work on *Eugen Oniegin* and to begin the orchestration of the Fourth Symphony, which he had started to sketch in April. But his return to Moscow, where Antonina was lovingly making a home for them, could not be postponed indefinitely. He went back, and for the two most hellish weeks of his life again tried to live with his wife. It was a gathering crescendo of terror and despair, during which he was unable to write a note. One night he stood waist-deep in the icy Moskva: he hoped to catch pneumonia and die, but his fine constitution defeated him. On October 6, he could stand Antonina's nearness no longer, and boarded the St. Petersburg train. His brother Anatol met him at the Nikolai Station, took one look at this hideously altered hysteric, and rushed him to the nearest hotel. There, after a cataclysmic nervous attack, the details of which Anatol forever kept secret, he lapsed into a two-day coma. As soon as he was somewhat recovered, he and Anatol left for Switzerland. To Nikolai Rubinstein and Modest was left the awful task of breaking to Antonina the news of her husband's seizure and the impossibility of his ever rejoining her. She heard Rubinstein's brutally unvarnished words calmly. Probably she did not take them as really final.*

Early in that ambiguous period that had given him both Nadejda and Antonina, Tchaikovsky had heard three large compositions of his given in Moscow, all of them of minor importance musically, and memorable only for their popularity. The first of these, written at Nikolai Rubinstein's request, to be played at a benefit concert for the Serbian victims of Turkish aggression, was the jingoistic, Pan-Slavic, and infectiously noisy *Marche Slave*. As the Russians were working themselves into that fine fever of indignation which was to fit in so well with their Tsar's desire for a war against Turkey, the piece was a huge success. It still is. Even Tchaikovsky was so carried away that he forgot his podium terrors, and consented to take the baton at a repetition of the *Marche*, the following February. So well did this go off that he thereupon decided to do more conducting—a decision that ended by making him something of a globe-trotter. Shortly after Tchaikovsky's un-

---

* Already partly psychopathic when she fell in love with Tchaikovsky, Antonina became odder and odder with the years. She wrote her husband long, rambling, and nonsensical letters, which never contained a single word of reproach. After a long career of free love (including the bearing of numerous illegitimate children), in 1896 she was confined in an insane asylum, where she died in 1917. For his own part, Tchaikovsky always spoke gently of the wretched creature, and blamed himself for the marriage.

expected resurrection as a conductor came *Le Lac des cygnes*, based on a poem by Pushkin, and produced at the Grand Theater on March 4, 1877. This gracious, pellucid, and rather empty composition, which clearly shows the influence of Delibes and the fashionable French entertainment music of the time, has a place in history as the forerunner not only of Tchaikovsky's own later and finer ballets, but also of a distinguished line of ballets by other Russian composers.

Five days after the opening of *Le Lac des cygnes*, Nikolai Rubinstein conducted the first performance of Tchaikovsky's *Francesca da Rimini*, based on the touching lines from the fifth canto of the *Inferno*. Although some have considered this temperately Lisztian tone poem superior to *Romeo and Juliet*, Tchaikovsky himself knew better. In 1882, in a letter to Balakirev, he said, "Both these things [an earlier tone poem, *The Tempest*, is also referred to] are written with merely affected warmth, with false pathos, with whipping-up of purely external effects, and are really extremely cold, false, and weak. All this arises from the fact that these productions did not *arise out of* the given subject, but were only written apropos of it, i.e., the birth of the music was not inward but fortuitous, external. The meaningless uproar in the first part of *Francesca* does not correspond in the least to the stupendous grandeur of the picture of the infernal whirlwind, and the sham exquisiteness of the harmony in the middle part has nothing in common with the inspired simplicity and strength of Dante's text." It is only fair to observe that Tchaikovsky was equally harsh with *Romeo and Juliet*: "I was all too painfully conscious of the complete lack of connection between Shakespeare's portrayal of the youthful passion of the Italian Romeo and my own bitter-sweet moanings." These quotations should go far in refuting the charge that Tchaikovsky lacked self-criticism.

When he arrived in Switzerland in October, 1877, Tchaikovsky had with him the scores of two partially completed works, *Eugen Oniegin* and the F minor Symphony. It is amazing that except during the weeks he had actually spent with Antonina, he had been working on them—in the case of the Fourth Symphony, passionately, for he intended it as a gift for Mme von Meck. That he had been able to compose at all was largely owing to her generosity, for she saved him from distraction by paying his most pressing debts and lending him money besides. Now, when his funds were so low that it seemed he might have to return to teaching before he was physically fit, Tchaikovsky received from her enough money to live on for several months. The generous woman was not content with this: some weeks later, he received a letter from her, stating that she was settling an annuity of six thousand rubles on him, and enclosing the first installment. The effect of this overwhelming good fortune, this unquestioning and undemanding kindness offered him as a musician by a woman who had unquestionably resented his marriage, was a splendid burst of creative energy unparalleled elsewhere in his career. In six months he completed the instrumentation of *Eugen Oniegin* and the Fourth Symphony, and composed the Violin Concerto and an extremely long Piano Sonata. Far from being a recluse while accomplishing all this, he gadded happily from one place to another, lighting at Clarens, Venice, Vienna, Milan, San Remo, Florence, and finally, in April, 1878, at Mme Davidova's estate at Kamenka. Here he finished the Violin Concerto before going on to the vast Von Meck house at Brailov, which had been placed at his disposal during Nadejda's absence. There he passed the summer like a great Russian landed proprietor.

In September, Piotr Ilyich returned to Moscow: it was exactly a year after the darkest hours of his marital tragedy. He wanted at once to give up his Conservatory job, but his hands were momentarily tied, as Rubinstein was at the Paris Exposition conducting the Russian music—an honor Tchaikovsky had refused. On Rubinstein's return, he resigned at once, and resumed that roving life that lasted, with few settled intervals, until his death, fifteen years later. He was fretful, fearful lest Antonina track him down (which she managed to do on at least one occasion), and annoyed that the performance of the F minor Symphony, which had been composed with such loving care, had not noticeably increased his Moscow reputation. It is difficult to understand why this extraordinarily attractive composition was not taken to the heart at once. Very gradually it made its way through the world. As late as 1897, over twenty years after it was composed, James Huneker, a passionate Tchaikovskyan, wrote, "Western ears are sometimes sadly tried by the uncouth harmonic progressions and by the savagery of the moods of this symphony." Today it ranks high in popularity.*

The composition of the F minor Symphony was so closely identified with Tchaikovsky's regard for Mme von Meck that he and she always referred to it as "our symphony": as it reflected their common pessimism, it is a good description. The Fourth is unique among his symphonies in having a detailed program, which he wrote out in response to Nadejda's request. Like Beethoven's Fifth, it opens with a fate motive,† and this Tchaikovsky called the germ of the entire composition. The first movement pictures futile efforts to escape from tragic reality into a dreamworld, which is rudely shattered by the irruption of the fate motive in a savagely acrid key. The second movement is a flight into the past—an obbligato to evening reminiscences: "It is bitter, yet so sweet, to lose oneself in the past." The scherzo consists of "capricious arabesques, intangible forms, which crowd the mind when one has drunk a little wine, and feels rather giddy." The finale explores a very Russian idea: "If you can find no reasons for happiness in yourself, look at others. Go to the people." But Tchaikovsky confesses finally that "my description is not very clear or satisfactory. Here lies the peculiarity of instrumental music: we cannot analyze the meanings. 'Where words leave off, music beings,' as Heine has said." Thus, it is with a Parthian shot at the rising school of program musicians that Tchaikovsky ends his description of what was in his mind while composing the F minor Symphony.

Whether or not it was because the two masters conceived of fate in different aspects, it must be admitted that Tchaikovsky's fate motive is more eloquent, more ominous, more truly fatalistic than Beethoven's. But instead of evolving an entire movement from it, he merely states the motive with unmistakable vigor, and begins a series of attempts to forget its implications. The first movement, which is a kind of half-valse built up into rhapsodic episodes of shrewdly varying vitalities, is of boundless rhythmic interest. De-

* In the WQXR poll (footnote, page 194), the Fourth stood last in the popularity rating of Tchaikovsky's last three symphonies. Tchaikovsky was a heavy favorite in this poll, taking third, fifth, and seventh places with the Fifth, Sixth, and Fourth Symphonies respectively. In the entire poll, he ran second to Beethoven, and well ahead of Wagner and Brahms, who ran practically nose and nose for third place.

† He frankly confessed that "my work is a reflection of Beethoven's Fifth Symphony. . . . If you have failed to understand it, that simply proves that I am no Beethoven—on which point I have no doubt whatever."

spite its fragmentariness to the eye (it is, in reality, a series of variations), the yearning, predominantly chromatic character of the melodies gives it a very real unity. The second movement is one of Tchaikovsky's finest inspirations, its rambling narrative main theme one of poignant, nostalgic beauty. The scherzo is a structural masterstroke: its nervous, insistent plucking, with marvelously calculated points of rest, is a perfect foil to the languors and reminiscence of the second movement and to the lusty, forthright strength of the finale. The total effect of the Fourth Symphony is one of almost perfect integration, and shows Tchaikovsky in full command of his powers. He never bettered this performance, for the Fifth and Sixth Symphonies are not better in quality, only different in kind. And in one respect—the achievement of large architectural balance—the Fourth is his most nearly perfect work.

Russia gave Tchaikovsky, at this period, little more than polite response to his efforts, and it is not strange that he spent much of his time in foreign parts, usually returning home to spend the summer in the Russian countryside he came increasingly to love. The chill success of the F minor Symphony was only a sample of the real neglect and painful slights the composer had to endure, even in the case of his best work. For instance, the splendid Violin Concerto, which he had dedicated to Leopold Auer, was carelessly put aside by that fiddler: he found it too difficult to struggle with, and was not sufficiently interested to work it up. Uglier still was the reception that *Eugen Oniegin* got when it was presented by the Conservatory students at Moscow on March 29, 1879, for though Nikolai Rubinstein and some other distinguished musicians were devoted to the music, Anton, who had come specially from St. Petersburg for the *première*, withheld his praise. The audience gave Tchaikovsky a personal ovation, but was merely polite to *Eugen*. Tchaikovsky's disappointment over this rebuff was assuaged, five years later, when the Tsar ordered it performed at the Imperial Opera in St. Petersburg. A slight flurry of popularity followed, and on several occasions Tchaikovsky made long journeys as far afield as Prague and Hamburg to conduct it.

Almost thirty years ago, the Metropolitan staged *Eugen Oniegin* seven times in two successive seasons, but has not revived it since. This is doubtless wise, for with all its moments of romantic charm and gentle melancholy, it is only intermittently dramatic. What we hear of it over the air and on records is a shrewd sampling of the best moments of what Tchaikovsky thought his best opera. It is pleasant enough music (Bernard Shaw implied that it is *The Bohemian Girl* of Russia, and suggested that the hero's name might best be spelled O'Neoghegan), but completely lacks the power and urgency of Tchaikovsky's finest orchestral music. He was not completely at ease when writing for the voice. He composed dozens of songs, some of them popular, and one of them—a setting of Goethe's commonplace *Nur wer die Sehnsucht kennt*—something that cannot be escaped. Had he written nothing else, he would rank a step or two below Massenet. His songs, more than any other class of his compositions except his trivial salon pieces for piano, point up the sad fact that this rigid self-disciplinarian began to eye himself askance only after the deed was done. Tchaikovsky's output of trash is equaled among first-rank composers only by Sibelius'.

Traveling from one gay capital or resort town to another (precisely what Tchaikovsky continued to do) was in certain respects detrimental to the character of his music. Always fatally facile, prone, too, to fall under the spell of others as fatally facile as himself, he picked up a characterless way of writing—a real international idiom—that allowed him to grind out rigmarole that did nobody any harm and himself no good. Anyone who had been to Paris, and had sat drinking lemonade in the Pincian Gardens, could have written the *Capriccio Italien*. Similarly, anyone with a flair for shattering mass orchestration, enough counterpoint to combine the *Marseillaise* with the Tsarist anthem, and a feeling for a good, swingy march, could have turned out the "1812" Overture, with its Russianism spread on too thick to be true.

The year 1881 laid heavy toll on Tchaikovsky's emotions. In February, his setting of Schiller's *Die Jungfrau von Orleans*, though received rapturously by a brilliant first-night audience at the Maryinsky Theater in St. Petersburg, was unmercifully but justly drubbed by the critics, led by César Cui. In April, Nikolai Rubinstein, his difficult, overbearing, but loyal friend, died at the early age of forty-six. Tchaikovsky's easy tears were roused, and there is no doubt that he was deeply touched. By the end of the year he was working on a trio for piano, violin, and cello—a combination he loathed—because he wished to honor Rubinstein's memory with a small, personal type of composition. An amusing instance of

Tchaikovsky's harmless deceptiveness is his writing Mme von Meck that he was composing the trio because she liked that sort of music so much.*

Although the A minor Trio is extremely long, this finest of Tchaikovsky's chamber works consists of but two movements, the first an elegy, the second a series of variations on a folk melody he and Rubinstein had heard during a happy picnic in the country nine years before. Each of the variations represents a facet in Rubinstein's character or an incident in his life. The concluding section, so extended as to seem like a third movement, is a whirl-wind of angry grief, and ends with an andante lugubre in which the selfsame rhythm as that of Chopin's *Marche funèbre* suggests that it may represent the funeral of "the great artist" to whose memory the trio is dedicated. The A minor Trio is a fine, eventful composition in Tchaikovsky's sincerest and most personal vein. It has few dull moments. In short, it is more thankful in performance than certain chamber works by recognized masters of the medium, played only because of the revered names attached to them.

Tchaikovsky was in Rome in November, 1881, when he heard that Adolf Brodsky had had the courage to make his Vienna debut as soloist in the long-neglected Violin Concerto. Not only was the Concerto in D extremely difficult, but it was a novelty, and to dare the austere Vienna press with a novelty not by Brahms was indeed rash. In shocked and vengeful mood, Eduard Hanslick, the self-appointed guardian of music's most sacred shrine, proceeded to rip the concerto to pieces in an article full of *Alt-Wien* billingsgate—a piece of gratuitous vituperation that Tchaikovsky brooded over until the day of his death. Brodsky, however, was not discouraged: he said that he was tempted to go on playing the concerto forever, and so not only won away the dedication from Auer, but also earned the composer's enduring gratitude. Time has proved that Hanslick and his colleagues were as flagrantly wrong about Tchaikovsky as about Wagner.

The D major is not only one of the most popular violin concertos ever composed, but it is one of the best. Its difficulties are for the

---

* At this time, Mme von Meck retained a private trio, the pianist of which was a nineteen-year-old Frenchman, Claude-Achille Debussy. Tchaikovsky never met "our little Bussy," as she called him, but influenced him indirectly, for Debussy's first published composition was a piano arrangement of selections from *Le Lac des cygnes*.

performer, not for the hearer, and it thus has an immediacy of appeal the more learned fabrications of Beethoven and Brahms cannot pretend to. It does not attempt as much—perhaps—but succeeds without qualification. It would be a misnomer to speak of the significance of the Concerto in D: it is primarily a sensuous work, to be enjoyed for the opulence of its melodies, its tireless rhythmic variety and vigor, and its bold but sensitive coloring. The violin has a lot of work to do, but work always peculiarly suited to its genius. The only disappointment the D major offers is the orchestral introduction, which is pompous but niggardly. But once the solo instrument has entered on the sweep of a broad cantilena, this unhappy first impression is permanently banished. The theme of the first movement has the character of a romantic song, and that its permutations should transfer it from the latitude of love to that of sheer exuberance might seem tasteless. The answer is that it does not: what happens seems inevitable and utterly germane. The brief canzonetta, a charming interlude of melancholy cast, is a needed moment of rest before the violent dynamics of the finale, as mighty in its high spirits and earthy jollity as a Beethoven kermis. In analyzing it, Rosa Newmarch said exactly the right thing: "Tchaikovsky has built a movement the brightness and infectious gaiety of which would probably have delighted Beethoven as much as it shocked Hanslick." It is clear that those who speak of Tchaikovsky as exclusively morbid and self-pitying have slept through his Violin Concerto.

After Rubinstein's death in 1881, the directorship of the Moscow Conservatory had been offered to Tchaikovsky, though it must have been an open secret that toward the end of his professoriate there Rubinstein had valued him rather as a composer than as a teacher. At any rate, Tchaikovsky refused: he was too attached to his roaming life to give it up. For the next six years, his biography is simply a record of his wanderings. He composed, of course, but nothing that added notably to his stature as an artist. One of the largest and most neglected works of this period is the Second Piano Concerto. Possibly the chief reason why it is never heard is that both the violin and cello have important solo passages—not important enough to make it a triple concerto, but too much so for the average pianist's comfort. The score is interesting, even if excessively long, and might well claim the attention of some enterprising virtuoso. *Manfred* is a vast symphonic pastiche—a musico-literary work patterned after Berlioz' *Symphonie fantastique*, even down to the *idée fixe*. Its neglect is not much to be deplored. To these listless years also belong several weak operas that are quite unlikely to be resurrected. One of them—*Vakula the Smith* rewritten and rechristened *Oxana's Caprices*—was performed in the United States in 1922 to a politely amused audience. Really popular is the delightful suite for orchestra called *Mozartiana*, a pretty tribute to Tchaikovsky's favorite composer, done in antique style.

With nothing in his past few years to shore up his title of composer except a gusty symphonic poem, some flabby operas, and a few delicately scented nosegays, it is not surprising that in April, 1888, Tchaikovsky was asking, "Have I written myself out? No ideas, no inclination?" But the very next sentence in this letter: "Still, I am hoping to collect materials for a symphony" indicates that he has entered upon a new stage of his career. Briefly, in January, 1888, as the result of a very successful appearance as a concert conductor in St. Petersburg the year before, he began the first of that series of ambitious conducting tours that carried him to such cultural outposts as New York, Philadelphia, and Baltimore, and ended by making him one of the most famous people alive. The first taste of this glory was tonic to him. Everywhere he was feted, and bigwigs thronged his concerts. At Leipzig, where he conducted a Gewandhaus concert, he met Brahms and Grieg and a shoal of lesser notabilities from the pages of Grove. At Prague, Dvořák sought him out, while at Paris Gounod, Massenet, and Paderewski were among his visitors. London ignored his social existence, but received his music enthusiastically. Reflecting on his growing fame, and sensible of the new artistic duties it involved, Tchaikovsky returned to Russia, and retired to a comfortable country estate a pension from Alexander III had helped him to purchase. Within four months he had completed the Fifth Symphony. With a charming irony, he dedicated it to the venerable Theodor Avé-Lallemant, manager of the Hamburg Philharmonic Society, who had severely lectured him for his lack of German musical training. On November 17, Tchaikovsky conducted the *première* of the E minor Symphony in St. Petersburg. So lukewarm was the public reaction that a short time later the volatile composer was writing dejectedly, "Am I done for already?" and himself railing against his new symphony.

Today the Fifth is not only the most popular of Tchaikovsky's symphonies, but is probably exceeded in public affection only by two or three other symphonies. With some important modifications, it follows the pattern of the F minor Symphony, particularly in that a fate motive binds the movements together, though here (and this may explain people's preference for the Fifth over the Fourth) Tchaikovsky uses the device with increased dramatic power. The first movement has an ambiguous stamp, blending gloom with a certain nervous gaiety, and using a somber, darkling palette with burnished highlights and smoky depths. The second movement, marked to be played "with all freedom," begins with a plaintive, yearning melody for solo horn that has made it a salon favorite in transcriptions. It works up gradually into an attack of public sobbing that would be embarrassing if it were not so effective musically. The third movement is not the usual tricky scherzo at which Tchaikovsky so excelled: a waltz, it begins questioningly, tentatively, almost listlessly, but develops fleetness and excitement until the first mood returns, only to be cut off sharp by a hint of the fate motive. The fourth movement is a stumbling block to those who assert that Tchaikovsky always took refuge in despair, for this tremendous, varirhythmed essay in mighty orchestration is one of the great yes-sayings in all music. Its effect, after three movements of predominant melancholy, is powerful beyond description. Had Tchaikovsky died right after completing the E minor Symphony, his biographer would be forced to conclude that he had found some ennobling way out of his soul sickness.

When Tchaikovsky went on his second European tour in 1889, he somewhat reluctantly included the Fifth Symphony in his concerts, only to find that it grew on acquaintance. When he played it in Hamburg, Brahms came to town especially to hear it. The finale was too much for him; the other movements he liked mildly. The rest of the year passed more or less uneventfully for Tchaikovsky, a lazy summer at his country place producing nothing beyond the orchestration of *The Sleeping Beauty*, a ballet commissioned by the Imperial Opera earlier in the year. It was given in the Tsar's presence the following January, and Tchaikovsky, who was himself enthusiastic about the music, was cast down by the perfunc-

tory "very nice" that issued from the imperial lips, and by the
tepid applause from the public. The light and charming music,
some of which had been composed for a playlet given by Tchaikovsky's small nieces and nephews at Kamenka, rapidly gained
ground, and is still popular, though the ballet itself has disappeared except in a briefer form known as *Aurora's Wedding*. What
vexation he suffered over the first reactions to *The Sleeping Beauty*
was more than made up for by the enormous ovation given to his
last full-length opera, *Pique-Dame*, completed just before his fiftieth
birthday. This was an all-Tchaikovsky product, for the libretto
was by Modest, who adapted it from a Pushkin story. The vogue
of *Pique-Dame*, like that of *Eugen Oniegin*, ceased about a quarter of
a century ago.

Unhappily for Tchaikovsky's peace of mind, *Pique-Dame* had not
yet been performed, and thus he could not know what tidy
royalties he would earn from it, when, early in October, 1890, the
most important relationship in his life suddenly collapsed. He was
in Tiflis visiting his brother Anatol when the blow fell: Mme von
Meck wrote him that her finances were perilously involved, and
that she was discontinuing his annuity. This was bad enough, but
worse, the letter sounded like farewell. As she was always com-
plaining about money matters, Tchaikovsky was prepared to believe that she really was in serious straits, even though she had
sent him an unusually generous check some months before. However, stopping in Moscow en route to superintend the rehearsals of
Pique-Dame in St. Petersburg, he received the startling information
that Nadejda's description of her money losses was so exaggerated
as to be a lie. He then knew that she was merely finding a way to
break with him. Although they had never spoken to each other,
even on the several occasions when they had accidentally met in
public places, they had in thirteen years of constant correspondence built up an intimacy that had all but one of the elements of a
love affair. It is not remarkable that Tchaikovsky, with his capacity for disillusionment, found in Nadejda's defection a parable
of the basic falseness of even the best of humanity. He never recovered: within a few months he became an old man.

We naturally wonder what led Mme von Meck to take this
callous measure. No really satisfactory answer is forthcoming.
Possibly she had heard of her protégé's homosexuality. More prob-

ably the death of her favorite son caused this neurotic woman to feel that Tchaikovsky was an indulgence for which she had sinfully neglected her family. A final factor in this baffling situation is that in 1890 Mme von Meck was a hopeless consumptive with but three years more to live.

The excellent financial results of *Pique-Dame* did not free Tchaikovsky from a frantic feeling that his income was seriously impaired, and that he could turn down no offer. He even spoke bitterly of having to apply for "some well-paid post." He accepted a commission from St. Petersburg for a one-act opera and a ballet; he agreed to conduct one of the modish Concerts Colonne at Paris; finally, he overcame his fear of long journeys, and at young Walter Damrosch's invitation signed up for an American tour. Almost before he had crossed the Russian frontier, he was engulfed by a wave of homesickness. Nor could his first French triumph cheer him. At Paris, the day before he sailed for the United States, he read in a newspaper of his beloved sister's death. For a moment, he was on the verge of turning back. He conquered this impulse, and on April 27, 1891, arrived in New York. He spent his first evening in America alone in his hotel room, crying. But his appearance at the opening concert of Music (now Carnegie) Hall, on May 5, cheered him immensely. With a pardonably exaggerated reaction to the unquestioning cordiality of the Americans, he wrote, "I'm ten times more famous here than in Europe." He took the United States to his heart, and except for persistent homesickness thoroughly enjoyed himself. After conducting four concerts in New York and one each in Philadelphia and Baltimore, he made the grand tour of Washington and Niagara Falls, was regally entertained by Andrew Carnegie, and was back in Russia by the end of May.

Tchaikovsky wanted to settle down in the country, and for a few months was able to do so, working on the compositions he had promised St. Petersburg. Then, almost against his will, but driven by his money mania and his profound unhappiness, he began another concert tour. At Paris, in February, 1892, he was so overcome by nostalgia and apathy that he canceled the rest of the tour, and fled back home. He had promised the Russian Musical Society a new work for a St. Petersburg concert on March 19, but having none at hand, quickly orchestrated a few numbers from the ballet he was composing. Thus the famous *Nutcracker Suite* came into being. At the concert, every number had to be repeated, and so the suite was started on its career as Tchaikovsky's most consistently popular nonsymphonic orchestral work. For this group of clear-cut miniatures, each of which is like a child's conception of a fairyland scene, he provided witty and delicately tinted orchestration. Some of it sounds like music Victor Herbert might have written if he had been a more gifted artist. The *Nutcracker* was the first work by a major composer in which the celesta, with its dainty tinkling tone, was used. The novelty of its effect in the *Dance of the Sugarplum Fairy*, on which Tchaikovsky banked so heavily, is now, of course, lost. The charm of the entire suite, however, has proved extraordinarily durable. It is curious that from the very beginning the *Nutcracker* failed as a workable ballet. At its *première*, on December 17, 1892, it was given along with the one-act *Iolanthe*, Tchaikovsky's last opera. Both just escaped being hissed.

But with the exception of the *Nutcracker-Iolanthe* debacle, the winter of 1892–3 was a series of personal accolades, the chief being Tchaikovsky's appointment as a corresponding member of the French Academy. He witnessed the huge success of *Pique-Dame* at Prague, as generous with its applause as in the days of Gluck and Mozart, and gave a highly acclaimed concert at Brussels. But his letters to Russia, written mostly to his nephew Vladimir ("Bob") Davidov, are almost casual about his triumphs, and vibrate with nameless fears and physically painful longings for the little house he had lately purchased in the quiet town of Klin, near Moscow. In January, he was once more on Russian soil, but before he could retire to Klin to complete a symphony he had started the year before, he had to attend a music festival in his honor at Odessa. Here he submitted to the ordeal of having his portrait done by one Kuznetsov. It is an old man who looks out at us—a bent old man with a tragic face and sparse white hair, his bitter, full-lipped mouth emphasized rather than concealed by the white mustache and beard. The piercing blue eyes look us through and through. Modest testified that the portrait was a speaking likeness.

Now, at last, he could go to Klin. There would be peace until May, when he had agreed to go to England to accept an honorary degree from Cambridge. He looked over the sketches for his new symphony, and found them mechanical and cold. So he put them aside, and took up some ideas that had come to him while in a French railway carriage. With lightning speed, he composed the sixth of his symphonies. To Bob Davidov, he wrote in an exultant mood: "You cannot imagine the joy it gives me to know my day is not yet done. . . ." In May, he went to England, and on June 1 conducted the London Philharmonic in his Fourth Symphony. Saint-Saëns presented a symphony of his own on the same program, but was quite overshadowed by the enthusiasm for Tchaikovsky. Eleven days later, along with Saint-Saëns, Max Bruch, and Boïto—Grieg was to have been of the company, too, but was absent—he received a music doctorate from Cambridge.

Back at Klin, Tchaikovsky finished orchestrating the Sixth Symphony late in August, and wrote his publisher one of his few self-satisfied reports: "On my word of honor, never in my life have I been satisfied with myself, so proud, so happy to know that I have made, in truest fact, a good thing." There was some discussion as to what the new symphony should be called. Modest suggested "*Tragique*" as the proper descriptive adjective. Tchaikovsky demurred, and Modest's next idea was "*Pathétique*," which delighted the composer. On October 28, he conducted it at St. Petersburg, and it is ironical that the only one of his symphonies the composer spoke of with unreserved pleasure should have been received with a chill lack of understanding. After the performance, Rimsky-Korsakov asked his friend whether the B minor Symphony had a program. Tchaikovsky said yes, but that it was secret. As it is dedicated to Bob Davidov, with whom he shared his own and Modest's secret, one possible program may easily be conjectured. Havelock Ellis has flatly called the Sixth Symphony the "homosexual tragedy."

Early in November, Tchaikovsky, who for some years had complained of what he called "heart cramps" and "nervous dysentery," awoke one morning after a gay evening, feeling ill. He brushed aside Modest's offer to summon a doctor, saying that a bottle of Hunyadi Water would fix him up. Instead, he drank a glass of unboiled tap water—a rash act in cholera-infested St. Petersburg. That night he was seriously ill, and the hurriedly summoned specialists pronounced him dying of cholera. Except for one slight rally, he sank rapidly, enduring the suffocation and thirst characteristic of the disease. The end came on November 6,

1893. He died reproachfully muttering the name of Nadejda Filaretovna.

Wild rumors began to circulate. About a fortnight after Tchaikovsky's death, a memorial performance of the *"Pathétique"* was given that was marked by wild acclamation of what was already beginning to be called the "Suicide" Symphony. Of course, these sensationalists and hysterics were wrong in their suspicion that the composer had taken his life. But they were right in a larger sense: the Sixth Symphony is an epitome of Tchaikovsky's biography, wherein his vices and virtues are ranged side by side. Here are all his faults, too glaring to be denied—gross sentimentality, inability to avoid the commonplace, unhealthy self-pity, overfervid emotionalism. Against these are his fertile melodiousness, his wide gamut of orchestral color, ranging from the rawest primes to the most delicate tints, his genius for knowing what instruments can do, the sweep of his rhythms, and the satisfying eloquence of his mighty climaxes. It is possible honestly to dislike something in each of the movements of the Sixth Symphony—the first for its tearful repetitiveness, the second for its petty waywardness, the third for its bombastic and vulgar spunk, and the finale for its neurotic self-revelation—but it will necessarily be an ambivalent dislike. For the symphony gathers compelling power as it moves along, and its dynamic sweep is not to be denied. The cold mathematician tells us that the whole is equal to the sum of its parts, but Tchaikovsky has proved that musically this can be false. In its totality the Sixth Symphony has a strength and a beauty that multiply rather than add together the strength and beauty of the separate movements. It is pointless to prate of vulgar tears, willfulness, bombast, and morbidity when the ocean is coming straight at you.

Chapter XX

Claude-Achille Debussy

(St. Germain-en-Laye, August 22, 1862–
March 25, 1918, Paris)

CLAUDE DEBUSSY, *musicien français"* was the way the greatest of French musicians was wont, in his last years, to sign his name. Gabriele d'Annunzio called him "Claude de France." Debussy was so French, and what he did was so French, that it is unprofitable to compare him with his musical contemporaries in other countries. Of course, no modern composer, with his unparalleled opportunities for hearing the music of all times and all countries, can fail to be influenced somewhat by the work of foreign musicians. But in Debussy's case that influence was singularly small. He took something from Russia, something from the Far East, and even a little from Spain, but these borrowings have been exaggerated in attempts to find a simple explanation for the exoticism that still clings to his music. Actually, the key to that exoticism lies nearer home, and is much simpler. Debussy broke with the German and Italian traditions that, between them, had run music for two hundred years, and wrote French French music. If he still sounds strange to us, that is partly because our ears are pro-German or pro-Italian.

Debussy was not only French, he was Parisian. When he was only twenty, Nadejda von Meck described him to Tchaikovsky as "Parisian from tip to toe, a typical *gamin de Paris*," and in some ways Debussy was the *boulevardier* of fiction. The Paris into which he was born was in most respects as barren artistically as the Germany Schumann laughed to scorn in the famous retrospective preface to his collected *Zeitschrift* articles. The Germany of 1833 was in the short-lived doldrums between the waning of classicism and the emergence of romanticism. The Paris of 1862 was in a deeper trough: except in literature, it was impossible to get even a Pisgah sight of the great efflorescence that was to begin in the eighties. Many of the lions of romanticism were either dead or dying. Lamartine, who had sponsored the movement in France, was an unburied corpse. However, Hugo was still to write masterpieces, and Baudelaire, the Goncourts, and Flaubert were to be reckoned with. Painting and music were the derelicts. Delacroix, the friend of Chopin, was on his deathbed, and so was the hope of romanticism in painting. The recognition of Daumier was yet to come, and the impressionists were still to perform. The academicians were in the saddle. In music, though Berlioz was still alive, the same situation obtained. The composers of *Faust* and *Mignon* were great in the land, and Auber and Offenbach were not far behind. Conforming to the rules as interpreted by the pundits was notoriously the only way to success, and (as Berlioz had found out) true originality meant being an outcast. Or, with the proper strength, it meant breaking the tradition—as Debussy did—and dying the most respected composer in France.

The art of Debussy is an aristocratic art, but his origins were definitely middle-class. In the days of his slightly affected and supercilious youth, he laid tacit claim to noble blood by pretending that his patronymic was De Bussy. Actually, the name had been Debussy for generations, and his parents kept a china shop at St. Germain-en-Laye. Here in sight of Paris, Achille-Claude* was born on August 22, 1862. Even as a baby, he had a mighty forehead, but with such projecting temples that in later life he wore his hair so as to hide them. Fortunately for his chances of getting a start in life, his father's sister, Mme Roustan, was the mistress of Arosa, a rich banker, and it was this lighthearted and artistic couple who acted as godparents at his belated christening in 1864. When the little china shop failed the next year, and the Debussys had to move to a scrubby artisans' suburb, his godparents temporarily adopted the child. While with them, he acquired that taste for the luxuries of life which never left him, and which even conditioned his art. Before he was seven, the fates were engaged in a tug of war over his future: his father wanted him to become a sailor; the boy himself, fascinated by Arosa's collection of modern paintings, yearned to be an artist; his aunt settled the matter by taking him to an old Italian piano teacher.

In 1870, the moody little boy must have been vaguely aware of the preparations for Napoleon III's disastrous war against Prussia and her allies. But he was already too enthralled by the sounds he

---

* Early in life, he called himself Achille. But he came to think of it as a silly name, and reversed his Christian names. He ended up as plain Claude Debussy.

could make on the piano to pay even a precocious child's heed to the outside world. Furthermore, a remarkable woman now took an interest in him. Mme Mauté de Fleurville exhaled the glamour of great memories: she had been the friend of Balzac and De Musset, and a pupil of Chopin. She knew Wagner. She was Paul Verlaine's mother-in-law. Debussy's talent was obvious to her, and she eagerly offered to prepare him for the Conservatoire. This took three years—long enough for him to have absorbed from Mme Mauté de Fleurville the essence of everything she could hand on to him from Chopin. And like Chopin, but more precociously (for he was barely out of his musical swaddling clothes), Debussy became an explorer of unorthodox harmonies. If his teacher thought about it at all, she must have known that life in the Conservatoire presided over by the pedantic and moribund Ambroise Thomas would not be easy for this born rebel. When he appeared there, in October, 1873, it seemed at first as if his fellow students would complicate the situation by ragging him about his strange appearance. For with Arosa respectably married, and no longer interested in Mme Roustan's charms, Debussy was back on his parents for support, and had to wear shabby clothes.

Debussy's eleven years at the Conservatoire were one round of difficulties, due chiefly to his independent and mocking spirit and his already marked originality—difficulties he met, quite logically, in a very cavalier manner. He was lucky in his *solfège* teacher, Albert Lavignac, a progressive young man who was soon to become a leader of the French Wagnerians. Not only was Lavignac moved to answer the boy's unconventional questions reasonably, but he found his own faith in the sanctity of rules seriously shaken by them. Within a few years, Debussy was at the head of the school in *solfège*. In sharp contrast was his experience in other classes, which were presided over by men twice Lavignac's age. Antoine Marmontel took him in piano. Here, unhappily for his parents' dream of a virtuoso son who would be a good moneymaker, Debussy did not shine. For some years a state of war existed between him and Marmontel, who was angered by his pupil's waywardness and improvising idiosyncrasies. In 1877, the fifteen-year-old boy managed a second prize in piano-playing, but thereafter failed to place. He fought his bloodiest battles in the harmony class of Émile Durand, a ninth-rate academician who was bored by music and detested the very idea of teaching. As a prize in harmony was prerequisite to going on to a composition class, Durand temporarily checkmated Debussy's most cherished wish by giving him no recognition whatsoever. It was only by getting honors in score-reading that he gained his wish.

The year 1880 was a lucky one for Debussy. Not only could he look forward to becoming a composition student, and thereby a candidate for the Prix de Rome, but he had by this time won Marmontel's solid regard. He was therefore his piano master's choice when Nadejda von Meck, who was luxuriating with her large family and entourage at one of the Loire châteaux, asked the Conservatoire to send her a pianist for her private trio, a teacher for her children, and a four-hands partner for herself. That summer Debussy saw Italy and Switzerland in style, and was thoroughly introduced to the music of Tchaikovsky. Mme von Meck thought "my little Bussy" a nice lad, but was not overly enthusiastic about his musical gifts. She liked him well enough to ask him to Russia in the summers of 1881 and 1882. That much is certain. The existence of two unpublished compositions signed "Debussy, Moscow, 1884" indicates that he was also there that year, and possibly other times. As he himself never mentioned these Russian experiences, and the references to him in the Von Meck letters are scanty, this matter is apt to remain obscure. One cannot help wondering what would have become of Debussy if the Von Meck girl to whom he proposed had accepted him, and he had settled down in Moscow.

Meanwhile, in the autumn of 1880, Debussy had entered Ernest Guiraud's composition class at the Conservatoire. During the next four years his principal efforts were directed toward gaining the Prix de Rome, the highest award in the gift of the Académie des Beaux-Arts, carrying with it a considerable subsidy for four years' study at the Académie de France in Rome. He made three tries, getting the second-prize gold medal at the last, but the now un-known compositions he submitted were judged too immature for the big honor. In 1884, he handed the judges the manuscript of *L'Enfant prodigue*, a cantata or, as he called it, "lyric scene." This time, twenty-two of the twenty-eight judges voted for him. Fore-most in his praises was Gounod, who loudly declared the cantata a work of genius. But the genius was Massenet, to whom Debussy was at this time little more than a sedulous ape. *L'Enfant prodigue* shows some dramatic flair, but has the peculiar cloying effect of much second-rate nineteenth-century French music. There is a minimum of Debussy himself in it, and it may be that the kindly Guiraud, mindful of the academic minds with which the Prix de Rome juries were packed, had advised him not to be naughty.*

The composer of *L'Enfant prodigue* had already written songs that are still sung. Among the dozen or so composed in the eight years between 1876 and 1884, some of which he revised later, we find the favorite *Beau Soir*, *Mandoline*, and *Fantoches*. The first of these is almost pure Massenet, though slightly more etherealized, but in the two settings of Verlaine, Debussy was at least borrowing more judiciously: this time he went to Berlioz, and the result is something magic in a small way. Many of these songs carry dedications to a Mme Vasnier, a delightful misunderstood wife in whose home Debussy made himself easy in the early eighties. It seems that M. Vasnier carried his misunderstanding of his handsome wife to the point of not realizing that she was having an affair with her accompanist. In fact, he was on excellent terms with Debussy, who found the comfortable Vasnier home much more attractive than his parents' dingy quarters in Clichy. Even after going to Rome, he corresponded with the Vasniers for some time, but soon other interests claimed him, and the friendship came to an end.

Debussy was idling on one of the Seine bridges when a friend tapped him on the shoulder, and breathed, "You've won the prize." He was crushed by the good news: "Believe me or not, I can assure you that all my pleasure vanished! I saw in a flash the boredom, the vexations inevitably incident to the slightest official recognition. Besides, I felt I was no longer free." In this antagonistic mood, he went to Rome in January, 1885. He disliked the city, hated the weather, and despised the restrictions of the Villa Medici, where the prizewinners lived and worked. The wide, open spaces of his living quarters, which he referred to as an "Etruscan tomb," aggravated the newcomer's loneliness. The food was bad—no trifling matter to this precocious gourmet. He poured out his dejection in long letters to the Vasniers. He made a few friends, met

---

* It has often been said that Debussy developed his essential style late. There is some truth in this, and it may have been that the seeming tardiness was due to his following the advice of Guiraud and other mistaken friends.

droves of notables. One day, at the home of Giovanni Sgambati, Cardinal von Hohenlohe, as a tactful gesture toward the young French laureate, induced the famous Italian pianist to sit down with Liszt, and play Saint-Saëns' two-piano *Variations on a Theme of Beethoven.* Another day, Debussy made the long pilgrimage to Sant' Agata, and chatted with Verdi while the old man puttered in his garden. Through Leoncavallo he met Boïto, who seemed to him more like a man of letters than a composer. Most Roman music either bored or annoyed him: the operas of Donizetti and the early efforts of Verdi reigned supreme. The Masses of Palestrina and, even more, those of Di Lasso, exalted him, but his most intense pleasure was playing over Wagner scores, particularly *Tristan.* In 1885, and for some years after, Debussy was a passionate Wagnerian.

Early in 1886, the atmosphere of the Villa Medici became too much for Debussy, and he fled to Paris. Doubtless, he hoped to turn his back on that hated Renaissance structure forever, but someone (probably Vasnier) persuaded him that he was foolishly throwing away his big chance. In April, he was back in Rome. The rest of the year was given over to grinding out an *envoi de Rome*—the stipulated yearly proof that the laureate was not wasting his time. Debussy had already made two attempts to compose one in 1885, but had abandoned them in desperation at having to write music to order. Now he took up one of them—*Zuleïma,* an adaptation for orchestra and chorus of lines by Heine—and finished a truncated version by October. The very next month, he began *Printemps,* also for orchestra and chorus, the inspiration for which had come from Botticelli's *Primavera.* The first of these was unmitigatedly damned by the Paris committee, and Debussy, who cared little for it himself, destroyed the score. *Printemps* fared somewhat better with the academes, though they took exception to the key in which it was written and to the humming chorus. In the official report on *Printemps* there occurred, probably for the first time in connection with Debussy, the word "impressionism." It was used to deride him, just as it had been used, ten years before, to deride a now world-famous group of painters.

Before the spring of 1887, Debussy made his final resolve not to finish out three years in Rome. Somehow or other, the committee was prevailed upon to accept his return to Paris, though this did not exempt him from submitting a third *envoi*. He threw himself thirstily into the artistic life of Paris, acquired a green-eyed mistress, cherished the Pre-Raphaelites, and became an intimate of the more outrageous literary circles. Mallarmé and the *symbolistes* welcomed him at their famous Tuesday evenings. From these associations and predilections came the inspiration for his last *envoi*, a setting of a French condensation of Dante Gabriel Rossetti's *The Blessed Damozel*. Before completing it, Debussy made a trip to Bayreuth in true pilgrim spirit, and swam rapturously in the murky sea of *Parsifal*, large doses of which he injected into *La Damoiselle élue*. Between the patches of thinned-out Wagner and the echoes of Franck, there was enough Debussy in it to at least put the committee in a questioning frame of mind. They referred to its "systematic vagueness" and lack of form, but admitted a certain poetic quality and charm. It is a work of exquisite taste, with much lovely pastel color, though too faithful to Rossetti for modern ears. Debussy's melodies swoon and languish with the poetry. *La Damoiselle élue* is an immature work. But, as Oscar Thompson has pointed out, it is "full of harmonic prophecies that no subsequent generation can fail to recognize."

The year 1889 was of salient importance in Debussy's artistic development, less for what came from his pen than for the influences to which he was subjected. A second pilgrimage to Bayreuth resulted in his beginning to look at Wagner with a coldly judicious eye: he was thrilled by the music of *Tristan*, but began to question his idol's theories of music drama. Once he had begun to doubt, recantation of his early enthusiasm followed fast until, by the time he himself began to compose *Pelléas et Mélisande*, he was in arms against Wagner's conception of the stage. As Wagner receded, Mussorgsky loomed as an ever more important influence. After returning from Bayreuth, Debussy got hold of a score of *Boris Godunov* (strangely enough, it belonged to Saint-Saëns, who was to lead the opposition to Debussy), and began studying it and playing it over to his friends. *Boris* implemented his flight from Wagner, for he saw that a frankly episodic opera could produce quite as integral an effect as Wagner's continuous and repetitive web. From Mussorgsky, too, he received certain harmonic hints, though none so germinative as those he got simultaneously at the Exposition Universelle of 1889–90. The music of the Javanese and Annamite orchestras—more particularly, the percussion group that accompanied the Javanese dancers—held him enthralled. The subtle, complicated rhythms, the harmonies that had never heard of Occidental textbooks, and the feline, insinuating coloration made something in his own nature respond, and opened more widely the vista of a music he dreamed of creating.

Debussy's immediate attempt at an opera may be classified as his protest against Wagnerism. Taking a libretto by Catulle Mendès, entitled *Rodrigue et Chimène,* he wrote three scenes of a melodramatic opera, and then gave it up. It was too Wagnerian. Debussy, though his opinions had changed, could not get Brangäne's potion out of his blood. Although elements that are now called Debussyan are recognizable in many small works that belong to the late eighties and early nineties, the composer was not yet in full command of his new resources, had not yet developed his peculiar idiom sufficiently to use it in a large work. These were essentially years of study and experimentation, of highly selective response.

Debussy did not crowd himself: he was too much a Parisian of the epoch to do that. To an outsider, to all but a handful of his friends, he seemed little more than a carefree *boulevardier* saved from stereotype only by his aristocratic and delicate tastes. He did his share of gossiping in the artists' cafés, usually in the company of Gabrielle Dupont, who remained his mistress through thick and thin until just before his marriage in 1899. Poor Gaby of the Green Eyes could not expect to hold her Claude forever, for apart from his congenital inclination to stray, she had little more than her physical charms with which to hold him. Once he became engaged to a young singer, another time he had an affair with a society woman. But he always returned to Gaby until the time he began to find her eyes "steely" and her companionship totally unstimulating. In 1891, Erik Satie, the talented and sardonic Mephistopheles of modern French music, became another of Debussy's café familiars. Satie, with his taste for the miniature and his loathing of the oversized and pompous, was instrumental in dissipating whatever traces of Wagnerism his friend retained. In later years, Satie's searing humor was to be turned against Debussy's programmatic titles. At first, however, he played the role of an intelligent interlocutor, and subtly directed Debussy's attention to the traditions of French music. The idea, once widely current, that

Satie strongly influenced Debussy's harmonic style is quite without foundation.

The period of meditation and search began to bear fruit as early as 1892, when Debussy embarked on the composition of two of his most characteristic works. One of them, *Prélude à l'Après-midi d'un faune*, was finished within two years. The other, which grew out of his happening upon a Maeterlinck play in a bookstall, and took ten years of false starts and revisions, was his only completed opera, *Pelléas et Mélisande*. Before finishing *L'Après-midi*, Debussy got his first taste of public reaction to some of his extended compositions. *La Damoiselle élue*, which should have been performed at the Conservatoire in a concert of his three *envois*, had its *première* elsewhere because Debussy had quarreled with the committee. Fortunately, the Société Nationale decided to present it at its concert of April 8, 1893. The critical reaction was mixed, Colette's caustic husband, Henri Gauthier-Villars ("Willy") being in the van of the scoffers. He referred to the composer as "Fra Angelico Debussy" and to the cantata as a "symphonic stained-glass window." In December of the same year, the Ysaÿe Quartet, at another Société Nationale concert, gave the first performance of a string quartet, to compose which Debussy had temporarily laid aside both *L'Après-midi* and *Pelléas*. This G minor Quartet, which is always called the First Quartet, though Debussy never completed another, was frowned upon by purists, but was acclaimed by many influential musicians, some of whom might have been expected to resent its break with cut-and-dried quartet tradition. In general, Debussy took the criticism calmly, but was wounded when his friend Ernest Chausson stood aloof. "I shall write another quartet for you," he wrote Chausson, "entirely for you, and I shall try to give dignity to my forms." There is, perhaps, a trace of irony in the last phrase.

The G minor String Quartet is the most distinguished piece of chamber writing in the French repertoire. Comparatively speaking, it is, for Debussy, an essay in abstract music. There is no doubt that working (however freely) with the string quartet—that most rule-bound of musical media—somewhat curtailed the expressiveness of the idiom he was engaged in perfecting. What weaknesses the quartet has are traceable to the respect Debussy sporadically showed to the old sonata formula of quartet construction, and it is precisely in the last movement, when the pull of convention became overpowering, and the *révolté* felt called upon to write true counterpoint, that the String Quartet approaches the stilted. One cannot help hazarding the guess that the mature Debussy would have carried to their logical conclusion the full implications of the cyclic form, and written the quartet in one movement. Although Debussy's only contact with César Franck had been as a short-term student in an organ class, here he was strongly influenced by the Belgian, who had devoted much of his creative energy to exploring the possibilities of cyclic form. At the beginning of the third movement, Franck's voice may even be heard, though fortunately not for long. In harmonic texture, in understanding of instrumental timbres, in a sensuousness unusual for the medium, the String Quartet is unmistakably Debussyan. The fragments of exquisite and caressing melody, the mixed, unsettled harmonies, the elegant attention to the personalities and versatilities of the instruments—all these testify to Debussy's tacit repudiation of the old-fashioned idea that the string quartet is par excellence the vehicle for the expression of lofty philosophical ideas. The G minor Quartet was Debussy's first important manifesto that, as far as he was concerned, music is to be enjoyed for itself and for the pictures and sensations it evokes.

And, after making every allowance for the difference of the media, what an advance Debussy registers toward his ideal of sensuous music in a work performed the very next year! The *Prélude à l'Après-midi d'un faune*, "orchestral eclogue after the poem by Stéphane Mallarmé," is, in the exact sense of those frequently misused words, a tone poem. Just as Mallarmé's lines are an idealess evocation of summer warmth and a faun daydreaming of the only delights he can know, Debussy's shimmering score is a musical gloss on this Theocritan afternoon. There is no real programmatic connection between the two works: this is mood music, and pretends to nothing more. Nijinsky's well-known choreography of the faun and the nymphs came from the poem and his own imagination, not from details in the music. Debussy disliked the ballet, and wrote of it with scarifying scorn: "It is ugly: Dalcrozian, in fact." Few will quarrel with the proposition that Nijinsky's descent to realistic detail fatally marred the quality Mallarmé tried to convey. Debussy has actually improved upon Mallarmé. Not only is the creation of the mood of *L'Après-midi* easier for music than for poetry, but Debussy had become the subtlest master of sensuous effect in music. The chromatic pleasings of the flutes, the rustlings and light pluckings of the harps, the warming sunlight of the strings and horns—all these conjure up the very feeling of a young and ancient world. What a relief it must have been in 1894 to have this vision of a sun-intoxicated Latin pagandom after the gross, glowering, and heavily philosophical magnificences of *Der Ring des Nibelungen*!

When *L'Après-midi* was first performed on December 22, 1894, at least the audience of the Société Nationale liked it, for it had to be repeated. As usual, however, the critics divided, largely along lines of age. Debussy's admirers found in it a proof that he had finally arrived; his enemies quite as much a proof that he was a hopeless case. The important thing was that in the struggle against a smothering tradition he now became a battle cry, often on the lips of people who had not the vaguest notion of what he was trying to do. Within a decade, *L'Après-midi* found its way around the world, but until just after the World War it was considered extremely daring. It then became, and has remained, the best known of Debussy's compositions.* But *L'Après-midi* was, at least in scale, a small work, and the Debussyans immediately began to clamor for something that could be used as an antidote to the Wagnerism poisoning the wellsprings of French music. Naturally, what they most wanted was the opera Debussy was known to be writing. But hurry was fatal to his best intentions, and when pressure became unendurable in 1895, he tore up in disgust a first, probably completed, version of *Pelléas*—an action that showed not only artistic integrity but also a clear realization of the high quality of what was asked of him. It showed courage, too, for he was so poor that grinding out a couple of potboilers would have been not only pardonable but reasonable.

Of course, the eight years intervening between *L'Après-midi* and the first production of *Pelléas* were not devoted exclusively to polishing that opera. In 1893, Debussy's acquaintance with the exotic Pierre Louÿs ripened into intimacy. The more one knows of Debussy, the more one realizes that he chose his friends with some of

* At least, that is, until 1938, when Debussy joined the immortals who have made the grade in Tin Pan Alley. In that year, his piano salon piece *Rêverie*—always negligible—lost what little distinction it had in becoming *My Reverie*, the hit song of the year.

the calculation Horace Walpole had used, in a more inhuman, pavonine way, in choosing his correspondents. Ever the self-conscious, aristocratic eclectic, he went through life adding to the scanty culture his deficient education had given him. Louÿs was a scholar with a dilettante's air, a pundit who posed as a mere elegant taster of culture. Rome and Greece and the Orient were at his fingertips: he used this quite profound knowledge to decorate his pornographic writings. Debussy definitely came under Louÿs' spell for a number of years, and absorbed many of his esthetic ideas. In 1897, he set three of his friend's notorious *Chansons de Bilitis*, a sequence of Lesbian love poems. Already, he had composed many fine songs, even a few great ones. Yet, with rare exceptions, these early songs are more reflective of other men's music than is the instrumental work contemporary with them. After Massenet had served his turn, Debussy wrote, in the *Cinq Poemes de Baudelaire* (1887–9), French cousins to Wagner's *Träume* and *Schmerzen*—splendid, heavy-colored songs not unworthy of their lyrics. But with the *Ariettes oubliées* (1888), he returned to Berlioz, his early master in the song. These are less opaque, extraordinarily simple and calmly wrought. Debussy never achieved a more pellucid wash than *Il pleure dans mon coeur*, a more guileless statement than *Green*. These are the works of a perfectly deceptive sophistication so sure of itself that it can risk a sly touch of sentimentality. As Verlaine moods, nothing better can be imagined. In 1892, Debussy tried his hand at setting some prose lyrics of his own manufacture: the results are machine-made and clumsy—epitaphs, if anything, of a transient lack of taste.

For Louÿs' *Chansons de Bilitis* Debussy surpassed himself. *La Flûte de Pan*, *La Chevelure*, *Le Tombeau des naïades* are, as poetry, negligible fake paganism; as songs, they have the remote, static beauty of a frieze about to be given life. Some such music whispers on the surface of Keats' Grecian urn. The *Chansons de Bilitis* are somewhat cold, incalculably distant, but extremely beautiful. The songs that came after them are something of an anticlimax. Then suddenly, in 1910, in three truly magnificent settings of Villon, Debussy found a new side of his lyrical nature. The *Trois Ballades de François Villon* show no marked technical difference from their predecessors, but are informed by a passion, a vigor, a sheer masculinity, if you will, that are unparalleled in his work. The musician in Debussy did not have to change to produce these: he had, as a man, to develop to the point of wanting to set Villon, and his musical sensitivity did the rest. The *Trois Ballades* register a human advance: despite the rollicking humor of the *Ballade des femmes de Paris*, these are, in total effect, a tragic triptych—the creation of a man not far from the end of his tether.

Debussy's care in his choice of friends was not matched in his love life. At least, apparently not. One may be permitted to wonder what had kept him generally faithful to Gaby for more than ten years, and equally, what induced him to leave her for a respectable little dressmaker whose sole qualities seem to have been an amiable disposition and a sort of wistful prettiness that reminded him of Mélisande. It is true that by the time he married this appealing Rosalie Texier, he no longer cared even physically for Gaby. It is also true that the girl he married on October 19, 1899, was virginal and unspoiled—attributes that appealed strongly to the sensualist Debussy. He was soon to discover that she represented the zero point as an intellectual companion, and nothing is more telling of this aspect of their six years together than that Debussy dedicated not a single published composition to her. From a financial point of view, the marriage was a risk: Debussy's tiny income rested precariously on a few piano lessons, an occasional order for a transcription, and a few coppers from royalties. On his wedding day he had to give a lesson in order to get enough money to pay for the traditional wedding breakfast and tickets to a circus. With a true Bohemian touch, the Debussys boasted that they had literally spent their last sou so that it could be said they had begun their married life with no money at all.

It has been loosely asserted that "Lily-Lilo," as Debussy called Rosalie, was the direct inspiration of the two large works he completed within three years of his marriage. Simple chronology refutes this idea. The second—and final—version of *Pelléas et Mélisande* was well advanced when he met Lily. As for the *Nocturnes*, though her name appears on the first page of the complete manuscript, they were begun years earlier as violin and orchestra pieces for his friend Eugène Ysaÿe, and in the published version for orchestra alone are dedicated to Georges Hartmann, Debussy's publisher. The unhappy tradition of playing only the first two of the three *Nocturnes* was instituted on December 9, 1900, when *Nuages* and

Fêtes were played at the Concerts Lamoureux. An opportunity to judge the *Nocturnes* as a whole was not afforded until October 27 of the following year, when *Sirènes* was also played. A key to the unity they undeniably have comes from Debussy himself: "The title *Nocturnes* is to be interpreted here in a general and, more particularly, in a decorative sense. Therefore, it is not meant to designate the usual form of the nocturne, but rather all the various impressions and the special effects of light that the word suggests." In short, they are neither the classical *notturni* of Haydn and Mozart nor the languorous night pieces of Chopin. The most obvious thing about the *Nocturnes* is their relation to impressionist painting: Debussy may even have borrowed their name from Whistler. Specifically, *Nuages* has been likened to Monet, *Fêtes* to Renoir, and *Sirènes* to Turner. It is easy to quarrel with these analogies, particularly the last, for *Sirènes* is reminiscent rather of the vasty emptinesses of Ryder. As contrasting moods, as contrasting evocations of light effects, these *Nocturnes* are unique in music. Among them, *Fêtes* is perhaps the most moving; the slow and mysterious entrance of a procession halfway through it is an utterly magical moment, as breathtaking each time one hears it, as suddenly surprising, as the modulation after the first fortissimo in Beethoven's Fourth Concerto.

By the time of the *Nocturnes*, the critics were so inured to Debussy's strange antics that they no longer commented overmuch on his technical innovations. They did not even blast his use of female voices as wordless instruments in *Sirènes*—an experiment that never quite comes off, and is mainly of historical interest. In fact, they were, on the whole, enthusiastic. One of them caught the very essence of Debussy's esthetic: "M. Debussy does not demand of music all that she can give, but rather, that which she *alone* is capable of suggesting." When, at the Paris Exposition of 1900, France herself had extended recognition to the composer by ordering some of his music performed at the official concerts, it was not likely that the sycophantic press would long hold aloof. A useful proof of Debussy's increasing weight in French music came in 1901, when he was invited to contribute articles to *La Revue blanche*. He accepted, for he had something to say, and the articles would be paid for. Appropriately, his first column appeared on April Fool's Day, for he was to become the G. B. S. of Parisian musical reporting. For thirteen years, in various journals, sometimes under the pseudonym of "Monsieur Croche, Antidilettante," sometimes under his own name, he was to harry the graybeards of all ages. When M. Croche's mocking, acid voice was first heard, the storm over Debussy's music had quietened, in his own bailiwick, to a deceptive lull, but as it was to break loose with unexampled violence in a year, it was all to the good that he had some share in directing public taste in the interim.

By the beginning of 1902, *Pelléas et Mélisande* was complete. It had been Debussy's intention merely to present it privately at the house of Comte Robert de Montesquiou, the wealthy eccentric whom both Huysmans and Proust took as a model for their most noisome characters. To his delight, in 1897 André Messager, a conductor at the Opéra-Comique, showed the incomplete score to the management, and it was accepted at once. Maeterlinck had already expressed his willingness to have Debussy set his play. Everything seemed ready when Albert Carré, director of the Comique, caused a scandal by giving the role of Mélisande to a young American singer by the name of Mary Garden. Debussy had previously promised the role to Maeterlinck's common-law wife, Georgette Leblanc, who had created Mélisande in the stage play. The Belgian dramatist was incensed at what he considered Debussy's trickery. Actually he had merely promised something he now lacked authority to give. It almost came to a duel, but Maeterlinck finally contented himself with rushing into print with a diatribe against Debussy and the management of the Comique. Carré was not to be bluffed. Rehearsals went on as scheduled, though certain members of the orchestra assumed part of Maeterlinck's grudge. The *répétition générale* was disturbed by heckling and unfriendly laughter. As a rumpus, the first performance, on April 30, 1902, equaled the Paris *première* of *Tannhäuser*. Almost all the critics, and more than half the audience, were vocally hostile. Miss Garden's American accent was jeered at, and her fine interpretation ignored. Nor did the other members of the cast—one hundred per cent French though they were—get more polite treatment. That audience wanted Debussy's scalp.

By the terms of his reaction against Wagner, Debussy had created a thoroughly non-Wagnerian opera in spirit. He could not afford, however, to ignore the techniques Wagner had added to opera, and selected from them just enough to allow one to say that *Pelléas* could have been composed only after Wagner had lived. Most obvious of these borrowings was the leitmotiv, from which Debussy evolved, as Vincent d'Indy said, "a series of pivot themes . . . the function of which is to send out harmonic rays in all directions, rays that serve to present the musical speech in the ambience suited to it." In other words, Wagner's leitmotiv serves constantly to advance the action, Debussy's pivot theme to concentrate the atmosphere. For *Pelléas* is an opera of atmosphere, of extended poetic evocation. A story unfolds, scrupulously Debussy follows the Maeterlinck text. Possibly too scrupulously. Maeterlinck's shadowland and twilight people call for a music of understatement. The score of *Pelléas* whispers: the orchestration is thin and restrained, the vocal line hardly different from ordinary speech. The result is that a work whose component parts are as disjointed as sections of a dream has also the incongruous unity of a dream. *Pelléas* has a oneness of atmosphere that is at once its strength and its weakness. It ensorcels, but it also emanates *tedium vitae.* It is a decadent opera, an opera of the nineties.

To Debussy's surprise, *Pelléas* bucked the harrowings of the press, and became first a cult, and then a staple of the repertoire. Enough of the old *fin de siècle* spirit was left in the world to make the opera the darling of an influential group of *précieux.* And when its purely cult appeal faded out, the fragile, poetic Mélisande of Mary Garden kept it a favorite wherever she sang. With her disappearance from the stage, *Pelléas* is heard less often, except in France. The rare concert performances of instrumental excerpts prove how indissolubly Debussy wedded music to words and action. This music, which in a stage version glimmers so exquisitely, definitely needs the words and action from which it grew: heard alone, it is all but meaningless and thoroughly monotonous. Paradoxically, though a more integrated opera does not exist, it needs a great singing actress like Garden to hold it together. Unless another such arises, Debussy's opera may disappear entirely at a not too distant date.

The success of *Pelléas* projected its composer into public life far more than he liked. He became a famous man, and France took cognizance of his eminence by giving him the Legion of Honor. His more feverish admirers were dubbed the *Pelléastres*, and were derided in print and caricature for their extravagant absorption, much as the Wagnerians had been pilloried by Beardsley. For a time this most personal, most intimate of composers, this aloof man who valued his privacy above everything else, was threatened with the destiny of a *chef d'école*. He had a bad attack of nerves, and retired to the country. As Lily was with him, this did not help much, for already that period was beginning which was to end with him confessing that the mere sound of her voice made him want to scream. He sketched the libretto of a new opera from Poe's *The Devil in the Belfry*, thought vaguely about another based on *As You Like It*, and did nothing about either. He did not hanker too much after further success at the Comique. He was ill, however, of something more destructive of peace than even success could be, and when an extended orchestral work—*La Mer*—did not progress as he had hoped,* he decided to leave Lily, whose personality was by this time revealed to him in all its flatness. It was one thing to write an opera about Mélisande, another to live with her. He fled to the arms of Emma Bardac, an attractive woman of the world and fine singer. Of somewhat ambiguous personality, she was already the wife of a rich banker and the mistress of Gabriel Fauré, an excellent composer who has never had his just deserts.

Lily took Debussy's desertion hard: she tried to kill herself with a revolver. He went to see her at the hospital, but never went back after being assured that she would not die. He had come to hate her, and never saw her again, though she outlived him fourteen years. He was living openly with Emma Bardac: Fauré protested, but not her husband—he was enjoying himself with an actress, and was inclined to tolerance. In this scandal, the public and most of Debussy's friends sided with Lily, and it was whispered that he was fortune hunting. There seems to be a core of truth to this idea, but when Emma's money evaporated, Debussy remained faithful, and went on dedicating compositions to her until the end. In October, 1905, she bore him a daughter after Lily had divorced him, but unfortunately before she had obtained her own divorce.

---

* His now unhappily forgotten *Rapsodie pour saxophone et piano* fared even worse. Begun in 1903 at the insistence of Mrs. Elisa Hall, a Boston lady who believed that playing what Debussy called "this aquatic instrument" was good for her health, it languished for years, and was finally delivered in incomplete form in 1911. Roger-Ducasse orchestrated it in 1919, and it was heard for the first time more than a year after Debussy's death.

Thus Claude-Emma, the beloved "Chouchou" of the doting father Debussy rather surprisingly became, was illegitimate. It was not until months later that Emma was free, and the marriage could take place. Bardac had tricked Emma into believing that she would receive an annual alimony of fifty thousand francs. When he failed to live up to his promise, there ensued a series of lawsuits that threw a lurid light on the motives of the three interested parties. These were fruitlessly protracted, outlasting Debussy, and ending only in 1934 with Emma's death.

The period of Debussy's marital vicissitudes was not musically unproductive. Aside from a Verlaine song suite he dedicated to Emma in 1904, the delightfully archaic *Danse sacrée et danse profane* for harp and strings, and the most ambitious of his orchestral works, *La Mer*, from these years date the earliest of the pieces that have entitled Debussy to be called the greatest composer for the piano since Chopin. When the semiofficial pianist of modern French music, Ricardo Viñes, played the suite *Pour le piano* in January, 1902, no new piano pieces had come from Debussy for ten years. Although some of those early pieces attained, and have kept, a great popularity—who does not know *Rêverie* and *Clair de lune?*— the enthusiasm that greeted Viñes at the Société Nationale showed that the public was ready for something more advanced than the Massenet salon pieces Debussy had been composing. As a writer for the piano, he evolved slowly. When he had all but attained full stature in songs and orchestral work, he had not yet begun to think in his peculiar piano idiom.

Pour le piano had a hint here and there, but it was not until January 9, 1904, when Viñes played *Estampes*, that Paris heard a Debussy who had caught up with himself. He had also caught up with Maurice Ravel, whose *Jeux d'eau*, containing many of the technical devices Debussy quietly annexed for his own very different purposes, had been performed two years before. Each of the three *Estampes* shows a separate influence: *Pagodes* reflects the Oriental impressions Debussy gained at the Exposition Universelle four years before; the *Soirée dans Grenade*, besides having to own an almost fatal relationship to a Ravel habanera now incorporated in the popular *Rapsodie espagnole*, actually echoes Debussy's early fondness for *Carmen* and Lalo; *Jardins sous la pluie*, finally, draws on two old French folk songs. But Debussy does not borrow—he transmutes. *Estampes* is the creation of a refined and delicate stylist, with the temperament of a Chopin subjected to modern influences. Chopin makes poetry with the piano, Debussy paints with it. The very title of his next two suites—*Images**—tells much of his point of view. Two of them—significantly, the most popular, possibly the most successful—are visual evocations, one of reflections in the water, the other of lacquered goldfish on a Japanese plate.

Debussy's esthetic predilection for water scenes, which one can discover merely by running through the titles of his separate pieces, now manifested itself in a vast tripartite orchestral work, *La Mer*. His actual experience of the sea was from the shore and from the deck of a Channel boat, but the great empty spaces of ocean as they change under light and wind compelled his imagination. After initial difficulties, enhanced by the brewing emotional storms of his domestic life, he took up *La Mer* again, and finished it during two of the most harried years of his life. But completing it was only half the battle with *La Mer*. The score frankly baffled its first conductor, and there was a violent demonstration against it at the *première* on October 15, 1905. So wretched was this performance that *La Mer* was not repeated for two years: it is this second hearing, conducted by the master himself, that dyed-in-the-wool Debussyans persist in referring to as the *première*.

The three divisions of *La Mer* are *De l'aube à midi sur la mer*, *Jeux de vagues*, and *Dialogue du vent et de la mer*. Nevertheless, despite these subtitles, this is not descriptive music. There is no reason why it should be: titles do not constitute a program. When Erik Satie wisecracked about the first movement, that he liked "the part at quarter past eleven," he was attacking Debussy's sometimes too specific titles rather than implying that the music was realistic. For *La Mer* is an imaginative response to thoughts about the sea and its moods, not a wave-by-wave description. Because Debussy conceived poetically of the sea, *La Mer* is necessarily a large and masculine work. Without sacrificing the sensuous delicacy of his perceptions or the subtly tapering color of *L'Après-midi* or *Nocturnes*, he had widened his scope to include big orchestral effects he had never before needed. The shattering climaxes of *La Mer* are

---

* Series I (1905) contains *Reflets dans l'eau*, *Hommage à Rameau*, and *Mouvement*; Series II (1907) *Cloches à travers les feuilles*, *Et la lune descend sur le temple qui fût*, and *Poissons d'or*.

unique to that composition only because Debussy never again felt called upon to use them.

There is a hint of more formal disposition of materials in *La Mer*: Debussy returns to a partial use of cyclic structure, and even occasionally develops a theme in a recognizably classical way. Also, *La Mer* progresses as much by longer melodic statements than are usual with Debussy as by the fusing and flowing of harmonies and the vicissitudes of rhythmic swirl. Debussy called it "three symphonic sketches": the effect is that of a symphony, and it is indeed much more clearly a whole than many a classical symphony. The more one hears this great poem of the sea, the more one realizes that *La Mer* is Debussy's masterpiece precisely because it adds to his decorative and mood-evocative qualities a powerful and satisfying emotional impact.

After *La Mer*, five years elapsed before a new orchestral composition by Debussy was played. The dropping off of his wife's income created a financial crisis in the small house near the Bois de Boulogne, for his own income was still meager—a bit from royalties, a bit from journalism. He had, much against his will, to trade on his fame as a composer to get, as conductor and pianist, engagements for which he was not fully equipped. Like Chopin, he played beautifully and with a distinctive style peculiarly suited to his own music, but so softly that he could barely be heard beyond the first few rows of a large concert hall. As a conductor, he was nervous and stiff, and if he got through an entire concert brilliantly, it was a happy accident. Yet he was well liked in both capacities. His appearances in Austria, Hungary, Italy, Belgium, Holland, and Russia were marked by excellent press notices and cheering audiences. But it was London that welcomed him most warmly, just as it had taken widely to his music before Paris gave it other than a cultish response. His second English tour had a tragic ending. Too ill to finish it out, he had to return home to consult specialists, and they told him he was suffering from cancer. Although he lived nine years more, Debussy became less active, and was never for long free of pain. Yet he continued his concertizing until the war, by which time his royalties were sufficiently large to support him in modest style.

Fortunately, these hectic years of making ends meet were free of domestic troubles. He may not have been passionately in love

with Emma, but he was on excellent terms with her. The focus of
the menage was Chouchou, who seems to have delighted her father
from the very day of her birth. The child had some slight musical
talent, which both amused and pleased Debussy. It was to her that
in 1908 he gave *Children's Corner*, with the dedication, "To my dear
little Chouchou, with her father's affectionate apologies for what
follows." Both the name of the suite and the titles of the six separate pieces are in English—for no explicable reason. The first of
them, *Doctor Gradus ad Parnassum*, is a wonderful parody of the
Clementi *Gradus* with which generations of children have struggled, and of a child playing it. *Jimbo's Lullaby* (Debussy's charming
misspelling of Jumbo, Barnum's big elephant) has a clumsy, childish humor. *Serenade for the Doll* and *The Little Shepherd* are pretty,
but not so effective as *Snow Is Dancing*, a miniature of exquisite
sharpness. The sixth of the *Children's Corner* is the ever-popular
Golliwog's Cake-Walk, which combines a malicious quotation from
Tristan with an elegantly rollicking adaptation of American rag-
time. Almost without exception, these little pieces exhale a personal warmth, a gentle humor that is rare in Debussy. Like Schumann's *Kinderscenen*, they are about the child's world, but scarcely
for the child himself.

In 1908, too, after Oscar Hammerstein had successfully presented *Pelléas et Mélisande* to New York for the first time, the Metropolitan Opera, not to be outdone by the dashing impresario of the
Manhattan Opera House, decided to approach Debussy with a
commission for another opera. One New York newspaper had
pronounced *Pelléas* "exquisite but creepy," another "a study in
glooms." The public reception had been ambiguous, even uncom-
prehending, but it had been just enthusiastic enough to warrant
Giulio Gatti-Casazza trying to get an option on the operas Debussy
was rumored to be composing. Debussy refused to promise a setting of Bédier's *Le Roman de Tristan*, but reluctantly took Gatti-
Casazza's eagerly proffered two thousand francs for an option on
The Fall of the House of Usher and *The Devil in the Belfry*. He had,
after several years, resumed work on the last, and told Gatti-
Casazza that its quite un-Faustian Devil would be a whistling, not
a singing role. These, in addition to a projected opera on Orpheus,
were allowed, after sporadic and halfhearted work, to lapse. Debussy's languid efforts to compose a second opera may indicate a

deep-seated dissatisfaction with *Pelléas* as well as a fear that his genius was not wholly suited to the demands of the stage. Some years later, after Nijinsky had given his notorious interpretation of the Faun in *L'Après-midi*, Debussy, rather against his better judgment, was persuaded to collaborate with the famous Polish dancer in *Jeux*, the best of three ballets he tried his hand at in something more than a year.* The music is deft but vapid.

One more stage work remains to be mentioned—the controversial *Le Martyre de Saint-Sébastien*. In 1911, Gabriele d'Annunzio gave Debussy a rush order for incidental music to a mystery he had written for the eccentric *diseuse*, mime, and dancer, Ida Rubinstein. Despite serious ill health, Debussy worked at top speed on the sketches, turning them over to Caplet for orchestration. The music, which is still performed in concert version, consists of a prelude to each of the five acts, occasional orchestral comment within the acts, and choral and solo-voice passages. As soon as notices of the performance were posted, the Archbishop of Paris issued a pastoral letter commanding his sheep to stay away from the *première* on May 22, 1911, and denouncing *Le Martyre* as offensive to Christian consciences. At once, Debussy and D'Annunzio— a Catholic in good standing—rushed into print in its defense.

These blasts and counterblasts could not have much affected the fate of a smart Ida Rubinstein first night. It was the death of a cabinet minister on the morning of the *répétition générale* that provided the scandal. On the grounds of public mourning, the government tried to exclude everyone except the press, upon which the rest of the invitees attempted to storm the hall. The garish publicity attending these tasteless events raised the first-night audience's hopes to a level that the sprawling, chaotic performance failed to satisfy. After the first astonishment at the sort of splendid shambles the combined talents of D'Annunzio, Debussy, Ida Rubinstein, Bakst, and Fokine could concoct, the audience settled back in boredom. Even Mlle Rubinstein dancing the Saint could not wake them. *Le Martyre* was a fiasco. All that survives of this expensive indulgence of a spoiled society entertainer is the set of religiosensual pieces made from it—music that is resplendent at times in an almost Straussian way, music that harks back to the Church

* *Jeux* was the only one of these he completed. *Khamma* was completed by Charles Koechlin, *La Boîte à joujoux* by André Caplet.

modes, but is not the less a commentary on the panoply of religion rather than a revelation of its spiritual essence. The best explanation of Debussy's part in this tawdry venture that did not even satisfy prewar café society is that he needed the money.

Possibly the explanation of Debussy's indifferent setting of D'Annunzio's overwrought text lies in the fact that he was writing to order and in a hurry. The history of his three ballets bears this out. His dawdling with Gatti-Casazza's commission emphasizes it. Yet, the same years, as anyone knows who has heard the piano *Préludes* and the orchestral *Images*, produced work of most exquisite finish, matured point of view, and abounding musical fruitfulness. By a curious vagary of selection, only one of the three *Images* is ever played. *Rondes de printemps* and *Gigues* are not far below *L'Après-midi* in loveliness, though technically they are more varied in color and harmony, and are more precisely outlined. They are stark Debussy, but it is a calculated starkness, implicit in the materials on which they are based—French folk music in *Rondes* and Scots folk dances in *Gigues*. They will never be as well known as *Ibéria*, the third of the *Images*, which has a greatness that smites one.* But that two large compositions of Debussy's maturity should be completely neglected is a telling comment on the incuriosity of orchestral conductors. And yet, except that it uses scraps of characteristic Spanish melody and rhythm, the constantly played *Ibéria* has no more surface attractiveness than *Rondes* or *Gigues*. The explanation of its popularity lies elsewhere. With all its color, its searching use of the resources of the modern orchestra, it remains somewhat difficult of access, and needs several hearings to reveal its full beauty. In this respect, it stands in salutary contrast to many of Strauss' symphonic poems, which give their all at a first devastating hearing, and pale thereafter. The inner vibrations of *Ibéria* are radiating centers of pure emotion: *Ibéria* is a tragic and deeply felt evocation of the passing show of life. Its three movements,† as clearly as the three sections of *La Mer*, are interrelated

---

* After *Ibéria* and *Rondes de printemps* were first performed, on February 20 and March 2, 1910, respectively, one Gaston Carraud attacked Debussy in a vitriolic article, asserting that the source of his genius was drying up. To the discomfiture of those who for years had been trying to set up Ravel as head of a group officially in opposition to Debussy, the younger man, angered by this unwarranted jet of venom, for once sought the limelight he loathed with a warm defense of Debussy.

† The tripartite division of *Ibéria* into *Par les rues et par les chemins, Parfums de la nuit,* and *Au matin d'un jour de fête* explains Edward Lockspeiser's (at first) astonishing state-

and cumulative in effect. If, as has been suggested, Debussy was influenced by the piano suite *Iberia* of the Spanish composer, Isaac Albéniz, he has subtilized and enriched his borrowings quite beyond recognition.

Without Debussy's large orchestral works, the modern repertoire would be deprived of some of its most precious color. Without his twenty-four piano *Préludes* (1910–13), the lack would be far more serious, for some of them have achieved places for themselves among those most popular of popular pieces—encore music. Most of the *Préludes* are delicious *morceaux* raised above triviality by their confectioner's unfaltering taste, perfect sense of the proportions of small things, and sharp inventiveness. Here, more than any place else in Debussy, is the work of a pupil of a Chopin pupil. Even the most trifling of them is grateful to play and to listen to, so purely pianistic is their texture. Only an insensitive could overlook this patent fact, and dare to transcribe them for another medium. There is no use pretending, however, that most of the *Préludes*—*La Fille aux cheveux de lin*, *La Danse de Puck*, *Brouillards*, and *Bruyères*, for instance—are anything but impressionistic miniatures. Nor are *Minstrels*, *General Lavine—Eccentric*, and *Hommage à S. Pickwick, Esq., P.P.M.P.C.*, anything more pretentious than cousins of *Golliwog* and music for Chouchou. And in the second book, there are a few that have no other function than filling out the traditional twenty-four.

But in both books of *Préludes* there are several of large dimensions and weightier import. *Ce qu'a vu le vent d'ouest* works up into a hurtling fury that seeks out the piano's full volume. *La Cathédrale engloutie* shows how brilliantly Debussy could have succeeded had he wanted to be a really programmatic composer: bells toll and echo, a Gregorgian chant is heard, first in the open air, then as it might sound coming from the bottom of the sea. There is a pretty story that Debussy was inspired to compose *La Puerta del Vino* by a picture postcard Manuel De Falla, always his admirer, often his debtor, had sent him. As Oscar Thompson has pointed out, the clashing keys of this fine, dancelike piece foreshadow the polytonality of postwar music. *Ondine* conjures up the mermaid's watery

---

ment that there are five orchestral *Images*. This division into three of one part of a three-part suite suggests that Debussy was inordinately fascinated by triptychs. He published seven groups of three songs, five piano suites in three parts, and three orchestral works similarly divided.

domain. No better way of hearing the basic difference in style between Debussy and Ravel can be found than by listening to their separate responses to the idea of Ondine, that favorite water sprite of French legend. Debussy's is sensuous, flowing, liquid; Ravel's is cold, clear, *pointilliste*, the glitter of spray. The last prelude in Book II is *Feux d'artifice*. By far the longest of the twenty-four, almost maliciously difficult, it is one of the most truly picturesque works in the virtuoso's repertoire. If anything so artificial as fireworks can be said to have an inner nature of their own, Debussy has found it, and put it on paper.

Book II of the *Préludes* was the last important composition Debussy finished before August, 1914. The outbreak of the World War shattered what long suffering had left of his once resilient spirit. For a time he could do nothing. The successive disasters of the Allied armies made him rage impotently that he could not join in the struggle to save the France he worshiped. In October, he was writing, "If I had the courage, or rather, if I did not dread the inevitable blatancy natural to that type of composition, I should like to write a *Marche héroïque*." His old mocking spirit reasserted itself momentarily in an afterthought: "But I must say I consider it ridiculous to indulge in heroism, in all tranquillity, well out of reach of the bullets." The next month he straddled the dilemma by composing an oddly dove-tinted work in honor of the then revered Albert of the Belgians—*Berceuse héroïque*.

To add to Debussy's distress of body and mind, his finances were in sad shape. His royalties were good, but too much of them was earmarked for Lily's alimony. His publisher, Jacques Durand, generously advanced considerable sums against future royalties, and it was to pay off these loans that Debussy took on the editing of part of the complete Chopin Durand was bringing out to replace German editions. Toward the end of 1914, there were some indications that he was on the verge of a new burst of creativeness. He said that he wanted to work to prove that no matter what happened, French thought would not be destroyed. The first signs of this activity were the *Six Épigraphes antiques* for piano duet. Being adaptations of old sketches for a second series of *Chansons de Bilitis*, they did not require the concentrated effort of completely new work. They are, however, charming if slight works of a cold and archaic loveliness. They are notable for their starkness of line, and for an absence of those washes of color to which, in Debussy, we are accustomed. It is this difference from his preceding work that has encouraged certain critics to point to the *Épigraphes* as proof that his creative energies were in decline.

But by June, 1915, when he began the first book of *Études*, Debussy had somehow uncovered a new lode of fertility that was to produce in rapid succession, besides the twelve *Études*, the two-piano suite *En Blanc et noir*, and two chamber sonatas. It seems probable that the *Études* grew out of his restudying of Chopin. Certain it is that he approached them with the same imaginative freedom as Chopin, and that his use of precise indications of what each study is—*Pour les tierces, Pour les huit doigts, Pour les notes répétées* —indicates no sacrifice of poetic intensity. Writing of them in wry, deprecatory vein, he said in part, "You will agree with me that there is no need of making technique any sadder than it is, that it may seem more serious; and that a little charm has never spoiled anything. Chopin proved that, and makes this desire of mine very rash, I realize. And I am not dead enough yet not to know the comparisons that my contemporaries, confreres, and others will not fail to make, to my disadvantage." In short, Debussy himself conceived of the *Études* as a finger technique without tears.

The *Études* are not in the class, nor are they intended to be, of Chopin's masterpieces, though they are frequently as difficult. "You break your left hand in them," Debussy confessed, "in gymnastics almost Swedish." Walter Gieseking, a few years ago, proved that a pianist whose hands know no terrors could use several as attractive, sure-fire novelties. The sad thing, of course, is that they remain novelties. For the *Études* are the very spirit of Debussy, crystallized, refined, classicized even. They have exquisite definition, a sharpness without angularity. One element is lacking, and it is this, no doubt, that has argued against their popularity. That element is sensuousness. It is as if the war had burned out Debussy's interest in the senses, and driven his genius to express itself in the most closely reasoned musical intellection. And yet, by a miracle, the charm he hoped to achieve is there. Of much the same character as the *Études*, and quite as worthy of performance, are the three pieces called *En Blanc et noir*. One need not refer to their elaborate and rather obscure programs in order to enjoy them.

Late in 1915, the rapid spread of Debussy's cancer necessitated a painful and weakening operation. From this he never recovered. For more than a year he did not even attempt to compose. Only his humor, a tragic ghost, remained. He wrote to Durand in June, 1916, "Claude Debussy, writing no more music, has no longer any reason to exist. I have no hobbies. They never taught me anything but music. That wouldn't matter if I wrote a great deal, but to tap on an empty head is disrespectful." When he finally summoned the will to rouse himself, it was to produce an unexciting sonata for violin and piano. He appeared as the pianist when it was first performed on May 5, 1917. André Suarès has left us an unforgettable picture of the master's farewell to Paris: "His complexion was the color of melted wax or ashes. In his eyes there was no flame of fever, only the dull reflections of silent pools. There was not even bitterness in his gloomy smile." He was beyond the reach of morphine and radium; a second operation did him no good. There was nothing left but to die. From late in 1917 on, he never left his house. The last act of a man whom the war had led to affix *musicien français* to his signature was to apply for a vacant chair at the Académie des Beaux-Arts, the organization with which he had so often crossed swords. He could scarcely sign his name. Eight days later, on March 25, 1918, he died. In the confusion of a Paris in range of German guns, he was given a funeral almost as hurried as Mozart's. What few had time to realize, or wit to foresee, was that these poor remains had been animated by the most fructifying spirit in twentieth-century music.

Chapter XXI

Richard Strauss

(Munich, June 11,1864–September 8, 1949, Garmisch)

IN 1911, a bland-faced, blue-eyed, middle-aged Bavarian, who was then the most famous composer in the world, put the finishing touches on one of the most effective operas ever written. Behind him stretched, like the peaks of—well, not the Himalayas, but the Alps—a series of notable works with which he had asserted his right to the mantle of Liszt and the crown of Wagner. After penning the most challenging orchestral pieces of the dying century, he had veered sharply to create three of the most talked-of operas of the new. He had produced a handful of master songs. He was forty-seven years old: he had conquered the world, and he still had the world to conquer. Since 1911, besides more than forty songs, he has composed two ballets, a long symphony, and ten operas. Among these later works, there is not one that has added the fraction of an inch to his stature. Rather, by their patent inferiority, by their manufactured quality, they have cast suspicion on his early works. This is manifestly unfair. The fair thing is to treat Richard Strauss as a man who died in 1911. One of the most fascinating, if finally insoluble, problems in music criticism is to try to discover the causes of his premature demise.

Strauss is doubly puzzling because both his beginning and his end are extraordinarily mediocre. There is little to detain us in the youthful career of this well-educated son of Franz Strauss, first horn player of the Munich Hofoper, and Josephine Pschorr, scion of a wealthy brewing family. He was an alarming child prodigy from the age of five. Within ten or eleven years he had composed a large number of pieces, including a serenade for wind instruments that Von Bülow liked well enough to play with the Meiningen orchestra. At the age of sixteen, he dashed off a symphony that was duly performed by the sainted Wagnerian conductor, Hermann Levi. If one looks long enough at any music, he can find whatever he is looking for. So some have looked at these Strauss *juvenilia*, and found wondrous hints of the epics to come Actually, by Strauss' own confession, they were pretty, neoclassic imitations.

In one way only did they hint at the composer of *Till Eulenspiegel* and *Elektra*: they are enormously clever. Obviously, it was quite absurd for a young fellow with so much musical *savoir-faire* to waste his time in a university. Accordingly, he quit school in 1883.

Luck was with Strauss. He met exactly the right people to establish him and help him break with his respectable past. The first of these beneficent deities was Von Bülow, who was bowled over by the lad's sheer adroitness. Without training, Strauss was already an astute conductor: had not Von Bülow seen him face the veterans of the Meiningen band, and conduct his own wind suite without a hitch, though he had never before wielded a baton? Needing an assistant, Von Bülow impulsively took Strauss on. Shortly after, he resigned, and his aide found himself, at twenty-one, leader of a famous orchestra. Had Von Bülow stayed on, this plastic youth might have docilely followed his chief, and run up his flag on Brahms' masthead. For that matter, there is a tinge of Brahms in some Strauss works of this period. But even before Von Bülow had left, Strauss had come under the influence of Alexander Ritter, a man thirty years his senior, whose comparatively humble position as a violinist in the orchestra was offset by the loftiness of his musical connections. Having married Wagner's niece, Ritter was hand in glove with the Music-of-the-Future crowd at Bayreuth. It was Ritter who, after whispering into Strauss' ear the facts of life about *Zukunftsmusik*, convinced him that the successors of Liszt and Wagner—he conceded Berlioz, too—would conquer the world. Strauss was tempted, and he fell. Doffing the somber weeds of the Brahms sect, he assumed a coat of many colors. The ease with which he made this change is one clue to the mystery of Richard Strauss.

Although while still in his teens he had composed several quite remarkable songs that showed him not unaware of Wagner, the first large composition in which Strauss toyed with revolution was *Burleske*, a fantasy for piano and orchestra he lived to regret, but which, significantly, is the earliest of his compositions still played. It is shilly-shally, genuflective to Brahms, but casting sheep's-eyes at Bayreuth and Weimar. But it is dynamic, it is energetic, it has a hint of the briefly great Strauss. Later, he himself called it "sheer nonsense": it is not quite that bad—or quite that good.

Strauss' next large work, the program symphony *Aus Italien*, written after he had given up the leadership at Meiningen for an assistant's job at Munich, revealed that he had reached Berlioz in his flight from neoclassicism. Still timidly clinging to the traditional phases of the classical symphony, he imposed upon them a specific literary program they were not fitted to enact. The result is a spotty hybrid, in parts fine to listen to, but not coming off as a whole. He had not yet discovered that the tone chronicler and psychologue must completely throw over the whole machinery of first and second themes, counterstatement, development, recapitulation, and coda, and make—or adapt—a free form of his own. In more ways than one, *Aus Italien* is inept. There is, for instance, that unfortunate quotation of the melody of Luigi Denza's *Funiculì, funiculà*, in the belief that it was a genuine Italian folk song. This is the sort of mistake the Strauss of a few years later, whose music prides itself on its cosmopolitanism and sophistication, would never have made. Even in *Aus Italien* he should have known better: it was composed after a trip to Italy.

Strauss was still fumbling for the heaven-made form in his next work, *Macbeth*. Here for the first time he used the expression "tone poem." But *Macbeth* is not a true tone poem: it is an adaptation of the classical sonata form, with its structure relaxed just enough for the purpose of musical portraiture. Sometimes Strauss achieves an uncanny insight into Macbeth's tortured mind, sometimes he writes a beautiful passage. Rarely does he fuse the two. However, he learned quickly. The very next year, 1888, he summarily threw off whatever shackles remained, and came out with one of his most characteristic and successful orchestral pieces. *Don Juan* is a miracle. As far as cogency of form is concerned, Strauss never bettered it. Nor did he often orchestrate more magnificently or with surer taste. *Don Juan* is a whirlwind under control, and never did Strauss compose more heroic music. The themes and rich contrapuntal harmony are not only beautiful in themselves, but admirably perform their function of carrying forward the story and of examining the state of Don Juan's soul. The frantic quality of the hero's search is given ironic emphasis by the sense of impending catastrophe that hovers over the music from the very beginning. In a few strides, Strauss has succeeded in creating an opera without words, cleverly adapting for solo orchestra Wagner's concept of a continuously unfolding music drama. *Don Juan* has immediate im-

pact as drama, whether or not the listener knows the Lenau poem
on which it is based.

In musical idiom, particularly in the use of discords, *Don Juan*
went Wagner one better. The first-night audience at Weimar, who
knew their Liszt and had at least a fashionable smattering of Wagner, easily followed Strauss. The critics did not. They accused *Don
Juan*, by implication, of being a work of original genius: they found
it formless, needlessly cacophonous, full of deliberate shockers.
They did not mention that it was the logical successor of Liszt's
symphonic poems and Wagner's musical speech. When Hanslick
deigned to mention *Don Juan*, he did indeed call Strauss a Wagnerian: it was the worst word he could think of. He might better
have spared his virulence for the longer *Tod und Verklärung*. It consists of the thoughts and memories of a dying man, his death, and
his transfiguration. Some of this supplies good material for musical
treatment, some does not. The result is patchwork, which, however, is not at first apparent. It takes several hearings of *Tod und
Verklärung* to get past the powerful enchantments of the bravura
technique, the breath-taking mastery of the orchestration. Then
the arid spots are revealed. It seems that they occur precisely at
those points where the program is too abstract, too religio-philo-
sophical, for Strauss' alchemy. But a worse charge can be leveled
against *Tod und Verklärung*: with all its grandiloquence, its celestial
harpstrings, its exalted sermonizings, we come away with the uneasy feeling that we have looked in on the last moments of a
stuffed shirt. For the first time a suspicion flits across the mind that
Strauss is a musical genius with a small soul. And here, perhaps,
is another clue to the mystery of Richard Strauss.

Tod und Verklärung is dated 1889; Strauss' next large composition
was not completed until 1893. This lull in the creative activity of
an extraordinarily fertile man can be attributed partly to a change
in his worldly position, partly to ill health. In Munich he had little
to do—he was only second assistant conductor—but when, in October, 1889, he was called to Weimar as director of the court opera,
he became a very busy man. He was not content with the mechanical resurrection of war horses, but eagerly sought for new stage
works, the most notable of which was Humperdinck's *Hänsel und
Gretel*. Of course, Wagner was a heavy staple. Against this he set
a rollicking presentation of *Die Fledermaus*. He was in constant de-

mand for concerts and festivals, for he was already a rather famous man. In 1890, a signal honor awaited him at Eisenach: he was invited to conduct the Allgemeine Deutsche Musik-Verein in world *premières* of *Tod und Verklärung* and *Burleske,* in which the fantastic Eugen d'Albert played the solo part. The very next year, Strauss' own transfiguration was accomplished: Cosima Wagner invited him to assist at Bayreuth, and three years later he conducted several performances of *Tannhäuser* there. It was then that Wagner's maddening lady exclaimed: "Well, well, so modern, yet how well you conduct *Tannhäuser!*" Strauss' reverence for Wagner went beyond the limits of good sense: though he customarily conducted sitting down, he always stood when the music was Wagner's.*

In 1892, Strauss' health was so bad that his doctor ordered a long vacation without work of any kind. He set out, and for a time rambled happily. From Greece, he went on to Egypt, and there his conscience began to bother him. As a professional composer, he had, except for a small sheaf of songs, been marking time for several years. Cairo was the scene of a historic decision: on December 29 he began to compose his first opera, and two months later, under the shadow of the massive colonnades of Luxor, he completed the first act of a medieval German opera called *Guntram.* Evidently, Strauss' muse was not allergic to scenery, for the second act is dated from an equally un-Teutonic Sicilian villa. Back home, and once more in good health, he finished the opera at his charming chalet in the Bavarian Alps. Presented at Weimar in 1894, this Wagnerian pastiche was received with scant approval. The composer did not attempt another opera for six years.

The heroine of *Guntram* had been sung by Pauline de Ahna, a well-born Bavarian girl who later in the year was the Elisabeth in the *Tannhäusers* Strauss conducted at Bayreuth. They were married the same year. Frau Strauss had not been very distinguished in opera, but under her husband's tutelage she became an excellent lieder singer, and did much to help popularize his songs. By the middle nineties, many of his best ones had been written, and though he has since tripled his output, he has never excelled the finest of his early songs. Strauss is not to be ranked with Brahms

* What Henry T. Finck happily called Strauss' Wagnerolatry had a mystical tinge. In 1891, when he was all but dead of a lung complaint, he one day expressed a wish to die. But he reconsidered. "No, before I do," he said, "I should love to conduct *Tristan.*"

and Hugo Wolf, much less with Schubert and Schumann. Most of his songs are flawed in various ways: they are pretentious, or bombastic, or expressively inept; the heaviness of the accompaniment often overshadows the voice; sometimes they are mere technical exercises. They are perhaps worst when Strauss tries to set a humorous or folksy lyric. But when something in the lyric—whether in itself good or bad poetry—set his imagination aflame, he could deliver a masterpiece. Such is *Ständchen*, whose passionate lyrical grace is poignantly intensified by a somber-colored middle section. Such, too, is *Morgen*, an idyl of contemplative beauty, which is matched in loveliness by a song similar in mood, the earlier *Allerseelen*. The ecstatic *Cäcilie*, the glimmering *Traum durch die Dämmerung*, and the serenely peaceful *Ruhe, meine Seele* could not well be spared from the pitifully limited literature of great songs. And *Die heiligen drei Könige aus Morgenland*, of solemn joy and apocalyptic rapture, is one of the most magnificent songs ever written.

Shortly after his marriage, Strauss went back to Munich, first as *Kapellmeister*, and finally, after Levi's retirement in 1896, as general music director. Von Bülow's death had left the Berlin Philharmonic without a leader, and Strauss, who had become one of the most sought-after conductors, tried for a while the experiment of commuting between Munich and Berlin. His health suffered, and he had to hand his Philharmonic baton to Artur Nikisch, the Hungarian genius who was to make the Berlin organization one of the crack European orchestras. Nikisch, who was not a composer, could juggle Berlin with Leipzig, and do full justice to both the Philharmonic and the Gewandhaus.

But in 1895, Strauss was engaged simultaneously on two more tone poems. *Till Eulenspiegels lustige Streiche* was the first completed. Till is the sort of fellow who is much loved by modern composers: he has his analogue in Zoltán Kodály's Háry János and Serge Prokofiev's Lieutenant Kijé. Strauss sets him and his fourteenth-century environment before us in a brawling, lusty, and bawdily witty score that is as far as possible removed from the heavenly visions and lugubriousness of *Tod und Verklärung*. *Till* is, after more than fifty years, one of the most complicated scores in existence (Strauss' orchestra was getting larger and larger), but so powerful was the impetus of its issuance from Strauss' imagination that, with all its episodes, it gives the effect of a perfectly described parabola. Hanslick, still savage against *Wagnerismus*, attacked *Till* with cold fury: "It is a mistake to look on this immoderate and masterless chase of pictures as an overflowing of youthful creative power. . . . I can see in it only the exact opposite: a product of subtly calculated decadence." The huge orchestral battery he thought might better be used to call up "the English war in the Transvaal than as an illustration of episodes in the life of a poor vagabond." But as it was precisely "an overflowing of youthful creative power," *Till* is as fresh today as the day of its first performance in 1895.

Almost exactly a year after the *première* of *Till*, Strauss conducted at Frankfort another vast tone poem. *Also sprach Zarathustra* is a tribute to Nietzsche. Strauss, just after the first performance, went to some pains to clarify his intentions. "I did not," he asserted, "intend to write philosophical music or portray Nietzsche's great work musically. I meant to convey musically an idea of the development of the human race from its origin, through the various phases of evolution, religious as well as scientific, up to Nietzsche's idea of the superman." As one can see, there is nothing modest about Strauss' aims. Rather the contrary. Here are definite signs of megalomania, which unmistakably constitute another clue to the mystery of Richard Strauss. Just as the conversation of a megalomaniac is apt to teem with banalities that have been accepted without question by their creator simply because they are his own, so the music of a megalomaniac is apt to be full of boring rodomontade. Not only does *Zarathustra* fail to cohere, but some of the separate sections into which it is far too easily divisible are shockingly flat. Such, for instance, is the silly Viennese waltz, intended as the climax of the piece. As a superman's dance, it is incredible. *Zarathustra* is a jumble, all the more tragic because magnificent music jostles the sensational and commonplace. Such a fabric does not long endure, and *Zarathustra* is already all but disappearing from the concert repertoire.

Zarathustra, evidently composed on a downswing, was followed in 1897 by a masterpiece as different in conception and form from its predecessor as that was from *Till*. As Cecil Gray has pointed out, the particular form of each of Strauss' large orchestral works is shrewdly calculated to the nature of the program. Thus *Macbeth*, *Don Juan*, and *Zarathustra* are adaptations of the Lisztian symphonic poem, since the psychological development that supplies the subject matter of these works is best expressed through the mechanics of theme transformation. *Till Eulenspiegel*, primarily a drama of action told in episodes, uses the rondeau, with the return of the main theme after each secondary theme has been introduced. Finally, in *Don Quixote*, Strauss, with exquisite appreciation of the essential conflict in Cervantes' great book, *i.e.*, the disparity between the real and the ideal, chose the classical variation, subjecting an originally noble theme to the most distorting adventures. In another sense, *Don Quixote* is a disguised cello concerto, for that instrument is given the task of speaking for the hero. The viola, too, gets considerable work, for it is made to utter the forthright comments of Sancho Panza. *Don Quixote* has as much dynamic energy as *Till*, but does not achieve the consistent musical beauty of that rogue's-epic. It is marred by touches that are merely realistic, and which add nothing musically. The once notorious wind machine, intended to give verisimilitude to the ride through the air, is a case in point. These are small details, however, in a work that is really new. In its admixture of humor and pathos, and as a whole, *Don Quixote* is extraordinarily moving. It is obvious that even the composer has been affected by his material. The deathbed scene is perhaps the most sheerly beautiful music Strauss ever composed.

The critics were annoyed because Strauss had based one of his tone poems on the anarchistic Nietzsche, and they were even more infuriated by the cacophonous superrealism of certain parts of *Don Quixote*. His next gesture was to offend a much wider group: he based an epic of a hero's struggles on his own life. Lest anyone should mistake who the hero was, he quoted ostentatiously from his own works, which of course were supposed to represent the hero's achievements. People resented the bad taste of *Ein Heldenleben*: they could not know that the way Strauss' career has turned out would make the bad taste seem even more flagrant. At the time of the first performance of *Ein Heldenleben* in March, 1899, however, it rallied a valiant army of champions, and such men as Romain Rolland and James Huneker were temporarily robbed of their critical senses by its vast plan,* excessive noise, and technical

---

* Its sections are, in condensed form, The Hero, The Hero's Adversaries, The Hero's Helpmate, The Hero's Battlefield, The Hero's Works of Peace, and The Hero's Flight from the World and Self-Development.

wizardry. Rolland's dithyrambs are worth quoting—as awful examples, if nothing else: "I had a strange feeling of giddiness, as if an ocean had been upheaved, and I thought that for the first time in thirty years Germany had found a poet of Victory." Of the Hero's Battlefield, Huneker wrote with a touch prophetic of Hollywood: "Such an exposition has never been heard since Saurians roared in the steaming marshes of the young planet, or when prehistoric man met in multitudinous and shrieking combat."

Ein Heldenleben has worn badly: it seems incredible now that even those who heard it fifty years ago could not see that it was constantly collapsing and falling over on its side like a backboneless leviathan. In the passing years, the little dead areas have spread until they now blotch the work like a devitalizing fungus. Strauss' ingenuity has outwitted itself: the combination of twenty-four themes in one contrapuntal web now sounds like commonplace music with wrong notes; the battle scene is tedious rather than exciting, and the love music sounds suspiciously like the smug sentimentality of the fireside instead of a noble and elevated passion.

Just before completing *Ein Heldenleben*, Strauss had relinquished his position in Munich for the chief conductorship of the Berlin Hofoper. At first, he had a hard time of it. Wilhelm II did not care for modern music, and showed no interest in his conductor's plans. Running the opera according to the Kaiser's whims was not sufficient for a man with the abundant artistic vitality that Strauss, despite the sad evidence of decline in *Ein Heldenleben*, still had. He wanted to put on a series of orchestral concerts of modern music, and as the only symphonic organizations in town were in the hands of Nikisch and Felix Weingartner respectively, he had to create a new orchestra for his purpose. Thus the Tonkünstlerorchester came into being. Its programs were, from the first, ambitious, and notable for exhibiting their conductor's catholicity of taste. One of his first ventures was to present all the symphonic poems of Liszt in chronological order. He played his own works, somewhat to the Kaiser's annoyance, and gave the Berlin *premières* of compositions by Tchaikovsky, Bruckner, Elgar, Hugo Wolf, Gustave Charpentier, Vincent d'Indy, and Charles Martin Loeffler, then an obscure violinist of the Boston Symphony Orchestra.

At the same time, by accepting the presidency of the Allgemeine

Deutsche Musik-Verein, the society Liszt had founded to foster the advancement of modern music by means of annual festivals, Strauss tended to put off the day he could sit down and start another large composition. His programs put him in no danger of being forced to resign by his energetic constituents, who had kicked out his predecessor for daring to include Brahms in concerts that were supposed to be modern. Paradoxically, he aroused opposition among the very modernists he was trying to help when, with a few others, he founded the Genossenschaft Deutscher Tonsetzer to fight for composers' rights to get reasonable royalties on performances. Some of the little men were afraid that if royalties were made an issue, they would not be performed at all. But the Genossenschaft won the battle despite them.

When Strauss simply made the time for himself, and broke silence in 1901, it was with a long one-act fantastic opera, *Feuersnot*. In a way, this was his method of working off a grudge and getting a forum for his rebuke to the Munich critics who had reviled Wagner in the sixties and himself a quarter of a century later. Pointedly, the scene is laid in thirteenth-century Munich (the analogy to *Die Meistersinger* escaped no one), though the story is actually borrowed from an obscene Dutch legend. The Valhalla motive of the *Ring* is quoted; there are puns on the names of Wagner and Strauss. Even Wagner himself had not carried the warfare into the camp of the critics more vigorously than Strauss was doing. Musically, *Feuersnot* is a blend of two tendencies that were becoming increasingly easy to isolate in Strauss' idiom: the use of the materials of folk music and a most complex orchestral polyphony. In *Feuersnot*, it is perhaps the former that gains the upper hand, and leaves the more enduring impression. It is very far from the earnest Wagnerism of *Guntram*, and clearly foreshadows the exquisite lyricism of *Der Rosenkavalier* of a decade later. Unfortunately, perhaps because it is almost devoid of action, *Feuersnot* has not held the stage outside Germany. Its single American production took place in Philadelphia in 1927, when Nelson Eddy played the relatively unimportant role of Hämmerlein. Alexander Smallens, a notable resurrector of neglected works of merit, was responsible for the production, and conducted.

Strauss had worked off his grudge in *Ein Heldenleben* and *Feuersnot*, but he had not yet exhausted his autobiographical vein.

This time, however, he was in a comfy mood. For to 1903 belongs the *Sinfonia domestica*, one of the most embarrassing works in the history of music. Those who found Strauss absurd as a hero now found him fatuous as a father. The *Sinfonia* is nothing more than a day spent in the Strauss household, which turns out to be quite as tedious as any other German household. The clock strikes seven, the baby squeals in its tub (for by this time Strauss had an heir), a crowd of doting relatives coo their appreciation, the Strausses register conjugal felicity. To such no doubt worthy emotions and (to Strauss) interesting incidents we are treated for an hour. All the technical ingenuity in the world does not compensate for the almost unalleviated poverty of musical invention in the *Sinfonia*. Except for a certain structural conciseness, it is an utterly negligible work. When it was first performed, some kind people explained it by saying that perhaps Strauss was trying to pull his audience's leg.

But those who thought that the *Sinfonia domestica* indicated that Strauss had burned himself out were in for a shock. In fact, his next large work was altogether shocking. It was *Salome*, whose prolonged *succès de scandale* did more to put Strauss on the map for the general public than all his previous works put together. It was based on Wilde's *Salomé*, which in its original play form had had a tremendous vogue among the Germans, who tended to regard it as a creation of sweeping genius that transcended any objections based on breach of the moral code. When Strauss' opera was first given at the Hofoper in Dresden on December 9, 1905, the fashionable audience received it with hysterical acclamation. But the next morning the newspapers were ominous: the moralists were in arms—at their van, within a few days, His Imperial Majesty Wilhelm II, the patron of Leoncavallo. Necrophily had seemed all right in the play, but given explicit sensual attractiveness by Strauss' music, it proved too strong a dish for imperial and other stomachs.

Yet, audiences loved *Salome*, and soon, despite the enormous difficulties of the score, it was given all over Germany. It was successfully kept out of England by the censor, but rapidly spread to most of the other civilized countries of the world. In New York, after a semipublic dress rehearsal and one performance, the opera was withdrawn because the directors of the Metropolitan Opera and Real Estate Company protested to Heinrich Conried, the impresario. Most of the newspapers acted like outraged Aunt Mabels, but the Brooklyn *Eagle* was scathing: "As to the mind and morals, they were diseased. Not to emphasize disgust, their state was one of decomposition far advanced. As to the music, it fits. It makes worse that to which nothing but music could have added degradation." Two years later, Oscar Hammerstein staged *Salome* without dire results, even though Mary Garden played the part of Herod Antipas' naughty daughter for all it was worth. At last, in 1934, the Metropolitan plucked up courage, and tried it again. No one of any importance protested. During the 1938–39 season the most discussed opera of modern times—Dance of the Seven Veils and all—was given three times to packed houses.

Much of the ornate seductiveness and aphrodisiac leer of *Salome* having vanished with the years, it is possible to view Strauss' score with some measure of critical calm. First, it is superb theater— energetic, swift-paced, dramatic. In this respect, Strauss never did a better job, though *Elektra* may have more vertiginous climaxes. Technically, the old magician is back, refreshed and renewed. While the strongly contrasted characters are cunningly projected by the music, the vocal parts are in themselves generally undistinguished and feeble: underneath them is the fabric of a continuous and expressive orchestral web. This is, indeed, nothing but a logical next step after *Parsifal*—a tone poem with words. It is invariably the wonderful, shifting temper of the orchestra that lends significance to the vocal line, and fire to the static, jeweled words. The effect of *Salome* is fine, nay, it is overpowering. It is only when it is examined too closely (as the Dance of the Seven Veils is through constant isolated performance) that its jewels are seen to come from Woolworth's, its veils to be cheesecloth, and even the Baptist's gory head on the platter becomes nothing but a papier-mâché prop. Just as the refined perversities of the Herods begin to sound like the Saturday-night excesses of a bourgeois family, so the magnificent, glittering score inevitably begins to seem like old musical commonplaces traveling under fanciful assumed names. It is fair, perhaps, to assume that Strauss realized all this in 1905, and banked his all on the grand effect.

It seemed that in *Salome* Strauss had done the ultimate in musical shockers. But on January 25, 1909, the New York *Sun*'s Dresden correspondent wired his paper: "The seemingly impossible has been accomplished: *Salome* has been outdone." For a modernized version of Sophocles' *Elektra* by the aristocratic Viennese littérateur Hugo von Hofmannsthal, Strauss had brewed a hellbroth of cacophony, psychopathic passion, and tragedy. Compared with it, *Salome* was a pleasantry by a spoiled child. For one hour and fifty minutes, the singers shouted and screamed to make themselves heard through an all but impenetrable mesh of sound made by a tremendous modern orchestra. Poor Elektra was on the stage almost all the time. It was no wonder that Mariette Mazarin, the first New York Elektra, fainted after the performance. That energetic woman, Ernestine Schumann-Heink, who created the role of Klytemnestra at the world *première* in Dresden, resigned after one night of it. She told Henry T. Finck that during rehearsals Strauss had shouted at the conductor: "But, my dear Schuch, louder, louder the orchestra; I can still hear the voice of Frau Heink!" As *Elektra* represented Strauss' most advanced conception of the Wagnerian music drama, and harmonically was very daring (looking toward certain ultramodern experiments that Strauss himself did not choose to pursue, but which were later made by Schönberg, Alban Berg, and Anton von Webern), the critics fell on it with whips and scorpions. Many of them, including men of genuine perspicacity, called it ugly, and washed their hands of it. Its composer was, by implication, called a madman and a criminal.

In 1937, Rose Pauly came to New York, and with the Philharmonic-Symphony Orchestra and some confreres gave a concert performance of *Elektra* that was by all odds the outstanding artistic event of the season. Like *Salome*, *Elektra* was no longer a musical shocker, but unlike the earlier opera, it vibrated with life. And, far from being ugly, it proved to be a work of constantly welling-up musical beauty. Paradoxically this score—really far more complex than *Salome*—is also more singable, and the vocal line frequently has an intrinsic beauty that has its own telling effect in the rush toward catastrophe. By its symptoms of lasting vitality, *Elektra* is without question the finest tragic opera composed since the death of Wagner.

Strauss could well afford to laugh at the old-line critics who heard in *Salome* and *Elektra* nothing but discord. He could merely show them his bankbook, and watch the expression on their faces.

His publisher had paid him $15,000 for *Salome*, $27,000 for *Elektra*. When Oscar Hammerstein imported the latter, his take on *Salome* had been so impressive that he thought it no risk to buy the American rights for $10,000, and to pay Strauss $18,000 in advance royalties. From the beginning of the twentieth century on, Strauss' compositions were exceedingly popular, and he was becoming a rich man. His income was swelled by the vast number of calls made upon him as a conductor. Having appeared in almost every important European city, in 1904 he went to the United States at the invitation of Hermann Hans Wetzler, who had got a symphony orchestra together almost solely for the purpose of giving a Strauss festival, to culminate in the world *première* of the *Sinfonia domestica*. At the four concerts, almost all the tone poems were played, and David Bispham and Frau Strauss presented fourteen of the songs. The orchestra men found Strauss a severe taskmaster: he required fifteen rehearsals of the *Sinfonia* before he was satisfied. New York held somewhat aloof—the critics were definitely nasty. But Strauss' inland tour was a brilliant success, particularly in Chicago, where Theodore Thomas' advocacy of his music had prepared an audience with unusually sophisticated ears. Winding up in New York, however, Strauss became involved in an odd controversy when he gave two concerts at Wanamaker's. He was straightway accused of degrading art by appearing in a department store. His response was curt and to the point: "True art ennobles any hall, and earning money in a decent way for wife and child is no disgrace—even for an artist." He had received $1,000 for his two appearances.

Strauss' official status kept pace with his finances. In 1908 he was created director general of the Berlin Hofoper. Honors rained upon him: governments decorated him, and in 1910 Germany made him a member of the Akademie. By 1911 he had become by all odds the world's most famous musician, and the announcement of a new opera from his pen was awaited with curiosity by the sensation-seeking public, and with eagerness by music lovers. This time, the former was disappointed, for *Der Rosenkavalier*, though its morals are far from spotless, is neither morbid nor sensational. "This time I shall compose a Mozart opera," Strauss had announced, and he kept his promise. Von Hofmannsthal had provided him with a libretto brimming over with intrigue, and successfully flavored with the eighteenth century, quite as much in its vulgarities as in its delicacy and charm. Strauss' score is the tasteful comment of a true man of the world. Without sacrificing the externals of his idiom, he has miraculously imported to it an old-time character. *Der Rosenkavalier* is a string of gloriously allur- ing waltzes connected by a glittering musical thread. The finest comic opera since *Falstaff*, it has often a warmth, a persuasive sincerity that, except for certain pages of *Till Eulenspiegel* and *Don Quixote* and a few songs, is foreign to Strauss. Salome and Elektra are presented with an intense objective verity that makes them seem to live. Yet, they are only seen from without: in *Der Rosen- kavalier*, at least in the music devoted to the Marschallin and Baron Ochs, Strauss abandons exteriorization, and builds his characters from the vantage ground of their inner realities. It has been said that three hours and a half of a comic opera is too much, and that in this one Strauss' old betrayer—the commonplace— shows itself. There is a measure of truth in these strictures: all but a tiny handful of operas would be the better for cutting, and cer- tainly there are banal sections in *Der Rosenkavalier*. But the score abounds in beauty. An opera that is in its totality instinct with life, and that contains such strokes of genius as—to name but two of many—the scene of the presentation of the silver rose in Act II and the third act trio, is indeed a worthy swan song.

Der Rosenkavalier was produced at Dresden on January 26, 1911. Everything in this score pointed to Strauss' being at the height of his powers. The next year came incidental music to Molière's *Le Bourgeois gentilhomme*, with the miniature opera *Ariadne auf Naxos* tucked away in its folds, and containing a *scena—Grossmächtigste Prinzessin*—that is the most taxing music composed in recent times for coloratura soprano. *Ariadne*, which Strauss later separated from its Molière association, sounds like a clever modern parody of Mozart, but shows an undeniable falling off. People said pleasantly that it was but a temporary decline. After 1912, however, there were many Strauss *premières*, and his well- wishers were kept waiting. Strauss was now borrowing without restraint from the styles of others. In *Ariadne auf Naxos*, as Cecil Gray said, "Mozart dances a minuet with Mascagni, and Handel with Offenbach. . . ." In *Die Frau ohne Schatten* (1919), again (like *Ariadne*) with a Hofmannsthal libretto, Gray found "Wagner . . .

reconciled to Brahms, and Mendelssohn to Meyerbeer." *Die Frau* was received with ominous coldness.

With *Intermezzo* (1924) Strauss again tried the Wagnerian trick of writing his own libretto, doubtless because this "bourgeois comedy with symphonic interludes" is based on a little incident in his own life. It is a series of set numbers designed for *bel canto* singing and connected by a sort of amiable *Sprechstimme*. This, too, failed to please, and four years were to pass before he tried again. This time he returned to Hofmannsthal for the ponderous pseudoclassical text of *Die aegyptische Helena* (1928), the latest Strauss opera imported by the Metropolitan. This static and unoriginal music was a disaster, and Strauss never again attempted anything so elaborate. Significantly, when he returned to the boards five years later it was with *Arabella* (1933), an opera so light that it could properly be labeled a musical comedy. It contains many delicious pages, the best of them evoking the champagne atmosphere of *Der Rosenkavalier*. The composer of this sparkling frivol was nearly seventy years old.

In 1935 Strauss made a tactical mistake. Despite Hitler's rise to power, he set a libretto—*Die schweigsame Frau*—by Stefan Zweig, a Jew, who had derived its story from Ben Jonson's *Epicoene, or The Silent Woman*. Three weeks after the *première* of this excessively noisy opera on June 24, 1935,* he resigned from the presidency of the Reichsmusikkammer, an office he had accepted in 1933 from the hands of Paul Josef Goebbels. He adduced advanced age as the reason for his action, but no one believed him. He was temporarily out of favor, and *Die Schweigsame Frau* was withdrawn. Strauss certainly did not improve his position with the regime when he refused to furnish new incidental music for *A Midsummer Night's Dream*, confessing that he could not better Mendelssohn's. But he was soon rehabilitated. With *Friedenstag*, given at Munich in July, 1938, he pleased the Nazis, though this political morality play glorifies peace. In October, Strauss himself was glorified when *Daphne* (like *Friedenstag*, in one act) was given before an audience packed with Nazi officials. The following year, on Strauss' seventy-fifth birthday, he was personally congratulated by Hitler, who journeyed to newly conquered Vienna to hear a revival of *Friedenstag*. After

---

* Zweig's name is said to have been omitted from the program.

that Strauss composed at least two more operas (*Der Liebe der Danae*, 1940, and *Capriccio*, 1942); a Second Concerto for Horn and Orchestra (1943—the First dated from 1884); and *Metamorphoses*, a half-hour's nonentertainment for string orchestra completed in 1945. This last was composed in memory of Beethoven, a reminiscence of whose "*Eroica*" Funeral March is by far the best thing in it. Finally came the charming, surprisingly youthful Concerto for Oboe and Orchestra (1946).*

Meanwhile, the ex-magician continued to live. He was still news, if only for the reason that he was the most eminent musical has-been alive. But he was definitely not news in the way he had been. Strauss, it could safely be predicted, would never spring another of his shattering surprises, and now his composing only made trouble for bibliographers. A mild-mannered, stoop-shouldered, rather sleepy old gentleman, he supported his existence at Garmisch in the Bavarian Alps, and later in a dingy Swiss boardinghouse, exercising his tireless pen and living—and composing—on his memories. They were not precisely inglorious. In addition to being the composer of three or four superb tone poems, three magnificent operas, and a dozen master songs, was he not director emeritus of both the Berlin and Vienna operas, as well as the retired head of the Berlin Hochschule?

But poverty routed him out of his retirement. With his fortune in Germany destroyed and his foreign royalties impounded, Strauss accepted an invitation to visit Paris and one from Sir Thomas Beecham to visit England. On October 5, 1947, he sat in the royal box at Drury Lane Theatre wearing a tattered coat while Sir Thomas conducted *Don Quixote*. After the performance he responded to the loud plaudits of the crowd by going to the stage and saying feebly: "*Merci, Merci!*" Shortly thereafter he returned to the Continent. He had disappeared from the great world forever. On September 8, 1949, he died at Garmisch.

It seems certain that Strauss' place in the history of music is

* The Second Horn Concerto was first heard in America on October 18, 1948, when the Little Orchestra Society, Thomas K. Scherman conducting, played it in New York with Anthony Miranda as soloist; *Metamorphoses* received its American *première* on the Columbia Broadcasting System's notable program Invitation to Music on March 19, 1947, when it was conducted by Leopold Stokowski; the Oboe Concerto was also first heard in America on CBS when it was performed by Mitchell Miller as soloist with the Columbia Concert Orchestra, Daniel Saidenberg conducting, on February 1, 1948.

secure. But as time goes on, it becomes clearly manifest that though he looked forward to certain modernisms that have since borne fruit, he himself did not noticeably change the face of his art. For he was the end of a tradition—the afterglow of Liszt and Wagner—rather than the beginning of a new. There is, perhaps, some obscure connection between this fact and the mystery of his final decline after 1911. There is about all but the best of his achievement a feeling of applied modernism, a suggestion of shocking the bourgeois—a tendency that by the second decade of this century had become very old-fashioned. Charlatanism vitiates most of his work, and it is patent that a flair for the sensational is not a quenchless source of inspiration. Also, Strauss was a career man. More than any other great figure in music, Rossini excepted, he was as much businessman as musician. It is probable that the final key to his failure lies in his richly successful career. If he had only had Rossini's perfect sense of timing, and had known that his masterpieces were written, he would have served himself better. People today would be saying, "Ah, if Strauss had only composed another opera . . ."

Chapter XXII

Jean Sibelius

(Tavastehus, December 8, 1865—
September 20, 1957, Järvenpää)

FOR many years the careers of Richard Strauss and Jean Sibelius showed what seemed to be salient contrasts. Strauss at thirty-five was already the most famous of living composers, but after *Der Rosenkavalier* (finished 1911) he wrote no further masterpieces, though several of his later operas have been seriously underestimated. Sibelius at thirty-five was esteemed in his own Finland, and had been played in Germany, but was otherwise unknown. With creativity apparently undiminished he marched through his sixtieth year (his Seventh Symphony was finished in 1924). While Strauss kept on disappointing his admirers, Sibelius went on from triumph to triumph. Yet, after 1925 he published little of importance. What made him international news until his death was the persistent legend that he had finished an eighth symphony and was even working on a ninth. The legend did not turn into fact. Nevertheless, a study of Sibelius' attitude toward his art may help to explain the phenomenon of his long and satisfactory fruitfulness, and may also give some clue to the mystery of the seeming disorientation of Strauss's later years. Here the effective words—"satisfactory" and "unrewarding"—are both used to suggest the responses of sophisticated listeners with a tendency to plot ideal graphs.

The fact that Sibelius came out of Finland has given many a very distorted picture of the man and his music. This is based on the misconception that Finland is full of igloos and Eskimos—a country of savages who somehow manage to pay their bills. With this are associated the ideas that there are no proper conservatories of music there, and that Sibelius began composing without previous instruction. Thus, he has been pictured as an intuitive, a primitive—a sort of musical *douanier* Rousseau. Actually, Tavastehus, where he was born in 1865, was, though necessarily insular and limited in its outlook, a center of some culture. Its mixed Finnish, Swedish, and Russian population of about four thousand supported an ambitious concert season, during which such artists as the violinist Wilhelmj and the pianist Sophie Menter felt themselves well repaid for visiting there. Sibelius grew up in a home where music was a commonplace. Far from being untaught, he had a very tolerable grounding in piano and violin, later attended the Helsingfors Academy of Music, and, after convincing himself and others that he had talent, went abroad to finish his studies.

Sibelius came of good middle-class stock, on both sides of mixed Finnish and Swedish blood. This eldest son of Battalion Surgeon Christian Sibelius and Maria Charlotta Borg was elaborately christened Johan Julius Christian, but of this string of names the composer retained only the first, Frenchifying it into Jean in imitation of a much-admired uncle. Dr. Sibelius died when Jean was less than three years old, and consequently the child was brought up by his mother, assisted by a flock of female relatives. As there was a piano at hand, he picked out little tunes at an early age, and began to receive formal instruction on that instrument at the age of nine. He got the general idea of violin-playing by himself, and his first composition—*Drops of Water* (written at the age of ten)—was a pizzicato duet for violin and cello. He much preferred the violin to the piano, but did not begin to study it seriously until he was fifteen. Meanwhile, he led the healthy, active life of a growing boy, but delighted more in the poetic aspects of nature than most children. With his brother and sister as cellist and pianist respectively, he soon founded a family trio that played Haydn, Mozart, and Beethoven. He and his sister also tried over a Mendelssohn violin and piano sonata, but: "I was so thoroughly impregnated with the classical spirit that I could not bear the piece."

In 1885, the young Sibelius, with an average diploma from the Tavastehus preparatory school, went to Helsingfors in no very enthusiastic mood. His family could think of no other than an official's career for him, and so had sent him to the capital to study law. By this time, however, the young man whose life was being disposed of so cavalierly was determined to become a great violinist. For that reason, rather than to study composition, he began taking lessons at the Academy of Music even during his first term at the University of Helsingfors. As Sibelius fluctuated between duty to his family and an interest in music that was growing by leaps and bounds, one of his uncles, finding in the youth's room a law text whose dust-covered jacket told the tale of months of neglect, cut the Gordian knot by saying, "After all, Janne, it would be best for you to devote yourself entirely to music, seeing that study does not interest you any more than this." So, after a summer vacation reading and playing, he returned to Helsingfors in the fall of 1886 to study composition at the Academy of Music under its well-known director, Martin Wegelius.

Sibelius' relations with the domineering Wegelius showed his early-developed independence of spirit and intellectual honesty. The director was a fierce *Zukunftsmusiker* and rabid Wagnerian, endowed with an intemperately crusading spirit. Sibelius was vastly uninterested in Wagner, and nothing Wegelius could say had any effect on him. Yet, the two got on together, and the instruction bore fruit. For some time Sibelius led what he himself described as "a double life," which meant nothing more criminal than manufacturing rather textbookish pieces for the severe scrutiny of his master and, on the sly, working out his own ideas in less conventional compositions. In this latter activity, he was much stimulated by powerfully felt reactions to nature and omnivorous reading, particularly of Homer and Horace, Björnson and Strindberg. After three years of hard work, he received a hint from Wegelius to go ahead and write as he pleased. The results were a workmanlike string suite and a string quartet that were played when he was graduated from the Academy. The critical press, led by the influential Karl Flodin, was enthusiastic. It was at once perceived that a new note had been sounded in Finnish music, which had previously been cultivated with more industry than inspiration. It was further seen that this young man might well put Finland on the bigger map of European music. Accordingly, a scholarship was provided, and he was packed off for graduate studies in Berlin and Vienna.

Sibelius did not like Berlin, and German—at least, Prussian—culture did not seem to him either so broad or so deep as Finnish. Albert Becker, the highly respected expert in theory and composition, was a stiff, punctilious pedant whose angularities of character presented more obstacles to Sibelius than did, perhaps, the motets and fugues he was set to analyzing. However, Wegelius had recommended Becker, and Sibelius took his medicine. "But I could not resist the feeling," he confesses, "that all the time I was dealing with things that belonged to the past, and at times my patience almost failed." Far more important in his development was his introduction to fine symphonic music. True, Helsingfors had a symphony orchestra, but a feud between its conductor, Robert Kajanus, and Wegelius was so inflamed that the latter's students were forbidden to go to its concerts. It is odd that the otherwise independent Sibelius respected this absurd ban. In Berlin, he made up for this unnatural abstinence by attending Von Bülow's concerts, at one of which he saw Strauss take a bow after the playing of *Don Juan*. Years later, he remarked to Strauss that this once revolutionary work seemed positively classical in the light of his later compositions, and was astonished when Strauss murmured thoughtfully, "At that time I had not yet divided the violins. . . ."

When Sibelius had first taken ship for Germany in September, 1889, a fellow passenger had been a young Finnish painter, Eero Järnefelt, son of a distinguished general. Together they had grown enthusiastic over the prospects of Finnish art, explored the hopes of Finnish nationalism, and discussed the *Kalevala*, the great collection of bardic verse that had been pieced together earlier in the century to form a national epic. Returning to Finland in the summer of 1890, Sibelius spent a great deal of time at the Järnefelts, and before leaving for Vienna in the autumn had plighted his troth to his friend's sister Aïno. Robert Fuchs, to whom soon after his arrival in Vienna he was directed by Hans Richter, gave him regular instruction in orchestration. Goldmark, though at the summit of his ephemeral fame, consented to give him a few pointers in composition.

When Sibelius returned home for good in 1891, he found Finland in a ferment of extremely self-conscious nationalism. The Tsar's government had begun curtailing the rights of the grand duchy, suppressing newspapers, interfering with freedom of speech, and making itself generally obnoxious. From the purely political aspects of Finnish opposition Sibelius held aloof, but he participated enthusiastically in the artistic movement that worked tacitly with the patriots by nurturing a really native art. He began this collaboration by composing a huge five-movement symphonic poem with voices called *Kullervo*, after one of the more lugubrious heroes of the *Kalevala*. When it was performed on April 28, 1892, it had an instant success. Even the critics liked it. As *Kullervo* exists only in manuscript, and has apparently never been given outside Finland, we must perforce be content with the word of responsible music critics who have examined the score and pronounced it a masterpiece. Sibelius himself, though fond of the work, was not entirely satisfied with it, and therefore it was not performed again during the composer's lifetime.

Fortunately, we have a frequently played work of approximately the same period—*En Saga*, a tone poem written at Kajanus' request after the success of *Kullervo*. It affords (though Cecil Gray correctly points out that Sibelius is not always so "dark and wintry") an excellent—and easy—introduction to his music. It contains elements of style that he was to modify but not essentially to change. Those who know him well recognize instantly his unique orchestral color, obtained in part by reliance on woodwind ensemble, sudden irruptions of brass, and long pedal points used for much the same purpose as the sustaining pedal in piano compositions. Here are the long-persisting, stubborn rhythms in which he delights; here, too, the acrid, sometimes parched harmonies, often widely and daringly spaced, and depending for their effect more than is usual on instrumental timbres. These are combined, in *En Saga*, to produce a somber legend of the folk, with occasional glints of campfire and armor, highspotted by a climax like a battle, dying away in a few pages of elegiac beauty.

In June, 1892, Sibelius married Aïno Järnefelt, and went on his honeymoon to the sparsely populated district of Karelia. Life there was really as primitive as outsiders fancy Helsingfors to be: it is a peasant land, where Sibelius heard, for the first time, the extremely ancient folk songs on which many had supposed *Kullervo* to be based. He was often suspected of being a self-conscious folk composer, in much the same sense as Smetana and Dvořák were. This notion is absurd. Those who know Finnish folk music deny its resemblance to anything in Sibelius, and the composer himself was frankly puzzled by the charge that he either quoted or imitated it. His undeniable national quality is something far more subtle and difficult to understand—call it atavism or gene inheritance, if you will. Reduced to its most sensible terms, this nationalism is merely the translation into music of a very sensitive nature lover's response to the lakes and forests of his native land and to the magical and heroic aspects of its traditional literature.

From the fall of 1892 on, Sibelius began a long-persisting routine of life, spending three seasons of the year in Helsingfors teaching, and enjoying the brief, hot Finnish summer in a wooded country district. Until 1897, when his financial position was somewhat improved, life was far from easy for this fortunately rugged man: sometimes he taught as many as thirty hours a week—a heavy program for anyone with a primary passion for creative work. Kajanus, now his stanch friend, had made a job in the orchestral school of the Philharmonic Society expressly to help Sibelius out. Both there and at the Academy of Music, Wegelius' stronghold, he taught theory. Meanwhile, he composed songs, piano pieces, incidental music for plays, and miscellaneous orchestral works. Even though it produced the four *Legends* for orchestra, including first versions of *The Swan of Tuonela* and *Lemminkäinen's Home-Coming*, this period did not register any important advance over *En Saga*. In fact, these five years are more remarkable for quantity than quality, for Sibelius never held with the idea that a composer can compose too much. Although his vigorous iteration of this point of view must be taken with a saving grain of salt, it explains the presence of the merest ephemera in the catalogue of his works. No composer has ever been less sentimental and more realistic about his art. To Sibelius, there was something absurd about not constantly pursuing your profession just because you could not turn out a masterpiece every time you touched pen to paper. And if you made money by these second- and third-rate flights, well— so much the better. Sibelius would have been the last to claim that *Karelia* and the incidental music to *King Christian II* were high art: the first is good fun (rather in the Enesco manner), and the second has a certain pictorial felicity.

It might be supposed that foreign travel would be reflected in the music of a man so sensitive to nature's moods as Sibelius. But he took the Italian tour in 1894 without absorbing any Latin color whatsoever: his *Aus Italien* was never written. On his way back from the South, he stopped briefly in Bayreuth at the insistence of his bellicosely Wagnerian brother-in-law, Armas Järnefelt. He suffered through *Lohengrin* and *Tannhäuser*, but refused to suffer through *Parsifal*. Sibelius often declared, "Wagner has never meant much to me." As the composer of only one opera (and that tossed off, and produced privately), Sibelius could hardly be considered an authority on the subject. Still, as a great composer, he must be listened to with attention. "I still place Verdi higher than Wagner" is another of his heresies, with its dry coda: "Opera is, after all, a conventional form of art, and should be cultivated as such." This dictum explains both why Sibelius was not a Wagnerian, and why he did not cultivate opera. He did not smuggle a single bar of Bayreuth into Finland. The swan that glides with such ominous and inhuman serenity on the dark waters of Tuonela is not remotely related to Lohengrin's faithful bird. The cold mist that pervades this evocation of the Finnish Hades, blurring and masking all the contours, is the creation of an orchestral color as inhibited and fastidious as that Debussy used in *Nuages*. Almost rhythmless, *The Swan of Tuonela* has only fragments of melody, achieves its effect by suggestion. Its companion piece (for Sibelius recast only these two of the *Legends*), *Lemminkäinen's Home-Coming*, is less impressive. It has high spirits, a rough *brio*, but no magic.

In 1897, the newspapers began a campaign to have the Finnish Senate give Sibelius a money grant to ease the strain on his energies. Accordingly, with surprising promptness, he was voted an annual stipend of about four hundred dollars. Let the reader ponder this sum of money, lest he has been imposed upon by the favorite story that a government grant allowed Sibelius to take it easy for the rest of his life. A man with a wife and daughters, and whose reputation, though already heroic, was confined to a small, relatively poor, and subjugated country, could not live on his royalties plus four hundred dollars. He did, however, relinquish his most onerous duties, and devote longer sustained periods to composition. At the age of thirty-four, he began his first symphony: he had waited for maturity, and the work went easily. Within a few months it was down on paper—the E minor that was the first of a line of symphonic masterpieces that have been called, by Sibelius' most enthusiastic admirers, the greatest since Brahms, or even since Beethoven. Given its *première* at Helsingfors on April 26, 1899, it was literally and figuratively the last nineteenth-century symphony. With far more reason than had led people to call Brahms' First Beethoven's Tenth, this might have been called Tchaikovsky's Seventh. It abounds in Tchaikovskyan echoes, and is, indeed, the most derivative of Sibelius' large works. But these are the echoes of a natural-born symphonist, about to speak *in propria persona*. He did not have to struggle with the form as Brahms did. There is no padding, a minimum of awkwardness. And the symphony has the native bigness, the breadth of shoulder needed to sustain its un-Sibeliuslike melodrama. Still a bit timid in its traditional patterns, yet it is a remarkable first try.

It so happened that the First Symphony came almost stillborn into the world, for on the same program was a choral work, also by Sibelius, that for nonmusical reasons aroused the audience to unbridled excitement. Ostensibly nothing more than a setting, for men's and boys' voices, of a Swedish pseudoclassical poem, *Song of the Athenians* was a political harangue devised to inflame the Finns, and yet get past the ever more oppressive Russian censors. Even without the aid of words, Sibelius could forge a potent weapon against tyranny, for that is really how *Finlandia* was conceived. In November, 1899, a series of celebrations, outwardly fostered for newspaper pension funds, but actually for the writers whose pens had been tireless in the cause of Finnish independence, was given throughout the country. For the gala fete at Helsingfors, Sibelius composed several numbers to accompany historical tableaux, only one of which—*Finlandia*—has survived. Known first simply as *Finale*, it was played in that, and several other, disguises. As late as 1904, for instance, it was masquerading in Russia as *Impromptu*. With the exception of the *Valse triste*, the most widely popular of Sibelius' compositions, it is stirring, noisy, and empty—good made-to-order patriotic music of the "1812" Overture variety. There is more apparent reason for its popularity than for that of the *Valse triste*, which is simply a respectable waltz that could have been written by any one of a hundred composers. It no doubt served its purpose adequately in a death scene in *Kuolema*, a play by Arvid Järnefelt, another of Sibelius' gifted brothers-in-law.

In the summer of 1900, the Helsingfors Philharmonic went on an extensive tour, with Kajanus as conductor and Sibelius as his assistant. Within a month the orchestra gave concerts at Stockholm, Christiania, Göteborg, Malmö, Copenhagen, Lübeck, Hamburg, Berlin, Amsterdam, Rotterdam, Brussels, and Paris. Sibelius was well represented in the repertoire, and the beginning of his European fame may be said to date from this series of concerts. That autumn he was notified that the Allgemeine Deutsche Musik-Verein was placing two of his orchestral *Legends* on the programs of its next festival.

Gratified by this recognition, Sibelius went to Italy with his family. At Rapallo, where he settled for the spring, he composed the Second Symphony, which today is not only the favorite among his extended orchestral works, but is one of the most frequently played of all symphonies. Aside from the rich romantic fruitiness of the finale, it is a very characteristic work. The opening movement is built up of simple, attractive motives, which, as first presented, have no special distinction. As the movement progresses, we gain insight into one of the salient features of Sibelius' method of symphonic architecture: the relating and transforming of apparently uncongenial fragments of sound into a beautifully integrated fabric. Quite as much as his peculiarly personal orchestration, quite as much as the sobriety of his coloring, this device is a hallmark of a Sibelius symphony. "Nothing, from a purely technical point of view," Cecil Gray says, "is more remarkable in the entire range of symphonic literature than the way in which the composer, having presented in the exposition a handful of seemingly disconnected and meaningless scraps of melody, proceeds in the development section to breathe life into them and bring them into relation with one another." In the last movement of the Second Symphony this device is used to create one of the most triumphant paeans in modern music.

In comparison with the big work that followed it, the Second Symphony has many holdovers from the nineteenth century. The Violin Concerto, composed in 1903 and revised in 1905, is in every sense an unconventional work. Although thankful to the virtuoso, it is never a mere display piece, and throughout has essentially musical interest. Only in the second movement (incidentally, the least satisfactory of the three) does it more than casually bow to traditional concerto forms. Having evolved a whole new battery of technical means in the Second Symphony, Sibelius did not, as a less discriminate and sensitive artist might, force all of them on the concerto, but selected just those which seemed germane to the balance of forces. Of the three movements, the first is at once the most startling and most attractive: cadenza and all, it is clearly a whole of exactly the duration required to expound its material. For Sibelius at his best shared with Beethoven, his idol, an infallible sense of timing. It is no small triumph to know exactly when to break off a rhapsody (precisely what this first movement is), especially when in an access of sustained beauty. Unhappily, Sibelius did not know when to stop in the second movement, which at times comes close to maundering. He got into stride again in a final allegro that is one of his rare flights of humor. The vigorous and appealing quality of this section of the concerto is more interesting to the listener than the enormously skillful juggling of rhythms by which it is achieved. Owing to the unadventurousness of great violinists, the concerto was one of the most recent of Sibelius' works to find wide favor. To Jascha Heifetz go thanks for his magnificent and successful championing of this long-neglected masterpiece, which in its revised version had been auspiciously ushered into the world in 1906 under the baton of Richard Strauss, with Karl Halîr, a member of the Joachim Quartet, as soloist.

In 1904, Sibelius began to have grave misgivings about remaining in Helsingfors. There were far too many demands on his time, and he ingenuously confessed: "I was too sociable to be able to refuse invitations that interfered with my work. I found it very difficult to say no. I had to get away." He vacillated between the idea of moving to a large European capital, where he could be isolated in the crowd, and that of living in the country. As was probably inevitable, he chose the latter, for practical as well as spiritual reasons. He built a house two miles from a railroad station called Järvenpää; practically in the forest, and near the shore of a lake, this rural solitude was yet only a short trip from Helsingfors. He lived there the rest of his life. For him it was an entirely satisfactory choice. Nor could his devotees argue with it, for from Järvenpää, with its wild and beautiful environs, came a string of works that showed Sibelius had absorbed strength from his native soil. Here, far from cosmopolitan influences, he was not tempted, as was Stravinsky, the greatest of his younger contemporaries, to thin out his creative energies in fashionable frittering. There were no fads, artistic or otherwise, in Järvenpää.

As soon as he moved into his country home, Sibelius began a third symphony. This proved to be a three-year job, which was interrupted by several trips and the composition of various shorter works. Most of these are of passing interest only. Take *Pelléas et Mélisande*, for example. This incidental music for the Maeterlinck play is dreamy and delicate, but Sibelius was not at his best on a miniature canvas. Nor does the conscious Orientalism of *Belshaz-zar's Feast*, another suite of incidental pieces, seem a natural ges-ture. This is watered-down Sibelius. But in 1906 he returned to the *Kalevala* for inspiration, and the result was the intensely character-istic *Pohjola's Daughter*, a symphonic fantasy that is, perhaps, the most rigidly programmatic music he ever composed. The spinning maiden, the rainbow on which she sits, her taunting of the hero, and his baffled rage and furious leave-taking—these and a few other elements of the program must be grasped before the music can be appreciated to the full. At times the sumptuousness of the music is reminiscent of Strauss, though the color and accent are totally different. *Pohjola's Daughter* has the impact of an epic frag-ment: it is a heroic tale set in a splendid landscape. Although rela-tions between Finland and Russia were more strained than ever, Sibelius journeyed to St. Petersburg to conduct the *première* of this extremely Finnish piece at one of the concerts established by Alex-ander Siloti.

On September 25, 1907, Sibelius, for the first time in several years, conducted a concert of his own works in Helsingfors. *Poh-jola's Daughter* and *Belshazzar's Feast* were enthusiastically received, but the high spot of the program was the Third Symphony, which he had completed the same summer. In light of the desperately compressed emotion of the symphony that was to follow it, the C major is a lull before the storm—a moderate, tempered, and pre-dominantly happy composition. With its diminished orchestra and contracted size, Sibelius had begun to move away from the easy largess of his first two symphonies. There is a compensatory gain in the direction of depth and concentration. It is significant that he now unleashes the brasses only for climaxes. As has been suggested above, the C major stands in the shadow of the Fourth, but further-more, it is a truly lightweight work. For all its easy allure, it is a collection, skillfully assembled, of tendencies that were to be real-ized in later symphonies. Not unnaturally, there is a tentative quality to the Third Symphony, suggesting that Sibelius is still feeling his way toward what can be called his *ars nova*, and is not quite sure what his final direction will be. It is this lack of assured-ness that makes it a not altogether satisfying composition to listen to.

Early in 1908, an ear-and-throat infection that had been worry-ing Sibelius for some years became acute. At first, he had been afraid that he might lose his hearing. When that fear was dissipated, one quite as frightful took its place: there was ground for believing that his throat trouble was cancerous in origin. He went under the knife in Helsingfors, but to no avail. In those days, the greatest professors of the surgical art were Germans, and accordingly Sibelius went to Berlin and submitted to a series of no fewer than thirteen operations at the hands of a gray and revered specialist. After this dreadful experience, he was not improved. "Finally," Sibelius says, "the old man gave it up, and handed the operation over to his assistant, a young man with sharp features and a steely look, the personification of ability and energy. He lowered his instrument into my throat, and found the bad place. A strong jerk, a shout of triumph: 'Now I've got it!'—and he pulled out the instrument. I was released from torture."

Although his physical suffering was thus ended, Sibelius continued to worry. Might not the tumor that had been excised give place to a true cancerous condition? Who could tell? It seems that troubles of all sorts conspired to put Sibelius in a gloomy and self-questioning frame of mind. As he wandered over the map of Europe, conducting concerts of his works, his ills pursued him. It was inevitable that this mood should be mirrored in his music. This spiritual malaise was so intense that he felt forced to express himself in a more intimate medium. The result was the string quartet *Voces intimae*, in five brief, almost gnomic movements. Completed in London in March, 1909, this shows a mature handling of string-quartet forces, but there is little doubt that its interest is more biographical than musical. It can be dismissed (though not scornfully) as another way station on the road to the Fourth Symphony. Its first three movements grope and come to no decisions: there is frank confession here, confession of near-desiccation. But the fourth movement plucks up courage, almost as if sluggish blood had begun to course freely, and this interesting composition ends on a small but assured yea. Sibelius needed to express himself just this way, but he showed wisdom by not pursuing the string quartet any farther. His genius needed plenty of elbow room, even in its moments of greatest concentration.

In the fall of 1909, much of Sibelius' anxiety was a thing of the past. Clearly, a vacation was indicated. So, with his painter brother-in-law, Eero Järnefelt, he once more braved the wilds of

Karelia. This time winter was coming on, and they experienced a variableness of weather they never forgot. While Järnefelt painted, Sibelius reveled in the wild scenery of white cliffs, wind-swept lake, and dark forest. Speeding patches of cold sunlight raced before the sharp wind that sometimes brought bursts of hail. This was tonic to Sibelius, who exposed himself to every peril his doctors had warned him to avoid. After returning home and playing with a few small compositions, he plunged into his Fourth Symphony. Less than a year later, this most controversial of all his works was finished. On April 3, 1911, he conducted its *première* in Helsingfors.

The first audience that heard the Fourth Symphony was friendly but baffled. The critics, also in the same dilemma, wrote inconsequentially of it. One of them said that he could not explain the work at all except as a series of Karelian landscapes, and proceeded to furnish a convenient Baedeker for the perplexed concertgoer. This obtuseness angered the composer, who for once felt called upon to explain himself. He did not deny that the A minor had assimilated some of his reactions to the wild north country, but he did deny that it was a picture album. It dealt, he said, with the eternal problems of suffering mankind as he himself had experienced them. This explanation cleared up a misunderstanding, but did not make the Fourth easier to understand. Those who had warmed to the symphonic poems and the first three symphonies might well feel themselves betrayed by this superficially unattractive work, though some must have known what was coming if they had listened closely to *Pohjola's Daughter*, the Third Symphony, and *Voces intimae*. The A minor dispenses entirely with purely sensuous attractions, makes its points rapidly and concisely, and uses harmonies that do not float in one ear and out the other. To those who pillow themselves on dulcet melodies and savor the delights of sweet repetitiveness, the elliptical and Spartan Fourth makes no concessions. In one sense, it exacts more from the listener than even the most complex of classical symphonies: it is possible, for instance, to let the mind wander momentarily, and yet enjoy to the full the surpassing beauty of the "Jupiter" Symphony. The Fourth allows no such leeway.

There are those who do not admit Sibelius to a place among great composers. But even some of those who do, say that the

Fourth Symphony is a mistake, a sport, a momentary lapse quite off the line of his development. They interpret its sparseness as poverty of inspiration, its abruptness and angularity as deliberate experimentation that does not come off. They say that it relies solely on technical interest, and therefore does not excite the emotional catharsis that is the end result of a great work of art. Scornfully quoting Sibelius' own remark that whereas other composers gave the world champagne, he offers cold, clear water, they retort that Sibelius himself is at his best dispensing champagne. Nevertheless, its admirers claim a very lofty place for it, and have not hesitated to compare its fundamental quality to the daemonic concentration of Beethoven's last quartets. Certainly, it is, like them, distilled down to an essence. Partisans of the Fourth Symphony say that, far from not touching the emotions, it descends deep into their remote, rarely touched sources. They say that its peculiar language, its savage speech, is well worth the learning, for it reveals important things that could not otherwise be said. Finally, they claim that it is a tragic masterpiece—one of the few spiritual talismans of the twentieth century.

The habit of dividing the products of artists' lives into neat little periods is almost always silly, but it must be admitted that the A minor Symphony closed one phase of Sibelius' life. Henceforth he was not to pursue the gnomic saying or the spiritual epigram. It was as if *Voces intimae* and the Fourth Symphony had solved certain personal problems in his own life, and left him free to develop more objective tendencies that were also implicit in his earlier work. Again, in such compositions as the tone poems *The Bard* and *Luonnotar*, he sent up trial balloons that reached modest heights, but four years were to elapse before another symphony (the form we must necessarily regard as the decisive focusing of his interests) told his precise direction. Meanwhile, his pastoral life at Järvenpää was interrupted by increasingly frequent tours and visits abroad. In 1912, he was offered a chair at the Vienna Conservatorium, but what might have been a temptation eight years before, when he was sick of the social demands his Helsingfors friends made upon him, was now refused without a second thought. A request, the next year, that he compose a special orchestral work for the Litchfield, Connecticut, June festival was accepted enthusiastically, particularly as it was accompanied by a generous invitation to come to America and conduct it in person.

On May 16, 1914, Sibelius sailed for Bremen, whence he embarked for the United States. In his luggage was the score of *The Oceanides*, the new tone poem he had reserved for an American *première*. He went at once to the estate of Carl Stoeckel, who sponsored the Litchfield festivals, and who had been responsible for the invitation. At the first rehearsal, the orchestra, composed of fine players from New York and Boston, struck him as the best he had ever led. The countryside delighted him—"the sort of district in which Leatherstocking formerly dwelt and had his being."

On June 3, the festival opened before an audience of invited guests (Stoeckel was afraid that commercializing Litchfield might turn it into a second Bayreuth). On that day the offering was *Messiah*. The next day, Sibelius conducted an entire program of his own works: *Finlandia*, *Pohjola's Daughter*, *King Christian II*, and *The Oceanides*, the last a grim picture of a churning northern ocean. Typical of the enthusiasm Sibelius aroused was Henry E. Krehbiel's bracketing of him with Strauss and Toscanini as the three indubitable musical immortals he had seen in the course of fifteen years. The climax of Sibelius' American visit came, after several trips in his host's private Pullman, when Yale bestowed on him an honorary doctorate of music. Professor Wilbur L. Cross, later Governor of Connecticut, read the citation, which concluded in the following lofty strain: "What Wagner did with Teutonic legend, Dr. Sibelius has done in his own impressive way with the legends of Finland as embodied in her national epic. He has translated the *Kalevala* into the universal language of music, remarkable for its breadth, large simplicity, and the infusion of a deeply poetic personality."

In late June, the Finnish master left the shores of the United States, gratified by his reception, and promising to return for a transcontinental tour the following year. But he had scarcely reached home before the World War broke out, and his second American visit never took place. Before the end of 1914 he had begun work on another symphony, which proved more stubborn of perfection than anything he had ever composed. At first, Sibelius was comparatively unaffected by the war, though it was annoying to have performance fees and royalties stopped by his German publishers.* Like most people, he believed that the war would be brief. To enlarge his straitened income, he made extensive tours of Norway and Sweden, and composed a number of trivia for quick sale. Despite these distractions, the Fifth Symphony was completed, in a first version, late in 1915. It was performed on Sibelius' fiftieth birthday, which had been declared a national holiday. The composer himself conducted the concert, which climaxed a gala day. But he was not satisfied with his new symphony. In October, 1916, he revised it, and this second version was played. Even then, it was not precisely what he had in mind. More wrestling with the recalcitrant material followed, and it was not until 1919 that the third, and final, version was achieved.

The Fifth Symphony is not a controversial work. It is easily approachable, teems with quite recognizable melodies, and is only mildly discordant. Big, assertive, extroverted, the E flat major is the Second's glorious heir. While the Fourth can almost invariably make its most telling points *mezza voce*, the Fifth raises its voice with the naturalness of uninhibited emotive speech. There is still some argument as to whether the long section leading to the first obvious break is one movement or two. One principal theme dominates this entire section, but entirely new material surrounds this theme in the second part. Clearly, it is unimportant whether this section is to be called one or two movements: what is important is that it foreshadows that technique of agglutination that was, a decade later, to result in the vast one-movement world of the Seventh Symphony. The unity of the beautiful andante (the second or third movement, depending on your point of view) is achieved by a set rhythmic pattern: various melodies play upon this rhythm, with an eeriness of effect suggesting the unvaried variability of a narrative epic. Here, if anywhere, Sibelius dons warlock's robe, and reads the runes. Discreetly lost in the accompaniment, and droned in octaves by the double basses, is a positively banal theme that has an unfortunate resemblance to *O, Dry Those Tears*, the masterpiece of Teresa del Riego. By some obscure alchemy, this galumphing motif, helped along by one other equally mediocre melody, be-

---

* Finland (as a part of the Russian Empire) was not at this time a party to the Bern Convention that protects international copyright. Sibelius, however, by selling his works first to German and English publishers, managed to obtain an ever-growing royalty income.

comes the motor of one of Sibelius' most stupendous and exciting climaxes.

Until the March, 1917, revolution, which established the provisional government of Miliukov and Kerensky, Finland had been relatively untouched by the war. At first it seemed that she would benefit by the collapse of the tsarist system. For one thing, her representative form of government was restored to her. But the Kerensky regime was short-lived, and the Finns had little sympathy with the Leninists. On December 6, 1917, they accordingly declared their independence, which was at once recognized by several foreign countries, and confirmed, in March, 1918, by the treaty of Brest-Litovsk. But the Communists were not disposed to see Finland slip away from Russia's orbit, and soon the little country was swarming with Red Guards. Resistance stiffened under White Russian and German leadership, but the Reds were not finally ousted until the end of April, in a battle that took place at Sibelius' birthplace, Tavastehus. Then followed a White terror, during which reprisals were carried out in a grimly sanguinary manner. It was not until July, 1919, that the White hooligans were dispersed, and an orderly government was established under predominantly Social Democratic control.

Sibelius' part in these gory events was as passive as a Finnish Gandhi's, but there was no doubt that as a nationalist he could only view the Reds with abhorrence. In February, 1918, his house was repeatedly searched, and he was virtually a prisoner. Finally, after fearing for his life, he was allowed to take his family to Helsingfors. There they nearly starved to death. Sibelius himself lost almost forty pounds during the weeks the besieged Reds doled out a bread-and-water diet to Whites and White sympathizers. An entry in his diary shows that he regarded these events with horror, but as an artist: "The crescendo, as the thunder of the guns came nearer, a crescendo that lasted for close on thirty hours and ended in a fortissimo I could never have dreamed of, was really a great sensation."

And it was during these grisly happenings that he was struggling with the final shape of the Fifth Symphony, working on a sixth, and planning a seventh. Already, in a letter written two days after the battle at Tavastehus, he was describing the revised Fifth as "triumphal," the Sixth as "wild and impassioned" (which it is not), and the Seventh as epitomizing "joy of life and vitality." At fifty-three, Sibelius had a resilience that could go unscathed through revolution and bloodshed. After the troubles were all over, he quietly returned to Järvenpää, and finished the Sixth Symphony. The horrors he had seen had not embittered him or made him love his country the less. In 1920, when he was offered the richly paid directorship of the Eastman School of Music in Rochester, New York, he refused it with as little compunction as he had felt in turning down the Vienna chair so many years before.

The Sixth Symphony was not finally completed until 1923, and, though a creature of the turbulence of 1917–19, shows few traces of its chronological lineage. A feckless, almost insouciant creation, it has attracted much highfalutin respect from competent authorities. "The chief interest of the work is formal," Cecil Gray has said. Perhaps that is what is wrong with it. It is, for the most part, down-right dull—Sibelius' "Pastoral" Symphony, in fact, in number and attractiveness. Without austerity, it is nevertheless as hard to get hold of as the Fourth, and quite lacks the Fourth's intensity. Possibly the fact that it is a late work has blinded some to the equally obvious fact that, of all Sibelius' symphonies, the Sixth has the least to say. In view of its neutral color and tame personality, Sibelius' description of it as "wild and impassioned" (written before much of the symphony was complete) sounds flatly misleading. One can only suppose that he saved these fervors for the Seventh.

On March 2, 1924, the Seventh Symphony was completed. This the composer had at first called *Fantasia sinfonica*, doubtless because it is in one movement only. By the letter of a textbook definition, it is probably not a symphony at all, though with some freedom it can be analyzed as one. The important thing is that it follows the spirit. It is as compact, and quite as unadorned, as the Fourth, but it is more varied in mood, uses a wider color and volume gamut, and is more approachable after a few hearings. Luminosity has been claimed for the Sixth; it is really this second C major Symphony that has it. Sibelius had now discarded the last shreds of romanticism in his music and, allowing for the inevitably modern constituents of his idiom, had achieved a purely classical symphony. The classicism at which he had arrived represents, not a mimicry of the past, but a natural growth. In short, Sibelius is a classicist, not a neoclassicist. There is no lack of emotional connotation in the Seventh (any more than in a Mozart symphony)—but it is connotation only. Everything is sublimated. The drama that is presented, struggled through, and solved is the drama of the themes themselves. Sibelius has said, "I am the slave of my themes, and submit to their demands." Here they have freed him entirely from the fuzziness and grandiloquence of much nineteenth-century music. Yet, simplified, restrained, essenced out though the Seventh is, it is very far from art for art's sake, and is an intensely moving composition.

The Seventh was the last symphony from Sibelius' pen, which until the middle twenties of this century was very active. As 1931 approached, Serge Koussevitzky, a masterly interpreter of Sibelius, announced hopefully that the Eighth Symphony would be played during the fiftieth-anniversary celebration of the Boston Symphony Orchestra. But the work did not show up. It was said that it had been completed, but there was also a rumor that it was not to be heard during the master's lifetime. All this was conjecture: Sibelius, who did not hold back in talking of other composers and their work, invariably refused to discuss what he himself was doing. Of the several smaller orchestral works he published after the Seventh Symphony, only one—*Tapiola*—has gained a wide audience. Tapio is the forest god of the Finnish pantheon, and *Tapiola* breathes the spirit of his forest home without actually being program music. It shares the classic temperateness, the reasonableness of the Seventh Symphony, and represents the final stage of tone-poem evolution as Sibelius conceives it. Like *La Mer*, it suggests the infinitudes of nature without revealing the particular.*

Sibelius, who lived out his long life at Järvenpää in what is little more than a large log house on the edge of the Finnish forests, was regarded in his country as a living demigod. On December 8, 1925, his sixtieth birthday was again a national holiday, marked by nationwide celebrations and concerts of his music. On that day, he received the highest decoration in the gift of the Finnish government, and was granted the largest state annuity ever given to a private citizen of Finland. Ten years later, his seventieth birthday was made the subject of similar rejoicings, which, however, had a

---

* Commissioned by the Symphony Society of New York, *Tapiola* received its world *première* under Walter Damrosch on December 26, 1926.

slightly different tone. Within that decade he had become one of the most frequently played of composers, and it was obvious that his country had an immortal. On his eightieth birthday, in 1945, congratulations from all parts of the non-Communist world flooded Järvenpää. Much the same celebration ensued on his ninetieth birthday, and no doubt the more sanguine looked forward to the composer's being present on his own centenary. Without having given to the world another major work for more than thirty years, Sibelius died at Järvenpää on September 20, 1957. It is said that the only unknown manuscript discovered among his papers was a trifle tossed off half a century before. The final word seems to be that Sibelius, untouched by the fads and fancies of contemporary fashion in music, worked unflaggingly to develop to the full the gifts that he had and at a certain point had nothing more to say.

Chapter XXIII

Igor Stravinsky

(Oranienbaum, June 17, 1882–   )

AFTER twenty years of shadowboxing, Igor Stravinsky still retains the crown of modern music. He retains it because there are none to dispute his supremacy. Sibelius, though using as many modern means as he needed, was at heart a traditionalist who had found the essence of classicism. There have been challengers, more or less serious, whom Stravinsky has not even had to vanquish, for they have eliminated themselves simply by not getting into the heavyweight class. First it was Ravel, then Falla; even the mathematician Schönberg was once spoken of as a dangerous rival. The weary king retains his crown, but unless he shows his royal will shortly, it will be time to declare the throne vacated, and a democracy established.

There is between Stravinsky's career and that of Richard Strauss a parallel so tragically close that one wonders whether a twentieth-century composer can live fully in the world, and yet come to the fullest fruition. They both started out tepidly with Brahmsian echoes: Strauss, as the better-taught man, produced his academic symphony at an earlier age than Stravinsky, who merely dabbled in music until his early twenties. Both quickly spouted revolutionary works, threw off fireworks for a couple of decades, and then fizzled out, though in different ways. Strauss' creative energy dried up. Stravinsky, always an experimentalist, continued to experiment. But for a number of reasons, his later experiments have been too often experiments. By a strange coincidence, their careers as composers that matter stopped just short of their fiftieth year. Neither of them possessed the staying power of a Haydn, a Wagner, a Sibelius—a Verdi. Still, there is the ghost of a chance that Stravinsky may come through with another masterpiece. It is still too early to write his epitaph.

In many respects, Stravinsky's early life was conventional for a major Russian composer. The second- and third-rate Russian musicians were prodigies, and went early to academies of music; the geniuses came late to music, and ended up by teaching themselves.

594

The Five were young-gentleman dilettantes who entered music by the back door. Tchaikovsky, though he eventually acquired a solid academic grounding, did not start formal training until after his twentieth year. Stravinsky, not having Tchaikovsky's overmastering urge to devote himself to music, in 1905 docilely finished a law course at the University of St. Petersburg because his mother wished him to. The next year, his mind still not made up about becoming a professional musician, he married his second cousin.

There is something incredibly lackadaisical, something whimsical, about Stravinsky's inability to grow up. At this time, he was a typical gifted futilitarian from a Chekhov play. Yet, his background was musical. His father was an opera singer of some renown, and his mother knew music at least well enough to enjoy reading opera scores. Not the least surprising thing about Stravinsky is that he was no prodigy. His parents viewed his childish musical efforts with indulgent amusement: they did let him study the piano, but he had to pick up the rudiments of harmony and counterpoint by himself. Soon he tried compositions of his own—little more than written-down improvisations. But it is uncertain how long his musical maturity would have been delayed if he had not met Rimsky-Korsakov's son at the university. In 1902, while traveling in Germany, Stravinsky, by his chum's wangling, got to show the pedantic master some of his *juvenilia*. Rimsky was not enthusiastic: he advised the boy to go on with law and, if he wished, to take private lessons in harmony and counterpoint. He unbent enough to offer to look at any future pieces by his son's friend. Five years were to elapse before Stravinsky, having done everything the great pundit asked of him, and having frequently consulted him about his confessedly desultory work, showed Rimsky a large composition that his adviser thought fit to be performed.

Stravinsky's Opus 1 and Opus 2—respectively a symphony and a song cycle with orchestral accompaniment—are rarely given. By 1908, however, he was at work on three compositions that have, in some form or other, kept a precarious hold on public attention. The first was an opera, *Le Rossignol*, with which he struggled, off and on, for six years. The second was the orchestral *Scherzo fantastique*. The last was a little tone poem called *Feu d'artifice*, which he sent to Rimsky on his daughter's wedding, as the master had expressed an interest in its composition. "A few days later," Stravinsky says in his autobiography, "a telegram informed me of his death, and shortly afterwards my registered packet was returned to me: 'Not delivered on account of death of addressee.'" In honor of his teacher, he then composed a *Chant funèbre*, the score of which vanished during the Russian Revolution.

The *Scherzo fantastique* and *Feu d'artifice* were the means of bringing fame and fortune to their composer, for in the audience at the Siloti concert where they were first performed on February 6, 1909, sat the greatest talent scout of the century—Serge Diaghilev. Something in these fast, crackling pieces, with their knowing echoes of Paul Dukas' popular *L'Apprenti sorcier*, enthralled him. With his usual impetuosity, Diaghilev instantly commissioned Stravinsky to orchestrate a Chopin nocturne and valse, to be used in the forthcoming performance of the Ballet Russe's version of *Les Sylphides*. Stravinsky was made. His adaptations turned out to be most satisfactory, and later that year the impresario telegraphed him to compose a completely new work for the Ballet Russe's 1910 season at the Opéra.

The result of Diaghilev's confidence in his find was *L'Oiseau de feu*, the first real modern ballet. Not only did it inaugurate Diaghilev's custom of commissioning entire ballets, but it set the precedent of the composer consulting both the choreographer and the *décor* artist during the course of composition. The brilliant Opéra audience that made the opening of *L'Oiseau de feu*, on June 25, 1910, the notable event of the Paris season saw, in effect, the perfectly functioning collaboration of Stravinsky, the choreographer Fokine, and the scene painter Golovin. Thamar Karsavina was the Firebird, Adolf Bolm the Prince. We who have too often seen a tired version of *L'Oiseau de feu*, with faded sets and bedraggled costumes and bored dancers, can scarcely imagine the incredible glamour of the original production. Stravinsky, who was making his first visit to Paris, found himself famous overnight—the most feted hero of smart Paris society. For years *L'Oiseau de feu* remained a favorite of balletomanes, and spread Stravinsky's name across the world. Shortly after the *première*, he made a selection of excerpts from the ballet, and this rather hasty business served for some years as an orchestral suite. In 1919, however, he reorchestrated and re-edited the suite, and his carefully constructed potpourri is, even thirty years later, his most popular concert piece. Abounding in vivid color, romantic melodies, and easy, fruity emotion, *L'Oiseau de feu* is as ingratiating as *Scheherazade*. Only the *Dance of Katschei*, the fourth of the five sections of the suite, might hit the conservative in the midriff: its irregular pounding rhythm and jagged harmonies, the sheer physical excitement of this diabolic music—all foreshadow the cometlike anarch of *Le Sacre du printemps*. The rest of the suite might be not quite first-rate Rimsky. It is fading rapidly. But fortunately, it was the *Dance of Katschei* that the composer was to use as a springboard.

While composing *L'Oiseau de feu*, Stravinsky toyed with the idea of doing a ballet based on the ancient pagan rites of his native land. He discussed the matter with the painter Roerich, but the difficulties of the task deterred him momentarily. Keeping it cubbyholed in his mind, he turned to another idea he found equally fascinating—the composition of a large orchestral work with an important piano part. Speaking of how this unnamed piece happened to develop into *Petrouchka*, Stravinsky has written, "In composing the music, I had in my mind a distinct picture of a puppet, suddenly endowed with life, exasperating the patience of the orchestra with diabolical cascades of arpeggios." As soon as he played over the manuscript to Diaghilev, the impresario, though he had been expecting to hear the pagan ballet music of which rumors had reached him, was excited, and persuaded his friend to enlarge it to ballet size. Wandering across Europe, from Switzerland to France, and from France to Russia and Italy (for Stravinsky, like all Russians, is a tireless traveler), the composer, adding touches to *Petrouchka* along the way, finally settled down in Rome, and completed the score on May 26, 1911, three weeks before his twenty-ninth birthday.

Only eighteen days later, Diaghilev sumptuously mounted *Petrouchka* at the Châtelet in Paris. Again a galaxy of talents gave added éclat to a new ballet by a man who was already hailed as one of the first of living composers. This time Nijinsky danced the Clown, Bolm was the Moor, and Karsavina the apex of the tragicomic triangle. It was admitted at once that a perfect ballet had been written, the principal reason being that nowhere before or since has such wholly danceable action been allied to such vividly illustrative music. While previous composers had generously borrowed Russian material, Stravinsky, with the help of the learned

and sensitive Alexandre Benois (despite his name, also a Russian),
had, in this tale of a St. Petersburg carnival, caught the very essence of theater Slavdom.

In the *Dance of Katschei*, a new voice had been heard, but it was
still uncertain what that voice would say. *Petrouchka* ended all
doubt. It was undeniably an anarch's voice, but hostility was not
yet aroused. This anarch was an amusing one. Yet, the leap from
L'Oiseau de feu to *Petrouchka* is immensely wider than that from *Petrouchka* to the next ballet Stravinsky wrote—that ballet which
literally caused a riot, and organized powerful forces against his
music. In *Petrouchka* gone are the romantic melodies and charming
Rimskyan harmonies. In a work just as brimful of color, Stravinsky
has primitivized his palette. The raw, sharp color of *Petrouchka* has
its analogue in the choppy, mechanized rhythms, which tend to
dominate among the various musical elements. Stravinsky broke
even more violently with the past in the harmonies. For the first
time, a composer wrote simultaneously in two clashing keys. The
effect, far from being ear-shattering, is strange, acrid, deliciously
different. Bitonal counterpoint is being born under our very noses,
but we scarcely notice it, much less damn it, for, as Gerald Abraham
has shrewdly noted, "Both contrapuntal strands are absurdly easy
to follow."

In 1921, Stravinsky "began a task which enthralled me—a transcription for the piano which I called *Trois Mouvements de Pétrouchka*.
I wanted this to provide piano virtuosos with a piece having sufficient scope to enable them to add to their modern repertoire and
display their technique." Those who have heard Arthur Rubinstein, to whom the *Trois Mouvements* is dedicated, play it, will
realize how perfectly the composer has succeeded. The transcription is one of the few notable large pieces of post-Debussyan piano
music. In addition to being a work of distinction and beauty, it
illustrates the changed point of view from which postwar composers considered the piano. No longer the vehicle of fluctuant,
cloudy impressionism, of curtains of sound, it began to be treated
as a percussion instrument—something that could be properly
thumped, banged, struck, and otherwise attacked. Now a projector of significant noise, it might be considered a congeries of
small drums tuned to various pitches. This conception has led to
the anarchic extravagances of Henry Cowell, and has its golden

mean in Prokofiev, in Stravinsky's Concerto for piano and wind orchestra (1923), Capriccio (1929), Concerto for two unaccompanied pianos (1935), and Sonata for two pianos (1944).

After *Petrouchka* was produced, Stravinsky returned to Russia and his idea of a pagan ballet. He stayed there until winter in order to complete the scenario with Roerich, after which he moved to Switzerland, to Clarens, almost sacred to him because it had often sheltered his hero Tchaikovsky. There, after other visits to Paris, Bayreuth (which moved him to irreverent laughter), and Russia, he finished *Le Sacre du printemps* in March, 1913. He looked forward to the staging of this very complicated ballet with trepidation, for the choreography had, at Diaghilev's insistence, been entrusted to the maladroit care of Nijinsky. His worst fears were realized. Nijinsky was both incompetent and unreasonable, and though the *corps de ballet* was working against a deadline, his inability to follow the bar-by-bar significance of the score took the form of demanding an absurd number of rehearsals. "Although he had grasped the dramatic significance of the dance," Stravinsky writes, "Nijinsky was incapable of giving intelligible form to its essence, and complicated it either by clumsiness or lack of understanding. For it is undeniably clumsy to slow down the tempo of the music in order to compose complicated steps which cannot be danced in the tempo prescribed. Many choreographers have that fault, but I have never known any who erred in that respect to the same degree as Nijinsky." Despite all the resulting contretemps, the invitation dress rehearsal went off well.

Not so the *première*. The first performance of *Le Sacre du printemps*, at the Théâtre des Champs-Elysées, on May 29, 1913, was a scandal unmatched in the annals of music. Jean Cocteau, the star reporter of smart Paris, so describes it: "Let us now return to the theater in the Avenue Montaigne, while we wait for the conductor to rap his desk and the curtain to go up on one of the noblest events in the annals of art. The audience behaved as it ought to; it revolted straight away. People laughed, booed, hissed, imitated animal noises, and possibly would have tired themselves out before long, had not the crowd of esthetes and a handful of musicians, carried away by their excessive zeal, insulted and even roughly handled the public in the loges. The uproar degenerated into a free fight.

"Standing up in her loge, her tiara awry, the old Comtesse de

Pourtalès flourished her fan and shouted, scarlet in the face, 'It's the first time in sixty years that anyone's dared to make a fool of me.' The good lady was sincere: she thought there was some mystification."

The cause of all this disturbance was the most beautiful, the most profoundly conceived, and most exhilarating piece of music thus far composed in the twentieth century. By some odd freak of genius, Stravinsky, a straitlaced devotee of Greek Catholicism, had become an earth-worshiper, and written a hymn of pantheistic exaltation. For *Le Sacre* is in truth exactly what Stravinsky called it: an act of faith. A skirling bassoon melody ushers us into the primeval world of Scythia, long before Christianity came to give it history. Now, technical analyses of music are too often nothing but the most unpalatable dry bones, but it happens that Nicolas Slonimsky, analyzing *Le Sacre* in his invaluable chronicle, *Music Since 1900*, manages to communicate the very essence of this masterpiece.

Part 1: Kiss of the Earth, opening with a high-register bassoon solo, the tune being derived from a Lithuanian song; *Spring Fortune-telling*, in stamping duple time; *Dance of the Womenfolk*, on a melody within the range of a fifth, characteristic of Stravinsky's stylized Russian thematics; *The Game of Kidnaping*, brusque and crude, with unperiodic explosive chords; *Spring Rounds*, a syncopated march-tune, opening and closing with six bars of serene folk song in unison; *Game of Two Cities*, polytonal and polyrhythmic; *Procession of the Oldest and Wisest Men*, with a stultifying persistent figure in the brass; *Dance of the Earth*, in triple time with unperiodic blasts against a quartal motto on a firm pedalpoint C. *Part 2: The Great Sacrifice*, opening with a tortuous introduction in subdued orchestral colors; *Mysterious Games of Young Maidens*, in a polyharmonic major-minor mode, in soft coloring, ending in an eleven-times-repeated chord in heavy beats; *The Glorification of the Chosen*, in uneven meters, with the eighth-note as a constant, dynamically and rhythmically vitalized into a frenzied dance; *Evocation of the Ancestors*, slow and elementally crude; *Rites of Old Men, Human Forebears*, on D as a keynote, with a sinuous chromatic English-horn solo against a rhythmic duple-time motion; *Great Sacred Dance*, in ternary form with a sixteenth-note as a constant in the first and third part and eighth-note rhythm in the middle section; *Sostenuto e Maestoso*, with a quarter note as a unit, in triplets or duplets, interrupted by a quotation from the *Sacred Dance*, which finally returns in constantly changing meters of 1, 2, 3, 4, 5 sixteenth-notes in a bar, until, after a scratch of a Cuban *guiro*, used here for the first time in European orchestral music, and a fertilizing run of the piccolo, the orchestra comes to rest on the key-note D. with the tritone-note G sharp on top.*

The *Great Sacred Dance*, in which the scapegoat maiden dances herself to death, is the high-water mark beyond which the brutal modern technique has not gone, possibly cannot go. Its constantly changing rhythms thudded out in screaming, searing discords engender a physical agitation in the listener that is closely akin to sexual excitation, acting chiefly on atavistic, deeply veneered strata of being. Music, beginning with the rewritten Venusberg scene from *Tannhäuser*, and proceeding through *Tristan und Isolde* to much of Strauss and the now unheard tone poems of Alexander Scriabin, was tending inevitably to this glorification of the physical, and for decades was busily stripping away veil after veil of respectability. Once Stravinsky had completed the process, imitators were quick to take a hint. For instance, Prokofiev's clever but derivative *Scythian Suite* came a year later than *Le Sacre*. But gradually, music (largely under Stravinsky's own tutelage) has been turning away from these scandals to desiccated forms of experimentation which, momentarily at least, seem to remain localized in the laboratory of the past. It is not a little odd that Stravinsky, whose pantheistic vision reduces Wordsworth's or Thoreau's to spongecake, should have become the leading medium in those ectoplasmic spinnings-out which have thus far characterized the career of musical neo-classicism. Because *Le Sacre* is Stravinsky's overtowering masterpiece, everything he has done since is necessarily something of an anticlimax. But the anticlimax is most depressing when he is in full flight from the genii he uncorked in *Le Sacre*, and retreating headlong into the arms of Tchaikovsky, Pergolesi, Handel, and Bach. As his artistic remorse becomes unbearable, it may be that he will go farther, and retreat into Palestrina, Des Prés, and Jubal.

Before Stravinsky went off into those experiments in pure rhythm which were clearly prognosticated by *Le Sacre* he completed the opera he had begun in 1908. He had written but one act of *Le Rossignol* then, and it was only in 1914 that he found time to compose the last two acts. Meanwhile, a lot of water had gone under the bridge, and there was a huge disparity between the

* Quoted by kind permission of Mr. Slonimsky's publishers, W. W. Norton and Company.

styles of Act I and Acts II and III—far more disparity than was required by the change in scene and mood in the Hans Christian Andersen fairy story. Although Diaghilev gave *Le Rossignol* a sumptuous mounting, the opera was not a success. Then Diaghilev suggested staging it as a ballet. But Stravinsky said no: he would, instead, take material from the last two acts, and adapt it as a symphonic poem that could be used for a ballet. This was *Le Chant du rossignol*, a glittering simulacrum of real Chinese music, the composer's last fling with the musical paintpot. Hereafter his color was to be applied gingerly and, in many places, to be reduced to black and white. *Le Chant du rossignol* is attractive picture-book music, and is unduly neglected.

Beginning with *Trois Pièces pour quatuor à cordes*, composed in 1914, for nine years Stravinsky sent forth from his studio a series of small compositions that have the air of being experiments with one or more aspects of musical technique. As these bloodless fragments appeared, they were greeted by Cocteau, Boris de Schloezer (who had constituted himself Stravinskyographer extraordinary), and other less talented but equally thuriferous critics with clouds of incense that simultaneously gave the occasions a religious tinge, and served to obscure the paltriness of the music. According to these official communiqués from the Étoile sector, it seemed that Stravinsky had always just completed a masterpiece that would alter the whole face of music. In 1918 it was *L'Histoire du soldat* that was crowned by the Académie Cocteau; in 1920 it was *Pulcinella*, in 1922 *Le Renard*. *Le Soldat* and *Renard* were experiments in timbres and rhythm; *Pulcinella* was an experiment in melodies (since Stravinsky had so few of his own he used Pergolesi's). Poor, half-starved things that they were, they have scarcely had the energy to last thirty years. The best parts of them, the parts when they are suddenly galvanized into life, are evidence that at moments Stravinsky realized he was a Russian. The one-act *Mavra* (1922), for instance, delightfully echoes Glinka and Tchaikovsky.

In a somewhat different category is *Les Noces villageoises*, a secular ballet-oratorio, first performed in Paris in June, 1923. This tale of a Russian village wedding, though it began as more experimentation in timbre and rhythm—Stravinsky discarded several instrumentations (including one with mechanical pianos, which were found impracticable) before hitting on the final one—ended up as something far more formidable. It is scored for four pianos, seventeen percussion instruments, solo voices, and chorus. Some have called *Les Noces* Stravinsky's masterpiece. It is, for perhaps half its length, as exciting as a tribal chant. After that, its lack of color palls, its insistent rhythms numb rather than excite, and the voices distort the delicate balance of timbres. They become overprominent, inescapable, exacerbating. It may be said that it was exactly this maddening iteration at which Stravinsky was aiming: if so, he has succeeded. But whereas *Le Sacre* maddens and exhilarates, *Les Noces* maddens and leaves you exhausted. This is sensationalism pure and simple, and it is all very cleverly done. In *Les Noces* Stravinsky has interpreted the idea of catharsis not as a purging of the blacker humors, but as a draining of vitality. It is precisely a deathly work.

Stravinsky's feverish search for the new, constant change of technique, and bald refusal to repeat himself make the comparison with Picasso inevitable. Both are expatriates from countries with strong folk traditions: both men became Parisians and, by extension, internationalists. Here the comparison ends. Picasso is a tireless experimenter in new techniques and new styles, and has as wholly discarded his Spanishness as Stravinsky his Russianness. But the painter, though he may not produce an immortal work of art each time he changes his manner, shrewdly knows that the new canvases can be accepted or rejected at a glance by the sophisticated eye, which, after all, is the only eye he paints for. The musician contrarily has failed to realize that the sophisticated ear has a limit of toleration. It can take in an almost unlimited amount of discord, polyrhythm, atonality, and novel timbre, but it cannot, will not, endure for long the musical analogues of a Picasso puzzle. Stravinsky's refusal to admit this handicap of a temporal art is odd if not stupid. His later compositions have a limited meaning to the unaided ear, however sophisticated: to be fully understood, they would need perfectly trained groups of listeners, each equipped with a full score. Obviously, this is not one of the desiderata of a sensual art.

With *Les Noces*, Stravinsky's interest in the nerve-twisting possibilities of rhythmic pulse culminated. Worse was to follow. Having devitalized his audiences in *Les Noces*, he now proceeded to devitalize himself. His principal aim in most of the compositions he has written since 1923 seems to have been to make them sound as little as possible like those on which his reputation had been founded. It has been a difficult task, but in some of them he has done it flawlessly. The composer's retreat into the past—away from both his achievements and his experiments—began with the *Octuor* (1923), and by the time of the Piano Sonata, the following year, he no longer looked over his shoulder. A landmark, or a tombstone, along this tragic road of misguided genius is *Oedipus Rex*, a pompous, turgid, and altogether prolix opera-oratorio, after Sophocles—and Handel. Cocteau made a fine translation of the Greek play into French, and then his version was translated into Latin by the Rumanian poet, Jean Daniélou.

Let us hear Stravinsky's own explanation of this piece of what the old Comtesse de Pourtalès would have been justified in calling "mystification": "What a joy it is to compose music to a language of convention, almost of ritual, the very nature of which imposes a lofty dignity! One no longer feels dominated by the phrase, the literal meaning of the words. . . . The text then becomes purely phonetic material for the composer. He can dissect it at will and concentrate all his attention on its primary constituent elements—that is to say, on the syllable. Was not this method of treating the text that of the old masters of austere style?" The answer to Stravinsky's rhetorical question is no. Stravinsky was using Latin because it was denatured of meaning; Palestrina (who may fairly be taken as one of the "old masters") was using Latin because it was fraught with the most profound meanings and emotions he knew.

It seemed, in the two ballets that followed *Oedipus Rex*, that Stravinsky was faced with complete loss of creative potency. *Apollon Musagète* is an inane group of musical statuary, *Le Baiser de la fée* a nosegay of weakest scent "inspired by the Muse of Tchaikovsky," and quoting some of Piotr Ilyich's most sentimental trivia. But in 1929 came the Capriccio for piano and orchestra that could, at the moment, have been interpreted either as a sign of real life or as the last galvanic spasm of a dead man. There is a quality in it that might be called a memory of emotion: otherwise, the Capriccio is facile, clever, and pallid. The hope that the Capriccio was indeed a symptom of life was quickened the next year—1930—when the Brussels Philharmonic Orchestra gave the world *première* of the *Symphonie de psaumes*. Stravinsky, with a complete lack of humor,

had put on the title page "composed for the glory of God and dedicated to the Boston Symphony on the occasion of the fiftieth anniversary of its existence."* It is a setting for chorus and orchestra
of Latin versions of the thirty-eighth, thirty-ninth, and fortieth
Psalms, the first two fragmentarily, the last *in toto*. As Stravinsky is
an intensely religious man, it seemed reasonable to suppose that he
would have written deeply felt religious music, which—despite his
many pronouncements against emotional content in music—might
move the listener as well as the composing artist. Actually, except
in those portions when his sheer musical talent momentarily released him from the grip of his own esthetic, the *Symphonie de
psaumes* must be chalked up as just another experiment. For two
movements, the good things are spaced closely enough to make it
impressive, and occasionally moving, as nothing of Stravinsky's
had been since *Les Noces*. The third movement has been dismissed
by some critics as sentimental trifling: this would in itself be egregious in a setting of the fortieth Psalm. But the sad truth is that
even the sentimentality is not genuine. It rings about as true as
the halo Del Sarto put about the head of his peasant mistress
when he was manufacturing a religious picture.

Despite its lapses, its blotches of bad taste, the *Symphonie de
psaumes* kept hope alive for the patient. After all, he was only
forty-eight years old. In October, 1931, Stravinsky went to
Berlin to conduct the *première* of his Violin Concerto, his first
big instrumental composition for several years. The soloist was
the American violinist Samuel Dushkin, who for a long time was
to be closely associated with him, rather in the role of violinist
extraordinary. This quietly forbidding composition, interesting
for its variety of technical resourcefulness, again minimized expressiveness. In 1941, combined with George Balanchine's most
self-consciously mannered choreography, the Violin Concerto,
metamorphosed into a ballet called *Balustrade*, came close to
creating a riot at the last of its few New York performances.
Balustrade soon vanished from the repertoire (despite the worshipful regard of a few), and the Concerto itself is almost never
revived.

In 1932, again for Dushkin, Stravinsky produced his Duo

---

* Naturally, Dr. Koussevitsky was to have had the privilege of first presenting the
Symphonie to the world. But he fell ill, and the Brussels group got ahead of him.

Concertant, one of the most impressive offerings of his neoclassic muse. This extremely difficult five-movement piece for violin and piano, which more recently has been brilliantly interpreted by Joseph Szigeti, shows the composer momentarily losing his war against expressiveness. Was it not inevitable, finally, that he—who had omitted strings from his Piano Concerto eight years before as being "too expressive"—should surrender inadvertently to their romantic seductions? It was but a half-surrender: especially in the first four movements of the Duo Concertant the idiom and esthetic are still astringent. And in the final movement —a Dithyrambe—the exalted, hieratic mood that is achieved reserves a classicist's dignity.

Still exploring the violin, Stravinsky, with Dushkin as his colleague, arranged for violin and piano parts of the Divertimento he had fashioned earlier from the score of Le Baiser de la fée. In the process, he refined the original inspiration and strengthened its expression, though it is still a trifle embarrassing to hear Tchaikovsky's Humoresque anatomized by modern harmonies. A parallel operation was performed on the corpus vivendi of Pulcinella, giving to that witty commentary on Pergolesi a new and different life in a piece for violin and piano called Suite italienne. Whatever the separate virtues of these various enterprises, only the Duo Concertant manifested continuing creativeness.

In 1933, at the request of Ida Rubinstein, Stravinsky set André Gide's version of the Homeric Hymn to Demeter as Perséphone, a melodrama in three parts for orchestra, chorus, tenor, and a female speaking voice. Stravinsky himself conducted its première at the Paris Opéra. When people began to discuss and criticize, he said: "There is nothing to discuss or criticize." Then, explaining that Perséphone was "a sequel to Oedipus Rex, to the Symphonie de psaumes, to the Capriccio, the Violin Concerto, and the Duo Concertant—in short, to a progression from which the spectacular is absent," he proceeded to instruct the critics. "One does not criticize anybody or anything that is functioning," he said. "A nose is not manufactured; a nose just is. Thus, too, my art." But a critic's business is precisely to notice whether anybody or anything is functioning ill or well, and a critic may properly observe that *Perséphone* is a vast bore despite its distinguished ancestry.

Stravinsky's return to the ballet, signalized by the *première* of *The Card Party* at the Metropolitan Opera House, New York, on April 27, 1937, was almost as disappointing as *Le Baiser de la fée* nine years earlier. This entertainment "in three deals," representing the actual course of three poker hands, is as trivial, and not nearly so charming, as Delibes' most obscure and forgotten ballet. On the other hand, Stravinsky's acceptance of a commission to compose a band accompaniment for the frolics of Ringling Brothers-Barnum & Bailey's elephants led, in 1942, to some amusing results. Billed as "Fifty Elephants and Fifty Beautiful Girls in an Original Choreographic Tour de Force," this diversion was directed by George Balanchine, staged by John Murray Anderson, and costumed—down to the pachyderms' vast pink tutus—by Norman Bel Geddes. Newspaper reports had it that the elephants, unable to follow the intricacies of the score, expressed their dislike of it in some subtle elephantine way. In truth, the music was all but lost in the pervasive clamor of the circus. But Stravinsky, always economical with every composed measure, revised it for symphony orchestra as *Circus Polka*.

The elephant ballet was a far cry from the savagery of *Le Sacre du printemps*. Stravinsky's next alliance with commercial entertainment had a happier outcome. To Billy Rose's order he fashioned, for a lamentable revue entitled *The Seven Lively Arts*, a score for displaying the talents of Alicia Markova and Anton Dolin. What audiences at the refurbished Ziegfeld Theatre in New York heard in 1944 was snippets of the entire suite. Divorced from the *longueurs* incident on Dolin's boring choreography, *Scènes de ballet* easily established its autonomy. It is average latter-day Stravinsky with a few moments of graciousness (scarcely a Stravinskyan quality) in the midst of its clever aridities.*

Between *Circus Polka* and *Scènes de ballet* Stravinsky had, however, composed one of his most satisfactory and sensitive ballets—*Danses concertantes*. Written in 1942, heard the next year in

---

* Not very clever is the *Ebony Concerto* written in 1945 for the jazz orchestra of Woody Herman. The music suffers from a case of borborygmus so bad that early death is almost certain.

concert form (it was originally conceived as a sort of *concerto grosso* for twenty-four virtuoso string players), and not finally danced until 1944, this music gave Balanchine the perfect medium for a profound and consistently adult exploitation of abstract ideas. *Danses concertantes* is not only a Balanchine masterpiece; it is also Stravinsky's most successful solution in neoclassic style of the problem of communication. It shows him still primarily intellectual, but passionately so. The human is not easily abstractable from this music, but it glows with a white radiance.

Less human, and at times forbidding, is *Dumbarton Oaks*, a concerto grosso in E flat for chamber orchestra that Stravinsky composed in 1938 to celebrate the thirtieth wedding anniversary of Mr. and Mrs. Robert Woods Bliss, after whose Washington, D. C., manor house it was named. Chiefly a series of experiments in rhythms and timbres, this scholarly *pièce d'occasion* not inappropriately had its first hearing in a house that has since become the chief seat of Byzantine studies in America. Like Byzantine art, *Dumbarton Oaks* can fascinate those whose sophistication is tempted only by the most recondite flavors.

In 1940, Stravinsky returned to the symphony, a form he had not worked with for almost thirty-five years.* The fiftieth anniversary of the Chicago Symphony Orchestra was to occur in 1941, and the Symphony in C was composed to celebrate that event. Far from being festive, it is reserved and elegant, a formal and deliberate reminiscence of the classical symphony. But, as Virgil Thomson wrote, ". . . in spite of his almost academic intentions, the Russian ballet-master in him does take over from time to time. Indeed, what breath the piece has is due to the incompleteness of its voluntary stylization." All in all, the Symphony in C is true caviar to the general, and the rumor that Stokowski's playing it on the air caused his break with the NBC Symphony Orchestra is all too plausible.

Dedicated "to the Philharmonic-Symphony Society of New York as an homage and appreciation of my twenty years' association with that eminent institution," the Symphony in

---

* The *Symphonie de psaumes* need not be excepted: it is *sui generis*. The Symphonies for wind instruments in memory of Claude Debussy (1920) do not, in the ordinary sense, constitute a symphony at all.

Three Movements followed the Symphony in C five years later (1945). Ingolf Dahl, Stravinsky's friend and associate, had professed to find in the Symphony in C irony, wit, and playfulness. In strains reminiscent of the panegyrics of Boris de Schloezer and Jean Cocteau, he wrote of the Symphony in Three Movements: "But now it is not the *kothurnus* of Greek tragedy on which the composer stands, as in *Oedipus Rex* or Duo Concertant, but the soil of the world of 1945. One day it will be universally recognized that the white house in the Hollywood hills [where he now lives with his second wife, the first Mme Stravinsky having died some time before] in which this Symphony was written and which was regarded by some as an ivory tower was just as close to the core of a world at war as the place where Picasso painted *Guernica*." Anyone who has seen *Guernica* and heard the Symphony in Three Movements may decide for himself on the merits of this comparison, which nevertheless says nothing about the music itself. Its fury, unlike Picasso's, lacks validity, and the self-consciousness of its technical efficiency too often impinges upon the sympathetic listener.

For a man who was certainly the most gifted composer of his generation, the rest of Stravinsky's recent output is mostly a tally of trivial and disappointing essays and rearrangements. The Sonata for Two Pianos is among the best of his later inventions, of immense interest to the musical exegete. But in works like *Four Norwegian Moods* (1942), originally intended for a Broadway review, and the Ode composed in 1943 in honor of the late Mme Nathalie Koussevitzky, Stravinsky falls below those standards which, however chill and arid, are by their very loftiness somehow admirable. The *Four Norwegian Moods* are full of half-dissolved saccharin: it is truly astonishing that they could have come from Stravinsky's pen.

The Concerto in D for strings (1946), composed for a chamber group in Basle, and therefore often referred to as the "Basle" Concerto, again showed that the patient was by no means dead. It has one quality conspicuously lacking in the works that immediately preceded it: vitality. Yet it was not of the quality to prepare the hopeful watchers for the truly remarkable flare-up that took place in 1947. Using the much-used story of Orpheus and Eurydice (its very time-eaten substance gave edge to the challenge), Stravinsky concocted the beautiful and touching score of the ballet *Orpheus*. By his infallible sensitivity to the nature of the dance, he again triumphantly proved himself a great man of the theater, his perfect adjutant being one equally sensitive to the nature of music—the great choreographer George Balanchine. Here, better late than never, is a mellow Stravinsky, in effect willing to admit that his battle against expressiveness has been lost, a battle against his own nature, as *Orpheus* proves. The Stravinsky of five years before would never have composed these tender, pleading musical strophes, so suave and yet so persuasive. The elegance to which he had seemingly bade farewell is one of the positively cohesive elements of the score. As presented by Ballet Society in New York on April 28, 1948, it was one of the great occasions of the modern theater.

The simile Stravinsky-as-patient should not be pressed too far, for it would necessitate calling the Latin Mass for mixed chorus and ten wind instruments (1948) a relapse. Truly it is a crabbed piece, musically more Byzantine than Latin in its stiff lack of recognizable contour and plastic mobility. At its American *première* on February 26, 1949, it was sung twice, but did not seem any more accessible at the repetition. Perhaps *Orpheus* has supplied the final necessary proof that Stravinsky only comes fully to life in the ambiance of the theater. If so, his collaboration with the Anglo-American poet Wystan Hugh Auden on an opera may have great results. The theme is derived from Hogarth's great series of pictorial satires, *The Rake's Progress*. The vividness and variety of the material seem in advance peculiarly suited to Stravinsky's adaptability as a theatrical artist, and his first setting of English words should prove an interesting experiment. It is said that the opera may come to production in 1951.

It is fascinating to ponder the strange arc of Stravinsky's career. Many explanations have been advanced, all with grains of truth in them. Stravinsky is a complex personality, and it is not easy to chart the future course of his career or explain the vagaries of his past. Some have said that Diaghilev acted as his Svengali, and that Stravinsky's vitality waned with Diaghilev's. There are those who say that quite the opposite was the case, and that, by focusing Stravinsky's attention on rhythm (the prime requisite of ballet music), Diaghilev precipitated the drying up of his creative powers. They insist that Stravinsky had little melodic gift to start with, and that rhythmic preoccupation sapped that little. There can be no doubt, too, that expatriation hurt Stravinsky. Russians must go back. Even the Paris-loving Turgeniev went back, and we have seen the onetime internationalist Prokofiev returning to the Soviet Union with happy results. But the Russian Revolution completed Stravinsky's estrangement from his native land. He became a French citizen in 1934, an American citizen in 1945.*

The natural tendency in discussing the composer of music so frequently dehumanized, is to forget the personal element completely. Yet Stravinsky is by no means a Martian. There are plenty of Americans who remember his first visit to our shores in 1925, when he seemed like a herald angel, like the harbinger of a new dispensation in art. Despite his unpoetical resemblance on the podium to a trained seal, one was tempted to say of the composer of *Petrouchka* and *Le Sacre*, "I too have once seen Shelley plain." Since the fall of 1939 he has been domiciled in America—a little, hurried man, awkward in his gestures and looking myopically from behind horn-rimmed spectacles Alas, alas! we should have seen it on his first visit: Stravinsky looks like a businessman, and nothing else. It is difficult to think of him as the composer of indubitable masterpieces, even more difficult to think of him as holding the future of music in his (much photographed) hands. But when he takes up the baton, and begins to conduct *Orpheus*, he declares that some of the future of music still belongs to him.

* Stravinsky may have been looking forward to his American citizenship when, in 1942, he made an arrangement for orchestra of *The Star-Spangled Banner*. A puzzled Boston Symphony audience tried vainly to co-operate in its *première* at Symphony Hall, Boston, on January 14, 1944, but the plot line soon got beyond their powers. Apparently Stravinsky had approached the anthem reverently. "I gave it the character of a real church hymn," he explained, "not that of a soldier's marching song or a club song, as it was originally. I tried to express the religious feelings of the people of America." Nevertheless, he had offended the mores of Massachusetts: Boston Police Commissioner Thomas F. Sullivan warned him that he had made himself liable to a $100 fine under an old state law forbidding rearrangements, in whole or in part, of the national anthem. No action was taken, but Stravinsky did not again invite the law—his *Star-Spangled Banner* has not been heard since.

Index

A

À travers Chants (Berlioz), 360
Abraham, Gerald (1904–), 598
Academic Festival Overture (Brahms), 494
Acis and Galatea (Gay), 65
Adam, Adolphe-Charles (1803–56), 368
Adams, Henry (1838–1918), 243
Adams, John Quincy (1767–1848), 243
Addison, Joseph (1672–1719), 60
Aeneid (Virgil), 367
Aeschylus (525–456), 85
Agoult, Charles, Comte d' (1816–?), 341
Agoult, Marie-Catherine-Sophie de Flavigny, Comtesse d' (Daniel Stern) 1805–76), 244, 329, 377, 378, 379, 380, 381, 385, 389, 431
Aguado, Alexandre-Marie (1784–1842), 240, 243
Ahna, Pauline de, see Strauss, Pauline (De Ahna)
Aïda (Verdi), 461, 462–463, 465
Aix-la-Chapele, Peace of, 81
Albani, Alessandro, Cardinal (1692–1779), 90
Albéniz, Isaac (1860–1909), 20, 388, 552
    Iberia, 552
Albert I, King of the Belgians (1875–1934), 553
Albert, Prince of Saxe-Coburg-Gotha, the Prince Consort (1819–1861), 284, 289, 423
Albert V, Duke of Bavaria (1528–1579), 15, 16, 18
Albert, Eugene d' (1864–1932), 388, 560
Alboni, Marietta (1823–1894), 246
Albrechtsberger, Johann Georg (1736–1809), 168
Alceste (Gluck), 93–94, 98, 105, 138
Alexander the Great, King of Macedon (356–323), 159
Alexander I, Tsar of Russia (1777–1825), 236
Alexander II, Tsar of Russia (1818–1881), 460, 514, 518
Alexander III, Tsar of Russia (1845–1894), 522, 523-524
Alexander VI (Rodrigo Borgia), Pope (1431–1503), 6
Alexander's Feast (Dryden), 72–73
Allegri, Gregorio (1582–1652), 130
    Miserere, 130
Allgemeine musikalische Zeitung (Leipzig), 256, 560, 564-565, 581
Also sprach Zarathustra (Richard Strauss), 562

Almanach de Gotha, 11, 29, 321
"Alto" Rhapsody (Brahms), 535
Alva, Fernando Álvarez de Toledo, Duke of (1508–1582), 192
Ambrose, Bishop of Milan, St. (340–397), 3, 20
Amélie (last name unknown), 371
Ancient Mariner, The (Coleridge), 411
Andersen, Hans Christian (1805–75), 602
Anderson, Mr., 423
Anderson, Emily, 129
Anderson, John Murray, 607
Anhalt-Cöthen, Prince Leopold of (1694–1729), 33, 34, 35, 37, 38
Anne, Queen of England (1665–1714), 59, 61–62
Anne, Empress of Russia (1693–1740), 43
Annunzio, Gabriele d' (1864–1938), 529, 550, 551
Antigone (Sophocles), 283, 285
Après-midi d'un faune, L' (Mallarmé), 538
Arcadian Academy, 57
Aristotle (384–322), 329
Arnaud, Abbé François (1721–1784), 97
Arnim, Bettina Brentano von (1785–1859), 178, 191, 192, 272, 366
Arnold, Matthew (1822–1888), 329
Arnould, Madeleine-Sophie (1744–1802), 96
Arosa, Achille-Antoine, 530, 531
Artôt (de Padilla), Désirée (1835–1907), 505–506, 512
As You Like It (Shakespeare), 545
Asleep in the Deep (Petrie), 7
Athalie (Racine), 284
Auber, Daniel-François-Esprit (1782–1871), 222, 320, 355, 405, 457, 530
Auden, Wystan Hugh (1907–), 610
Auer, Leopold (1845–1930), 518, 520
Auf Flügeln des Gesanges (Heine), 278
Augsburg Confession, 270
Augusta, Empress of Germany (1811–1890), 428
Augustus II, King of Poland, see Saxony, Friedrich Augustus I, Elector of
Augustus III, King of Poland, see Saxony, Friedrich Augustus II, Elector of
Aurora's Wedding (Tchaikovsky), 524
Auvergne, Antoine d' (1713–1797), 96
Ave Maria (Schubert), 250, 251, 262
Avé-Lallemant, Theodor (1805–1890), 522
Avenarius, Cäcilie (Geyer) (1813–?), 397

B

B minor Mass (Bach), 38, 40, 42, 45-47,
   49, 78, 288
Bach family, 23, 24
Bach Gesellschaft, 22–23
Bach, Anna Magdalena (Wilcken)
   (1701–1760), 35, 38, 44, 52
Bach, Johann Ambrosius (1645–1695),
   24
Bach, Johann Christian (1735–1782),
   35, 52, 127, 136
Bach, Johann Gottfried Bernhard
   (1715–1739), 49
Bach, Johann Sebastian (1685–1750),
   14, 18, 21, 22–52, 53, 55, 63–64, 65,
   69, 70, 76, 82, 84, 104, 124, 153–154,
   160, 161, 165, 201, 207, 272, 273,
   275, 281, 282, 283, 289, 291, 294,
   315, 324, 372, 380, 396, 446, 464,
   469, 470, 472, 479, 486, 501, 510,
   601
   B minor Mass, 38, 40, 42, 45-47, 49,
      78, 288
   "Brandenburg" Concertos, 36–37, 63,
      76
   Capriccio on the Departure of His
      Beloved Brother, 27
   Chaconne, see Partita for violin
      alone (2nd)
   Christ lag in Totesbanden, 47
   "Coffee" Cantata, 47
   Concerto, four claviers and orchestra,
      38
   Concerto, three claviers and orches-
      tra, 282
   Ein feste Burg ist unser Gott, 47
   English Suites, 36, 37
   French Suites, 26, 36, 37, 38
   "Goldberg" Variations, 49
   Gott ist mein König, 28
   Gottes Zeit ist allerbeste Zeit, 31
   Italian Concerto, 26, 38
   Kunst der Fuge, Die, 51, 200
   Magnificat, 39–40
   Musikalisches Opfer, 50
   Partita for violin alone (2nd), 37
   partitas, clavier, 36, 37
   Passacaglia, C minor, 30
   St. John Passion, 40–42, 46, 47, 63–64
      Es ist vollbracht, 41
   St. Matthew Passion, 18, 37, 38, 40,
      41, 42–43, 46, 47, 64, 78, 272–273,
      288
   Singet dem Herrn, 154
   Sonata, violin and piano, C major,
      460
   Streit zwischen Phoebus und Pan,
      Der, 47–48
   Toccata and Fugue, D minor, 29
   "Vivaldi" Concertos, 28
   Wachet auf, 47

Bach, Johann Sebastian—(Continued)
   Was mir behagt, 32
   Well-Tempered Clavichord, The,
      35–36, 37, 49, 51, 65, 165, 294, 315,
      324, 330
Bach, Karl Philipp Emanuel (1714–
   1788), 23, 29, 41, 49–50, 52, 104, 105,
   117, 123, 124, 125, 127, 131, 132, 142
Bach Maria Barbara (Bach) (1684–
   1720), 28, 30, 35, 44
Bach, Wilhelm Friedemann (1710–
   1784), 29, 35, 41, 44, 45, 49, 50, 70, 82
Backer-Gröndahl, Agathe (1847–1907),
   141
Baini, Abbé Giuseppe (1775–1844), 275
Bakst, Leon Nikolaevich (1868–1924),
   550
Bakunin, Mikhail Aleksandrovich
   (1814–1876), 416
Balakirev, Mili Alexeivich (1837–1910),
   506, 515
Balanchine, George (1904–   ), 605, 607,
   608, 610
Ballet Russe (Diaghilev), 596, 599, 602
Ballet Society (New York), 610
Ballo in maschera, Un (Verdi), 457–458
Balustrade (Stravinsky-Balanchine), 605
Balzac, Honoré de (1799–1850), 239-
   240, 320, 329, 362, 531
Banck, Carl (1809–1889), 299
Barbaia, Domenico (1778–1841), 220,
   229–230, 234, 235
Barber of Seville, The (Rossini), 226,
   230–232, 233, 240, 242, 243, 246, 247,
   370, 466
Barbier, Henri-Auguste (1805–1882),
   355
Barbier de Séville, Le (Beaumarchais),
   230
Barbier von Bagdad, Der (Cornelius),
   383, 384
Bardac, M., 545, 546
Bardac, Emma, see Debussy, Emma
   (Bardac)
Bardi, Giovanni, Conte del (1534?–
   1612?), 85
Barezzi, Antonio (1787–1867), 446, 447,
   458, 461
Barezzi, Margherita, see Verdi, Mar-
   gherita (Barezzi)
Barnum, Phineas Taylor (1810–1891),
   68, 387, 549
Bastien und Bastienne (Mozart), 128
Baudelaire, Pierre-Charles (1821–1867),
   530, 540
Bauernfeld, Eduard von (1802–1890),
   255
Bavaria, Karl Theodor, Elector of
   (?–1799), 138
Bavaria, Maximilian III Josef, Elector
   of (?–1777), 125, 132
Beard, John (1716?–1791), 72

Beardsley, Aubrey (1872–1898), 545
Béatrice et Benedict (Berlioz), 349, 368, 369, 370–371
    overture, 370
Beaumarchais, Pierre-Augustin Caron de (1732–1799), 147, 230, 231
Beauvais Cathedral, 261
Becker, Albert (1834–1899), 576
Bédier, Joseph (1864–1938), 549
Beecham, Sir Thomas (1879–), 572
Beer, Jakob Liebmann, see Meyerbeer, Giacomo
Beethoven, Johann van (1740?–1792), 163, 164, 165, 166
Beethoven, Johann Nikolaus van (1776–1848), 171, 173, 193, 205
Beethoven, Karl Kaspar van (1774–1815), 171, 173, 174, 192, 197
Beethoven, Karl van (1806–1858), 197–198, 205
Beethoven, Ludwig van (1712–1773), 163
Beethoven, Ludwig van (1770–1827), 22, 46, 49, 65, 107, 115, 118, 122, 141, 142, 143, 149, 151, 152, 159, 160, 161, 162–207, 215, 216, 221, 236, 241, 242, 249, 251, 252, 255, 258, 262, 264, 266, 278, 279, 291, 296, 300, 302, 303, 304, 307, 317, 328, 337, 341, 344, 346, 347, 352, 356, 360, 362, 365, 366, 372, 374, 375, 379, 380, 382, 394, 395, 399, 402–403, 422, 423, 440, 446, 466, 469, 471, 474, 481, 489, 501, 510, 517, 521, 542, 572, 575, 580, 582, 587
    "*Adieux, Les,*" Sonata (Opus 81a), 190, 191
    "*Ah! perfido,*" 188
    "*Appassionata*" Sonata (Opus 57), 182, 206
    Battle of Vittoria, The, see *Wellington's Victory*
    "Battle" Symphony, see *Wellington's Victory*
    Choral Fantasy, 188
    "Choral" Symphony, 191, 192, 193, 194–195, 196, 202, 277, 302
    concertos for piano and orchestra
        1st, C major, 169–170, 188
        2nd, B flat major, 169
        3rd, C minor, 142, 178–179
        4th, G major, 185–186, 542
        5th ("Emperor"), E flat major, 185, 186, 207
    Concerto for violin and orchestra, D major, 186–187, 287, 472, 521
    Coriolanus Overture, 192
    "Diabelli" Variations, 49, 200
    Egmont, incidental music, 192, 278, 400
    Egmont Overture, 192

Beethoven, Ludwig van—(*Continued*)
    "Emperor" Concerto for piano and orchestra, 185, 186, 207
    "*Eroica*" *Symphony,* 179–181, 188, 194, 206, 236, 572
    "*Eroica*" Variations, 49
    Fidelio, 182–185, 196, 221, 241, 383, 400
        "*Abscheulicher, vo eilst du hin,*" 185
    Fidelio Overture, 184
    Geschöpfe des Prometheus, Die, 171, 180
        overture, 171
    Grosse Fuge (Opus 132), 207
    "*Hammerklavier*" Sonata (Opus 106), 198–200
    "Harp" Quartet (Opus 74), 207
    "Kreutzer" Sonata for violin and piano, 206
    Leonora, see *Fidelio*
    "Leonora" Overture, 1st, 183–184
    "Leonora" Overture, 2nd, 184
    "Leonora" Overture, 3rd, 183, 184, 185
    Mass, C major, 188
    Missa solennis, 200–202, 203, 401
        "*Et vitam venturi,*" 202
    "Moonlight" Sonata (Opus 27, No. 2), 175, 181, 191
    overtures
        Coriolanus, 192
        Egmont, 192
        "*Fidelio,*" 184
        "Leonora," 1st, 183–184
        "Leonora," 2nd, 184
        "Leonora," 3rd, 183, 184, 185
        "Prometheus," see *Geschöpfe des Prometheus, Die*
    "Pastoral" Symphony, 188, 190, 194, 277, 491
    "*Pathétique*" Sonata (Opus 13), 170
    quartets for strings, 587
        Opus 18, 206
            No. 4, 206
        Opus 59 ("Rasoumovsky"), 185, 186, 206, 207
            No. 1, 206–207
        Opus 74 ("Harp"), 207
        Opus 95, 207
        Opus 127, 205–206, 207
        Opus 130, 205–206, 207
        Opus 131, 205–206, 207
        Opus 132, 205–206, 207
        Opus 135, 205–206, 207
    "Rasoumovsky" Quartets (Opus 59), 185, 186, 206, 207
    Rondo, G major, for piano (Opus 51), 175
    Septet, E flat major (Opus 20), 171
    sonatas for piano
        Opus 2, 170

Beethoven, Ludwig van—*(Continued)*
  sonatas for piano—*(Continued)*
    Opus 10, 170
    Opus 13 (*"Pathétique"*), 170
    Opus 26, 181
    Opus 27, No. 1, 181
    Opus 27, No. 2 ("Moonlight"), 175, 181, 191
    Opus 31, No. 2, 181, 182
    Opus 31, No. 3, 181, 182
    Opus 53 ("Waldstein"), 182
    Opus 57 (*"Appassionata"*), 182, 206
    Opus 78, 191
    Opus 81a (*"Les Adieux"*), 190, 191
    Opus 90, 199
    Opus 101, 198–199
    Opus 106 (*"Hammerklavier"*), 198–200
    Opus 109, 198–199, 200
    Opus 110, 198–199, 200
    Opus 111, 198–199, 200
  Sonata for violin and piano (Opus 47) ("Kreutzer"), 206
  symphonies, 170–171, 399–400, 423
    1st, C major, 171, 178, 188
    2nd, D major, 179, 188
    3rd (*"Eroica"*), E flat major, 179 181, 188, 194, 206, 236, 572
    4th, B flat major, 187, 188–189, 196, 279
    5th, C minor, 185, 188, 189–190, 194, 517
    6th ("Pastoral"), F major, 188, 190, 194, 277, 346, 491
    7th, A major, 191, 192, 193, 194–195, 196, 202, 277, 302
    8th, F major, 192, 193, 195–196, 199, 202
    9th ("Choral"), D minor, 194, 199, 202–204, 352, 365, 401, 402, 407, 414, 422, 437, 440, 490–491
  "Battle," see *Wellington's Victory*
  "Waldstein" Sonata (Opus 53), 182
  Wellington's Victory, or the Battle of Vittoria ("Battle" Symphony), 193–194, 215
  writings
    "Heiligenstadt Testament," 170–174, 176
    letter to the "Immortal Beloved," 176–178
Beethoven, Maria Josefa (Poll) van (1714–1775), 163
Beethoven, Maria Magdalena (Keverich) van (1747–1787), 163–164, 165–166
Beethoven, Therese (Obermeyer) van (?–1828), 205
Beethoven, Theresia (Reiss) van, 197
Beggar's Opera, The (Gay and Pepusch), 64, 69, 74, 78

Beiden Grenadiere, Die (Schumann), 303
Beidler, Isolde (Wagner) (1865–1919), 431
Bekker, Paul (1882–1937), 202, 203–204
Belgiojoso, Princess Cristina (Trivulzio), 378, 381
Bellini, Vincenzo (1801–1835), 241, 294, 320, 337, 403, 448, 502, 507
  Capuletti ed i Montecchi, I, 507
  Norma, 294, 320, 448
  Sonnambula, La, 294
Benchley, Robert (1889–1945), 220
Benedict, Sir Julius (1804–1885), 218, 221–222
Benedict XIV (Prospero Lorenzo Lambertini), Pope (1675–1758), 90
Bennett, Sir William Sterndale (1816–1875), 298, 311, 486
Benois, Alexandre Nikolaevich (1870–   ), 598
Benvenuto Cellini (Berlioz), 350, 352, 353, 355–356, 365, 383; see also *Carnaval romain* overture
  overture, 355
Béranger, Pierre-Jean de (1780–1857), 352
Berg, Alban (1885–1935), 568
Berlin, Irving (1888–   ), 234
Berliner Musik-Zeitung, 165
Berlioz, Harriet Constance (Smithson) (1800–1854), 325, 341, 342, 343, 345, 346, 347, 348–349, 352, 359, 360, 362, 366, 371, 376, 383, 385, 391, 423, 424, 507, 522, 530, 533, 540, 557, 558
Berlioz, Louis (1834–1867), 349, 352, 353, 359, 366, 371
Berlioz, Louis-Hector (1803–1869), 189, 225, 241, 279, 282, 297, 320, 325, 326, 338–373, 376, 383, 391, 423, 424, 507, 522, 530, 533, 540, 557, 558
  Beatrice et Benedict, 349, 368, 369, 370–371
    overture, 370
  Benvenuto Cellini, 350, 352, 353, 355–356, 365, 383; see also *Carnaval romain* overture
    overture, 355
  Captive, La, 352–353
  Carnaval romain overture, 355, 356, 360; see also *Benvenuto Cellini*
  Cinq mai, Le, 352, 359
  Corsaire overture, 360
  Damnation de Faust, La, 360–361, 362, 365, 371, 383; see also *Huit Scènes de Faust*
    "*Immense nature*," 361
    Dance of the Sylphs, 361
    Minuet of the Will-o'-the-Wisps, 361
    Rákóczy March, 360
    Roi de Thulé, Le, 361
    "*Voici des roses*," 361

Berlioz, Louis-Hector—*(Continued)*
  Dernier Jour du monde, Le, 354
  Derniers Instans de Marie Stuart, Les,
    350
  Dix décembre, Le, 368
  Enfance du Christ, L', 364–365, 366–
    367, 369, 373
    Fuite en Égypte, La, 364–365, 367
      overture, 367
      Adieu des bergers, L', 367
      Repos de la Sainte-Famille, Le,
        367
    Songe d'Hérode, Le, 367
    Arrivée à Saïs, L', 367
  fantasy for orchestra, chorus, two
    pianos, on Shakespeare's *Tempest,*
    346–347, 350, 351; see also *Lélio*
  Francs-juges, Les, 342, 343, 349, 359
    overture, 343, 349
  Grande Messe des morts, see Requiem
  Harold en Italie, 346, 350, 351–352,
    356, 383
  Herminie, 343
  Huit Scènes de Faust, 343, 360; see
    also *Damnation de Faust, La*
  Impériale, L', 368
  Lélio, 343, 347, 348, 350–351, 369,
    372
    fantasy on Shakespeare's *Tempest,*
    346–347, 350, 351
  Mass (early), 341, 342
    Resurrexit, 342, 354
  Menace des francs, La, 364
  Mort de Cléopâtre, La, 343, 350
  Mort de Sardanapale, La, 346
  Mort d'Orphée, La, 342
  Nuits d'été, 352–353
    Absence, 352–353
    Au cimetière, 353
    Ile inconnue, L', 353
    Spectre de la rose, Le, 352–353
    Villanelle, 352–353
  Prise de Troie, La see *Troyens, Les*
  potpourri on Italian airs, 340
  quintet for flute and strings, 340
  Requiem *(Grande Messe des morts),*
    353–355
    Offertory, 355
    Tuba mirum, 354, 355
  Révolution grecque, La, see *Scène
    heroïque*
  Rob Roy overture, 348
  Roi Lear overture, 348
  Roméo et Juliette, 343, 356–357, 361,
    365, 370, 373, 507
    Grand Fete at the Capulets', 357
    Love Scene, 357
    Queen Mab Scherzo, 357
  *Scene heroïque: La Révolution grec-
    que,* 342

Berlioz, Louis-Hector—*(Continued)*
  Symphonie fantastique, 341, 342, 343–
    346, 347, 348, 359, 369, 371, 383,
    391, 522
    "Marche au supplice," 346, 347
  Symphonie funèbre et triomphale,
    358
  Te Deum, 363–364
    Judex crederis, 363–364
    Tibi omnes, 364
  Tour de Nice, Le, see *Corsaire* over-
    ture
  Troyens, Les, 343, 367, 368–370, 373
    Chasse royale et orage, 370
    "Inutiles regrets," 370
    Marche troyenne, 370
    Prise de Troie, La, 369
    Troyens à Carthage, Les, 369
    "Vallons sonore," 370
  Troyens à Carthage, Les, see *Troyens,
    Les*
  Waverley overture, 342, 343
  writings
    À travers chants, 360
    Grotesques de la musique, Les, 360
    Mémoires, 348, 360, 363, 366
    Soirées de l'orchestre, Les, 360
    *Traité de l'instrumentation et
      d'orchestration* (Opus 10), 360
    *Voyage musical en Allemagne et
      en Italie,* 306
Berlioz, Louis-Joseph (1776–1848), 339,
  340, 341, 353, 363
Berlioz, Marie - Antoinette - Joséphine
  (Marmion) (1781–1838), 339
Berlioz, Marie - Geneviève (Martin,
  called Recio) (1814–1862), 359, 360,
  362, 366
Bertin, Louise-Angélique (1805–1877),
  353
  Esmeralda, 353
Bertin family, 353, 354, 356
Bethlehem (Pennsylvania) Bach Festi-
  val, 46
Bethmann, Johann Philipp, 431
Billington, Elizabeth (1768–1818), 116
Billroth, Theodor (1829–1894), 493, 500
Bishop, Sir Henry Rowley (1786–1855),
  362
Bismarck-Schönhausen, Otto Eduard
  Leopold, Prince von (1815–1898),
  437, 486
Bispham, David Scull (1857–1921), 569
Bizet, Georges (Alexandre-César-Léo-
  pold) (1838–1875), 218, 388
  Carmen, 511, 546
Björnson, Björnsterne (1832–1910), 576
Blanchard, Sophie (Armant) (1778–
  1819), 213
Blessed Damozel, The (Rossetti), 535
Bliss, Mr. and Mrs. Robert Woods, 608

Blom, Eric (1888-   ), 137, 153
Blossom Time (Romberg), 248, 261
Bohemian Girl, The (Balfe), 519
Böhm, Georg (1661–1733), 25
Boïto, Arrigo (1842–1918), 233, 361, 450, 451, 456, 460, 464, 465, 466, 467, 468, 527, 534
    Mefistofele, 465
Bolm, Adolf (1884-   ), 596, 597
Bonaparte, Jérôme, King of Westphalia (1784–1860), 190
Bonaparte, Joseph, King of Naples and Spain (1768–1844), 193
Bonaparte, Princess Mathilde-Letitia (1820–1904), 245
Bonaparte, Napoleon-Joseph-Charles ("Plon-Plon"), (1822–1891), 385
Bordoni, Faustina, see Hasse, Faustina (Bordoni)
Boris Godunov (Mussorgsky), 535
Borodin, Alexander Porphyrievich (1833–1887), 506
Borromeo, St. Carlo (1538–1584), 7, 10
Boston Symphony Orchestra, 110, 564, 592, 605, 611
Boswell, James (1740–1795), 372
Botticelli, Sandro (1447?–1510), 331, 534
Boughton, Rutland (1878-   ), 31
    Immortal Hour, The, 31
Bourgeois-gentilhomme, Le (Molière), 570
Bragança, João de, Duke of Lafoens (1719–1806), 95
Braham, John (1774–1856), 223
Brahms, Caroline (Schnack) (1824–1892), 482, 486
Brahms, Johann Jakob (1806–1872), 470, 471, 482, 486
Brahms, Johanna (Nissen) (1789–1865), 470, 482, 483
Brahms, Johannes (1833–1897), 22, 49, 152, 181, 187, 206, 251, 263, 292, 297, 301, 304, 309–310, 311, 328, 338, 366, 444, 469–501, 510, 517, 520, 521, 522, 523, 557, 560, 565, 571, 580
    chamber music, 480–481
        Quintet, piano and strings, F minor (Opus 34), 480, 481
        Sextet, strings, G major (opus 36), 481–482
        sonatas, clarinet and piano (Opus 120, 480
        Trio, piano, violin, and cello, B major (Opus 8), 480
    choral
        Deutsches Requiem, Ein, solo voices, chorus, and orchestra, organ and libitum (Opus 45), 478, 482–484

Brahms, Johannes—*(Continued)*
    choral—*(Continued)*
        Rhapsody ("Alto"), alto solo, male chorus, and orchestra (Opus 53), 485
        Triumphlied, chorus and orchestra, organ ad libitum (Opus 55), 486
    concertos
        piano and orchestra
            1st, D minor (Opus 15), 477–478, 487, 490, 495
            2nd, B flat major (Opus 83), 495–496
        violin and orchestra, D major (Opus 77), 187, 493–494, 521
        violin, cello, and orchestra ("Double") (Opus 102), 498
    orchestra alone
        Hungarian Dances (arrangements of three piano duets), 484
        overtures
            Academic Festival (Opus 80), 494
            Tragic (Opus 81), 494–495
        serenades, 477, 490
            A major (Opus 16), 477
        symphonies, 489–492
            1st, C minor (Opus 68), 478, 489, 490–491, 492–493
            2nd, D major (Opus 73), 489, 491, 493
            3rd, F major (Opus 90), 491–492, 493, 497
            4th, E minor (Opus 98), 489, 492, 497, 499,
        Variations on a Theme by Josef Haydn (Opus 56a), 49, 487–488, 490
    piano solo, 500
        ballades, 474
            D minor ("Edward"), (Opus 10), 474
            G minor (Opus 118), 501
        capriccios
            B minor (Opus 76), 500
            G minor (Opus 116), 501
            of Opus 76, 500
        Hungarian Dances (arrangements of piano Duets), 484
        intermezzos
            A minor (Opus 76), 500
            C major (Opus 119), 501
            E flat minor (Opus 118), 500
            of Opus 76, 500
        rhapsodies
            E flat major (Opus 119), 500–501
            of Opus 79, 500
        Scherzo, E flat minor (Opus 4), 473
        sonatas, 473
            C major (Opus 1), 473-474

Brahms, Johannes—*(Continued)*
  piano solo—*(Continued)*
    sonatas—*(Continued)*
      F minor (Opus 5), 474
      F sharp minor (Opus 2), 474
    variations
      and fugue on a theme by Handel
        (Opus 24), 49, 478–479, 487,
        492, 500
      on a theme by Schumann (Opus
        9), 474–475
      on a theme by Paganini (Opus
        35), 479
  piano duets
    Hungarian Dances, 484
    Liebesliederwalzer (with mixed
      vocal quartet) (Opus 52), 485
    sixteen waltzes (Opus 39), 484
    A flat major, 484
  songs, 473, 488–489
    Sapphische Ode (Opus 94), 488
    Vergebliches Ständchen (Opus 84),
      488
    Von ewiger Liebe, 488
    Wiegenlied (Opus 49), 482, 484,
      488
  variations, 181, 479, 487
Brandenburg, Christian Ludwig, Margrave of (1677–?), 36
"Brandenburg" Concertos (Bach), 36–37, 63, 76
Brandenburg, Sophia Charlotte, Electress of (1668–1705), 54
Brandt, Caroline, see Weber, Caroline (Brandt) von
Brantôme, Pierre Bourdeilles de, Abbé de (1540?–1614), 15
Braun, Peter, Baron von, 183
Breitkopf and Härtel, 415
Brendel, Franz (1811–1868), 310
Brenet, Michel (Marie Bobillier) (1858–1918), 109
Brentano, Bettina, see Arnim, Bettina (Brentano) von
Breughel, Pieter (1525?–1569), 195
Breuning family, 166, 168
Breuning, Hélène (von Kerich) von (1750–1838), 166
Breuning, Stephan von (1774–1827), 183, 197
Britannia, Rule the Waves, 194
Broadwood, John, and Sons (London), 198
Brockes, Barthold Heinrich (1680–1747), 41, 63
Brodsky, Adolf (1851–1929), 520
Brosses, Charles, Président de (1709–1777), 87
Browning, Elizabeth (Barrett) (1806–1861), 329
Browning, Robert (1812–1889), 210

Bruch, Max (1838–1920), 494, 527
Bruckner, Anton (1824–1896), 266, 564
Brühl, Count Karl Friedrich (1772–1837), 217
Brunswick, Therese von (1775–1861), 177
Buckingham, George Villiers, Duke of (1628–1687), 209
Bull, Ole Borneman (1810–1880), 275
Bülow, Cosima (Liszt) von, see Wagner, Cosima (Lizst von Bülow)
Bülow, Franziska von, 438
Bülow, Hans Guido von (1830–1894), 366, 385, 387, 388, 414, 421, 424, 430, 431, 432, 433, 434, 435, 469, 470, 486, 489, 494, 497, 498, 510, 556, 557, 561, 577
Bulwer-Lytton, Edward George Earle Lytton, Baron Lytton (1803–1873), 408
Bunyan, John (1628–1688), 33
Buononcini, Giovanni Battista (1672–1750?), 67–68, 69
  Astarto, 67
Burlington, Richard Boyle, Earl of (1695–1753), 61, 67
Burney, Charles (1726–1814), 15, 32, 83, 114, 126, 129
Buxtehude, Dietrich (1637–1707), 24, 25, 27, 29, 30, 55, 510
Byrd, William (1540–1623), 59
Byrom, John (1692–1763), 68
Byron, George Noel Gordon, Baron (1788–1824), 292, 307, 350, 376

C

Calzabigi, Raniero da (1714–1795), 91, 93, 94, 95, 101, 137
Camille, see *Dame aux camélias, La*
Canons (near London), 64, 66
Caplet, André (1878–1925), 540
Capriccio Italien (Tchaikovsky), 519
Carissimi, Giacomo (1605–1674), 25
Carlyle, Thomas (1795–1881), 335
Carmen (Bizet), 511, 546
Carnarvon, James Brydges, Earl of, see Chandos, James Brydges, Duke of
Carnaval (Schumann), 279, 296, 297, 298, 301, 303, 474
Carnaval romain overture (Berlioz), 355, 356, 360; see also *Benvenuto Cellini* (Berlioz)
Carnegie, Andrew (1837–1919), 525
Carnegie Hall (New York), 364, 525
Caroline of Anspach, Queen of England (1683–1737), 73
Carraud, Gaston (1864–1920), 551
Carré, Albert (1852–1938), 543
Carus, Ernst August, 293
Caruso, Enrico (1873–1921), 460

Carvalho, Léon (1825–1897), 369, 425, 427

Casanova de Seingalt, Giovanni Jacopo (1725–1798), 149, 175

Catherine II, Empress of Russia (1729–1796), 101

Cavour, Camillo Benso, Conte di (1810–1861), 459

Cellini, Benvenuto (1500–1571), 350

Cenerentola, La (Rossini), 233

Cervantes de Saavedra, Miguel (1547–1616), 33, 218, 338, 563

Chaliapin, Feodor Ivanovich (1873–1938), 232

Chamberlain, Eva (Wagner) (1867–?), 431, 433

Chamberlain, Houston Stewart (1855–1927), 422

Chamisso, Adelbert von (1781–1838), 302

Chandos, James Brydges, Duke of (1673–1744), 64, 66

Chansons de Bilitis (Louÿs), 540

Charles VIII, King of France (1470–1498), 6

Charles IX, King of France (1550–1574), 15, 16

Charles X, King of France (1757–1836), 238, 239, 240, 241, 242, 245, 339, 376

Charles, Ernest (1895–   ), 75

Charlie Is My Darling, 284

Charlotte of Mecklenburg - Strelitz, Queen of England (1744–1818), 127

Charpentier, Gustave (1860–   ), 564

Chateaubriand, François René, Vicomte de (1768–1848), 320

Chaucer, Geoffrey (1340?–1400), 4

Chausson, Ernest (1855–1899), 537

Chekhov, Anton (1860–1904), 595

Cherubini, Maria Luigi Carlo Zenobio Salvatore (1760–1842), 214, 222, 223, 239, 270, 278, 319, 338, 340, 342, 359, 371, 375, 469
Deux Journées, Les, 278

Chezy, Helmine (von Klencke) von (1783–1856), 220, 258

Chicago Symphony Orchestra, 608

Children's Corner (Debussy), 549

Chopin, Frédéric-François (1810–1849), 35, 150, 217, 225, 263, 275, 279, 292, 297, 301, 311, 314–337, 349, 351, 376, 377, 380, 392, 394, 477, 500, 502, 520, 530, 531, 542, 547, 548, 552, 553, 554, 596
ballades, 332
　1st, G minor (Opus 23), 332
　2nd, F major (Opus 38), 332
　3rd, A flat major (Opus 47), 332
　4th, F minor (Opus 52), 332
Barcarole in F sharp major (Opus 60), 334

Chopin, Frédéric-François—(Continued)
Berceuse in D flat major (Opus 57), 334
concertos for piano and orchestra, 319
　1st, E minor (Opus 11), 319
　2nd, F minor (Opus 21), 319
　Variations on "Là ci darem," 150
études, 324–325, 554
　12th, C minor ("Revolutionary") (Opus 10, No. 12), 324–325
　18th, G sharp minor (Opus 25, No. 6), 324
　22nd, B minor (Opus 25, No. 10), 324
　three supplementary, 325
Fantaisie in F minor (Opus 49), 332-333
"Fantaisie-Impromptu," see impromptus, 4th
impromptus, 332
　1st, A flat major (Opus 29), 332
　2nd, F sharp major (Opus 36), 332
　3rd, G flat major (Opus 51), 332
　4th, C sharp minor ("Fantaisie-Impromptu") (Opus 66), 325, 332
Marche funèbre, see sonatas, 2nd
mazurkas, 323–324
nocturnes, 327–328
　7th, C sharp minor (Opus 27, No. 1), 328
　13th, C minor (Opus 48, No. 1), 328
　15th, F minor (Opus 55, No. 1), 500
polonaises, 322–323
　3rd, A major ("Militaire") (Opus 40, No. 1), 322
　5th, F sharp minor (Opus 44), 323
　6th, A flat major ("Heroic") (Opus 53), 323
　7th, A flat major (Polonaise-Fantaisie), 323
preludes, Opus 28, 330–331
　2nd, A minor, 331
　4th, E minor, 331
　5th, D major, 331
　6th, B minor, 331
　7th, A major, 331
　15th, D flat major ("Raindrop"), 331
　16th, B flat minor, 331
　19th, E flat major, 331
　20th, C minor, 331
　23rd, F major, 331
scherzos, 328–329
　1st, B minor (Opus 20), 328
　2nd, B flat minor (Opus 35), 328

Chopin, Frédéric-François—(Continued)
Sonata for cello and piano in G
minor (Opus 65), 335
sonatas for piano
1st, C minor (Opus 4), 331
2nd, B flat minor (Opus 35), 331–
332, 334
3rd, B minor (Opus 58), 334
valses, 321–322
D flat major ("Minute") (Opus
64, No. 1), 322
C sharp minor (Opus 64, No. 2),
322
Variations on "Là ci darem" for
piano and orchestra (Opus 2), 317,
319
Chopin, Justina (Krzyanowska) (1782–
1861), 315
Chopin, Ludwika (1807–1855), 315,
336
Chopin, Nicolas (1771–1844), 315, 334
"Choral" Symphony (Beethoven), 191,
192, 193, 194–195, 196, 202, 277, 302,
352
Chorley, Henry Fothergill (1808–1872),
246, 279, 383, 450–451, 454
Chrysander, Friedrich (1826–1901), 84
Cibber, Susanna Maria (1714–1766), 78
Cimarosa, Domenico (1749–1801), 229
Cinti-Damoreau, Laure (1801–1863),
334
Clement VIII (Ippolito Aldobrandini),
Pope (1535–1605), 17
Clement XIV (Lorenzo Ganganelli),
Pope (1705–1774), 130
Clement, Franz (1780–1842), 187
Clementi, Muzio (1752–1832), 139, 549
Gradus ad Parnassum, 549
Clésinger, Solange (Dudevant) (1828–
1899), 334, 335
"Clock" Symphony (Haydn), 122
Cocteau, Jean (1891–   ), 599–600,
602, 609
Colbran, Isabella Angela, see Rossini,
Isabella (Colbran)
Colette, Sidonie-Gabrielle (1873–   ),
537
Colles, Henry Cope (1879–1943), 35
Collin, Heinrich Josef von (1771–1811),
192
Colloredo, Hieronymus Joseph Franz
von Paula, Graf von, Archbishop of
Salzburg (1732–1806), 131, 135, 137,
138–139
Cologne, Maximilian Franz, Elector
(1756–1801), 165, 166, 167
Cologne, Maximilian Friedrich, Elec-
tor of (?–1784), 163
Colonna family, 8

Columbia Broadcasting System, 572
Columbia Concert Orchestra (New
York), 572
Comédie humaine, La (Balzac), 240
Conried, Heinrich (1855–1909), 567
Constantine Pavlovich, Grand Duke
(1779–1831), 316
Consuelo (George Sand), 105
Cooper, James Fenimore (1789–1851),
266
Corelli, Arcangelo (1653–1713), 57, 75
Weinachtskonzert, 75
Coriolanus (Von Collin), 192
Cornelius, Peter (1824–1874), 355, 366,
383
Barbier von Bagdad, Der, 383, 384
"Coronation" Concerto (Mozart), 155
Corsaire overture (Berlioz), 360
Così fan tutte (Mozart), 154–155
Costa, Sir Michael (1808–1884), 84
Council of Trent, 7, 9–10, 12, 19
Couperin, François le grand (1668–
1733), 25, 65
Cowell, Henry Dixon (1897–   ), 598
Creation, The (Haydn), 119–120, 121,
122, 153, 244
Croche, M., pseudonym of Claude-
Achille Debussy, 542
Cross, Wilbur Lucius (1862–1948), 588
Crystal Palace (London), 237
Cui, César Antonovich (1835–1918),
506, 511
Cumberland, William Cumberland,
Duke of (1721–1765), 80
Cuzzoni, Francesca (1700–1770), 67, 68,
69, 72
Czerny, Karl (1791–1857), 159, 293, 317,
375

D

Dahl, Ingolf, 609
Dalcroze, see Jaques-Dalcroze, Émile
Dame aux camélias, La (Dumas fils),
381, 454, 455
Damnation de Faust, La (Berlioz),
360–361, 362, 365, 371, 383; see also
Huit Scènes de Faust
Damoiselle élue, La (Debussy), 535, 537
Damrosch, Walter Johannes
(1862–   ), 364, 525, 592
Daniélou, Jean, 604
Dannreuther, Edward George (1844–
1905), 325, 435
Dante Alighieri (1265–1321), 515
"Dante" Symphony (Liszt), 381, 393
Daumier, Honoré (1808–1879), 530
David, Ferdinand (1810–1873), 283,
285, 287, 290

Davidov, Lev Vasilevich (1837–1896),
512
Davidov, Vladimir Lvovich ("Bob")
(1871–1906), 526, 527
Davidova, Alexandra (Tchaikovskaya)
(1842–1891), 503, 508, 512, 516, 525
Davidsbund, 219, 297
Debussy, Claude-Achille (1862–1918),
190, 218, 308, 370, 393, 440, 467,
500, 520, 529–555, 580
ballets
    Boîte à joujoux, La (completed
    by Caplet), 550
    Jeux, 550
    Khamma (completed by Koechlin)
    550
cantatas and choral works
    Damoiselle élue, La, solo voices,
    chorus, and orchestra, 535, 537
    Enfant prodigue, L', soprano,
    tenor, and baritone, 532–533
    Printemps, female voices, 534
    Zuleïma, 534
chamber music
    Quartet ("First"), strings, G
    minor, 537–538
    Rapsodie pour saxophone et piano
    (orchestrated by Roger-Ducasse),
    545
sonatas
    cello and piano, 554
    flute, viola, and harp, 554
    violin and piano, 555
incidental music
    to *Le Martyre de Saint-Sébastien*,
    550–551
operas
    Pelléas et Mélisande, 150, 535, 537,
    539, 541, 542–543, 549, 550
    Rodrigue et Chimène (unfin-
    ished), 536
orchestra
    Berceuse héroïque, 553
    Danse sacrée et danse profane,
    harp and strings, 546
    Images, 551
        Gigues, 551
        Ibéria, 551–552
        Rondes de printemps, 551
    Mer, La, 545, 546, 547–548, 551,
    592
    Nocturnes, 541–542, 547
        Fêtes, 542
        Nuages, 541, 542, 580
        Sirènes, 542
    Prélude a l'Après-midi d'un faune,
    537, 538–539, 547, 550
piano solo, 546
    Children's Corner, 549

Debussy, Claude-Achille—*(Continued)*
piano solo—*(Continued)*
    Children's Corner—*(Continued)*
        Doctor Gradus ad Parnassum,
        549
        Golliwog's Cake-Walk, 549, 552
        Jimbo's Lullaby, 549
        Little Shepherd, The, 549
        Serenade for the Doll, 549
        Snow is Dancing, 549
    Clair de lune, 546
    Estampes, 546–547
        Jardins sous la pluie, 546
        Pagodes, 546
        Soirée dans Grenade, 546
    Etudes, 554
        Pour les huit doigts, 554
        Pour les notes répétées, 554
        Pour les tierces, 554
    Images, 547
        Book I, 547
            Hommage à Rameau, 547
            Mouvement, 547
            Reflets dans l'eau, 547
        Book II, 547
            Cloches à travers les feuilles,
            547
            *Et la lune descend sur le
            temple qui fût*, 547
            Poissons d'or, 547
    Pour le piano, 546
    Préludes, 551, 552–553
        Book I
            Cathédrale engloutie, La, 552
            Ce qu'a vue le vent d'Ouest,
            552
            Danse de Puck, Le, 552
            Fille aux cheveux de lin, La,
            552
            Minstrels, 552
        Book II, 553
            Brouillards, 552
            Bruyères, 552
            Feux d'artifice, 553
            General Lavine—Eccentric,
            552
            Hommage à S. Pickwick, Esq.,
            P.P.M.P.C., 552
            Ondine, 552–553
            Puerta del vino, La, 552
    Rêverie, 539, 546
piano duet
    Six Épigraphes antiques, 553–554
two pianos
    En blanc et noir, 554
songs, 533
    Ariettes oubliées, 540
        Green, 540
        Il pleure dans mon coeur, 540

Debussy, Claude-Achille—*(Continued)*
  songs—*(Continued)*
    Beau Soir, 533
    Chansons de Bilitis, 540, 553
      Chevelure, La, 540
      Flûte de Pan, La, 540
      Tombeau des Naïades, Le, 540
    Cinq Poèmes de Baudelaire, 540
    Fantoches, 533
    Mandoline, 533
    Trois Ballades de François Villon,
      540–541
      Ballade des femmes de Paris, 541
Debussy, Claude-Emma ("Chouchou")
  (1905–?), 545–546, 549, 552
Debussy, Emma (Bardac) (?–1934), 545,
  546, 548, 549
Debussy, Manuel-Achille (1836–?), 530,
  531
Debussy, Rosalie ("Lily-Lilo") (Tex-
  ier), 541, 544, 545
Debussy, Victorine (Manoury)
  (1836–?), 530, 531
Defoe, Daniel (1661?–1731), 64
Delacroix, Ferdinand-Victor-Eugene
  (1798–1863), 320, 336, 337, 342, 530
Delany, Patrick (1685?–1768), 78
Delibes, Léo (1836–1891), 511, 515, 607
  Lakme, 157
  "Bell Song," 157
Del Riego, Teresa, 589
  O, Dry Those Tears, 589
Dent, Edward Joseph (1876–   ), 190,
  221
Denza, Luigi (1846–1922) 558
  Funiculì, Funiculà, 558
Des Prés, Josquin, see Josquin Des
  Prés
Dessoff, Felix Otto (1835–1891), 492
Dettingen, battle of, 79
Deutsches Requiem, Ein (Brahms),
  478, 482–484
Deutschland über Alles, 119
Devil in the Belfry, The (Poe), 545,
  549
Devrient, Eduard (1801–1877), 273
Diabelli, Anton (1781–1858), 200, 259,
  375
Diaghilev, Serge Pavlovich (1872–
  1929), 596, 597, 599, 602, 610–611
Dichterliebe (Schumann), 303
Dickens, Charles (1812–1870), 336
Dido and Aeneas (Purcell), 59, 86
Dies irae, 345
Diet of Worms, 23
Dietsch, Pierre-Louis-Philippe (1808–
  1865), 428
Ditters von Dittersdorf, Karl (1739–
  1799), 111, 145

Doles, Johann Friedrich (1715–1797),
  154
Dolin, Anton (Patrick Healey Kay)
  (1905?–   ), 607
Don Carlos (Schiller), 451
Don Carlos (Verdi), 460–461
Don Giovanni (Mozart), 101, 149–151,
  152, 165, 263, 278, 317, 345, 400, 401
Don Juan (Richard Strauss), 558–559,
  562, 577
Don Quixote (Cervantes), 466, 563
Don Quixote (Richard Strauss), 563,
  570, 572
Donizetti, Gaetano (1797–1848), 226,
  359, 380, 414, 502, 534
  Favorita, La, 359
  Lucia di Lammermoor, 226, 362
Dorn, Heinrich (1804–1892), 201, 295,
  297, 301, 303, 401, 406
Dowson, Ernest Christopher (1867–
  1900), 342
"Drum Roll" Symphony (Haydn), 402
Dryden, John (1631–1700), 72, 73, 77,
  206
Du Barry, Marie-Jeanne Bécu, Com-
  tesse (1746–1793), 99
Duboeuf, Estelle, see Fornier, Estelle
  (Duboeuf)
Ducré, Pierre, composer invented by
  Berlioz, 364
Dukas, Paul (1865–1935), 596
  Apprenti sorcier, L', 596
Du Locle, Camille (1823–1903), 462
Dumas, *père*, Alexandre (1802–1870),
  320, 342, 349
Dumas, *fils*, Alexandre (1824–1895),
  381, 454
Dunciad, The (Pope), 61, 280
Dunstable, John (1370?–1453), 4–5, 59
Dunstan, Archbishop of Canterbury,
  St. (925?–988), 4
Duplessis, Marie (1824–1846), 381
Dupont, Gabrielle ("Gaby"), 535, 536,
  541
Duprez, Gilbert-Louis (1806–1896), 355
Durand, Émile (1830–1903), 531–532
Durand, Jacques (1865–1928), 553, 555
Dürbach, Fanny, 502
Dushkin, Samuel (1898–   ), 605, 606
Dvořák, Antonin (1841–1904), 509, 578
  Symphony No, 5, E minor ("From
  the New World"), 509

E

Eagle (Brooklyn), 567
Eastman School of Music (Rochester),
  591
Eddy, Mary Baker (1821–1910), 128
Eddy, Nelson (1901–   ), 565
"Edward" Ballade (Brahms), 474

Egmont, Lamoral, Count of (1522–1568), 192

Egmont (Goethe), 192

"1812," overture solennelle (Tchaikovsky), 194, 519, 581

Ein feste Burg ist unser Gott (Luther), 23, 274

Einstein, Alfred (1880–   ), 90, 92, 118, 134

Elektra (Richard Strauss), 99, 228, 557, 567, 568, 569, 570

Elgar, Sir Edward (1857–1934), 564

Elijah (Mendelssohn), 228–289, 290

Eliot, George (Mary Anne Evans) (1819–1880), 329

Ellis, Henry Havelock (1859–1939), 527

Elsner, Joseph (1769–1854), 316, 318

"Emperor" Concerto (Beethoven), 185, 186, 207

Enesco, Georges (1881–   ), 579

Enfance du Christ, L' (Berlioz), 364–365, 366–367, 369, 373

Enfant prodigue, L' (Debussy), 532–533

En Saga (Sibelius), 578, 579

Entführung aus dem Serail, Die (Mozart), 101, 129, 137, 139, 140, 154

Epicœne, or The Silent Woman (Jonson), 571

Erdmann, Georg (1681–?), 43

Erlkönig, Der (Schubert), 250, 251, 254, 259

Ernani (Verdi), 449–450, 451–452

Ernesti, Johann August (1707–1781), 48

"Eroica" Symphony (Beethoven), 179–181, 188, 194, 206, 236, 572

Essays in Musical Analysis (Tovey), 338

Esterházy, Prince Antal (Pal Antal) (?–1794), 111

Esterházy, Count János (1775–1834), 141, 256, 261

Esterházy, Countess Karolin (1805–1851), 261

Esterházy, Prince Miklós Jozsef (1714–1790), 107–108, 109, 110–111, 113, 141

Esterházy, Prince Miklós II (1765–1833), 102, 118, 122

Esterházy Prince Pál Antal (?–1762), 106, 107

Esterházy family, 168, 375

Euclid (fl 300 B.C.), 153

Eugénie, Empress of the French (1826–1920), 461

Eugen Oniegin (Pushkin), 513

Eugen Oniegin (Tchaikovsky), 513, 515, 516, 518–519, 524

Euryanthe (Weber), 220–221, 222, 224, 225, 236, 258

Evans, Edwin, Jr. (1874–1945), 480

Exposition of 1851 (London), 237, 365

Exposition Universelle of 1855 (Paris), 363, 368, 456

Exposition Universelle of 1878 (Paris), 516

Exposition Universelle of 1889–90 (Paris), 535

Exposition Universelle of 1900 (Paris), 542

F

Fact and Fiction about Wagner (Newman), 397

Fall of the House of Usher, The (Poe), 549

Fall Wagner, Der (Nietzsche), 436

Falla, Manuel de (1876–1946), 20, 552, 593

Falstaff (Verdi), 370, 466–467, 570

Fantasiestücke (Schumann), 301, 302, 303, 500

"Farewell" Symphony (Haydn), 109–110, 117

Farinelli (Carlo Broschi) (1705–1782), 72, 87, 88

Fauré, Gabriel-Urbain (1845–1924), 545

Faust (Goethe), 343, 495

Faust (Gounod), 36, 391, 507, 530

"Faust" Symphony (Liszt), 381, 385, 393

Faustina, see Hasse, Faustina (Bordoni)

Fausts Höllenfahrt, 212

Feen, Die (Wagner), 401, 402, 403, 425

Ferdinand I, Emperor of Austria (1793–1875), 300, 360

Ferdinand I (IV of Naples), King of the Two Sicilies (1751–1825), 235

Ferrand, Humbert (?–1868), 349

Ferrara, Alfonso II d'Este, Duke of (1533–1597), 15

Festin de pierre, Le (Molière), 91

Fétis, François-Joseph (1784–1871), 320, 324, 347

Fidelio (Beethoven), 182–185, 196, 221, 241, 383, 400

Field, John (1782–1837), 322, 327–328

Fieschi, Giuseppe Maria (1790–1836), 353, 354

Finck, Henry Theophilus (1854–1926), 560, 568

Fingal's Cave (Mendelssohn), 274, 275, 276, 284, 291, 470

Finlandia (Sibelius), 581, 588

Firmian, Carl, Count, Governor-General of Lombardy (1716–1774), 129, 130, 131

"Fischer, Der" (Goethe), 350

Five, the, 506, 594

Flaubert, Gustave (1821–1880), 314, 329, 530

Fledermaus, Die (Johann Strauss), 559

Flegeljahre (Jean Paul Richter), 295

Fliegende Holländer, Der (Wagner), 408, 409–411, 414

Flodin, Karl (1858–1925), 576

Fokine, Mikhail (1880–1942), 550, 596

"Forellen" Quintet (Schubert), 257

Fornier, Estelle (Duboeuf) (1797–?), 342, 371

Forza del destino, La (Verdi), 459–460, 461

Foundling Hospital (London), 81–82

Francesca da Rimini (Tchaikovsky), 515

Francis II, Emperor of Austria (1768–1835), 119, 121

Franck, César-Auguste (1822–1890), 345, 509, 535, 538
Symphony, D minor, 509

Franck, Salomo (1659–1725), 31

Francs-Juges, Les (Berlioz), 342, 343, 349, 359
overture, 343, 349

Franz, Robert (1815–1892), 251, 297

Franz Josef, Emperor of Austria (1830–1916), 387, 498–499

Frederick, King of Sweden (1676–1751), 31–32

Frederick II ("the Great"), King of Prussia (1712–1786), 50, 97, 126, 154

Frege, Livia (Gerhard) (1818–1891), 290

Freischütz, Der (Weber), 212, 216–217, 218–220, 221, 223, 258, 269, 399, 411

French Revolution, 154, 180, 268

Frescobaldi, Girolamo (1583–1643), 30

Freud, Sigmund (1856–1939), 475, 496, 502

Fricken, Baron von, 296, 298

Fricken, Ernestine von (1816–?), 296, 297, 298

Friedheim, Arthur (1869–1932), 388

Friedrich I, King of Württemberg 1754–1816), 211–212

Friedrich Augustus I, King of Saxony (1750–1827), 215, 216, 217

Friedrich Augustus II, King of Saxony (1797–1854), 285, 408, 409, 414

Friedrich Wilhelm II, King of Prussia (1744–1797), 146, 154

Friedrich Wilhelm III, King of Prussia (1770–1840), 203, 214

Friedrich Wilhelm IV, King of Prussia (1795–1861), 283, 285, 286, 302, 416

Fuchs, Robert (1847–1927), 577

Funiculì, Funiculà (Denza), 558

Fürnberg, Karl Josef, Baron von, 105, 106

Furtwängler, Wilhelm (1886–   ), 39

G

Gade, Niels Wilhelm (1817–1890), 289, 305, 311

Galitzin, Prince Nikolai Borissovich (1794–1866), 201

Galuppi, Baldassare (1706–1785), 75
Toccata, 75

Gand-Leblanc, Marie-François-Louis, Bailli du Rollet (1716–1786), 95–96

Gänsbacher, Johann (1788–1844), 210, 212

García, Manuel del Popolo Vicente (1775–1832), 231

Garden, Mary (1877–   ), 543, 544, 567

Garibaldi, Giuseppe (1807–1882), 459

Gates, Bernard (1685–1773), 70

Gatti-Casazza, Giulio (1869–1940), 549, 551

Gauthier-Villars, Henri ("Willy") (1859–1931), 537

Gautier, Théophile (1811–1872), 320, 353

Gay, John (1688–1732), 61, 65, 69

Gazette musicale (Paris), 363, 364

Gazza ladra, La (Rossini), 234

Geddes, Norman Bel (1893–   ), 607

Geneviève, St. (422?–512), 306–307

Genossenschaft Deutscher Tonsetzer, 565

Genoveva (Schumann), 306–307, 383

Georg, Elector of Hanover, see George I, King of England

George I, King of England (1660–1727), 57, 61–62, 63, 67, 69

George II, King of England (1683–1760), 69, 70, 72, 73, 78, 79, 80

George III, King of England (1738–1820), 83, 102, 116, 127

George IV, King of England (1762–1830), 114, 116, 193, 238, 375

Gerusalemme liberata (Tasso), 60, 98, 343

Geschichte der Kunst des Alterthums (Winckelmann), 90

Gesellschaft der Musikfreunde (Vienna), 260, 264

Gesner, Johann Matthias (1691–1761), 44, 48

Gewandhaus (Leipzig), 39, 279, 282, 284, 285, 286, 287, 288, 289, 290, 298, 303, 307, 366, 399, 429, 477, 483

Geyer, Cäcilie, see Avenarius, Cäcilie (Geyer)

Geyer, Johanna, see Wagner, Johanna (Pätz)

Geyer, Ludwig (1779–1821), 397, 398, 399

Gibbon, Edward (1737–1794), 51

Gibbons, Orlando (1583–1625), 59

Gibson, Edmund, Bishop of London (1669–1748), 71

Gide, André (1869–   ), 606

Gieseking, Walter (1895–   ), 181, 554

Gilbert, William Schwenk (1836–1911), 31, 465

Girl of the Golden West, The (Puccini), 227

Glinka, Mikhail Ivanovich (1803–1857), 506, 602

Gluck, Christoph Willibald, Ritter von (1714–1787), 68, 76, 85–101, 124, 129, 136, 137, 138, 141, 167, 340, 365, 369, 383, 414, 422, 450, 526
  Alceste, 93–94, 98, 105, 138
    "*Divinités du Styx,*" 94
    Overture, 94
  Antigone, 90
  Armide, 98–99
  Artaserse, 88
  Don Juan, 90–91
  Echo et Narcisse, 100
  Ipermestra, 88
  Iphigénie en Aulide, 96–98, 414
    overture, 97
  Iphigénie en Tauride, 99–100, 101, 185, 340
  Orfeo ed Euridice, 91–93, 94, 97–98
    "*Che farò senza Euridice,*" 92
    chorus of Furies, 92
    "Dance of the Blessed Spirits," 92
  Orphée et Eurydice, 98
  Paride ed Elena, 94–95
    "*O del mio dolce ardor,*" 95
  Roland, 99

Gluck, Marianne (Pergin), 89–90, 96, 100, 101

Gluck, Marianne (1759–1776), 96, 101

God Save the King, 119, 194

Goebbels, Paul Josef (1897–1944), 571

Goethe, Johann Wolfang von (1749–1832), 28, 93, 127, 151, 178, 191–193, 213, 249, 250, 251, 252, 270, 274, 275, 343, 350, 361, 362, 366, 382, 399, 485, 519

Goldberg, Johann Gottlieb Theophilus (1720–1760), 49

Goldman Band (New York), 358

Goldmark, Karl (1830–1915), 493, 577

Golovin, M., 596

Goncourt, Edmond–Louis de (1822–1896), 530

Goncourt, Jules-Alfred de (1833–1870), 530

Gonzaga, Ferdinand, Viceroy of Sicily (1507–1557), 14

Gossec, François-Joseph (1734–1829), 98

Gotha-Altenburg, Augustus, Duke of (1772–1822), 215

Gott erhalte Franz den Kaiser (Haydn), 119, 122

Götterdämmerung, Die (Wagner), 420, 425, 435, 440, 443, 512; see also *Ring des Nibelungen, Der*

Gottschalk, Louis Moreau (1829–1869), 324

Gounod, Charles (1818–1893), 36, 361, 385, 391, 507, 522, 530, 532
  Ave Maria, 36
  Faust, 36, 391, 507, 530

Gradus ad Parnassum (Clementi), 549

Gramophone Shop Encyclopedia of Recorded Music, The (Darrell), 250

Granvelle, Antoine Perrenot, Cardinal de (1517–1586), 15

Graupner, Christoph (1683–1760), 38

Gray, Cecil (1895–), 370, 391, 562, 570–571, 578, 582, 591

Greco, El (Domenico Theotocopuli) (1548?–1625), 18

Gregory I, Pope, St. (540?–604), 4

Gregory XIII (Ugo Buoncompagni), Pope (1502–1585), 13

Gregory XVI (Bartolommeo Alberto Cappellari), Pope (1765–1846), 449

Grétry, André-Ernest-Modeste (1741–1813), 243
  Richard Coeur-de-lion, 243
    "O Richard! O mon roy!" 243

Grieg, Edvard Hagerup (1843–1907), 142, 522, 527

Grillparzer, Franz (1791–1872), 266

Grimani, Cardinal Vincenzo, 58

Grimm, Friedrich Melchior, Baron von (1723–1807), 127

Grisi, Giulia (1811–1869), 244

Grob, Therese (1798–1875), 261–262

Grotesques de la musique, Les (Berlioz), 360

Grove, Sir George (1820–1900), 203, 259, 262, 522

Guernica (Picasso), 609

Guicciardi, Contessa Giulietta, 175, 177

Guillard, Nicolas-François (1752–1814), 99

Guiraud, Ernest (1837–1892), 532, 533

Gutenberg, Johannes (1397?–1468), 5

H

Hass, Alma (1847–?), 141

Habeneck, François-Antoine (1781–1849), 347, 407

Hadow, Sir William Henry (1859–1927), 204, 244, 333, 494

Haffner, Marie Elizabeth, 135

Haffner, Sigmund, Burgomaster of Salzburg (1699–1772), 135, 144

"Haffner" Symphony (Mozart), 144, 149

Halévy (Levy), Jacques-Fromental-Élie (1799–1862), 355

Halíř, Karl (1859–1909), 583

Hall, Elisa, 545

Hamilton, Emma, Lady (1765?–1815), 130

Hamilton, Sir William (1730–1803), 130

Hamlet (Shakespeare), 273, 342, 399, 451, 495

"*Hammerklavier*" Sonata (Beethoven), 198–200

Hammerstein, Oscar (1847–1919), 549, 567, 569

Händel, Dorothea (Taust) (1652?–1730), 53, 63, 70

Händel, Georg (1622–1697), 53–54

Handel, George Frideric (1685–1759), 21, 22, 24, 37, 41, 51, 53–84, 86–87, 88–89, 98, 102, 105, 114, 116, 119, 124, 127, 142, 153, 157, 205, 264, 277, 279, 281, 283, 289, 291, 316, 382, 396, 478, 486, 510, 570, 601, 604

  Acis and Galatea, 65
  "O ruddier than the cherry," 65
  Agrippina, 58
  Alcina, 72
  Alessandro, 68–69
  Alexander Balus, 80
  Alexander's Feast, 72–73
  Allegro, il Penseroso, ed il Moderato, L', 77
  Almira, 56
  Aria con variazioni, B flat major, 478
  Athalia, 71
  Birthday Ode, 61
  Chaconne, G major, 65
  "Chandos" Anthems, 64–65
  Concerti grossi, 76
  Deborah, 71
  Dettingen Te Deum, 79
  Esther, 71
  Firework Music, 81, 84
  Funeral Anthem, 73
  Giulio Cesare, 68
  Haman and Mordecai, 66, 70–71
  "Harmonious Blacksmith, The," 65, 75
  Hercules, 80–81
  Israel in Egypt, 76–77, 277
  "The people shall hear," 77
  Jephtha, 80, 82
  "How dark, O Lord," 82
  "Waft her, angels," 80
  Joshua, 80, 119
  "Oh, had I Jubal's lyre," 80
  Judas Maccabaeus, 80, 81
  "Glory to God," 80
  "Largo," see *Serse*
  Messiah, 53, 76, 77–79, 81–82, 83, 84, 119, 120, 153, 288
  "Hallelujah" Chorus, 55, 78
  "He shall feed his flock," 78
  "I know that my Redeemer liveth," 78
  "The people that walked in darkness," 142
  "Worthy is the Lamb," 78
  Nero, 56

Handel, George Frideric—(*Continued*)
  Occasional Oratorio, 80
  Ode for St. Cecilia's Day, 77, 316–317
  Ottone, 67
  Passion, 63–64
  Pièces pour le clavecin, 65
  Poro, 70
  Radamisto, 66–67
  Resurrezione, La, 57
  Riccardo Primo, 57
  Rinaldo, 60–61, 98
  "*Cara sposa*," 60
  "*Lascia ch'io pianga*," 60
  Rodrigo, 56, 57
  Samson, 79
  Saul, 76, 77
  Dead March, 76
  Semele, 79
  "Where'er you walk," 79
  Serse, 74–75
  "Largo" ("*Ombra, mai fu*"), 55, 74–75, 302
  Susanna, 80
  "Ask if yon damask rose be fair," 80
  Tamerlano, 68
  Teseo, 61, 66
  Theodora, 80
  Trionfo del tempo e del disinganno, Il, 57
  Triumph of Time and Design, The, 57
  Utrecht Te Deum, 61
  Water Music, 62–63, 75, 81

Handel Commemoration (1784), 83

Handel Gesellschaft, 84

Handel Society (London), 84

Hanover, Prince Ernst Augustus of (Duke of York) (1674–1728), 57, 58

Hänsel und Gretel (Humperdinck), 559

Hanslick, Eduard (1825–1904), 433, 493, 495, 520, 521, 559, 562

Hark, Hark, the Lark! (Schubert), 249, 251, 263

"Harmonious Blacksmith, The" (Handel), 65, 75

Harold en Italie (Berlioz), 346, 350, 351–352, 356, 383

Hartmann, Georges (?–1900), 541,

Harzreise im Winter (Goethe), 485

Haschka, Lorenz Leopold (1749–1827), 119

Hasse, Faustina (Bordoni) (1693–1783), 44, 68–69, 72, 87

Hasse, Johann Adolf (1699–1783), 41–45, 72, 87, 88, 112, 125, 132

  Artaserse, 72, 76, 88, 131

Hastings, Warren (1732–1818), 116

Hausmann, Robert (1852–1909), 498

Haussmann, Baron Georges-Eugène (1808–1891), 427

Haydn, Franz Josef (1732–1809), 88, 101, 102–123, 124, 128, 140, 141, 142, 143, 144, 145–146, 152, 153, 155, 159, 162, 167–168, 169, 170, 171, 180, 181, 188, 191, 196, 207, 212, 217, 227, 229, 244, 252, 253, 293, 317, 327, 382, 396, 402, 446, 487, 542, 575, 594
   "Chasse, La" Symphony, 117
   "Clock" Symphony, see "Salamon" No. 11
   Creation, The, 119–120, 121, 122, 153, 244
     "The Heavens are telling," 120
     "With verdure clad," 120
   "Drum Roll" Symphony, 402
   "Farewell" Symphony, 109–110, 117
   Fedeltà premiata, La, 112
   Gott erhalte Franz den Kaiser, 119, 122
   Isola disabitata, L', 112
   "Oxford" Symphony, 105, 114, 117
   piano sonatas, 122
   "Russian" Quartets, 111
   "Salamon" Symphonies, 117–118
     2nd, 114
     5th, 117
     11th ("Clock"), 122
   Seasons, The, 120–121
   string quartets, 122–123
   "Toy" Symphony, 122
Haydn, Maria Anna (Keller) (1729–1800), 106, 110, 121
Haydn, Michael (1737–1806), 128, 130, 209
"Haydn" Quartets (Mozart), 145, 146
Haym, Nicolo (1679–1729), 61, 66
"Hebrides" Overture (Mendelssohn), 274, 275, 276, 284, 291, 470
Hegel, Georg Wilhelm Friedrich (1770–1831), 272
Heidegger, John James (1659–1749), 66, 70, 71, 72, 74
Heifetz, Jascha (1901–), 132, 583
"Heiligenstadt Testament" (Beethoven), 170–174, 176
Heine, Heinrich (1797–1856), 23, 219, 244, 272, 301, 302, 320, 321, 329, 517, 534
Heldburg, Helen Franz, Baroness von (morganatic wife of Grand Duke Georg of Saxe-Meiningen), 497
Heldenleben, Ein (Richard Strauss), 563–564, 565
Helsingfors Philharmonic Orchestra, 577, 581
Hempel, Frieda (1885–), 220
Henri III, King of France (1551–1589), 16
Henrici, Christian Friedrich (Picander) (1700–1764), 42

Herbeck, Johann Franz von (1831–1877), 260
Herbert, Victor (1859–1924), 526
Heritage of Music, The (H. J. Foss, editor), 160
Herman, Woody, 607
Hernani (Hugo), 320, 449
"Heroic" Polonaise (Chopin), 323
Hérold, Louis-Joseph-Ferdinand (1791–1833), 320
   Zampa, 320
Herrmann, Bernard (1911–), 75–76
Herz, Henri (Heinrich) (1806–1888), 296, 311
Herzogenberg, Elisabeth (Von Stockhausen) von (1847–1892), 484–485, 495, 499
Herzogenberg, Baron Heinrich von (1843–1900), 484
Hesse-Cassel, Karl, Landgrave of (1670–1730), 31
Hill, Aaron (1685–1750), 60
Hiller, Ferdinand (1811–1885), 280, 282, 286, 306, 308, 311, 317, 326, 346, 347, 383
Hitler, Adolf (1889–1945), 208, 571
Hoffman, Ernst Theodor Amadeus (1776–1822), 213, 219, 399
Hofmannsthal, Hugo von (1874–1929), 568, 569, 570, 571
Hogarth, William (1697–1764), 74, 82, 610
Hohenlohe, Gustav Adolf, Cardinal (1823–1896), 386, 534
Hohenlohe-Schillingfürst, Prince Konstantin von (1828–1896), 385
Hohenlohe-Schillingfürst, Princess Marie (Sayn-Wittgenstein) von (1837–1920), 385, 386
Hohenzollern, house of, 36
Holy Alliance, 236
Holz, Karl (1798–1858), 205
Home, Sweet Home (Sir Henry Bishop), 232
Homer (circa ninth century B.C.), 480, 576
Homme armé, L', 12
Horace (Quintus Horatius Flaccus) (65–8 B.C.), 451, 576
Horst Wessel Song, 119
Hugo, Victor (1802–1885), 282, 320, 342, 349, 353, 449, 451–452, 529–530
Huguenots, Les (Meyerbeer), 245, 409
Huit Scènes de Faust (Berlioz), 343, 360; see also Damnation de Faust, La (Berlioz)
Humbert I, King of Italy (1844–1900), 468
Humboldt, Baron Alexander von (1769–1859), 272, 316
Hummel, Johann Nepomuk (1778–1837), 293, 294, 317

Humperdinck, Engelbert (1854–1921), 442, 559

Hänsel und Gretel, 442, 559

Huneker, James Gibbons (1860–1921), 301, 322, 324, 328, 444, 516–517, 563, 564

Hungarian Rhapsodies (Liszt), 391-392

Hünten, Franz (1793–1878), 296, 311

Hunter, John (1728–1793), 115

Hüttenbrenner, Anselm (1794–1868), 255, 256, 260, 264

Hüttenbrenner, Josef (1796–1882), 256

Huysmans, Joris Karl (1848–1907), 543

I

Ibéria (Debussy), 551–552

I'm Always Chasing Rainbows (Carroll), 325

'Immortal Beloved," letter to the (Beethoven), 176–178, 344

Incoronazione di Poppaea, L' (Monteverdi), 85–86

Indy, Vincent d' (1851–1931), 178, 544, 564

Inferno (Dante), 515

Ingres, Jean-Auguste-Dominique (1780–1867), 320

Innocent VIII (Giovanni Battista Cibò) Pope (1432–1492), 5

Invitation to Music (CBS), 572

Invitation to the Dance (Weber), 208, 212, 217

Interior Causes of the Exterior Weakness of the Church, The (Sayn-Wittgenstein), 386

Iphigénie en Aulide (Gluck), 96–98, 414

Iphigénie en Tauride (Gluck), 99–100, 101, 185, 340

Isabella II, Queen of Spain (1830–1904), 380

Ismail Pasha, Khedive of Egypt (1830–1895), 462

Israel in Egypt (Handel), 76–77, 277

Italiana in Algeri, L' (Rossini), 229

"Italian" Symphony (Mendelssohn), 276-277, 284, 291

J

Jackson, Andrew (1767–1845), 321

James II, King of England (1633–1701), 61

Janina, Countess Olga, 387–388

Jaques-Dalcroze, Émile (1865–), 538

Järnefelt, Aïno, see Sibelius, Aïno (Järnefelt)

Järnefelt, Armas (1869–), 579

Järnefelt, Arvid (1861–), 581

Järnefelt, Eero Nikolai (1863–1937), 577, 585–586

Järnefelt, General, 577

Jeanrenaud, Cécile-Charlotte-Shopie, see Mendelssohn-Bartholdy, Cécile (Jeanrenaud)

Jeanrenaud, M., 281

Jeanrenaud, Mme, 281

Jennens, Charles (1700–1773), 77

Jephtha (Handel), 80, 82

Joachim, Joseph (1831–1907), 187, 282, 289, 310, 311, 364, 366, 388, 470, 472, 473, 478, 480, 484, 493, 494, 498

Joachim Quartet, 480, 498, 583

Jockey Club (Paris), 321, 428

John the Divine, St., 10

Johnson, Samuel (1709–1784), 83

Jommelli, Niccolò (1714–1774), 76

Jonson, Ben (1572?–1637), 63, 571

Josef II, Holy Roman Emperor (1741–1790), 93, 128, 139, 140, 141, 147, 148, 151, 154, 155

Joseffy, Rafael (1852–1915), 388

Joshua (Handel), 80, 119

Josquin Des Prés (1444?–1521), 5–7, 20, 395, 601

Masses, 1st book of, 6

Journal des débats (Paris), 353, 360, 363, 373

Judas Maccabaeus (?–160 B.C.), 80

Judas Maccabaeus (Handel), 80, 81

Julius III (Giovanni Maria del Monte) Pope (1487–1555), 8

Jullien, Louis-Antoine (1812–1860), 362

Jungfrau von Orleans, Die (Schiller), 519

"Jupiter" Symphony (Mozart), 153, 586

Juvenal (Decimus Junius Juvenalis) (60?–140), 129

K

Kajanus, Robert (1856–1933), 577, 579, 581

Kalevala, 577, 584, 588

Kalkbrenner, Friedrich (1788–1849), 123, 320

Karsavina, Thamar Pavlovna (1885–), 596, 597

Kayserling, Baron Karl von, 49

Kean (Dumas *père*), 451

Keats, John (1795–1821), 266, 540

Keiser, Reinhard (1674–1739), 54–55, 56

Kemble, Charles (1775–1854), 221–222, 273, 342

Kent, Victoria, Duchess of (1786–1861), 224

Kerensky, Alexander Feodorovich (1881–), 590

Kind, Johann Friedrich (1768–1843), 216

Kinderscenen (Schumann), 302, 308, 549

King Lear (Shakespeare), 451, 455, 465
"King of Prussia" Quartets (Mozart), 146
Kinsky, Prince Ferdinand Johann Nepomuk (?–1812), 190, 197, 255
Kiss Me Again (Herbert), 7
Kleine Nachtmusik, Eine (Mozart), 149
Klopstock, Gottlob Friedrich (1724–1803), 96
Knobel, Theo, 285
Köchel, Ludwig von (1800–1877), 134
Koczwara, Franz (?–1791), 194
   Battle of Prague, The, 194
Kodály, Zoltán (1882–   ), 561
Koechlin, Charles (1867–   ), 550
Körner, Karl Theodor (1791–1813), 215
Koussevitzky, Nathalie (Ushkov), 609
Koussevitzky, Serge Alexandrovich (1874–   ), 110, 592, 605
Krehbiel, Henry Edward (1854–1923), 588
Kreisler, Fritz (1875–   ), 494
Kreisleriana (Schumann), 301, 302, 500
Kreutzer, Léon, 364
"Kreutzer" Sonata (Beethoven), 206
Kuhnau, Johann (1660–1722), 38
Kuznetsov, N. D., 526

L

Lablache, Luigi (1794–1858), 320, 337
Lac des cygnes, Le (Tchaikovsky), 515, 520
Lachner, Franz (1803–1890), 431
Lady of the Lake, The (Scott), 262
La Harpe, Jean-François de (1739–1803), 99
Lalla Rookh (Moore), 304–305
Lalo, Victor-Antoine-Édouard (1823–1892), 546
Lamartine, Alphonse-Marie-Louis de (1790–1869), 393, 529
Lambert, Constant (1905–   ), 488
Lang, Margarethe, 212, 213, 214
Lange, Aloysia (Weber) (1760–1839), 136, 137, 139, 141
Lange, Josef (1751–1831), 139
Larrivée, Henri (1737–1802), 96-97
Lasso, Orlando di (1530?–1594), 9, 12, 14–18, 20, 25, 119, 278, 395, 534
   Gustate et videte, 17
   Lagrime di San Pietro, 17
   madrigals, 5th book of, 17
   motets, 1st book of, 15
   seven penitential psalms, 18
Last Judgment, The (Michelangelo), 45
Laussot, Eugène, 418
Laussot, Jessie (Taylor) (?–1905), 418
Lavigna, Vincenzo (1777–1837), 446

Lavignac, Alexandre-Jean-Albert (1846–1916), 531
Lawrence, Thomas Edward (1888–1935), 396
Leblanc, Georgette (1875–1941), 543
Lee, Vernon (Violet Paget) (1856–1935), 100
Legouvé, Gabriel-Ernest (1807–1903), 353, 380
Legros, Joseph (1730–1793), 96, 97
Lehmann, Liza (1862–1918), 75
Leipzig, battle of, 193
Lélio (Berlioz), 343, 347, 348, 350–351, 369, 372
Lenau, Nikolaus (1802–1850), 559
Leo, Leonardo (1694–1744), 278
Leonardo da Vinci (1452–1519), 8, 14, 159, 168
Leoncavallo, Ruggiero (1858–1919), 534, 566
"Leonora" Overtures (Beethoven)
   1st, 183–184
   2nd, 184
   3rd, 183, 184, 185
Leopold II, Holy Roman Emperor (1747–1792), 155, 156
Lepanto, battle of, 10
"*Les Adieux*" Sonata (Beethoven), 190, 191
Lesueur, Jean-François (1760–1837), 189, 340, 341
Levi, Hermann (1839–1900), 402, 442, 443, 556, 561
Lewes, George Henry (1817–1878), 329
Leyer und Schwert (Körner), 215
Lichnowsky, Prince Karl (1756–1814), 153, 168, 169, 175, 186, 191, 197, 206
Liebesverbot, Das (Wagner), 404–405, 407, 425
Lind, Jenny (Mme Otto Goldschmidt) (1820–1887), 287, 289, 290, 450
Linley, Thomas (1756–1778), 129
"Linz" Symphony (Mozart), 143, 144, 149
Lippe, Prince Leopold of (1821–1875), 476
Lippe, Princess Friederike of (1825–?), 476
Liszt, Adam (?–1827), 375, 376
Liszt, Anna (Lager) (?–1866), 375, 376, 377
Liszt, Daniel (1839–1859), 378, 381, 385
Liszt, Blandine, see Ollivier, Blandine (Liszt)
Liszt, Cosima, see Wagner, Cosima (Liszt von Bülow)
Liszt, Franz (Ferenc) (1811–1886), 28, 169, 185, 200, 225, 244, 245, 266, 275, 282, 290, 297, 300, 304, 305,

Liszt, Franz (Ferenc)—(Continued)
310, 320, 322, 323, 324, 325, 326,
329, 330, 333, 338, 345, 347, 349,
351, 353, 355, 356, 360, 361, 365,
366, 367, 371, 374-394, 414, 417,
418-419, 420, 425, 431, 435-436,
437, 438, 443-444, 472, 473, 478,
486, 487, 511, 534, 556, 559, 564,
565, 573
chorus, soloists, and orchestra
Christus, 392
Masses, 392
"Coronation," 387
Psalm XIII, 392
St. Elisabeth, 389, 392
opera
Don Sanche, 375
orchestra
symphonic poems
Mazeppa, 393
Orpheus, 393
Préludes, Les, 393
Tasso, lamento e trionfo, 391,
393
symphonies
"Dante," 381, 393
"Faust," 381, 385, 393
organ
Ad nos ad salutarem undam
(Meyerbeer), 391
piano
Années de pèlerinage, 377, 391
Au bord d'une source, 392
Au lac de Wallenstadt, 392
Tre Sonetti di Petrarca, 392
Auf Flügeln des Gesanges (Men-
delssohn), 278
Don Juan Fantaisie (Mozart), 391
Études transcendantes, 380
Fantasia on Niobe (Pacini), 378
Grand Galop chromatique, 380
Harmonies poétiques et religieuses
Bénédiction de Dieu dan. la
solitude, 393
Hungarian Rhapsodies, 391
2nd, 391-392
Deux legendes, 393
Saint-François d'Assise predicant
aux oiseaux, 393
Saint-François de Paule mar-
chant sur les flots, 393
Liebestraum, A flat major, 392
Rigoletto Paraphrase (Verdi), 391
Soirees de Vienne (Schubert), 391
Sonata in B minor, 391, 392
Waltz from Gounod's Faust, 391
piano and orchestra
concertos, 392
Little Orchestra Society (New York),
572

"Little Russian" Symphony (Tchai-
kovsky), 508-509, 511
Lobkowitz, Prince Ferdinand Philipp,
88
Lobkowitz, Prince Josef Franz (1772-
1816), 168, 190, 197, 198, 255
Lockspeiser, Edward (1905-   ), 551-552
Loeffler, Charles Martin (1861-1935),
564
Lohengrin (Wagner), 286, 413, 416, 418-
419, 420, 425, 429, 430, 512, 579
Lohenstein, Daniel Casper von (1635-
1683), 48
London Music in 1888-89 as Heard by
Corno di Bassetto (Shaw), 142
Loon, Hendrik Willem van (1882-
1944), 194
Louis XI, King of France (1423-1483),
5, 6
Louis XII, King of France (1462-1515),
6, 396
Louis XIII, King of France (1601-
1643), 455
Louis XIV, King of France (1638-
1715), 86
Louis XV, King of France (1710-1774),
32, 108, 127
Louis XVI, King of France (1754-1793),
95
Louis XVIII, King of France (1755-
1824), 339
Louis-Philippe, King of France (1773-
1850), 243, 318, 335, 339, 353, 362, 376,
380
Louÿs, Pierre (1870-1925), 539, 540
Loyola, Ignatius, St. (1491-1556), 19
Lucrezia Floriani (George Sand), 334
Ludwig I, King of Bavaria (1786-1868),
275, 432
Ludwig II, King of Bavaria (1845-1886),
429-431, 432, 435, 436, 437, 438, 441
Lully, Jean-Baptiste (1632-1687), 86,
98
Luther, Martin (1483-1546), 7, 23, 46,
275
Ein feste Burg ist unser Gott, 23, 274
Lüttichau, Wolf Adolf August Baron
von (1786-1863), 415

M

McCormack, John (1884-1945), 79
Macbeth (Shakespeare), 495
Macbeth (Verdi), 450, 461
Maeterlinck, Maurice (1862-1949), 537,
543, 544, 583
Maffei, Contessa Clara (?-1886), 451,
464, 466
Mahler, Gustav (1860-1911), 184
Mahmúd II, Sultan of Turkey (1785-
1839), 237
Malbrouck s'en va-t-en guerre, 194

Malibran, Maria Felicità (García) (1808–1936), 273, 320
Mallarmé, Stéphane (1842–1898), 535, 538
Mälzel, Johann Nepomuk (1772–1838), 192, 193–194, 196
Manchester, Charles Montagu, Duke of (1656–1722), 57
Manfred (Byron), 307
Manfred (Schumann), 306, 307, 312
Manzoni, Alessandro (1785–1873), 461, 463
"Manzoni" Requiem (Verdi), 463–464
Marcellus I, Pope, St. (?–309), 10
Marcellus II (Marcello Cervino), Pope (1501–1555), 8
Marchand, Louis (1669–1732), 32
Marche slave (Tchaikovsky), 514
Margaret, Archduchess of Austria, 19
Margherita, Queen of Italy (1851–1926), 468
Maria, Holy Roman Empress (?–1603), 19
Maria Feodorovna, Tsarina of Russia (Sophia Dorothea of Württemberg) (1747–1828), 101, 111
Mariage de Figaro, Le (Beaumarchais), 147
Maria Theresa, Empress of Austria (1717–1780), 93, 98, 103, 110, 126, 127, 128, 130, 131, 138, 157, 165
Marie Amélie, Queen of France (1782–1866), 335
Marie Antoinette, Queen of France (1755–1793), 93, 96, 98, 136
Mario, Cavaliere di Candia (Giovanni Matteo) (1810–1883), 244
Markova, Alicia (1911?–), 607
Marlborough, John Churchill, Duke of (1650–1722), 67
Marks, G. W. pseudonym of Johannes Brahms, 471
Marmontel, Antoine-François (1816–1898), 531, 532
Marschner, Heinrich August (1795–1861), 298, 400, 402, 403
Marseillaise, La (Rouget de Lisle), 23, 519
Martha (Flotow), 414
Martin, Marie-Geneviève, see Berlioz, Marie (Recio)
Martin, Sotera Vilas, 360
Martini, Giovanni Battista (1706–1784), 129
Martyre de Saint-Sebastien, Le (D'Annunzio), 550
Martyre de Saint-Sebastien, Le (Debussy), 550–551
Marxsen, Eduard (1806–1887), 471
Mascagni, Pietro (1863–1945), 184, 570
Massenet, Jules-Émile-Frédéric (1842–1912), 500, 519, 522, 532–533, 540, 546

Mattei, Stanislao (1750–1825), 227
Mattheson, Johann (1681–1764), 55–56
Cleopatra, 55
Mauté de Fleurville, Antoinette-Flore (Chariat) (?–1884), 531
Mavra (Stravinsky), 602
Maximilian II, Holy Roman Emperor (1527–1576), 15, 19
Mayrhofer, Johann (1787–1836), 255
Mazarin, Mariette, 568
Measure for Measure (Shakespeare), 404
Meck, Nadejda Filaretovna von (1831–1894), 512–513, 514, 515–516, 517, 520, 524–525, 528, 529, 532
Medea (Euripides), 495
Medici, house of, 15
Medici, Catherine de', Queen of France (1519–1589), 16
Medici, Ferdinand de', Grand Duke of Tuscany (1663–1713), 56
Medici, Giovan Gastone de' (1671–1737), 56
Méditations poétiques (Lamartine), 393
Mefistofele (Boïto), 465
Méhul, Étienne-Nicolas (1763–1817), 215
Joseph, 215
Mein Leben (Wagner), 398, 403, 433, 436
Meistersinger, Die (Wagner), 47, 370, 419, 426, 432–434
Melba, Nellie (Mitchell) (1861–1931), 237
Mémoires (Berlioz), 348, 360, 363, 366
Mendelssohn, Moses (1729–1786), 267–268
Mendelssohn - Bartholdy, Abraham (1776–1835), 268, 270, 277, 278, 280
Mendelssohn-Bartholdy, Cécile-Charlotte-Sophie (Jeanrenaud) (1819–1853), 267, 281, 284
Mendelssohn-Bartholdy, Fanny Cäcilie (1805–1847), 268, 289
Mendelssohn-Bartholdy, Felix (1809–1847), 22, 39, 120, 151, 185, 187, 207, 219, 241, 244, 263, 264, 267–291, 297, 298, 300, 301, 303, 304, 305, 306, 310, 312, 316, 320, 321, 326, 328, 343, 347, 359, 382, 416, 421, 423, 460, 483, 571
Antigone, incidental music, 283, 285
Athalie, incidental music, 284
"War March of the Priests," 284
Auf Flügeln des Gesanges, 278–279, 290
concertos, piano and orchestra
1st, G minor, 275
2nd, D minor, 281
Rondo brillant, 278
concerto, violin and orchestra, E minor, 187, 287, 291

Mendelssohn-Bartholdy, Felix—(Continued)
"Consolation," 290
Elijah, 288–289, 290
"It is enough," 289
"O rest in the Lord," 289
Fingal's Cave, 274, 275, 276, 284, 291, 470
"Hebrides" Overture, see *Fingal's Cave*
Hochzeit des Camacho, Die, 270
Hymn of Praise, see *Lobgesang*
"Italian" Symphony, 276–277, 284, 291
Lieder ohne Worte, 263, 275, 290, 291
Lobgesang (Hymn of Praise or "2nd" Symphony), 282-283
Meeresstille Overture, 279
Midsummer Night's Dream, A, incidental music, 285–286, 291, 571
Funeral March, 286
Intermezzo, 286
Nocturne, 286
Overture, 271–272, 275, 276, 285, 286, 291
Scherzo, 286
Wedding March, 286, 290
Oedipus Coloneus, incidental music, 283
overture
Fingal's Cave, 274, 275, 276, 284, 291, 470
"Hebrides," see *Fingal's Cave*
Hochzeit des Camacho, Die, 270
Meeresstille, 279
Midsummer Night's Dream, A, 271–272, 275, 276, 285, 286, 291
Ruy Blas, 282, 286, 291
Schöne Melusine, Die, 278
"Trumpet," 277
piano solo
Capriccio brillant, 275
Lieder ohne Worte, 263, 275, 290, 291
Prelude and Fugue, E minor, 291
Rondo capriccioso, 291
Songs Without Words, see *Lieder ohne Worte*
Variations sérieuses, 291
"Reformation" Symphony, 274, 275
Rondo brillant, piano and orchestra, 278
Ruy Blas Overture, 282, 286, 291
St. Paul, 278, 280, 281, 321
"But the Lord is mindful of His own," 280
Schöne Melusine, Die, Overture, 278
"Scotch" Symphony, 274, 284, 285, 291
Songs Without Words, see *Lieder ohne Worte*
"Spring Song," 290

Mendelssohn-Bartholdy, Felix—(Continued)
symphonies
1st, C minor, 269, 274
2nd, B flat major (*Lobgesang*), 282-283
3rd, A minor ("Scotch"), 274, 284, 285, 291
4th, A major ("Italian"), 276–277, 284, 291
5th, D minor ("Reformation"), 274, 275
"Trumpet" Overture, 277
Mendelssohn-Bartholdy, Leah (Salomon) (1777–1842), 268, 281, 285
Mendelssohn-Bartholdy, Paul (1813–1874), 269, 283, 288
Mendelssohn - Bartholdy, Rebecka (1811–1858), 269
Mendès, Catulle (1841–1909), 536
Menter, Sophie (1848–1918), 388, 574
Menuhin, Yehudi (1917–   ), 132
Mer, La (Debussy), 545, 546, 547–548, 551, 592
Merelli, Bartolommeo, 447, 448
Mérimée, Prosper (1803–1870), 320, 329
Mesmer, Franz Anton (1733–1815), 128
Messager, André-Charles (1853–1929), 543
Messiah (Handel), 53, 76, 77–79, 81–82, 83, 84, 119, 120, 153, 288
Metastasio (Pietro Trapassi) (1698–1782), 88, 91, 93, 95, 104, 131, 147, 156
Méthode des méthodes pour le piano (Fétis and Moscheles), 324
Metropolitan Opera and Real Estate Company (New York), 566–567
Metropolitan Opera House (New York), 184, 228, 237, 465, 518, 549, 566–567, 571, 607
Metternich-Sándor, Princess Pauline (1836–1921), 427, 428
Metternich-Winneburg, Prince Clemens (1773–1859), 119, 236, 375
Meyerbeer, Giacomo (Jakob Liebmann Beer) (1791–1864), 150, 212, 238, 243, 270, 275, 301, 311, 319, 337, 347, 357, 359, 362, 383, 385, 391, 405, 406, 407, 409, 413, 417, 421–422, 427, 428, 461, 462, 571
Huguenots, Les, 245, 409
Prophète, Le, 391
"*Ad nos ad salutarem undam*," 391
Michelangelo Buonarroti (1475–1564), 14, 45, 364
Midsummer Night's Dream, A (Mendelssohn), 271–272, 275, 276, 285–286, 290, 291, 571
Midsummer Night's Dream, A (Shakespeare), 271, 285, 571
Mignon (Thomas), 530
Mikado, The (Gilbert and Sullivan), 465

"Militaire" Polonaise (Chopin), 322

Miliukov, Paul Nikolaevich (1859–1943), 589

Miller, Mitchell, 572

Milton, John (1608–1674), 77, 79

"Minute" Waltz (Chopin), 322

Mirabeau, Honoré-Gabriel Riquetti, Comte de (1749–1791), 268

Miranda, Anthony, 572

Missa Papae Marcelli (Palestrina), 8, 10, 12, 13, 14, 18

Missa solennis (Beethoven), 200–202, 203, 401

Mohammed (570?–632), 20

Moke, Mme (mother of Mme Camille Pleyel), 347, 348, 371

Moke, Marie, see Pleyel, Marie (Moke)

Molière (Jean - Baptiste Poquelin) (1622–1673), 91, 98, 570

Mona Lisa (Leonardo da Vinci), 10

Monet, Claude (1840–1926), 542

Montagu, John Montagu, Duke of (1689–1749), 81

Montesquiou, Comte Robert de (1855–1921), 543

Monteverdi, Claudio (1567–1643), 25, 85–86

   Incoronazione di Poppaea, L', 85–86

Montez, Lola (1818–1861), 381, 431

"Moonlight" Sonata (Beethoven), 175, 181, 191

Moore, Thomas (1779–1852), 304

Morlacchi, Francesco (1784–1841), 215, 216, 217, 409

Morzin, Count Ferdinand Maximilian von, 106

Moscheles, Ignaz (1794–1870), 158, 269, 280, 282, 288, 290, 294, 295, 297, 317, 324

Moszkowski, Moritz (1854–1925), 388

Mottl, Felix (1856–1911), 369

Mozart, Constanze (Weber) (1763–1842), 139, 140, 143, 145, 148, 149, 155, 157–159, 209

Mozart, Karl Thomas (1784–1858), 275

Mozart, Leopold (1719–1787), 124, 125, 126–127, 128, 129, 130, 131, 132–134, 135, 136, 137, 138, 139, 143, 144, 145, 164, 396

Mozart, Maria Anna (Pertl) (1720–1778), 125, 127, 129, 135, 136

Mozart, Maria Anna ("Nannerl") (1751–1829), 125, 126, 127, 128, 129, 143

Mozart, Wolfgang Amadeus (1756–1791), 14, 22, 24, 45–46, 90, 101, 107, 112–113, 117, 118, 124–161, 162, 164, 165, 167, 69, 70, 171, 181, 183, 188, 195, 196, 207, 209, 212, 214, 227, 229, 231, 234, 244, 251, 252, 254, 258, 262, 269, 270, 275, 291, 293, 300, 317, 320, 327,

Mozart, Wolfgang—*(Continued)* 345, 355, 365, 372, 380, 382, 383, 391, 394, 396, 446, 471, 490, 522, 526, 542, 555, 569, 570, 575, 592

   Bastien und Bastienne, 128

   Clemenza di Tito, La, 156

   concerto, flute, harpsichord, and orchestra, C major (K.299), 136

   concertos, piano and orchestra, 142–143

     E flat major (K.271), 135

     A major (K.414), 143

     B flat major (K.450), 143

     A major (K.488), 143

     C minor (K.491), 143

     D major ("Coronation") (K.537), 155

   concerto, two pianos and orchestra, E flat major (K.365), 137

   concertos, violin and orchestra, 132

   "Coronation" Concerto, piano and orchestra (K.537), 155

   Così fan tutte, 154–155

   Don Giovanni, 101, 149–151, 152, 165, 263, 278, 317, 345, 400, 403

     "Il mio tesoro," 150

     "Là ci darem," 150, 317

     minuet, 15, 270

   Entführung aus dem Serail, Die, 101, 129, 137, 139, 140, 154

   fantasia, piano, C minor (K.475), 141–142

   Finta giardiniera, La, 132

   Finta semplice, La, 128

   "Haffner" Serenade, 135

   "Haffner" Symphony (K.385), 144, 149

   "Haydn" Quartets, 145–146

   Idomeneo, Rè di Creta, 137, 138, 156

   "Jupiter" Symphony (K.551), 153, 586

   "King of Prussia" Quartets, 146

   Kleine Nachtmusik, Eine, 149

   "Linz" Symphony (K.425), 143, 144, 149

   Lucio Silla, 131

   Missa brevis, F major (K.192), 134

   Missa brevis, D major (K.194), 134

   Mitridate, Rè di Ponto, 130

   Nozze di Figaro, Le, 143, 147–149, 231, 278, 370

     "Voi che sapete," 148

   "Paris" Symphony (K.297), 144

   "Prague" Symphony (K.504), 149

   quartets, strings, 145–146

     G major ("Haydn") (K.387), 146

     D minor ("Haydn") (K.421), 146

     C major ("Haydn") (K.465), 146

     "Haydn" Quartets, 145, 146

     "King of Prussia" Quartets, 146

   quintet, strings, G minor (K.516), 160

Mozart, Wolfgang—*(Continued)*
 Rè pastore, Il, 132
  "*L'amerò, sarò costante,*" 132
 Requiem, D minor, 155–156, 157,
  158–159, 337
  Kyrie, 159
  Lacrymosa, 158
 Schauspieldirektor, Der, 146–147
 Sinfonia concertante (K.364), 137
 Sogno di Scipione, Il, 131
 sonatas, piano, 142
  A minor (K.310), 142
  A major (K.331), 142
 symphonies, 143–144, 151–153
  D major ("Paris") (K.297), 144
  C major (K.338), 137
  D major ("Haffner") (K.385), 144,
   149
  C major ("Linz") (K.425), 143, 144,
   149
  D major ("Prague") (K.504), 149
  E flat major (K.543), 144, 152, 490
  G minor (K.550), 152–153
  C major ("Jupiter") (K.551), 153,
   586
 Veilchen, Das, 141
 Zaïde, 137
 Zauberflöte, Die, 129, 145, 155, 156–
  157, 355, 394
  "*Bei männern, welche Liebe
   fuhlen,*" 157
  "*Der hölle Rache,*" 157
  "*In diesen heil'gen Hallen,*" 157
  "*O Isis und Osiris,*" 157
Mozart and Salieri (Rimsky-Korsakov),
 158
Mozart: The Man and His Works
 (Turner), 160
Much Ado About Nothing (Shake-
 speare), 368
Müller, Wilhelm (1794–1827), 250, 272
Müllerlieder (Wilhelm Müller), 250
Murat, Joachim (1771–1815), 229
Murdoch, William (1888–1942), 331,
 479
Music Since 1900 (Slonimsky), 600–601
Musical Times, The (London), 363
Musset, Louis-Charles-Alfred (1810–
 1857), 329, 531
Mussorgsky, Modest Petrovich (1838–
 1881), 346, 372, 506, 535
 Boris Godunov, 535
 Night on Bald Mountain, A, 346
My Reverie (Clinton), 539

N

Napoleon I, Emperor of the French
 (1769–1821), 121, 163, 180–181, 186,
 190, 196, 211, 213, 228, 229, 268, 292,
 339, 352, 363, 372, 445

Napoleon III, Emperor of the French
 (1808–1873), 245, 339, 363, 368, 385,
 427, 428, 457, 486, 530
National Broadcasting Company, 108
NBC Symphony Orchestra, 608
Neefe, Christian Gottlob (1748–1798),
 165, 167
Nelson, Horatio, Lord (1758–1805), 130
Neri, St. Filippo (1515–1595), 10–11, 13
Nerval, Gérard de (Gérard Labrunie)
 (1808–1855), 342, 343
Neue freie Presse (Vienna), 433
Neue Zeitschrift für Musik (Leipzig),
 296–297, 300, 305, 310, 473, 478, 486,
 489, 500, 529
Neumann, Angelo (1838–1910), 441
New Friends of Music (New York), 118
New Philharmonic Society (London),
 365
Newcastle, Thomas Pelham-Holles,
 Duke of (1693–1768), 66
Newman, Ernest (1868–   ), 343, 396–
 397, 398, 402, 404–405, 419
Newmarch, Rosa (Jeaffreson) (1857–
 1940), 521
Newton, Sir Isaac (1642–1727), 61
Nicholas I, Tsar of Russia (1796–1855),
 380
Nicolai, Carl Otto (1810–1849), 448
 Lustigen Weiber von Windsor, Die,
  448
Nietzsche, Friedrich (1844–1900), 398,
 436, 562, 563
Night Thoughts (Young), 293
Nijinsky, Waslav (1889–1950), 538, 550,
 597, 599
Nikisch, Arthur (1855–1922), 39, 388,
 561, 564
Niobe (Pacini), 378
Noces villageoises, Les (Stravinsky),
 602–603, 605
Nocturnes (Debussy), 541–542, 547
Norma (Bellini), 294, 320, 448
Nostits, General, 215
Notre-Dame de Paris (Hugo), 353
Noverre, Jean-George (1727–1810), 90
Nozze di Figaro, Le (Mozart), 143, 147–
 149, 231, 278, 370
Nur wer die Sehnsucht kennt (Goethe),
 521
Nutcracker, The, ballet and suite
 (Tchaikovsky), 525–526

O

O, Dry Those Tears (Del Riego), 589
Oberon (Weber), 212, 222, 223–224
Obreskov (Potocka), Countess, 336
Ode for St. Cecilia's Day (Dryden), 77
Ode to Joy (Schiller), 202
Oedipus Coloneus (Sophocles), 283

Offenbach, Jacques (1819–1880), 229, 240, 530, 570
Oh! Susanna (Foster), 7
Oiseau de feu, L' (Stravinsky), 596, 597
Okeghem, Jean de (1430?–1495), 5, 20
Ollivier, Blandine (Liszt) (1835–1862), 377, 381, 385, 386
Ollivier, Émile (1825–1913), 385
Orange, William V, Prince of (1748–1806), 127
Oratorians, 10
Orfeo ed Euridice (Gluck), 91–93, 94, 97–98
Orlando di Lasso, see Lasso, Orlando di
Orpheus (Stravinsky), 609–610, 611
Otello (Verdi), 233, 464–465, 466, 467
Othello (Shakespeare), 232, 464, 465
Ottobuoni, Cardinal Pietro (1667–1740), 57
"Oxford" Symphony (Haydn), 105, 114, 117

P

Pachelbel, Johann (1653–1706), 25
Pachmann, Vladimir de (1848–1933), 381
Pacini, Giovanni (1796–1867), 378
Niobe, 378
Paderewski, Ignace Jan (1860–1941), 381, 522
Paganini, Nicolò (1782–1840), 26, 264, 272, 275, 317, 326, 349, 350, 356, 376, 377, 479
Paisiello, Giovanni (1740–1816), 231
Barbiere di Siviglia, Il, 231
Palatine of the Rhine, Karl Theodor, Elector (1733–1799), 135, 209
Palestrina, Giovanni Pierluigi da (1525?–1594), 3, 8–14, 15, 17, 18, 19, 20, 22, 46, 52, 85, 162, 275, 278, 446, 534, 601, 604
Assumpta est Maria, 12–13, 18
Improperia, 9
Masses, first book of, 8
Masses, fourth book of, 13
Masses, seventh book of, 13
Missa Papae Marcelli, 8, 10, 12, 13, 14, 18
Tu es pastor ovium, 12
Papillons (Schumann), 295, 297, 301
Paradise Lost (Milton), 119
Parry, Sir Charles Hubert Hastings (1848–1918), 51
Parsifal (Wagner), 369, 390, 422, 435, 441, 442–443, 535, 567, 579
Pasta, Giuditta (1798–1865), 294, 320
"Pastoral" Symphony (Beethoven), 188, 190, 194, 277, 346, 491
'*Pathétique*" Sonata (Beethoven), 170

"*Pathétique*" Symphony (Tchaikovsky) 517, 518, 527, 528
Paton, Mary Anne (1802–1864), 223
Patti, Adelina (Baroness Cederström) (1843–1919), 232, 245, 246
Paul I, Tsar of Russia (1754–1801), 101, 111
Paul IV (Giovanni Pietro Caraffa), Pope (1476–1559), 8–9
Paul V (Camillo Borghese), Pope (1552–1621), 7
Pauly, Rose (1905?–), 568
Pedro II, Emperor of Brazil (1825–1891), 438
Pélissier, Olympe, see Rossini, Olympe ·(Pélissier)
Pelléas et Mélisande (Debussy), 150, 535, 537, 539, 541, 542–543
Pelléas et Mélisande (Maeterlinck), 537, 582
Pepusch, Johann Christoph (1667–1752), 64, 69
Beggar's Opera, The, 64, 69, 74, 78
Pergolesi, Giovanni Battista (1710–1736), 244, 278, 600, 601, 606
Stabat Mater, 244
Petite Messe solennelle (Rossini), 242, 246
Petrarch (Francesco Petrarca) (1304–1374), 15, 17
Petrouchka (Stravinsky), 597–598, 599, 611
Pfeiffer, Tobias, 164
Pfistermeister, Franz von (1822–1912), 429
Philadelphia Exposition of 1876, 437
Philharmonic Society of London, 203, 364
Philharmonic - Symphony Orchestra (New York), 568
Philharmonic-Symphony Society of New York, 608
Philip II, King of Spain (1527–1598), 19
Piave, Francesco Maria (1810–1876), 452, 456
Picander, see Henrici, Christian Friedrich
Picasso, Pablo (1881–), 603, 609
Piccinni, Niccola (1728–1800), 99, 136
Iphigénie en Tauride, 99
Piccioli, 504
Pietists, 28
Pique-Dame (Tchaikovsky), 524, 525, 526
Pirro, André (1869–), 36
Pitt, William (1759–1806), 102
Pius IV (Giovanni Angelo de' Medici) Pope (1499–1565), 7, 9, 10
Pius V (Michele Ghislieri), Pope, St. (1504–1572), 10

Pius IX (Giovanni Maria Mastai-Ferretti), Pope (1792–1878), 246, 384
Planché, James Robinson (1796–1880), 222
Planer, Amalie, 406
Planer, Natalie (Bilz) (1826–1886?), 403
Plato (427?–347 B.C.), 3
Pleyel, Camille (1788–1855), 348
Pleyel, Marie-Félicité-Denise, called Camille (Moke) (1811–1875), 346, 347–348, 365, 368–369
"Plon-Plon," see Bonaparte, Napoleon-Joseph-Charles
Poe, Edgar Allan (1809–1849), 545, 549
Pohjola's Daughter (Sibelius), 584, 586, 588
Pohlenz, Christian August (1790–1843), 285
"Polish" Symphony (Tchaikovsky), 208, 509, 511
Polzelli (Franchi), Luigia (1760–1832), 110
Pompadour, Jeanne-Antoinette Poisson, Marquise de (1721–1764), 127
Ponte, Lorenzo da (1749–1838), 147, 149, 154, 234
Pope, Alexander (1688–1744), 61, 66
Porpora, Niccola (1686–1766), 72, 73, 76, 104–105
Potocka, Countess Delphine (1807–1877), 327, 337
Pourtalès, Comtesse de, 599–600, 604
Prélude à l'Après-midi d'un faune (Debussy), 537, 538–539, 547, 550
Préludes, Les (Liszt), 393
Pre-Raphaelites, 535
Primavera (Botticelli), 534
Prince Regent, the, see George IV, King of England
Prokofiev, Serge Sergeivich (1891–), 561, 599, 601, 611
Scythian Suite, 601
Promessi sposi, I (Manzoni), 461
Prophète, Le (Meyerbeer), 391
Proust, Marcel (1871–1922), 543
Prussia, Amalia, Princess of (1723–1787), 126
Prussia, Princess Augusta of, see Augusta, Empress of Germany
Prussia, Frederika Charlotte Ulrika, Princess Royal of (Duchess of York) (1767–1820), 154
Puccini, Giacomo (1858–1924), 227, 465
Girl of the Golden West, The, 227
Purcell, Henry (1658–1695), 59, 63, 86
Dido and Aeneas, 59, 86
Pushkin, Alexander Sergeievich (1799–1837), 158, 513, 515, 524

Q

Quinault, Philippe (1635–1688), 98

R

Racine, Jean (1639–1699), 96, 284
Radziwill, Prince Valentin, 321
Raff, Joseph Joachim (1822–1882), 366, 367
"Raindrop" Prelude (Chopin), 331
Rake's Progress, The (Hogarth), 610
Rameau, Jean-Philippe (1683–1764), 75, 89, 95, 124, 370, 372
Tambourin, 75
Raphael (Raffaele Sanzio) (1483–1520), 14
Rasoumovsky, Count Andreas Kyrillovich (1752–1836), 185, 206
"Rasoumovsky" Quartets (Beethoven), 185, 186, 206, 207
Ravel, Maurice-Joseph (1875–1937), 218, 346, 546, 551, 553, 594
Jeux d'eau, 546
Ondine, 553
Rapsodie espagnole, 546
Rè pastore, Il (Mozart), 132
Recio, Marie (Marie-Geneviève Martin), see Berlioz, Marie (Recio)
"Reformation" Symphony (Mendelssohn), 274, 275
Reicha, Anton (1770–1836), 341
Reinecke, Karl (1824–1910), 483
Reinhardt, Max (1873–1943), 393
Reinken, Johann Adam (1623–1722), 24, 25, 34
Rellstab, Heinrich Friedrich Ludwig (1799–1860), 250
Rembrandt Harmenszoon van Rijn (1606–1669), 80
Reményi, Eduard (1830–1898), 366, 472, 484
Renoir, Pierre-Auguste (1841–1919), 542
Requiem (Grande Messe des morts) (Berlioz), 353–355
Requiem ("Manzoni") (Verdi), 355, 463–464
Reszke, Édouard de (1853–1917), 237
"Revolutionary" Etude (Chopin), 324–325
Revue blanche, La (Paris), 542
Rheingold, Das (Wagner), 420, 422, 424, 425, 441; see also Ring des Nibelungen, Der
"Rhenish" Symphony (Schumann), 309
Richard I ("the Lion-Hearted"), King of England (1157–1199), 69
Richter, Hans (1843–1916), 433, 435, 437, 493, 497, 499, 577
Richter, Jean Paul Friedrich (1763–1825), 293, 294, 295
Ricordi, Giovanni (1785–1853), 447
Rienzi (Wagner), 402, 408–409, 410, 411, 413, 414, 415, 425

Rienzi, the Last of the Tribunes (Bulwer-Lytton), 408

Rigoletto (Verdi), 391, 449, 450, 452–453, 454, 455, 460, 463

Rimsky-Korsakov, Nikolai Andreievich (1844–1908), 158, 218, 506, 508, 510, 527, 595–596, 597
  Mozart and Salieri, 158
  Scheherazade, 597

Ring des Nibelungen, Der (Wagner), 225, 226, 241, 384, 419, 420, 422, 423, 424, 426, 429, 430, 433, 435, 436–440, 442, 512, 539, 565

Ringling Brothers–Barnum and Bailey Circus, 607

Ritter, Alexander (1833–1896), 557

Ritter, Franziska (Wagner) (1829–1895), 557

Ritter, Julie (1795–1869), 418, 424

Ritter, Karl, 424

Road to Xanadu, The (Lowes), 397

Rob Roy overture (Berlioz), 348

Robinson, Anastasia (1698?–1755), 67

Rodrigue et Chimène (Mendès), 536

Roerich, Nikolai Konstantinovich (1874–   ), 597, 599

Roger-Ducasse, Jean-Jules (1873–   ), 545

Rohan, Prince Louis de (1734–1803), 110

Roi Lear overture, *Le* (Berlioz), 348

Roi s'amuse, Le (Hugo), 452

Rolland, Romain (1866–1944), 54, 563, 564

Roman de Tristan, Le (Bédier), 549

Romeo and Juliet, overture-fantasia (Tchaikovsky), 506–507, 515

Roméo et Juliette (Berlioz), 343, 356–357, 361, 365, 370, 373, 507

Rosamunde, Fürstin von Cypern (Schubert), 258–259

Rose, Billy (1899–   ), 607

Rosenkavalier, Der (Richard Strauss), 565, 569–570, 571

Rosenthal, Moriz (1862–1946), 388

Rossetti, Dante Gabriel (1828–1882), 535

Rossi, Giovanni Gaetano (1828–1886), 237

Rossignol, Le (Stravinsky), 595, 601–602

Rossini, Anna (?–1827), 226–227, 229, 230, 235, 240

Rossini, Gioacchino Antonio (1792–1868), 219, 220, 221, 222–223, 224, 226–247, 248, 249, 258, 270, 281, 296, 319, 375, 383, 385, 446, 452, 460, 461, 463, 464, 466, 511, 573
  Almaviva, ossia L'inutile precauzione, see *Barber of Seville, The*
  Barber of Seville, The, 226, 230–232, 233, 240, 242, 243, 246, 247, 370, 466

Rossini, Gioacchino—*(Continued)*
  Barber of Seville, The—*(Continued)*
    "Lesson Scene," 370
    Calumny Song, 232
    "*Largo al factotum*," 226, 232
    overture, 232
    "*Una voce poco fa*," 232
  Cambiale di matrimonio, La, 227
  Cenerentola, La, 233
    overture, 233
  Comte Ory, Le, 240
  Donna del lago, La, 235
  Elisabetta, Reghina d'Inghilterra, 230
  Gazza ladra, La, 234
    overture, 234
  Italiana in Algeri, L', 229
    overture, 229
  Maometto II, 239
  Moïse, 239–240
  Mosè in Egitto, 239, 466
  Péchés de viellesse, 246
    Hygienic Prelude for Morning Use, A, 246
    Miscarriage of a Polish Mazurka, 246
  Petite Messe solennelle, 242, 246
  Pietra del paragone, La, 228
  Plaint of the Muses on the Death of Lord Byron, The, 238
  Scala di seta, La, 228
    overture, 228
  Semiramide, 236–237
    overture, 237
  Siège de Corinthe, Le, 239, 241
  Signor Bruschino, Il, 228–229
  Stabat Mater, 242, 243–244
    "*Quis est homo*," 246
  Tancredi, 229, 246
    "*Di tanti palpiti*," 229
    overture, 229
  Viaggio a Reims, Il, 238
  William Tell, 234, 241–242, 243, 246, 334
    "*Asile héréditaire*," 242
    overture, 237, 242, 373
  Zelmira, 235

Rossini, Giuseppe (1759–1839), 226–227, 240

Rossini, Isabella Angela (Colbran) (1785–1845), 230, 232, 234–235, 236, 237, 240, 243

Rossini, Olympe (Pélissier), 243, 245, 246

Rothschild, Baron Jacques de (1792–1868), 321

Roubilliac, Louis-François (1695–1762), 74

Rousseau, Henri ("*le douanier*") (1844–1910), 574

Rousseau, Jean-Jacques (1712–1778), 96

Roustan, Mme. (Octavie de la Ferron-
nière), 530, 531
Royal Academy of Music (London), 66,
68, 69, 70
Rubini, Giovanni Battista (1795–1854),
320
Rubinstein, Anton Grigorievich (1829–
1894), 201, 298, 371, 486, 504, 505,
506, 518
Rubinstein, Arthur (1886–   ), 598
Rubinstein, Ida, 550, 606
Rubinstein, Nikolai Grigorievich
(1835–1881), 371, 504–505, 506, 508,
509, 512–513, 514, 516, 518, 519, 520,
521
Rudolf Josef Rainer, Archduke of Aus-
tria, Cardinal (1788–1831), 190–191,
197, 200, 255
Rungenhagen, Carl Friedrich (1778–
1851), 276
Ruskin, John (1819–1900), 160
Ruspoli, Francesco Maria Capizucchi,
Prince, 57
Russian Gazette, The, 510
Ruy Blas (Hugo), 282
Ruy Blas Overture (Mendelssohn), 282,
286, 291
Ryder, Albert Pinkham (1847–1917),
542

S

Sachs, Hans (1494–1576), 413, 429
Sacre du printemps, Le (Stravinsky),
189, 599–601, 603, 607, 611
Saidenberg, Daniel (1906–   ), 572
Saint-Saëns, Charles-Camille (1835–
1921), 94, 245–246, 372, 388, 438, 527,
534, 535
    Caprice on Airs de Ballet from Al-
    ceste (Gluck), 94
    Variations on a Theme of Beetho-
    ven, two pianos, 534
Saint-Simon, Claude-Henri, Comte de
(1760–1825), 376
Sainte-Beuve, Charles-Augustin (1804–
1869), 245, 329, 342
St. John Passion (Bach), 40–42, 46, 47,
63–64
St. Matthew Passion (Bach), 18, 37, 38,
40, 41, 42–43, 46, 47, 64, 78, 272–273,
288
St. Paul (Mendelssohn), 278, 280, 281,
312
Salieri, Antonio (1750–1825), 101, 122,
147, 158, 167, 252, 317, 375
    Danaïdes, Les, 101
Salome (Richard Strauss), 566–567, 568,
569, 570
Salomé (Wilde), 566
Salomon, Johann Peter (1745–1815),
113, 114, 119

"Salomon" Symphonies (Haydn), 114,
117–118, 122
Sammartini, Giovanni Battista (1701–
1775), 88, 129
Samson (Handel), 79
Samson Agonistes (Milton), 79
Sanborn, Pitts (1879–1941), 229
Sand, George (Aurore Dudevant)
(1804–1876), 105, 227, 329–330, 331,
333, 334–335, 378, 381, 385, 389
Sarto, Andrea del (1486–1531), 605
Satie, Erik-Alfred-Leslie (1866–1925),
536–537, 547
Saul (Handel), 76, 77
Saxe-Meiningen, Grand Duke Georg
of (1826–1914), 497
Saxe-Weimar, Carl Friedrich, Grand
Duke of (1783–1853), 365
Saxe-Weimar, Ernst Augustus, Duke
of (1688–1748), 26, 33
Saxe-Weimar, Prince Friedrich Ferdi-
nand Constantin of (1758–1793), 397
Saxe-Weimar, Prince Johann Ernst of
(1696–1715), 26
Saxe-Weimar, Johann Ernst III, Duke
of (?–1707), 26, 33
Saxe-Weimar, Karl Alexander, Grand
Duke of (1818–1901), 384
Saxe-Weimar, Karl August, Grand
Duke of (1757–1828), 397
Saxe-Weimar, Wilhelm Ernst, Grand
Duke of (1662–1728), 26, 29, 30, 31,
32, 33, 37
Saxe-Weissenfels, Christian, Duke of
(1681–1736), 32, 44
Saxe-Weissenfels, Johann Georg, Duke
of, 53
Saxony, Christiane Eberhardine, Queen
of Poland and Electress of (?–1727),
40
Saxony, Friedrich Augustus I ("the
Strong"), Elector of (Augustus II,
King of Poland) (1670–1733), 39, 40,
45, 329
Saxony, Friedrich Augustus II, Elector
of (Augustus III, King of Poland)
(1696–1763), 45, 49, 50
Sayn-Wittgenstein, Princess Carolyne
von (1819–1887), 333, 367, 368, 381–
382, 384, 385, 386, 387, 389, 393, 437
Sayn-Wittgenstein, Marie von, see
Hohenlohe - Schillingfürst, Princess
Marie
Sayn-Wittgenstein, Prince Nicholas
von (1812–1864), 386
Scala di seta, La (Rossini), 228
Scalchi, Sofia (1850–?), 237
Scarlatti, Alessandro (1659–1725), 56,
57, 76, 112
Scarlatti, Domenico (1685–1757), 57, 65,
124, 380

Schauffler, Robert Haven (1879–   ),
  475
Scheherazade (Rimsky-Korsakov), 597
Scheibe, Johann Adolf (1708–1776), 47–
  48
Schelling, Ernest (1876–1939), 194
  Victory Ball, A, 194
Scherman, Thomas K. (1916–   ), 572
Schikaneder, Emanuel (1748–1812),
  155, 156, 183
Schiller, Johann Christoph Friedrich
  von (1759–1805), 28, 202, 204, 241,
  252, 519
Schloezer, Boris de (1884–   ), 602,
  609
Schmidt, Johann Christoph, 63
Schnabel, Artur (1882–   ), 495
Schnack, Fritz, 482, 486
Schnorr von Carolsfeld, Ludwig (1836–
  1865), 430
Schnorr von Carolsfeld, Malwine (Gar-
  rigues) (1825–1904), 430
Schober, Franz von (1798–1883), 254,
  255, 266
Schönberg, Arnold (1874–   ), 5, 568,
  594
Schopenhauer, Arthur (1788–1860),
  398, 421, 439
Schott, B., and Sons, 427–428
Schrattenbach, Sigismund von, Archbishop of Salzburg (?–1772), 125, 128,
  131
Schröder-Devrient, Wilhelmine (1804–
  1860), 400, 408, 409, 410, 412, 415
Schroeter, Mrs. John Samuel, 115, 116
Schubart, Christian Friedrich Daniel
  (1739–1791), 133
Schubert, Anna (Kleyenböck) (1783–
  1860), 253, 256
Schubert, Ferdinand (1794–1859), 264,
  266, 300
Schubert, Franz Peter (1797–1828), 141,
  205, 221, 236, 248–266, 291, 294,
  295, 296, 297, 300, 303, 310, 380,
  391, 488, 561
  operas and incidental music
    Fierrabras, 258
    Rosamunde, Fürstin von Cypern,
      258–259
    Zwillingsbrüder, Die, 255
  piano solo, 262–263
    fantasias
      C major ("Wanderer"), 262, 263
      G major (sonata-fantasia), 262,
        263
    impromptus, 263
    Moments musicaux, 263
      F minor, 259
    sonatas, 262–263
      A minor (Opus 42), 262
      A major (Opus 120), 262
      A major ("Grand"), 262

Schubert, Franz Peter—(Continued)
  piano solo—(Continued)
    sonatas—(Continued)
      B flat major ("Grand"), 262
      G major (sonata-fantasia), 263
      "Grand" Sonatas, 262–263
    waltzes, 263
  quartets, string, 257–258, 263
    A minor, 258
    D minor ("Tod und das Mäd-
      chen"), 258
    Quartettsatz in C minor, 257
  quintets
    piano and strings, A major ("For-
      ellen"), 257
    strings, C major, 258, 263
  songs, 249–251, 254
    Am Meer, 251
    Atlas, Der, 250
    Ave Maria, 250, 251, 262
    Doppelgänger, 250
    Du bist die Ruh', 251
    Erlkönig, Der, 250, 251, 254, 259
    Forelle, Die, 257
    Gretchen am Spinnrade, 254
    Hark, Hark, the Lark!, 249, 251, 263
    Schäfers Klagelied, 256
    Schöne Müllerin, Die, 250
    Schwanengesang, 250, 263
    Stadt, Die, 250
    Ständchen, 250
    Tod und das Mädchen, 258
    Who is Sylvia?, 251, 263
    Winterreise, Die, 250, 263
  symphonies
    5th, B flat major, 254, 260–261
    7th (9th), C major, 264–265, 286,
      300
    8th, B minor ("Unfinished"), 260–
      261
    "Grand," C major (?), 262
Schubert, Franz Theodor Florian
  (1763–?), 252, 253, 254, 256, 266
Schubert, Ignaz (1785–1844), 252
Schubert, Maria Elisabeth (Vietz)
  (1756–1812), 253
Schuch, Ernst von (1846–1914), 568
Schumann, August (1773–1826), 292–
  293
Schumann, Clara Josephine (Wieck)
  (1819–1896), 245, 279, 282, 294, 296,
  298, 299–300, 301, 302, 304, 305, 306,
  307, 308, 309, 310, 311, 325, 401, 414,
  473, 475–476, 482, 485, 488, 497–498,
  499
Schumann, Eduard (?–1839), 300
Schumann, Emilie, 292
Schumann, Felix (1854–1879, 493
Schumann, Johanna Christiana (Schna-
  bel) (1771–1836), 293, 294, 298
Schumann, Julie (Contessa Radicati di
  Marmorito) (1845–1872), 485

Schumann, Marie (1841–1929), 499
Schumann, Robert Alexander (1810–
    1856), 22, 36, 143, 150, 201, 212,
    225, 251, 263, 273, 279, 285, 287,
    291, 292–313, 319, 323, 326, 331,
    342–343, 355, 359, 360, 369, 380,
    382–383, 414, 473, 474, 475, 476,
    477, 482, 483, 486, 489–490, 491,
    499, 500, 529, 561
  Album für die Jugend, 301, 306,
    307–308
  Carnaval, 279, 296, 297, 298, 301,
    303, 474
  Concerto for piano and orchestra,
    A minor, 306, 307, 312
  Davidsbundlertänze, Die, 201
  Études symphoniques, 296, 298
  Fantasiestücke, 301, 302, 303, 500
  Faust, scenes from, 309
  Genoveva, 306–307, 383
    overture, 307
  Kinderscenen, 302, 308, 549
  Kreisleriana, 301, 302, 500
  Manfred, incidental music, 306, 307,
    312
  overtures
    Genoveva, 307
    Manfred, 307, 312
  Papillons, 295, 297, 301
  Paradies und die Peri, Die, 304–305
  piano compositions, 301–302, 313
    Album für die Jugend, 301, 306,
      307–308
    Carnaval, 279, 296, 297, 298, 301,
      303
    Davidsbundlertänze, Die, 301
    Études symphoniques, 296, 298
    Fantasie, C major, 301, 302, 337,
      338
    Fantasiestücke, 301, 302, 303, 500
    Kinderscenen, 302, 308, 549
      Träumerei, 291, 302
    Kreisleriana, 301, 302, 500
    Papillons, 295, 297, 301
    sonatas, 302
      F minor, 299, 302
    Studien nach Capricen von Pa-
      ganini, 295
    Waldscenen, 308
    Vogel als Prophet, 308
  quartet, piano and strings, E flat
    major, 304
  quintet, piano and strings, E flat
    major, 304, 312
  "Rhenish" Symphony, 309
  songs, 302–303, 312
    Beiden Grenadiere, Die, 303
    Dichterliebe, 303
    Erstes Grün, 303
    Ich grolle nicht, 303
    Lotusblume, Die, 303

Schumann, Robert—(Continued)
  songs—(Continued)
    Nussbaum, Der, 303
    Widmung, 303
  "Spring" Symphony, 303
  symphonies, 303–304, 312
    1st, B flat major ("Spring"), 303
    3rd, E flat major ("Rhenish"), 309
    4th, D minor, 303
    G minor (fragment), 295, 303
    Waldscenen, 308
Schumann, Rosalie (?–1833), 295
Schumann-Heink, Ernestine (1861–
    1936), 251, 280, 568
Schwarzenburg, Karl Philipp, Prince
    zu (1771–1820), 119
Schweitzer, Albert (1875–), 24, 37
Schwind, Moritz von (1804–1871), 255,
    261
"Scotch" Symphony (Mendelssohn),
    274, 284, 285, 291
Scotti, Antonio (1866–1936), 460
Scott, Sir Walter (1771–1832), 235, 262
Scriabin, Alexander Nikolaievich
    (1872–1915), 600
Scribe, Agustin-Eugène (1791–1861),
    240, 405, 406, 407, 455, 456, 457
Seasons, The (Haydn), 120–121
Seasons, The (Thomson), 120
Sechter, Simon (1788–1867), 265–266
Sembrich, Marcella (Praxede Kochan-
    ska) (1858–1935), 157
Semiramide (Rossini), 236–237
Senefelder, Aloys (1771–1834), 209
Senesino (Francesco Bernardi) (1680?–
    1750?), 67, 68, 70, 72
Seven Lively Arts, The (musical re-
    view), 607
Sforza, house of, 5
Sgambati, Giovanni (1841–1914), 388,
    536
Shakespeare, William (1564–1616), 77,
    182, 192, 206, 232, 249, 251, 271, 273,
    285, 342, 346–347, 350, 356, 357, 361,
    368, 399, 404, 464, 465, 466, 507, 515
Shaw, George Bernard (1856–), 118,
    141–142, 157, 180, 271, 289, 292, 312,
    394, 419, 465, 481, 483, 519, 542
Sheridan, Richard Brinsley (1751–
    1816), 129
Sherlock Holmes (Conan Doyle), 397
Sibelius, Aïno (Järnefelt), 577, 578
Sibelius, Christian (?–1868), 575
Sibelius, Jean (1865–), 291, 519, 574–
    593, 594
  chamber music
    Drops of Water, violin and cello,
      575
  quartets
    strings, B flat major, 576
    Voces intimae, strings, 585, 586,
      587

Sibelius, Jean—*(Continued)*
 chorus
  Song of the Athenians, male voices,
   581
 concerto for violin and orchestra,
  D minor, 582–583
 orchestra
  Bard, The, 587
  En Saga, 578, 579
  Fantasia sinfonica, see 6th Symphony
  Finale, see *Finlandia*
  Finlandia, 581, 588
  Impromptu, see *Finlandia*
  incidental music
   to *Belshazzar's Feast,* 584
   to *King Christian II,* 579, 588
   to *Kuolema,* 581
    Valse triste, 291, 581
   to *Pelléas et Mélisande,* 583–584
  Karelia, overture and suite, 579
  Kullervo (with voices), 577–578
  Legends, 579, 580, 581
   Lemminkäinen's Home-Coming,
    579, 580
   Swan of Tuonela, The, 579, 580
  Luonnotar, 587
  Oceanides, The, 588
  Pohjola's Daughter, 584, 586, 588
  string suite, 576
  symphonies
   1st, E minor, 580–581
   2nd, D major, 582, 589
   3rd, C major, 583, 584, 586
   4th, A minor, 574, 584, 585, 586–587, 589, 591
   5th, E flat major, 589–590
   6th, D minor, 590, 591
   7th, C major, 589, 591–592
   8th, 592, 593
  Tapiola, 592
Sibelius, Maria Charlotta (Borg), 575
Siebold, Agathe von, 481–482
Siegfried (Wagner), 420, 424, 425, 435, 436, 440; see also *Ring des Nibelungen, Der*
Siegfried Idyl (Wagner), 436
Signor Bruschino, Il (Rossini), 228–229
Siloti, Alexander (1863–1945), 388, 584, 596
Simone Boccanegra (Verdi), 456, 457, 464
Sinfonia domestica (Richard Strauss), 566, 569
Sistine frescoes (Michelangelo), 10
Sistine Madonna (Raphael), 13
Sitwell, Sacheverell (1900–), 380, 389
Sixtus V (Felice Peretti), Pope (1521–1590), 12
Skarbek, Count Gaspar, 315
Skarbek, Countess Gaspar, 315

Sleeping Beauty, The (Tchaikovsky), 523–524
Slonimsky, Nicolas (1894–), 600–601
Smallens, Alexander (1889–), 97, 565
Smart, Sir George (1776–1867), 223
Smetana, Bedřich (1824–1884), 388, 578
Smith, John Christopher (1712–1795), 63
Smithson, Harriet, see Berlioz, Harriet (Smithson)
Société Philharmonique (Paris), 364, 365
Soirées de l'orchestre, Les (Berlioz), 360
Sonnambula, La (Bellini), 294
Sonnleithner, Ignaz, Edler von (1770–1831), 259
Sonnleithner, Josef (1766–1835), 183
Sonnleithner, Leopold (1797–1873), 259
Sophocles (497?–405 B.C.), 370, 568, 604
South Wind (Douglas), 16
Spaun, Josef von (1788–1865), 252–253, 255
Speaks, Oley (1876–1948), 75
Spinoza, Baruch (1632–1677), 12
Spohr, Ludwig (Louis) (1784–1859), 190, 213, 220, 288, 307, 410, 423
Spontini, Gasparo Luigi Pacifico (1774–1851), 214, 215, 218–219, 238, 270, 316, 347, 365, 409, 413
 Fernand Cortez, 214
 Olympie, 218–219, 347
 Vestale, La, 214, 365
"Spring" Symphony (Schumann), 303
Squire, J. H., Celeste Octet, 392
Stabat Mater (Rossini), 242, 243–244
Stamitz, Johann Wenzel (1717–1757), 135
Ständchen (Schubert), 250
Steele, Sir Richard (1671–1729), 60
Steffani, Agostino (1654–1728), 58–59
Stendhal (Marie-Henri Beyle) (1783–1842), 234, 248, 320
Stern, Daniel, see Agoult, Marie, Comtesse d'
Stiedry, Fritz (1883–), 118
Stirling, Jane Wilhelmina (1804–1859), 335, 336, 337
Stockhausen, Elisabeth von, see Herzogenberg, Elisabeth von
Stockhausen, Julius von (1826–1906), 480
Stoeckel, Carl (1858–1925), 588
Stokowski, Leopold (1882–), 36, 572, 608
Strauss, Franz (1822–1905), 556
Strauss, Johann (1825–1899), 103, 151, 217, 321, 485, 505
 Fledermaus, Die, 559
Strauss, Josephine (Pschorr), 556

Strauss, Pauline (De Ahna) (1863–1950), 560, 569

Strauss, Richard (1864–1949), 91, 99, 123, 190, 251, 285, 303, 345, 346, 391, 466, 492, 497, 550, 551, 556–573, 574, 577, 583, 588, 594, 601

concertos

Burleske, piano and orchestra, 557, 560

1st, for Horn and Orchestra, 572

2nd, for Horn and Orchestra, 572

for Oboe and Orchestra, 572

incidental music

to Le Bourgeois-gentilhomme, 570

operas

Aegyptische Helena, Die, 571

Arabella, 571

Ariadne auf Naxos, 570

Grossmächtigtse Prinzessin, 570

Capriccio, 572

Daphne, 571

Elektra, 99, 228, 557, 567, 568, 569, 570

Feuersnot, 565

Frau ohne Schatten, Die, 570-571

Friedenstag, 571

Guntram, 560, 565

Intermezzo, 571

Liebe der Danae, Die, 572

Rosenkavalier, Der, 565, 569-570, 571

Salome, 566–567, 568, 569, 570

Dance of the Seven Veils, 567

Schweigsame Frau, Die, 571

orchestra

Also sprach Zarathustra, 562

Aus Italien, 557–558, 578

Don Juan, 558–559, 562, 577

Don Quixote, 563, 570, 572

Heldenleben, Ein, 563–564, 565

Macbeth, 558, 562

Metamorphoses, 572

Serenade, wind instruments, 556

Sinfonia domestica, 566, 569

Symphony, D minor, 556

Till Eulenspiegels lustige Streiche, 557, 561–562, 563, 570

Tod und Verklärung, 559, 560

songs, 560–561

Allerseelen, 561

Cäcilie, 561

Heiligen drei Könige aus Morgen-land, Die, 561

Morgen, 561

Ruhe, meine Seele, 561

Ständchen, 561

Traum durch die Dämmerung, 561

Stravinsky, Feodor (1843–1902), 595

Stravinsky, Mme (composer's second wife), 609

Stravinsky, Igor Feodorovich (1882–   ), 123, 208, 509, 594–611

ballets

Apollon Musagètes, 604

Baiser de la fée, Le, 604, 606, 607

Card Party, The, 607

Danses concertantes, 607–608

Noces villageoises, Les, 602–603, 605

Oiseau de feu, L', 596, 597

Orpheus, 609–610, 611

Petrouchka, 597–598, 599, 611

Pulcinella (after Pergolesi), 602, 606

Sacre du printemps, Le, 189, 599–601, 603, 607, 611

Great Sacred Dance, 601

Scènes de ballet, 607

chamber music

Baiser de la fée, Le, arrangement violin and piano of Diverti-mento from, 606

Duo Concertant, violin and piano, 605–606, 609

Dithyrambe, 606

Histoire du soldat, L' (seven in-struments), 602

Octuor, 604

Suite italienne, arrangement for violin and piano of excerpts from Pulcinella, 606

Trois Pièces pour quatuor à cor-des, 602

concertos

Capriccio, piano and orchestra, 599, 604, 606

piano and wind instruments, 599, 606

violin and orchestra, 605, 606

Mass (Latin), 610

operas

Mavra, 602

Oedipus Rex (opera-oratorio), 604, 606, 609

Rake's Progress, The, 610

Renard, Le, 602

Rossignol, Le, 595, 601–602

orchestra

Baiser de la fée, Le, Divertimento from, 606

Chant du rossignol, Le, 602

Chant funèbre, 596

Circus Polka, 607

Dumbarton Oaks, concerto grosso in E flat major, 608

Concerto ("Basel"), strings, in D major, 609

Ebony Concerto, 607

Feu d'artifice, 595, 596

Four Norwegian Moods, 609

Ode, 609

Stravinsky, Igor—(Continued)
  orchestra—(Continued)
    Oiseau de feu, L', suite from, 596–
     597
      Dance of Katschei, 596, 597
    Perséphone (with chorus, tenor,
     female speaking voice), 606–
     607
    Scherzo fantastique, 595, 596
    Star-Spangled Banner, The, or-
     chestration of, 611
    Symphonie de psaumes (with
     chorus), 604–605, 606
    Symphony in C, 608, 609
    Symphony in Three Movements,
     608-609
    Symphony, E flat major, 595
  piano solo
    Sonata, 604
    Trois Mouvements de Pétrouchka,
     598–599
  two pianos
    Concerto for two unaccompanied
     pianos, 599
    Sonata for two pianos, 599, 609
  song cycle, mezzo-soprano and or-
    chestra (Faune et la bergère, Le),
    595
Stravinsky, Katerina Gabriela (com-
  poser's first wife), 609
Strepponi, Giuseppina, see Verdi, Giu-
  seppina (Strepponi)
Strindberg, Johan August (1849–1912),
  576
Stuart, Charles Edward, the Young
  Pretender (1720–1788), 79–80
Suarès, André (1866–), 555
Sullivan, Sir Arthur Seymour (1842–
  1900), 31, 259, 465
  Mikado, The, 465
Sullivan, Thomas F., 611
Sun, The (New York), 567–568
Supervia, Conchita (1899–1936), 233
Suppé, Franz von (1819–1895), 409
Süssmayr, Franz Xaver (1766–1803),
  156, 158, 159
Swan of Tuonela, The (Sibelius), 579,
  580
Swieten, Baron Gottfried van (1734–
  1803), 153, 158, 168
Sylphides, Les, 90, 322, 596
Symphonie de psaumes (Stravinsky),
  604–605, 606
Symphonie fantastique (Berlioz), 341,
  342, 343–346, 347, 348, 359, 369, 371,
  383, 391, 522
Symphonie funèbre et triomphale
  (Berlioz), 358
Symphony Society of New York, 592
Szigeti, Josef (1892–), 132, 606

T

Tadolini, Giovanni (1793–1872), 244
Taglioni, Marie Sophie (1804–1844),
  300
Taine, Hippolyte–Adolphe (1828–
  1893), 245
Talleyrand–Périgord, Charles-Maurice
  de, Prince of Benevento (1754–1838),
  196
Tamburini, Antonio (1800–1876), 244
Tannhäuser (Wagner), 24, 291, 311,
  368, 383, 384, 385, 411–413, 414, 415,
  417, 420, 423, 425, 427, 428, 430, 433,
  543, 560, 579, 601
Tapiola (Sibelius), 592
Tasso, Torquato (1544–1595), 60, 98,
  229, 343
Tasso, lamento e trionfo (Liszt), 393
Tate, Nahum (1652–1715), 77
Tausig, Carl (1841–1871), 388
Taylor, Chevalier John (1703–1772),
  51, 82
Tchaikovskaya, Alexandra (Assière)
  (1813–1854), 502
Tchaikovskaya, Alexandra, see Davidova, Alexandra (Tchaikovskaya),
Tchaikovskaya, Antonina Ivanovna
  (Miliukova) (1849–1917), 513–514,
  515, 516
Tchaikovsky, Anatol Ilyich (1850–
  1915), 502, 512, 514, 524
Tchaikovsky, Ilya Petrovich (1795–
  1880), 502, 503, 504, 506
Tchaikovsky, Modest Ilyich (1850–
  1916), 502, 512, 514, 524, 526, 527
Tchaikovsky, Piotr Ilyich (1840–1893),
  118, 187, 194, 206, 208, 304, 338,
  345, 371, 399, 438, 498, 502–528,
  529, 532, 564, 580, 595, 599, 601,
  602, 604, 606
  ballets
    Aurora's Wedding, 524
    Lac des cygnes, Le, 515, 520
    Nutcracker, The, 525–526
    Sleeping Beauty, The, 523–524
  chamber music
    quartet, strings, D major, 508
     "Andante cantabile," 508
    trio, strings, A minor, 519–520
  concertos
    piano and orchestra
     1st, B flat minor, 509–510, 511
     2nd, G major, 521–522
    violin and orchestra, D major,
     187, 516, 518, 520–521
  operas, 508
    Eugen Oniegin, 513, 515, 516, 518–
     519, 524
    Iolanthe, 526
    Joan of Arc, 519
    Oxana's Caprices, 522

Tchaikovsky, Piotr—(Continued)
  operas—(Continued)
    Pique-Dame, 524, 525, 526
    Vakula the Smith, 507–508, 522
    Voyevoda, The, 505
  orchestra
    Capriccio italien, 519
    Francesca da Rimini, 515
    Manfred Symphony, 522
    Marche slave, 514
    Mozartiana, 522
    Nutcracker Suite, 525–526
  overtures
    –fantasia Romeo and Juliet,
      506–507, 515
    solennelle, "1812" 194, 519, 581
  symphonies
    1st ("Winter Daydreams"), G
      minor, 505, 509
    2nd ("Little Russian"), C minor,
      508–509, 511
    3rd ("Polish"), D major, 208,
      509, 511
    4th, F minor, 208, 507, 513–514,
      515, 516–518, 523
    5th, E minor, 194, 498, 517, 518,
      522–523
    6th ("Pathétique"), B minor,
      517, 518, 527, 528
    Manfred, 522
  Tempest, The, 515
  piano solo
    Humoresque, 606
    sonata, G major, 516
    Souvenir de Hapsal, 507
    Chant sans paroles, 507
  songs
    Mezza notte, 503
    Nur wer die Sehnsucht kennt, 519
Te Deum (Berlioz), 363–364
Telemann, Georg Philipp (1681–1767),
  38, 54, 125
Tempest, The (Shakespeare), 182, 347,
  350, 351
Terence (Publius Terentius Afer)
  (190?–159? B.C.), 272
Teresa de Jesús, St. (1515–1582), 18
Terry, Charles Sanford (1864–1936), 48
Texier, Rosalie, see Debussy, Rosalie
  (Texier)
Thackeray, William Makepeace (1811–
  1863), 62
Thaïs, St. (4th century), 306
Thalberg, Sigismond (1812–1871), 300
  305, 317, 378
  fantasia on Rossini's Moïse, 378
Thayer, Alexander Wheelock (1817–
  1897), 168
Theatrical Register (London), 82
Theocritus (3rd century B.C.), 539

Theodora, Empress of the East (508?–
  548), 69
Thomas, Charles-Louis-Ambroise
  (1811–1896), 530, 531
  Mignon, 530
Thomas, Theodore (1835–1905), 569
Thompson, Oscar (1887–1945), 535, 552
Thomson, James (1700–1748), 120
Thomson, Virgil (1896–), 608
Thoreau, Henry David (1817–1862),
  601
Three Blind Mice, 144
Thun, Count Johann Josef (1711–
  1788), 143, 144
Tibbett, Lawrence (1896–), 457
Tichatschek, Joseph Aloys (1807–1886),
  408, 410, 412
Tieck, Ludwig (1773–1853), 220, 416
Till Eulenspiegels lustige Streiche
  (Richard Strauss), 557, 561–562, 563,
  570
Times, The (London), 274
"Tod und das Mädchen" Quartet
  (Schubert), 258
Tod und Verklärung (Richard Strauss),
  559, 560
Tolstoi, Count Lev (1828–1910), 160
Tonkünstlerorchester (Berlin), 564
Toscanini, Arturo (1867–), 108, 220,
  228, 467, 588
Tovey, Sir Donald Francis (1875–1940),
  12, 76–77, 88, 143, 184, 195, 221, 276,
  338, 370
"Toy" Symphony (Haydn), 122
Toye, Francis (1883–), 303, 449
Tragic Overture (Brahms), 494–495
Traité de l'instrumentation et d'or-
  chestration (Opus 10) (Berlioz), 360
Traviata, La (Verdi), 454–455
Treitschke, Georg Friedrich (1776–
  1842), 183, 185
Trent's Last Case (Bentley), 397
Tristan und Isolde (Wagner), 47, 150,
  384, 390, 399, 412, 418, 424, 425, 426–
  427, 429, 434, 534, 549, 560, 601
Trovador, El (Gutiérrez), 451, 453, 456
Trovatore, Il (Verdi), 453–454, 455,
  460, 463
Troyens, Les (Berlioz), 343, 367, 368–
  370, 373
Turgeniev, Ivan Sergeievich (1818–
  1893), 482, 483, 611
Turner, Joseph Mallord William (1775–
  1851), 542
Turner, Walter James Redfern (1889–
  1946), 160, 220–221, 340, 354, 355,
  370, 372
Two Gentlemen of Verona (Shakespeare), 154
Tyers, Jonathan (?–1767), 74

U

"Unfinished" Symphony (Schubert),
   260–261
Universal Exposition of 1862 (London), 460

V

Vaisseau fantôme, Le (Dietsch), 428
Valois, house of, 15
Variations sérieuses (Mendelssohn), 291
Vasnier, M., 533, 534
Vasnier, Mme, 533
Vauxhall Gardens (London), 74, 81
Verdi, Carlo (?–1867), 445, 453, 461
Verdi, Giuseppe Fortunio Francesco
   (1813–1901), 230, 233, 241, 245,
   247, 338, 355, 370, 383, 445–468,
   534, 580, 594
operas
   Aïda, 461, 462–463, 465
      "Celeste Aïda," 463
   Aroldo, 457
   Ballo in maschera, Un, 457–458
      "Eri tu," 457
   Don Carlos, 460–461
      "O Carlo, ascolta," 461
      "O don fatale," 461
   Ernani, 449–450, 451–452
      "Ernani, involami," 449–450
   Falstaff, 370, 466–467, 570
   Finto Stanislao, Il, see Giorno di
      regno, Un
   Forza del destino, La, 459–460, 461
      "Pace, pace," 460
      "Solenne in quest'ora," 460
   Giorno di regno, Un, 448, 466
   Iago, see Otello
   Lombardi alla prima crociata, I,
      449, 451
   Luisa Miller, 450
   Macbeth, 450, 461
   Maledizione, La, see Rigoletto
   Masnadieri, I, 450
   Nabucodonosor (Nabucco), 448–
      449, 453
   Oberto, conte di Bonifacio, 447,
      451, 466
   Otello, 233, 464–465, 466, 467
      "Ave Maria," 465
      "Salce, salce," 465
   Rigoletto, 391, 449, 450, 452–453,
      454, 455, 460, 463
      "Caro nome," 452–453
      "La donna è mobile," 453
      quartet, 453
   Simone Boccanegra, 456–457, 464
   Stiffelio, 457
   Traviata, La, 454–455
      "Ah! fors è lui," 455
      "Di Provenza il mar," 455

Verdi, Giuseppe—(Continued)
   operas—(Continued)
      Traviata, La—(Continued)
         Drinking Song, 455
         "Sempre libera," 455
      Trovatore, Il, 453–454, 455, 460,
         463
         "Ai nostri monti," 454
         Anvil Chorus, 454
         "Il balen," 454
         Miserere, 454
         "Stride la vampa," 454
      Vêpres siciliennes, Les, 456
      Vespri siciliani, I, 456–457
   Requiem ("Manzoni"), 355, 463–464
   string quartet, E minor, 463
Verdi, Giuseppina (Strepponi) (1815–
   1897), 447, 449, 451, 453, 458, 459,
   460, 466, 467
Verdi, Luigia (Uttini) (?–1851), 445,
   453
Verdi, Margherita (Barezzi) (1821–
   1840), 446, 447, 448
Verlaine, Paul (1844–1896), 531, 533,
   540, 546
Vernet, Émile-Jean-Horace (1789–
   1863), 243, 347, 348
Verona, Congress of, 236
Vestale, La (Spontini), 214
Vestris, Gaëtan Apolline Balthasar
   (1729–1808), 97
Vestris, Lucia Elizabeth (1797–1856),
   223
Viardot–García, Michelle Ferdinande
   Pauline (1821–1910), 334
Victoire Mme (1733–1799), 127
Victor Emmanuel II, King of Italy
   (1820–1878), 457
Victoria, Queen of England (1819–
   1901), 224, 284–285, 289, 307, 379,
   389–390, 423–424
Victoria, Agustín de, 18
Victoria, Tomás Luis de (1540–1611),
   13, 14, 18–20, 73
   Canticae beatae Virginis, 20
   Officium defunctorum, 19, 73
Victory Ball, A (Schelling), 194
Vienna, Congress of, 196
Vigny, Comte Alfred-Victor de (1797–
   1863), 342
Villon, François (1431–1464?), 540–541
Viñes, Ricardo (1875–   ), 546
Virgil (Publius Virgilius Maro) (70–
   19 B.C.), 367, 369
Vitoria, battle of, 193
Vivaldi, Antonio (1675?–1743), 26
Vogl, Johann Michael (1768–1840), 254–
   255, 256, 259, 262
Vogler, Abbé Georg Josef (1749–1814),
   210, 212, 217
Voltaire, François-Marie Arouet de
   (1694–1778), 97, 128, 229

Voyage musical en Allemagne et en Italie (Berlioz), 360

W

Wagenseil, Georg Christoph (1715–1777), 126
Wagner, Adolf (1774–1835), 398
Wagner, Albert (1799–1874), 398, 401
Wagner, Carl Friedrich (1770–1813), 397, 398
Wagner, Cosima (Liszt von Bülow) (1837–1930), 378, 385, 387, 389, 390, 403, 422, 424, 431, 432, 433, 435, 436, 443, 444, 475, 476, 560
Wagner, Eva, see Chamberlain, Eva (Wagner)
Wagner, Isolde, see Beidler, Isolde (Wagner)
Wagner, Johanna (Pätz) (1774–1848), 221, 397, 398, 399, 400
Wagner, Johanna (1826–1894), 412, 415
Wagner, Minna (Planer) (1809–1866), 403–404, 405–406, 407, 409, 410, 414, 416, 417, 418, 420, 422–423, 424, 428, 429, 438, 451
Wagner, Rosalie (1803–1837), 398, 401, 402
Wagner, Siegfried (1869–1930), 431, 435, 444
Wagner, Wilhelm Richard (1813–1883), 17, 22, 24, 47, 91, 123, 151, 194, 212, 221, 224, 225, 226, 241, 242, 245, 246 276, 279, 288, 290, 291, 295, 297, 304, 306, 307, 308, 310, 311, 338, 339, 345, 357, 359, 360, 361, 368, 371, 383, 384, 385, 387, 389, 391, 395–444, 445, 450, 451, 452, 456, 461, 462, 469, 475, 478, 479, 486, 510, 512, 517, 520, 531, 534, 535, 536, 540, 543–544, 556, 557, 558, 559, 560, 565, 570, 571, 573, 576, 579, 580, 594
  instrumental compositions
    American Centennial March, 437
    Faust, seven scenes from, 401
    Faust Ouvertüre, Eine, 407
    Kaisersmarsch, 437
    overture, B flat major, 401
    Siegfried Idyl, 436
    symphony, C major, 401, 443
  operas
    Feen, Die, 401, 402, 403, 425
      overture, 402
    Fliegende Holländer, Der, 408, 409–411, 414, 415, 424, 430
      "Die Frist ist um," 411
      overture, 410, 411
      Senta's Ballad, 411
      Spinning Chorus, 411
    Götterdämmerung, Die, see *Ring des Nibelungen, Der*

Wagner, Richard—*(Continued)*
  operas—*(Continued)*
    Liebesverbot, Das, 404–405, 407, 425
      overture, 405
    Lohengrin, 413, 416, 418–419, 420, 425, 429, 430, 512, 579
      Bridal Chorus, 286, 413, 419, 434
      prelude, 419
      Wedding March, see Bridal Chorus
    Meistersinger von Nürnberg, Die, 47, 370, 419, 426, 432–434
      Dance of the Apprentices, 434
      Preislied, 434
      prelude, 434
      quintet, 434
      "*Wahn! wahn!*," 434
    Novice de Palerme, La, see *Liebesverbot, Das*
    Ollandese dannato, L', see *Fliegende Holländer, Der*
    Parsifal, 369, 390, 422, 435, 441, 442–443, 535, 567, 579
      Good Friday Spell, 443
      prelude, 443
    Rheingold, Das, see *Ring des Nibelungen, Der*
    Rienzi, 402, 408–409, 410, 411, 413, 414, 415, 425
      overture, 409
    Ring des Nibelungen, Der, 225, 226, 241, 384, 419, 420, 422, 423, 424, 426, 429, 430, 433, 435, 436–440, 442, 512, 539, 565
      Götterdämmerung, Die, 420, 425, 435, 440, 443, 512
        Siegfried's Funeral Music, 440
        Siegfried's Rhine Journey, 440
      Rheingold, Das, 420, 422, 424, 425, 441
        prelude, 422
      Siegfried, 420, 424, 425, 435, 436, 440
        Waldweben, 440
      Walküre, Die, 420, 422, 424, 425, 440, 441
        Brunnhilde's Immolation Aria, 440
        Liebeslied, 440
        Ride of the Valkyries, 440
        Wotan's Farewell, 440
    Siegfried, see *Ring des Nibelungen, Der*
    Tannhäuser, 24, 291, 311, 368, 383, 384, 385, 411–413, 414, 415, 417, 420, 423, 425, 427, 428, 430, 433, 543, 560, 579, 601
      Bacchanale, 413
      Elisabeth's Prayer, 413
      "Evening Star," 291, 413, 434

Wagner, Richard—*(Continued)*
  operas—*(Continued)*
    Tannhäuser—*(Continued)*
      Festmarsch, 413
      Hymn to Venus, 412
      overture, 413
      Pilgrims' Chorus, 413
      Venusberg Scene (original), 412, 426
      Venusberg Scene (Paris), 428, 601
    Tristan und Isolde, 47, 150, 384, 390, 399, 412, 418, 424, 425, 426–427, 429, 434, 534, 549, 560, 601
      Liebesnacht, 426, 427
      Liebestod, 426
      prelude, 427
      prelude to Act III, 427
    Walküre, Die, see *Ring des Nibelungen, Der*
  songs, five, 424
    Schmerzen, 540
    Träume, 424, 540
  writings
    Hochzeit, Die, 401
    Judenthum in die Musik, Das, 421, 422, 423
    Junge Siegfried, Der, 420
    Leubald, 399, 400
    Mein Leben, 398, 403, 433, 436
    Oper und Drama, 422
    Siegfrieds Tod, 420
    Vaisseau fantôme, Le, 408, 428
Wailly, Armand-François-Léon de (1804–1863), 355
Waldstein, Count Ferdinand von (1762–1823), 166, 167, 168
"Waldstein" Sonata (Beethoven), 182
Wales, Frederick Lewis, Prince of (1707–1751), 71, 72, 73
Walewski, Comte Alexandre-Florian-Joseph (1810–1868), 385
Walküre, Die (Wagner), 420, 422, 424, 425, 440, 441; see also *Ring des Nibelungen, Der*
Walpole, Horace, Earl of Orford (1717–1797), 540
Walsegg, Count Franz von, 159
Walsh, John (?–1736), 60
"Wanderer" Fantasia (Schubert), 262, 263
Wanhal, Johann Baptist (1739–1813), 111, 145
Wartburg (Eisenach), 23–24, 411, 412
Wasielewski, Joseph von (1822–1896), 292
Water Music (Handel), 62–63, 75, 81
Waterloo, battle of, 142
Waverley overture (Berlioz), 342, 343
Weber, Aloysia, see Lange, Aloysia

Weber, Carl Maria von (1786–1826), 135–136, 150, 208–225, 226, 233, 236, 238, 258, 269, 270, 271, 293, 296, 343, 365, 369, 399, 400, 402, 403, 409, 411
  Abu Hassan, 213
  Conzertstück, 208, 218, 219, 274, 365
  Drei Pintos, Die, 218
  Euryanthe, 220–221, 222, 224, 225, 236, 258
    overture, 208, 219
  Freischütz, Der, 212, 216–217, 218–220, 221, 223, 258, 269, 399, 411
    "Durch die Wälder," 220
    "Leise, leise," 220
    overture, 208, 221
  Invitation to the Dance, 208, 212, 217
  jubilee cantata, 217
  Kampf und Sieg, 215
  Leyer und Schwert, 215
  Masses, 208
  Oberon, 212, 222, 223–224
    "Ocean, thou mighty monster," 223
    overture, 208, 224
  overtures, 423
  Preciosa, 218
  Rübezahl, 210, 211
  Sylvana, 212–213, 214
  symphonies, C major, 211
  Turandot overture, 208
  Waldmächen, Das, 210, 212
Weber, Caroline (Brandt) von, 213, 214, 216, 217, 218, 219, 222, 223, 224
Weber, Constanze, see Mozart, Constanze (Weber)
Weber, Franz Anton von (1734?–1812), 209, 210, 211, 212, 213
Weber, Fridolin (1733–1779), 135–136, 139
Weber, Genofeva (Brenner) von (1764–1798), 209
Weber, Marie Cäcile (?–1793), 139
Webern, Anton von (1883–1945), 568
Wegelius, Martin (1846–1906), 576, 579
Weingartner, Felix (1863–1942), 388, 564
Weinlig, Christian Theodor (1780–1842), 401
Wellington, Arthur Wellesley, Duke of (1769–1852), 193, 236, 238
Well-Tempered Clavichord, The (Bach), 35–36, 37, 49, 51, 65, 165, 294, 315, 324, 330
Wesendonck, Mathilde (Luckemeyer) (1828–1902), 423, 424–425, 429, 438, 451
Wesendonck, Otto (1815–1896), 423, 424, 425, 427, 429, 438, 441
Wetzler, Hermann Hans (1870–1943), 569

Whistler, James Abbott McNeill (1834–1903), 542

Who is Sylvia? (Schubert), 251, 263

Wieck, Clara Josephine, see Schumann, Clara (Wieck)

Wieck, Friedrich (1785–1873), 279, 293–294, 295, 296, 297, 299–300, 301, 400

Wilde, Oscar Fingal O'Flahertie Wills (1856–1900), 566

Wilhelm I, Emperor of Germany (1797–1888), 438, 486, 566

Wilhelm II, Emperor of Germany (1859–1941), 564

Wilhelm Tell (Schiller), 241

Wilhelmj, August Daniel Ferdinand Victor (1845–1908), 440, 574

William V, Duke of Bavaria (?–1626), 16, 17

William Tell (Rossini), 234, 241–242, 243, 246, 334

Winckelmann, Johann Joachim (1717–1768), 90

"Winter Daydreams" (Tchaikovsky), 505, 509

Wittelsbach, house of, 15

Wodzińska, Countess Marja (?–1896), 327, 328, 329

Wodziński, Count, 327

Wojciechowski, Titus, 317, 318

Wolf, Hugo (1860–1903), 303, 488, 561, 564

Wood, Sir Henry J. (1869–1944), 84

Wordsworth, William (1770–1850), 163, 601

Wotton, Tom S., 363–364

WQXR (New York), 194, 517

Würth, Karl, pseudonym of Johannes Brahms, 471

Württemberg, Eugen, Duke of (1758–1822), 211

Württemberg, Ludwig, Duke of (1756–1817), 211

Wyzewa and Saint-Foix (Teodor de Wyzewa and Georges de Saint-Foix, *W. A. Mozart, Sa vie musicale et son oeuvre, de l'enfance à la pleine maturité*), 132

Y

Young, Edward (1683–1765), 293

Young Pretender, see Stuart, Charles Edward

Ysaÿe, Eugène (1858–1931), 541

Ysaÿe Quartet, 537

Z

Zachau, Friedrich Wilhelm (1663–1712), 54, 63, 82

Zaremba, Nikolai Ivanovich (1821–1879), 504

Zauberflöte, Die (Mozart), 129, 145, 155, 156–157, 355, 394

Zelter, Carl Friedrich (1758–1832), 269, 272, 273, 276

Zweig, Stefan (1881–1942), 571

Zywny, Adalbert (1756–1842), 315, 316